PERSONALITY AND LEARNING THEORY

*"When man's knowledge is not in order,
the more of it he has, the greater will be his confusion"*

HERBERT SPENCER

Raymond B. Cattell, Ph.D., D.Sc., London University, is one of the world's leading personality theorists and researchers. As Distinguished Research Professor at the University of Illinois for thirty years he spearheaded a team of internationally acclaimed scholars in their innovative, pioneering research on personality and motivation. This work has been heralded for its creative contributions to personality concepts, psychometric advances, behavioral genetic methods, and clinical, social, and cultural research.

Among Dr. Cattell's many awards are the Darwin Fellowship, the Wenner Gren Prize of the New York Academy of Sciences, distinguished foreign honorary membership in the British Psychological Society, and presidentship of the Society of Multivariate Experimental Psychology. Among his 35 books are the *Handbook of Multivariate Experimental Psychology*, *Personality and Social Psychology*, *Prediction of Achievement and Creativity*, *Abilities: Their Structure, Growth and Action*, and *Meaning and Measurement of Neuroticism and Anxiety*. He has made over 400 contributions to scientific journals.

Personality and Learning Theory (Volumes 1 and 2) is the crowning work of one of this century's most distinguished psychologists. He has undertaken to heal the gulf between personality theory and learning theory which has troubled many, but so far has been comprehensively attacked by none. This two-volume work may well be remembered as the point at which learning theory, in a new synthesis, turned a corner into a more profitable and potent structured learning theory.

Volume 2, building on the personality theory and structures presented in the first volume, unravels the learning principles by which these structures are acquired.

PERSONALITY AND LEARNING THEORY

Volume 2

A Systems Theory of Maturation and Structured Learning

Raymond B. Cattell

Distinguished Research Professor in Psychology, Emeritus;
University of Illinois

SPRINGER PUBLISHING COMPANY

New York

Springer Publishing Company, Inc.
200 Park Avenue South
New York, N.Y. 10003

80 81 82 83 84 / 10 9 8 7 6 5 4 3 2 1

Library of Congress Cataloging in Publication Data (Revised)

Cattell, Raymond Bernard, 1905-
    Personality and learning theory.

    Bibliography: p.
    Includes index.
    CONTENTS: v. 1. The structure of personality in
environment. --v. 2. A systems theory of maturation
and learning.
    1. Personality. 2. Learning, Psychology of.
1. Title. [DNLM: 1. Personality.
2. Personality development. 3. Learning.
4. Psychological theory. BF698.C366p]
BF696.C323   155.2   79-594
ISBN 0-8261-2120-9 (v. 1)
ISBN 0-8261-2121-7 pbk. (v. 1)
ISBN 0-8261-2124-1 (v. 2)
ISBN 0-8261-2125-X pbk. (v. 2)

Printed in the United States of America

CONTENTS

Preface   vii

CHAPTER 1
Genetic, Maturational Interactions with Learning   1

CHAPTER 2
The Dynamic Calculus Foundations of Learning Theory   63

CHAPTER 3
Learning Defined: The Integration of Reflexological
and Structured Learning Concepts   157

CHAPTER 4
The Action of the Primary Learning Laws
within a Dynamic Structure   217

CHAPTER 5
Matrix Analysis (APA, PLA, and DPA) of the Learning
of Structure and Process   291

CHAPTER 6
The Acquisition of Integrating Structures and Their Action
in a Systems Theory of Personality   359

CHAPTER 7
The Systems Theory of Personality, Society, and Culture   461

Bibliography   589
Author Index   625
Subject Index   633

The general plan of this two-volume work has been discussed in the preface to the first and needs only brief recapitulation and extension here.

The first volume deals with personality and environment *in being*, without the strategic measurement of which no further science of maturation and personality learning can be established. It has dealt with trait structures, with the dynamics of environment in relation to the existing structures, with the flow of states and processes, and with the methodological problems of psychological relativity, that is, of separating observed and true data.

This second volume moves on, logically, to all that has to do with the growth and change of personality, beginning with behavior genetics in maturation, continuing through structured learning on a basis of dynamics, and so to a systems theory of organization of the individual personality and of the personality within the cultural environment.

The contribution in this second volume is more theoretically speculative than in the first, due to insufficient experiment by learning theorists in the domain of the new structured learning theory. It will be more "controversial" than the first volume because it attempts the Herculean task of bringing personality theory and learning theory together and steps into the midst of a no-man's land where one is shot at from both sides. Since the purpose of a preface is to express frankly personal views I shall in a moment describe the irrational resistances to this integration with perhaps indiscreet sincerity. But first we have a greater peril than these difficulties between personality and learning theorists to deal with, namely, the flood of barbarism that would attack both of these empires of genuine scientific culture.

Psychology as a science has long been like a ship with a professional crew of 100, together with 1,000 tourists who are permitted into the engine room and throng the bridge, pushing at the wheel and scribbling on the navigation charts. Every man is a psychologist, and the market of books and magazines plays up to this belief. Even within the universities the "psychologist" rather than the "psychono-mist" prevails. Educators realistically recognize a curriculum that calls for two types of courses in psychology. On the one hand a type of course is needed for some millions of undergraduates who will take at most one or two such courses as part of a liberal educa-tion. On the other, a different type is needed for some mere thou-sands who are studying psychology as a science and who will be the professional psychologists and research leaders of the future. I must grant that *perhaps* the former should be given a primarily human-istic approach, catering to diverse nonscientific interests. However, many would-be-popular books omit any treatment of *how the given conclusions* ("He is lazy because his mother did not show affection when he was two") *are reached methodologically*. This leaves the future "educated" citizen, of a society in which psychology is part of the general scientific orientation, sadly lost. What a professional psychologist must nevertheless object to is that the commercial en-ticements and promotions of publishers, to which too many academ-ics succumb, lure the young pre-professionals themselves into using the same bestsellers and swallowing the same pap as the dilettanti. Other areas of university study, such as medicine and engineering, for example, are able, by clearer separation of amateur and professional, to avoid this dangerous dilution and contamination of the early ed-ucation of their professional students.

The diversion of students from a treatment—disciplined, experi-mental, mathematical, conceptually-precise and imaginative—that will alone advance our science, is aided by a fifth column within the city. These are the many rococo, verbose "theoretical" writings, unrefer-red or unreferrable to any testable mathematical (or other exact) model. These might have been expected to disappear in the thirties, but they still appear perennially, as in this year's *Current Personali-ty Theories'* appeal to the market. There is no bulwark against these commercial exploitations of the student's naiveté except the discon-cerning academic teacher. The excess of verbiage over the number of dependable predictive laws and effective research methods that can be taught is fantastic. That is why I have quoted Spencer on page ii, and why my whole aim has been to reduce the domain of my dis-course to exact formulations, even though in some cases still hypo-thetical, that are testable.

Because of these values and aims there is risk that reviewers, contrasting this book with psychology texts more journalistic in ex-pression, may at first pronounce it as too difficult for the under-graduate. Admittedly it has equations and diagrams (although inspec-tion will surely show that they are simpler than those that under-graduates in chemistry, physics, engineering, or psychology typically have to study). I am convinced that the teacher in psychology today is, on the one hand, underestimating the students' capacities, and, on the other, underestimating the amount and quality of study and supplementary explanation that a teacher typically needs to give to a good assigned textbook. If we believe that psychology students are as bright as chemistry students, this book should be understandable to any serious student of psychology, whether a senior undergraduate major or a graduate.

By analogy with the cultural phases noted by anthropologists, psychology today is surely best described as in transit from the nomadic to the agricultural stage. It moves as from an economically weak and little coordinated hunting-and-fishing activity to a systematic harvesting of experimental data and the construction of growing "cities" of integrated, testable theory. This concept may give added meaning to my implication above that psychology is still too often the careless hunting ground of the loosely speculative theorizers who distract so many students from careful theory construction and exact models. The areas in which psychology has most clearly entered the second cultural phase, and built up some firm and architectonic growth, are those of psychometrics and learning theory. Here the giants of the new age in this century—Galton, Spearman, Thurstone in the one, and Wundt, Pavlov, Hull, Mowrer, Spence, Anokhin, Tolman, and Skinner in the other—have conceived great models. In both of these "cities," mathematical and experimental researches have successfully reared edifices—perhaps still of modest height, but offering consistent, dependable laws, and hard-headed reasoning.

We can admire these two edifices and yet have to admit that they have remained strangely and grievously mutually segregated. I have suggested that current reflexological concepts, neat and intelligently scientific in intention, confine learning in too tight a hide of basic axioms. There is some quality of perfection there, but there is an old adage that "Perfection is finality, and finality is death"! My estimate, supported in argumentation in the text, is that the strictly peripheral (*S-R*) framework for learning concept development and the constrictions to a reflex arc model has served its purpose and achieved most of what is ultimately possible on that basis. Thoughtful reflexological learning theorists are themselves publishing articles aware of the limitations of the existing model. But the momentum of verbal habit and loyalty to a school may stand in the way of their followers acquiring the concepts, terms, and perspectives necessary to augment existing theory, such as I have aspired to develop here.

Personality theory, as developed clinically and psychometrically, even with the concepts sharpened and renovated, as in Volume l here, is equally in need of change and extension. That is why I have, at risk of some charges of speculation, introduced developments of the dynamic calculus and of systems theory creating fundamentally new learning concepts, which I have ventured to call *structured learning theory*. I cannot hope that this transcendance of artificial boundaries will be examined by the general run of learning theorists truly on its merits, but the open-minded response to its launching at the International Congress of Psychology, in London and in Moscow, suggest that a sufficient number will be intrigued by its possibilities.

Science has suffered many unnecessary setbacks from imprecise and ambiguous terminology. An historian of science can realistically claim that sometimes a bad term has done more damage than a bad theory. Beginning with an undue faith in and concern with introspection, the psychology of Brentano, Kulpe, Mach, Titchener, and, to some extent, Wundt and others, flourished academically until Galton, Spearman, Pavlov, McKeen, Cattell, Watson, Woodworth, and others in diverse fields came to realize that the only truly scientific psychology had to be based on *observed behavior* and concepts derived therefrom. There the basic concept of *reliability* could be introduced, through the possibility of having more than one observer (the introspector). This movement is properly called *behavioral psychology*. Unfortunately, in an empire-building movement, Watson tried to pre-empt "behaviorism" for a much narrower concept—reflexology. Still more unfortunately, a number of psychologists, with perhaps even less historical and methodological perspective than Watson, mechanically repeated this malapropism.

Clearly, what, for lack of a better name, we may call the *reflexological, or S-R, model* is only one of several models and areas of behavioristic research. The psychometry of individual differences, much social psychology, and broader varieties of learning study all methodologically embrace the behaviorist approach. Much of psychometry, and all physiological, social, group dynamic, motivational, and personality psychology are thus today behavioristic in the correct sense. Certainly my own work in the last three areas over the last 50 years has held strictly to a behaviorist basis. To say that it is now too late to correct the observations of the unscholarly, and to call for precision in the distinction of "behavioristic" and "reflexological" is arrant conservatism and a counsel of despair. Much pointless debate and many astigmatisms of perspective could be avoided if the term "reflexological" were used to designate the Pavlov-to-Skinner form of learning theory, and "behavioristic" for all forms of psychology which, in contradistinction to Bertrand Russell, for example, insist on psychological concepts being based on checkable behavioral observations.

The essential issue which I take up in the text, in hybridizing personality and classical reflexological learning theory, is that of expanding the *S-O-R* in place of the *S-R* model. Both are only special models within behaviorism, but it is anyone's guess whether a majority or a minority of those in the Watsonian reflexological tradition could be counted today as having explicitly moved on from the reflexological *S-R* model to the *S-O-R* model, which the personality theorists mentioned above set out to introduce forty years before them.[1]

Scientists, being human, are dogged by social and emotional attachments, but in order that intellectual progress, sometimes of a threateningly revolutionary kind, may eventuate, definite attempts must be made to allow for personal biases. My experience in speaking of structured learning themes at meetings convinces me that the first obstacle to bringing personality and learning theory together lies in the above inbred psychometric and reflexological professional attachments. But a second difficulty, which the reflexologist has rightly pointed out, lies in the vagueness of much that has been written under the label of personality theory. It is my conviction, expressed in this book, that a good weld can be made between the two only if both are developed and expressed in precise models. The theory that integrates them must begin with explicit assumptions, and must issue in equations quantitatively testable.

After this appeal for well-defined models I must with some embarrassment beg for understanding regarding a type of latitude I have had to practise in my algebraic presentations. It has been my aim to have the consecutively developed formulas, equations, and measuring instruments stand as hostages for the genuineness of my theory—as well as concrete leads to the research designs by which the theories can be empirically tested. But I do not claim that they always have the precision, yet, of formulations of theory in more established sciences. Experiment is not yet so advanced in the structured learning and dynamic caclulus fields that a full operational definition can always be given. Nor could I afford, with so much to cover, to delay the reader with meticulous definitions of all postulates and conditions that would ultimately need to be set down. And the completeness of equations as to subscripts, terms irrelevant to the immediate exposition, and others, is not at such a level of polish as would be appropriate for an article in *Psychometrika*, *M.B.R.*, or the *British Journal of Mathematical and Statistical Psychology*. For example, in a prototype equation for the main model in a given area all subscripts are usually given initially, but later, in more widely embracing relationships, they would clutter the picture and are dropped as understood. The general reader will not miss them and the expert psychometrist will have no difficulty in filling them in. I have, in fact, in some areas moved to what might be called a style of "schematic" equations, trimmed of conditional clauses, because I am writing primarily for the psychologist rather than the psychometrist as such.

A central illustration of this is the factor specification equation, which normally contains specific factors and error terms. But after once instancing the latter for statistical completeness, I have dropped them, assuming that the common sense and convenience of the reader will prefer this economy of the "understood." Similarly, I have omitted the i subscript for an individual's score when it is understood we are speaking of individuals generally.

As to statistical postulates the general psychologist may not be much interested in them, and the alert psychometrist can fill them in for himself. For example, I have not modified the usual factor-analytic symbols in shifting from unit length factors to real base factor analysis. Space has dictated that I leave the chiaroscuro of the picture to be filled in by the psychometrist and by those who would carry the given special conceptual development further. At any rate, I hope it can be said that I have indulged in no wanton pedantry here of formulas for formulas' sake. Each equation is included only when judged indispensable to ensure that some relationship or theoretical concept verbally introduced is fully understood as to its implications for a model.

There is another sense in which I have had to live with rough edges and incompleteness in the theoretical development of Volume 2, in contrast to Volume 1. Outside such traditional areas of psychometric activity as the abilities, sophisticated multivariate experimental work, *especially of a manipulative kind*, is still rare. It is rare in the personality domain and virtually absent from reflexological learning research. My oft-repeated tenet that in theoretical development empirical laws best arise from deep immersion of the thinker in the data of his field has had to be abrogated more than I can happily tolerate. Occasionally, I have had to fall, not with the usual pride of a conjuring trick but with apology, into some rather bold borrowing of remote analogies in theory building. As I have discussed elsewhere (1966) psychologists sometimes make an untutored use of the term theory. Some recent writers on "personality theory" have stated explicitly to their readers that Eysenck, Guilford, and I, for example, are as atheoretical in personality as Skinner has said he is in learning theory. The last I must leave to speak for himself, but inasmuch as the three first mentioned make considerable use of multivariate methods, intrinsically and closely bound to patterns and concepts, I believe the difficulty lies in the failure of free-wheeling theoretical writers (Royce is one of several brilliant exceptions), to understand the need to tie down most "pattern" concepts in operational, multivariate, experimental findings. When they speak of our "empiricism" some of these would-be theoretical writers clearly do not realize, for example, that factor analysis is an hypothesis-testing as well as an hypothesis-creating tool. But the misunderstanding goes deeper, as shown by whole books on theory (such as the perennials instanced above) that weave elaborate verbal theories out of unchecked, unquantified, and statistically quite inadequate clinical notes, and that fail to state theories in the form of a genuine model, mathematical or otherwise.

Good instructors recognize by now that students in psychology are, relative to those in other sciences, peculiarly exposed to emotional, myth-making, and scientifically regressive modes of thinking. They presently need to be aroused with clear ideas of method and the nature of theory, such as will lead them to use the latter term more sparingly and precisely. Above all they need to recognize the simple truth that viable theories, however stated, cannot rest on the thin air of personal introspection. Newton's laws and the theory of gravity were possible only because of the extensive ordering of astronomical data by Kepler and Tycho Brahe, and anyone too impatient with the checked and ordered data in their extensive notebooks would never have crossed the bridge to real theory as Newton did.

In my 1946 *Description and Measurement of Personality* I stressed to students the importance of intimate daily immersion in a field of data and of a listening ear to what laws Nature has to tell us. A perusal of the actual course of scientific advance in any relatively new field will show that workers with this life style, rather than that of self-appointed pure theorists (whose specialization is often nothing more than an avoidance of the tough challenge of realistically pursuing the unraveling of nature's puzzles), has produced valid theory. However, although the jungle of speculation has since given way to the outlines of a city, the verbal theorizers seem still prone to erect their tents, inconveniently and perhaps in naive unawareness, in city streets where the traffic of precise theory and measurement has long become brisk.

While abiding by the *spirit* of this approach in theory, I have already confessed that in Volume 2, in contrast to Volume 1, I have not been able always to stand by the *letter*. Experiments following the new perspectives and rather complex multivariate methods of structured learning theory are yet so few that, like the initial hypotheses of a shrewd detective, my formulations have had to be based on scant, but hopefully significant, bits of evidence. At least, however, the formulations point to definite experiments for the adventurous student to undertake.[2]

As to the accessibility of evidence, some reviewers of concepts advanced by my colleagues and myself have justifiably complained about its being scattered in journals of many countries, published from Tokyo to London and to Calcutta, and across journals in many psychological speciality areas, from experimental to clinical, physiological, social, educational, behavioral, genetic, developmental, and other sources. Recently, Wardell (1976) threw up his hands at "myriad contributions" he had to pursue in his survey of these pieces of evidence, over some 400 articles. Among other things, therefore, this book represents a major effort at a comprehensive bibliography and at offering a more definitive integration than heretofore, of the terms and ideas involved, proceeding as far as the present stage of research will justify.

Despite the scattered publication, and the sometimes transformed and not easily recognized application of the same principles and findings, as addressed to the differing interests of the above-mentioned applied fields, some synthesis has occurred. The recent appearance of several books on personality theory shows that perceptive psychologists have not failed, even before the present explicit integration, to recognize the research plan and the developing theory that have run through the fifty years of multivariate experimental publications, from 1928 to 1978. The reader who wishes further perspective from seeing these theories reflected in the facets of many different viewpoints will find it most clearly in the books and articles of Arndt, Baughman, Brody, Buss, Cartwright, Dreger, Eysenck, Gorsuch, Hakstian, Horn, Lawlis, Levy, Liebert, Loehlin, Nesselroade, Pervin, Sell's Behavioral Institute, and Royce's Centre for Advanced Theoretical Psychology. But like attempts to infer merely at ground level the deep-down shafts and corridors made by miners shrewdly in search of the richest ore, the writings of some others have penetrated little below the surface observations. Theoretical interpretations of our own work in relation to that of others, by Cartwright, Madsen, Loehlin, Horn, Bolton, Kline, Nesselroade, Dreger, Pervin, and others, have been particularly penetrating, and the reader may be interested to compare their formulations with those of various chapters in Volumes 1 and 2.

As regards the plan of the book itself, in terms of reading and teaching, the over-all aim has been to present, in concise definition and consolidating formulas, first, a comprehensive integration of the findings of quantitative, behavioristic, personality theory—as it has been achieved to date. Thus, beginning with states, types, and roles, Volume 1 proceeds to environmental perceptions, modulations, observer perturbation error, conflict, and, finally, to dynamic structure and the dynamic calculus.

On this foundation, the present Volume 2 turns to the theory explaining the rise of the above structure in terms of genetic and learning theories. As stated, it lacks—except for certain reflexological animal learning findings unfortunately not offering sufficiently close and dependable applications to personality—the desired breadth of experimental research foundations. The evidence, for example, on the change of behavioral indices in attitudes under learning; on the role of the U and I motivational components in unconscious and conscious motivation; and on the magnitudes of ergic investments in attitudes and sentiments from learning experiences rests on researches so far, countable on one's fingers. Yet to those close to such research the goodness of fit and ultimately the wider predictive power of this structured learning theory as a whole will surely be impressive.

It is well for the teacher using this book—and perhaps also for the general reader—to realize more explicitly the problems of assimilation that arise from the novelty of some concepts and the necessary new terms attached to them, as discussed below. The working concepts in structured learning are mainly in personality, and are well founded in that field. Any problems that arise are created at the interface with present "classical" learning theory, with clinical habits of thought, with bivariate experimental psychology, and at a few minor frontiers elsewhere. I hope I can convince the establishment in these fields that the demolitions and intrusions called for are not the wanton iconoclasms of some temperamental rebel. Perhaps my stand with the establishment in psychometry will allay that suspicion.

In some ways the chief departures here from currently widespread clinical theorizing in methodological stance show us to be shoulder to shoulder with those of the experimental psychologists and reflexological learning theorists. Although disagreements on legitimacy of evidence cleave us from the clinicians, our debates at the frontiers of the present domain with the two latter are conducted in a basic language of science shared by all. The issues are those of reconstruction of concepts on a multivariate basis, and where issues of method arise the reader can see for himself that they spring from this encapsulation of more conservative members of these latter traditions within bivariate designs.

Regarding the last point, a change that will surely be perceived more clearly in the history of psychology than is realized at present is this powerful transformation of ideas in experimental and learning fields, since 1950, through the impact of *multivariate* experimental designs (discussed more fully in the *Handbook of Multivariate Experimental Psychology*, 1966). It must be said that despite the congruity of multivariate and bivariate experimental methods in their objectivity, and manipulative control, the restriction of most reflexological learning theory to bivariate methods, in contrast to a joint use of both in the new, structured learning theory, has built around classical learning theory a Chinese Great Wall resisting invasion by many fertilizing ideas from outside. If this is doubted the reader may see for himself what amount of consideration is given in "regular," "official" current learning texts to, for example, the multivariate evidence for the existence of specific ergic structures; the role of measurable ergic tensions in quantifying reinforcement rewards; the existence, in humans, of massive but measurable sentiment structures that must be taken into account in rates of learning; the concept of a five-vector description of learning change; the existence of distinct U and I motivation components; the use of indices of conflict and related formulas in decision theory; and, finally, the whole notion of integration learning. Virtually none of these has been permitted to cross the frontier of classical learning theory.[3]

It behooves us also to consider problems of another frontier— that at which the transactions of the present structural theory occur with *general* experimental psychology. Here again relations are inadequate, and we conclude they are so largely because of the same lack of multivariate designs and concepts in most experimental psychology courses. As regards psychology department "sections" one must ask if "experimental psychology" is not an increasingly superfluous term, as *most* of psychology has become experimental. For that *APA* section is really defined, as far as the original antique province was definable, by such inessentials as being conducted in a laboratory building; using brass instruments; being relatively unconcerned with individual differences; and being by the traditions of its present occupants more confined to the accidental and non-essential particular combination of manipulative with bivariate conditions.

With all its emphasis on objectivity it has nevertheless worked with the door wide open to subjectivity when it defines its concepts by a single operation.[4] (Arousal may be low electrical skin resistance, but so also are anxiety, stress, and other distinct states.) By contrast, multivariate experiment has begun objectively at the beginning and derived its concepts of states, traits, and processes from *patterns* first established correlationally as unitary entities. Classical bivariate experiment has similarly proceeded with *a priori* definitions of such concepts as inhibitory action, apperception masses, drive, adaptation level, and others. The present approach questions whether starting with the general dictionary definition of, say, inhibition (which covers everything from the inhibitory action of chemicals on plant growth to the action of brakes on cars) is as useful a taking-off point for research in that domain as the discovery of the number and nature of situationally provoked or constitutionally provided behavior reduction patterns in human behavior. For example, the clear-cut and real-life-criterion-predictive patterns discovered in UI(T)17 and 21 (Volume 1, p. 106) is surely a far firmer starting point for experiments and theory concerning any concept of some unitary inhibitory action.

Actually, the connections even with what was once sequestered as experimental psychology, of the personality theory in this book, is extensive. Those broader connections have been missed by quite a number of bivariate experimenters through the latter being caught in a curious absurdity of bibliographies. A multivariate study that examines, say, the 3,160 relationships possible among some 80 chosen experimental variables (either in a process or an individual differences study) cannot possibly set out the names of the 80 variables in the title of the article or monograph! The result has commonly been that the assiduous experimentalist makes a journal survey of the titles indicating relationships of his particular bivariate, concrete interest, say, the absolute electric skin resistance in GSR experiments, collects perhaps 30 bivariate studies with skin resistance clearly in the title. The 30 relationships witnessed by these 30 studies are commonly on noncomparable samples, whereas had the researcher picked up a single multivariate study with 80 variables, he would have found 79 reported relationships of skin resistance made comparable by the same sample. Ten multivariate studies that he misses would thus yield incomparably richer and wider relations than the 30 bivariates he locates. Unfortunately, one has to read the articles themselves to find that they deal with the variable in question. Twenty years ago the present writer called attention to this unawareness in "A need for alertness to multivariate experimental findings in integrating surveys" (*Psychological Bulletin*, 1958, 55, 253-256), with perhaps some moderate success, though review articles show that joint multivariate and bivariate surveys of experimental findings are still uncommon.

One reason for the experimentalist's seldom looking over the fence into psychometry is his assumption that it is not objective because it often deals with self-evaluative questionnaires, rating scales, and the like. This has unfortunately been true of most of it in the past, as has the stereotype that it deals with individual differences rather than states and processes. But as to brass instrument objectivity of measurement the experimentalist who peruses Cattell and Warburton (1967) will see that over the years nearly 500 objective tests and nearly 2,000 forms of objective behavior measurement have been used, and that in this work, and that of Eysenck, Nesselroade, and others, this interest is not confined to individual differences but that processes, states, and motivations are now involved. As for reaching out in the opposite direction, from personality to classical experimental areas, the research referred to in Volume 1 has used virtually all of the measures and concepts in the mainstream of experimental psychology, and a number of similar measures beyond it. When Scheier and I (see Scheier & Cattell, 1961) studied 400 articles claiming to deal with anxiety measurement, we found at most six or eight experimentalist's objective, laboratory-type tests being used. But by inventing many others we ultimately derived a harvest of about 20 objective anxiety *state* measures evaluated and ultimately concept-validated against anxiety by multivariate experiment. Incidentally, the need to modify as many such tests as possible for group administration and to transform them into pencil-and-paper situations, often hides their essential identity, in principle and origin, with laboratory measures.

Despite these facts, and an energetic educational campaign by Eysenck to bring present multivariate concepts to the notice of bivariate experimentalists, I must confess that, as of the mid-seventies, the really fertile integration that I see as intrinsically possible is still largely to come. For example, Helson's fine experimental work on adaptation level and Witkin's perceptual work on field independence and style have never been substantially related, respectively, to the multivariate work on states (Chapter 5 here) and to the important general personality factor of ego standards UI(T)16 and independence, UI(T)19, which the phenomena they study respectively express. The trait of independence has an enriched theoretical meaning beyond a purely perceptual psychology "field" independence. For example, it demonstrated high genetic determination, predictive value in general educational performance, and diagnostic discrimination in psychology.[4] Such links the experimentalist will readily see as he reads further into the expanded discussion of such source traits as UI(T)19, UI(T)21, UI(T)24, and UI(T)28, when it will be evident that the traffic with experimental psychology and its concepts is in full development in the present integration.

It is, of course, natural, and repeatedly seen in the history of science, that distinct methodologies are like separate vortices, dragging as much into themselves as each can, but unable to contribute to a common progress until some much-resisted meddler forces them to flow in a common stream. If this book does even a little to show that quantitative personality theory and learning theory can be wedded to produce a new generation of concepts the effort will have been worthwhile.

Meanwhile, to speak candidly, the irrationalities and confusion that impede communication remain. Let us recognize, however, that the obstacles that arise in Volume 2 in building a clerestory on present learning theory, and in the creation of structured learning theory, are not entirely due to the objections of some of the present congregation to building disturbance. They spring from inadequate experimentation on the new concepts, due to the thinness of the ranks of the new generation of multivariate builders. Clear experimental evidence of the potency of structured learning concepts is going to call for (1) more researchers operating at a high technical level in multivariate designs, such as confactor analysis, for example, to demonstrate learning in the behavioral index changes posited in the specification equation; (2) development of higher validity in the measurement of ergic tension, arousal, activation, and so forth, defined as unitary factor loading patterns and used as dependent and independent variables in manipulation research; (3) a greater availability in psychology departments of comprehensive batteries of multivariate computer programs, extending beyond current psychometric software into algorithms needed for diversified multivariate experiment.

A word should be given in this preface about the nature of the theory itself as a species of theory, because nothing approaching philosophy enters the main text. Fortunately, under the title of systematology—the comparative study of theories and models—K. B. Madsen has recently (1977) made available a very expert and comprehensive statement of the relationship of present theoretical developments to others in psychology.

Although the above matters of method are discussed technically in the text it has seemed desirable to devote much of the preface to discussing them candidly in the broader context of the social realities of scientific movements. There remain for discussion here some deeper, epistemological questions on the nature of theory, for which the main text, intent on particular theories and their experimental bases, cannot turn aside.

Naturally, I have proceeded through most of this scientific treatise with an implicit acceptance of scientific determinism in relation to all events. However, on reaching Chapter 7 I pause to posit a limit to the scientific determinism of the social and biological sciences, because evolution constantly produces new emergents and patterns not entirely predictable from past forms and experiences. Even apart from any defects of understanding, the flow of never-repeating history denies to human prediction the ability to catch up with the novel event. Because this proposition cannot be checked practically, we cannot reach at present a decision as to whether it is theoretically correct. But in any case we have to accept the reality of Lloyd Morgan's concept of creative emergence, according to which a new integration possesses properties we see no way of predicting from the known properties of the ingredients. Regardless of what we choose to believe on this second issue, as practical psychologists we are left with the first problem—the logistic impossibility of assembling all relevant data in time to calculate the event (see Chapter 7). In this same broader statement of philosophical assumptions I wish to be clear that my position accepts determinism in present fields of investigation, so long as it continues reliable, and that there is no need to doubt it until it actually breaks down. Like physics, in the Bohr and Schrödinger principles of indeterminism, psychology may have eventually to accept a penumbra of phenomena only statistically and not individually predictable. But psychology has far to go before failure in its predictions need be attributed to anything more than the crudity of our concepts and measurement methods.

In this connection, however, I do not accept that division of psychological *science* into nomothetic and idiographic forms, a division popularized largely in Allport's discussions on personality. Science is entirely nomothetic, that is, a matter of universal principles. The dictionary tells us that idiographic means the study of the concrete, individual, unique case. Allport's and other recent use of it has given it the implication that the individual does not obey the usual general laws. The individual case, however, is a special combination of relations and properties to be understood through general nomethetic principles. The only sense in which a study can be idiographic is either in a purely descriptive or in an esthetic, not a scientific, sense, inasmuch as we experience a unique feeling at a unique event.

To complete this preface let us turn from the above consideration of this book's theoretical aims and perspectives to the practical questions of its use by the teacher and student. As implied earlier, it is a book primarily for graduate students (and professional psychologists), although I am convinced that with good teaching support it can readily be used with undergraduate majors. Indeed, I can scarcely imagine how a student can be qualified to enter on graduate work without an appreciable part of the methodological groundwork given here or in equivalent texts.

To read easily the reader will need: (1) basic psychological statistics extending at least to an acquaintance with multivariate thinking and the logic of factor analysis (but not necessarily to the detailed calculations); (2) a first degree of familiarity with existing personality theory, and particularly the concepts of temperament and dynamic structure from multivariate experiments; (3) corresponding familiarity with the existing main concepts of classical learning theory (actually, in this presentation I do go over (2) and (3) before proceeding, but earlier, more extended contact would help); (4) that intangible qualification, a disciplined mind, permitting the reader to absorb compactly-stated propositions, and to enjoy the unraveling of conceptual complexities. Unless this last is more thoroughly inculcated than in many present-day undergraduate programs, psychologists must surely soon encounter a day of reckoning when society demands proof of the worth of its technological claims, as a science, to direct therapy, education, and occupational selection. Eysenck, for one, has pioneered by asking bluntly, "Do psychiatrists or psychotherapists do any good?" and Hudson (1978) and Fischer (1976) among others have answered that it is highly questionable. The U.S. government has passed a law demanding that any psychological tests used shall demonstrate predictive criterion validity; but what of therapy? The vindication of psychology must come partly from more basic, less superficial research, but largely from a curriculum less clogged with pseudo, "make-work" scholarship, and more demanding of precise thinking and elementary calculation. Psychologists need to be challenged to meet some of the standards of physics, chemistry, and engineering students, who are required to read even relatively complex mathematics in their undergraduate texts because telephones have to work and bridges have to stand up. The price of true control and effectiveness by psychologists in clinic, school, and society is an earlier weaning of the undergraduate from merely verbal and sometimes almost anecdotal presentations, and a pedantry of names, in favor of more precisely expressed models and simple but real calculations.

To this plea for a good background for readers of books like the present must be added an appeal of a very different kind. It is possible to read not only popular texts, but even the classics of William James (and, to some degree, Freud) without much technical vocabulary. But, however simply one may wish to write, the fact today is that psychology has moved on to become a technical subject. Without long circumlocutions, and misleadingly vague popular terms, the newer quantitative and experimentally derived concepts cannot dispense with their concise language. In personality description, for example, there have nevertheless occurred irritated cries of objection to use of a new nomenclature that, no matter how steadily adhered to by myself and numerous colleagues in a hundred publications, transcends popular language. At the risk of repeating explanations, I must point out we have never initiated a new term unless a new concept has been operationally demonstrated for which no existing terms are adapted. Rapoport (in Ariete, S. *American Handbook of Psychiatry*, N.Y., Basic Books, 1973) has well argued "Common usage words are also heavy usage words: that is to say, they are rich in marginal, metaphorical meanings. It is here that the tendency to 'theorize' by juggling words in their various contexts is greatest, among those who are impressed but not disciplined by the spirit of the exact sciences." Both psychology and medicine deal with matters in which everyone is personally much interested. Medicine has learned the advisability of separating its technical concepts from popular ones by technical terms. Some psychologists, judging by their complaints, have not yet done so. Here, as in my other books, I have proceeded consistently to use the same symbols: for example, in referring by an index to established unitary traits I have kept to the alphabet for primaries but Roman numerals for secondaries in Q-data source traits. The same technical terms, for example, surgency, superego, premsia, exvia, and cortertia are consistently used for well-replicated patterns. When new factors are 12 times confirmed it is surely no presumption to assign to the new and well-replicated patterns appropriate new names.

As to advice on order of reading the chapters, the best order is that given. Except for well-trained personality students, it would be distinctly unprofitable, for example, to tackle Volume 2 on learning without first absorbing the concepts of Volume 1 on personality theory. The reader is particularly urged to study carefully the succinct summaries given at the end of each chapter. Finally, the bibliography has the double purpose of documenting the supportive scientific foundations as such and of opening to the reader more expanded explanations of matters often dealt with here in condensed fashion.

Documentation has thus been used most heavily for *research* sources, but hopefully also with adequacy concerning general reading expanding the various areas. To cut down on what threatened to become an enormous bibliography I have resorted to representing the articles and books of many eminent contributors by the one or two most prominent of their contributions, from which their other developments can readily be traced.

In teaching, since condensation has converged here on principles and models, the skillful teacher should prepare to put flesh on their bones by expanding on illustrations for which the text had no space. For example, in Volume 1, it would be of interest and help to the student to dwell on the psychological nature of the principle primary traits and states—on their clinical relevancies, and on the criterion relations found for them in applied psychology.

Finally, in this preface I am moved to express warm gratitude to those colleagues and graduate students who helped me to achieve a synoptic view of a breadth that any individual alone could scarcely hope to complete in accurate detail. Especially, I wish to thank certain young professors and older colleagues who combined painstaking thoroughness in knowledge of their fields with an openness to new viewpoints; as representative I would gratefully mention Heather Birkett, Dan Blaine, Ralph Dreger, and Art Sweney, and, outstandingly, John Nesselroade, John Horn, Sam Krug, John Sigudrson, and Larry Sine.

No author can be trusted to evaluate soundly the significance of his own book relative to those of others, but he may more reliably evaluate it relative to other books of his own, and here I can only say, as I did in Volume 1, that hitherto no book of mine has had so much thought and labor put into it or issued in so much that is new.

Raymond B. Cattell

NOTES

[1] One of the confusions is the uncertainty in modern reflexology itself as to whether it is dealing with an *S-R* or an *S-O-R* model. This is fully discussed in the text which follows, but one must point out that the suggestion around 1940 by the present writer, Woodworth, and some others that reflexology should adopt an *S-O-R* model was firmly ignored by leading learning theorists of the day on the ground that all concepts should be strictly peripheralistic, that is, rest on *S* and *R* observations alone. Berg (1973) has commented historically on this attempt to fill the learning theorist's black box—the organism—with substance from personality theory. He added that the idea was slow to be assimilated because it cut across movements of the day, and because it introduced new terms to distinguish new ideas. The history of science, particularly in aspects stressed by Kuhn (1950), convinces him that nothing but patience can be urged when schools so command their adherents. What is surely remediable, however, is the ambiguity of current reflexology on its present (late seventies) position regarding admitting personality traits as learning predictors. On the one hand, some representatives of the establishment itself assert that to criticize mere *S-R* formulations is to beat a dead horse. On the other, many leaders in learning theory join Skinner, when he says "There is an *O* term (organism property), but it is a black box about the content of which we can know nothing." My position has been that we can say a great deal about it, as Volume 1 should show.

Further, I would add that as a behaviorist I derive the structures in the box entirely from behavioral observations, not introspection. At the same time, I would be clear in view of the above mentioned semantic confusion begun by Watson, that as a psychologist who is a behaviorist I do not have to be merely a classical reflexologist. And although current reflexology may hedge on the question of how far it is willing to lean on the dynamic structure concepts of the personality theorist, our conceptual development will be more clear if we make a clean break between most learning theory based on *S-R*, and the present structured learning theory which not only explicitly takes the *S-O-R* position, but modifies all concepts through the rich influx of information which *O*, as a datum of personality theory, introduces. And in this connection I am also prepared to show that *O* structure is to be inferred from much *more* than *S-R* reflex behavior observations. Within the personality it rests, for example, on physiological evidence, state behavior change, the internal, ergic tension reinstatement of apperception masses, and so forth, and in representing the environment it introduces what I have called *ambient situations* (*k*'s in the various equations), as contrasted with the focal stimuli (h's), with which S-R has been alone preoccupied.

[2] The author, aware both of the loss of formulation of ideas and the injustice to able individuals from researches overlooked, would be deeply grateful to any readers who inform him (Psychology Dept., University of Hawaii) of studies inadvertently omitted that are relevant to these conclusions. He would also appreciate hearing of doctoral dissertations proposed as crucial experiments on basic issues in the dynamic calculus or structured learning theory.

[3] The problem in attempting to integrate the published results from so-called experimental psychology into the various multivariately established trait and state concepts resides almost entirely in different habits of thought with regard to adequacy of definition of a concept and perhaps, at times, of a theory. The fact that a bivariate experimentalist form of operationism rests on a one-aspect definition compared with that of the multivariate investigator. The former accepts some variable x, as a response *sufficiently representing* some verbally defined concept. Yet a single variable can practically never do so with a high degree of validity because a true concept (of any breadth of utility) is commonly represented by degrees of expression through *many* interrelated variables, expressed for example in the magnitude of their correlation and time relations. Thus as far as the relation of a concrete variable to a concept is concerned, multivariate experiment recognizes that although one variable can contribute its bit of meaning to a factor concept, the factor, recognized by the many variables involved, is more likely to throw light on that one variable than that one variable on the factor. It is the modified factor pattern that appears in a given domain, therefore, and not—in most cases—the original, subjectively-defined concept (which the bivariate experimentalist originally considered expressed in his first variable) that should *become* the concept under study. To many in the experimentalist tradition this requires a mental somersault.

[4] A criticism as extensive as these needs some concretization. I would instance first the rejection of multivariate analysis of human and animal learning, which my colleagues have encountered with such journals as the *J. of Experimental Psychology* and the *J. of Comparative Psychology*, purely on the grounds of being "inappropriate." The articles with Dielman (1974) experimentally analyzing rat motivation components is an example. And despite Cartwright and Cartwright (1970), for example, having called attention to the relevance to learning theory of *adaptation process analysis*, or the several publications by Barton, Butcher, the present writer, and others having shown the quite substantial importance of personality factors in a learning equation, conventional learning course texts omit this whole personality aspect of learning. A spot check of common learning texts also reveals no reference to the dynamic calculus concepts set out 20 years ago in such publications as the Nebraska and the Kentucky Symposia. It is especially surprising that the demonstration by Dielman and by Haverland of the complex structure of motivation in rats has not altered the simplistic descriptions of the measurement of rat motivation now current, by arbitrary single variables. Nor can one find in most rat learning texts reference to either Haverland's or Anderson's pioneering work in factorial discovery of the actual rat drive patterns.

The above may seem to imply that a text on learning theory is typically restricted to experiments on rats or pigeons, but in how many widely used learning or personality texts is experimental work on human personality change under learning included? (See Chapter 5 here.) Academic establishments of this kind should surely not take it ill if the holy circle drawn around their guild practices excites some satire by the major innovators, such as was expressed in similar situations in their sciences by Pasteur, Harvey, Mitchell, Galileo, and others defrauded by delays. As another concrete instance of difficulties in cross-fertilization I ascertain from Bolz and Korth that their studies (now published) using multivariate methods to ascertain temperamental dimensions in the behavior of dogs, and to check the behavioral differences of breeds of dogs were rejected overnight—presumably because of strangeness of method—by the chief journal concerned with animal experiment. (Operating on an obsolete and arbitrary definition of experiment as bivariate, they declared the work "non-experimental.")

PERSONALITY AND LEARNING THEORY

CHAPTER 1

GENETIC, MATURATIONAL INTERACTIONS
WITH LEARNING

1-1. Available methods for investigating inherited contributions to behavior
1-2. Basic genothreptic models for the interaction of chromosomal and environmental influences
1-3. Convarkin methods of investigation: The essence of twin and MAVA designs
1-4. Possible and probable varieties of correlation and interaction between heredity and environment
1-5. Parent-child and other family relations to be evaluated
1-6. A closer look at the psychological genothreptic interactions and the psychometric status of the components
1-7. Two models for genetic interaction in traits, leading to uncovering Mendelian mechanisms
1-8. Isolating score components in individuals and relating the magnitude of threptic variance to environmental influences
1-9. Summary

1-1. Available Methods for Investigating
Inherited Contributions to Behavior

Entering Volume 2, we cross the line from the foundation of personality-in-being, provided by Volume 1, to a wealth of questions as to how such a structure ever comes into existence. In pursuing this sequence we commit ourselves thoroughly to the scientific position that the study of change—whether through motivation or learning—cannot fruitfully proceed until we have located the structures and processes to be explained. There is frankly an implied criticism here that many developmental theories right up through the last decade have neither made sure that they are addressing themselves to known and measured structures, in generating their ideas, nor provided any basis for precisely checking theories. And though reflexological learning theory has respected experiment, its atomistic approach and lack of familiarity with multivariate structural findings leave its findings as featureless as desert sands. Change, after all, is always change in *something*, and that something can best be, for the sake of integrating personality and learning theory, a meaningful, established structure in behavior, measurable with psychometric validity.

Two possible misunderstandings of this position should be cleared before proceeding to developmental matters. First, our conception of structure-in-being, though precise, has not been a narrow one of fixed traits. It also involves states, processes, and a joint picture of personality and environment. Although the term "system theory" has rarely been introduced explicitly in Volume 1, and the control systems of personality remain to be discussed in this volume, yet the specification equation, and the matrix treatment of multiple interaction in Chapters 1, 5, and 7 lay a foundation for approaching systems theory in this volume. And although one has to begin, in projecting the action in a movie, with individual frames, each photographing an instant, as we began with cross-sectional exactitude here, yet our theory embraces the notion that there is no understanding of the whole without considering both the cross-sectional picture and the longitudinal flow.

It should also be recognized that in saying (as we do more explicitly later) that the atomistic laws of classical reflexology learning are not enough, we are not saying that they are not true. If we know the properties of grains of sand, one may at first be able to infer only the nature of desert topography. But one may also, with further steps, infer something about the property of concrete houses in which that sand is a stable ingredient. What is questionable is the attempt to extend the animal reflex learning laws to personality development by speaking of attitudes, sentiments, and other traits as being "conditioned," that is, by a mere semantic substitution treating these more complex structures as if they were just reflex response potentials.

However, before the study of development concerns itself with learning it has to consider genetic maturation. Putting genetics first is not ignoring the fact that genetic inner maturation interacts constantly over the years with environmentally determined learning. Yet the genetic potential is given in the newly conceived individual before ever learning begins, and it is appropriate, therefore, to have our first chapter deal with behavior genetics.

It is a truism that individual differences in any area of behavior ever analyzed by psychologists have been found determined both by genetic and learning influences. So much political cant has been written regarding the unimportance of genetic determination that one must urge the pre-exposed student to follow Dr. Johnson's advice to "clear one's mind of cant" and be prepared to follow the facts and arguments purely on their own merits. In the first place the relative magnitudes of genetic and cultural forces will assume very different perspectives according to one's position. One can depend on the expectation that a crab will behave like a crab and a dog like a dog on genetic grounds. On the other hand, it might be true, as some sociologists and cultural anthropologists argue, that different races of men can be taught any particular human culture with equal ease. There is thus no general answer to "the relative importance of heredity and environment." For example, if we ask how important heredity is relative to environment in deciding whether a person shall be a communist or a fascist, the answer is sure to be "only trivially" whereas in asking the same in regard to relative achievement in a common educational system the answer is "heredity has a significant role."

Even where one's primary interest is to find out how learning affects personality there are gains from first studying heredity and getting a perspective on the relative roles of each. For example, the discovery in several traits of a negative correlation within families between the deviation of a child from the sib mean due to heredity and that due to within family environmental differences led to a law of "coercion to the cultural mean" which could not very well have been reached without that finding. And as we shall see below, the fact that the nature-nurture variance ratio and the associated heritability quotient vary with the age of the group studied, and the social and racial setting, opens up avenues for determining the time and manner of incidence of various cultural influences.

Behavior genetics is thus an increasingly important and useful branch of psychology for learning as well as understanding heredity, and in recent years it has made great strides in its technical equipment. However, before encountering specific technicalities let us look broadly at the methods and areas of observation by which we can gather knowledge, and which are four in number:

1. *The clinical-genealogical method.* This method has led, over generations, to most discoveries of inheritance in the medical field and has been responsible for the initial insights also into the genetics of psychopathology. The method may be seen, in all its advantages and shortcomings, already in the classics of a generation ago, such as those of Blacker (1934), Blakeslee and Fox (1932), Bleuler (1933), Huntington (1927), Kallmann (1953), Ruggles-Gates (1946), Slater (1937) and is still effectively pursued in current articles and books, such as Sturtevant (1965), Rosenthal (1970), and

Darlington (1969). Scandinavian studies, in particular, have contributed much here by reason of their more thorough local genealogical records. At its most precise, the behavior observed is some well-defined symptom syndrome, such as Huntington's chorea or catatonic schizophrenia; at its loosest, it is a study of such uncertain matters as "inheritance of hot temper," not reliably measured. The aim has been so to trace the behavior over several generations that conclusions can then be drawn on the number of genes and the presence of dominant and recessive action, as brought out well in Falconer (1960), Li (1961), Cavalli-Sforza (1971), Sturtevant (1965), Waddington (1957, 1962), and others. Though the number of established *behavioral* connections by this method is decidedly less, and less definite, than for the several hundreds of connections found in physical medicine, the results of this method continue to be impressive as long as well-defined syndromes are taken. McKusick (1966), for example, listed over 1500 presumed Mendelian syndromes, forms of mental defect, and so on.

2. *The inheritance-manipulated animal method.* Here we have an advance into the measured behavior that is possible with animals, though occasionally categorical syndromes, for example, that in "waltzing" in mice, are used. The great advantage in method here, however, is the possibility of manipulating the patterns of matings. In the skillful hands of Broadhurst (1959), Tryon (1940), Rundquist (1933), Royce (1957), Royce and Covington (1960), Fuller and Thompson (1960), McClearn and DeFries (1973), Scott and associates (1959), Hall (1940), Thompson (1957, 1966), Yerkes (1940), and others, this has yielded, particularly in the last decade, some splendid results. But as far as assistance to *human* personality behavior genetics is concerned, the *specific* findings remain virtually untranslatable, due to lack of demonstrated comparability of the animal behaviors to replicated temperament and motivation factors in human beings.

3. *The physical link method.* This takes some physical feature the genetic mechanisms in the inheritance of which have become well understood (being usually easier to determine), and seeks to relate measured or categorical behavior to the physical features.

In the animal domain such connections are widely quoted by animal breeders, though the behavioral side is less precise than psychologists would demand. Workers in conditioning are well aware of differences in behavior between species and races. For example, Cattell and Dielman (1974) were unable to get certain behavior scores on hooded rats and Wistar strains into the same range, for learning treatments. Within the *same* species and strain Tryon (1940) was able to breed groups by selection that became virtually non-overlapping in performance. The finding that dogs classified purely by their temperament dimensions (Cattell & Korth, 1973) by taxonome (Cattell, Korth, & Boltz, 1973) on behavior, "sight unseen," yielded classes corresponding to physically classifiable breeds is also positive evidence of genes covering physique and behavior jointly.

In man some initial significant associations of this kind have been obtained with physical elements that are elements of racial features, such as eye color (Baker, 1974; Cattell, 1945; Cattell & Molteno, 1940), species and race differences (Loehlin, Lindzey, & Spuhler, 1975; Lindzey, 1965; Hess, 1958, 1959, 1962), body build (Kretschmer, 1925; Sheldon & Stevens, 1942), blood groups (Cattell, Young, & Hundleby, 1964; and Cattell & Brackenridge, in press). The heredity of finger print forms (Swan & Hawkins, 1978) promises another basis. Particularly interesting are the findings that certain physical and *functional* diseases are significantly related to temperament, for example, manic depression and peptic ulcer incidence (Aird, and others, 1954; Parker & Spielberger, 1961).

4. *The comparison of relatives, or convarkin methods.* (Convarkin is a useful contraction of what is fully spelled out as *con*trasting *var*iances among *kin*ship groups.) These studies take persons of varying distance and kind of family and living relationship. Using, generally, *measured* behavior, they seek by statistical analysis to determine the relative contribution of within- and between-family environment, and within- and between-family genetic variances, to an *observed* variance. There have been two main approaches: the older and much more used twin method, and the newer, more powerful, but more expensive, *MAVA (Multiple Abstract Variance Analysis)* method. The difference is as follows: (a) The twin method commonly compares the differences within pairs of identical with that within pairs of fraternal twins, as described below; (b) the MAVA method takes sibs (henceforth used for siblings) reared together, sibs reared apart, fraternal twins reared together and apart, continuing with measures through several other obtainable different relational "constellations," as described below. By comparing the within- and between-pair differences of pairs from these constellations, it aims to estimate a total of four genetic and environmental contributions as set out below.

All of the above methods have their appropriate roles in modern behavior genetics research. But as our concern is with features of *personality*, quantitatively conceived, and measured largely in the normal range, this chapter will be principally occupied with the last method—the all purpose convarkin method covering twin and MAVA designs.

1-2. Basic Genothreptic Models for the Interaction of Chromosomal and Environmental Influences

The models to be dealt with in this domain of interaction are at several levels. To the psychologist the most interesting is that expressing a theory of interaction of maturational and learning processes in *personality* development. To the sociologist and social psychologist the center of interest is the interaction of *whole cultures* with population genetic laws, that is, the laws governing distribution and evolution of gene pools in relation to mating customs, and so forth. To a third scientist—the molecular geneticist and the geneticist per se—the important thing is to find out how genes are situated on the chromosomes and through what chemical actions they produce their effects on the body.

The extent to which a model can be shaped and tested depends on the investigatory methods developed, and so models and methods must generally be considered together.

The problems of behavior genetics, determined in part by the nature of behavior, dictate a somewhat different sequence of methods and initial models from those of physical features. Many physical features, such as a blue eye, or an ear lobe, are either present or absent, and in most environmental ranges it makes sense to speak of some definable "phenotype." But in the domain of behavior the modifications are great and the distributions are continuous, so that a quantitative "scale" approach is the unavoidable alternative. The value which the researcher in human behavior genetics research initially seeks is a "heritability quotient" or a "nature-nurture ratio," each expressed as a percentage, and his models have to operate at the precision levels of his methods. A good deal later and further on he may have to apply this knowledge of ratios to the matters that interest the geneticist—such as the number of genes at work in the chromosomes, frequencies of polymorphic forms of a gene, degrees of dominance, locus, epistatic action, crossover effects, and so on. After this he may move to a further question: "How does the gene-determined progress of endogenous maturation, through the intermediate action of regulatory metabolites, such as enzymes, interact with environment to produce the final phenotype?" Having only the space of one chapter, we shall not concern ourselves with the genetic mechanisms in the parental chromosomes per se, or with the Mendelian unfolding of the genome into the genotype. Even if we did, it would today be largely speculation. There can be comparatively little or no connection worked out at this stage between gene structure and the psychometric, psychological findings, for the genotypic level of any individual on a factorial source trait is virtually certain to be related to the complex summative action of *many* genes; that is, it is the result of polygenic action. Only in a handful of connections of the "behavioral syndrome" type (for example, phenylketonuria, Klinefelter's syndrome, Down's syndrome) has it yet been possible reliably to tie psychological diagnoses to actual individual genes and gene doublings. Nevertheless, in Section 1-7 we will try at least to foreshadow some ways of going from the behavior-analysis, variance-percentage type to inferred gene mechanism action through the use of population genetic parameters.

Meanwhile, let us consider models that merely treat the genetic contribution as a "lump sum," being content for the time being to regard that contribution realistically as unspecified in regard to the particular gene mechanisms. With this aim, and considering a trait to be finally recognized and defined, as in Volume 1, and rendered validly scorable by a loading pattern on tests, we can break down any individual's score into two parts. That is to say, we consider anyone's actual score as a *summative* result of gene maturational action and environmental action (learning, for example) accumulating up to that time, as follows:

$$T_{ij} = g_{ij} + t_{ij} \qquad\qquad\qquad (1\text{-}1)$$

Here j is any trait, and we assume g, the *genetic* part, and t, the environmentally determined or *threptic* part, are similarly scaled. We are not free to put *any other* part into this simple model; for what is not from environment is from heredity, by mutually exclusive definition. However, we are free to play about with models of how they interact. Starting with the above simplest additive model, it will follow that $\sigma_{gj}^2 + \sigma_{tj}^2 = 1$, the variance of the trait in standard score. (That is to say, if we put our observed phenotypic variance in standard score, and assume $r_{gt} = 0$, the variances due to genetic and threptic sources—measured in our phenotypic unit—will add to one).

We will use the word *threptic* here and elsewhere, instead of the clumsy repetition of the long-winded "environmentally determined fractional" part. Though still in process of wider adoption, the term has a respectable Greek origin (like many more precise scientific terms) in Aristotle and Galen. It offers besides economy of diction an important conceptual clarification by separating, in measurement and discussion, *the variance of the environment itself* from *the variance in behavior that is attributable to the environment*. The ambiguity of the expression *environmental variance* has led to much misconception and miscommunication. Here *environmental variance* means a measure of variance on some environmental trait, for example, the size of the vocabulary in the child's family, and is an aspect of *ecometric* measurement as defined in Volume 1. By contrast threptic variance means the variance in (say) children's vocabularies due to a given environmental variance. In formulae, *threptic* will always be symbolized by a *t* subscript and *genetic* by *g*.

Less vitally but still usefully, this area of study could advantageously settle on a clear distinction of *genic* and *genetic*, reserving the former for the variance *in behavior* from genetic, physiological structure, and the latter for the actual genetic structural causes, thus:

	Heredity	Environment
Measured cause	Genic (Chromosomal)	Environmental (Ecometric)
Measured effects in behavior itself	Genetic	Threptic

Threptic, being clear of past associations, will be consistently used hereafter, but we shall not strictly pursue here the genetic and genic usage, which needs trial as to its practicality and acceptability.

A warning that seems to need to be made perennially is that assertion of a clean division into genetic, genically derived variance and threptic, environmentally derived variance is not an assertion that any given piece of behavior can be so dissected into corresponding concrete parts. Some assertions that behavior cannot be divided into genic and threptic percentages apparently assumed that particular parts of a total performance would be so allocated. What the first method and model we are about to follow actually does is to assign fractions of interpersonal variance in a group to heredity and environment. Only later can we approach the problem of what these fractions are *in a given individual* or where they predominate in parts of a trait.

Anyone familiar with mathematical models, in looking at equation (1-1), will at once ask, "Why addition rather than multiplication, and why is there not some term for possible *interaction* effects of heredity and environment?" The answer, as usual, is that we begin with the simpler model and pursue it unless, or until, forced to something more complex. Actually, there is not much doubt that sometimes the additive model is *not* adequate, and that some interaction term is needed for multiplicative effects of environment on heredity. For example, the well-known imprinting effect (Hess, 1958, 1959) shows that an environmental influence applied at some particular age and stage of maturation has a more powerful effect on the final level of the trait than if applied at another. In that case we would want a weight (a coefficient) for the threptic component that would be a function of age. What weight would go on each of two terms that are to be added depends on the scale units in which each is measured. There is no need here to digress into scaling problems so we will assume that at the age measured g and t are alike in standard scores and that T is also, so that g and t simply have weights for their relative importance in terms of variance for the given trait.

If we work to open up the next more complex model it would be one that introduces a nonadditive, interactive expression for the contributions from the two sources, as in the following equation:

$$T_{ij} = g_{ij} + t_{ij} + c \cdot g_{ij} \cdot t_{ij} \tag{1-2}$$

In this equation (where i means an individual's score), c is a constant giving a weight to the product term relative to the additive terms, and in which interaction is taken in its simplest form as a product—though more complex terms with exponents might conceivably still fit better.

Among more basic aspects of the use of such equations that need to be cleared of misunderstanding at the outset are the following four:

1. As just noted in passing, there must be some regard for the "scales" in which the terms are supposed to be measured in the above equations. As just stated the simplest approach is to assume that g and t are in standard scores, with coefficients added for their relative weights that will be consistent with a standard score of unity for T.

2. One should note (in this connection and in others) that there is a difference between *interaction* effects and *correlation* effects in any two sources of variance adding to a total variance. Curiously, this point is often obscure, in accounts of analysis of variance generally, and in genothreptic calculations in this field in particular. The existence of a correlation across the population between genic and threptic components will be evidenced in analysis of variance by the appearance of a significant interaction effect, that is, in high and low summed values (with a positive r) appearing with greater frequency than would be expected from a random relation of genetic and threptic "independent variables," even when the two sources are themselves uncorrelated. In short, we must distinguish between the end result in what are called "statistical interaction effects," demonstrated by simple addition being sufficient, and what we may call inherent "interaction effects" which may or may not be the main root of the observed statistical interaction. Statistical interaction outcomes may appear, either from true inherent interaction *or* from correlation of the two *effects* without causal interaction

between them. The latter still leaves the addition for an individual as in (1-1), namely:

$$T_{ij} = g_{ij} + t_{ij}$$

but the variance of T_j is no longer a simple sum of the g and t variances and becomes:

$$\sigma^2_{T_j} = \sigma^2_{g_j} + \sigma^2_{t_j} + 2r_{gt}\, \sigma_{g_j}\, \sigma_{t_j} \tag{1-3}$$

r_{gt} being the correlation between them.

Thus if, across the population, the contributions g_j and t_j in equation (1-1) are correlated, but, as in (1-1), do not interact mutually, then a new term will appear in total variance as a function of g_j and t_j, accounting for an observable statistical interaction effect. There is plenty of reason for believing that the genetic and threptic components *do* get correlated quite often, as shown in Section 1-3, so this term cannot be neglected.

3.   In concluding this statement of models, let us reiterate the remark above concerning the importance of being conceptually vigilant in distinguishing between the *threptic component* itself, that is, the result of the environment acting on the person's traits, and the *ecometric environment* range itself, which causes or is associated with that growth of threptic structure. One and the same ecometric environment—say, salary of parents—might affect the threptic contribution to two or more traits, but would do so at very different rates for the different traits, producing different threptic components. This should remind us, as our terms below are intended to do, that the quantities for threptic and environmental variables are two very different things. In general there *will* be considerable parallelism, though we must never assume an unquestioned linear rather than curvilinear relation of environmental *influences* and threptic *effects*. Furthermore, if environmental conditions and gene incidences are correlated across a given population, then threptic variance and genetic variance will also be correlated monotonically in the population with effects as in (1-3) above.

In the case of true inherent interaction, as in equation (1-2), the question naturally arises how the threptic score, now compounded in a genetic interaction, will mathematically relate to the environmental-influence score. The nicety of such equations we need not pursue here, but when we come to analyzing variance into two parts, we have to reach a rationale for splitting this product term if we want to talk of *total* genetic and *total* threptic components. As to the first, *inherent* interaction we have to note that it could be something happening in the genetic and environmental original sources themselves, as when, say, low intelligence in the parental heredity is related to low income, so that children tend to be simultaneously of lower intelligence genetically and exposed to more poverty, or it could be an interaction in the genic and threptic components in the individual, as when a dominant individual absorbs less instruction, even though genetic dominance and exposure to instruction are uncorrelated. The statistician's answer to the demand for an expression for distinct genic and threptic components, when they are related in interaction (whether inherent or correlational) is that the interaction term, say cg_jt_j must be equally shared between the genetic and threptic components, so that

Genetic contribution in person i's trait
$$j = g_{ij} + \tfrac{1}{2}cg_{ij}t_{ij} \tag{1-4a}$$
Threptic component in person i's trait
$$j = t_{ij} + \tfrac{1}{2}cg_{ij}t_{ij} \tag{1-4b}$$

The clinician's and the individual personality theorist's interest is of course in the individual, but in behavior genetics we are compelled to seek our ultimate understanding of the individual through first researching on the relations of genic and threptic components *in the group.* Instead of dealing with individual scores we deal with variance (the square of the standard deviation) of a trait in the group, and, incidentally, though true interaction can usually be conceived as happening in the individual, the covariance just discussed, $r_{gt}\sigma_g\sigma_t$, arises from the shape of things in the group. Variance on some trait from different sources in a group has the convenient property of being additive, so if the genic and threptic score elements in (1-1) above are uncorrelated in the group we can say that the total observed variance is the sum of genic and threptic variances, as in (1-5a), which is a simplification of (1-3):

$$\sigma_j^2 = \sigma_{g_j}^2 + \sigma_{t_j}^2 \tag{1-5a}$$

This is reached simply by squaring both sides of (1-1) (assuming the scores to be in deviations). The cross-term in (1-3) vanishes when there is no correlation of g and t. (Incidentally, we shall use Greek σ throughout, rather than the sample value s, for standard deviation because our basic propositions are best not entangled with sampling problems, which can come later in research method. If the gene endowments and environmental influences—and therefore the genetic and threptic components—are correlated, however, the covariance of these will add to the observed variance σ_j^2. Repeating (1-3) for immediate visual comparison with (1-6), and dropping the general trait symbol T, we have:

$$\sigma_j^2 = \sigma_{g_j}^2 + \sigma_{t_j}^2 + 2r_{gt}\,\sigma_{g_j}\,\sigma_{t_j} \tag{1-5b}$$

the covariance being expressed here as the correlation existing between g and t multiplied by the sigmas.

If we go from this to the fullest complication in the (1-2) model, namely, if we allow *both* some interaction and some correlation, then:

$$\sigma_j^2 = \sigma_{g_j}^2 + \sigma_{t_j}^2 + \sigma_{cgt}^2 + 2r_{gt}\,\sigma_{g_j}\,\sigma_{t_j}$$
$$+ 2r_{t_j\cdot cgt}\,\sigma_{t_j}\,\sigma_{cgt} + 2r_{g_j\cdot cgt}\,\sigma_{g_j}\,\sigma_{cgt} \tag{1-6}$$

This model permitting interaction may be a "safer" one than the simpler one, in that certain values are not set at zero but allowed to fall to zero if the solutions on empirical data prove them to be so. But we shall not pursue it further here because the MAVA analysis is already threateningly complicated, even with the simpler model, and in fact no one has yet worked out the way we would solve for (1-6) in actual research. Fortunately the data so far available suggests that the simpler model works.

1-3. Convarkin Methods of Investigation: The Essence of Twin and MAVA Designs

Because our concern is basically with personality theories and their associated models, it may not at first seem necessary that we pursue in much detail the methodological questions connected with actually reaching nature-nurture conclusions from empirical data. However, throughout this book, hypotheses and theories have justified their existence and form by having emerged from close observation of actual data relations. And, in any case, the true, operational meaning of any theoretical model is better understood if research procedures are included. A theory that cannot be investigated, or the method of investigation of which is not made clear by its exponent, is so much garbage in the scientific marketplace. Consequently, the method of reaching conclusions about the genothreptic model by the MAVA method (which is in its principles inclusive of the twin method) will now be set out briefly. The aim of the MAVA method (and its subdivision, the twin method) is to discover the underlying σ_g^2 and σ_t^2 components from actual measurement observations on the existing

σ^2's of various family groups, and it falls, of course, within the class of what we have called convarkin methods.

The MAVA (multiple abstract variance analysis) method was proposed in 1953 and carried forward in a number of theoretical papers (Cattell, 1953, 1960, 1963); substantive researches (Cattell, Stice, & Kristy, 1957; Cattell, Blewett, & Beloff, 1955; Loehlin, 1978; Cattell, Klein, & Schuerger, 1980) and critical evaluations (Jinks & Fulker, 1970; Loehlin, 1965). It can be applied to present-absent categorical data (as in all-or-nothing syndromes) as well as to continuous variables. It is one of the *two* main convarkin methods, for the historically older and more established "twin method" is also generically a convarkin method.

The twin method takes measures on a series of identical-twin and fraternal-twin pairs. In principle it also includes identical twins reared apart, although such pairs are so difficult to obtain that in practice measurement has not yet been achieved on even a barely sufficient sample. By *twin method* we shall understand definitively here the comparison of between-pair variance for (1) identicals and (2) fraternals, both raised in the usual family situation. By variance one means here that derived from the standard deviation of members of twin pairs from the "family mean" of the two of them—the values for the parents do not enter. Incidentally if the student wonders why we operate in a family only with the children he will see later that parent-child comparisons are confounded by the environment which created the parent personality not being the same as that which affects the children. If we want to speak of the effect of a given shared family environment, then it is the similarities and dissimilarities of the children that must be measured.

In calculation one compares either the intraclass coefficient, or the ratio of the obtained within- and between-pair variances, which is essentially the same thing. If members of a pair of identicals differ *only* by the environment and members of a pair of fraternals by both genetic variance within the family *and* environmental variance within the family, then it is possible by comparing the within-family (within pair) variances of these two types ultimately to compute a ratio of genetic to threptic variance (called N, for nature-nurture ratio) (or, alternatively, of genetic to total variance, called H, for heritability, as explained below). All of the four broader research approaches described here can be used either with precisely measured *continuous* variables, or with categorical observations instead. The latter, using such categories as "schizophrenic," "manic," "delinquent" in psychology, or "diabetic," or "hypertensive" in physical medicine, has actually been employed with greater frequency up to this point. The twin form of the convarkin approach, particularly, has been used with abnormal categorical syndrome data, as can be illustrated in recent work by Gottesman and Shields (1966), Kety and others (1968), Rosenthal (1970), and the earlier work of Kallman (1953) which brings out some of the methodological requirements.

Although within convarkin methods, the twin method has been far more used than the MAVA, because it is simpler in data gathering and because the MAVA method is relatively new, the method has unfortunate limitations. The principal limitations of the twin method are: (1) it tends to assume that the variance of within-family environmental influences between twins is the same as that characteristic of ordinary sib families generally; and (2), it successfully breaks down the variance *within* the family into components, but does not handle the genetic and environmental variances *between* ordinary families, that is, the variance among the family means. And for many purposes of social inference, it is the relative importance of heredity and environment *between* families (that is, across society) that is more important. To make this more clear let us note that by contrast the MAVA method posits *four* main sources of variance in cultures where the family exists as a parental pair and as an institution for raising children, as follows:

σ^2_{wg} = genetic variance within family from different combinations of parental chromosomal sources; represented as *wg* for "within genetic."

σ^2_{wt} = threptic variance *within* family from sources of *environmental difference* with respect to different children being treated differently within the family; *wt* stands for "within threptic."

σ^2_{bg} = genetic variance *between* the means of families of children from mean parental chromosomal sources; *bg* represents "between genetic."

σ^2_{bt} = threptic variance *between* family means related to differences of *environmental situation* of families; *bt* stands for "between threptic."

These have been called *abstract* variances, because they cannot be immediately, concretely measured as can, say, the actually measured variance from the differences of brothers. They have to be abstracted from the more direct measures. "Abstract" rather than "hypothetical" is used, because these are real, unquestionable sources of variance and only their magnitudes are matters for hypotheses. As stated below, the concrete variances are actually calculated with respect to *pairs* of children, either as difference between the members (within) or differences among the means of pairs (between). The within pair concrete variance for example is usually calculated from the difference of the two twins or sibs $(x_1 - x_2)$ rather than taking each from the mean. Over n families this variance is therefore $\Sigma^{2n} [(x_1 - x_2)/2]^2 /n$ (since n is the degrees of freedom in this case), which becomes $\Sigma^{2n} (x_1 - x_2)^2 /4n$.

The MAVA method thus begins by experimentally determining, for whatever source trait is the object of experiment, the concrete variances for each of a number of family *constellations* such as identical twins, fraternal twins, sibs reared together, sibs reared apart, and so on. As just stated this refers to families as defined by the *children*. And as an estimate for a larger number of children in a family can always be made from any *two*, we shall, for simplicity, suppose we always uniformly take a sample of two from each family of siblings. (If one wishes to take a sample larger than two, the calculation can be easily adapted to taking appropriate degrees of freedom for three, four, and so on.) An alternative hypothesis to accepting the above—which is that the within-family variance is independent of the number of children in the family—is to try the hypothesis that larger families may have a more varied internal environment psychologically. This could be tested, even if we uniformly take only two children as a sample, by doing so from families all of, say, size three and next from families all of, say, eight. Apart from this, the only difference in taking two, three, or more for testing is that the variance for the family is *statistically estimated* from different numbers, but it is the same variance.

Following the model in equation (1-5), in which some correlation of genetic and threptic components is admitted, we can, from first principles, write a series of equations in which the concrete, observed variance in each kind of family constellation, as estimated from two or more children, is broken down into abstract variances. The breakdown of concrete into abstract variances are as follows:

Within-Family Variances

For *identical twins raised together (ITT)*, we have:

Constellation 1:
$$\sigma^2_{ITT} = \sigma^2_{wt}$$

(1-7)

Here and later, the subscripts for the concrete experimental variances will repeat the title, for example, ITT represents identical twins raised together.

Constellation 2:

$$\sigma^2_{FTT} = \sigma^2_{wt} + \sigma^2_{wg} + 2r_{wt \cdot wg}\,\sigma_{wt}\,\sigma_{wg} \tag{1-8}$$

Here, with *fraternals raised together*, both within-family genetic and threptic variances enter, as well as a covariance term, because g and t may be correlated.

For *like-sex sibs raised together*, we have:

Constellation 3:

$$\sigma^2_{ST} = \sigma^2_{wt} + \sigma^2_{wg} + 2r_{wt \cdot wg}\,\sigma_{wt}\,\sigma_{wg} \tag{1-9}$$

Unless σ^2_{wt} is assumed different for sibs and twins, as it might be because the members of the former pair differ in age, this is identical to (1-8). *Some* difference of the σ^2_{wt} value from (1-8) might exist, however, even when sib scores are corrected for age differences. Indeed, such a difference has recently been demonstrated (Cattell, Klein, & Schuerger, 1980) requiring $wt \cdot t$ and $wt \cdot s$ to be centered.

Constellation 4:

$$\sigma^2_{SA} = \sigma^2_{wg} + \sigma^2_{wt} + \sigma^2_{bt} + 2r_{wg \cdot wt}\,\sigma_{wt}\,\sigma_{wg}$$
$$+ 2r_{wg \cdot bt}\,\sigma_{wg}\,\sigma_{bt} \tag{1-10}$$

This constellation consists of pairs of sibs in which each member of a pair is raised in a different family; therefore, *sibs apart, SA.*

These constellations will suffice to show the mode of analytic argument. We consider in each case whether genetic makeup and environment are the same in the two members of the pair or different. When different, we consider also the possibility of covariance terms, though experiment may show that they are zero.

We can go beyond these four equations to Constellation 5, unrelated pairs reared together; 6, half-sibs reared together; 7, half-sibs reared apart; and 8, the general population (genetically unrelated persons reared apart, that is, as random pairs) (see Cattell, 1960, and Cattell, Klein, & Schuerger, 1979, for detailed statements), as in Table 1-1.

Between-Family Variances

After examining the within-family concrete variances the analytical possibilities are continued by a series of between-family variances. By between families we mean the variance calculated among the *means* of the scores of members in each family—in this case kept to two for each family. In n such pairs the degrees of freedom will be $(n - 1)$. Repeating the order for within-family variance, we return to the constellation of identical twins raised together.

Constellation 1:
$$\sigma^2_{BITTF} = 2\sigma^2_{wg} + \sigma^2_{bt} + 2\sigma^2_{bg} + 2\sigma^2_{bt}$$
$$+ 2\sqrt{2} \cdot r_{wg \cdot wt}\, \sigma_{wg}\, \sigma_{wt} + 4r_{bg \cdot bt}\, \sigma_{bg}\, \sigma_{bt} \quad (1\text{-}11)$$

BITTF stands for between identical-twins-raised-together families.

Constellation 7:
$$\sigma^2_{BHSA} = \sigma^2_{wg} + \sigma^2_{wt} + \tfrac{1}{2}\sigma^2_{bg} + \sigma^2_{bt}$$
$$+ 2r_{wg \cdot wt}\, \sigma_{wg}\, \sigma_{wt} + 2r_{bg \cdot bt}\, \sigma_{bg}\, \sigma_{bt} \quad (1\text{-}12)$$

BHSA stands for between half-sibs-raised-apart families.

The above formulas are set out to show the principle of resolving the observable concrete variances, which are symbolized on the left, with capital letter subscripts, into the abstract variances on the right. The full array of possible equations, covering those eight constellations that research might find it practical to collect, consists of 16, as set out systematically in Cattell (1960). An illustration subset is given in Table 1-1. Algebraically one should note that we do not have as many as 16 independent equations, however, for the within- and between-family variances add to the same total population variance in certain cases. Not every sum of within and between variances adds to the empirically obtainable total population variance because the general population is not composed of, for example, identical or fraternal twins (only about 1 in 70 is a twin). If it were the total population variance would be significantly different from that we now get by taking people in the street at random.

The object of collecting these constellations, aimed to provide as many independent equations as possible, is, of course, to obtain enough simultaneous equations to solve for the various unknown abstract variances and the unknown correlations among the various deviations. For reasons of practical difficulty we need not enter into here, no investigator has yet obtained large enough samples on enough constellations to solve without approximations for all of these unknowns. And, although the psychological model we discuss here is guided by such experimental findings, we need not enter on further statistical technicalities. More important is the psychological and genetic reasoning by which the equations are put together. A typical set of analytical equations showing how the concrete variances are broken down into abstract variances is given in Table 1-1.

TABLE 1-1. A Set of Eleven MAVA Equations for Six Constellations, Showing How the Model Analyzes Concrete into Abstract Variances

$$\sigma_{ITT} = \sigma^2_{we'}\,\sigma^2_{we''}$$

$$\sigma_{FTT} = \sigma^2_{wh} + \sigma^2_{we'} + 2r_{wh\cdot we}\,\sigma_{wh}\,\sigma_{we'}$$

$$\sigma_{ST} = \sigma^2_{wh} + \sigma^2_{we} + 2r_{wh\cdot we}\,\sigma_{wh}\,\sigma_{we}$$

$$\sigma_{SA} = \sigma^2_{wh} + \sigma^2_{we} + \sigma^2_{be} + 2r_{wh\cdot we}\,\sigma_{wh}\,\sigma_{we}$$

$$\sigma_{UT} = \sigma^2_{wh} + \sigma^2_{we} + \sigma^2_{bh} + 2r_{wh\cdot we}\,\sigma_{wh}\,\sigma_{we} + 2r'_{we\cdot bh}\,\sigma_{we}\,\sigma_{bh}$$

$$\sigma_{UA} = \sigma^2_{wh} + \sigma^2_{we} + \sigma^2_{bh} + \sigma^2_{be} + 2r_{wh\cdot we}\,\sigma_{wh}\,\sigma_{we} + 2r_{bh\cdot be}\,\sigma_{bh}\,\sigma_{be}$$

$$\sigma_{BITTF} = 2\sigma^2_{wh} + \sigma^2_{we''} + 2\sigma^2_{bh} + 2\sigma^2_{be} + 2\sqrt{2}\,r_{wh\cdot we}\,\sigma_{wh}\,\sigma_{we''} + 4r_{bh\cdot be}\,\sigma_{bh}\,\sigma_{be}$$

$$\sigma_{BFTTF} = 2\sigma^2_{wh} + \sigma^2_{we'} + 2\sigma^2_{bh} + 2\sigma^2_{be} + 2\sqrt{2}\,r_{wh\cdot we}\,\sigma_{wh}\,\sigma_{we'} + 4r_{bh\cdot be}\,\sigma_{bh}\,\sigma_{be}$$

$$\sigma_{BNF} = \sigma^2_{wh} + \sigma^2_{we} + 2\sigma^2_{bh} + 2\sigma^2_{be} + 2r_{wh\cdot we}\,\sigma_{wh}\,\sigma_{we} + 4r_{bh\cdot be}\,\sigma_{bh}\,\sigma_{be}$$

$$\sigma_{BBF} = \sigma^2_{wh} + \sigma^2_{we} + 2\sigma^2_{bh} + \sigma^2_{be} + 2r_{wh\cdot we}\,\sigma_{wh}\,\sigma_{we} + 2\sqrt{2}\,r'_{we\cdot bh}\,\sigma_{we}\,\sigma_{bh} + \sqrt{2}\,r''_{bh\cdot be}\,\sigma_{bh}\,\sigma_{be}$$

$$\sigma_{BSF} = \sigma^2_{wh} + \sigma^2_{we} + \sigma^2_{bh} + 2\sigma^2_{be} + 2r_{wh\cdot we}\,\sigma_{wh}\,\sigma_{we} + 2r'_{we\cdot bh}\,\sigma_{we}\,\sigma_{bh} + 2\sqrt{2}\,r''_{bh\cdot be}\,\sigma_{bh}\,\sigma_{be}$$

Note 1. That *h* and *e* are used instead of *g* and *t* here; and the within family threptic variance for twins is written *we''* instead of *lot-t.*

Within-Family Concrete Variances

σ^2_{ITT} = identical twins raised tcgether

σ^2_{FTT} = fraternal twins raised together

σ^2_{SA} = sibs raised apart

σ^2_{ST} = sibs raised together

σ^2_{UT} = unrelated raised together

σ^2_{UA} = unrelated raised apart (pairs at random in general population

Between-Family Concrete Variances

σ^2_{BITTF} = **between identical twins raised together families** (means of 2 twins)

σ^2_{BFTTF} = **between fraternal twins raised together families** (means of 2 twins)

σ^2_{BNF} = between natural families (sibs together)

σ^2_{BBF} = between biological families (sibs raised apart)

σ^2_{BSF} = between social families (unrelated raised together)

Note 2. σ^2_{UA} has dependencies, or near dependencies, with other equations, notably σ^2_{ST} and σ^2_{BNF}, these being the within- and between-variances which add to the general population (if we assume the population is substantially made up of natural families).

Note 3. These equations do not assume, as in the twin method, that the within-family environmental difference is the same for identical twins, fraternal twins (same sex), and sibs (same sex). There is evidence that it is of increasing size in that order. Hence the different symbols *we'*, *we'*, and *we*.

To illustrate the thinking in the above equations a little more, let us consider some equations in more detail, beginning with fraternal twins (or ordinary sibs) raised together, as in constellation 2, equation (1-8) above. Between two members of the same family, obviously, no *between*-family difference, either genetic (σ_{bg}^2) or threptic (σ_{bt}^2) can enter. They differ only because of σ_{wg}^2 and σ_{wt}^2—the genetic difference of sibs (or fraternal twins) through different segregations of the parental genes, and the differences of environment that can be encountered in the family. To these must be added the covariance term shown in (1-8), because the possibility must be kept open that the genetic and threptic deviations from the mean may prove to be correlated. Thus equation (1-8) above says the obtained variance is the sum of only these three terms.

In constellation 4, the sibs raised apart have the usual genetic segregation variance existing between two sibs from the same biological family, and are in adopting families in which they occupy different environmental positions from the other members. Their difference of environment is, therefore, twofold: (1) the usual difference from positions within a family, namely, σ_{wt}^2, and (2) the social-familial atmosphere difference from the fact that they are in two different families, which thus involves σ_{bt}^2. However, there is no between-family genetic difference, σ_{bg}^2, as they come from the same biological family. Thus in equation (1-10) there are three variance terms. But what about covariance? The same covariance of scores with respect to *wg* and *wt* deviations can arise as in equations (1-8) and (1-9), for within *any* family a genetically different individual may come to be treated differently. Similarly, there can be a correlation of individual genetic status and between-family social status if adopting agencies, for example, tend to place orphaned children from higher-intelligence parents in adopting homes of high educational level. Thus $r_{wg \cdot bt}$ would not be zero, and a term is entered for it in equation (1-10).

Incidentally, a case such as this calls our attention to the possible subtleties of genetic-threptic correlations. In analysis of variance we are accustomed to the idea that there can be no correlation between an individual's deviation from his group mean and the deviation of the mean of his group (family here) from the grand mean. Here we are not restricted by all ANOVA assumptions, for families, in the first place, are not random groupings from the total population. And, as regards the abstract variance components, it *is* possible that such within-between correlations as $r_{wt \cdot bt}$, $r_{wg \cdot bt}$, will be significant. Such a psychologically meaningful $r_{wg \cdot bt}$ correlation has just been discussed (in equation 1-10), and others will be mooted in the discussion of correlations in the next section.

The reader penetrating deeper into this field will find it a useful exercise to try to account individually for the terms in the full list of equations such as are given in Table 1-1 (Cattell, 1960; Jinks & Fulker, 1970). He will then realize that over and above the questions concerning correlation, there are issues about the variances themselves. For example, there are arguments for using three different σ_{wt}^2 terms—namely, for identical twins, for fraternal twins, and for sibs—as their degrees of environmental difference could be systematically different. Additionally, the situations might be different for same- and opposite-sex sibs if our subjects are of different sex. There are also psychological and genetic arguments for different σ_{wt}'s and σ_{wg}'s when half sibs share the same father, that is, live with the father but not the mothers, and when they share the same mother; and so on.

At this point we realize that though the MAVA method has far greater resolving power than the twin method—notably on the between-family variances and their correlations—it yet can scarcely hope to provide—in view of practical costs—enough equations to solve for *all* the particularized, hypothetically different abstract variances and correlations to which we would like to give a chance of solution. Jinks and Fulker (1970), in pointing out the limitations of the twin method compared to what they call the "biometric method" (the latter is a special case of the MAVA method), have also recognized this cost problem of the large number of cases needed, and Eaves (1969) has discussed the practical sampling conditions needed for optimum efficiency. However, in terms of method and meaning, it suffices if we grasp that *the essence of the MAVA design is that it offers the possibility of solving for some four or more genothreptic unknowns, by four or more equations*, for each of which a concrete variance value can be experimentally obtained. It can be said without further ado that the most practicable design of MAVA experiment—called the *limited objectives* design—is to ask for solutions to six unknowns only. These are four variances—σ_{wg}^2, σ_{wt}^2, σ_{bg}^2, and σ_{bt}^2 — in which we make no distinction of several σ_{wt}^2's, the possibility mooted, for theoretical interest, above; and two covariances—namely, those in the correlations $r_{wg \cdot wt}$ and $r_{bg \cdot bt}$. Such a basic "six-unknown" solution is possible from various groups of six equations, the most practicable being those based on collecting data for constellations 1, 3, 4, 5, 6, and 7 (identical twins, fraternal twins, sibs together, sibs apart, unrelateds raised together, and general population [random pairs]). Solutions along these lines for various personality factors as measured by questionnaires and by objective tests are given by Cattell, Blewett, and Beloff (1955), Cattell, Stice, and Kristy (1957), and Cattell, Klein, and Schuerger (1980). The last goes to seven unknowns because of the mounting evidence that within-family environment is more varied for sibs than for twins.

1-4. Possible and Probable Varieties of Correlation and Interaction between Heredity and Environment

From the above and from the discussion below on standard errors of estimates, it becomes evident that no research short of a million-dollar endowment is likely to gather sufficient data on necessary constellations, for example, identical twins reared apart, half-sibs reared apart, to solve for a really refined and comprehensively open-minded assumption regarding all possible existent unknowns. Especially, we are likely to lack for some time knowledge of the correlations of the various influences. Although we cannot yet hope to get enough, and sufficiently large, constellation samples to solve for them, several theoretically important points can be brought out in discussing the nature of these correlations. The arithmetic of combinations tells us that if there are four components, then six correlations are possible among them (12, if we admit three varieties of within-pair threptic variance, as shown by the broken lines in Figure 1-1).

By the ordinary rules for analysis of variance, when deviations of individuals from the mean of their group are necessarily uncorrelated with the deviations of their groups from the group mean, the correlations in brackets in Figure 1-1 would have to be zero. Actually, even with our abstract variances, linear correlations of this kind are not possible, but, as discussed above, *curvilinear* correlations are, and, moreover, we can conceive of real-life conditions that would cause them.

Four instances of psychogenetically meaningful nonchance scatterplots concerning correlation of within-family and between-family deviations such as one would not normally encounter in ANOVA are shown in Figure 1-2. First, as regards environmental influences, we can imagine that in families on a higher anxiety level the children would be more dispersed in anxiety (by the modulator action rule) than in those on a low level, as shown in (*a*). Another instance is the probability that parents higher in educational level would give more diverse educational endowments to different members of their family, appreciating more sensitively their different capabilities. The reverse type of relationship would be illustrated in families bringing high, and more explicit, standards of discipline to bear. There we would expect the higher family level to go with less dispersion of lev-

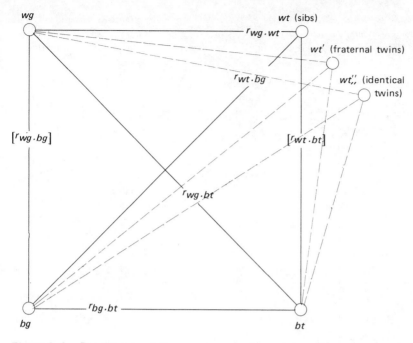

Figure 1-1. Possible correlations among genetic and threptic components.

el among the children, as in (*b*). The same pattern might happen if families with more affection are also careful to bestow it more evenly.

In the genetic field alone some similar types of curvilinearity possibly exist. For example, if, as Higgins, Reed, and Reed (1962) suggest, marriages are less assortive as to intelligence at lower levels of intelligence, the within-family genetic variance, arising from the ordinary genetic segregation of the parental genes for intelligence, would be less. Or, if assortiveness of mating in some trait were greater at middle levels, we might have a "double eta" relation, as in Figure 1-2(*d*).

Regarding the four more basic correlations discussed earlier, which are not so exceptional and would probably be linear, no psychologist should have any difficulty in thinking of influences that would produce significant correlations of the type $r_{wg \cdot wt}$ and $r_{bg \cdot bt}$, that is, within-family deviations of individuals *jointly* on genetic and threptic components, and between-family means also jointly on genetic and threptic components. A familiar instance is higher family intelligence of children genetically and more educated environment. Such correlations could arise from (1) a genetic difference causing, by some chain of connections, an environmental difference such as native intelligence leading to better environment; (2) an environmen-

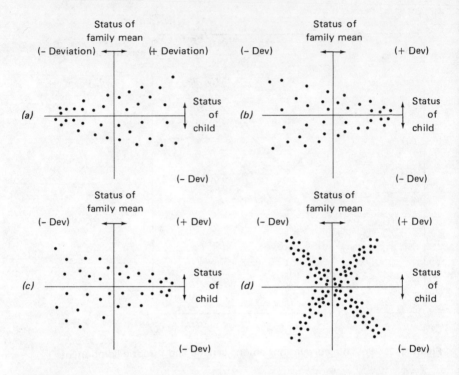

Figure 1–2. Forms of significant curvilinear correlation of genetic and threptic components.

Some major examples of forms of association of within- and between-family deviations (and therefore variances) which do not create correlations. Scattergrams illustrate hypothetical relations produced in variances. *(a)* and *(b)* in environmental influences; *(c)* and *(d)* in hereditary influences.

tal difference bringing about a genetic association, for example, an urban environment selecting individuals high on surgency, F; and (3) some influence that is not exclusively one or the other bringing about a change in both. Though brief, the following section will amplify explanation of the above possibilities.

1. Genetic Causation of Significant Associations of Environmental and Genetic Determiners

a. WITHIN-FAMILY

i. *Associations by migration.* Genetic endowment causes an individual to move into a certain kind of environment, as when a schizothyme temperament (factor $A-$) causes a person to take up such occupations as forestry or research physics. Experience of social situations is then reduced, so that schizothyme temperament and schizothyme-producing environment get correlated. There are migratory associations where the distinction of movement due to qualities in the individual and movement due to action by society becomes subtle. Does the bright school child go to the university or the university select bright students from high school? The effect may often be the same but the question of which takes the initiative may be important in determining correlations and limits.

ii. *Associations by shaping environment.* The genetic endowment results in environmental correlation in this case because it changes environment (as birds get extensive experience in a nest environment denied to, say, mammals). Countless examples of this nature can be cited in human life. A fairly subtle instance is the finding by Cattell, Blewett, and Beloff (1955) of an apparent tendency for a high-I-factor (tender-minded) person to create an environment that cherishes aesthetic development ($r_{we \cdot wh}$ = +0.10 to +0.50).

iii. *Associations through genetic factors producing particular responses from the environment.* From the social and the physical environment, a genetic endowment may itself provoke characteristic environmental treatment. The example found by Cattell, Blewett, and Beloff (1955) of negative $r_{we \cdot wh}$ for dominance suggest that society presents a more dominance-reducing environment to high- than low-dominance individuals. Shakespeare called this "trash for overtopping," referring to hounds, and boys call it "cutting down to size." In this general mode we must include the tendency of other people than the subject to select associates according to preferred characteristics.

b. BETWEEN-FAMILY

All three of the above operate here also, and an example combining them is the upward social mobility of families endowed with high intelligence. One might assume that correlations from (iii) would be smaller here than within families, because society does not know each family as well as a family knows its members. Conversely, (i) and (ii) should be larger, because there might be less error in the mean performance of a group than in the fate of a single individual.

iv. *Associations by differential survival.* If a certain genetic endowment favors survival, by differences in birth rate or in death rate, within a certain social environment, then $r_{bh \cdot be}$ correlations will ensue, by reductions of numbers in certain quadrants of the scatter plot. For example, because there is evidence that intelligent people survive longer, we would expect a correlation in an age-scattered adult population between genetic components of intelligence and amount of life experience.

2.   Environmental Causation of Significant Associations
of Genetic and Environmental Determiners

a.   WITHIN-FAMILY

In general, within-family correlations springing from an environmental source should be minor, as a child necessarily is born with his genetic endowment fixed, before within-family environmental differences can begin to operate. However, differential death rates might show environmental relations; for example, an overprotective attitude toward a child might favor his survival if he is of weak constitution. Such selection would increase the conjunction of overprotection with defective constitution.

b.   BETWEEN-FAMILY

All four mechanisms already listed under (1), genetic causation, can act here, but of course in the reverse direction, making environment the cause. Next, environment could act by natural selection. An environment stimulating migration could produce correlations, for example, the association of lower intelligence (assuming this means less successful farming) with migration to a city in times of agricultural distress. Environment can shape connections with heredity through sexual selection, say, if persons in a more neurosis-producing environment avoid neurosis-prone mates. It can act by birth-rate selection effects, as when educated families have fewer children. And it can produce differential survival, as in (1) (b) (iv). We would expect correlations from (2) to be trivial, as compared with those in (1) or (3).

3.   Common Causes Operating
on Both Heredity and Environment

a.   WITHIN-FAMILY

Only in the exceptional instance of something producing mutation (for example, radiation) simultaneously affecting heredity and environment could there be anything but a general zero correlation here. Such an uncommon instance would be Down's syndrome, occurring more in later-born children, who would also experience an environmental difference from earlier-born sibs because the parents are older.

b. BETWEEN-FAMILY

Many influences can simultaneously change environment and select for heredity between families. In a more refined analysis we could make claims for all four mechanisms noted in (1) (a). There can be deliberate selection by society, as when intelligent children are sent to college or delinquents to jail. Diseases may select simultaneously for both environment and heredity, as malaria does for debility and sickle-cell anemia and tuberculosis does for lower social status and leptosomatic-schizothyme constitution (Cattell, 1950c). Such various influences as social placement agencies or eugenic ideals may produce similar correlations; and, as Fisher pointed out (1930), dysgenic, competitive family restriction attitudes may become correlated with higher intelligence and other genetic qualities.

The above systematic analysis and classification of the possible varieties of genothreptic correlation may seem to the student somewhat unduly exhaustive—and exhausting! But psychologically and sociologically these are important for a true understanding of the makeup of the individual and the structure of society. They are essential also to understanding the interaction of maturation and learning in development.

A relation of particularly wide relevance is the social press that in Chapter 6 is called the *law of coercion to the biosocial mean.* We may note here that cultural pressures attempt to raise some personality qualities, such as honesty and intelligence (crystallized intelligence at least) toward the highest the individual can reach, in what could be called a *law of coercion to the cultural ideal.* (A term like coercion is necessary, for it is not only the school, but neighborhood pressures, and other cultural forces, that offer pressure.) In other traits, however, the net effect of many coercive influences—envy, convenience of uniformity, a desire to help the underdog—pressures individuals toward an approved *central or "average" norm,* which is defined both culturally and biologically. For example, people are educated not to be too shy or too forward, too interested in or too indifferent to the opposite sex, and so on. There are three or four independent sources of evidence for this pressure toward the mean, but we are concerned here with evidence offered by genothreptics. If a person is born, say, with excessive dominance of disposition, pressure is exerted by associates to keep him in his place, or, if unduly diffident, to "bring him out." In traits of the type where, by hypothesis, this occurs, we should find in MAVA analyses a *negative* correlation of genetic and threptic components.

Although the initial solutions for correlations made possible by the two or three pioneer uses of the MAVA method (Cattell, Blewett, & Beloff, 1955; Cattell, Kristy, & Stice, 1957; Cattell, Klein, & Schuerger, 1980) were on samples too small (500 to 1200 pairs) to define values with desirable certainty, the algebraic *signs* of the correlations that appeared were found to fit expectations as here discussed from psychological theory. For example, the $r_{wg \cdot wt}$ correlations for the dominance factor, E, are negative, suggesting a *within-family* tendency to suppress the dominant and encourage the assertiveness of the unduly submissive. And, there are signs that the *between-family* correlations of genetic and threptic components for dominance may be positive, supporting the existence especially of action of the type (1) (b) (ii) above. That is to say the assertive, achieving family may tend to move into a status position encouraging dominance ("Nothing succeeds like success"). Several significant r's of this type were found, though most genothreptic r's are negative.

Harder to understand are correlations of the "cross" kind, instanced in $r_{wt \cdot bg}$ and $r_{wg \cdot bt}$ in Figure 1-1. In the former instance an individual's exposure to some environmental influence within family is assumed to be associated with the genetic level of his family among families. A moment's reflection on the ANOVA discussion above will show that any such linear relation is logically impossible in ordinary families. But in adoptive families the child from a genetically intelligent family entering an average family is likely to get some special treatment because he will tend also to be above average for the host family. And, as regards $r_{wg \cdot bt}$, it is possible to be non-zero again, in adoptive or foster families, if placement agencies show any disposition to place a biologically more intelligent child, as regards his position in his old family, in a family of better intellectual standards than average.

In considering correlations some selection effects (differences of range) need to be recognized, if treatment of the problem is to be refined. These are examined elsewhere (Cattell, 1960). The type of issue arising is illustrated by asking whether $r_{wg \cdot wt}$ in adoptive families (unrelated reared together) can be considered to have the same value as in ordinary families, where the genetic range is smaller, or whether it might be expected to be *corrected* for the wider range of genetic components $(\sigma_{wg}^2 + \sigma_{bg}^2)$ in the adopting family whose members come from different families.

Finally, in this complex field of genothreptic relations we must be clear about the conceptually surprising assertion sometimes made that the level of environmental influence depends on the genetic qualities of the individual perceiving it and living in it. For example, it is said sometimes that an identical physicosocial environment is more intelligence-stimulating to the intelligent than an unintelligent child. Certainly, the soft thud of a falling apple in an orchard at Woolsthorpe meant something very different to the local farmer than to Isaac Newton. But this argument has confused two concepts— the ecometric and the psychometric. The distinction made in Volume 1, Chapter 6, between the ecometric and the psychometric environment, here comes to our help, for it reminds us that when we are talking about environment as an outer cause rather than an inner effect we must maintain a clear difference of concept and measurement. It is conceivable that the genetic and the threptic components will at times correlate when the genic and the environmental do not. If we adopt the more complex model in equation (1-2), admitting interaction, then the reasonable hypothesis can be tested that the same level of environment actually contributes more *to a trait* when the genetic components stand at a higher than a lower level. In dividing the interaction term of g and t equally between g and t (to get just two sources, as suggested above), then it will be found that the same environment is credited with more influence when the genetic component is larger. But when we recognize in this sense that the same, ordinary environment is "richer" for a natively intelligent than an unintelligent child, we are saying that the *threptic* component is made larger, but the *environment* is the same. In summary, our equation (1-2) explicitly recognizes that the environmental effect on the growth of a trait is sometimes greater when the genetic endowment is greater. Although the interaction model presents difficulties for research, there is little doubt that we shall have to adopt and explore it in some cases. The rise of the learned crystallized intelligence factor, g_c, from the largely genetic fluid intelligence, g_f, is a case of such interaction, and at present we hypothesize that a *product* relation of fluid intelligence and time spent in school seems called for (Cattell, 1971). So compelling is certain evidence for interaction—in such examples as the above and in imprinting—that the MAVA method needs to be extended to embrace it, and a tentative development to do so is given elsewhere (Cattell, 1973).

1-5. Parent-Child and Other Family Relations to Be Evaluated

As suggested earlier the student first meeting the nature-nurture methods and concepts often wonders why we do not, in the convarkin approaches, go to the obvious source of evidence presented by correlation of parents and children. The phrase "like parent like child" indeed expressed the popular idea that such resemblance is the main evidence of genetic action, although the more sophisticated student realizes that (1) such resemblance could be partly an effect of environment, and (2) heredity is responsible for some parent-child *differences* as well as similarities. The latter means that perfect genetic resemblance of parents and children is not to be expected from genetic laws. Instead, children are genetically different from either parent and from each other because of the segregational juggling of the genes of the two parents in different combinations for each child. Indeed, even the "mid-child" (average of all children) should not—because of genetic dominance and epistatic effects—be a precise replica of the "mid-parent." However, the main reason for caution in using parent-child correlations in investigating inheritance lies in the difficulty of incorporating in MAVA a term for the shared family environment. Such a term inserted in the equations above would be different for the two parents, whose backgrounds are different, and different from that family atmosphere that is shared by the children. Consequently we should introduce more new terms than we have equations to solve for, if we tried to use in the same MAVA set the concrete variances of parent-child differences. However, it is possible to get some extra leverage in equation solution from the parent-child relation from the geneticist's knowledge about the similarity of the *genetic* variance of parent-child and that of child-child. The fact is that when mating within the population is random the correlation (Jensen, 1978) of a parent and a child must (with simple, non-dominant genetic action) come out, genetically, to be the same as that between child and child, namely, +0.5. And if, more realistically, we accept that marriage is assortive, with a positive correlation of r_m between the genetic makeup of the parents, then the child-child correlation, $r_{cc \cdot g}$, becomes:

$$r_{cc \cdot g} = \frac{1 + r_m}{2} \qquad (1\text{-}13a)$$

as also does the genetic correlation of parent and child, $r_{pc \cdot g}$.

These reflections on the nature of the family environment per se focus on the fact that we are using the socio-biological family as the "cell" in the above analysis. One might ask "Why not use instead the school, or social class, or occupational group as the unit organism for comparing genetic with environmental variance?" The answer is, of course, that the family is a natural biological unit and still a social unit, and though one can conceive with and between genic and threptic components with respect to human variation in some trait expressed, say, in social classes, the investigation is impracticable for lack of a large number of such units or means to measure them. Finding the fraction of the observed variances within and between, say, church congregations or social classes, that result from environment or heredity would certainly be valuable for social psychology. But it is at once apparent that we can give no simple definition of what we expect the abstract genetic variance to be in such groups and therefore what the remaining, environmental variance should be.

The genetic story of parents and children is well known to geneticists, but what happens in social classes is a branch of population genetics that is still obscure. Moreover, to solve by simultaneous equations, we must be able to analyze the observed variances into terms that repeat themselves in several equations. This is not possible for the genetic parts of the large social groups just considered. More fodder for MAVA analysis nevertheless exists in such new family constellations as parent-child, cousin-cousin, uncle-nephew, and other such "families" (including even the offspring of incestuous father-daughter relations). For, by genetic principles, we can express the within and between genetic variances in these cases in terms of the basic σ^2_{wg} and σ^2_{bg} of the normal family in the familiar MAVA equations, thus getting new-constellation concrete variances without multiplying unknown abstract variances. The *environmental* similarity shared by, say, uncle and nephew, is another matter, but some of the family environments, by approximation, might be considered the same as in other MAVA constellations.

A very thorough treatment of the relations to be expected on scores among various relatives from genetic mechanisms alone will be found in Burt and Howard (1956), Jinks and Fulker (1970), and Mather and Jinks (1975). For example, with random mating, the genetic correlations of one parent with one child is .50, which, as shown in equation (1-13) above, is the same as that to be expected between two sibs. Certain conditions however must hold for this to be so and we cannot therefore extend the use of the σ^2_{wg} and σ^2_{bg} of the main MAVA immediately in further MAVA equations for parent-child values. (As implied above, two simplifications are made in saying $\sigma^2_{bg} = \sigma^2_{wg}$: (1) no dominance or sex linkage is recognized, and (2) no assortiveness of mating of parents is assumed.) If dominance is admitted, then Burt and Howard calculate the r for sibs is .53 and .55 for parent-child genetic ($r_{pc \cdot g}$) correlations; and if assortiveness (positive resemblance of parents) were to reach perfection, parent-child correlation would reach .67. The appropriate estimate of the effect of some degree of assortiveness is:

$$\sigma^2_{bg} = \sigma^2_{wg}\left(\frac{1 + r_m}{1 - r_m}\right)$$

$$(1\text{-}13b)$$

where r_m is the genotypic correlation. As Cattell and Nesselroade (1967) and Jinks and Fulker (1970) have suggested a formula can be used for deriving from this latter an estimate of the actual genetic coefficient of spouse similarity.

By relating the genetic resemblance in the less-common constellations to that in our standard family, for example, by knowing that the genetic $r = .25$ for nephew-uncle and $r = .125$ for first cousins, these constellations could be empirically used to extend the MAVA equations (without disabling their usefulness through any defect of adding as many new unknowns as equations). This assumes that we work out some solution to the problem mentioned above of estimating the relative environmental resemblance in the lives of cousins, nephews, parents, and children in some ratio relation to that of sibs. Admittedly, to give meaning to such environmental resemblances—especially in terms of our familiar σ_{bt}^2 and σ_{wt}^2—is at present rather impractical, though we can foresee a possible sociological calculus of environmental elements in common in such special family constellations relative to those shared in the core family. Of course, if a researcher has social-work resources to seek far enough he or she can collect instances where, say, uncle and nephew are of much the same age and happen to be brought up in the same family. In a set of such families fitting this valuable new constellation, and within- and between-family environmental terms—σ_{wt}^2 and σ_{bt}^2—would be the same as in the rest of the equations and the genetic terms would be simple known fractions of the regular genetic terms.

Among all the constellations it is, naturally, the ordinary parent-sib interrelation that is of greatest interest to the clinician and, as "the family," to the sociologist. Both for the present genetic analysis and for other psychological reasons it would be desirable to find some way of quantifying the typical shared environmental variance. (The shared genetics of parent and child is, in the simple case, σ_{wg}^2.) The problem is that in seeking the effect of environment on parent-child trait resemblance the formative effects for the child are in the present family and those for the parent in a family a generation back. One way to conceive this is to assume the typical within-family variance to be the same in both families and the parent-child differences variance therefore twice the ordinary within-family differences. Another is to consider a between-family environmental difference term entering into their difference, although if family tradition is carried on the term would not be as big as the usual between-family variance. So recondite a problem can be discussed but not solved, with full statement of assumptions, in the present space. However, if we write the shared formative within-family effect on variance with a double prime, as $\sigma_{wt''}^2$, to indicate difference from the usual

σ_{wt}^2 expression, and write the one-parent-one-child concrete variance as σ_{pc}^2, we can summarize the relation by:

$$\sigma_{PC}^2 = \sigma_{wg}^2 + \sigma_{wt''}^2 + 2r'_{wt''wg}\,\sigma_{wg}\,\sigma_{wt''} \tag{1-14}$$

$$\sigma_{BPCF}^2 = \sigma_{wg}^2 + \sigma_{wt''}^2 + 2\sigma_{bg}^2 + \sigma_{bt''}^2$$
$$+ 2r'_{wg\cdot wt''}\,\sigma_{wg}\,\sigma_{wt''} + 4r'_{bg\cdot bt''}\,\sigma_{bg}\,\sigma_{bt''} \tag{1-15}$$

Here *PC* stands for the concrete parent-child variance and *BPCF* for the variance between parent-child means (across families). For, as in every other constellation, two equations are derivable—within and between families—but as they are in general not independent, both cannot be used, and unless we further assume that $r'_{gt''} = r_{gt}$, we cannot get a solution for $\sigma_{wt''}^2$.

1-6. A Closer Look at the Psychological Genothreptic Interactions and the Psychometric Status of the Components

The concepts concerning four basic genothreptic components, and of their interactions and correlations, have been developed above in the context of research operations and an exact model. It remains to polish up some psychometric qualifications, on the one hand, and further meaning of the psychological and genetic mechanisms, on the other. In this section the psychological and metric issues are discussed.

The value σ_{wt}^2 has been referred to as within-family threptic variance. This is one of several points where distinguishing between threptic and environmental (ecometric, to be precise) variance avoids misconceptions. For although this value is the environmentally determined (threptic) behavioral variance among sibs *within* a family, it would be a mistake to assume that the ecometric variance from which it springs is that occurring *only* within the family. That is to say, the part of the total within-family variance that does *not* result from the genetic segregation effects on the genetic endowment from parents does not arise from environmental differences children encounter purely within the family environment. One sib in the family may go to this school, another to that; one will move in a younger peer group circle, and another in an older one. Already, in fact, the within-family threptic variance is partaking of effects of some between-family general environmental differences, selectively encountered by the children.

When we look at the between-family threptic component, there is similarly some duality of origin. The features of the environment more obviously causing the differences and similarities in the threptic component between families are those the sociologist sees as existing at the time, such as income, class, neighborhood, religious affiliation. Additionally, there is something we can perhaps designate "family atmosphere," created both by what the parents bring from the past history of their families and by what the personalities of the children produce. The first of these additions we will dismiss relatively briefly as a fusion of the family value traditions in which the two parents were brought up. It includes the contributions from the personality profiles of the parents, and the interactions of these profiles, in conflict and in harmony.

The second component in the joint family atmosphere, the mutual contributions of the children as peers, is probably the most substantial part of the family environment of a child. The personalities of the other children contribute both to the within- and the between-family environment parts of the variance. Whether a child is brought up, for example, with good-natured sibs ($A+$ on affectia) or aloof and morose ($A-$) companions is surely likely to make a decided difference in the environmental ecometric influence, and therefore on the threptic component. The heredity of one child is thus part of the environment of the others—which must call for still further analysis of initially obtained MAVA values.

Thus we might expect that greater similarity of heredity in sibs will conduce to their environment within the family being more similar. Certainly it will be more similar than if they were out in the wide world and more similar in assortive than random mating. Thus genetics will account, at one remove, for some of the between-family and within-family *environmental* variance features.

Initial genetic differences also may operate to increase within-family environmental variance. For example, if one child is naturally talkative, another may become more silent; or if one is submissive, the other may become more dominant. This we might call the "Brazil nut effect," inasmuch as two adjacent nuts within the constraining outer casing usually show a bump on one corresponding to a depression on the other ("A pessimist is someone who has lived with an optimist"). It is true, however, that virtually all empirical studies of personalities of sibs and parents show *positive* "concrete" correlations of traits of any pair in the same family. But this is probably because the heredity component predominates. (In the case of the parents, where positive husband-wife correlations are usual [Barton & Cattell, 1973; Cattell & Nesselroade, 1967] it has a different source in mutual selection for compatibility.) No analysis seems yet to have been made comparing a more assortive mating with a less assortive set of families to see if larger within-family genetic variance goes with larger σ^2_{wt}. (Parenthetically we agree here with the practice of several behavior geneticists in shortening "assortative" to "assortive" in its meaning for mating.)

However, the present writer has recently obtained results on several traits in which the final, concrete, within-family variance for unrelated children reared together (adoptive families) exceeds that between pairs in the general population taken at random. That is, it actually exceeds the general population variance. This suggests that the larger within-family genetic variance $\sigma^2_{wg} + \sigma^2_{bg}$, in this constellation) has blown up the within-family environmental variance in the covariance form, because of a large r_{tg}. Finally, one must alert the reader to the fact that despite the term "within-family threptic variance" for σ^2_{wt} the differences of twins and still more of sibs, from this source, will arise partly from differences outside the family, for example, from the sibs going to different schools, mixing with different peer groups, and so on.

All that we can be sure of at this point is that there are complex effects additional to the main ones considered in our equations above. Psychoanalysts, for example, have argued that the force of the human need for a distinct identity is so great that identical twins raised together will attempt to magnify whatever threptic differences begin to be produced between them. If true, the differences between them in the environmentally produced component—and this is their only difference—should be greater than in the environmental component distinguishing two people taken at random and brought up together. Actually, as results for our adoptive cases show, there is no support in the data for this psychoanalytic conjecture, and, indeed, identicals seem to experience more similar environmental effects than do sibs.

Another interesting, but complicating, probability is that *the genic traits of one family member act as environment upon another.* Of course, it is possible in a purely theoretical analysis to set up a figure like Figure 1-4, in its separate genic and threptic parts upon every trait in the mother, the son, and the daughter, on both genetic and threptic components and both directly and indirectly, for example upon the son through effects on the mother. But the gathering of empirical data necessary for this is so complex that it can scarcely be contemplated at the moment. A beginning has nevertheless been made with a path coefficients scheme by Rao and Morton (1974) and Rao, Morton, and Yee (1976).

It is part of this interesting, probably true, but forbiddingly complex possibility that when two people are part of one another's environment, the full understanding of their difference on trait X

cannot be reached without also taking into account other traits, Y, Z, and so on. For example, sib A's level on anxiety may produce effects on sib B's level on, say, sociability. This obviously calls for analyzing MAVA data in more than one trait at a time. That some such cross-trait interactions actually exist in families is shown by the existence of significant correlations between a husband's score on one kind of trait with a wife's scores on a different kind of trait. These correlations are different from the ordinary correlation of factors across a set of unrelated individuals, as Table 1-2 illustrates. (See the husband-wife studies by Cattell & Nesselroade, 1967; Barton & Cattell, 1973; Jensen, 1978).

The above has perhaps indicated some of the subtleties of environmental action that enter into what is finally measured in the MAVA model in simple or more complex form. Further developments in both the genetic and environmental models are made in Sections 1-7 and 1-8. Meanwhile, however, there are possible misunderstandings to be cleared up in regard to the main model itself, which can best be tackled by looking at the psychometric procedures in getting the concrete variances. Let us consider first the fact as studied in the first part of this book, that traits fluctuate, yielding trait-change factors—which perhaps grade into states (Volume 1, Chapter 5). (Chapter 5 was concerned more with establishing that the *patterns* of such trait change factors are the same as those of the traits themselves, but here our concern is with the quantitative effect of a given degree of trait fluctuation on the estimate of the trait's heritability.) If by a trait score we mean the central tendency of the score taken over days, weeks, and months, then a heritability quotient calculated from a single measurement can be shown to have overestimated the effect of environment. It has included momentary fluctuation as if it were part of some steady, systematic effect of environment on the trait level. The variance allowance for this unreliability is best made at the level of estimating the concrete variances, by making a correction for fluctuation, but in certain equation combinations it cancels out.

To be clear about this we must remind the reader of certain general concepts and formulae in test psychometry briefly touched on in Volume 1. Elsewhere (Cattell, 1973; Cattell & Warburton, 1967) the distinction has been made between the *dependability coefficient*, r_d (test-retest consistency, immediately), and the *stability coefficient*, r_s. (Consistency taken over some longer interval over which the trait is likely to fluctuate.) A concept quite distinct from test unreliability can be derived from these two coefficients, namely *trait fluctuation*. The coefficient of trait constancy (obverse of trait fluctuation) may be written as follows:

$$r_{tc} = 1 - \frac{\sigma_f^2}{\sigma_t^2} \qquad (1\text{-}16)$$

where σ_f^2 is the fluctuation variance and σ_t^2 is the true (interindividual) variance on the trait. It can be shown that this r_{tc} value is calculable from:

$$r_{tc} = \frac{r_s}{r_d} \qquad (1\text{-}17)$$

In other words, the true concrete variance we need as the basis for calculating the abstract genothreptic variances can be obtained as:

$$\sigma_t^2 = \sigma_o^2 - \sigma_e^2 - \sigma_f^2 \qquad (1\text{-}18)$$

where t is the true variance, o the concrete, observed variance, e the measurement error variance, and f the trait fluctuation. The alternative to calculating from these variances is to attempt to get the original concrete trait score per person as nearly correct as possible from the beginning by taking for each person an average across a dozen or so retestings with the battery. This labor the present writer has never attempted, though it might give more confidence than correcting, as in equation (1-17), from single obtained r_d and r_s values.

Additionally, when the differences between sibs, from which σ_o^2 is calculated, are involved, the scores need to be corrected for the

TABLE 1-2. Relations of Traits of Husbands and Wives Showing Direct and Cross-Trait Connections on Primary Traits (on 16 PF)

Wife	Husband						
	A	B	C	E	F	G	H
A	*.16*	-.26	-.40*	-.32	-.44**	-.18	-.58**
B	.28	*.31*	.67**	-.06	.08	-.02	.41*
C	-.12	.04	*.32*	.02	-.18	.14	.02
E	-.03	.21	-.31	*.13*	-.10	-.40*	-.36*
F	-.19	-.04	-.11	-.15	*.23*	-.25	-.29
G	.21	.30	.04	.22	.14	*.33*	.14
H	-.15	-.23	.15	-.20	-.15	-.06	*.23*

From Cattell and Nesselroade, 1967. Illustrated by first seven primaries only. (Remainder p. 353, op. cit., 1967.)
*Significant at $p < .05$.
**Significant at $p < .01$.

natural age trend in the factor (as is done in converting mental age to an IQ) before subtraction, in order for sib differences to be comparable with those of twins and other groups. Note that this age correction does not eliminate the greater difference between sibs than twins that results from their being raised at different epochs in the parent life, the social movement of the times, and other differences of circumstance. Indeed, when the full set of MAVA equations is used, so that different terms, σ^2_{wt} and $\sigma^2_{wt'}$, can be evaluated for the twin and the sib within-family variances, it does not surprise us to find that the latter (apart from the Brazil nut effect) is twice as large.

Among other sources of error, sometimes unregarded, is the fact that true siblings considered separated from birth, and adopted children considered living together from birth, are often not started in the new living constellation until they are actually a year or more old. Further, it is sometimes suggested (Fulker, 1971) that environmental differences may enter into the very testing itself, in differences of attitude toward tests or in motivation in the test situation. This, if it repeats itself (as would be expected) for the same child, is better considered as lack of validity rather than of reliability. This turns our attention to the second problem in the meaning assigned to the concrete variances—that connected with the concept validity of tests.

The *concept* validity (sometimes called construct validity; but see Cattell & Warburton, 1967) of a test or battery is its correlation with the concept involved, for example, intelligence or anxiety, as defined operationally by the pure factor. The variance in the battery itself is pure factor variance and specific factor variance (the latter an unwanted intrusion) to the magnitude defined by the validity coefficient. Consequently, if both validity *and* the above test dependability (inverse of error) and trait fluctuation are taken into account, the true concrete variances for use in MAVA need to be pared down still further than in equation (1-18), as follows:

$$\sigma^2_t = \sigma^2_O - \sigma^2_s - \sigma^2_e - \sigma^2_f \tag{1-19}$$

σ^2_s being now the specific factor variance.

Because failure to correct for s, e, and f will result in all concrete variances entered in MAVA being larger than they should, we may wonder whether most results so far reported for convarkin methods (particularly the reported twin-method calculations, in which neglect of these concepts is almost universal) have been biased in one direction. Actually, the answer will depend on the constellation or constellations used, as in some cases the errors in the concrete variances will cancel; but probably the effect of neglecting these corrections has generally been to give an *overestimation* of environment. (See Loehlin, 1976.) Let us consider concretely the usual twin method—ids and frats comparison—and wrap up the three sources of error in equation (1-19) in the expression σ_u^2 for intrusive *"unwanted* variance." Then:

$$\sigma_{ITT}^2 = \sigma_{wt}^2 + \sigma_u^2 \tag{1-20a}$$

$$\sigma_{FTT}^2 = \sigma_{wt}^2 + \sigma_{wg}^2 + \sigma_u^2 \tag{1-20b}$$

or, with correlation existing, too:

$$\sigma_{FTT}^2 = \sigma_{wt}^2 + \sigma_{wg}^2 + 2r_{wg \cdot wt}\,\sigma_{wg}\,\sigma_{wt} + \sigma_u^2 \tag{1-20c}$$

The estimate of σ_{wg}^2, by subtracting (1-20a) from (1-20b), is unimpaired, but the N (nature-nurture) ratio is reduced, becoming:

$$\frac{\sigma_{wg}^2}{\sigma_{wt}^2 + \sigma_u^2} \tag{1-21}$$

instead of:

$$\frac{\sigma_{wg}^2}{\sigma_{wt}^2}$$

which it should truly be. The nature-nurture ratio, if we use the slightly more complex model in equation (1-20c) (using the equal division of the covariance, as discussed above) becomes:

$$N = \frac{\sigma_{wg}^2 + \frac{1}{2}(2r_{wg \cdot wt}\,\sigma_{wg}\,\sigma_{wt})}{\sigma_{wt}^2 + \frac{1}{2}(2r_{wg \cdot wt}\,\sigma_{wg}\,\sigma_{wt}) + \sigma_u^2} \tag{1-22}$$

which is again an underestimate, though not so bad. Whenever the twin method has been used without allowance for invalidity, fluctuation, and error, our conclusions about genothreptic action have thus been biased generally toward an excessive estimate for environmental contribution. In the MAVA method with four or five constellations, the distortion would not always be in this direction, but would vary according to the equation. But even there, the common errors of method, some unavoidable, have so far almost certainly, in the main, tended to give us overestimates of environmental relative to genetic effects, and need to be watched as to their impact on psychological theory.

While tidying psychometric indices in relation to genothreptic concepts, we must also take a closer look at the use of the heritability, H, and nature-nurture ratio, N, concepts themselves. It suffices to make this examination in terms of H, because the corresponding modifications in N can be made from the values reached in H, by

$$H = \frac{N}{N + 100} \quad \text{or} \quad N = \frac{H}{100 - H} \tag{1-23}$$

(assuming N and H are given as percentages).

Incidentally, psychologists would be well advised to use the symbol H rather than h^2 for heritability, as the latter invites constant confusion with trait communality, h^2 —a risk that nonpsychological geneticists are only just beginning to encounter. (And there is no need, just because the value deals with ratios of variances, to carry the "squared" appendage in the index itself.) However, we still need to indicate which of two or three possible H's any reported H value means. In the first case, as in results from twin research (comparison of ids and frats), it is concerned with within-family variances, and should be written:

$$H_w = \frac{\sigma^2_{wg}}{\sigma^2_{wg} + \sigma^2_{wt} \, (\, + 2r_{wg.wt} \, \sigma_{wg} \, \sigma_{wt})} \tag{1-24}$$

Whether the covariance term, in parentheses, should be included is debatable. The present writer, Moran, and others consider H better defined without.

The reader will see the essential meaning of this most quickly if he or she considers the expressions in parentheses dropped. However, the original model has always supposed that correlation of genetic and threptic components is possible, and in that case the estimate of the total population variance would be made by taking the straight genetic and threptic variance and adding to it the genothreptic covariance.[1] Contrasted with the above within-family heritability, we now have:

$$H_b = \frac{\sigma^2_{bg}}{\sigma^2_{bg} + \sigma^2_{bt} \, (\, + 2r_{bg.bt} \, \sigma_{bg} \, \sigma_{bt})} \tag{1-25}$$

Note, $r_{bg.bt}$—the correlation of genic and threptic components between families—has b subscripts to distinguish it from $r_{wg.wt}$ in equation (1-24).

This between-family heritability could be, and generally is, a very different value from H_w, and several blistering sociological arguments have arisen simply because the two were confused. Finally, we have the value most useful to the population geneticist and the best summary for most psychologists' statements. In this the within-and between-genetic variances are thrown into a total genetic variance, and similarly for the threptic variance:

$$H_p = \frac{\sigma^2_{wg} + \sigma^2_{bg}}{\sigma^2_{wg} + \sigma^2_{bg} + \sigma^2_{wt} + \sigma^2_{bt} \left(+ 2r_{wg.wt}\,\sigma_{wg}\,\sigma_{wt} + 2r_{bg.bt}\,\sigma_{bg}\,\sigma_{bt} \right)}$$

$$(1\text{-}26)$$

This total population (H_p) value has no covariance in the numerator because no linear covariance is possible, and we have kept tentatively only the two most undisputed covariance terms in the denominator which, however, by the definition we prefer can be dropped. This is not the end of the story for the H's, for, in addition to the above, geneticists recognize what they call a broad and a narrow heritability. Narrow heritability, H_n (in genetics texts commonly written h^2) states what is commonly called the "additive genetic variance" as a fraction of the total observed "phenotypic" variance. Broad heritability (H here) in such texts written H^2, is the ratio of *total* genetically-caused (genic) variance to *total* observed variance. The distinction can be made only if we have knowledge, or are prepared to make assumptions, about the Mendelian genetic mechanisms at work. Broad heritability, as will be seen in Section 1-7, is a compound of variance from simple additive action of genes, along with dominance effects, gene interaction, and linkage effects. The last three are sometimes called *epistatic* effects. At this stage of research, when we simply want to discover heritability values empirically, further assumptions about genetic mechanisms do not yet concern us and the value we are interested in is H. However, we should take note that heritability has particular meanings in H_w, H_b, H_p, H_n, and H, some of which become identical under special conditions. From this point the reader can well pursue critical statistical refinements in Loehlin (1965, 1978), Kempthorne (1969), Eaves (1969), Cavalli-Sforza and Bodmer (1971), McClearn and De Fries (1973), Vandenberg (1965), and others.

Finally, in this review of the meaning of threptic components and environmental effects it is well to remind the reader that H and N (where $N = H/(100 - H)$ are stated as empirical values *tied to a particular range of environment* (cultural and natural) and to a particular *range of genetic endowment*—racial composition—existing in a given population. Also, it is well to remember (though this assumes we give more precise meaning to terms than in popular speech) that the terms *innate* (for genetically given); *inherited* (as a relation to parental genetics); and *constitutional* are not synonymous, and confusion will arise if they are not distinguished. Their relations and the more precise meanings we can give to them are shown in Figure 1-3. Although genetic mutations are uncommon, we must note, as in Figure 1-3, that the individual's innate endowment can contain more than can be inferred from inheritance from the parental genes. The innate-inherited distinction is important also because, apart from mutation, there is still the fact that what the child inherits is not immediately uniquely definable by the parental genotypes because of the chromosomal re-shuffling. If inheritance is defined by resemblance to parents, then it is always imperfect because the child gets only a selection from the parental genes.

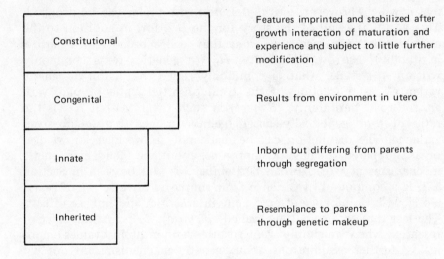

Figure 1-3. Relation of concepts of constitutional, congenital, innate, and inherited.

These   four terms are used approximately iin popular speech but can be given precise meanings as shown. "Constitutional" lacks the operational precision of the others and requires an arbitrary drawing of limits.

Occasionally the fact that heritability, H (or the N value) has a precise value only for a particular cultural-racial population has caused it to be spurned by some writers, for example, J. Hirsch (1973) as if it thereby lost scientific importance. A deeper insight will show that the relativity does not detract from its usefulness in practice or in basic science. A biologist's account of, say, the flora and fauna of South America, or an astronomer's study of the radiations of a particular star are also purely local, but when integrated with other such knowledge they generate universal scientific laws. Just so, as we shall see, the H and N values for a particular racio-cultural population become the logical stepping stones to deeper generalizations.

But even on the immediate practical level, since the variations in H and N are in fact small, the numerical advice one gets from such a value is useful. Thus both the clinician and the educator get guidance from the given values in their population as to what they can and what they cannot hope to change very much by the therapeutic and educational resources available in the culture. "Available in the culture" is an important clause, for these environmental resources, such as the school, the clinic, the family may—or may not—be appreciably manipulable. When we go on to define relations of range of threptic contributions to range of actual ecometric environment, it becomes possible, by a ratio between them, to talk of the "teachability" or plasticity of a trait, by which we mean the extent to which it can be altered by deliberate *manipulation* of given environmental ranges. Because every trait has some plasticity, enthusiasts have argued that the nature-nurture ratio is a figment that can be substantially overridden. It is doubtful that it can be much altered when effects arise from *the culture as a whole.* For the resources of a society are always limited, as part of a system (Chapter 7), as also are those of the individual, who has only so much energy and 24 hours in a day. Attempts to bring intensive environmental treatment to bear simultaneously on a whole range of "cultural desirables" therefore almost certainly will result in little movement of presently naturally occurring nature-nurture ratios. However, nothing is to prevent an individual bringing the balancing of a billiard cue on his nose to supreme levels of skill if he is willing to spend 10 hours a day on it and neglect everything else. The importance of environment as shown in the H and N values is thus not any final value but the value existing at an effective equilibrium of energy disposal within society itself.

As will become more evident below, the differences of H or N values for different cultures and different ages of population in the same culture could be very instructive. As to age, not only is it incorrect operationally to identify "inborn" by what is evident in behavior at birth, but also to continue that stereotype into the expectation that H—the contribution of heredity to the variance—will be greater in younger than older populations. Indeed, the latter question brings us to an extension of discussion of the interaction mechanisms in Section 1-6 that could well be taken up at this point. It concerns the main model for the longitudinal, *cumulative* interaction of heredity and environment.

Let us first look at the contributions statistically. As a first crude generalization one might argue that since the genetic part is given once and for all, but environment goes on acting cumulatively, the function of variance due to environment should increase in *H* and *N* values taken in later years. This overlooks two modifying principles (1) that the hereditary components go on for the whole lifetime, unfolding by maturation. (For example, sex life at adolescence, and certain diseases, such as Huntington's chorea, appear quite late in life—the latter as a simple Mendelian dominant.) (2) That if a given number of influences exist in life to raise or lower a trait, a short interval will tend tó contain a more biased value of them than a long interval. For example, the experience of bereavements in children of 10 is likely to have a larger variance than for people of 50. In general, if we consider, say, a child of 5 compared with a man of 50, and we treat the effect of each year on a given trait as the toss of a coin, it is obvious that over the 50 years the older person has more likelihood of an even break than the child, who has only 5 chances; that is, *the ratio of sigma to mean will be lower in the older group.*

But further principles enter into determining the *H* ratio which modify this purely statistical first principle: (1) the evidence of far greater susceptibility to environment in early life, shown for example by imprinting. These effects tend to endure into later life, but they would seemingly tend to make the *H* ratio lower in early age groups. (2) The action of a principle which we may call environmental stochastics or chain effects in deviation. Thus a person who has an accident which injures his sight may become more liable to another accident and the individual who damages his social reputation and is put in a disadvantaged situation thereby may be more forced to other acts damaging his social reputation further. We have opened up here a considerable set of issues, but as far as the nature-nurture question is concerned we must close it with the generalization that these stochastic chain effects from environment can be classified as of two kinds. (a) Those, like the accident case above, or such cases as the psychoanalyst designates by "a repetition compulsion," where the tendency to further environmental consequences is something *within* the individual. An early environmental trauma may set up a compulsion to generate a similar environment or continue with the same problem. In popular terms, "As bends the twig so grows the tree." (b) Those where the effects are due to the critical social position into which the individual gets himself. These *external* effects arise partly because associates like and expect an individual to go on dependably in the same way—good or bad. A respectable man has little chance of "making good" in a gang of crooks, and vice versa. What happens to a man who becomes alcoholic is normally likely to make him more alcoholic and so on.

The operational quantification of genic and environmental influences may eventually give reliable credence and precision to these principles, but all we can say at present is that principle (2) might result in environmental variance effects being magnified with age, whereas our first considerations would lead us to expect, contrariwise, that *H* would be higher with age. In any case, the determination of *H* differences in regard to specific age, sex, culture, and race differences is a lever to open up understanding of both genetic and environmental action.

1-7. Two Models for Genetic Interaction in Traits, Leading to Uncovering Mendelian Mechanisms

As stated initially, the complex research to discover nature and nurture variances ultimately has further objectives than simply determining the *H* and *N* values themselves for particular source traits in particular populations. Advance in knowledge of these would, it is true, throw a flood of light on present personality theories, dismissing some and building others to greater clarity, and it would help practical counseling and clinical practice. But determination of the magnitude of the components is only the beginning of two further research steps: (1) explaining the discovered genic-threptic variance relationships genetically in terms of the genome (the set of genes and their Mendelian action), and (2) relating the obtained threptic variances to measurable variances in important features of our physical and cultural environment.

Behavior genetics has had to be content so far with location in terms of specific genes for only a few syndromes of a pathological kind. The professional geneticist has been accustomed, since Mendel's time, to relating particular phenotypic characters in animals and plants pretty definitely to inferred individual genes. Consequently, the geneticist has been somewhat taken aback methodologically by his inability to do this in research in human behavior genetics. Except for a few all-or-nothing phenotypes, like Huntington's chorea, Down's syndrome, or color-blindness, which still can be studied by the clinical-genealogical method, the geneticist has been forced to aim at more modest objectives. One reason some definite behavior syndromes can be brought into the compass of obvious Mendelian mechanisms is that the existence of the genotype is in these cases *not masked by environmental effects*, to the extent that its identity is lost as would have been the case even with Mendel's peas, if varieties of soil had been potent enough to produce graded intermediates of dwarf and tall plants. Even in the more concrete physical domain, the identification of genes and mode of gene action gets frustrated in such traits as human stature, which are more like psychological traits in being determined by numerous small gene effects. Indeed, in most behavioral variables, even the perception of some step-like gene action by as few as half a dozen genes is denied us, for the smoothing action of environment on even a fairly discontinuous histogram of frequencies of genetic values hides the latter within a continuous distribution curve.

As regards intelligence, for example, proposals for accounting for genetic variance by as few as six to 10 genes have been seriously argued, but most investigators agree with Burt and Howard (1956, p.95) that genetic "differences in intelligence are determined by a large number of genes, segregating in accordance with Mendelian principles and each producing effects that are small, similar and cumulative." Nevertheless, an open mind must be kept for the possibility that other traits are genetically simpler.

In this connection the question has often been mooted (Cattell, 1965; Loehin & Vandenberg, 1968; Royce, 1957; Thompson, 1957, 1966, Vandenberg, 1962) whether factor analysis (as a device for locating independent influences by means of simple structure) might be able *directly* to separate the contribution of one gene from that of other genes and environmental influences. The answer is that in principle it could, but that in practice, if we roughly estimate that humans have 10,000 genes, and there are also, say, 1,000 different environmental learning sources, the smallest set of variables needed to locate 11,000 factors would be about 30,000. Thus although the "factors" (genes) of the geneticist and the factors of the psychologist *could* theoretically be brought into line, as the same entities (as argued in (1) below) the fact is that except in the case of a few massive genes, the technical difficulties defy present resources to reach them. On the other hand, the factoring of identical- and fraternal-twin differences, in the manner of Loehlin and Vandenberg (1968), can separate genetic factors that are the result of cumulative (polygenic) action.

However, we must attempt to penetrate the relations to actual genes, even though subtle and difficult methods are demanded. There are four such that we may consider as future possibilities.

1. Models with Heritability Applicable
   to the Whole Factor Pattern as Such

a. THE FACTOR TRAIT IS A GENE EXPRESSION

Here, because a gene usually shows pleiotropic action affecting several behaviors at once, a factor (if alleles are reasonably equal in frequency) *could* correspond, as just discussed above, to a single large gene. In that case the value of H for such a factor would prove to be 1.0—though allowance would have to be made for the factor score estimate being contaminated by threptic elements. That is to say, the factor analysis would simply pull out as a factor the expression of a single gene or gene complex, like any other set of correlated manifestations emanating from a single source. Any environmental variance on these marker variables would go off into different, environmental factors. Thus this source trait would prove, on MAVA analysis, to be wholly genetic ($H = 1.0$), except for the attenuation of trait-score estimation by specifics. In this case no environmental trait pattern need exist as a *corresponding* pattern. The environmental-effect source traits would be entirely independent and different. For example, the gene might define a general auditory ability source trait, and a threptic-factor in that area of variables might cover some auditory skills forming essentially a different pattern of language listening skills, based, moreover, on visual sources as well. What have been called "provincial powers," p's, in the triadic theory of ability structure (Cattell 1971) might well prove to be such sensory and purely genetic components. In the same areas the "agencies" (primary abilities) and capacities (higher-order factors) would be considered as relating to special learning impacts produced by institutional patterns.

b. THE GENETIC COMPONENT IS MULTIGENIC,
    BUT APPEARS AS A SINGLE UNITARY NATURE—
    NURTURE-DEVELOPED GENIC SOURCE TRAIT:
    THE EIDOLON THEORY

In the second model, 1(b), not exclusive to the first, we suppose, instead of the genetic and threptic contributory factors making different patterns on the variables, that they share similar loading patterns. That is, the genic pattern and the acquired pattern correspond, like a box and its lid. At first this may seem an improbable pattern, but it is at any rate what we truly suppose to be happening when we take a source trait and divide it into nature and nurture components. However, already existing empirical structural analyses suggest that the occurrence is not so improbable as one might expect. One begins to theorize therefore that there may be some special reasons for this similarity being brought about. The best-explored instance is found in the fluid and crystallized general intelligence factors, which were long assumed to be just one factor, Spearman's g. Their similarity is accounted for by the investment theory, which states that g_c is created by the learning investment of the largely innate g_f pattern in the higher skills the culture requires us to learn. It is possible that an innate endowment in a personality trait like surgency (F) likewise tends to gather around it social skills appropriate to its expression and therefore loading much the same variables as initially express the innate pattern.

We are compelled then to ask, Can *most* known unitary source traits properly be regarded each as a composite of two such similar patterns—one genetic, one threptic—the latter arising as warmth produces leaves in the pattern of a tree or the tradewind produces cloud masses in the shape of high Pacific islands? The question is vital, for if we are to talk with any sense about a heritability H_x for a particular unitary source trait X, then the threptic portion of the variance-covariance *must* logically be calculated from essentially the same pattern of variable loadings as the maturing genetic part. In the present state of our ignorance, with the g_c-g_f relation as the only captured example, we can only hope that research will be intensively directed to possible isomorphisms of the genetic and threptic parts in primary and secondary personality factors.

This first "box-and-lid" model, which regards the genetic part as polygenic and the threptic part as taking the same form, requires subtheories as above to account for the similarity of patterns seen in descriptive taxonomy. Our first theory would be that the threptic part arises—as in g_c and g_f—by a special interaction effect of the innate pattern with environmental opportunities (Cattell, 1971). That is to say, a genetic pattern accumulates threptic developments rather uniformly across its expressions, as say the fissure pattern in a cliff face becomes the pattern of growth of ferns, or thirty children develop thirty desks and books in a classroom, or the patterns in an offset printing pick up ink. For the acquired, threptic part of a trait to follow the genic part with little change of loading pattern we must suppose exposure to the environmental expressions to be equally available to all persons and relatively "passive" in its action, so that the genic pattern loadings determine the threptic pattern loadings. This will not happen if there are strong institutional patterns independently in the culture. If, for example, visualation capacity is used both in say, spelling and sculpture, and children train differentially in these, we shall not get a set of visualization-acquired skills forming a factor uniformly over visualization activities. Statistically the acquisition of a threptic pattern similar to the genic pattern may be analyzable as an additive or a non-additive interaction effect. For example, theory at present says crystallized intelligence is a product term of fluid intelligence and school opportunity, and statistically this creates a third factor, not to be accounted for as a simple sum of fluid intelligence and schooling—a new dimension. Alternatively, the relation *could* be a simple additive one, the learning increments being a function of the genetic scores alone (see Cattell, 1971, p. 336), though not necessarily the same function for each element of the pattern. A fuller discussion of such relations is developed in relation to learning theory in Chapter 5, notably in the concept of the *successive investment* model as developing threptic from genetic patterns, and also in the analysis of change curves into maturational (genetic) and learning (threptic) components.

Yet another theory to account for geno-threptic parallelism of trait pattern is one that assigns a more active part to environment. Here we suppose that the culture somehow recognizes the form of genetic talents and builds artificial superstructures on them within the given form. Thus the human capacities that make language possible are enhanced, by the cultural construction of dictionaries, into Thurstone's V factor with definable H and N ratios (Vandenberg, 1962). Possibly Broca's language area in the brain (genetic) and Thurstone's V factor are the genetic and genetic-plus-threptic aspects of the same entity.

2. Unrelated, Overlapping Cumulative Genetic and Threptic Factors: The Independence Model

The hypothesis here extends from that of a single large gene appearing as a genic trait factor (Model 1(a) above) only in that it does not suppose the genetic factor pattern to result from a single gene, but, instead, from the cumulative action of several genes that tend to influence the same variables and to be present or absent (to various degrees) as a gene complex. Otherwise, the model is similar in supposing that factor analysis will discover separate genetic and threptic patterns with no particular alignment in their overlap on variables. As to causes of this distinctness, we may speculate that the gene accumulations follow some evolutionary direction fixed by millions of years of genetic selection before the advent of agricultural and urban civilizations (8000 B.C. on). The institutional skill demands of the latter must be such that the threptic parts of traits developed *quite* differently, as novel learning patterns, imposed by more recent culture. In this case N ratios would be meaningless (except for single variables or for surface traits) since genic and threptic could not refer to the same source trait pattern. Every factorially discoverable source trait would be either wholly genetic or wholly environmental in origin. The present writer has elsewhere (1973) pointed to some tendency for a U-shaped distribution to become evident in histograms of H values for an extensive sample of source traits, which were examined by the MAVA method (Cattell, Blewett, & Beloff, 1955; Cattell, Stice, & Kristy, 1957; Cattell, Klein, &

Schuerger, 1980). When blurring of values by error is allowed for, we may conclude that some personality factors, notably B (gf), intelligence; F, surgency; I, premsia; UI(T)19, independence; UI(T)17, general inhibitory control; and UI(T)21, exuberance (see Chapters 2 and 3 in Volume 1) are wholly genetic, whereas others, for example Q_1, radicalism; Q_2, self-sufficiency; UI(T)24, anxiety and UI(T)31, wariness could be wholly environmental, when contamination of the score estimates is allowed for.

An alternative experimental approach to finding factors and then determining their H or N values, in the case of this second model has been proposed and illustrated by Vandenberg (see Loehlin & Vandenberg, 1968). It proceeds by factoring the within pair differences of identical and fraternal twins separately. The former should yield only environmental factors, the latter both environmental and genetic factors (the latter not being necessarily of single gene origin, however). The Loehlin-Vandenberg results are promising for illuminating the segregating model. Factor analytically, the situation is exactly analogous to trait and state factors appearing side by side in an R-technique analysis, and requiring a dR-analysis to show which are states. It might be thought that ordinary R-technique factor analysis would be capable of separating the two parts, in the case of the organic model, but technical difficulties would arise in rotating such "cooperative factors" (see Cattell, 1961, 1977; Gorsuch, 1974) to complete separation and, later, in assigning distinct scores to each. Nevertheless, the existence of such organic, saucepan-and-lid patterns deserves research attention, and to pinpoint this special model, the term *eidolons* has been suggested (Cattell, 1973) for the two members of such pairs of factors because they image each other in pattern.

Some interpretation of trait genetic and learning development in terms of the above models may be expected soon, and can already be instanced in the fluid and crystallized intelligence model. In the more distant future the use of a *population comparative* MAVA method—which contrasts the obtained genetic variances across diverse racial and family relationship populations—may lead to a mapping of some Mendelian mechanisms, but at present we must be content with gross variance solutions.

In this second *unrelated genic and threptic pattern* model the possibility will also arise that the independent genic and threptic factors that sum their effects in a particular variable or surface trait will stand sometimes at the same and sometimes at different strata levels. For example, it is possible that the second-strata factors QI, exvia, and QIV, independence, are wholly genetic. Thus in exvia, for example, the primary "stubs"—A, F, H, Q_2—after the secondary has been taken out could be wholly environmental additions. The converse—that primary stubs are genetic and secondaries are environmental organizers—is also possible but not easy to check psychometrically because the second-order factor at present has to be estimated through the first orders (see Chapters 2 and 3, Volume 1). Consequently, it follows that the H or N values for exvia per se will be roughly an average of those for A, F, H, and Q_2 components. However, if the second-order loadings turn out to be heavier on the primaries that have higher H values (or the converse) a lead toward an answer is possible. Space forbids our expanding on the technicalities of this approach, but at least it is evident that if the primary stubs are, in fact, wholly genetic in nature, then current practices of reporting H and N ratios for such secondaries as exvia and anxiety are in the region of fiction, for these second orders could be wholly environmental, and their genetic ratios could be wholly a product of stub primary factor heritabilities. Conversely, they could be wholly genetic and given their threptic variance by environmental stubs.

As more data accumulate, and are intelligently analyzed with respect to the above two possible models, it may well transpire that instances of the different modes of action and the two main models will be discovered. Whichever model applies, it continues to be a strategically better research plan to enter upon investigation of heredity in behavior genetics in terms of discovered factors, primary and secondary, than by scattering research over innumerable arbitrary bits of behavior. The latter are indeed infinite, and unless some accident has led us to the conviction that one particular "bit" is wholly hereditary (which is most unlikely), it is unprofitable to pursue so endless an inventory.

When all is done that the behavior geneticist can do in investigating continuous source trait variables, he finishes, as with stature in man or milk yield in cows, with a statistical estimate. This is most likely to be an H or N ratio, or, what is better, a statement of an estimate of the actual magnitudes of the genetic variances, σ_{wg}^2 and σ_{bg}^2, in given racial populations. But the professional geneticist, as we pointed out, cannot stop there. He yearns to get understanding in terms of the actual chromosomal positions and Mendelian mechanisms. He wants to discover the substrate of chromosomal action: the number and nature of genes involved, the actions of dominance, linkage, epistasy, pleiotrophy, and so forth. And as molecular genetics is advancing, he will also want to know through what chains of enzyme action initiated by the genes the inner maturation proceeds (in interaction with environment).

Even if it were appropriate in a book on personality and learning to follow this trail into the technical fastnesses of genetic mechanisms, asking how degrees and types of chromosomal action in conception would affect the genetic variances of parents, sibs, half-sibs, and so forth, it would at present do us little good. For virtually no findings with humans—as distinct from lower animals—are available on these matters in the psychological field. The reader must therefore be referred to the excellent expositions of principles in Mc-Clearn and De Fries (1973); Burt and Howard (1956); Broadhurst (1959, 1967); Falconer (1960); Jinks and Fulker (1970); King (1965); Lerner (1968); Li (1955); Loehlin, Lindzey, and Spuhler (1975); Mather and Jinks (1971); Waddington (1956, 1962); and others.

However, we may pause to note that the methodological path from established genetic variances, in continuous measures, to knowledge of gene mechanisms has almost certainly got to be through what is called population genetics, or through particular genealogical studies, because predesigned experiments in human matings are, shall we say, very unlikely! In the population genetics approach, by obtaining the first- and second-generation genetic variances for parents and offspring with varying degrees of relation of parents ("crosses"), such as random-related marriages, first-cousin marriages, uncle-niece marriages, and varying degrees of parental assortiveness, we may hope to accumulate data from which talented population-genetics statisticians, inspired in the tradition of Fisher, Haldane, Mather, Jinks, Morton, Rao, Wright, and Malecot, can provide inferences of genetic mechanisms.

Meanwhile, we can at least investigate, preparatory to such further analyses, the extent to which the above models are empirically supported. For ease of reference we have given to the "box-and-lid" model the distinctive name of the *eidolon* theory (eidolon, from the Greek for image) because the threptic additions to the trait variance shape up as an image of the genic propensities. Whenever the H value is middling, around .50, it is reasonable to conclude that this must be at work. And perhaps extremely good factor analytic technique will someday split each of the components—box and lid—into two highly cooperative factors (for cooperative factors see Cattell 1978). On the other hand when we get factors that yield heritabilities of .90 or .10 we may suspect what we have called the *independence* model, and examine the possibility that error of estimate is sufficient to account for the source trait pattern not being 100% one or the other, that is, that we are separating genetic and threptic by factor analysis alone.

1-8. Isolating Score Components in Individuals and Relating the Magnitude of Threptic Variance to Environmental Influences

We have suggested that the path toward linking genic variance with genetic mechanisms will be found, in the case of continuous variables, through finding the genic variance of various populations—sibs, twins, parent-child, cousin, and uncle-niece matings, etc. Thus, by *comparative MAVA*, with further developed population-genetic theorems, inferences can be attempted regarding number of genes, dominance, epistacy, etc.

There are two other promising products that rest on new uses of *comparative MAVA* that need to be considered in the present section because of their vital interest to the personality theorist. One is the isolation of the genetic and the threptic contributions *in a given individual*—a matter of great interest to the clinician and the educator. The other is the quantitative *relating of threptic increments to increments in a variety of environmental features.* In other words asking what ecometric features (for example income level, length of schooling, experiences of marriage) are responsible for the threptic variances.

A naive investigator, unaware of genetic principles, often asserts, when he has obtained a correlation between some trait in a child and some attitude or behavior of the parent (say, child neuroticism and parental conflict), that he is elucidating a causal connection between parent conflict and child neuroticism. As the following discussion on path coefficients shows, this is far from being correct in *any* such correlation situation: the causal paths can be in all directions. Further, such conclusions are specifically misleading in the genothreptic perspective because the correlations immediately obtained are between environment and *the sum of the genetic and threptic contributions in the child, not with the threptic, environmentally caused part of the trait itself.* As it turns out, the determination of the genothreptic components in an individual and the determination of threptic effects from various specific ecometric causes hinge on the same development, and hence are handled together in this section.

The correlation of the genic, chromosomal measures (if we had them) with the total observed, phenotype variance in a trait T would be the square root of the fraction of T's variance that is genetic, that is, $r_{T_g}^2 = \sigma_{wg+bg}^2$. (This assumes genic variance in the population is a linear function of genetic variance.) Likewise $r_{T_e}^2 = \sigma_{wt+bt}^2$, assuming threptic variance in the trait a linear function of outer total environmental variance acting on the trait, and total variance 1.0.

Our aim now is to take some theoretically interesting aspect of the total environment, e, which feature we may call e_y, and find out what its correlation is with that portion of the trait T_x that is environmentally produced, and which we will call t_x. This will be less than 1.0, because t_x is also contributed to by other environmental features, which could be symbolized by e_a, e_b, and so forth. (For example, number of sibs, parental income, and number of books in the home, might all correlate with an individual's acquired score on the V primary (verbal ability).)

One might think to solve for r_{te_y} by partialling out the genetic part of T from the correlation of e_y with T_x as a whole, but looking at the requirements for a partial correlation one sees that $r_{e_y \cdot g}$—the correlation of e_y with the purely genetic part of T—is unobtainable. However, if we may assume that there is no correlation of the genetic and environmental contributions to T, as in our initial equation (1-5a) above, then a comparatively simple solution is possible, since r_{Te_x} is calculable and r_{Tt}, squared, as seen above, is the ratio of threptic to total variance (and known to us also as $1/N$). Thus:

$$r_{t_x e_y} = \frac{r_{Te_y}}{r_{T_x t_x}} \tag{1-27}$$

If this were worked out for a sufficient number of environmental features, the correlations among which one would know, a multiple R would reveal as shown in (1-29) how much of the total environment acting causally on a particular trait has been mapped.

A more satisfactory solution can be obtained through a radically different but arduous approach recently published by the present writer (1974). It derives from a general statistical proposition (McNemar, 1962) that if across n groups the correlation of the *sizes of variances* on two variables, a, and b, in these groups is r_{ab}, then, if the groups can be considered randomly chosen from a larger population, the correlation of scores on a and b *within any group* (and in the population) will be r_{ab}.

Now, although it would be a major experimental undertaking, it will ultimately be possible, by MAVA, to determine the differing variances for many groups on the threptic part of a trait σ_t^2, and also on the environment σ_e^2, for some given feature, for example, parental salaries, climatic temperatures, years of schooling—for such values are in principle obtainable. If t_x is the threptic part of a trait x, and e_y is a given external environmental feature y, then we are saying:

$$r_{t_x \cdot e_y} = r_{\sigma_{t_x}^2 \sigma_{e_y}^2} = \frac{\overset{N}{\Sigma} \sigma_{t_x}^2 \cdot \sigma_{e_y}^2 / N - \overline{\sigma}_{t_x}^2 \overline{\sigma}_{e_y}^2}{\sigma_{\sigma_{t_x}^2} \cdot \sigma_{\sigma_{e_y}^2}} \tag{1-28}$$

where N is the number of groups, and $r_{t_x \cdot t_y}$ is $r_{t_x e_y}$ in (1-25), calculated in the new way.

As suggested above, the determination of $r_{t_x e_y}$ by either method leads to an estimation of how much of the effective environment has been located, through evaluating and multiple correlation of the form:

$$R_{t_x(e_1 \ldots e_n)} = b_1 r_1 + b_2 r_2 \ldots b_n r_n \qquad (1\text{-}29)$$

where the r's are the correlations calculated as in equation (1-25) or (1-26) and the b's are multiple regression weights calculated in the usual way, from the correlations among the "outside" environmental features 1 through n. It is up to the psychologist, by hunch, theory, or trial and error to find the features of the environment most potent in accounting for the threptic part of the given personality trait, which are, therefore, capable of raising R in equation (1-30) close to unity.

It is on this multiple R, and on measures of the real features in the individual's environment, that we eventually depend for our estimate of any individual's total threptic trait score, by the regression:

$$x_{ti} = b_1 e_{1i} + b_2 e_{2i} + \ldots + b_n e_{ni} \qquad (1\text{-}30)$$

the e_i's being the ecometric scores of individual i on the environmental features.

The determination of these b's could, incidentally, become an iterative procedure. For, having determined important b's, we could correlate the obtained estimated individual x_t values directly with individual e_y values. When significant correlations are obtained, an improved estimate of x_t would ensue, and permit a third round of more accurate correlations with environmental elements.

As mentioned, some environmentalist assertions and also some political derogations of the value of behavior-genetic findings have been made, to the effect that, as H-values will vary from population to population, they lose scientific importance. It will now be seen from the above that precisely the opposite is true. It is through studying these variations, by the comparative MAVA variance correlation (CMVC) method (Nesselroade & Reese, 1973, p. 123), that new domains of evidence are opened up. Among these we find also the possibility of assigning genetic and threptic component scores to a single individual. For if we know the environment component x_{ti} above we also know, by subtraction, the individual's genetic component, x_{gi}. Such values should be helpful not only in Mendelian relation inferences but also in applied psychology in clinics and elsewhere.

The CMVC approach provides, as it were by a by-product, a methodology of relating environmental learning features and conditions to learning gain (threptic variance) unconfounded with maturational, genetic difference. It is true that in full controlled experiment such bias does not arise. But in the majority of experiments, reporting observed differences in level between occasions does not get the required answer. Yet almost all generalizations, for example, about the relation of family background and "ensuing" child characteristics, are now reported on that basis of calculation.

At the very least, equation (1-27), or its development for correlated threptic and genetic components, should be used; but for complete solutions we need to move into path coefficient methodology, which has been well developed recently in its genetic context by Rao, Morton, and Yee (1976). Path coefficients, p's, are essentially quantitative variance contribution hypotheses including also the direction of causal action. (See introduction by C. S. Li, 1976, Rao, Morton and Yee, 1976, and a design for combination with factor analysis by Cattell, 1978, p. 425.) So far these models do not include feedback loops, except for a recent unpublished article by Loehlin (1979). But typically they are intended to explain action in networks as instanced in Figure 1-4. In any such network there is usually freedom to hypothesize a number of different variance contributions along the paths that would work out consistently with the experimentally obtained correlation values. Ancillary experiment, or special knowledge beyond the obtained correlations, is therefore usually necessary, to choose the best-fitting path coefficient values– p's—for a given set of obtained r's. In Figure 1-4 the proposed values have not been written in beside the arrow paths, which are shown simply to bring out the possible extent of path coefficient action.

Because space precludes a detailed examination and discussion, we will let Figure 1-4, concerned centrally with a midparent and two sibs, tell the tale of possible causal actions. Such action is analyzed in terms of separate possible effects from the genetic and threptic components of each person. As the arrows in the figure show, the observed parent-child correlation could result from the parents' genes being passed to the child directly; from the effect on the child's threptic component of the parents' genetic characters directly and through the sib; from the threptic component of the parents' traits affecting the threptic component of the child's trait and so on. As an instance of a long-circuited effect we may take the case where the parental genes affect the child's genes, which result affects, by interaction, the child's threptic component, which affects the parents' threptic component, which affects the child's sib's threptic component, the behavior in which affects the child's own threptic component. The paths in this instance are shown by the

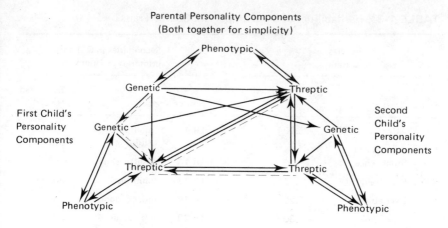

Figure 1-4. Interpreting family member correlations by terms of genetic and threptic sources.

Arrows to the phenotype are twoway to permit *equation* of phenotype with genetic plus threptic components. The interrupted lines correspond to the instances discussed in the text.
After Rao, Morton, and Yee (1976).

dashed lines in Figure 1-4. Such chains may be a nightmare to the serious user of a methodology that in principle permits adequate analysis, but Rao's tests of fit may make it practicable.

As in all our analyses in this area it is important to keep an eye on the assumptions made in the model, for example, whether interaction is or is not assumed between genetic and threptic components, so that the limiting conditions in each calculation are kept in mind.

As to actual heritability coefficients for particular source traits, the reader is referred to a summary for Q-date measures in Cattell (1973) and for T-data to Cattell and Schuerger (1978). For intelligence the most recent summary is in Loehlin, Lindzey, and Spuhler (1975). Results from the recent 1,800 case studies by Cattell, Schuerger, and Klein (1980) are summarized in Table 1-3.

1-9. Summary

1. As we turn to the study of personality change, we recognize first that methodologically it has to be based on prior accurate description of personality structure at any given moment, as approached in Volume 1. Second, it has to be conceived as determined by both

TABLE 1-3. Heritabilities of Some Important Source Traits

Primaries; in Q-data		Secondaries in Q-data; primaries in T-data		
Source Trait	Estimated H	Source Trait		Estimated H
A Affectia	.50	UI 1	Intelligence (Fluid)	.65
B Crystallized Intelligence	.60	UI 16	Assertive ego	.36
C Ego strength	.42	UI 17	Inhibition	.40
D Excitability	.25	UI 19	Independence	.30
E Dominance	.30	UI 20	Evasiveness	.60
F Surgency	.55	UI 21	Exuberance	.45
G Super ego	.15	UI 23	Mobilization-vs.-regression	.30
H Parmia	.45	UI 24	Anxiety	.30
I Premsia	.55	UI 25	Realism	.35
J Zeppia	.70	UI 26	Narcissism	.40
L Protension	.55	UI 28	Asthenia	.25
M Autia	.40	UI 32	Exvia	.50
N Shrewdness	.25	UI 33	Discouragement-vs.-sanguineness	.40
O Guilt proneness	.30			
Q_1 Radicalism	.10			
Q_2 Self sufficiency	.35	These figures average earlier studies and the recent studies of Cattell, Klein, and Schuerger (1980).		
Q_3 Self sentiment	.55			
Q_4 Ergic tension	.55			

inner maturation, genetically present, and by change through environmental impact, the former being the special theme of this chapter.
2. Our understanding of maturational processes themselves depends initially on our determining how much of a trait at a given age and in given circumstances is genetically determined. For such determination, four main methods are available to behavior geneticists: the clinical-genealogical, the animal-manipulative, the physical-associative, and the convarkin methods. Some apply to all-or-none phenotypic features, some to continuous variables.
3. The convarkin methods (acronym for *con*trasting *var*iances in *kin*ship groups) are the classical twin method and the newer MAVA method, and both are particularly apt for the personality psychologist, who deals largely with continuous variables.

4. The basic models possible for the coaction of genetic and environmental influences are two: (a) the simple additive model, and (b) the interactive model. The latter introduces a third term, consisting of a weighted genetic-environment product (in the simplest formulation). By weighting the latter at zero we revert, of course, to (a). Alternatively, by weighting the two additive terms at zero, we have a formula with nothing but interaction. We must distinguish between this true psychogenetic interaction and mere statistical interaction in the ANOVA sense. The latter is simply a statement that something more than addition occurs in the combined outcome of the two numbers, but the origin can be either this true *interaction* in the model or *correlation* of the two additive elements, which can occur in (a), producing more high and low values in the dependent variable than would be expected. Although nothing we know argues against (b), and some observations argue for it, yet in this first pursuit of MAVA (itself sufficiently complex), we have followed the simpler additive model (plus covariation) as an approximation. Elsewhere it has been argued that a MAVA solution is possible, however, even with the more complex model.

5. The *multiple abstract variance analysis* (MAVA) method takes six or more family constellations—twins, sibs, unrelated children reared together, sibs reared apart, and so forth. It then equates—in as many equations as there are obtainable constellations—the experimentally reached concrete (intra- and inter-pair) variances for each constellation to a set of theoretical abstract components into which the former can be broken down. These "unknown" abstract values are σ_{wg}^2, σ_{wt}^2, σ_{bg}^2, σ_{bt}^2, $r_{wg.wt}$, and $r_{bg.bt}$, plus possible $\sigma_{wt'}^2$ and $\sigma_{wt''}^2$ within-family environmental variances special to twins and adopted children. Although the MAVA method demands large samples, it is able to yield values for the genothreptic correlations and for between normal-family variances not attainable by the twin method.

6. The determination of as many as five or six possible non-zero correlations between hereditary and environmental deviations has great importance for personality theory and learning. They include "straight" correlations, $r_{wg.wt}$, $r_{bg.bt}$; "adoption" correlations, $r_{wg.bt}$, $r_{wt.bg}$; and curvilinear correlations, $\eta_{bt.wt}$, $\eta_{wt.bt}$, $\eta_{bg.wg}$, and $\eta_{wg.bg}$. A systematic presentation has been given of the causal actions, in both directions, which can theoretically be investigated as producing these correlations.

7. The heritability of a trait, written H, is the ratio of the genetically determined to total variance, whereas the nature-nurture ratio, N, is that of genetic to threptic variance (whence, if percentages for H are used, $H = 100N/(N + 1)$). The psychologist distinguishes this H in the total population from H_w, defining the ratio for within-

family variance, and from H_b, the ratio when family means (between-family observations) are involved. The geneticist also distinguishes the ratio for additive gene action, h^2 ("narrow heritability"), from H^2, when dominance, epistacy, linkage, and other such effects are included ("broad heritability"); H_n and H have been used for these terms here, for uniformity. However, this analysis referring to genetic mechanisms does not immediately concern the psychologist.

8.   Further refinements of genothreptic concepts require recognition that sources of within-family threptic variance do not lie wholly in the family; that other constellations than child-child pairs may be brought into MAVA analyses, notably parent-child pairs and uncle-nephew pairs; that trait fluctuation and measurement unreliability can affect the H estimate, though psychologists can correct for these; that II and N are purely relative to racio-cultural groups; and that a distinction of variance of environment itself from variance of environmentally-produced (threptic) components is essential. Clarification can be ensured on the last issue by calling the former "environmental" and the latter "threptic" (hence e and t as distinct subscripts in the equations).

9.   Strategically, it seems best to concentrate behavior-genetics research on source traits (unique factors) rather than on an infinity of narrow, highly-specific variables. Two distinct theoretical models could relate genes to factors: (1) That in which we recognize the whole source-trait pattern as a genetic expression of (a) a single gene of high pleiotropy or (b) of a collection of genes operating additively specifically in the given case. We may call this the *genetic-threptic independent action model, for it supposes each discovered source trait* is either entirely genetic or entirely threptic (from a single environmental institutional learning pattern) and that they act with irregular overlap on all behaviors. Ergs and sentiments fit this model of wholly innate and wholly learned factor patterns. (2) The *eidolon* model in which the factor-analytically discovered source trait is perceived as a "box-and-lid" combination of isomorphic genetic and threptic loading patterns. It is hypothesized that the pattern of the genetic trait is the source of the threptic image, through determining or encouraging environmental contacts and the acquisitions of appropriate, consistent, learned behaviors. This leads to a threptic variance pattern (the "lid"), isomorphous with the genetic factor. Model (2) is illustratable today by fluid and crystallized intelligence, and probably by most instances where heritability, H, is in the middle range. In model (1) it is possible, with trait factors *wholly* genetic or *wholly* threptic, only to divide variance into N and H ratios for specific variables, the N's and H's for traits being 0 or 1.0; whereas in Model 2 it is logical to consider a nature-nurture ratio for a source trait as a whole.

The distribution of H values from the present pioneer studies on source traits sometimes suggests a bimodal form. If we consider the high and low extreme values to depart from 1.0 and 0 only because of error of estimate Model 1 may be considered supported for several source traits.

10. Even with continuous measures and presumably multigenic action the behavior geneticist aspires ultimately to understand the basis of genes and genetic mechanisms accounting for the experimentally determined genetic variance contribution to a trait. One avenue would open up if we could estimate the genic endowment of a particular individual and use this in genealogical and other calculations. The individual's genetic component can be estimated by elimination if we can determine his particular threptic endowment (rather than a general population-variance value). This aim and that of determining correlations between objective (ecometric) features of environment and the purely threptic part of a trait hinge on the same approach. Two means of reaching the correlation of the threptic component of a trait, t_x, with an environmental feature, y, are proposed ($r_{t_x e y}$ = $r_{Txey} \cdot r_{Txty}$ and the CMVC method).

If $r_{t_x e y}$ can be determined for the chief environmental features, and we can measure these features for a given individual, a multiple R from e_a, e_b, e_c, and so on, should give an estimate of the total threptic part of his trait. Such individual scores on t, the threptic part and g, the genetic part, would be useful not only to genetic research but to counseling and clinical practice with individuals.

11. In seeking to unravel genetic mechanisms human behavior geneticists are denied the manipulative matings, such as back-crosses, available to animal geneticists. They may, however, (a), by social search find enough instances of special matings, for example, niece-uncle, naturally occurring; (b) utilize, as research advances, the genealogical method on individual genetic estimates obtained as in (10) above; (c) compare genetic variances obtained by applying the MAVA method to the above less usual matings—first cousins, uncle-niece, and so forth. Comparative MAVA results with population-genetic theorems may yet expose genetic mechanisms.

12. The interaction of genetic and environmental influences within the family is highly complex making the transition from known correlations to causal action quite difficult. Causal hypotheses can best be stated in terms of *path coefficients*, the correctness of the hypotheses in which can be tested by comparing the inferred correlations from the path coefficients with those actually obtained. Ultimately the answer to most hypotheses cannot rest on twin or MAVA experiment in one population but requires planned comparative MAVA studies with differently chosen populations. In particular, for clinical

and educational purposes, we now need to determine H and nature-nurture correlation values at many age levels and in changing cultural conditions.

NOTES

[1] There are other possibilities of division on which consensus has not yet been obtained. One is to divide the covariance in the proportions presented by the two variances themselves. For certain uses of the results this would be the same as proceeding simply with σ^2_{wg} and σ^2_{wx}. Another is to treat the total observed variance as if it were a criterion score predicted by weights on the two variances. In that case we have $B_g r_g$ as the contribution of the genetic part, B being the loading (weight) and $B_t r_t$ as that of the threptic part, allowance being made in B for the different variance of the two "factors" by using B instead of b.

CHAPTER 2

THE DYNAMIC CALCULUS FOUNDATIONS
OF LEARNING THEORY

2-1.   *Attitudes, subsidiation chains, and a taxonomy of attitudes*

2-2.   *The dynamic lattice and the main means for its investigation*

2-3.   *The origins of sentiments and evidences of their structures*

2-4.   *The mode of action of sentiments and ergs, and the concept of ergic investment*

2-5.   *The relations among drive strength, need strength, ergic tension, and arousal*

2-6.   *The calculus of decision, conflict, and integration*

2-7.   *Integration and impulse control: Self-sentiment, ego, and superego structures*

2-8.   *Definition of the ego structure as integrating and evaluating capacity*

2-9.   *Summary*

2-1. Attitudes, Subsidiation Chains, and a Taxonomy of Attitudes

With this chapter we pass on, from that part of human development that relates to maturation, to the study of all that comes with learning. The treatment of learning in the individual will cover four chapters. Chapter 2 is decidedly innovative. Chapter 3 reviews existing classical learning theory, and Chapters 4 and 5 go to new findings and formulations in structured learning theory—a theory linking learning with the personality structure findings in the first volume of this book.

The *dynamic calculus* is a branch of psychology that introduces calculation into motivation, drive strength, conflict, decision, and control mechanisms, that is, into all that has been studied as dynamic psychology. There are other fragmentary developments of quantitative formulation in dynamic psychology, but the dynamic calculus (summarized in Cattell & Child, 1975) offers the most complete, conceptually and empirically integrated system.

It may not be immediately demonstrable or self evident that

dynamics is a necessary foundation for learning theory. There are forms of cognitive learning, such as memory for nonsense syllables, and of classical Pavlovian conditioning, which at first seem little involved with motivation, but we shall hope to show that it is the central principle in all learning. Certainly the emotional learning in personality growth forces the personality theorist to consider motivational phenomena as central.

Personality learning, under various rubrics, has been irrationally divided between clinicians, notably Freud (1920) and Jung (1911), on the one hand, and reflexological learning theorists from Pavlov (1928, 1955) to Skinner (1938) on the other. Yet in modern multivariate experiment the accidental historical separation through these schools has been transcended in a new development in which the objectivity of the latter is combined with the breadth of the former, in a consistant and adequate system called *structured learning theory*. One foundation of that development lies in classical learning theory and the other in structural dynamics, a first statement of the elements of which was given in Volume 1, Chapter 4.

These elements must be briefly reviewed here as we pass on in this chapter to a full exposition of the dynamic calculus. In Chapter 4, Volume 1, evidence was given that the strength of motivation—of interest in a course of action—can be measured by a variety of objective-test devices that resolve into seven *primary* and two (possibly three) *secondary* motivation component factors: U, unintegrated and I, integrated. When the spectrum of human interests is measured by a wide sample of attitudes (defined in stimulus-response terms as interest in a course of action in a given situation) a relatively limited number of *dynamic structure* factors are found to be enough to account for the underlying motivation strength in the majority of human actions. On examination of environmental content these dynamic structure traits are found to be of two distinct types: *ergs*, which are innate drives, as seen in other primates, and *sentiments* or *engrams*, which are acquired patterns learned in relation to social institutions by reinforcement, and the unitary character of which is isomorphous with that of the institutions in the culture from which we learn.

It is important to distinguish at the outset between the *motivational component* (m.c.) factors that appear among *devices* for measuring motivation strength, in *any* dynamic interest content or area, and the *dynamic structure* factors which define interest areas (ergs such as sex or fear, sentiments as to home, job, religion). It has been shown that whether we measure an array of attitudes largely in the U (unintegrated) or the I (integrated) m.c. devices the same dynamic structures always emerge. We shall systematically, as in

Chapter 4, Volume 1, refer to the m.c. secondaries by U and I, and the classes of dynamic structure factors by E's for ergs and M's for engrams (acquired sentiments and what psycho-analysis calls complexes).

In animal experiments (Cattell & Dielman, 1974) the devices for measuring manifestations of the m.c.'s (motivation components) are such behaviors as speed of running on a straight part of a maze, muscular pressure on a door, or frequency of bar pressing, but in humans the measures have so far been taken to live in a less merely concrete world, consisting of symbols or signals of the life behavior rather than the life behavior itself. We must, indeed, never forget in comparing animal and human experiment that humans live in a world of symbols to an altogether higher degree than animals. For example, a person's interest in say photography is measured by his taking ambiguous words in certain ways in word association (for example, "shot" in a photographic sense); by his eye movements to a set of exposed pictures; by his GSR response to verbal stimuli dealing with cameras; by the facility with which he produces synonyms for the ideas concerned, and so on. The full *interpretation* of the distinct motivation components that appear in these interest responses and reaction potentials is a hot subject among researchers in this field, but there is no doubt about the nature and number of distinct m.c. factors (primaries α, β, γ, δ, etc.; secondaries U and I). The dynamic structure factors, ergs and sentiments, have proved far more easily recognizable. This brief survey of the dynamic calculus concepts as far as they were covered in Chapter 4, Volume 1, can be examined more fully as to its experimental foundations in Cattell and Horn (1963), Cattell, Radcliffe, and Sweney (1963), Cattell and Child (1975), Pervin (1975), Lindzey and Hall (1975, 1978) and others. The recent confirmation of m.c. primary and secondary structures by Cattell, Lawlis, McGrath, and McGraw (1978) is particularly relevant.

The variables that have been correlated and factored in finding dynamic structure have been attitudes, defined in Volume 1, Chapter 4, in stimulus-response terms. At this point we propose to examine the structure of attitudes from a different viewpoint and by different methods enriching the concept by clinical observations and the classical learning notion of the chain reflex.

It is a conclusion of everyday life observation, brought to some greater clarity by the clinicians, that any attitude action is directed to some intermediate subgoal on the way to another subgoal and ultimately to a consummatory ergic goal. The interest in the given attitude-interest and its response potential and action drop as the organism approaches the subgoal. Almost invariably, however, the condition produced on reaching the given subgoal situation provides a necessary stimulus and the necessary permitting condition for some new attitude response to arise so that action continues to a further subgoal, en route to the ergic consummatory goal. Murray (1937) expressed this by saying the first attitude *subsidiates* to the second, and we shall continue to use this useful term. Subsidation thus implies two things: that some satisfaction is given to the first attitude on reaching the subgoal, and that the use and effective action of any attitude subsequent to the subgoal is rendered possible by the creation of suitable new stimulus conditions produced when the first attitude reaches its subgoal.

The above paragraph treats subsidiation descriptively rather than explanatorily. The methods employed by clinicians to recognize the chain are either simply to ask a subject "Why do you do this?" or to use such devices as hypnotism, free association and dream analysis or location (in behavior therapy) of cognitive elements maintaining the behavior. As regards explanation, we shall have to ask in Chapters 3 and 4: (1) "Is there a new reinforcing reward at each subgoal?" (2) "If so, is that reward a pleasurable further arousal of excitement, conditioned by past experience, or is it a reduction of need-strength tension?" (3) "Is there not some cognitive representation of the ultimate consummatory goal all along through the series of subgoals to "glue" the successive steps together in a single functional whole?" Tentatively we answer yes to (1), and to the first part of (2), and to (3).

It will be noticed that a chain of attitudes in subsidiation is analogous in form to the reflexologists' "chain reflex." At first one might say that the difference of scale and the absence of motivation in the reflex makes them in reality very different; but as far as the latter is concerned we shall attempt to show below that there is a very small but real satisfaction in the discharge of an innate reflex, and indeed that an innate reflex is a "mini-erg" and that this accounts for the chain acquisition. A full demonstration of this "dynamic" in a reflex requires more sensitive means of measuring changes in satisfaction level than we yet have. But, if supported, this dynamic similarity would increase the similarity of a subsidiation tract to a chain reflex. However, in any case, the over-all parallel is very rough for other reasons: (1) The situation and the response course of action in the *attitude* are typically truly complex *molar* behavior, not the micro behavior of a reflex per se; there is a quantum leap between the two phenomena. (2) The attitudes in a chain (or lattice) tract do not necessarily have their behavior bound in an immediate time sequence. The attitude action "I will do this work to increase my bank balance" and the succeeding "Having a bank balance, I will

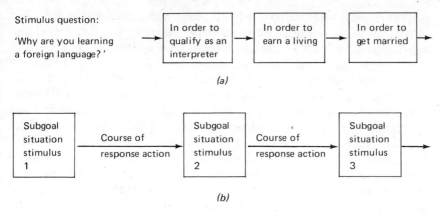

Figure 2-1. A simple subsidiation chain.

(a) Example; *(b)* diagrammed.

buy a car" can usually operate separately in time—and even inversely with a trusting bank manager! (3) It is not just the *response* itself to A_1 that triggers attitude A_2 in the lattice (as it does the next reflex in a chain reflex), but also the provision of a suitable *environmental condition* reached through action A_1 and possibly other contributors. As to (1), we recognize that Pavlov had no difficulty in very concretely demonstrating chain reflexes. Fortunately, strict reflexologists, not given to promiscuous theorizing by verbal analogy, have rightly hesitated to consider the sequences of molar attitude courses of action as defined in the dynamic calculus to be nothing more than a chain reflex explicable in the reflex framework, and have confined the chain reflex to small, relatively narrow bits of behavior. Multivariate experimental methods, capable of recognizing and measuring broader patterns in processes, are necessary to bridge this gap from the reflex to the attitude chain. In short, it is a gap not to be bridged by facile verbal identities, and we must be prepared eventually to recognize some important qualitative differences between the micro and the macro processes.

As mentioned, the discovery of such a chain structure as is shown in Figure 2-1 is initially by life observation, or, with a self-aware and frank person, by asking, "Why do you want to do that?" at each step. The answers will lead, eventually, to biological, ergic goals—eating, security, sex, etc.—as final needs beyond which no further goal can be stated. The part of the chain close to the ergic consummatory goal we shall call *proximal*, and the part most remote (and usually most recently learned), *distal*. For although we have naturally just followed above the subsidiation chain toward the proximal end, the learning growth over years in the life situation moves distally, adding new attitudes at the end of the chain, subsidiating to what is already there. Such additions are caused by the complexity of civilized life, which, in education, recognizes the danger, cost, or brutality of direct paths to ergic goals and seeks to bring about safer, more effective, but more long-circuited behavior. For example, the attitude in Figure 2-1, "Intend to learn a foreign language," will almost at once require one more distal attitude added than is there indicated, namely, "I intend or wish to register at a college," and still another, "I must get a part-time job to pay the fees." Similar distal growth is also commonly built into animal experiments when, for example, a rat is first taught to get food by pressing a lever, and then to open a door to get to the lever, and so to other preliminaries in a chain of subgoals.

The temporal stability of the habit system in a chain of attitudes in an individual is, of course, dependent on the stability of features in the life environment. There must exist a continuing capacity of each course of action to lead to and build up a subgoal suitable for the next attitude to take off from, and powerful enough to act as a stimulus for it. The latter connotes among other things that the ultimate goal remains unsatisfied by any other approaches. Indeed, we must on no account forget the postulate basic to the dynamic calculus that the maintenance of an engram in being depends on its continuing habitually to direct behavior to the goal. All other influences on learning and the maintenance of memories are subsidiary to this. Reflexological generalizations from animal learning, although initially strictly mechanical, have begun to address themselves to *apparent* teleology. Though we do not accept teleological causation as such, teleological goal seeking is true *descriptively* though explained later here in ordinary causal terms, by a special model.

Writers, for example, Woodfield (1976), in the teleological school argue that the rewarding value of the basic ergic goal is *somehow* passed down the subsidiation chain of subgoals. So do reflexologists, but they do not agree on the mechanism involved. McCorquodale's version of Tolman's verbal notion as $S_1 R_1 \rightarrow S_2$ can be considered one statement of the subsidiation principle. Among the paradigm laws that have some relevance to our subsidiation chain concept are secondary and higher-order conditioning and secondary reinforcement (Skinner, 1969). The former, in which a conditioned stimulus to R is used as the basis for conditioning a new stimulus to the same R in secondary conditioning seems a very weak force, hard to push beyond the third order, and therefore not very applicable to subsidiation learning. The latter, which supposes that each successive stimulus (going backward) acquires some capacity to evoke a fractional goal response (Hull), with accompanying reward, is feasible. However, in Chapter 4, here, a radically different solution for reward passing down the subsidiation chain, as a theory of "pleasant arousal," is proposed, from the dynamic calculus.

In animal (rat) learning the clear demonstration of the rise of such chains goes fairly far back to Saltzman (1949) and Napalkov (1959). The latter's work we may take as support for the *third* principle in the dynamic calculus. This third principle (more analogous to Newton's first) says "motivation strength . . . persists . . . unless," and means that apart from influences covered by the second empirical law, *the motivation strength remains the same throughout a closed tract*, for example, a single tandem chain. There exist, however, certain influences, which make the first law in practice only an "ideal" asymptote. These are various frictions, uncertainties of perception, and errors and failures in dependable reward, and interruptions in passing motivation down the chain. In human life it is obvious that "there is many a slip twixt the cup and the lip" and that a given distal performance leads only to a *probability*, appreciably less than unity, that it will lead to the ultimate goal satisfaction. However, for the present we will leave the question open as to whether the motivation strength, and the accompanying rate of learning, decline distally because of intermittence of reward alone, or for other reasons, including a possible inherent principle of fading with sheer time distance.

As just stated we must realistically take note that the attitude course of action as we take it in humans, and the laws connected therewith, might differ in some important way from the reflexological chain and hence from the empirical laws in animal experiment. This would be largely because *the attitude stands at a more macroscopic, less molecular level than the single reflex response*, and because humans are reacting far more to abstract cues and symbols. However, the micro- and macrostructures may be regarded as joining up organically in the end, in that we can see a hierarchy of mental sets operating in the attitude, without change of nature, right down to specific behavioral "reflex" responses. In such an attitude as, "I want to do better in school work," we see sets that diversify in particular situations, such as deciding to go to library more often, being more careful in taking notes, and so on, and ultimately express themselves in atomistic reflex actions, such as turning the pages of a book. Or again, the attitude, "I want to play more outdoor sports" has subattitudes, "I want to arrange more tennis games" and "I want to swim regularly," and these in turn include more specific "mental sets" down to a reflex-response level. Whatever has been learned about the chain reflex, therefore, is helpful to understanding some part of the subsidiation chain of attitude actions.

Inevitably, once we follow the hierarchy of sets above a molecular reflex level (see Harlow, 1949), there arises some arbitrariness in deciding *at just what level we will cut into the hierarchy* of acts to justify speaking of some sort of organic unity or even autonomy in the process entity chosen. We would argue that what we have called the attitude unit in Volume 1, Chapter 4, is the best compromise between seeking structure in behavior too molecular to be structurally meaningful (or too multitudinous to be encompassed), on the one hand, and on the other hand turning to such structures as sentiments, which, although apparently suitable for the transactions of clinicians, are patterns of so vast a nature that they cannot easily be immediately caught as observable, operationally-measurable variables. Somewhere we must begin with the "bricks" of the building, small enough to observe, to measure, and to use in calculations, and from which the shape of the total structure can be determined. For this the attitude seems the least arbitrary of "bricks."

In defining an attitude, in Volume 1, Chapter 4, as a readiness for response by a specified course of action to a specified stimulus situation, we recognized that the release of the actual behavior is likely to be episodic and contingent rather than absolutely regular and automatic in temporal sequence. Its actual release is determined in part by the degree of deprivation of the ergic satisfaction to which the attitude subsidiates, in part by the strength of the triggering stimulation, and in part by the wisdom of restraining expression to the right moment. The last—the appropriateness of inhibitions—is most characteristic of humans. These circumstances of stimulation and control are likely to introduce temporal fluctuation in the strength of the motivation components by which the attitude's strength is measured in an objective test, for example, word association, reaction time, or projection. The motivational component measures of an attitude may in fact turn out to be indicators of these different situational determiners of attitude strength.

There has been some tendency to criticize multivariate experiment using attitudes to determine dynamic structure on the grounds that most of the research has not measured actual attitude *performance*, such as time, money, and so forth, expended on the course of action, but has depended on GSR, memory, fluency, etcetera, in response to symbols of that activity. These measures, however, yielding the seven primaries discussed in Volume 1, Chapter 4, may well be providing *richer* information than the "criterion" does about the above diverse parameters of the attitude strength. A keen football player reminded of his team by a photograph or headline may be revealing by reactions to these symbolic stimuli more clearly "How much I would love to be playing," than by starting to run or kick a ball then and there. Nevertheless, it has been important to demonstrate, in the early motivation-component studies, that the responses to symbolic stimuli in symbolic manner did indeed correlate as hypothesized with the actual "criterion" behavior. The pioneer researchers (Cattell, Radcliffe, & Sweney, 1963) found that actual attitude courses of action, as measured in money spent on an interest, time spent, and so on, correlated well with the perceptual and symbolic behavior.

Because such attitude measurements are the very foundation of all the superstructures we are about to discuss, it behooves us at this point to make a more complete study of the attitude unit itself, and incidentally to remind the student of the difference of the functional attitude as here defined from a miscellany of existing usages of attitude. It has been noted that the strength (reaction potential) of one and the same attitude can be measured by any one of the seven primary motivation components or by the U and I secondaries. It is reasonable to suppose that these distinct measures correspond to various features in the natural history of the attitude and the particular type to which it belongs in a taxonomy of attitudes.

The meaning of an attitude as defined in the dynamic calculus belongs in the stimulus-response category, and its parts are expressed in the paradigm "In this situation I want so much to do this with that" (Chapter 4, Volume 1). This definitely sets aside the pollster's "for or against a person or object" use of attitude, but it still needs at some time to have brought into relation with it the almost endless set of meanings indicated in more or less vague verbal definitions in some sociological and psychological literature. It is, indeed, both a popular and a battered term, and the reader must be careful not to forget the particular use here.

Nothing approaching a scholarly review of numerous classifications in the literature will be attempted here (see Levine, Chein, & Murphy, 1945; Sherif, Sherif, & Nabergill, 1965; Fischbein 1967). However, many older definitions of attitude are scarcely relevant to the new stimulus-response definition offered. For example, even so obvious an a priori division as between a verbal and a nonverbal attitude is not apt when both verbal and nonverbal behaviors have been shown correlationally to be integral parts of any attitude unity. Indeed, the finding of motivation components shows that verbal and nonverbal behaviors sometimes load the same component, so that this a priori verbal versus nonverbal distinction is in various ways less important than other α, β, γ, δ, etc. distinctions. On the other hand, there is promise in Fischbein's (1967) introduction of the effect of "normative beliefs" in describing a difference between action and behavioral intention. Nevertheless, as will be seen below, this is more parsimoniously explained by bringing a loading on the self-sentiment into every attitude action, for this precisely imparts and estimates the effect of belief systems. Setting many a priori classifications aside, and keeping strictly to the S-O-R model as used here, and to the central definition that the attitude strength is the strength of potential or intended behavioral action, we still encounter the need for some subdivisions in a taxonomy of attitude "types."

Chiefly in such a broad taxonomy we shall recognize three *dimensions* of attitude classification. Our hypothesis—and it is little more at present—is that these dimensions may prove to be related operationally to m.c. measurements and other properties of attitudes. They are (1) a dimension from *more-conscious* to *less-conscious* attitudes; (2) *recently acquired* to *long-acquired (indurated)* attitudes (this will also mean distal distance in the dynamic lattice); and (3) *fully exercised* and *general-behavior-integrated* to *latent and unrealized attitudes*. For example, an important attitude for Mr. A might be, "I would like to see newspapers that practice deception censured." He may at some time have seen factual evidence that the *Daily Trumpet* is deliberately suppressing certain news, but has never brought the two things together in his mind and so does not establish his latent real attitude to the *Daily Trumpet* until the connection is called to his attention. A lot of people, according to experiments using cognitive consistency of syllogisms as a personality test (Hundleby, Pawlik, & Cattell, 1965; Coan, 1974; see also related concept in Rokeach, 1960, Festinger, 1962, and Rotter, 1966), have many latent attitudes that may arise only when a logically and situationally implied linkage arises or is forced upon them. The suggestion above that some possible taxonomic differences in length of time established, degree of consciousness established, age at which acquired, latency or non-latency, and so forth, will show up in different relative strengths of the seven discovered primary components has unfortunately so far not been investigated.

Conscious versus unconscious, as usual, has diverse meanings in psychology, but here we shall refer to two senses of unconscious: (1) the individual does not know he has a certain attitude or (2) he knows he has it, but cannot consciously understand to what it subsidiates. An example of the latter would be a phobic symptom such as the attitude, "I cannot bear to be in a small room." It is something the individual is fully aware of, but its rational and situation connections to other attitudes have been broken, a psychoanalyst would say, by repression, and only fragmentary rationalizations keep it in any cognitive connection. Other attitudes, especially prejudices, illustrate attitudes an individual may not even know that he has.

Some writers, giving brief introductions to the nature of *U*- and *I*-component batteries, have seemingly identified the former with unconscious and the latter with conscious and overt. However, this attractive traditional alignment is not entirely correct, for the *U* and *I* components apparently have a difference primarily rooted in degree of *integration* into the cognitive association system, which, it is true, is also *associated* with degrees of consciousness, but is only secondarily a degree of consciousness.

The latest information on the *U* and *I* structures, in the form of mean patterns from three researches each on several attitudes, is shown in Table 2-1.

In terms of projections on test devices *U* expresses itself particularly in autism, fantasy, verbally stated interest (as in most verbal attitude scales), GSR response, low memory for cues and distortion of reasoning. *I* expresses itself, through β (ego) and γ

TABLE 2-1. The Secondary Motivation Components, Unintegrated, Integrated

Primaries	Secondaries		
	U Unintegrated	*I* Integrated	A[*]
α	44	05	-07
β	10	53	06
γ	11	41	-14
δ	27	12	-05
ϵ	37	-04	29
ζ	03	05	34
η	22	06	-13

Studies as collated by Cattell, 1979.
[*]The third factor, derived from the research by Cattell, Lawlis, McGill, and McGraw (1978) is contingently labelled A for anxiety–conflict. It is of comparatively small variance and is not included in most motivation strength measurement, being only once replicated.

(super ego) in knowledge of the area, word association, warm-up speed, super-ego projection, and rate of learning in the area. "A" is as yet insufficiently defined but appears in impulsive decision, speed, muscular tension in decision, and certain "complex indicators."

2-2. The Dynamic Lattice and the Main Means for Its Investigation

It is a fact of life and learning, in any culture, that certain situations, which we call subgoals, serve as intermediate stages not just for one ultimate ergic consummatory goal only but for several. A very central instance is the situation-subgoal of keeping some credit in a bank, for from this situation attitude courses of action to several ergic goals, say, eating, avoiding danger, or looking after one's children, can be started. Conversely, several attitude courses of action, may contribute to one subgoal. In the above case attainment of the bank balance situation is helped by doing more work, keeping down income tax, economizing on recreation, and so on.

The result is that the structure among human attitudes is not just a series of simple subsidiation chains, of the type just discussed in Section 2-1, but rather what has aptly been called a *dynamic lattice*, as illustrated in Figure 2-2. Its main features are subgoals and ultimate ergic goals, with crisscrossing attitude chains between. The precise way in which such a lattice is learned is a matter for study in Chapters 3 and 4 for our concern is initially the structure itself and next how research can unravel and put together that structure. One must recognize at once that reward, producing reinforcement at intermediate stages, and somehow deriving from the ultimate consummatory ergic goals, will be involved in the learning.

For the initial analysis we shall consider the lattice to be in equilibrium. That is to say, the individual has learned that certain responses to subgoal stimuli generally lead to certain other subgoals and at last to final ergic goals, and *his interest strengths in the courses of action have become proportional to the magnitudes of satisfaction reliably, habitually gained* through them. This might be called our *second law of psychodynamics*, and it carries further our first law, given earlier, that *a course of action will be learned and will remain in action only so long as it leads to ultimate ergic satisfaction.* Incidentally, that does not mean only visceral satisfaction, for there are ergs such as curiosity, escape (fear), gregariousness, and self assertion, the goals of which are purely to reach a certain *psychologically satisfactory situation*, such as security, the presence of company, the mastery and control of some challenging situation. These we shall call nonviscerogenic ergs, and we must not overlook their more subtle action when considering the above law.

The first basic law of psychodynamics draws much support from the clinical observations of Freud and others, as well as from the findings of animal experiment. However, the quantitative multivariate research designs now opening up in the dynamic calculus are almost certain in the near future to put this law on a firmer quantitative basis and to generate secondary modifying laws. Thus, although our position is incompatible with Allport's principle of absolute "functional autonomy," that is, that "habit" makes an action persist even when it no longer leads to ergic goals, it is likely that the age of attitude connections and their distance distally in the lattice will modify the *degree* of their quantitative dependence on the magnitude of ultimate subsidiation to satisfaction at an ergic goal. Parenthetically, it is likely that many apparent instances supporting Allport's principle are due to new ergic goals becoming attached to the old behavior as the original goals fall out.

The research possibilities of discovering the ergic satisfaction invoked in a specific course of action will soon be discussed. But we may note even at this early point that the quantification thereof will be in the v and the s coefficients of the specification equation as used in equation (6-6), p. 239, Volume 1. They are attached, of course, to the E (ergic tension level) and M (engram, sentiment) traits, as defined in equation (4-3), p. 158, Volume 1. These express, for a given erg, the degree of stably continuing satisfaction, v, and the arousal in anticipation of satisfaction, s, respectively, for a given course of action. The hypothesis can be tested by asking if the rise and decline in strengths of action performance is a function of the rise and decline of these values.

The simplest statement of the dynamic lattice, as given in various books over the last 15 years, is as in Figure 2-2, but some modifications will be mentioned later that are required to this simple introductory, basic form.

The essential features of the statement of the basic lattice model are as follows:

1. The pervasive presence of attitude subsidiations (the direction of successive action being predominantly, and in ultimate total outcome, from left (distal) to right (proximal), finishing with the *ergic goals*).

2. The feature of two (or more frequently several) attitudes joining in producing certain situations that are *subgoals* appearing as nodes in the network.

3. Acceptance of the definition of a subgoal that is simul-

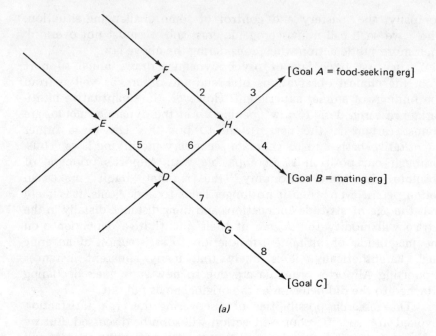

(a)

Figure 2-2. The dynamic lattice structure.

(a) (above) Essential form;

   A, B, and *C* are final ergic goals;

   D, E, F, G, and *H* are subgoal stimuli;

   1 to 8 are attitudes forming the subsidiation chain.

   Thus, attitude 1 could be "I want to qualify as an interpreter"; attitude 2 could be
   "I want to earn a living"; attitude 3 could be "I want to eat"; attitude 4 could
   be "I want to get married."

(b) (opposite) Exemplified in some psychological attitudes, sentiment subgoals, and ergs.

taneously the *result* of actions leading to it and the required provocative *situation*, at once permissive and stimulating, for several different attitudes that "take off" from the subgoal node. As will be seen later the decision as to which of the latter ongoing, stimulated attitudes is followed will depend on which of several focal stimuli are most active there. When speaking of a given subgoal (node, in the lattice) the converging attitudes may be called the *serving*, or *contributing*, attitudes and those following the subgoal the *evoked* attitudes, relative to the given subgoal. The subgoal is a whole ambient situation, with several possible specific attitude provoking stimuli within it and the condition of these at the time will decide which of the evoked attitude paths will be followed.

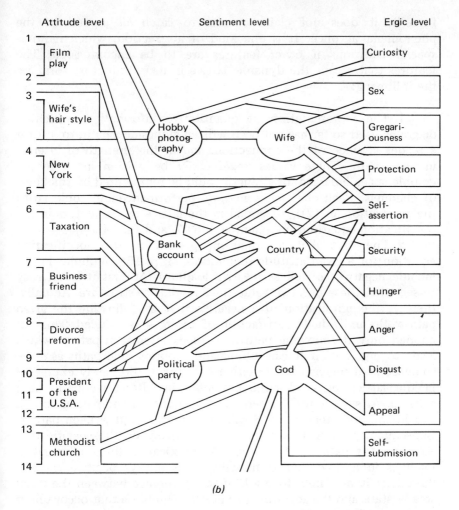

(b)

4. All attitude paths in the lattice eventually subsidiate to ergic-tension-reducing consummatory goals.

5. The more distal parts are generally the last to be added by learning, whereas the more consummatory courses of action are generally established first, being immediately proximal to ergic goals.

6. There is a tendency to a dendritic form, with manifold "rootlet" structures of a more complex kind toward the distal end.

7. As a consequence of the above, each ergic goal will be served by a variety of attitude paths and each attitude will subsidiate to a variety of ergs.

The lattice is drawn in Figure 2-2. Like an abstraction in any other scientific model (for example, Faraday's "tubes of magnetic force"), it does not claim or aim to catch *all* aspects of the phenomena at once. It is one kind of abstraction, which requires special additions if other features are to be encompassed. The features that escape the dynamic lattice in its introductory form are the following:

1. The representation of quantitative information, which in diagrams used so far has not been written alongside a path, to inform a reader at once of the connections *and* of the strength of interest in each path. These values *could* easily be written in, were the graphic space enlarged, or strength could be represented by thickness of channels. Each channel is an a_{hijk} performance and could (with the reservation in (2)), be coded in the lattice by its vectors in the specification equation, for example, the v's, and s's, for a_{hijk}.

2. The fact that information, present in the specification equation for a given attitude (equation 4-3, p. 158, Volume 1) will include negative as well as positive loadings. At first it is not easy to see what these negative values mean in lattice structure. Actually, there is the implication of a negative that by following the given path x the individual's satisfaction of an erg A is reduced. This can happen only if following path x weakens interest in path w which leads to erg A or if it can inhibit and suppress such paths as w by some control mechanism. In either case this is ultimately expressed in the lattice by a cleavage presented by alternative paths at a subgoal. At such a node, where path x leads to A and path w to B, a rise in the ergic tension of B will favor path w and weaken path x. Consequently, B will tend to load negatively on the specification equation for path x. If it seems paradoxical to think of negative loadings in a flow that is thought of as always positive (in one direction) it may help to think of the difference between the usual steady state and the adjustments between equilibria that occur under special conditions. Thus we can imagine the pull of B on path w becoming so great as to bring the flow in x to a standstill, or even to a reversal in which "I do *not* want to follow path x" becomes positively loaded on B to the extent that the individual reverses his behavior. It is certainly possible to have a reversed arrow (negative contribution) of, say, one arrow among several positively converging on a subgoal, indicating (with conflict) "I want to avoid this subgoal situation." In principle, therefore, every specification equation for an attitude path could have written into it negative loadings expressing the ergs fed by the attitudes to which it is an alternative. The specification equation is thus not a simple statement of the positive flow in a lattice path but includes also regard for the effects of the path in relation to other paths.

3. On closer examination of particular instances we have to recognize that the flow (in terms of the hydraulic model) is not uniformly from distal to proximal parts of the lattice. There will be many recursive links. For even many positive attitudes will curve back to earlier subgoals, producing positive and negative feedbacks that are, in part, largely circular. For example, the interest ensuing on a bank account will also contribute to that account, in a positive feedback. Conversely, the presence of a well-stocked liquor cupboard may be a stimulus detracting from the individual's capacity to keep it filled, and thus offering negative feedback. As usual, in a stable network as posited here, loop systems that bring catastrophic lack of equilibrium would not long remain and need not be considered. However, we must recognize that these retroacting courses of action, at present omitted from Figure 2-2, greatly complicate the research task of mapping the lattice.

4. The points at which intermediate satisfaction occurs are depicted as a number of subgoal nodes. However, it happens fairly often that some kind of action itself—say, swimming or arguing—is a satisfaction. Thus, on the one hand, a man may play golf with the goal of preserving his health, which may subsidiate to ergic goals of security, selfassertion, sex, and so forth; but, on the other, there is also direct ergic satisfaction in the activity itself, though it may be hard to define what ergs are involved in the esthetics of fresh air and being on a beautiful golf course. This satisfaction in the action itself rather than some situational goal is a subtle, little-investigated, dynamic phenomenon. The dynamic lattice can handle this by making the activity itself a subgoal (after all, skiing is a noun) with some subsequent paths proceeding to a direct ergic satisfaction and some to further subgoals. ("I like skiing because I enjoy exercise and because it brings me into the company of Miss X.") The problem of representing multiple satisfactions in the lattice from one course of action is in fact a general one, requiring, as just indicated, that the lattice include split paths, one branch going directly to ergic goals and another to several subgoals.

5. The position of the ergs in the lattice is clear, but a problem arises in the proper depiction of sentiment structures. Sentiments are sometimes defined by objects like "my car," and environmental objects as such are at present not represented in the lattice, although the *maintenance* of an object *is* a subgoal situation. If a sentiment reaches the usual degree of conscious recognition, so that maintaining the home or a socially appreciated job function becomes a goal in itself then it is reasonably clear that such a sentiment structure is represented in the lattice as a subgoal node. However, later discussion here suggests that it may also take other forms.

Granted that measurable attitudes can be seen to link themselves in a general lattice pattern, the next question, is, "By what methodology do we uncover this structure?" A lattice structure, like the corresponding representation of trait structures (including dynamic traits) by means of factor-loading patterns, can represent either a *culture-common* or an individually *unique* pattern. Whichever is involved, psychology seems at present to have three main ways of discovering the structure, each throwing some light on its nature from a slightly different angle.

1. *Clinical procedures.* For purposes of only rough quantitative statements and relatively low reliability of conclusions, we can follow the methods clinical psychology has long used: free association, hypnotism, shrewd inference from daily behavior, dream analysis, and noting the nature of change produced by therapeutic intervention.

2. *Factor-analytic experiments, including checks on path coefficients.* The multivariate but nonmanipulative experimental approach we have taken so far, and which has been the means of discovering ergic and sentiment structures provides the necessary evidence in the form of specification equations for each of the pathways in the lattice. These, however, still have to be fitted together like pieces in a jigsaw puzzle. The beginning here is therefore the experimental measurement and factoring of the strengths of many attitudes sampled across the lattice, objectively measured. In common-trait analysis the experimental correlations will be those of R-technique and in the search for unique patterns those of P-technique. The factor-analytic findings may then suggest hypotheses to test by path-coefficient analysis (Wright, 1954; Morton, 1974) and the inferences from general network relations (Kleinrock, 1964). Naturally this quantitative information offers a totally new level of accuracy and of certainty (in terms of checks, available in replicated experiment) relative to the clinical approach.

3. *Manipulative experiments.* When feasible, such experiments bring blockages and facilitations of attitude paths to bear in tactical relation to hypotheses concerning alternative and complexly related courses of satisfaction and alternative subgoal structures. In this method we use inferences that depend on the same principles as in hydraulic or electric networks. These find expression here in what may be called the *fourth law of psychodynamics,* which could be stated as, *"The motivational strength (defined as readiness to respond) in a path* X *which shares subsidiation to a subgoal* A *with an alternative path,* Y, *will, if the further paths evoked beyond* A *remained unchanged, vary inversely with that of* Y." This has some-

times been called the principle of equivalents in clinical psychology, where X and Y are often equivalent symptoms used at different times to lead to the satisfactions of subgoal A. Other guiding principles of search can be added to this, pursuing the hydraulic model. For example, if attitudes A and B both weaken together when the action of an attitude C is blocked, we may infer that A and B alike subsidiate to C or are paths from a C subgoal.

The reader should be reminded again that in applying the three investigatory methods described above—or at least the two latter, more exact and experimental ones—we suppose, for the simplest handling, that we are investigating a system *in equilibrium*, which means that the environment is for the time being held constant and that the individual has settled down to some steady compromise adjustment of his wants therein. In these circumstances the strength of interest (motivation) in a course of action is measured, if in life actions, by the frequency and readiness to respond, and if in objective tests by scores on the batteries for the total *(U* and *I)* motivation components discussed above. Until we penetrate further in this and the next chapter into the dynamics of learning, we can suppose simply that that strength as written in equation (4-3), p. 158, Volume 1, is the sum of two classes of terms appropriately weighted: (1) M's that are strengths of sentiment structures. These M's record the magnitude of engramming actually achieved, which, residing in the memory storage, is a function of past frequency and regularity of reward satisfaction from the course of action, and (2) E's, ergic tensions (need strengths) existing at the time. A product relation of M and E, as in the partly analogous Hullian "habit strength" and "drive" model, is also possible, but these weighting and multiplying issues need not be discussed in regard to the lattice.

If we compare the two precision methods of uncovering the lattice—that of multivariate experiment ((2) above) by nonmanipulative factoring of attitude strengths (by R- or P-technique) as attitudes exist at a given moment, and that of (3), manipulative experiment, which blocks or changes rewards—we see certain advantages and disadvantages in each. The factor analysis will tell us dependably, by the loadings in the specification equation for each particular attitude, to what ergs, involved in what degree, the given attitudes subsidiate. These are rows in the factor matrix. And if alternatively we look at the figures in the columns of the factor-pattern matrix they will tell us, with respect to any given erg, which attitudes subsidiate to it.

But these answers in a given matrix covering a sample of attitudes have to be fitted together with the data from others if we are to get the complete picture. For typically, the sample of attitudes used cannot include the whole lattice, but only some irregular cross-section of it. It is irregular especially in level (distal-proximal position) of cross-section because, not knowing at the outset the subsidiation sequences, we cannot choose for experiment an exact "temporal homogeneous" cross-section comprising only attitudes that stand at just the same distance from the ergic goals. In fact, our choice might include, unknowingly, two attitudes that stand in immediate sequence in a chain, though afterward there would be evidence to reveal this in the high correlation of strengths of the two and their great similarity of factor pattern in a row of the factor matrix. Details of this derivation of lattice structure from matrices cannot be pursued here. In principle, by collating factorings of overlapping sets of attitude variables, and by invoking also hypothesis-testing, path-coefficient factor analysis (Cattell, 1978) it should prove possible to map a lattice pretty completely by this approach. It offers an area for fascinating technical developments.

The alternative of exploring the lattice by manipulation can be illustrated by Figure 2-3. If, in Figure 2-3, the attitude course of action 1 is blocked, then, if the ergic tension demand of erg X is considered constant, there will be a tendency to find ways to *increase activity*, motivation, and satisfaction, in paths 2 and 3. Figure 2-2(b) depicts an analysis of the other main feature in a lattice—a subgoal with *serving* and with served (or *evoked*) attitudes. Here blocking or facilitating of one or more of the evoked attitudes, 4, 5, or 6 will in general lead to a corresponding reduction or facilitation of reactivity, likely to be shared, across the serving contributory attitudes 1, 2, and 3, and vice versa. Conversely, a constriction, by difficulties, of attitude 1, for example, could uniformly reduce 4, 5, and 6. Incidentally, even with such small examples it could be shown that a variety of conditions and solutions exist, and certain network flow principles could be developed. However, it is not our purpose at this point to do more than indicate that manipulation can lead to inferences about connections according to definite "hydraulic" principles.[1]

In animal research, blocking and facilitating manipulations could include, on the one hand, the physical blocking of a maze path, and, on the other, the removal of obstacles and shortening of paths in a maze. Change of difficulty and of ease of satisfaction need, of course, only be relative and partial in order to explore the relations. In human research such manipulation—at least of important existing life satisfaction paths—is not normally possible, which is one reason why factor methods need to be well developed (Method 2 above). But a *relative* blocking and facilitation can be

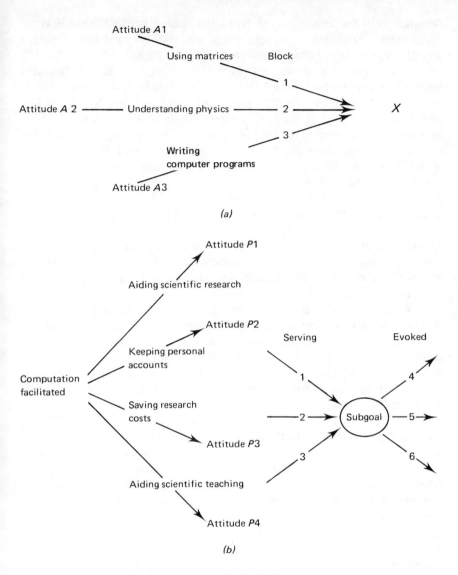

Figure 2-3. Exploration of lattice manipulatively.

(a) Joint subsidiation to subgoal; *(b)* Joint dependence on subgoal situation stimulus.

achieved by such methods as supplying incomplete or biased information (as is daily done, for example, by mass media, to favor certain courses of political and social action). Thus, in the simplest physical example, if Smith is accustomed to prefer route X in getting home from business, and is informed that X has traffic jams or floods, we infer and discover from his taking route Y that it is an "equivalent behavior," though a less commonly used one, relative to path X, and that both subsidiate to the same goal.

A complete treatment of methods of analysis of the dynamic lattice remains to be worked out in a complete mathematical model. This can be checked with precision, incidentally, only as the properties of the attitude measures themselves become further clarified. At present what we may call the *hydraulic* and the *electric-network models* offer guidance (see Kleinrock, 1964, on networks). The former uses the already formulated laws, and to some extent the formulae, concerning pressure and rate of flow in a system of channels, for example, pipes carrying any fluid. The flow is here the analogue of degree of motivation persisting (adjusting to satisfaction habitually obtained) in the given course. The model suffices to illustrate our first dynamic law: behavior persists only as long as there is subsidiation to a consummatory goal (an "outlet," on the hydraulic system). It also illustrates the fourth dynamic law: that of "equivalents."

The usefulness of the hydraulic model in mapping the lattice has been illustrated in note 1. The need for such introductory models to be refined to our particular area, psychodynamics, is brought home by the differences in formulae that would appear, in detail, between the hydraulic and the electric-conductor network model. The latter involves, for example, a fall of potential with distance in different metal conductors. This latter, we shall conclude later, needs to be embodied as a fifth psychodynamic principle; modifying the third (that *the strength of interest along a straight isolated chain is the same at all points,) by "There is in general a specific decline with distance from the goal resulting from secondary influences."* The dynamic lattice, in addition to such a decline of motivation analogous to that of electrical potential, may prove to require still further modifying principles. We can perhaps reasonably expect in the near future the development of an effective mathematical model, in the style of hydraulic and electrical models, but using learning (engramming) parameters for guiding investigation of the dynamic lattice and expressing its properties.

2-3. The Origins of Sentiments and Evidences of Their Structures

Although sentiment factor patterns have been replicated with great reliability, and are shown by factor analysis to have substantial weights in the specification equations for many common attitudes, there are problems in their representation in the lattice that can be solved only by understanding the manner of their acquisition. We shall study the problem of acquisition of sentiments twice: immediately here in brief, and in depth after considering more learning principles (Section 5-4).

The problem is, of course, that of accounting for the rise of a functionally unitary structure. Three experiential sources for the rise of sentiment structures have been mooted in the framework of the dynamic calculus by the present writer, by Child (Cattell & Child, 1975), Horn, Sweney, Dielman, Barton, Nesselroade, Bartsch, and others working in the calculus. They are (1) The experiencing of a common learning schedule fixed in environment by the set of loaded attitudes; (2) an inherent common growth agency; and (3) A common subsidiation to a preexisting sentiment—the "budding" process, as we may call it.

Principle 1: The Common-Learning Schedule

This principle supposes that the correlation of many attitude strengths indicated in a simple-structure factor arises because the environment provides that all members of the attitude set tend to be exercised with equal frequency and reinforced with equal reward in given life positions. Some persons occupy the culture-susceptible position (to meet a given institution) much more than others (see Volume 1, Section 6-10), so that, across people, a correlation arises throughout the attitude set.

What operates on people in the given position can be (1) a well formed social institution; (2) the characters of an object requiring concern, (3) a cultural sub-group, for example, peers, or even (4) the mere material geography of a region. Thus a church institution exposes its members with standard frequency to singing hymns, listening to sermons, praying, and contributing to charities. An object, such as a car, forces an individual to have attitudes and skills concerning tires, traffic laws, gear changing, the price of gasoline, and the behavior of other drivers. An individual who has a car will differ from one who has not on the strength, simultaneously developed, of *all* of these attitude actions and skills. And an individual with a sentiment for London, compared to one who has not, will differ in knowing where the theaters are, in enjoying sunset across the Embankment, and in a habit of listening to speakers at the Marble Arch corner of Hyde Park.

A sentiment founded on such experience of different exposures to an object (from a physical object to an institution) need not have a high degree of conscious, logical, and emotional coherence of its parts. Elements could be there, with statistically significant relations to the whole, that had no organic or certainly no consciously perceived unity with others. It could even be that the stimulation of one such element would not arouse the others. Some of the reinforced attitudes might have no more meaning than Skinner's "superstitious learning." For instance, if a certain congregation could reach its church only by climbing a rope ladder, attitudes and skills concerning rope ladders would correlate with more strictly religiously elevating habits. Similarly in driving a car an individual may experience no conscious connection between his style of putting pressure on the brake pedal and his appreciation of traffic signs. Yet both are more developed in the driver than in a nondriver, and across the population will correlate in a "sentiment to a car" factor.

Principle 2:   Action of an Inherent Growth Agency

By contrast to the external occurrence of common degree or frequency of excitation and/or reward in the common schedule origin, action of an inherent growth agency supposes connections established by processes *in the individual*. These may turn out to be several, but probably two are most marked. The notion of a unitary trait emerging by what has been called an *agency* or *aid* (Cattell, 1971) has the clearest support in the ability field. In that area some logical dependency of several skills on a particular "discovery," as illustrated, for example, by Piaget's work, leads to all of them being developed with approximately equal speed. Thus Thurstone's N primary ability, which loads performances of addition, subtraction, multiplication, and division could, it is true, appear partly because these skills are taught together (illustrating a common schedule, as above). But their correlation can also be conceived as manifesting inherent logical dependencies—something in the mind of the subject—that bring about simultaneous growth in the grasp of all.

Elsewhere (Cattell 1971), the mechanism has been discussed in more detail whereby abilities and interests may grow together in a single pattern through an agency. A child who finds himself dexterous is more likely to acquire a sentiment for sports than is a clumsy, short-sighted child. But abilities cannot create sentiments unless some enveloping interest is also there. Perhaps the best perspective on present knowledge suggests that we consider abilities, in the strict ability sense of agency or aid, as only a partial and, usually, late shaping influence in the rise of sentiment patterns. But there are other inherent unity-producing agencies than abilities, notably in the dynamic realm.

The true analogue of the ability factor "agency" in the dynamic realm is the cognitive linking of the elements of a sentiment through coexcitation, a process we do not study fully until Section 3-1, but which describes the rise of a unity through its parts experiencing excitation at the same moment (repeated). One of the few reflexological learning theorists to grapple with the personality learning problem, Staats (1975), has used Pavlovian conditioning of emotions to explain the spread of motivation when he speaks of what we would here define as a sentiment. This seems close to the mark, but not entirely correct. One criticism that may be clearer later is that Staats uses the Pavlovian (*CRI*) conditioning of an emotional experience (the existence of which no one can doubt) to explain an association with motivation (conation), which we argue at more length elsewhere is a different entity from an emotion. The present writer (1929), collating thousands of introspections on emotion (affect) and on conation (effort, impulse, drive) in association with GSR magnitudes, found very significant differences between the GSR response magnitudes with reports of conative and affective experiences. Aveling (1926) early confirmed this with other GSR experiments. Nevertheless, in some quite recent writings, a careless switching of properties goes on, confusing affective and conative (drive) phenomena and causal actions. Since this distinction was well drawn by Aristotle and the Scholastics without the reference to apparatus, they might be excused a little cynicism over the modern intellect.

At this point we must anticipate a later (Chapter 5) refinement of the concept of learning by conditioning into (1) coexcitation effects and (2) means-end (operant conditioning) neural learning. To see how these operate in sentiment acquisition we shall assume that many sentiments (perhaps most, in contrast to complexes) become *conscious as to their objects*, and symbolized by words (my career is, say, *mathematics*, my hobby, *sailing*). By the coexcitation of various matters having to do with mathematics, stimulated cognitively when "mathematics," as a symbol, is mentioned, the cognitive connection network of recall in a sentiment is created whereby when one part is stimulated the other parts come nearer to the threshold of consciousness. Because coexcitation (fusion in contiguity) without reward seems of lower potency than the reward learning principle we may doubt that this is sufficient to account for the powerful unity observed. However, the *frequency* of co-appearance in the outer world, generally used in, say, rat conditioning, is, in humans, only a small fraction of the totally experienced cognitive coincidences. Humans constantly turn over ideas, and cognitive links between symbols and other ideas or memories can occur by contiguity with very great frequency. The individual with a sailing hobby daydreams about his sailing experiences and talks with others. (Like the retired Menelaus he may have "sacked a hundred Troys twixt noon and supper" binding events more than the experience of Troy itself did.)

Once again we must remind the student, whose understanding of classical learning is based largely on animal learning experiment, of the huge cognitive activity gap between man and rat. Because of this gap we shall reason, when we come to a fuller discussion of learning, that much of the unity of a sentiment arises from the relatively feeble connection-establishing power of coexcitation (CRI) being followed up by means-end ($CRII$) reward, well distributed by cognitive insight into the reward connections and repeated with great frequency in reminiscence. The evidence in Chapter 4 from P- and R-techniques, and other evidence (Alker, 1972, Cattell, De Young, & Horn 1978), undoubtedly shows that a sentiment tends to be *cognitively activated* as a whole, just as it shows that an erg tends to be *aroused* as a whole, that is, in all attitudes loaded, and these unities have to be accounted for. The argument for what we have called an inherent growth process of the unity we see in a sentiment is, therefore, that attitudes *a, b, c, d* are found correlated not because of an external schedule of common degrees of reinforcement (as in the common schedule principle 1 above) but because of a growth of cognitive connections in the individual, then or later, that ensures the spread of local reinforcement of any part to the whole.

Principle 3: Common Subsidiation, or "Budding"

The third and last principle can be seen in perspective if we remember that learning of the means-end type depends both on the *strength of the drive* (level of need) and the *magnitude of the reward*. Principle 1 hinges on a common reward magnitude through features of the environment. Principle 3 assumes, instead, that a correlation arises through the attitudes in the set being infused with a common dynamic strength which ensures a certain communality of reward for a different reason. That common level produces a tendency to common strength of reward and of reinforcement regardless of whether reward is itself distributed equally by environment to the various elements (or occurs in the action Principle 1, where equal schedules of frequencies and rewards extend across the unitary set). Obviously this third principle of common internal need strength is the mechanism we have already supposed to produce the correlation among attitudes marking an *erg*. But now, instead of an ergic goal equally motivating all of a set of attitudes and producing a factor, we are supposing that some already established subgoal, for example a desire for money, offers the common reward strength which brings a set of attitudes into a common (sentiment) factor.

Granted that a large subgoal is the essence of a sentiment structure we are therefore saying that this third process is one of "budding" in which a large sentiment generates another as a subsidiary subsidiating to it. In the realm of social structure a close analogy to this action would be when a large automobile company sets up a steel-smelting subsidiary to meet its needs. In fairly conscious human procedures an example would be when a professor with a strong sentiment for chemistry decides that he needs high facility in reading the literature in German. He then infuses a whole set of learning attitudes and skills connected with the German language with the uniformly high motivations accumulated behind his main sentiment to chemistry. (Those motivations we shall later define as the *ergic investment*.) Probably such a development (as illustrated by subgoal 1 in Figure 2-4, p. 91) is usually conscious and the transfer of motivation deliberate. But regardless of that feature the important point is that a whole set of attitudes becomes simultaneously roughly equally motivated by subsidiation to an existing sentiment investment of definite strength. And because different persons do this to different degrees and have different strengths in the original parent sentiment, an independent new factor will become evident in the form of positive intercorrelations among all of the new subsidiating set of attitudes and skills.

Reflexological learning theorists at this point may see some aptness, in regard to Principle 2, of their *stimulus generalization* findings—that is, the extension of a type of response learned to X to many situations like X. There is an analogy here, but the actual process as observed in animals refers, by comparison with a sentiment, to a microprocess. Simple stimulus similarity is trivial in breadth of effect in humans compared to the insight, logical connections, and deliberate recognition of what stimuli will lead to the same rewards that we have argued operate in cognitive *coexcitation* (*CE* learning). Indeed, it cannot be too strongly stressed, in comparing the fragmentary sentiments of animals or very young children with the highly organized patterns we find in adults, that the human capacity to relate cognitively, to handle symbols, and to develop broad concepts is alone capable of producing the highly integrated cognitive-emotional structures we encounter in the discovered sentiment factors. In summary, the sentiment reached by Principle 2 is a closely woven cognitive structure, such that the activation of one part is likely to activate all, and the acquisition of which often proceeds in a logical conceptually conscious manner, establishing linkages by cognitive coexcitation.

The usual scientific ideal of reaching a monistic principle may incline us to ask if the above three causes of emergence of a sentiment factor could be brought to a single explanatory principle. We ask this partly because, when looking in the dynamic lattice, we see only one kind of structure—a subgoal node—that could correspond to the sentiment factor. (In the lattice we see only two types of structure: the attitudes converging on each ergic goal, and those converging on or diverging from the various acquired subgoals appearing as large nodes in the lattice.)

Conceivably, of course, research will unearth other lattice structures besides sentiments and ergs. But empirically we see, in each sentiment structure so far appearing as a factor, a cluster of loaded attitudes having obvious relation to some object—a physical object such as a car, an institution such as a church or nation, or an abstract conception such as mathematics. Characteristically, the evoked attitudes from this nodal "stimulus and goal object" lead to a diversity of ergic satisfactions, as indicated in the ergic loadings. We are inclined to conclude, therefore, as earlier that a sentiment factor represents a subgoal node in the lattice, which is both the permission and the stimulus for a set of diverse attitudes leading to and evoked by it. This subgoal may not always be consciously perceived, as in a young child who goes to church without any unitary conceptions of the church. But the existence of the object is nonetheless the condition of the unity of the various satisfactions. Indeed, this instance may illustrate the close interaction—sometimes in a succession—of the three different learning mechanisms, for the church sentiment may begin as a *budding* from the parental (home) sentiment, continue as a common reinforcement schedule pattern, and be cemented by an inherent perception of logical connections. The child acquires church practices initially to please his parents and receive their rewards; institutional behaviors are then simultaneously rewarded by the institution itself; and later he consciously recognizes the church as an object and his attachment to it as a distinct part of his self-concept and self-sentiment.

It must be remembered that the structural appearance of the

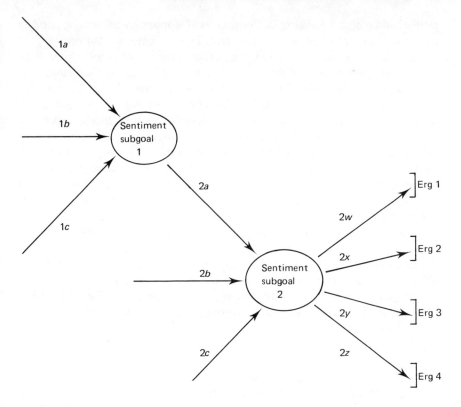

Figure 2-4. Structure of a sentiment as a subgoal.

sentiment in the dynamic lattice is still hypothetical, the manipulative experimental explorations indicated above not having yet been performed. The assumed relation of correlation to structure may be illustrated in Figure 2-4, where the longer sentiment subgoal 2 might be "Being accepted as a good member of this church congregation." The smaller subgoal, 1, might illustrate the budding principle just described, say, as the subgoal "To be accepted as an effective member of the church choir."

As a subgoal the sentiment subgoal 2 permits and evokes a whole series of designated attitude satisfactions, which lie proximally from it in the lattice, as shown by $2w$, $2x$, $2y$, and $2z$ in Figure 2-4. Attitudes $2a$, $2b$, and $2c$, which bring about the condition at subgoal 2, are concerned with preserving and maintaining the existence of situation 2. As some individuals will have a high development of 2 in their lives and others a low development, we may expect a positive correlation of strengths over the whole set of attitudes—the serving attitudes $2a$, $2b$, and $2c$ and the evoked, $2w$, $2x$, $2y$, and $2z$—though conceivably some loading difference will appear between the serving attitudes and the evoked attitudes. These same attitudes will, of course, also be loaded on the ergs (four in this case) to which they subsidiate. Subgoal 1 is introduced here simply as an illustration of the budding principle. The three attitudes serving it, $1a$, $1b$, and $1c$, will tend to correlate positively because their sum must equal $2a$, and $2a$ will vary in strength from person to person. In the structure of the lattice we would expect from the experimental results to date (for example, as embodied in the Motivation Analysis Test of Cattell, Horn, Sweney, & Radcliffe, 1964) perhaps comparatively few large sentiments. These are exemplified in the findings of a sentiment attached to home, school, nation, particular close relatives such as mother or brother, job, various hobbies, and so forth, and a large number of smaller attachments. These patterns will depend on the culture, and we would hypothesize that such factors in the end will be decidedly more numerous than the ergs, though in present lists they are about the same in number, and, incidentally, equally predictive of real-life performances. (See Cattell & Child, 1975; Pierson, Barton, & Hey, 1964; and developments by Sweney, 1969.)

2-4. The Mode of Action of Sentiments and Ergs, and the Concept of Ergic Investment

In Chapter 4, Volume 1, ergs and sentiments were treated simply and solely as resting on the empirical basis of factors found to fit a specification equation, contributing to the estimation of an attitude-strength score. In Section 2-3 above we anticipated a later discussion on how sentiments can be acquired by learning, but we mentioned this topic here mainly to fill out the properties of a sentiment (or other engram) as a structure in being. That structure we see as a network of cognitive connections that enable the ergic satisfactions of the sentiment to be reached through an integrated functioning of its attitudes. In the next step here—relating the functioning of ergs and sentiments—some principles yet to be clarified in Chapter 5 must momentarily be accepted as assumptions.

One such main assumption is that the strength of any response performance is a function partly of a motivation strength at the time, which we will denote by D (for dynamic element) and partly of a cognitive connection in memory, which we will denote by G (for engram[2]) which mediates between the environmental perception and the excitation of the erg. Omitting at this stage any consideration of scaling, or whether the function would better be a product than a sum, we may state the basic postulate in the formula:

$$A = D + G \qquad\qquad (2\text{-}1)$$

where A is the strength of the act (response performance). (Incidentally it will be noted that this basic division into some drive-like concept on the one hand and a habit formation on the other has entered into a number of learning theories, most clearly in Hull's system as "drive strength" and "habit strength." Later developments here, however, are very different.)

This formulation we shall soon surpass, as insufficient. Yet for lack of respect for the elementary distinction it makes between *performance gain* through learning, on the one hand, and *structural learning change* or engramming, on the other, countless discussions and even research designs, have gone astray. The first is a measure of actual performance, as in A, or gain of performance ($A_2 - A_1$) or dA; the second is the relatively permanent change produced in the engram system, which may subsequently operate with *any* motivation linked to it. It is this second which is to be called the actual learning. Thus a rat may run a maze quicker (gain in A) either because the first experience modified G, or because D happens to be greater, or both.

Research, mainly as reported in Chapter 4, Volume 1, already permits us confidently to expand D and G into many terms, D becoming the series of E's (such ergs as sex, fear, food seeking), and G the series of M's (such sentiments as to home, religion, self), each weighted in the specification for the given A or the given gain in A. An erg, by definition, does not change its pattern of motivational support or its inherent need level, by *learning*, but it does change its degree of involvement (v in the specification equation) and the extent to which it is modulated (aroused) by a given situation—its s in the specification. An M, on the other hand, will change through learning both in its structural nature and its v and s involvements.

Let us leave for the moment what learning does to E and M, as such, because there are some special problems about E, and study instead the general development of equation (2-1) as a series of duly weighted E's and M's. The weights are initially b's, behavioral indices, obtained experimentally as factor loadings on variables. From Chapter 7, Volume 1, we recognize, however, that there are operations for breaking down the b's into v's and s's (the latter being modulators, increasing *arousal* level in the E's and cognitive *activation* level in the M's). The v's can be broken down further into p's (perceptual skill weights) and e's (execution strength) later if need be. Meanwhile we shall break down the experimentally given *b* no further than into *v*, the involvement index, and *s*, the modulator. The former expresses how much a unit of ergic tension (in the case of E's) or activated sentiment strength (in the case of M's) affects the resulting behavior, a_j, made in response to focal stimulus *h* (in an ambient situation *k*). The reader will recognize that we are using the *v*, *s*, *p*, and *e* terms with the definitions and experimental ascertainment of their values given in Volume 1, Chapters 5 and 6, equations (5-3), (5-8), and (6-10). Here we merely remind him briefly of those precise meanings by the above, and by pointing out that s_k, the modulator index for an ambient situation *k*, says how much the ambient situation *k*, relative to the average of ambient situations, augments or contracts the ergic-tension levels or the sentiment-activation levels, before they act in behavior with the potency defined by *v*.

Although we are not ready yet to commit ourselves precisely to learning laws, it is certain we must recognize that both *v* and *s* are coefficients that normally represent results of past experience. However, we must also keep open the possibility, in the case of ergs that a fraction of the value of each behavioral index can reside in innate, racially-acquired connections. The v_{hj} (which can be either positive or negative) dictates that, say, an ergic tension E_x meeting stimulus *h* will tend to discharge itself by the action *j*, because *j* has previously proved rewarding. It will do so to an extent v_{hj}, as calculated from the performance. The s_k dictates that, because a raised excitation of the need E_x by situation *k* has in the past brought behavior that ended in drive satisfaction, the need now responds by increased arousal on meeting *k*. (Note E is used for *need strength*, E for the *ergic tension level* derived from it.)

In the case of E's we must defend the until recently unpopular position just stated that part of the v_{hj} and s_k values may be innately given. In regard to the fear erg, for example, there is evidence that it responds to large, strange, fast-moving objects, to darkness, and to pain, without any prior conditioning. (There is even evidence that young chimpanzees react with innate fear to a perception as specific as that of a snake.) Consequently we reiterate that *we must admit the existence of cognitive structure in all animals that nevertheless is not acquired engram structure.* And in every piece of behavior we must admit that there is some hidden, innate reactivity, contributing to the total performance, small though it may be relative to the learned reactivity.

In this connection, the massive evidence of the sociobiological researches of Wilson (1975) and his colleagues, if not the ethological studies of Tinbergen, McDougall, and Lorenz, must surely by now have laid to rest the aberration which began 50 years ago with Watson (1914) and certain sociologists denying any role to innate behavioral propensities. Those of us who endured through this period of popular suppression, nevertheless made little progress, until the factor analytic demonstration of ergic tensions methodologically substantiated the concept of propensity, innate drive, or erg, E, and appropriately introduced it into the behavioral equation. Here, stating a simplified introductory level of the dynamic calculus, we have put ergic tensions and the acquired engrams which permit their stimulation in cultural settings, into a plain additive model, soon to be developed in product terms. However, we must at this point explicitly recognize that the cognitive connections that release ergic needs are not entirely confined to the M's. There must be innate cognitive connections also for any erg which for the moment, until ME products are introduced, we shall consider and write as one with the E term, since they have no action apart from E. There will, however, be a different behavioral index for this connection from that for the acquired connection of any erg with a given situation. This implies that in most cultural situations to which a person has learned to react there is already some vestige of an innate reaction. The person avoids a recklessly driven truck both because he knows of people killed in the street by such and because he is innately set to fear large, swift-moving, loud objects. He makes love to his wife because all the sentiments built up in marriage contain subsidiation to the sex erg, but also because of certain primitive stimuli to sexual activity. Consequently, in considering a vsE term in the specification equation it is important to recognize that it is qualified by involvement, v, and modulation, s, indices that spring from two sources, and can be rearranged thus:

$$vsE = (v_g + v_t)(s_g + s_t) E \tag{2-2}$$

where g and t represent genetic and threptic components. (Let the reader be reminded that threptic means not the environmental influence, but the component *in a trait* resulting from environmental determination.) Whether the augmentation of the learned (v_t and s_t) values for ergs and sentiments should be ascribed to classical or instrumental conditioning or both can be left for later discussion.

Now, although a human attitude performance or a rat barpressing performance at any moment admittedly must have past engramming, G, and present drive, D, as components, as in equation (2-1), the law of their combination does not necessarily require the most simple additive form there given. Indeed, at this point we must raise some momentous questions regarding our model. We have obviously been compelled by the factor-analytic evidence to accept a duality of factors—E's representing innate ergic forces and M's representing acquired patterns. The latter seem to be largely cognitive. There is some suggestion in the preliminary evidence that the U motivational component, with its physiological and other expressions, better records ergic tension, and that the I, the integrated component, with its cognitive activities, better measures M. Unfortunately for confident further theoretical advance at this point no one has yet demonstrated that the variance from the U motivation component (with its drive-like physiological loadings) is greater in the E factors while that from the I is greater in the sentiment factors. Certainly no data has been presented that shows E factors disappearing in factoring the I mode of measurement and the M's disappearing in U data. Since all known valid motivation measurement devices contain both, though in very different proportions, it will require particularly refined factor analytic experiment to show just what is happening. But on the present rough evidence we lean to the theory that I will be found to predominate in M's and U in E's.

And at this point we are compelled, by psychological not factor analytic considerations, to suggest that the truly representative equation must contain a product term of M and E. As far as the ergic level is raised by the usual learned channels the effect must be proportional to the development of M, and some kind of product—at simplest ME—would be necessary. Later we shall present an argument for a reverse direction of action in which the level of an ergic tension excites the cognitive association previously connected with it—as a wave of hunger makes a man think of dinner. Without pausing to discuss that here let us note that we are, in terms of the mathematical form of the model, proposing to add an EM and also what may be called an ME term to the existing E and M terms.

The addition of these "hybrid" terms is such a radical alteration of the model that before pursuing it further we should ask if it will fit at all the existing multivariate experimental evidence on which the first, simpler model was propounded. The fact is that so far research produces only E and M factors, and in a much smaller number than would be required if every E, forming a product term with every M, required a new factor. However, in the first place, it has been empirically demonstrated by Bargmann and others (see Cattell, 1977) that the factor model and analysis procedure are handy in the sense that they will still produce, in the form of an additive model, as an approximation, apparently linear, additive factors when we know that in the data they really relate as products. Second, if the scaling properties of variables are uncertain, the factor analytic finding could be reconciled with either the earlier or the later model.

To recognize this, let us look at the specification equation we now typically get, reducing the situation to one E and one M, as follows:

$$a_{hjk} = b_{hjke} \, \mathrm{E} + b_{hjkm} \, \mathrm{M} \tag{2-3}$$

Then, squaring, we have:

$$a_{hjk}^2 = b_{hjke}^2 \, \mathrm{E}^2 + 2b_{hjke} b_{hjkm} \, \mathrm{E} \, \mathrm{M} + b_{hjkm}^2 \, \mathrm{M}^2 \tag{2-4}$$

In other words, if the raw scaling of our variable were $a^{1/2}$ in relation to the true scoring, a, we should get a solution as in (2-3) when the true state of affairs should be as in (2-4). It is thus not at all unlikely that our present results, appearing as in (2-3), are compatible with the existence and discovery—when more sensitive scaling methods are used—of a structure like that in (2-4).

In an introductory way we have stated that two product terms are probably necessary, ME and EM. Let us next consider how the behavioral indices would be attached to them. Both, incidentally, are products of what we broadly call emotional learning, in that they involve new attachments of emotional, motivational responses. In the ME case the question arises whether the behavioral indices should be attached to the stimulating M term, as in:

$$a_{hjk}' = v_{hjm} s_{km} \, \mathrm{M} \, (\mathrm{E}_1 + \ldots + \mathrm{E}_p) \tag{2-5a}$$

(Taking a_{hjk}' as only one part of the total a_{hjk} and omitting i's) or whether the involvement of the ergs should be considered as quantitatively peculiar to them as in (where M is now a given M_x):

$$a_{hjk}' = v_{hjx} s_{kx} \, \mathrm{M}_x \, (g_{x1} \mathrm{E}_1 + \ldots + g_{xp} \mathrm{E}_p) \tag{2-5b}$$

Here the g_{x1}, g_{x2}, etc., values have the new meaning of permanent invoker modulators, that is, they show the extent to which the given sentiment arouses (g for "generates") the given erg, as part of the permanent structure of the sentiment, regardless of any particular situation k.

For the sake of clarity regarding all future use of symbols, let us alert the reader that *he is likely to encounter the symbol ME in future in two contexts that require distinction, namely, ME as a product of two factor (trait) scores, as in these equations, and ME as a symbol for means-end learning, or* CR*II.* The accident of symbolization is unavoidable, and the difference of reference is so clear from the contexts that ambiguity can scarcely arise—but its possibility should be watched.)

A vital addition—though perhaps a controversial one—has now been made to the general dynamic specification equation, which can be expressed, stripped to essential form, as:

$$a_{hjk} = \sum_{x=p}^{} b_{hjkx} E_x + \sum^{y=q} \sum^{x=p} b_{hjkm} M_y E_x$$
$$+ \sum^{x=p} \sum^{y=q} b_{hjkx} E_x M_y + \sum^{y=q} b_{hjky} M_y \qquad (2\text{-}6)$$

omitting *i*'s and the weights from (2-5b) and (2-7) which make ME different from EM).

The EM term will later (Chapter 5) be given more discussion than we can give it immediately. It hypothesizes that the rise in ergic tension of a particular erg, E_x, is capable of activating a cognitive system, M, with which it has been associated. Thus if the ergic tension level of, say, fear, is elevated by some accidental event unconnected with any sentiment—say a frightful airplane crash—there will be a tendency to evoke and activate those sentiment systems—say religion or concern for family and insurance—that have in part been acquired under the influence of an emotional need for security. The same phenomenon is often seen in emotions tending to reinstate images and cognitive memories acquired in some previous experience of the same emotional state (Weiner, 1966; Hess, 1959; Kimble, 1967; Lazarus & Fonda, 1957). It is also evident from everyday experience that the rise of a certain emotional need often evokes two different cognitive sentiment systems that in the past have been instrumental in satisfying it, causing a cognitive-emotional conflict of sentiments.

If we consider that a different sentiment will be activated to different degrees (*f*'s, below) by a given erg, then the EM in (2-6) should take the reciprocal form of (2-5b) in which we shall suppose that the initial arousal of E is by both an innate s_{k1} and some acquired modulation, s_{k2}.

$$a'_{hjk} = v_{hje} (s_{k1e} + s_{k2e}) E (f_{e1}M_1 + f_{e2}M_2 + \cdots + f_{eq}M_q) \qquad (2\text{-}7)$$

Here a'_{hjk} will be expressing a largely cognitive aspect of interest, especially measurable by the *I* factor in m.c. measures, and *f*'s are the "flow" capacities of E to activate M's.

This last observation reminds us that although we shall often use a_{hjk} for interest strength in the course of action a_j, that strength will have both ergic, U, and cognitive, I, components, in different proportions. In fact we are reminded also that a_{hjk} as typically measured and used in experimental work (Birkett & Cattell, 1977; Horn, 1966; Sweney, 1969) is always a composite measure of both U and I components that would be expected to yield both E and M terms. Any total attitude strength measure, in short, would have cognitive components such as would come from the straight M measures and from their E-derived forms in (2-7), as well as drive strength measures such as come from the innate E stimulation and the M-derived E in (2-6). Incidentally, it remains to be experimentally demonstrated whether using pure U and pure I measures of a_{hjk} will drop out respectively the M and the E patterns, as looking at a red and green diagram now through a red and now through a green filter will drop out respectively the green and red patterns.

A full specification equation must thus include not only the arousal of an E by features of the environment it is innately set to respond to in $v_{hje}s_{ke}$ E, and the activation of the cognitive M as such, in $v_{hjm}s_{km}$ M, through its learned associations, but also two interaction terms, ME and EM. The first expresses the power of the sentiment to arouse and draw upon ergic energy, and the second the capacity of a need to bring closer to consciousness—or into consciousness—the cognitive elements previously associated with its satisfaction.

Both of these terms will be composite and have vector form. Every sentiment has an *ergic investment*, which we shall study in more detail elsewhere (p. 104), and which denotes quantitatively by a vector, the ergs to which it ultimately subsidiates, and through which, therefore, it draws its energy to respond (response potential). The weights for this vector we have represented by g's—*generators*—such that g_{mxey} is the coefficient stating how much a unit of sentiment strength in sentiment M_x is capable of generating (in E units) motivation from E_y. Since the sentiment will in general itself be activated to a new level by its ambient situation the ME in full will be:

$$v_{hjy}s_{ky}M_y(g_{y1}E_1 + g_{gy2}E_2 + \cdots + g_{yp}E_p) \qquad (2\text{-}8a)$$

and $(g_{y1}, g_{y2}, \ldots g_{yp})$ will represent the *ergic investment* of M_y in a series of *generator* values.

Conversely, if we accept the law that a mood—an ergic tension level—tends to make easier the retrieval of cognitive elements associated with it, a series of *influence values*, f's, can be calculable showing how much a unit increase in need strength will tend to evoke a given sentiment. Just as the ergs that are served (subsidiated to) by a sentiment may be called its *ergic investment*, so the sentiments that, in a given culture, are the various means to a particular ergic goal may be called the *sentiment mandate* of that erg. (The factor analyst will perceive the connection with columns in the concept of the factor mandate matrix. Cattell, 1962, 1978). The terms of the sentiment mandate vector we may call *access* or *flow* values and represent by *f*'s. Thus the EM term in the dynamic specification equation would contain the sentiment mandate vector for the given E as follows:

$$v_{hjx} s_{kx} E_x (f_{x1} M_1 + f_{x2} M_2 + \cdots + f_{xq} M_q) \qquad (2\text{-}8b)$$

A path to the experimental determination of the generator (*g*) values has been indicated in describing (p. 104) a proposed calculation for the ergic investment of a sentiment. In principle the sentiment mandate of a given erg could be determined by the same approach, substituting the column of loadings of an erg for that of a sentiment and choosing the sentiment loadings that go with the highest ergic loading. However, future experiment will doubtless refine this crude initial approach, and also make fresh approaches through possible direct solutions for equation (2–8) below.

We now see that the dynamic specification equation (the behavioral equation minus the ability and temperament modality terms) must take on a fairly complicated appearance as shown in:

$$a_{hjk} = \overset{x=p}{\Sigma} v'_{hjx} s'_{kx} E_x + \overset{x=p}{\Sigma} v_{hjx} s_{kx} E_x (f_{x1} M_1 + \cdots + f_{xq} M_q)$$

$$+ \overset{y=q}{\Sigma} v_{hjy} s_{ky} M_y (g_{y1} E_1 + \cdots + g_{yp} E_p)$$

$$+ \overset{y=q}{\Sigma} v_{hjmy} s_{ky} M_y \qquad (2\text{-}8c)$$

The *i*'s are omitted from trait terms, and the reader will recognize that the *innate* E connections are given by a v' and an s' because they would be different from the *acquired* effects on E in the second term. Strictly, this second term must be considered to come from the internal appetitive and constitutional effect on the E level, as well as environmental stimulation, so that s_{kx} deals with internal s'_{ky} effects as well as the usual external situations. However, as we admit later *systems* designs (feedback) the E levels in the second term will be considered also as subject to feedback from the E generators in the third term. The s_{ky} in the third term is unlike the ergic case, the same as in the fourth. However, v_{hjy} is different, namely,

v_{hjmy}, because the effect on behavior of the third term is likely to be different from that of the purely cognitive activation in the fourth term. It will be noted that the essence of (2-8c) is that every erg interacts with every sentiment (often, however, very minimally) and reciprocally every sentiment with every erg, and that the a_{hjk} will typically have both cognitive and dynamic elements, which a comprehensive measurement should seek to include.

We now need to put on a more formal basis certain concepts with which we have been concerned for some time, namely, the difference between the unactivated *need* strength, E, and the actual *ergic tension* level in any normally stimulating ambient situation that we may represent by E. Further we need to give term and symbol to the difference between these two values, especially to the generated arousal that we can represent as E. These and the corresponding differences of the activated and unactivated sentiment engram are set out once and for all in Table 2-2.

Further considerations will suggest the hypothesis that in some respects the E, E, and E have the same properties and in others properties which, at least quantitatively, deserve different values (and similarly for M, M, and M).

The question arises first in regard to the feedback effect just mentioned, to which we must give some attention even before we launch into a full systems theory treatment. As mentioned, the E in the second term in (2-8c) is partly an internally generated value and partly the consequence of feedback from the arousal of E's by the activated M's in the third term. Representing it for the moment as E_{x2}, to indicate a secondary phase, we recognize that its value is:

$$E_{x2} = (s'_{kx} + \overset{y=q}{\Sigma} s_{ky} M_y)\, E_{x1} \qquad (2\text{-}9)$$

TABLE 2-2. Symbols for Ergic and Sentiment Derivatives

E	Need strength in the individual without stimulation
E	Ergic tension strength at a given moment from various external stimulations
E	Amount of arousal, such that E $+$ E $= E$
E	Drive strength as a constitutional feature (see equation 2-12)
M	Sentiment strength as engrammed
M	Sentiment strength at a given time of activation
M	Amount of activation

(The M_y value in the third term is also augmented by what is going on in the fourth, but in that case it can be directly represented.)

This feedback will require eventually that we move on from the ordinary specification equation into a systems theory model. However, since observation tells us that we do not have a run-away acceleration here, but that a_{hjk} rises and stabilizes itself at some level, there must be some control system we have not yet introduced to make the ordinary specification a reasonable approximation. This introduction of controls, because of the need to prepare background, we shall defer to Chapter 6.

Meanwhile we should pause to make clear a psychological fact: the difference we have made between s'_{kx} and s_{kx}. The former represents the arousal effect on an ergic tension of a situation k purely through unlearned *innate cognitive paths* that trigger its action. Since, as stated above, the lingering Watsonian tradition in psychology opposes recognition of this action we *might* perhaps feel called upon to emphasize its defense. Actually such emphasis seems today unnecessary and we shall refer the reader to ethologists, such as Lorenz (1966), Lorenz and Leyhausen (1971), experimentalists like Harlow and Harlow (1965) and Hess (1962), some "between the lines" in Mead (1942), and sociobiologists, such as Wilson (1975) for the highly convincing evidence that ergs have their own frameworks of innate connections. The sociologist or reflexological learning theorist can certainly no longer ignore this, but must soon seek means of incorporating it in behavioral theory as we do here. Our changed and ever-changing cultural environments may seem to make innate fear of the dark, or revulsion to snakes, or a preference of pink to blue in things to eat, irrelevant, for there are assumed no longer to be snakes in Manhattan, and with the food artists pink food is not necessarily less poisonous than blue. Moreover, the perceptual object in the innate link may be innately only roughly and flexibly defined. However, even with some learning modification (the ME term), the innate response may still add its quota to a total learned plus innate reaction in some largely cultural situation. Jung was very aware of this, as seen in his "archetypes" and the racial unconscious, and no perceptive psychologist can doubt that there is a rich field of investigation still to be approached in defining the underlying stereotypes of innate stimulators that humans possess. That is to say, there is programmed perceptual information in the innate erg similar to the acquired programming in the sentiments. The issue is in fact within the realm of experimental investigation by the methods of the dynamic calculus. Indeed it may be considered already partly answered by the finding that stimuli close to the consummatory goal retain high loadings on ergic factors as one takes different cultural populations, whereas the lower loaded, culture-bound stimuli and responses change. In the choice of measures for an erg we naturally keep a core of these consummatory behaviors for the sake of identification of the factor. But if one considers the whole *cultural* environment it is quite probable that the s'_{kx} values will play a relatively small part. What, for example, is the direct sex or hunger appeal of a pillow or a colored vase? Surely trivial and yet by remote perceptual resemblances not entirely absent, as the experiments by the Harlows (1965) demonstrate. And though the male sex erg may be strongly tied into the sentiment to the wife it is unfortunately a social fact that it can have a large s'_{kx} value for woman as such, with respect to which arousal no previous learning conditioning has taken place.

The aspect of sentiments now most in need of research is the precise nature of what we have described as their ergic investment, and represented a few pages back by the g or generator terms in equations (2-8a) and (2-8b), arranged as a vector. In general terms it has been defined as the ergic reactivity or energy that the sentiment as a whole can draw upon, and we have proceeded beyond this (Cattell, 1959; Cattell & Child, 1975) to a first suggestion for calculation, which we shall now refine. Incidentally, it brings out the reciprocity of two important concepts if we deal with the *sentiment mandate* of an erg, introduced above, at this same place, though the latter has its main relevance in the problem of memory retrieval.

In terms of observable behavior a sentiment is seen as a bunch of attitude courses of action, all much involved in reactivities and satisfactions centered on the particular sentiment object. They are operationally revealed by all of them showing significant loading on a single factor, M. However, as Table 2-3 illustrates, though uniform on the sentiment object they are commonly diverse on loadings on ergs. The loadings of an attitude on ergs represent, according to our dynamic calculus theory, the magnitudes of ergic satisfactions that course of action has come to offer, habitually. (Parenthetically, the loadings are actually tangents representing the rate of increase of satisfaction with increased attitude action, not absolute values. But, as we have argued earlier, when starting from a zero value these amount to the same thing, that is, $\overline{E} = b'a$, where $\overline{E}$ is total ergic satisfaction, a is the strength of a_{hjk}, and b' is the opposite regression to b, that is, of E on b.

Now in calculating the ergic investment of a sentiment we need to add the ergic satisfactions of all attitudes connected with it. In a first approach to this (Cattell 1959, Cattell & Child, 1975) the approximation was suggested of adding the loadings (or the

TABLE 2-3. Calculating the Ergic Investment and Strength of a Sentiment

Attitudes Loading Career and Self-sentiment	Factors (pattern)						
	Fear	Mating	Assertiveness	Narcism	Pugnacity	Career	Self-sentiment
I want:							
To control impulses	32	-07	-05	-12	14	-29	42
Never to damage self-respect	-10	-11	-08	17	-13	16	90
To maintain reputation	-22	-34	03	42	-29	-04	58
SS Never to be insane	05	23	06	09	14	06	84
A normal sexual adjustment	17	55	02	-07	22	28	47
To know myself better	44	13	01	-04	-09	-18	43
To look after my family	23	-19	-08	-02	-00	-08	16
To be proficient in career	37	10	69	11	22	19	45
Career To learn my job well	04	02	25	17	00	79	08
To stick to my job	13	05	-15	-61	-11	58	-11

Method 1. Simple addition of total ergic increments.

Career sentiment.

Fear	Mating	Assertiveness	Narcism	Pugnacity
.17	.07	.10	-.44	-.11

Self-sentiment.

Fear	Mating	Assertiveness	Narcism	Pugnacity
1.26	.30	.60	.54	.21

Method 2. Ergic contribution weighted by the loading of the attitude in the sentiment.

Career sentiment.

Fear	Mating	Assertiveness	Narcism	Pugnacity
.10	.04	.13	-.22	-.06

Self-sentiment.

Fear	Mating	Assertiveness	Narcism	Pugnacity
.43	.20	.29	.43	.71

Negative loadings denote loss of ergic satisfaction through the attachment. (In this case, because insufficient attitudes are taken for career, it ends negatively, which would not properly happen.) The total rather than the mean of attitudes is taken, but this presupposes that a stratified sample of attitudes has been used and that one sentiment genuinely has more attitudes strongly involved than another.

squares thereof, for variance contribution) for each erg over all attitudes significantly loaded on that sentiment. That calculation is shown in the two rows at I in Table 2-3.

However, a more precise calculation can be justified as follows. If attitude a_1 is loaded $b_1 = 0.8$ on the sentiment and attitude a_2 shows only $b_2 = 0.4$, the ergic investments of attitude a_2 are probably going to *other* sentiments in larger measure than those of a_1. The best estimate of how much of the ergic satisfaction in each case goes to the given sentiment is the product of the attitude's loading on the sentiment, M, and its loading on the erg, E, which we will write b_{e1} and b_{e2}, and suppose to be 0.3 and 0.5. Thus $b_1 b_{e1} = .24$ and $b_2 b_{e1} = .20$, and, from the activities in these two attitudes the sentiment will have a gratification on E of .24 + .20 = .44. In the end some further sophistication will be necessary in this addition according to such issues as possible use of the attitudes as alternates, the effect of correlation of attitudes upon the summation, and the relative magnitudes of ergs as ergs. But, until more experiment has groped into these avenues it would be academic to polish the model further.

What we finish up with is a vector of ergic involvements of the sentiment, as shown at II in Table 2-3. (Parenthetically, the more exact II is not so different from the approximate I, except in level, which as we shall see, needs modifying anyway.) If we grant that it is usual for a well organized sentiment to act as a whole, when activated, on all the ergs concerned, as symbolized on the ME term, then what we set out as the g, *generator*, terms in (2-8a) and (2-8c) are the same as the ergic investment vector, except for any scaling that may be necessary. (In equation 2-8c there was implicit the notion that the g's could be obtained appropriately scaled for a factor equation, by a sophisticated form of factor analysis, but the present channel of experimental evaluation is more direct and practicable.)

If we make the sentiment strength estimate over x attitudes, then any value g_{my}, for erg y in equation (2-8a) or (c) is:

$$g_{my} = \overset{a=x}{\Sigma} b_{ma} b_{ea} \qquad (2\text{-}10)$$

where a is any one of the attitudes, and m and e subscripts are sentiment and erg. The resulting vector of g values will then need to be scaled to meet the variance requirements of a factor analytic equation, if used in (2-8). From this vector we can sum to a scalar quantity representing the total ergic investment of the given sentiment. If all ergic factors are of the same size it will be as in (2-11), but if we are dealing with real base factoring or with individual differences, the ergs will be of different sizes (with subscript i in the latter case) slightly complicating the expression. If we denote the ergic investment of a sentiment y as G_y, and any erg e, then summation across p ergs gives:

$$G_y = \sum^{e=p} g_{mye} \qquad (2\text{-}11)$$

(It will be noted this is an addition of variance since the product of two r's (loadings in this case), $b_{ma}b_{ea}$, is a variance fraction.)

Having stated the core of the ergic investment concept in an exact, though initially simplified, model, let us look at its relation to rougher ideas that have been around in psychology, and let us consider also some refinements that may be necessary. The concept has broad and important relevance. Social psychologists and sociologists can use it in a calculus of social dynamics (see Chapter 7), assessing the population investment in various institutions. Clinicians and educators will see its relevance to calculations in conflict of sentiments, control, and life achievement, as shown below. In psychoanalysis a rough equivalent for G_y has been employed in the notion of *cathexis* of an object, and indeed there is no obstacle in Freud's writings to permitting cathexis to grow into the investment concept (except that Freud did not recognize the since discovered ergs we have included in the g values). Part of the enrichment in G is that the emotional (ergic) quality of the cathexis is indicated by the profile of the vector and this ergic strength of a sentiment, G, is distinguished from the engram strength, M. More importantly in the contrast is that G integrates as a basis for dynamic calculations into the whole theory of the dynamic calculus, which cathexis and similar clinical notions do not.

In clinical and everyday life terms G represents the total satisfaction that a person would lose if its structure could somehow be surgically dissected out of his personality or if the object to which it refers—concrete or conceptual—should be taken out of his life. In this last statement, we recognize that *the existence of the given sentiment object is an absolute precondition for all the diverse attitude satisfactions, ergically evaluated, that are obtained through its existence.* Some inferences from this theory in experiment are the following: (1) Because total pugnacity (expressed in the emotion of anger) can be assumed to be a simple function of the magnitude of the amount of ergic tension frustrated, a measure of *pugnacity* arousal when the sentiment is threatened should be proportional to G's in Figure 2-5. (2) Because depression is (in part) a function of irretrievable ergic loss, it also should be proportional, in death or destruction of the sentiment object, to G. (3) *Conflict* measures and other related measures involving M_y (in its *external* relations) should also be positive functions of its G to the extent M is involved.

The reader will recognize that what we have just stated above algebraically can also be conveniently represented (and for visualizers made more clear) by the geometric representation in Figure 2-5. There (at (a)) out of 5 attitudes 2 are taken that load on sentiment x and 2 on sentiment y and the simple form of unweighted vector addition in ergic space (just two ergs here) to get total ergic sentiment strength, G, is used (a_1 is some attitude in the same ergic space but not loaded on either sentiment).

At (b) we are reminded of the more refined model in which the projection on the sentiment modifies the amount of ergic investment from the raw projection on the erg.

As to qualifying conditions and caveats on the basic concept, we should note that in the experimental basis of measurement the dynamic lattice points to the strength of a sentiment being the same in the attitudes converging on the node (which a sentiment is in the lattice), namely, the *contributory* attitudes, as in the *evoked* attitudes, which diverge from it. So it will not make any difference which we take in estimating the total ergic investment. This follows from what we have named as the third psychodynamic law. If for convenience we take the contributory attitudes closest to the sentiment subgoal they will (1) be the attitudes most highly loaded on the sentiment, and (2) sum, in their vector sum on ergs, to the total ergic satisfaction obtained through the existence of the sentiment. Parenthetically, according to equation (2-3) or (2-4), this ergic loading on each constituent attitude, as obtained from the factor analysis, will represent partly innate b's ($v_{hjk}s_k$'s) from the first—innate—term and partly the $v_{hjm}s_{km}$ values we actually seek to get from the second. Some approximation therefore attends the calculation now proposed, both because of this contamination and because the E's and M's obtained by factoring, as suggested in connection with equation (2-5), do not exactly fit the present model. In any case the exigencies of practice will almost certainly incline psychologists to the approximations of (a) taking only 3 or 4 attitudes most highly loaded on the given sentiment, and (b) giving them equal weight, as is done for example in the MAT instrument (Cattell, Horne, & Sweney, 1965).

A more theoretical problem that enters here concerns the implications for the above calculations with b's, of breaking down the b's into v's and s's (or, indeed, finally into p's, r's, and i's and s's). The v's are, of course, peculiar to a particular stimulus, h, and attitude action, j, whereas the s's represent a situational arousal, k, that may be related to several h's. When we add attitudes, as proposed,

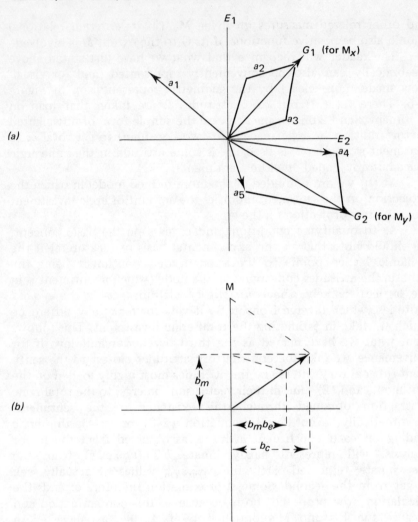

Figure 2-5. A sentiment as a vector combining ergic investment and engram strength.

In *(a)* the geometric vector calculation for the ergic investments, G_1 and G_2, of two sentiments, M_1 and M_2 are shown, each from two attitudes. $a1$ is an attitude loaded on these ergs but not on either of the sentiments.

In *(b)* the calculation is shown as modified by taking into account the loading of the attitude on the sentiment, as in the second method in Table 2-3. The investment of M in a particular erg E is shown geometrically by plotting just the two. The construction lines c_1, c_2, and c_3 (c_2 parallel to c_1) enable one to reach the ergic investment $b_m b_e$, which is the product of the two loadings (cosines).

it is appropriate that the v's should enter as well as the s's; so the use of the "global" b's above is correct, though special analyses might be conceived in which the summation of v's and s's separately is illuminating.

Finally, in considering the *ergic strength* of a sentiment G (not to be confused with its cognitive engram strength, M) or its vector unfolding in the ergic investment $(g_1, g_2, \cdots g_p)$, it is necessary to recognize the implications of the fact that sentiments frequently show partial subsidiation to one another in the dynamic lattice ("budding" is a clear instance). The question will thus arise whether we can thus segregate and unconditionally assign energy to a given sentiment, when its final ergic subsidiation is in general actually through *other* sentiments. When the water used to power Mr. A's mill proceeds downstream to power Mr. B's, we have to recognize that when the stream fails for A it fails for B. Yet, in this physical example, or that of two houses in series on an electric circuit, they have, within limits, partial independence. Beyond our third law of psychodynamics—that motivation tends to remain the same through a closed subsidiation chain—stands a law of modifying circumstances akin to the physical laws involved above, namely, that motivation gets less with increased goal distance. Consequently, it is desirable to measure the strength of a sentiment as it stands, without regard to the structural subsidiation to others, because, presumably, the ergic loadings reflect this goal distance. And the ergic investment values define the energy in that sentiment, without need to consider the subsidiations, though if the structure alters the ergic investment will alter. When a company goes bankrupt the director is no longer concerned with his scheme for a truly artistic renovation of the offices.

All kinds of social and clinical calculations of the role and importance, growth and decline of sentiments hinge on the G and M values, and the vector patterns of ergic investments. To turn next to broader theoretical interests, we must here look at the *reciprocal* relation of what we have studied, what might be called the "sentiment investment of an erg," meaning the vector of sentiment loadings that a single erg commands. For clarity we have called it the *sentiment mandate of an erg*, when setting out its vector in equations (2-7) and (2-8b) and suggesting a general mode of calculation. The more exact calculation is simply the reciprocal of the calculations, of $b_y b_x$ terms, illustrated in Table 2-3 *for a sentiment*. The calculation will lead to an equivalent to ergic strength of a sentiment G which total we shall label F and call engram command of an erg, and to the corresponding *vector* of f's which we shall call the sentiment mandate of an erg. Psychologically we introduced it as the activation of a set of sentiments by an erg—the EM term in the dynamic specification equation—now recognizing that each E will operate over several M's, by influence values, entered as f's, in the mandate, as calculated above.

About this engram-activating action there is still only a handful of adequate experiments. More precise knowledge is needed, both on this activation effect as it shows in total a_{hjk} motivations, and in the domain of retrieval and memory studies. Our hypothesis has been that arousal of an erg lowers the threshold for retrieval of certain memories, and that, in accordance with the development of cognitive networks in M's, this means that we can speak of an activation influence for an erg with respect to the totality of a particular sentiment as such. The concept obviously leans on the distinction between arousal states in ergs and activation states in sentiments, the latter purely cognitive and cortical. It *may* also ultimately turn out that the generators, g's, and influencers, f's, are essentially the *same* engram linkages able to operate (with some discount) in both directions.

Finally, a word is desirable on the need to keep conceptually separate the concepts in a sentiment of the engram strength, M, and the ergic strength, G, and, correspondingly, in an erg, of the ergic strength, E, and the engram command F. A sentiment contributes to any action both through its ergic investment (the second term in the general equation) and through the *cognitive* contribution by M itself (the fourth term). The vector for strength of a sentiment, if it is fully to describe the sentiment, should therefore project on *engram* coordinates of some kind, as well as the various *ergic* coordinates. This will be shown in the first place, of course, by part of the sentiment strength, like any a_{hjk}, recording itself in the motivation component scores that have a cognitive, integrated character. It will not usually show itself by any appreciable projection on *other* M coordinates, as there are projections on the E coordinates to give ergic investment, because most M's will be little correlated. However, these M correlations, second order M's and projections thereon could be revealing regarding the subsidiations among sentiments.

With these statements we shall leave for a while the structure of sentiments as such. Our main statements end that a quantitative description of a sentiment requires (1) An evaluation of the ergic investment vector that gives it its particular power, (2) Of the strength of the engramming itself which is derived from the estimate of pure M factor using cognitive component measures, and (3) Its subsidiation and competitive relations to other sentiments. The above equations are statements of essentials and ultimately need regard for various conditions and sub-definitions passed over in a first treatment.[3]

2-5. The Relations Among Drive Strength, Need Strength, Ergic Tension, and Arousal

The factor that is measured as an erg, by the totality of objective motivation devices, in the attitudes loading an erg, is strictly to be called an *ergic tension* measure, for it measures the tension level of a unitary erg *in a given condition of stimulation.* As we know more about the primary m.c.'s and the secondary (U and I) m.c.'s we may be able to say that some m.c.'s measure this arousal component in tension more than others; but at present we are speaking of an ergic factor as found in a combined battery of U and I devices. It must be regarded as the final expression of several causes that contribute to the ergic tension in a given situation on a given occasion and which we may hope experimentally to unravel. In this section we shall attempt to unravel into a proportion of components that must for the time being be called "hypothetical" but which is so broadly based on psychological observation that there can be little doubt of the initial soundness of their conceptual status. These concepts about the E and M roles will late be related to the motivational-component findings.

Let us remember that research in this field began by getting the dynamic structure factors from attitudes measured on U and I devices together, as a composite, but later it showed that the same patterns appear in attitude measures picked up factor analytically solely in U and I devices separately. A hypothesis (Cattell, 1959, 1965) that the nature of the integrated component, I, requires M's to appear with greater variance and emphasis in terms of I measures and for ergs to appear with greater variance in U measures, has been mentioned. However, because the attitudes necessary for measuring ergs always have some sentiment variance too (that is, both E and M terms are generally present) and because the devices for measuring U components always have some I variance and vice versa, the results required clearly to check the hypothesis would need an exceptionally well-planned, well-executed, large-sampled, factor-analytic experiment, such as has not yet been performed. Accordingly, in stating our best hypothesis we shall also entertain any alternative hypothesis regarding m.c.'s that seems promising.

The chief hypothesis we shall put forward is that the seven

or eight *primary* motivation components may have relation to dynamic components specifically within the ergic tension measure. A second hypothesis is the psychoanalytic one already stated, of α as id, β as ego component, etc., and, which is not entirely incompatible, granted certain psychoanalytic definitions, with our first hypothesis. A third alternative hypothesis, that the m.c.'s could be related to parameters of attitudes, such as conscious-versus-unconscious, old-versus-new, and so forth, has already been mooted in Section 2-1. The breakdown of components in ergic tension to which we now relate the m.c.'s was first proposed by the present writer (1959) without relation to m.c.'s. It posits in every erg a *need strength* which becomes an *ergic tension* through an arousing[4] stimulus situation, k, and the modulator s_k. This need strength is relatively fixed in an individual, though also partly determined by transient appetitive conditions. It has two components, a constitutional *drive strength* truly peculiar to the individual, and an *appetitive strength* depending on the contemporary balance of *gratification* and physiological *appetite-generation*. Let us now define these terms for further precise use, and in relation to the new hypotheses of possible motivation component identification.

Drive strength is the equivalent of a fixed trait, "constitutional" in nature. We use constitutional not as "hereditary," but, as defined in Chapter 1, that is as all that heredity and experience have left the individual with, as a steady characteristic, up to the point of observation or experiment. Drive strength may be briefly written $(C + H)$, where C is the genetic component and H is the effect of previous history, especially the early history of imprinting and those fixations (autoerotic, homosexual, and so on) that Freud explored so widely as fixations and regressions in regard to the total sex drive. If psychoanalytic observation is sound, however, these modifications by early history could affect the total basic strength of a drive and not merely some limited area of attachment.

Parenthetically, the reader should recognize that drive strength as we define it finally in equation (2-12) is not to be carelessly equated with say Hull's drive strength or any less precise definition but must be precisely understood on the basis of its ultimately assigned properties here. Beyond the hypothesized, relatively permanent, C and H components, what we are here calling the need-strength component (see equation 2-12), there exists in drive strength an appetitive component. That is to say, *current need strength* is the permanent *drive strength* plus the current *appetitive condition*.

Appetite strength is split into independent parts—physiological and behavioral—because many experiments on consummatory drive satisfaction (for example, on feeding through a fistula and copulation without ejaculation) indicate that if the innately given physiological demands are satisfied without satisfaction of the normally corresponding innate sequences of consummatory behaviors some tension to discharge the behavior still exists—and vice versa if behavior, but not physiology, is satisfied (Sheffield & Roby, 1950; Sheffield, Wulff, & Backer, 1951).

We must also suppose that for purely internal reasons connected with the passage of time—for example, falling blood sugar in the case of hunger—the physiological component in the need strength is not fixed but normally increases as a function of an internal clock.

Thus the appetitive level component, whether in the physiological or the behavioral component, is always a balance between some internal generation of drive strength and the external incidence of behavioral satisfactions or physiological gratifications. As far as the physiologically-generated drive is concerned we adopt the simplest assumption that it increases linearly with time from any given time-point, and that the effect of gratification conversely decreases linearly. Thus we would write the physiological component as $P \times t$, where t is time from a given origin, and the gratification as $G_p - btg$ (where b is a constant and tg this second time scale; that is time since last gratification). But to avoid cluttering, P and B are initially written in equation (2-12) "as taken at the given moment." Incidentally, to meet possible time findings we assume B also has a linear increase with time although there is yet no exact evidence of any temporary augmentation or change in the level of the need to get behavioral expression for a nonviscerogenic erg. Possible differences of viscerogenic and nonviscerogenic drives in equation (2-12) are discussed later. The subscripts p and b on G are for physiological and behavioral satisfactions respectively. With these sub-definitions the need strength at a given moment can be written:

$$\text{Need strength} = E$$
$$= \{(C + H) + [x(P - G_p) + y(B - G_b)]\} \quad (2\text{-}12)$$

where x, and y are merely scaling weights to bring the different kinds of measures to comparability. In short, (2-12) says present *need strength* is inherent "constitutional" drive strength, plus appetitive state strength. Our general model now hypothesizes that the actual *ergic tension* at a given moment is the product of this need strength and the stimulating power, s_k (possibly innately determined but generally arising from past experience) of the ambient situation k. Although in the statistical framework of the factor specification equation we have written, and shall regularly write, $E = s_k E$, we propose now to make a simple transformation to a new type of s_k, written S_k such that $(s_k + 1) = S_k$.

The reason for this is that we need to recognize the psychological fact that when stimulation, s_k, falls to zero there is still ergic tension from the original need strength. That is to say, the measures we use for attitude strength, such as spontaneous attention, fluency, or GSR do not seem to approach zero when stimulation itself is minimal and close to zero. Moreover, in animal observations, later, we shall formalize the concept of *spontaneous behavior* consistent with this view of behavior and the observation of perceptual manifestations existing at ordinary times for unstimulated need strength.

The theory that drive strength is not zero when stimulation is zero seems supported at the physiological level by such observations as those of Prosser (1959) on the crayfish, showing that large neurons do not wait to respond reflexly to a stimulus or to other neural messages, but have periodic spontaneous discharges. The phenomenon has since been recognized widely in neural action of most species. Skinner's use of the term "operants" for undefined stimuli that provoke random responses necessary for operant conditioning to act on might, in the light of this theory, be thought of as a superstitious word to avoid a new theory accepting *response without stimulus* (see Sheffield, 1951; Cattell, 1954). Throughout the study of drive we encounter evidence that relatively fixed action patterns of ergic response, such as studied by Lorenz (1966), Lorenz and Leyhausen (1970), Schludt (1963), and Tinbergen (1951, 1953) will at times "fire" with so little trigger action from the environment that it would be hard to deny the word "spontaneous" to them. Probably we deal with an asymptotic curve between response and stimulus and there may be no harm in speaking of extremely small stimuli to be called operants, if reflexologists wish to avoid committing themselves to "response without stimulus." But many indicators of need strength for example stomach movements when hungry, phantasy imagery, tremor, etc., that are short of actual external behavioral response undoubtedly exist to make need strength measurable before any external stimulus provokes ergic response. The only question that arises is whether the latent need strength, when provoked by a stimulus to become what we measure as ergic tension is in some way qualitatively changed. This difficult question will have to await further experiment. Meanwhile, to avoid having ergic tension vanish when all known stimulation is absent we shall meet the problem by supposing that an amount of "stimulus ground noise" always exists (perhaps analogous to the astronomers' basic cosmic noise?) which (in 2-13) we will call c. If we like to have ergic need strength at zero stimulation simply equal to need strength then c is placed equal to unity.

It is worthy of comment, incidentally, that the distinction we have made between viscerogenic and nonviscerogenic ergs here comes out strongly in the size of s_k. Nonviscerogenic drives depend markedly on the environment to bring their arousal from drive or need strength to a fair state of ergic tension, but viscerogenics do not, and depend more on the weight of x. At this point also we must be more precise about the concept of ergic *arousal*. By arousal we mean the increment in an ergic-tension measure that occurs when stimulation of the need strength rises above zero, that is, when s_k exceeds zero. (However, if c equals more than 1 there is already arousal in the E measure.) This concept becomes important in Chapter 4, when we make a distinction between need reduction and arousal reduction. Accordingly in terms of the above definitions of the constitutional component, C, gratification, G, and so forth, we can write the full origin of ergic tension as:

$$E = (c + s_k) \underbrace{\{ \underbrace{(C + H)} + \underbrace{[x(P - G_p) + y(B - G_b)]} \}}_{}$$

$$\underbrace{}_{\text{drive strength}} \quad \underbrace{}_{\text{appetite strength}}$$

need strength

ergic tension strength (2-13)

If the constant c is made statistically to be 1.0, the E can be separated into the original need strength and the arousal components in the observed ergic tension, as follows:

$$E = \{(C + H) + [x(P - G_p) + y(B - G_b)]\}$$

need strength

$$\{(C + H) + [x(P - G_p)\, y(B - G_b)]\}$$

arousal (2-14)

In accordance with the symbolism in Table 2-2 this can be condensed to:

$$E \quad = \quad E \quad + \quad E$$

ergic need arousal
tension strength (2-15)

The question naturally arises whether an analogous model exists for the strength of an activated sentiment, expanding the M = M + M we have met in Table 2-2. There is surely here, however, no constitutional component and no appetitiveness. There may, however, be some difference of property between earlier and later learned parts of an engram and between parts learned more by repetition, by strong and weak learning motivation, and by cognitive relation eduction as compared to association, and so forth. It is pointless to speculate on any concepts of this kind until evidence is available, and we shall stay with the three parts: the strength of the engram laid down, M, the activated state part, M, and the sum of these, M, except for a distinction shortly to be made between directly activated part s_{km} M and part activated through ergic tension s_{ke} EM.

It will be recognized that the E statement in (2-13) and the corresponding M statement stand for the first and last terms in (2-8c), that is, those in which the situational modulation acts directly on the erg or the sentiment. In the case of the middle terms in (2-8c) the activation of the sentiment is mediated by the arousal of ergs, and the arousal of an erg is mediated either by the activation of a sentiment or an innate activator expressing itself in s_{ke}. This involves nothing more than the insertion of an E and an M term after s_k in equation (2-13).

It will be noticed that we now have, in any attitude strength, derived from the above, as many as seven possibly different qualities of contribution. This total is reached if we admit that the constitutional need strength may have different properties from that due to viscerogenic, passing appetite, and that drive strength and need strength are different in quality and quantity, as supposed in equation (2-13).

Then we have distinct qualitative derivatives corresponding to the ergs and sentiments and their interaction as shown in Table 2-4.

It might be sheer coincidence that in any attitude measurement by all objective devices we have seven primary m.c.'s and seven sources here; but there are such similarities to the seven qualitative characters here that we shall tentatively put forward for experiment the theory that these are nothing other than the primary motivational components. The alignments and brief arguments for them are as follows:

α *component.* We hypothesize this to be M₂ the arousal of a sentiment through the action of an erg on a sentiment (M₂ = s_{ke} EM). Support for this is the predominantly ergic root of α manifestations and its prominence on the second order U, yet with a substantial cognitive content. The basic ergic "I want" or "id" nature is shown

TABLE 2-4. Components in an Attitude Response as Deduced from the Totality of Erg-Sentiment Action

1. Constitutional need strength with non-viscerogenic appetite*	E'	(ϵ)
2. Viscerogenic component in need strength	E''	(δ)
3. Arousal of erg from innate cognitive paths	$s_{ke}E = E_1$	(ζ)
4. Arousal of erg through sentiment activation	$s_{km}ME = E_2$	(η)
5. Engram strength of sentiment as such	M	(β)
6. Activation of engram by environment directly	$s_{km}M - M = M_1$	(γ)
7. Activation of sentiment through ergic tension	$s_k EM - M = M_2$	(α)

*It is possible to conceive of a split of the need strength in two or three ways according to equation (2-12). One would be to put the appetitive part (in the square brackets) in a category different from the fixed constitutional. Here, guided by indications of some separateness of the physiological appetite we have put this viscerogenic part $(P - G_p)$ separately as E''. To avoid excessive splintering we suppose that the constitutional and non-viscerogenic appetitive strength are one, represented as E'. Thus $E = E' + E''$, but this split is probably not relevant to the products of E such as 3, $s_{ke}E$, and 7, $s_{ke}EM$.

by the prominent loadings in autism, projection, and fantasy. But at the same time the loading pattern has considerable similarity to that of γ (Cattell, Lawlis, McGill, & McGraw, 1978) which we identify below with M_1, the amount of direct environmental activation of the sentiment (notice the high common loading, for instance, on criterion utility). Consequently with this cognitive content emphasis we identify it as sentiment activation due to ergic pressure. The largeness of the α factor may seem to give a larger role, incidentally, to ergic arousal determination of sentiment activity than one might *a priori* expect.

β *component.* The heavily cognitive loadings here (see Chapter 4, Volume 1) can leave little doubt that this is basically the engram contribution M in Table 2-4. The loadings particularly on information, warm-up speed, and persistence suggest a long-established cognitive interest.

γ *component.* This we interpret as the direct activation by environment of M above, that is, as $M_1 = s_{km}M - M$. The evidence of a raised activation of the engram is in speed of word-association, fluency on cues to action, regard for criterion utility, superego projection (This ought to be done), and some role in fantasy, autism, perseveration, and selective perception (Cattell & Child, 1975, p. 12).

δ *component.* This factor, the many physiological response associations of which have long been noted (size of GSR, decision speed, blood pressure changes—Cattell & Child, 1975, p. 13) along with a retroactive inhibition effect on current mental processes, we interpret as the physiological appetitive component in ergic tension, E'' in Table 2-4.

ε *component.* One has some hesitation in interpretation here, since this has formerly been interpreted by discussants as the "Freudian complex" contribution, on the basis of a combination of high GSR to stimuli along with forgetting of them. However, in the total framework it looks here like the straight constitutional and appetitive ergic strength component, E'. In recent work (Cattell, Lawlis, McGill, & McGraw, 1978) it continues low on cognitive expressions and negative in memory and reminiscence, but it has GSR associations and relations to various criterion results. For example, it is positively related to time and money spent on interest. This may indicate the basic pull of a sustained ergic interest.

ʃ *component.* This weaker component has loadings with negligible cognitive content consisting of decision speed, muscular tension, and impulsiveness. It could well be an ergic arousal component operating through purely innate and largely unconscious cues, that is, as E_1.

η *component.* The ergic tension from stimulation of ergs by sentiments one would expect to be large—in signs of ergic tension as such as well as in some of the cognitive triggering that should accompany it in the ME product. The present identification is therefore the least satisfactory of any, and one is tempted as an alternative to consider that α is a yet unsplit EM and ME combination. There *are* sentiment-like expressions here, in fluency on cues, general fluency on the interest, perceptual activity in hidden figures, persistence of activity, but none of the straight "desire" expressions one might expect in the stimulated ergic investments of the sentiment. The hypothesis is then very tentative.

The hypotheses are indicated in parentheses in Table 2-4. There should be no difficulty with this degree of operational definition in experimentally checking these hypotheses. For example, the viscerogenic component could be manipulated, in hunger, sex, and so forth. The degree of activation could be manipulated in the environment to study γ and η scores. The degree of fluctuation could be measured over time against α and ε measures, and so on. Meanwhile we do have replicated second order structures to look at (Cattell, 1979) and at places α, δ, ϵ, and η in the U factor, β, γ, some δ in the I, and ϵ and ζ in a third smaller factor. In terms of the present hypotheses that would classify EM, E'', and E_2 in unintegrated expressions (which would make good sense except for E_2). It would place M, M_1, and some E'' in integrated behavior, which would seem correct except for E''. The discovery of E' and E' together in the smaller third factor puts the constitutional strength of the erg and the strength of its innate arousal together, which matches a clear concept. Space forbids discussion of possibilities in regard to the two anomalies, the simplest resolution of which would be to exchange their identity, making η the viscerogenic component E'' and δ an ergic arousal through sentiment activation. The loading patterns of the above primary motivation components were given fully in Cattell, Horn, Radcliffe, and Sweney (1963) and more condensed in Volume 1, Chapter 4, while a recent re-check on the patterns is available in Cattell, Lawlis, McGill, and McGraw (1978).

2-6. The Calculus of Decision, Conflict, and Integration

Not a day passes but thousands of pages are read in books, magazines and the press in which psychiatrists and others explain the roots of conflicts and the motives behind various behaviors in the average man. Unfortunately for this important subject very little that an experimentalist can recognize has been done to place our knowledge of the common dynamic lattice prevalent in our culture on a firm footing of quantified specification equations. (The few R- or P-techniques that have ever been done often verify the speculations, for example that oral action in smoking, and listening to music load the sex erg, and that satisfactory sex relations satisfy the self-assertive erg and self-sentiment.) It is surely high time, however, that professional psychologists desisted from entertaining the public with these speculations and set out with comprehensive and serious research to ascertain the loading specifications on ergs and sentiments for the main activities in our culture.

In those attitude courses of action for which some mapping has been done it has now become possible to go further in the dynamic calculus to embrace the calculation of decision-making and the evaluation of conflict.

Let us consider conflict, with decision as a particular aspect. Conflict is implicitly between courses of action, as in attitude courses, but also as between ergs (and associated emotions) and sentiments, which *connote* actions. Under the rubric of decision theory and conflict the student will find writings somewhat oblique to the present. Decision theory, for example, is handled as a very clear theory that is cognitive and has to do with computers and games. That will join up with the dynamic calculus, but it is not our central concern here. Conflict, in animal experiment, is much nearer, but when treated as a conflict of *stimuli* it misses what the dynamic calculus conceives about the conflict of structures—of ergs and sentiments. Stimuli are involved, but as reflections of ergic goals and meanings.

When a given erg is dynamically aroused or an acquired sentiment engram cognitively activated, there are two kinds of conflict that can be studied. The archetypal reflexological conflict of Pavlov, in which hungry dogs reacted to ambiguous visual stimuli, is one the dynamics of which concerns the satisfaction or inhibition of a *single* drive—hunger. Here the conflict might seem to be correctly described as a conflict of stimuli—to satisfaction or nonsatisfaction. But in the normal situation conflict is both of stimuli and of drives (or sentiments). Directly or through sentiments it is a conflict between *different* ergic *goals*, because the stimuli are attached to different ergic goals. The strengths both of the drives and of the stimuli are then involved—the stimuli existing in the sense of the k in $s_k'E$ and $s_k ME$ in the last section. In the animal domain we now have fairly extensive and exact studies analyzing relative influences on action and learning of differing drive strengths and the reinforcement effect of particular stimuli (Sheffield 1965, 1966). The above attention to conflict of different drives, because it is most important in personality, does not overlook that there *can* be conflict in which only *one* drive is involved, with (a) two or more stimuli pointing to different paths or (b) one stimulus saying "stop" and one "go," as in Pavlov's classical conflict experiment. Animal experiment has concentrated, relatively, on that design (except such early work as that of Warden, 1931) but most conflict of stimuli is also one between drive goals. Even when two stimuli, and the indicated paths, lead to much the same ultimate goal they will still, as immediate actions with different side subsidiations to other ergs, have somewhat different vectors of E and M weights.

Here, to consider essentials and to set aside problems of purely cognitive uncertainty and confusion in decisions, we shall begin by considering that two cognitively clear stimuli evoke two clearly different courses of action with different dynamic goal satisfactions. The problem is to understand the decision in terms of the relative strengths of those anticipated previously learned satisfactions.

In real life and with humans the cognitive stimuli can be in physical, ecometric properties, highly similar. The difference between a reprieve and a death sentence is a few words. Generally there is at least an identity of the global situation, otherwise the individual would not be presented with a conflict at the same moment in space and time. In this connection, however, because our principal concern is with human personalities, whose conceptual capacities permit them to perceive different focal and ambient stimuli in the same general situation, we shall continue to use distinct h's (focal stimuli) and k's (ambient situations) applied to the two courses of action in conflict.

A distinction must be made at the outset between *active* and *indurated* conflict. (This distinction affects both goal and course of action conflicts.) In active conflict, which is our first case here, there are *two possible courses* of action, generally leading to two more or less different kinds of dynamic satisfaction, indicated by cues that will be constituted by different focal stimuli. The question of whether there are two different ambient situations (k_1 and k_2) as well as two different stimuli (h_1 and h_2) needs clarifying. It is usually the ambient situation rather than the stimulus which decides (by s_{ke} and s_{km}) what drive and sentiment purpose shall be evoked. According to our dynamic specification model, a given situation, k, fixes the ergic and sentiment goals and action. If there is conflict of goals at a given time and place it must be because the human capacity to conjure up images of situations not physically present has exposed the subject simultaneously to a concrete and a conceptual, or two conceptual situations. Incidentally, to say that he perceives the concrete situation in two ways will not do; for, as our analysis of perception in Chapter 6, Volume 1, asserts, the perception is given by the behavioral indices affixed to the traits (the p and s fractions of the index b). The nearest to a dual situation in the same concrete situation is dwelling in attention on different aspects of the situation; but most conflict of goals will be between two conceptual situations offering different ergic arousal and expectations of satisfaction. On the other hand, a conflict of means to the same situation-k-provoked, desired goal will frequently depend on which of two stimuli actually appears. If A is aroused by the situation to murder B his choice of action may depend on whether a pistol or a knife is conveniently at hand. *Active conflict* therefore can take two forms. In one there is only conflict over means, and the difference in equation (2-16) below is only in the h's; in the other there is conflict over goals (which will commonly *include* different means of action too) and this must be represented by different k's.

Indurated conflict (conflict to which the person has settled down in a compromise) implies on the other hand a single course of action, but some persisting conflict of desires in doing so. In such a habit the gain of a greater satisfaction in one erg has been possible only by some degree of denial of another, so that conflict of a certain kind may be seen still to be embodied in the agreed course of action. In setting out these two conflict forms in formulae, we shall not at present bother about some rather refined statistical qualifying conditions.[5]

In *active conflict* our assertion is that the outcome of the decision process will be determined by the relative strengths of the two courses of action, which can be calculated from the specification equation or objectively measured directly in a_{hjk}. Thus (reverting for simplicity to gross behavior indices, for example b's, instead of p's, e's, and s's) we have two alternative action courses, in this case also with different kinds of goal satisfaction, defined as follows:

$$a_{h_1 j_1 k_1} = \overset{x=p}{\Sigma} b_{h_1 x j_1 x k_1 x} E_x + \overset{y=g}{\Sigma} b_{h_1 y j_1 y k_1 y} M_y \qquad (2\text{-}16a)$$

$$a_{h_2 j_2 k_2} = \overset{x=p}{\Sigma} b_{h_2 x j_2 x k_2 x} E_x + \overset{y=g}{\Sigma} b_{h_2 y j_2 y k_2 y} M_y \qquad (2\text{-}16b)$$

There is no need for an i subscript, for the traits (E's and M's) here must be those of one and the same individual. (The form of these questions, if we consider the dynamic interaction terms, has been given in (2-3), but for studying conflict per se let us keep to the simpler form.) Equation (2-16) reminds us of the multiple determination by having p ergs and g sentiments.

If the experimental values hitherto obtained for b's, E's, M's, and so forth, in relation to habitual directions of decision in the individual's life (Laughlin, 1973; Sweney, 1969) are any indication we can predict that the decision will in general favor whichever a_{hijk} has the higher value by this calculation. Of course there will be other terms besides E's and M's in the behavior-specification equation, namely, ability and temperament traits, but the weights of the latter, at least, should be trivial, and the former, at least, would concern only how well the two actions are performed, if performed, not how much they are desired. If we wish to state prediction of decision outcome in the form of a probability, we have:

$$P_{1\text{-}2} = \overset{x=p}{\Sigma} (b_{x1} - b_{x2}) E_x + \overset{y=g}{\Sigma} (b_{y1} - b_{y2}) M_y \qquad (2\text{-}17)$$

Note that it is not possible to express this purely in loadings—b's—because the particular individual's particular ergic tensions and M's are also involved. *P* simply reexpresses the difference value, from knowledge of distribution of differences, in terms of a probability of decision for action 1 rather than 2.

Apart from indirect indications this proposition has so far only been investigated by Laughlin (1973), predicting from test measures of the attitudes to decisions in actual life situations and using *R*-technique values in comparing the decisions of individuals. In one form his results were inconclusive, which seemed traceable to some nonconformity of the life-situation "criterion" choice which he set up and the test room definition of the alternatives as measured. This might be partly remediable by setting up *several* repeated rather than just one life-situation choice, the better to average out equivalently to the over-all *symbolic* choice in the test measures. However, with further data Laughlin was able to predict life-situation decisions with moderate statistical significance. The whole domain of decision theory in relation to the dynamic calculus now calls for experiments extending decision research more realistically into common deliberations of everyday life, using whatever new light can be thrown by better measurement of distinct motivational components.

The direction of the decision taken is one thing; the amount of conflict in it another. Assessment of the amount of conflict needs to be approached in two ways: (1) By evaluating the magnitude of the dynamic forces (in $v_{hj}s_k E$ and M terms) known to be opposed either in active or indurated conflict, and (2) By an independent and empirical approach to bring order into the manifestations of conflict named in clinical psychology leading to setting up measurements for these. As far as the first approach, applied to active decision conflict, is concerned, the theoretical approach would suggest first that amount of conflict should be a function of the mean strength of the two forces in conflict, that is, a sum of $a_{h_1j_1k_1}$ and $a_{h_2j_2k_2}$ in (2-16a), (2-16b). Second, the existence and duration of conflict should be a function of the smallness of their *difference*, since it is when they are virtually balanced that hesitation and prolongation of the conflict occur. Third, the question will be raised whether when $a_{h_1j_1k_1}$ and $a_{h_2j_2k_2}$ lead to much the same ultimate E and M satisfactions, the conflict is as great as when they do not. The answer would seem to be, considering a person desperately hungry and having to choose between entering a restaurant by a side or a main door, that (provided each is equally certain) there is not the same degree of conflict as when two quite different ergic satisfaction patterns are pitted against one another.

A tentative formulation of conflict in *active* decisions is given in equation (2-18). This illustrates the need to give different weights,

w_1 and w_2 respectively, to (1) the mean magnitude of the contestants and (2) the smallness of their differences. Thus we get (with a_1 assumed larger than a_2):

$$c_a = w_1(a_{h_1j_1k_1} + a_{h_2j_2k_2})$$
$$- w_2(a_{h_1j_1k_1} - a_{h_2j_2k_2} + p) \tag{2-18}$$

(The c is kept lowercase to avoid confusion with C as ego strength.)

This assumes the stronger attitude, $a_{h_1j_1k_1}$, is placed first. The constant p has to be worked out to prevent the second term becoming unduly large with very small differences. The form of (2-18) is speculative, insisting only that conflict will be greater with stronger attitudes and with lesser difference between their strengths, and hypothesizing, incidentally, that w_2 will be smaller than w_1.

If we now turn to the component in active conflict which arises from difference of goals rather than merely of means we reach a model very similar to that more fully discussed below for indurated conflict. The magnitude of the difference of ultimate dynamic goal is represented by the differences of the loadings on dynamic traits, in which for addition, one might take the squares of the differences thus:

$$c_d = (b_{hjka1} - b_{hjka2})^2 + \cdots + (b_{hjkz1} - b_{hjkz2})^2 \tag{2-19}$$

where c_d is the dynamic conflict and the dynamic traits are an array from a to z. In the individual, as distinct from the common population equation in (2-19) the individual dynamic trait strengths would be inverted (as, for example, $(b_{hjka1} - b_{hjka2})^2 E_i$) since a disparity on a powerful drive means more than on a weak one.

Contrasted with active decision and active conflict so far discussed, we encounter next what has been called *indurated*, subconscious, latent, or built-in conflict. In this case a number of active conflict situations have been finally resolved in the life of the individual by a compromise course of action. How this compromise is learned, through *integrative* or confluent learning, is described in Chapter 5. All we need to know here, however, is that the individual has settled on some compromise course of action which, though *fully* satisfying neither of the original active conflict courses, maximizes, as far as he is able, the average joint satisfaction of all ergs and sentiments involved. It has repeatedly been shown (Cattell, 1950; Cattell & Baggaley, 1958; Cattell, Horn, Sweney, & Radcliffe, 1964) that most attitudes of most people are predominantly of this type. That is to say the analysis almost always shows the specification containing some negative along with positive loadings, as discussed briefly in the vector representation of attitudes in Volume 1, Chapter 4 and in Section 2-4 above.

The meaning of such an obtained negative value is shown in geometric terms in Figure 2-5 (p. 108). That diagram was set up primarily to illustrate the *vector summation of attitude strengths*, at once on *ergic* coordinates and *on engram coordinates*. These give respectively the total *ergic investment in an attitude (or sentiment)*, as discussed above, and the total *engram strength of an attitude or sentiment*. It illustrates, also, however, at a_1 and a_4 in Figure 2-5(a), attitudes that have negative projections, respectively on E_2 and E_1. What do these negative projections mean? They mean surely that the only courses of action discoverable to the subject for yielding major satisfaction on one erg tend to lose him satisfaction on some other. (Or, in the alternative regression, that greater expression given to a certain erg means reduction of activity on the attitude.) However, as the projections show, the gain on the accompanying erg is in each case greater than the loss on the first. In fact, as drawn here, the sentiment or attitude ends with positive gains in each illustration.

Because a regression coefficient may mean causal action in either direction, it could be, as just hypothesized, that a negative ergic loading sign means that a *reduction* of expression of the erg leads to an *increase* in the strength of the attitude. But various considerations suggest that the dynamic explanation in the alternative direction, as we finally accepted here, is more correct. That is to say, when this course of action is pursued, it leads to satisfaction of the positively loaded ergs and through environmental difficulties created by that action, to reduction (inhibition) of expression of the negatively loaded ergs. If now we sum the *negative* involvement, $(-v)$, and *negative* modulation, $(-s)$, values, over all p ergs and sentiments loaded on the attitude, writing these as $(-v)$ and $(-s)$, we should obtain a measure of the absolute loss by "internal friction" involved in the given attitude or sentiment, thus:

$$c_{hiks} = \sum^{x=p} (-v)_{hjx} (-s)_{kx} \qquad (2\text{-}20)$$

The subscript s on c here means *stable*, indurated conflict.

This is a first approach, assaying conflict for every person: that is, the average person in the sample. For a given individual, however, the dynamic trait strengths, the D's (D for dynamic traits: E's and M's) would have to go in. And unless we accept the questionable simplification of Hull's and other reflexological systems of assuming that there is only "general drive," ignoring the weights for different qualities and strengths of particular ergs, certain weights that may be empirically found for the conflict-producing quality of each erg should also go in.

Finally, it may seem desirable to express the conflict not as an absolute amount as in (2-19) and (2-20) but as a *fraction* of the total satisfaction in the given dynamic system attitude or sentiment. An equation simultaneously to bring the expression to fractional meaning, and to applicability to individuals (introducing the D_{xi} for the individual dynamic traits of persons) would be (the pluses being positive loadings):

$$c_{d \cdot hijk} = \frac{\overset{x=p}{\Sigma}(-v)_{hjx}(-s)_{kx}D_{xi}}{\overset{x=p}{\Sigma}(+v)_{hjx}(+s)_{kx}D_{xi}} \tag{2-21}$$

where c_d means indurated conflict and there are p dynamic traits (assumed, initially to be ergs, E's, but now recognized as any dynamic traits, D's). It is axiomatic that this index should not reach unity. Nor has it been found to do so empirically in any dynamic specification equation yet seen. For the individual would not then derive *any* satisfaction from that course of action. Consequently he would not have learned this unreinforced behavior in the first place, or, if having learned it under more positive motivation he would drop it as it drifted into such negative values. No attitudes experimentally studied in published researches have in fact shown more than a rather small fraction of negative values.

The conflict index has for initial simplicity been discussed in ergic projections only, though the D symbol normally embraces both E's and M's. The question may arise, however, whether the loadings on sentiments should also be included? Sentiments certainly do come into conflict. Indeed, the whole of literature, from Hamlet to the latest paperback novel, is full of graphic descriptions of such conflicts. How such conflict is to be represented will depend on whether the model of equation (2-4) without E and M interaction or (2-8c) with mutual interaction (EM and ME) has been followed. If we wish to be open minded and comprehensive of all possibilities, then, as in most analyses from this point on, we should stand by (2-8c). If two sentiments are in conflict, this gives two kinds of contribution from each sentiment, one from the ergic investment (aroused) of each and one from the cognitive activation (terms 2 and 4 in equation 2-8). The former will be easy enough to recognize, being emotional conflict, but what is meant by a conflict of the cognitive activations of two sentiments? Surely this also we experience, in the battle for attention to perceptions and for the retrieval of ideas which occurs when two sentiments are simultaneously stimulated. Indeed, the Freudian notion of repression describes just such action, though it is viewed as involving repression of forces of the "id" only, whereas our formula would involve both the ergic strength of the sentiment investments and the activated strength of the cognitive networks themselves.

The above indices of indurated conflict, in (2-16), (2-19), and (2-21), first considered for attitude conflict only can be applied, as Figure 2-5 shows, to any size of dynamic system. The dynamic trait may be an attitude, a subsentiment, a sentiment, and ultimately the c index could embrace what happens to the total personality. A clinician is generally most interested in the conflict in a sentiment, such as that to a mother, a wife, or husband, and so on. He or she often makes a substantial use of the concept of *ambivalence* and may be puzzled as to how this gets expressed in our quantitative concept of sentiment investment, where all the f weights are represented by *single* values (positive or negative). The answer is that these are the projections of *the final summed vector* of all the attitudes connected with the sentiment object. *Among* these several attitudes there can be conflict. One attitude to the mother may for example contain and express affection, whereas another may include the expression of hostility. The ambivalence will be accurately measured by the index for internal conflict for the sentiment, which can also be expressed vector-wise, instead of as a single sum as in (2-21), to display in what ergs the ambivalence lies.

Over and above the measure of conflict in a given sentiment the clinician also wants to assess conflict for the total personality. In fact, up to the present, it has been in regard to the total personality that the necessary experimental investigation of the relation of the conflict index to other conceptual measures has begun. Clinical considerations suggest that a more-than-average array of negative loadings in a stratified sample of a person's life attitudes (courses of action) implies maladjustment. A sum of this conflict index over all his interest-attitudes might thus be used as a precise operational statement of the degree of poorness of integration of the total personality. Indeed, the essential theoretical form of the dynamic calculus calls for total internal personal conflict to be so defined. All that is necessary is to have the index c_{hijk} in (2-20) (or as fraction in 2-21) determined for each of an agreed stratified sample of *total* life attitudes (hence c_t), and summed as follows:

$$c_{ti} = \sum^{hijk=h_n ij_n k_n} c_{hijk}/n \qquad (2\text{-}22)$$

where there are n attitudes or sentiments included. We must conclude that the higher this c_{ti} value is the more the individual's emotional learning has failed to discover effective compromise courses of action by confluent, integrative learning (with inhibition) that will come anywhere near maximizing (for the given environment) the possible ergic satisfactions. If we hypothesize that the need to make a break with reality—the rejection of reality perception—in a nonorganic psychotic, notably a schizophrenic, comes if the reduction of satisfaction in the real world goes beyond a certain critical point, then it would be expected that psychotics would turn out to be significantly higher than normals on the c_t index.

If psychotics and normals are factored together in R-technique the b (vs) values will be the same for both, because shared, being group values. Consequently only some oddity in particular combinations of b's and scores on D's (dynamic traits—actually ergs, E's, in these experiments, which is not theoretically expected) could produce differences in c_{ti}'s. Any attempt to check comparative conflict totals in this way would be useless. Instead the examination must be by P-technique, which alone can yield b's specific to the individual and which, of course, require about 100 occasions of measurement on each. The careful and lengthy task of getting P-technique comparisons of psychotics and normals was made by Williams (1958, 1959) and though he had to stop at no more than six cases of each kind (psychotic and normal), the c differences nevertheless proved significant in the expected direction at about the $p < .05$ level. His study also supported other theoretically expected relations as described below.

We have distinguished between *indurated conflict*, for which we might write c_d and action conflict, which we have written c_a. The total personality conflict has been expressed in indurated form though presumably a separate total personality conflict index could also be assessed in action conflict terms, following the same strategy of using a sample of current attitudes and summing the expression in (2-21) across them. Obtaining c_d and c_a would give a more total view of the individual's conflict. However, because the indices would have very different properties one (c_a) being transient in its magnitude and the other (c_d) more steadily characteristic of the individual, it would scarcely do to add them. Many a well-integrated and adjusted person could be high on c_a for temporary situational reasons. The c_d (more fully c_{dti}) index, on the other hand, should by all sanctions of the dynamic calculus model reflect poor personality integration. Consequently, we propose to stake one aspect of our definition of personality integration below on the operational definition of integration as the inverse, or, more simply, the complement, of indurated conflict, thus:

$$I_i = (1 - c_{dti}) \tag{2-23}$$

In the next section we shall explore the relation of total integration operationally so defined to other possible definitions and measures of integration.

Meanwhile let us examine the promised check on this dynamic calculus approach through comparing its results with those of direct examination of clinical signs of conflict. Clinicians, for example, have a substantial variety of behavioral signs they have long conceived as symptomatic of conflict. Although the statistical significance of measures on these clinical observations need not, in general, be doubted, yet until structural analysis has been done we have no right to consider they are all measuring the same thing—that is constitute a single dimension of conflict. A comprehensive and replicated exploration of this domain (Cattell & Sweney, 1964), using 20 commonly accepted diverse manifestations of conflict, showed, factor analytically that there exist some seven basically different kinds of expression of conflict. It indicated batteries of devices by which these underlying dimensions could be measured. The seven experimentally-thrice-checked factor patterns were labeled from content as follows: (1) exercise of willed suppressive action, with cognitive distortion; (2) sensitive avoidance of stimuli that threatened further provocation to conflict; (3) a pattern of responses as yet uninterpreted; (4) fantasy on solutions, mainly unreal; (5) enhanced activity of ego-control measures; (6) tension and sensitivity of a general kind, appearing largely at a physiological somatic level; (7) uninterpreted.

Incidentally, in this work two concepts were developed useful to the structured investigation of conflict and for further descriptive discussion here. They are the notions of *loci* and *foci* of conflict. The first is a socio-cultural concept of content area (family-versus-religion, peer group-versus-parents, and so forth). The second defines the internal psychological structures involved (between erg and erg, superego and erg, and so on). The obtained patterns of the seven primary modes of expression of conflict were found to be constant regardless of locus or focus.

At this point the similarity of the seven conflict manifestation factors to the m.c.'s in number and content (for about half the variables have similarity to the motivation strength measures) has struck several researchers, for example Krug (1977), with the thought that they may be the same. There is actually nothing amiss in this concept, for if there are varieties of motivation and the clash of two ergs or sentiments occurs, as is likely, across all of them, then there would be as many manifestations of conflict as there are of motivation. The possible alignment we have discussed of a, β, γ, and so on with EM, M, and M, and others in Table 2-2 offers no obstacle to this interpretation, for the frustration of E, M, ME, and so on might well produce different manifestations.

What prevents an organized solution at the moment is the strange absence from the conflict manifestation factors of any pattern—except possibly 2 or 6—that could be confidently interpreted as anxiety. For the overwhelming evidence of clinical psychology that conflict produces anxiety—and also pugnacity, depression and defense mechanisms—cannot be neglected. As to the defense mechanisms one extensive multivariate experiment (Cattell & Wenig, 1952) has verified that they have much the form described so lucidly by Anna Freud (1937), and that they have certain general personality factor associations. However, readers familiar with the necessary strategy of programmatic personality structure investigation by factor analysis will recognize that often (a) planned restriction of variables to a certain class must necessarily overlook other factors in the area requiring a different class, and (b) that conversely a factor usually seen in class A variables may nevertheless intrude into class B results, but not be recognized because of lack of the usual markers.

The pioneer multivariate research trails in this domain of the dynamic calculus—a vast domain of vast importance to psychology—are still pitifully thin. To attempt a hypothesis almost in a vacuum we would expect the relations in this area to be (a) that anxiety will appear as a second order factor among the seven conflict primaries, (b) that the defense mechanism factors will prove distinct and independent with respect to the conflict factors, representing a second stage, (c) that most of the m.c. factors—we would with some confidence name four at present—will be paralleled by conflict factors, but contain extra loadings (conflict) in the latter not needed to estimate the former. It is likely that the structure will resolve factor analytically by conflict factors of anxiety, anger (pugnacity), depression appearing as second order factors among the m.c. primaries, adding the extra conflict features we have noted. As we look at the conflict equations, for active (2-18) and indurated (2-21) conflict, and consider that what is there given by a total dynamic trait, D, could be split into E's, M's, EM's, ME's, and so forth we see that the single conflict index, c_a or c_d, could be more fully represented by a vector of differences (or negative loadings in the case of indurated conflict) on the E, M, EM, ME, and so forth terms that would be expected, if the above theory is correct, to correspond to scores on the conflict primaries.

Although the above structure rests on only a handful of researches, the stage is set for crucial experiments, since operational checks are clearly indicated. We have, in effect, three independently derived measures of conflict that should check. First, the theory of active and indurated conflict gives us estimates from equations (2-18) and (2-21). Secondly, the direct measurement of conflict manifestation primary factors gives us another, with which we may find anxiety as a second stratum conflict factor, now very validly measurable. A third measure of conflict comes from yet another direction, namely clinical use of the MAT by Sweney (1969), J. M. May (1964), Birkett & Cattell (1978), and others. Their studies have shown that conflict as rated clinically (or, again, when essentially evaluated by the dynamic calculus as above) shows itself by a significant excess of U- over I-component levels in measures taken in the area concerned. This is consistent with the meaning previously given to I as the integrated, conscious, expressed part of a dynamic trait. For U and I components may be regarded as drawing on a common energy source, and when the individual is unable to give integrated, adjusted, real-life expression (I component) to any drive, a comparatively large U component would be expected to pile up. The evidence on this diagnostic value of the U/I ratio is still largely clinical, but has been quantified in group comparisons (Cattell, Horn, Sweney, & Radcliffe, 1964). The design of experiments to produce or utilize separate variations in these different measures should be a challenge to resourceful clinical researchers.

2-7. Integration and Impulse Control: Self-Sentiment, Ego, and Superego Structures

Hopefully the experimentalist will not prejudge from this use of psychoanalytic terms that there is to be any reversion in this section to unchecked clinical methods! Multivariate experiment has brought advances in understanding and measurement of structure beyond what has been possible from either clinical observation or classical bivariate experiment. But well-checked factor-analytic research has undoubtedly brought solid evidence of ego, superego, and self-sentiment structures, and it has seemed reasonable to retain these clinical terms in their more precise, modern, operational reference in discussion here. In short, continuity of science and respect for earlier insight justify retaining these terms for the obviously similar patterns now found by R-, dR-, and P-techniques.

The study of the dynamic calculus leads inevitably from questions of integration and conflict in particular areas toward those of total integration and toward investigation of the ultimate controlling mechanisms, including the nature of the self. Indeed, what we have begun to discuss under the experimental investigation of conflict above is always begun in traditional clinical approaches on the assumption that the ego, the id, the superego, the censor, the defense mechanisms, and so forth, are the main actors in conflict. The enormous number of largely clinical volumes about control and the self structure constitute one of the largest extant bibliographical jungles, in which a conscientious historical appraiser might be lost forever. But although the issues are the most subtle that psychology faces, it is yet possible, as the work of Gorsuch (1965); Gorsuch and Cattell (1977); Horn (1966); Birkett (1979); Sweney (1969); and other multivariate experimentalists shows, to begin afresh with firm conclusions reached by sufficiently refined concepts and methods.

In the present section, we intend only to make a preliminary evaluation of the natures of these dynamic structures as such and their controlling action as a triumvirate. Their full action in a systems theory is reserved for Chapter 6, which studies also their acquisition through learning.

In the first place we note that in purely descriptive structural research such as we began to survey in Chapters 2, 3, and 4, of Volume 1, three structures have been located repeatedly that operate in what clinicians and shrewd qualitative human observers recognize as the general area of integration, control, and direction of impulse in human behavior. They are, in the Q- and L-data series, C, the ego-strength factor; G, the superego source trait; and Q_3, the self-sentiment. These patterns of behavior have stood up to repeated factoring and rotation in up to 28-dimensional space in Q-data and L-data factoring series (the L-data notably in the investigations of Digman, 1963, 1965, and Cattell, 1945, 1957, 1979). It seems at first curious that although G and Q_3 have appeared also very clearly in a third observation medium—the factoring of objective measures, yielding dynamic structure factors—C, until Birkett (1979) had not. But there is a reason, which we shall soon encounter. It should be noted that the asserted identity of G and of Q_3 across three media of observation does not rest just on meaning and concept, but is established experimentally by common factoring, across these media whereupon the particular markers in the three media correlate positively and load on the same factors (see, for example, Cattell, Pierson, & Finkbeiner, 1976).

The natures of Q_3 and G are clear both from their L- and Q-data (rating-questionnaire) *item content* (Cattell & Child, 1975, p. 99) and from their *predictive potencies* against everyday life criteria. The latter data are now very numerous (Cattell, Eber, & Tatsuoka, 1970). The former, Q_3, has to do with maintaining behavior fitting close to the person's adopted cognitive self-concept and satisfying the pressure of social expectations. That concept, whatever its other content, loads questions and attitudes concerned with the individual maintaining his social reputation and his self-regard concerning his capacity to control himself. For this reason it has been called the *self-sentiment;* it is the system of attitude actions centered on the self-concept and its maintenance, just as any other sentiment centers its attitudes on some other object.

In G we have strong support for the Freudian concept of the superego. The pattern concerns moral behavior and ethical standards. Moreover, it demands certain behaviors of the individual in the nonintellectual spirit of an emotional categorial imperative. In some methodologically less developed rating factorings G and Q_3 have been confounded, because they do in fact load some of the same social and ethical attitudes and behaviors—though for different motives—but all careful simple-structure studies pull them clearly apart. Psychologically, the distinction can be summarized in two words: "manners" in Q_3 and "morals" in G (with the understanding that manners means, broadly, attentiveness to social approval, and morals means the moral imperative values implanted in children in the culture of the time). The O (guilt proneness) factor has also sometimes been confused with G; but O seems to be a deep "oceanic" emotion as described in part by William James and by Dosteovsky, partly involved in religious feeling, and determining a strong emotional feeling of unworthiness, depression and guilt. Strangely it scores above average in convicted criminals as well as neurotics. Anyone who studies these and other factors in Chapter 2 or in detail in Cattell (1973), will have little difficulty in seeing G (rather than O or other factors) as the source of the essential moral effort and demand for standards of persistence in personality.

Before studying these "controllers" more carefully, let us study the proposition (Cattell, 1950) that these particular structures are not the whole story of cultural control and that a dependability vis-à-vis threats of upset by crude ergic impulsiveness is also given by an individual's whole acquired equipment of stable sentiments. When we say, however, that the normal array of sentiments—to home, job, hobby, country, and so forth—brings greater "predictability" by providing channels that chance ergic stimulations can follow, we must be careful to define this predictability and dependability more exactly in regard to a reference framework. For ergs themselves bring high predictability, too, if statistical predictability per se is all we are concerned with. For example, a roué with little sentiment for his wife can dependably be predicted to pursue every passing attractive woman; and the instinctual behavior of lower animals is highly predictable once we know the stimuli.

What an employer, a teacher, or a cultural institution means by saying that a man with many well-developed sentiments is more dependable is something quite different from scientific determinism. They mean that he will dependably respond to what constitute generally approved institutional stimuli, if dependably present, rather than respond to crudely instinctual stimuli sporadically scattered among the cultural stimuli. In terms of equation (2–8) we are saying that the largest weights in the specification equations have, by learning, shifted from the initial innately stimulated E term to the new ME term that follows. The innate connections have been swamped by the acquired M's. It is true, however, that this shift of energy expenditure from crude instinctual responses into channels provided and taught by the culture *will* also tend to bring greater integration, in the sense defined in equation (2–23). For by the insightful or trial-and-error experience of the culture, these provide ready-made channels, possessing a substantial probability of low indurated conflict—that is, of ultimate frustrations.

So long as a culture remains reasonably stable, therefore, the learning of sentiment systems of a general kind—not just the special controlling sentiments such as G and Q_3—will contribute to integration, besides increasing dependability in the sense that other people in the culture approve dependability. We see this cultural integration in comparing the child, or the hypothetical lone savage beloved of philosophers, with the matured, civilized adult. If we have a taste for literary reflections we see it in comparisons of the "wilder" characters in Gogol and Dostoyevsky with those of Victorian Europe in Dickens, Thackeray, and Galsworthy. What these sentiments to home, school, country, organized sport, and so forth do is provide prescribed engrammed paths of discharge for any erg "accidentally" strongly stimulated by any situation. When Pascal was disappointed in love, he found habitual paths capable of absorbing interest already available in the mathematics he had learned and loved since childhood. If a metaphor rather than a more exact model may for the moment be permitted to summarize this rather complex mechanism, we may say that the sentiments are flywheels that can absorb the changing inputs of ergic stimulation.

We can see that stability would be aided by adjustment of sentiment growth to a stable life environment, and if the culture is itself well integrated in the sense of having worked out the least punishing paths to maintain a healthy society with adequate expression for the individual, the individual who adopts the sentiments more completely will tend to be more integrated than one who does not. However, this contribution of sentiments to integration can go only a certain distance. One should not rashly equate amount of sentiment acquisition with the totality of integration, and certainly not with higher moral behavior. There are countless instances (Burt, 1923) of children brought up in criminal gangs whose sentiments are strong but morally inverted. The phenomenon of sentiments that do not fit the culture, or are incompatible with one another, is also behind the fact that any individual who is entirely shifted out of his usual cultural environment is likely to show both poor integration and antisocial behavior. This can be recognized in, for example, the erratic behavior frequently seen in persons so transported from their supporting and restraining environment, as in a normally faithful husband away in a distant city. In short, even when a person is within the usual environment, and still more when he or she is not, the existence of strong sentiments alone fails to offer any strong guarantee (1) that the behavior will be morally directed, at least beyond what is necessary to the satisfaction of the given sentiment in a watchful, normally policed society; and, (2) the avoidance of clashes among sentiments. An example of the first is that a man may have a powerful, lifelong sentiment to his country, and yet, setting aside a superego sentiment, behave to the rest of the world like Hitler; or a master passion for art, and yet behave like Cellini. Inasmuch as cultures survive by internal morality, *most* institutional sentiments will have *some* moral values built into them, for example the superego may not be the sole repository of moral values. But, as we shall see, a superego sentiment specifically concerned with moral values nevertheless seems to be necessary. The loadings we find for attitudes of moral sentiment indicate that invigilation by the superego brings on altogether greater access of moral direction than the rest of the sentiments achieve together. As to the second—sentiment inconsistency—because institutions clash in society, the corresponding sentiments may clash in the individual. Although they themselves are stable, inner structures, conflict will therefore arise among them in certain situations as when a good union member finds himself loyally tied to a dishonest labor politician. Thus they seem to require a "higher-level" integration by a regulation from the self-sentiment, superego, and ego. In their intrusion particularly we see that integration is more than a strong sentiment-structure acquisition.

No further reference need be made here to the evidence on the accuracy of factor determination, the loading patterns, and the interrelations of the C, G, and Q_3 source traits. These patterns and their criterion correlations are well known to the student and amply set out in the literature (Burdsal & Schwartz, 1975; Cattell, Eber, & Tatsuoka, 1970; Cattell & Horn, 1963; Cattell, 1973). Our task is now rather to ask how they bring about both greater integration and greater alignment with the values of the culture than is possible from general sentiment development alone. In so doing, note that though C results, until 1979, came only from questionnaires and ratings, our data for G and Q_3 can be taken also from objective motivation measurement of the G and Q_3 patterns in assemblies of attitudes, for example in the MAT and SMAT batteries. There we note that though a sufficient sampling of all life attitudes has not yet been experimented upon, present results argue for the self-sentiment having loadings on more attitudes than most other sentiments. This statistical indication that it has a "finger in the pie" of most other sentiments is supported by other sources of evidence of a psychological nature, for example, the clinical reports of conscious reference of problem behaviors to appraisal by the self-sentiment, the demands it makes at crucial moments of conflict, and the nature of the attitudes with high loading on the SS (as we shall henceforth symbolize it, for economy). As an integrator it is the keystone of the arch of sentiments, binding them in a necessary subsidiation to itself. It contains, in miniature, the other sentiments, so that if a man has a sentiment for photography, is a good husband, an officer in an important social club, and a patriot, these diverse individual sentiments are embodied in his final self-concept and sustained by the attitudes of self-regard. Proposed behavior is tested against this self-concept.

Classical writing making insightful though nonexperimental analysis of this self-concept action is to be found in the writings of William James and especially McDougall (1932) (and, indeed, in many first-rate novelists). Furthermore, considerable research was directed in the 1960s to the self-concept, for example, by Wylie (1961); Brookover and Gottlieb (1964); Purkey (1970); and Rogers (1960) and many clinicians. The concepts that cropped up centrally in that decade of self-concept concentration have been expressed as well as anywhere by the poet who wrote:

"There were three men went down the road,
    As down the road went he.
    The man they saw, the man he was, and
    the man he wished to be."
(We might add, "The man *he* saw.")

It would have been far more profitable to psychology if the almost exclusively cognitive and questionnaire work on the self-image or concept in that era could have been related to the dynamic calculus concepts, based on objective, stimulus-response, attitude course measurement, which was then emerging in the experimental literature. Unfortunately the clinical writing and the multivariate experimental streams remained separated. Whatever experiment was done clinically dealt only in cognitive questionnaires about the self-concept. As research now indicates, the importance of the cognitive self-concept—the M in the self-sentiment—is mainly that it is the target or subgoal of a strong system of attitudes, dynamically organized about this cognitive self-view, just as any other sentiment factor is about some other cognitive concept. For the dynamic calculus recognizes that the action system connected with this cognitive self-concept is, for personality, as distinct from studies in the psychology of perception, the more important adjunct of the cognitive entity itself. True, the cognitive concept will be related, in its content, to the nature of the attitude-action system. But objective motivation-measurement research to discover the boundaries of the unitary attitude system and to provide measurement of the dynamic strength of the sentiment is more vital than the partial glimpse of the structure given by the cognitive records alone.

The attitudes that consistently load the self-sentiment factor, both in objective motivation measures (alike in U and I components) and in the questionnaire response in the Q_3 factor, show (see Chapter 2 in Volume 1 here, and Cattell, 1973) concern for the health and safety of the physical self, for success in career, for mental health and good self control, for meeting the demands of the self-concept the individual happens to have adopted, and especially for social approval, a good reputation, and a morally respectable social record. In terms of ergic investment, the main subsidiations are to the need for security (fear), and the ergs of self-assertion ("achievement") and gregariousness (see Cattell & Child, 1975). The factor has a relatively small hyperplane count, showing that, relative to other sentiments, it covers rather a large sample of attitudes, affecting many with at least a slight degree of loading.

The hypothesis best interpreting these findings is that the preservation of the self—physically, economically, socially, and spiritually—comes to be perceived (or, at least, realistically experienced if only unconsciously appreciated) as a necessary precondition for satisfaction of virtually all other sentiments and ergic goals. If we ask how this sentiment is placed in the dynamic lattice, the answer from the present theory is that it must be distal to most of the lattice structure. That is to say, the self-sentiment consists of a set of attitudes the satisfaction of which is a necessary pre-condition for the satisfaction of most other sentiments and ergs.

This concept takes a starker view of the self-sentiment, socially and even biologically, than that it merely serves self-regard and self-direction. It argues that it is necessary for the very preservation of the individual. Self-regard might, if this were not true, call only for an ergic investment mainly from the self-assertive erg and the super-ego. But the finding that there are ergic investments of this senti-ment also in the fear erg, gregariousness, and so forth, points additionally to a more basic function in self-preservation and survival. Pointing this way also is the fact that in the comparative simplicity of the life of preliterate peoples, we see that a person ostracized from society may actually starve to death or die from depressive emotional deprivation. In our more free society the dependence of ultimate ergic satisfactions on maintaining socially approved behavior and a self-image that brings a good social reputation is less evident, but is visible to careful scrutiny. Appreciable motivation in the self-sentiment certainly comes, according to the empirical loading data, from attitudes such as, "I want to maintain a good social reputation" in order (subgoal) that "I can continue to be a success at my job" (career sentiment).[6] Admittedly, sheer *physical* preservation of the self is not so prominent, but there are also attitudes of maintaining physical and mental health, which reach clear expression of self-concern in the hypochondriac. Doubtless there are also retroactive subsidiation paths, as in the chain, "I want to be successful in my career" in order that "People may have a good image of me." But in the main we shall suppose that the self-sentiment is a broad structure around the developing (distal) end of the lattice, and therefore bound to subsidiate to and derive its dynamic strength from, a wide spectrum of ergs and sentiments.

The nature of the G factor, which, as we have stated, so closely confirms the psychoanalytic pattern as to deserve our continuing the name of the superego, is relatively straightforward. It is conscience, the urge to do the right thing by the values implanted early in life, accompanied by the gnawings of guilt when this is not done. The coverage in attitudes, questionnaire items, and ratings, is typically of intention to honesty, mature consideration of needs of others, readiness to face difficulties and complete job obligations, perseverance in good works, dependability, charity to others, and antipathy to vice (Cattell & Child, 1975). Relative to the clinical conception, the rating questionnaire and objective (motivation) test pattern of G has more emphasis than we might have expected on perseverance per se, though with duty as the main value involved in such perseverance.

The self-sentiment (*SS*) and superego (*SE*) come out as cooperative factors, agreeing in an overlap of loadings on self-control, maintaining reputation, condemnation of sloth and vice, and a few other attitudes. Our theory is that they support these attitudes for different reasons: the *SS* for social-self reasons, the *SE* from fundamental conscientious conviction. The two factors also correlate significantly positively. Incidentally, however, one should note that technically a correlation of two factors is quite different from their cooperativeness of loadings, though both exist between *G* and Q_3. The most appropriate inference from the correlation is that the *SS* subsidiates to the *SE* just as to a basic need, that is, in much the same way as it does to most of the ergs. The cooperativeness is simply due to society fostering *some* superego values.

In this and some other ways the *SE* has almost ergic dynamic qualities. Although the particular ethical injunctions of the *SE* may differ with cultures (but let us not overemphasize these showpieces of cultural anthropology at the cost of over-all realism), its demands have the quality of a need, and it is not much more easily manipulated consciously than are ergic goals. The psychoanalytic explanation of this deep-rooted quality is that it is introjected, under the love-fear motivation possible with a loving and strict parent, at so early an age, and with such strong imprinting effect, that it is partly unconscious and largely beyond rational conscious manipulation thereafter. Our first results on the genetics of various traits (Cattell, Blewett, & Beloff, 1955; Cattell, 1973; Klein & Cattell, 1978), however, also show an unexpectedly large genetic component in *SE*, which adds to its similarity to an erg. Its final detailed cultural form of expression is certainly acquired, but proneness to guilt and sensitivity to moral expectations have many qualities, as Kant recognized, in referring to "the categorical imperative," that come close to an innate or, at least, inflexible ergic quality. Thus the *SE* joins with the ergs in a broad spectrum of goals to which the *SS* subsidiates, giving the latter a wide and varied ergic investment.

The third structure in the control system—ego strength, *C*—appeared, until recently, as stated, only in two of the three media, *L*- and *Q*- data, but has now shown in a set of specific attitude loadings in motivation measures. One considers the possibility that this nonappearance means merely that the necessary attitudes have been omitted from objective devices. The care taken in spreading research over many attitudes made this seem unlikely, though one must recognize that, for the sake of practicable measurement, attitudes have had to be relatively specific in reference. If the goal of *C* can only be reached by such highly general attitudes as "I want to handle emotional conflicts of all kinds effectively" it is possible that the requisite attitudes for the factor have not been so well constructed in objective tests such as enter into MAT and SMAT. In L-data (see Cattell, 1946, 1950) C shows itself positively in behavior rated as mature, emotionally stable, and adjusted to reality, and at the negative pole as unstable, changeable, easily upset, and evasive of reality, as well as by use of many "defense mechanisms." In Q-data (see Cattell, 1973; Cattell, Eber, & Tatsuoka, 1970) $C-$ is characterized by a distressed awareness of being unable to cope (Lazarus, 1966), by lack of energy, by failure of willpower, and by wishing everything in the person's life were different from what it is and has been. It is the epitome of all that has been described clinically as ego weakness $(C-)$ as opposed to ego strength $(C+)$.

Fortunately, interpretation by no means has to rest on factor-loading content alone. Through well-planned educational, clinical, and industrial use of the factored questionnaires 16 PF, HSPQ, CPQ, ESPQ, all containing the C scale, and of the MAT (Motivation Analysis Test) employing the SS and SE factor measures, a very substantial scientific accumulation of criterion relations and experiments already exists. The reader is referred to systematic collations of the evidence (Cattell, Eber, & Tatsuoka, 1970; Cattell, 1973, pp. 58–190; Karson & O'Dell, 1976). Briefly, these find that low C is associated with alcoholism, prolonged unemployment, truancy, delinquency, and, especially, with practically every form of pathology, neurotic and psychotic. C is high, occupationally, in air-line pilots, nurses, administrators, and competition athletes; low in persons in protected occupations, for example, clerks, in artists, and in vagrants. It is high in leaders who get selected in small groups in competitive situations. It has a significant but low heritability (0.4).

Considerable criterion relevance has now appeared to help the interpretation of Q_3 and G also. The self-sentiment (Q_3 in Q-data, SS in the MAT) is higher in children from harmonious families. It effectively predicts school achievement over and above prediction from intelligence. It is low in criminals and gang delinquents, high in persons with low accident records, high in group leaders, increases with a history of steady employment and added responsibilities, and, curiously, with demanding experiences such as death of a friend or near relative, parental illness, and experience of an unhappy love affair (see Barton's analysis in Cattell, 1973). It also rises in depressives with recovery after ECT (May, 1970).

The superego (G in questionnaires: SE in objective motivation batteries) has the highest correlation, after intelligence, with school and other achievement. It correlates with hours given to work, with experiencing parental warmth and close guidance in upbringing, with *not* being a college dropout, with being an elected and effective leader in small groups, with belonging to some church or group with idealistic goals, and with absence of alcoholism and drug addiction. It is high in accountants, airline pilots and hostesses, executives, mechanics, priests, and time-study engineers; low in artists, journalists, and competition athletes. It increases with executive responsibilities and with marriage. It has a significant loading in specification equations found for school success (see above), freedom from automobile accidents, teaching success, and ratings as an effective psychiatric technician (Cattell, 1973, p.166).

It will be observed that in relating to certain behavioral criteria, for example, school achievement, being chosen as a group leader, as well as in observer ratings and questionnaire items, Q_3 and G continue to overlap in areas of action, though they are unquestionably distinct factors. Overlaps, for example, in positively predicting and determining dependability behavior, exist indeed among all three source traits, C, Q_3, and G. This is not surprising for we have chosen them for discussion here on observations of that kind. They show by their actions that they are the chief controllers that we have to consider in personality behavior. Nevertheless their modes of producing that controlled behavior are recognizably different.

Naturally we look with curiosity to see what organization appears among these traits at the second order of factor analysis. The answer is clear and consistent, from over a dozen researches, that Q_3 and G appear together strongly on a second-order factor that has been called good upbringing or control (QVIII or UI(T)17) and that otherwise loads only $F-$ (inhibition, desurgency), moderately, and C, positively but very slightly. It is presumably a statement that good upbringing tends simultaneously to build up both superego and self-sentiment, while also raising the general level of inhibition.

2-8. Definition of the Ego Structure as Integrating and Evaluating Capacity

Representing in the behavioral specification equation the controlling action of the self-sentiment, Q_3, and the superego, G, in providing counter-balances for inhibiting ergic impulses or conflicting sentiment habit response systems presents no new problems. They enter as sentiment (M) terms in a decision or conflict equation, pitting one source-of-response system against another, just as any other sentiment or erg does in producing the opposing loadings in equations (2-18) and (2-19) (p. 124). When the SS trait score for a person is high, and the s_k term exciting the self-sentiment system is large, the stimulated and possibly undesirable behavior expression of some erg or sentiment is put in competition with the wider satisfactions indicated as alternatives by the self-sentiment, so that the v and s weights of the latter either completely block, or reduce that erratic, ultimately unrewarding but appealing action. Possibly these self-sentiment activations are capable, by a mechanism not yet discussed, of augmenting the s_k value on the superego, aiding its appearance in action, as shown in the "control equation," (2-25).

By contrast to this restraining effect on the expression of dissident attitude actions that Q_3 and G exert by the usual fixed sentiment action, the controlling action of the ego structure, C, appears to be more complex. We have argued that the fact that C was only recently caught in attitude analyses suggests that the attitudes involved—if any—must be at once general and complex. From the questionnaire items that load C we would hypothesize that these very general attitudes might be caught by something like "I want to keep my desires and emotions in integration," "I want to 'size up' the reality of a situation and make my behavior conform to the conditions for best total and long distance reward."

The distinctness of ego in this respect from self-sentiment and superego might be succinctly summarized by a boy tempted to steal an apple. The ego would ask, "Do I want it enough to risk being caught and thus feel badly about myself?"; the superego would add guilt and say, "You must not do this"; and the self-sentiment would ask, "Does this fit what you and others expect of you?" At a feeling level, guilt and shame are the emotions that operate respectively with SE and SS structures. Clearly the aim of the ego is *control*, not merely as such, but in the interests of achieving the greatest satisfaction over a forseeable range of time and circumstances. It is hard to believe that it takes no heed of good and bad or other qualities of the dynamic structures that sue for its permission. But the evidence seems to be that these weights are taken care of by the SS and SE and that the ego simply notes their weighted strengths, observes the immediate environmental reality, and refers to the records of reward and punishment outcomes in past expression of those particular demands.

The puzzle of why C has only just appeared in multivariate experiment with objective attitude measures should not create unnecessary doubts as to its structural existence. One reason for certain absences, beyond the insufficient experiment with more generalized attitudes, might well be that there is little difference among individuals in *strength of desire* for control (such as would show up in motivation measures) and that what we catch successfully in questionnaires and ratings is differences in capacity to *achieve* control. The functional aim of the ego is *control as such*, in the interests of the greater happiness of the individual in a complex world and an *intention* to achieve this may show little variance. One must not lean too heavily on this possible root of the failure so far to get an individual difference ego factor in attitudes of desire for high control, for C appears when measures of competence to obtain that control are included, as Birkett (1979) is now doing in her factor studies of the ego. The manifestation of differences in capacity certainly show up readily in the Q- and L-reports and behavior ratings. That there exists some innate limits to capacity to integrate is shown, incidentally, by the large differences between animal species in delayed choice and similar inhibitory performances as well as by the heritability coefficient so far found in human differences for C (about 0.4). However, to call it a capacity does not mean that heritability has to be high, for its level could well be determined considerably by early training and trauma.

From these considerations C takes on more the characteristics of a decision mechanism, which grows not through reinforcement of particular attitudes as do simple sentiments, but by reinforcement in the novel sense of rewarding habits that tend toward *total* success in emotional control. The evidences of this acquisition belong to Chapter 5, as we are here concerned only with describing the actually operating structure as part of the dynamic calculus among structures. Thus, descriptively, C is a power operating in decisions, and with an "energy-economic" goal: the maximization of satisfaction, in relation to complex obstacles in outer reality, summed over a long enough period of actions and their consequences. We are forced to such metaphors in encompassing the due description of this complex structure as "a clearing house," receiving information simultaneously on the external situation and the strength of desires, and evaluating for a decision from reference to engrams recording the reinforcements and failures of past behavior. Its ultimate act is to exert its own resources and "call in" the resources of a suitable coalition when one dynamic system threatens to reduce long-term satisfaction by getting out of line.

That by present findings, fairly extensive, C is not made dependent on intelligence—at least is not correlated—does not fit too well with this emphasis on C as an information-resolving system. But this can be met by certain hypotheses when we turn to systems theory in Chapter 5. Meanwhile let us note that in any case, though the process may be partly conscious (especially when the standards of the self-sentiment and superego are brought onto the scales) much of its weighing of forces is presumably as unconscious, in learning and action, as the muscular tension compromises in skating or riding a bicycle.

Clinically it is very clear that the psychoanalytic concept of the ego is compatible with the present theory of C factor development and with the description and measurement of the unitary structure itself. As to development, clinical theory says the ego feeds on success in control. If, through trauma or encountering difficulties too great for its current stage of development, it fails to engineer the best total expression for the "id," and is pressured, then it resorts to rigid, poorly-adaptive defense mechanisms such as repression, projection, rationalization, or fantasy. This rigid defense, undertaken in panic, denies the ego any hope of eventually incorporating the dissident forces in itself, in some compromise expression among them suited to reality. Our genetic studies, as stated, indicate an appreciable genetic (H index = 0.4) endowment in the "raw material" of the ego, which presumably lies in some primal capacities to control emotional impulse (or maybe in weakness of emotional impulse!), that is, to sustain temporary blocking of satisfaction, and to tolerate and handle conflict at times of frustration. A good beginning in the genetic endowment may surely initially tip the scales in favor of less resort to patchwork defenses. A person starting with a higher endowment in these deferment and control capacities (for they indeed deserve the label of capacities, as much as do those in ordinary abilities) will experience, by positive feedback, more reinforcement of them ("To him that hath . . ."). The ego structure thus draws upon the total satisfaction of the organism to control—judiciously, but sometimes also by suppression or repression—the rebel sources of dissatisfaction. This is perhaps why reports of "generally dissatisfied" in self reports and "inability to cope" in observer rated trait elements are among the most highly loaded ratings on low ego strength, $C-$.

The nature of the ultimate controlling system in the dynamics of the individual is a question both of great practical importance and concern in the theoretical completion of the dynamic calculus. Research that would permit checking of inferences from the above hypothesis is, alas, still very scanty.

One inference from the above theory of C structure is that measures of over-all conflict should correlate negatively with C, and this is supported by the work of Williams (1959). Parenthetically, the following notation on this statement is in some difficulty because we have used c for conflict, yet in personality traits C is ego strength! However, since I has been defined (equation 2-23), as integration, by $(1 - c_I)$, where c_I is indurated conflict (equation 2-18), we are very simply saying:

$$C = I \qquad\qquad (2\text{-}24)$$

that is, that C and degree of integration should correlate fully.

A second inference is that fluctuant instability of the attitude system should be less, with high C—especially "catastrophic" readjustments. Operationally, this was tested by the present writer (1943) by taking a wide sample of attitudes from the "dynamic sphere," measuring their fluctuation across days, and correlating with ego-strength measures. This seismographic search for vibrations at the attitude surface as indicators of general instability at a deeper level paid off in the discovery of a significant negative correlation of attitude fluctuation scores with C measures. Das's work (1955) confirmed and extended this.

Although cognitive consistency is not identical with emotional consistency, it is obvious that emotional inconsistencies must result in cognitive inconsistencies. A third check on the C hypothesis was therefore to examine relations to measures of logical inconsistencies within a set of attitudes as held at any one time. Objective tests in this area require much subtlety of analysis, but such truly hidden syllogistic forms were constructed and used (Hundleby, Pawlik, & Cattell, 1965; Cattell, 1951; Coan, 1974; Cattell & Warburton, 1967), and found to act as valid, significant measures of C. Incidentally, the later work of Festinger (1962) on "cognitive dissonance" approaches this same concept, though his conceptual emphasis is on the cognitive rather than the dynamic consistency we conceive here to be the root cause of an appreciable fraction of cognitive dislocations. However, some of his findings could be quoted as support for the relation of realistic internal dynamic consistency to estimated behavior of an ego-strength type.

The gross clinical support for C as ego strength is emphatic and widespread, and as it is set out elsewhere we need not more than repeat here that numerous studies show C to be decidely low in all forms of psychopathology—neurotic, psychotic, addictive—but not in criminals.

Finally, we might expect to find behavioral evidence on the nature of ego strength in the objective test (T-data) structuring described in Chapter 3, Volume 1. Actually, however, this objective behavior factoring is at the moment somewhat confusing because it presents four factors with at first sight almost equal claims to representing ego strength, namely UI(T)16, UI(T)17, UI(T)23, and UI(T)25. Since all but UI(T)17 are significantly below normal

($p<.01$) for neurotics and psychotics, and high in good achievers and UI(T)17 has been identified with "good upbringing" and super-ego (QVIII) the field is reduced to three. All three of these factors indeed play a powerful role in and are highly diagnostic of psycho-pathology in general (Cattell & Scheier, 1961; Eysenck, 1960; S. B. G. Eysenck, 1956; Cattell & Tatro, 1966; Cattell, Schmidt, and Bjersted, 1972). UI(T)16 has been called "assertive ego," but has narcistic features not usually considered intrinsic to C, and expresses itself perhaps excessively in competition. UI(T)23, capacity to mobilize, has strong claims, appearing in measures of lack of suggestibility in the sway test, ability to speed up without excessive error, low motor rigidity. UI(T)25 shows itself in good contact with reality, and has been called by Eysenck the psychoticism factor, though actually three other UI factors are equally deviant in psychotics and UI(T)25 is well below normal in neurotics too. A possible resolution is that for some reason the ego strength structure lies at the second stratum in T-data, in the general pathology factor, T(II) Expansive Ego in Table 3–11, Volume 1, containing 16 and 23. (Factors TI and TVII also deserve investigation.) No definite answer can be given at present, but the factors themselves are definite enough at both the first and second order level, and research, with the now available *Objective-Analytic (O-A) Battery* should soon provide answers.

With these objective-test structures still requiring more criterion interpretation, though firm as such in experiment, one must at present turn to C as measured in Q- and L-data for the broadest basis. Over and above the half-dozen directions of inference checked for the C hypotheses above, there are actually several other important pointers to the nature of C factor, such as the discovery that it measure rises with age and experience (Cattell, 1973), and it moves upward (being low in clinical cases) under psychotherapy (Rickels et al., 1965, 1966; Hunt et al., 1959) and with respite from failures in emotional control. We suspect that it was of this successful response to challenges that Goethe spoke when he said, "Es entwickelt sich ein Charakter in den Strom der Welt," for it seems to grow by exercise in emotional decision—provided the decisions are largely successful, that is, tend to maximization of ergic expression. This concept of the ego will receive further consideration in Chapter 5 developing the final systems theory picture.

Meanwhile, we have to approach the best formulation possible today of the action of the C, G, and Q_3 triumvirate. To the extent that they recognized these separate structures such writers as All-port, James, and McDougall were inclined to a further belief that was little more than mystical, namely, that somehow they integrated into one structure—that of the ideally developed personality. (We cannot resist a comparison with the views of the early Christian church on the nature of the Trinity at the Council of Nicaea in 325!) Tolstoy's concept of "depersonalization"—which might be translated that ego and self-sentiment should dissolve in the superego, becoming one—expresses the same idea and ideal. The study of the truly exceptional cases (which in fact these writers surely represent) is beyond comment when we have so little firm knowledge about even the average person. But one must recognize that the factor-analytic evidence on possible merging of these structures, as found in the well-conceived and profound multivariate analyses of Horn (1966) and Gorsuch 1965; see also Gorsuch & Cattell, 1977), is that ego, superego and self-sentiment structures remain, *at all levels* in their development, obstinately distinct; though of course not unrelated in dynamic exchanges. As factoring is carried to higher orders, even on such a rich basis of value, sentiment, and personality variables as used by the above investigators, the superego continues to remain a distinct *factor structure*, though the self-sentiment may adjust its values increasingly toward G (be more factorially "cooperative") in the more developed personality. Even at the third factor analytic order the superego remains distinct, although (Chapter 5) it becomes increasingly negatively correlated with anxiety and therefore positively with ego strength. Several things thus point to an increasing correlational interrelationship of C, Q_3, and G in more developed, older personalities, deserving of more investigation. But in themselves the cooperating structures remain distinct.

At the second order (see summary of research in Cattell, 1973, p. 116), ego strength, C, has its main expression (about -.7) in the anxiety factor (QII). Q_3 has a similar role (but less: -.4) in anxiety. G and Q_3 fall together (with desurgency, F-, and humility, E-) in the good upbringing or control factor ($QVIII$) already described. There are two riddles in these findings still to be solved: (1) that C scarcely has any loading in $QVIII$ (which strongly loads G and Q_3. However, there are indications that in some age groups (7, 10, 14 years; Cattell, 1973, p. 104) it is slightly positively loaded though in others (mainly adult groups) the relation is zero; and (2) that the correlation of intelligence and ego strength is consistently around zero over all groups.

As to the first, a zero correlation could be the result of two opposing relationships. Good upbringing or Control ($QVIII$), on the one hand, might spare a child those traumas that, in unhappy families, injure C development. On the other hand—and here we listen to some wisdom in psychoanalysis—the superego (and the self-sentiment—this latter unknown to psychoanalysis) hedge the ego around with demands that make its growth more difficult. The evidence (Cattell, 1973, p. 116) seems to be that in the early years, in the cherishing environment of parental guidance, the good upbringing atmosphere favors G and Q_3 strongly, without these traits putting difficulties in the way of C development; indeed, the correlation is slightly positive. but when the individual is "kicked around" in the world later, and his conflicts that realistic behavior brings with G and Q_3 demands are unresolved, an embattled ego strength, C, advances *less* in the individual in proportion to the exactingness of his G and Q_3 demands.[7]

2-9. Summary

1. An attitude is a behavioral "intention" to a certain course of action—a *response potential*. In analyzing structure it is taken to be measured in response to a stable life situation. It can be dissected out, at a level of size appropriate for social meaningfulness and experimental convenience, from a hierarchy of mental sets, extending downward from attitudes to small reflex acts and upward to massive sentiments. A taxonomy of attitudes can be made on a basis of four or more dimensions, notably: *greater or lesser consciousness* of the goal of the attitude; *newness* of establishment versus *long induration* in terms of learning; presence or absence of a *social belief* system (as in Fishbein's paradigm); a state of *latency* versus *actual overt functioning*; and possibly others that also may have predictive value about the stability of the attitude and what we will obtain in measurement in motivation component strengths.

2. Any attitude is *ultimately* directed to the satisfaction of ergic goals, but meanwhile belongs to a *subsidiation chain* of attitudes, each aimed at bringing about a state of affairs called a subgoal, which is the condition for the stimulus activation of the next attitude in the chain toward the proximal ergic goals. As regards position relative to any one subgoal the distal attitudes may be called the *serving* or *contributory* attitudes, and those following the subgoal the *evoked* attitudes. The first dynamic principle encountered in this domain is that the motivation strength tends to remain at the same level in all of a series of attitudes subsidiated along any self-contained, isolated, tandem chain, because the final reward and reinforcement apply equally to behavior all along the chain. Later research may modify this by secondary laws describing reduction for distance and reduced expectancy (probability) of final reward.

3. However, all studies of human dynamic structure show that an isolated chain is an abstraction virtually never found as such. Chains actually crisscross in a *dynamic lattice*, in which subgoals are *nodes* and the ultimate proximal goals are specific ergic consummatory goals. The dendritic model of the dynamic lattice can be explored profitably as to theoretical fit by models from hydraulics and from electric networks, though only certain abstractions, with their mathematical forms, are likely to be fully appropriate. Positive and negative loadings of ergs on an attitude in a specification equation correspond to subsidiation *to* and cleavage *from* a course toward the erg so loaded. The three main ways of revealing the lattice structure are (a) clinical free association and insights (a rough and qualitative method); (b) combining inferences from the weights (*b*'s) obtained by factoring attitudes at several planned different cross-sections in the distal-proximal succession; and (c) manipulative studies, which observe the consequences in other attitudes of blocking or facilitating a given attitude course.

4. Of the two well-confirmed and differentiated types of *dynamic structure factor*, those we have defind as ergs are adequately explained as particular ergic tensions, corresponding to particular innate ergic goals related to primate instinct structures. But though the origins and natures of the second type—the sentiment engrams—are tolerably clear from learning principles, their relation to structure in the lattice, is not so easily to be stated. It seems that some are subgoals, bringing out correlations among the attitudes evoked by them, and among the contributories. A first review of origins of learned sentiment structures suggests three principles: (a) common reinforcement schedule; (b) an "agency" effect from spread by coexcitation, largely at the level of "mental experiment" with cognitive symbols; and (c) common dynamic subsidiation, or "budding." This means that each sentiment is likely to correspond either to a concrete or a social institutional and conceptual *object*.

5. The modulator, s_{ke}, for an erg defines how much the erg is *aroused* at subgoal k, and that for a sentiment, s_{km}, how much the cognitive associations in the sentiment are *activated*. The observed *ergic tension* of an aroused erg which is what we measure with most batteries can be broken down into a modulating stimulus effect from k and a preexisting *need strength* before stimulation. The need strength can in turn be broken down into a permanent *drive strength* and an *appetitive state*. As hypothesized here, the ergic tension is *not* at zero when there is no stimulation. but then equals the drive strength. The potency of sentiments and other engrams in affecting behavior can analogously be broken down into two (but no more) parts: A *steady* engram strength and an *activated* component. The

possibility of these components being identified with motivation components is discussed later.

6. Most learning theorists have broken down response *potential* (or actual response *strength*), to which it is ultimately a function) broadly into an *engram* (learned deposit, habit strength, memory storage) and a *drive* active at the time of response. At its simplest, the relation of the two is additive (though Hull tried a product), and the first factor-analytic results, producing E (ergic tension) and M (sentiment) terms, carry this tradition of two terms to further differentiation. However, various psychological considerations suggest that some product effects exist and these can, with varying ease, be considered to fit more sophisticated factorial models. Ultimately four types of term (besides any ability or temperament terms, of course) are accepted in the model of the dynamic specification equation here: pure E terms; pure M terms; a term in which an activated M arouses an erg (ME); and a term in which an aroused erg helps activate a sentiment (EM). In the specification equation it is now hypothesized that in the pure E arousal, $s_{ke}E$, the s_{ke} represents the modulation of E through built in (innate) cognitive connections to features of the situation that have meaning in past human evolution, whereas in s_{km}ME we meet the arousal of E through learned connections in the sentiment M, stimulated by s_{km} in the situation k_m.

7. The hypothesis is tentatively offered that the seven primary motivation components we find in objective manifestations of motive could correspond to the seven terms and combinations in the above four dynamic terms and their interactions (E', E'', E', E^2, M, M, and M_2), the first four being largely in the second-order factor U and the last three in I. Since present factor experiments yield only E and M terms the theory is reconciled with experiment by recognizing that the "hardy" factor model resolves products (EM and ME) into additive terms, as a first approximation. Consequently, calculation from factorial experiment alone of the loadings on the ME and EM terms would require more complex discussion than can be given here and at this time. A rough approach, with several assumptions, depends on *relations* between the E and M loadings on a given attitude, for example, on the E's and M's in a row of the factor-pattern matrix corresponding to an attitude.

8. From the ME and EM terms develops the concept of the *ergic investment of an attitude or sentiment*. It can be stated by a profile or vector of ergic weights expressing the tensions a sentiment can arouse and call on to effect its purposes. A sentiment's ergic investment magnitude is the main measure of its dynamic importance in the personality. The question of whether the formula given here for

calculating from the factor matrix a sentiment's ergic investment is correct can be checked by comparing a sentiment's investment magnitude so calculated with (a) the pugnacity, (b) the anxiety, and (c) the depression responses when the sentiment object is threatened or removed. A conceptual and calculatory distinction is drawn between the ergic investment in a sentiment and the engram strength of a sentiment, both being involved in defining the total strength, but the latter deals specifically with cognitive components in a sentiment's contribution to behavior.

9. A model for decision theory develops in the dynamic calculus. An individual's decision between two attitude courses in active conflict should be predictable from the difference of the action strength, $a_{h_2 i j_2 k_2} - a_{h_1 i j_1 k_1}$ given by their specification equations. Conflict is either *active*, as in making a decision between two such courses, or *indurated* and stable, as in a compromise course of action "permanently" adopted. In either case equations for both forms of conflict can be stated (c_a and c_d) and they apply equally to an attitude, to a sentiment, or to the total personality. As would be expected from theory, the c_d conflict index, and its obverse, an integration index, prove experimentally to be significantly different for psychotic patients and normals. The index of integration ($1 - c_d$) correlates significantly with questionnaire C measure for *ego strength*, with low fluctuation of attitudes, etc. Conflict indices also relate significantly to excess of U over I components in the area concerned, which can therefore also count as a conflict measure. The theoretical formula for total indurated conflict (and the $U - I$ measure) can now be checked by correlation with clinical manifestations of conflict as factored into some seven recognizable factors.

10. In the area of behavior commonly recognized as impulse control and general behavioral control, three personality factors have long been recognized as operative: (a) the self-sentiment, Q_3; (b) the superego, G (both Q_3 and G appear both in L- and Q-data and in objective motivation measures, for example, in the MAT and SMAT batteries); and (c) the ego-strength factor, C (yet replicated only in L- and Q-data). The superego (SE in the MAT, G in questionnaire) presents demands almost as imperative and unmodifiable as those of ergs, probably through being implanted and imprinted very early in life. The acquired self-sentiment (SS in MAT, Q_3 in the 16 PF) in part subsidiates to G, but mainly aims to keep the self-concept intact, as a social reputation necessary to satisfaction of all ergs.

11. The ego structure at present differs in experimental status from G and Q_3 in not yet being established additionally as a factor in objective motivation measures in attitudes. This could be because

the high generality of its attitudes has escaped the usual attitude sampling in experiment, or because its influence is so wide that no hyperplane exists for its resolution as a first-order factor. However, certain factors in T-data (UI(T)16, 17, 23, and perhaps 25) manifest the behaviors conceptually expected of the ego, for example, stability measured through fluctuation of attitudes, capacity to mobilize, to maintain performance under stress, to overcome habit rigidities. These, and measures of internal consistency (here cognitive dissonance, low conflict index, and so forth, provide a C measure, which, like C in Q-data, is very significantly below average in all neurotic and psychotic pathologies (Cattell, Schmidt, & Bjersted, 1972).

12. Although C, G, and Q_3 are demonstrable as functionally distinct unities, they do have interrelations as would be expected; for example, a cooperativeness of loading pattern arising from common action in control, and a correlation of G and Q_3 giving rise to a second-order factor (QVIII) of control, now shown to match UI(T)17, control, in T-data. Unlike the Freudian clinical conclusion, from neurotics, multivariate experiment finds G and anxiety (QII) significantly *negatively* related. However, this is in the general population samples and the contrast with psychoanalytic beliefs brings one more instance of the bias in basing general psychological conclusions on special pathological samples.

13. From the available multivariate experimental and clinical data one can recognize that C has some four major "panels" of action (1) to "sense" and collate evidences on the demand strengths of various dynamic traits (2) To examine both the real world and the memory storage for an appraisal of the consequences of various actions, and (3) To inhibit and control while the above deliberations are made, and (4) To control directly and indirectly (CET) when the decided action has to be implemented.

Its work is in part like that of an ability, operating a clearing house of impulses and consequences, and although it operates with all dynamic traits its largest business is with the self-sentiment (Q_3 or SS) and with the super ego (G or SE). The loadings of this triumvirate would be expected to grow larger than those on most other dynamic traits where educated control occurs.

14. In the general operation of dynamic traits in the lattice the dynamic calculus can recognize so far some 5 psychodynamic laws: (1) Response potential will be maintained in a course of action only so long as a goal exists at which it is rewarded. (2) Measures of interest-strength in a course of action in a stable system will be simply proportional to reward magnitude. (This may cover (1) as an extreme case.) (3) In any closed chain of subsidiated attitudes

the strength of interest, apart from secondary principle effects, will be the same at all points in the sequence. (4) Alternative causes of possible action after a subgoal will vary inversely in strength in the same individual over time, and (5) A secondary principle in (3) is that strength of interest in a closed chain will be less with distance from the consummatory goal, by inherent effects of imperfect memory and situational uncertainties of reward in past experience.

NOTES

[1] The use of hydraulic principles can be simply, indeed domestically, illustrated by the way the buyer of an old house can trace the hidden water-pipe connections in the walls by turning on various combinations of taps simultaneously, and observing how an increase in the flow from one is accompanied by a decrease in others. Electrical networks have many similar bases of inference.

[2] A sentiment, a complex, a mental set, a concept, or any other kind of acquired learned structure we have agreed to call an engram, and to represent by the letter M. An engram being acquired and entered into memory "storage" renders the organism's behavior different from before, even if motivation and incentive are held constant across the first and second occasions of examining learning.

Because of my belief that scientific discussion benefits by terms that are short, precise, and unambiguous, I would prefer *gramming* to engramming for the corresponding verb. An engram is something grammed. For the time being, from deference to custom, I continue here, however, with engrammed, but ultimately I hope it will be widely agreed that the shorter term, grammed, can be used.

[3] The multivariate experiment will perceive all kinds of qualifying comments necessary on such calculation, for which the general reader may not be ready. For example, we may seem to presume to speak in some connections of comparative *absolute levels* of ergic investment, when in fact we are supplied with magnitudes of *correlations* and *variance contributions*. The latter basis of calculation, however, will be found on further consideration not to disqualify the conclusions on relative magnitudes as used here. Second, we deal with b's instead of the values required by real-base factor analysis. This approximation has been explained. Third, we have by-passed the problem that, as we cannot take *all* attitudes, the introduction of a careful adequate method of taking stratified samples of attitudes could alone give meaning to "relative strength of sentiments" or to comparison of persons on their levels of integration. Last, we have assumed, in proceeding to a total score, that ergs are of equal strength. However, it is possible to give meaning to ergic-strength differences when the simpler standard factor model here is shifted to a foundation of real-base factor analysis.

[4] The use of the term *arousal* for an erg and *activation* for a sentiment, though adhered to from this point, must wait on the next chapter for a more precise justification. Note also that we consistently use the word *dynamic*

when some writers would use *emotional*. The confusion that arises when *affect* (emotion) is not distinguished from *conation* (dynamic drive) has already been discussed here, and reference made to the difference of GSR and other associations respectively to emotion and drive. In the introspective systems of psychology (Titchener, Meinong, Külpe, etc.) including that of the Scholastics, there was a useful term, *orexis*, to cover generically *affection and conation*. The term dynamic, though used here in an exact operational and behavioral basis (Cattell & Warburton, 1967), is the more common modern equivalent of orectic, including both emotional observations and the associated drive measures. However, the emotion is, relatively, an objectively hard-to-measure epiphenomenon, involving such introspective components as Lange and James (but scarcely Cannon) ascribed to it. The definition of *dynamic* rests, by contrast to orectic, depends entirely on behavior (Cattell & Warburton, 1967). The use of the term "emotional" as equivalent to "dynamic," instead of for what is only an introspectible and physiological side effect of conation, as still seems to occur in some writers (even in *S-R* reflexology) is a looseness bound to lead to misconceptions and unnecessary debates.

[5] The qualifications are (a) that for conflict in an individual the v's and s's would be those found in P-technique, specific to the person, not R-technique; (b) that real-base factoring, permitting difference in variance size of the factors is necessary; and (c) that comparing strengths on different motivation component factors, for example, the U's and I's, presents problems in experiment when the *content* of the two courses of action is different. It is true that if we use, for example, short distance memory (see Table 4-1, p. 132, Volume 1), GSR, decision time, word association, and so forth, these come in comparable units, and though individuals differ in endowment in any one vehicle (as some are generally more reactive on GSR than others), a total gathered from a sufficient variety of vehicles will attenuate such effects. The problem lies rather in equivalent sampling of the stimuli given in the test to measure the strength of the given attitudes. For example, in comparing strength of interest in sport with that in mathematics, is a picture of someone scoring a goal equivalent in relevance to one of an uncompleted solution for a quadratic equation? In principle, domains of proper relevance can be defined and stratified sampling procedures applied to choosing stimuli from them, but as yet, as Laughlin (1974) has shown, practical experiment has not reached this technical level.

[6] The writer is frequently asked what the relation of the "need achievement" of McClelland, Atkinson, et al. (1953) is to the self-assertive erg and the self-sentiment as established in dynamic calculus research. Unfortunately, these writers have never adequately factored the manifestations they posit to represent a "need achievement." However, one or two objective devices at least—projection and association—in their measures would permit testing alignment with the dynamic structure factors from objective motivation test devices set out in the MAT and SMAT, so convergence is possible. From content, the present writer would strongly argue that "need achievement" is *not* a unitary trait, and certainly not a pure need or erg. We might guess it is a summation mainly of the assertive erg and the self-sentiment. How much the achievement score relations to various criteria found by McClelland et al. will ultimately need to be reinterpreted as relating in different degrees respectively to the former or the latter remains to be seen. Meanwhile the concept validity even of the TAT scoring itself, against U and I general motivation strength factors remains unproven.

[7] A curious finding here, still needing confirmation, is that Q_3 is actually high while C low (as would be expected) in schizophrenics (Cattell, Eber, &

Tatsuoka, 1965). The theory there used to explain this phenomenon is consistent with an additive, supplementary use of C and Q_3 in a control equation here. In the pathological case cited, we hypothesize that with decay of ego strength in the schizophrenic (for whatever reasons pathology can explain) he has, over the years, built up compensations in use of Q_3. That is to say, he depends excessively (relative to the normal) on a conscious appeal to the cognitive self-ideal, Q_3, for control, where the dynamically normally developed person would employ C immediately, easily and unconsciously. An alternative explanation, of course, is that an onerously high development of Q_3 has *contributed* in the schizophrenic, to the difficulties that lead to decline of the C factor.

CHAPTER 3

LEARNING DEFINED:
THE INTEGRATION OF REFLEXOLOGICAL
AND STRUCTURED LEARNING CONCEPTS

3-1. *Separation of change relating to learning, volution, soma change, and situation change*

3-2. *Reflexological (or "reflex") learning theory: Methods and concepts in SS, CRI, and CRII paradigms*

3-3. *Possible broader approaches to learning: Introduction to concepts of structured learning theory*

3-4. *Initial statement of five basic laws of learning changes: 1. The coexcitation effect*

3-5. *Further laws of learning change: 2. Means–end; 3. Integration; 4. Ergic goal modification; 5. Energy saving*

3-6. *The five-vector description of learning change*

3-7. *A closer look, psychological and statistical, at the nature of structured learning*

3-8. *Summary*

3-1. Separations of Change Relating to Learning, Volution, Soma Change, and Situation Change

It is hoped that the reader of the next three chapters will have the usual general knowledge of classical learning theory, but without being so emotionally wedded to it, as it stands, that a substantial addition of new concepts cannot be absorbed. In this chapter it is proposed (1) to refresh the reader's memory on basic tenets of classical, *reflexological learning theory;* (2) to introduce some revisions; and (3) to begin integration with an independent stream of new concepts from personality, which constitute *structured learning theory.* Subsequent chapters will develop this integration further, with the aid of the dynamic calculus advances discussed in the last chapter.

At the outset it is necessary to define the distinctions between learning and other changes over time. This is not academic pedantry, for many observations on learning are confused through confounding it with other sources of change, or through assuming that the area we call learning theory is responsible for all change. The latter may be true in a "roped off" area of animal learning but it is not true of human personality change in the physical and social world.

In the first place, the perspectives we gained in Chapter 1 should remind us that in human development genetic maturation is quantitatively about as important as learning in accounting for individual differences. Maturation can be separated conceptually, methodologically, and quantitatively from learning. Hopefully no one will caution us with the stale platitude that this is a "false dichotomy" because "in actual development they constantly interact." The only dangerous falsity in human development theory is putting all development down to one cause only, as when some ethologists think of hereditary patterns as immutable influences, or when Watson asserts he can make doctors and lawyers out of individuals with subnormal IQ by suitable conditioning. Let us recognize that certain maturations cannot take place without experience, and certain learning, for example, the beginning of education of sexual emotions, without maturation. Methods of investigating quantitatively the important interactions of genetic and threptic developments by determinations of H (heritability) and N (nature-nurture) ratios, repeated over a sequence of age intervals, have been discussed in Chapter 1.

In recognizing the genetic component we must not forget (so much work having been done on children only) that this internal clock is responsible for the changes of *involution* as well as those of maturation. The single term *volution* (meaning "an unfolding"—from inner sources) has therefore been suggested to cover *both*. Volutionary processes thus occur over the whole age curve. This is not suggesting that the processes of involution (in which, for example, we must include the loss of hearing acuity, and [see Horn & Donaldson, 1976, 1978; Baltes & Schaie, 1978] of fluid intelligence after the age of about 25) are a simple reversal of maturation; but only that they are highly alike in introducing parameters of behavior change, clearly physiologically tied, and independent in origin of those of learning.

Second, let us note that if learning is given its usual relatively precise meaning, as developed below, volution and learning *still* do not cover the whole of behavior change. There is a third source of change, which, for lack of a better and shorter term, we shall call the *somatic experience effect*, or *soma change*. Here we consider behavior changes from such things as a blow on the head, a vitamin-rich diet, the aftermath of influenza, and the *physical* effects of alcoholism, diabetes, or severe emotional upset. Regardless whether the causative agent is psychological or physical, its effect is not through learning, but through structural, hormonal, or neural somatic changes, which produce behavior changes not connected by any ordinary learning laws with the experience.

Yet another separation of learning from change in general hinges on the contrast of oscillatory fluctuations with steady trends. Let us set aside the latter, whether in learning or volution or somatic experience, from those that are reversible and sometimes cyclic, the latter being designated a fourth change category of *function fluctuation*. It suffices to summarize this logical clarification in Table 3-1.

Finally, we must draw the distinction between two concepts for lack of which general discussion sometimes gets snagged, namely, *structure* and *behavior*. We recognize, however, that even without any structural changes there are frequent changes of behavior. Any fixed, long-accumulated responsiveness potential (habit strength) constituting the organism's present *structure* constantly encounters different stimuli and different incentives. Both the upper and the lower halves of Table 3-1 deal with behavior change, but the lower half refers to structure held constant, with behavior changing from passing changes in inner and outer situations, whereas in the upper

TABLE 3-1. Causal Varieties of Behavior Change

A. Behavior Change from Structural Change

Essentially irreversible change, change with trend amounting to change in structural *disposition* itself	Not Environmentally Caused	Volution	maturation / involution
		Learning	
	Environmentally Determined		
		Somatic change experience	

B. Behavior Change Without Structural Change

Reversible, possibly cyclical change	Not Environmentally Caused	Function fluctuation with physiological, appetitive, and other inner instabilities
	Environmentally Determined	Change with situation

half we have inferred that the behavior change means structural change too.

A well-known instance in learning experiment of the possible confusion of these occurs in the finding that rats learning at reward level X are able to perform as well as those learning at reward level $2X$, if suddenly shifted to a $2X$ reward level. Here initially the behavior under X and $2X$ reward was different, and the first conclusion was that the structural gains must be different; but later researchers concluded behavior was different only because the *situational* incentive was different; that is, the learning, as engramming, was actually the same. This we discussed in the last chapter on distinguishing between *performance* change and *learning*, the former being a function of E and M and the latter only of M. It is proposed in this chapter to set aside from our study all but true learning, defined as a *structural* change (but as structural change through other than direct somatic change, Table 3-1). Later we shall speak of a learning structure as an engram, to distinguish it from other, possibly innate, structures. Although change through somatic experience is important, it has not seemed worthwhile at the present scarcely organized state of research in that field to devote space to it. And the reversible changes that occur with change of stimulus and ambient situation are taken just as a special aspect of learning study because they are merely the pulling out of suitable new responses, with situation change, from an already learned repertoire of engrams of adaptive responses.

3-2. Reflexological (or "Reflex") Learning Theory: Methods and Concepts in *SS, CR*I, and *CR*II Paradigms

Concentrating therefore on *learning change as such* we propose to look at the classical description of such change with a renaissance eye. Reflexological learning has concentrated largely on Pavlovian and instrumental conditioning to explain the attachment of new stimuli to old responses and new responses to old stimuli (and, of course, new to new). The whole development is couched in terms of "stimuli" and "responses," which constitutes what has been called a *peripheralistic* class of theory because it confines its observations and constructs to these entities visible in the environment, peripheral to any conception of determiners within the organism. As anyone familiar with the history of science will recognize it is *possible* (1) that not all the relations conceivable in a peripheral approach have yet been examined by researchers; and (2) that formulations *outside* the peripheral S and R constructs (and derived from wider behavioral observations) may have great importance for the further advance of learning theory. We shall be alert to both possibilities. But let it be said immediately regarding the latter possibility that personality theorists see very important forms of learning that still need to be added to any learning theory comprehensive of what we defined here and in Chapter 1 as personality learning change. Personality theorists want to know particularly what laws need to be involved to account for *the rise of the many types of personality structure*—traits, states, and processes—that they have discovered and found useful in behavioral prediction. They want to know more about what is broadly called "emotional learning"; about the gains in what the dynamic calculus has measured (Chapter 2) as integration; about the manner in which changes occur in the elements of the specification equation (traits and behavioral indices); and even about the acquisition of the less definite and presently poorly measured entities of the clinical world such as repression and reaction formation.

As any scientist looks at classical learning, as represented largely by reflexology, he must be impressed by the rigor with which it has been pursued. But are the S and R "reconnectings" all that we need to explain all phenomena of learning? It is just possible that such events as have just been mentioned—for example the rise of unitary trait structures; the phenomena of emotional learning: an increase in measured personality integration; the changes in specification equation behavioral indices, modulators, and trait levels; and a large number of other important events perceived by personality researchers and clinical psychologists may need additional principles.

The CRI and CRII paradigms (to use Skinner's notation respectively for the classical and operant, instrumental, conditioning principles) have justified themselves thoroughly in explaining specific bits of human behavior and especially in accounting for animal learning. But the more alert student is aware that enthusiastic reflexological writers have carried CRI and CRII over to complex human behavior in what are little more than metaphorical uses. When we talk about conditioning the self-image or reducing inner conflict by extinction procedures, the inferences claimed from reliable experiment with more narrow behaviors to these more global structures become indefensible. Cautious reflex-learning researchers, like Deese and Hulse (1967), for example, are aware of this and stress the difference between the "microscopic" research on actual reflexes such as Pavlov studied and the "macroscopic" scale of much human behavior.

We shall return to this micro-macro scale difference in several connections, sometimes with hope of bridging it by certain existing principles. But reflexological learning principles of classical conditioning as they stand will be applied here only with circumspection and with alertness to a possible need for a superstructure of new principles. Probably the most imaginative attempt to bridge to personality growth was Mowrer's (1938, 1960) use of animal experiments to simulate psychoanalytic personality concepts. That this ingenious work was not viewed as adequate by, and followed up by, reflexologists, and certainly not by personality theorists, seems to have been due to deficiencies in level of development on both sides, but mainly centered on the fact that personality psychometry—the factor analytic discovery and measurement of well defined traits— was not available to bridge the gap from a reflex response to a trait.

Let us begin with due tribute to the existing reflexological findings and the theoretical framework within which they are conceived. And first we may check whether, as asked above, a full use has been made of the possible S and R relations in a peripheral system. Table 3-2 begins this examination by examining the sheer logical possibilities of stimulus-stimulus and stimulus-response connections (response-stimulus and response-response being ruled out for the moment as logical possibilities that are "unreal"). Classical learning theory has worked with a fourfold table, as shown, formed by cutting across SS and SR with two types of learning, essentially contiguity and reward.

In classical reflexology the thoughtful student is compelled constantly to be asking whether he is dealing with descriptive or with explanatory laws. The line between description and explanation in science is inherently an uncertain and therefore a subjective one, subject to the illusions of the expositor's ambition or caution. His ambitions sometimes tell him he is explaining when he is only describing. Many classical learning theorists have recently been more content to consider that in CRI and $CRII$ they actually deal with descriptive categories and laws. In rendering in Table 3-2 a survey of the essential reflexological (we might call them "S-R connective") learning categories, probably the conceptually correct conclusion is that we are operating at the descriptive level. The table sets out those categories recognized under one title or another by the chief figures in learning theory to date.

Because our purpose in this book is to make developments beyond classical learning theory, following from its marriage to the dynamic calculus and personality theory of the preceding chapters, the review of reflexological principles in the present chapter must necessarily be stark—a view of the ground not of the building we are about to erect on it. Obviously we must assume the student has the usual training in that field, so that we can proceed by condensed

TABLE 3-2. Paradigms of Reflexological Learning Theory in Its Language of Connection of Peripheral Observables, S and R[a]

Mechanism[b] (or "principle") used to explain strengthening of connection		S-S	S-R
	Contiguity (temporal contingency)	S-S (1) Purely contiguity connection	S-R (2) Classical conditioning, *CR*I
	Reward[c] (contingent on the response)	S-S (3) Completion learning[d] implicit contiguity with reward too	S-R (4) Instrumental or operant conditioning, *CR*II

[a]Emphasis on one or another of these four paradigms as a basis for most or all learning has been, historically, placed on (1) by Morgan and Tolman; on (2) by Guthrie and Estes; on (3) by Schlosberg; and on (4) by Hull, Miller, Sheffield, and, in proportion to (2), Skinner.

[b]The question arises whether these should be called paradigms or laws. The difference between paradigm and mechanism (or laws) is discussed fully in the text, but it should be pointed out briefly here that a paradigm is a particular *pattern of arrangement of S and R contingencies,* for example, temporal sequences, repeatedly used by the experimenter. There are four here, but there could be others. A law concerns an underlying mechanism that accounts causatively for the rise of observed learning associations (engrams) when stimuli and response opportunities are presented in these paradigm orders; we shall argue that there are just five laws (Section 3-4 and Table 3-5), of which three are most basic.

[c]Reward rather than reinforcement is used here, not only for brevity but because reinforcement is an ambiguous term, meaning sometimes "rewarded," in other uses "strengthened" (see p. 181). Here *reinforcement* is "strengthening," and *reward* is one cause of reinforcement. Reward subsumes "punishment," as deprivation of desired reward (see p. 240).

[d]The category of completion learning may be strange to the classical learning theorist. It means the additional learning when two cognitive experiences are brought together through the *perception of a special relation* between them. Whether the reward is the usual dynamic (ergic) one when such a relation is perceived remains to be discussed.

schemas, like Table 3-2. Such summarizing tables will be clarified by notes under them rather than text discussion, their aim being simply to indicate what we consider the firm part of that theory from which we begin new construction.

It will be recognized that quadrant (1) in Table 3-2 has origins older than the reflexology of Pavlov and Watson, at least as far back as J. S. Mill, Reid, Bain, and the English associationist school, who recognized that the repeated contiguous (simultaneous or immediately successive) presentation of two words established a memory bond between them. Learning through stimulus-stimulus contiguity was brought to a most explicit principle by Lloyd Morgan, and has been invoked in countless experiments on memorizing word series, and so forth (Kimble, 1967; Underwood, 1966). It finally comes up, in pattern-construction form, in Tolman's (1948) argument that animals learn by developing a "cognitive map," and in various assertions that the other learning principles are not sufficient without this purely cognitive stimulus-connecting form of learning.

The upper right quadrant of Table 3-2, in which the connection is made between stimulus and response, is best known to students as the classical conditioning of Pavlov, though Lloyd Morgan was equally explicit—but less experimental—about it. By this device, and this alone, Guthrie and followers sought to explain all learning (adding that any new *S-R* connection also had the property of obliterating an old one). Staats (1975) recently has used it almost exclusively in determined (but this writer would claim simplified) explanations of personality growth and social learning. Thorndike, the comprehensiveness and adequacy of whose contribution to learning seem still not evaluated at their fundamental worth by the Watsonian type of reflexologist, introduced, besides the rather obvious law of exercise, the *law of effect*. The latter he stated in a weaker and stronger form theoretically, the weaker assumption being that learning is simply the consequence of a response that brings pleasure, and the stronger involving notions of what we here call dynamic engramming effects. Below we shall argue that Pavlov's classical conditioning (CRI) is not entirely distinct from means-end learning but includes a form of dynamic reward, *besides* contiguity. The argument, briefly, is that even a reflex has "a need to discharge" when defined more broadly. In that connection we may note that Thorndike's "weaker principle" of effect or reward was regarded by him as operative in what Pavlov called simple conditioning (CRI). And even at this introductory stage let us remind the reader of the above differentiation of descriptive and explanatory laws, and that for the time being, at least, we shall regard CRI and CRII as laws locked descriptively into *paradigms of experiment* rather than explanatory principles. That is, they describe simply what happens if one sets up an experiment repeatedly in a quite particular way. For example, in CRI we are simply saying descriptively that an unconditioned reflex stimulus and response preceded by a fraction of a second by a new stimulus leads to the new stimulus provoking the old response. The distinction of paradigm and principle or law will be more fully discussed later.

The lower right quadrant, (4), in Table 3-2 covers Thorndike's (1932, 1935) law of effect and related phenomena, and has been for some time academically known in reflexology by the rather cumbersome terms "instrumental conditioning" and "operant conditioning." (Later we must regretfully argue, in view of dangers in their present habitual usage, that the expressions involve a conceptual as well as a semantic contortion.) CRII has been treated by some important learning theorists as the main learning principle, indeed, it was almost entirely on this reinforcement, by drive reward, operating on response actions (the latter happening as they might), that Hull (1951, 1952) built his finely reasoned and precisely stated superstructure of learning principles.

Finally we come to quadrant (3), in Table 3-2, to find that it has been left almost completely uninhabited by learning in the reflexological tradition (except by, for example, Schlosberg). It supposes that the connection of a perception of one stimulus with perception of another (with no response whatever involved) can be made into an established connection by reward. We shall return to the question of what actually operates in these upper- and lower-left quadrants, and whether they really differ, as we encounter later certain possible principles labelled "coexcitation," "fusion," "cognitive completion reward," and "hidden dynamic reward."

Meanwhile, let us return for a moment to the issue of whether the logically ("mathematically") *possible* combinations of the peripheral elements—a topic normally bypassed as of little interest in learning theory—might have some psychological meaning. Actually both RS and RR have seemingly been invoked occasionally in explanations. Thus Hull's "fractional anticipatory goal response" permits a response, acting by proprioceptive feedback, to become a stimulus; but that is actually RSR; and the stimulus connection was, according to Hull, not learned. To make such a "machine" of a paradigm work we would have to both push and pull, so to speak. However, an RS connection is often considered in processes that could not go on unless a certain response reliably led to a required outer stimulus or became itself a stimulus to a new response. Because the RS question will be taken up in more refined senses later, and because in the form in which it is often badly stated, it *sadly drags in confusions of the word stimulus with inner experience, drive, and even, simply, "cause,"* let us drop it at this point. (Parenthetically, the stretching of the term "stimulus" in some reflexological literature to all kinds of *causes*, in a constant "renaming" game, is a prime cause of obfuscation of principles.)

As regards the possible RR connection, it is necessary in passing to clear the misapprehension that Spence's (1956) "RR psychology" refers to what we are now speaking of. Spence's label was an attempt to demarcate a whole domain of psychology seen by the reflexologist as *not* what interested him—namely individual differences. It repeats the distinction made by the present writer (1946, 1950, 1966) and later by Cronbach (1957) between cross-sectional, organism-structure research (as on traits in Volume 1 of this book) and longitudinal, process-structure research (perception, learning) as in Volume 2. Their cleanest and most fundamental separation, operationally and conceptually, is achieved by differentiating the two main score matrix facets (or grids) in the data box (Chapters 6 and 7 in Volume 1).

Returning from this digression to RR in the true present sense, we recognize that we are asking whether learning connections can be or have been investigated between two responses being made simultaneously (if that is possible) or in immediate succession. For the present, having noted the possibility, we shall leave a contingent answer to the more esoteric experiments in which reflex research abounds. The origins may be debatable but there is no question of an R_1-R_2 *correlation* being a possibility, that is, as a regular covariance of strength of two virtually simultaneous responses. As will be seen in structural learning, in the case when an individual is higher than another simultaneously in his making of R_1 and R_2 responses, we trace it to a conditioning schedule that *independently* raised these responses on stimulus-response potentials $S_1 R_1$ and $S_2 R_2$. The next question is whether this may produce a functional connection as well as a correlation.

The great bulk of reflex experiment has, of course, been in quadrants (2) (CRI) and (4) ($CRII$) in Table 3-2. But there has been a thinner stream of work more recently on the S-S quadrant—(1) in Table 3-2. It takes the form of ideas of "observational learning," and "mental experiments"—at least in mammals—and extends from Brogden (1939) and Razran's (1956, 1957) principle of "sensory preconditioning" to Bandura's (1962) "modelling."

A preoccupation of learning theorists for two generations in connection with the Table 3-2 concepts has been either to make a very clear conceptual separation of CRI and $CRII$ (Trappold and Overmeier, 1972; Heston and Iverson, 1978) or to bring them under a single principle. Monism is a justifiable, or at least respected, obsession in science and philosophy, and, conceivably, simplification *is* possible here. Some, like Guthrie and Estes, have tried to reduce all to CRI; others, like Hull and, at times, Mowrer, have brought all to $CRII$. To most experimentalists, as experimental *paradigms* rather than explanatory principles, the two have stayed distinct, as here expounded. Recognizing that neither reduction of all to CRI or

*CR*II has been successful, we question whether these *paradigms* are also true *principles* and so we set out later in this book on another way of "cutting the pie." Leaving these *CR*I and *CR*II lines of research, with their rich harvests in the classical experimental tradition, we should glance at the interesting developments in *statistical* learning theory. These are seen especially in Estes (1958), and Estes, Burke, and Atkinson (1957), and go back in principle to Guthrie's (1952) idea of selection of a stimulus through the potency of "areas in common," to various environmental experiences. The work of Estes, Atkinson, and others has resemblances, in its sensitivity to statistical frequency effects, to several formulations embedded in personality theory in Volume 1, Chapter 6, concerning frequencies and varieties of environmental exposures in regard to sentiment formation. Indeed, there are close methodological similarities in this kind of learning approach to notions in Tables 6-2 to 6-5 and Figures 6-4 and 6-5 in Volume 1 concerning the principles of explaining how repeating elements in situations acquire particular v and s values for dynamic traits.

With this perhaps unduly condensed review of the concepts guiding classical learning theory we turn in the remaining chapters to the new development over the last 10 to 15 years of what has been called *structured learning theory*. To distinguish classical learning by something more than its age and tradition, we shall continue to designate it *reflexological* or, more briefly, *reflex*, learning theory, because the use of peripheral concepts of stimulus and response bound by a reflex—literal or figurative—in the organism has always been its *central* model.

Our aim is now to develop precise functional connections between structured and reflex theory in a new integration across learning theory. In doing so we shall, at least in this chapter, be compelled to examine the findings of reflex learning theory at particular points in more detail and more extensively than in the above review (Table 3-2). In this the purpose will be to restructure and reinterpret a few of the reflex principles themselves, in the interests of better integration with personality learning.

A constant and explicit feature of the remodeling will be the use of definite concepts of structure within the organism—the existing traits—both as *determiners* and *products* of learning. (Hence the appropriate term, structured learning.) Thus structured learning prominently differs in going beyond the attempt of classical reflex learning to handle everything by observations and concepts based only on *peripheral* elements—stimuli and responses—and filling what some reflexists have called an empty "black box"—the organism— with potent machinery. Note that in expressly designating classical learning "reflexology" we are attempting also to disentangle the confusions created by calling it "behaviorism" (see p. vii). Our own structural approach is entirely behavioristic rather than introspective, as, indeed, most psychology has been since about 1880. That is to say, the structures with which we deal, and attempt to establish in the organism, are *inferences* from behavior itself. (This applies to all except Q'-data, personality factor constructs, for example.) We may nevertheless refer to the action in the upper tier of Table 3-2 as a contiguity of cognitive *experiences* rather than of stimuli, for, in these days of refined electronics and brain chemistry, conscious experiences yield cerebral behavioral indicators, for example, EEG records.

Let us remind the reader also of the other difference of approach just indicated above, namely that we shall consider CRI, $CRII$, and certain other reflex-research findings initially as *paradigms* rather than laws or principles. To pursue this further we wish to make a threefold distinction among certain research concepts (1) *paradigms*, (2) *empirical laws* or replicated data relations, and (3) *explanatory principles* or theories. A paradigm is a regularity observed in data when an experiment is repeatedly set up in a certain form. If connections on house wiring were so set up that pressing a certain switch turned off light A and turned on B, this would be a predicting paradigm, but not properly a scientific empirical law. An empirical law would involve a generalization that holds over several varied circuits and conditions, such as Ohm's law. And an explanatory principle might concern the flow of electrons. Again, in astronomy a statement about what happens to the shadow of the gnomon on a sundial when placed at various angles to the vertical describes a paradigm; Kepler's recognition of elliptical paths for all planets was an empirical law, and Newton's law of gravity was an explanatory principle. By this perspective CRI and $CRII$ could be considered paradigms, though $CRII$ might approach an empirical law.

When Pavlov chose, shrewdly but arbitrarily, to observe results on giving a new stimulus certain fractions of time before an unconditioned reflex stimulus he studied a paradigm. For he set up a restricted and rather unusual type of learning situation, which might be expected to catch only one of many possible ways in which fundamental learning laws might express themselves. Similarly, $CRII$ is a paradigm stating that a response to some accidentally present stimulus, when it happens to be followed by reward, increases the likelihood of that response being made to that stimulus again. It is easy to see that quite a number of other and more diverse experimental set-ups and sequences could be devised and repeated as the standard mode of investigation. For example, one could always give a reward immediately before a stimulus, or give several stimuli in a row, or have the response attached by previous experience to strong or weak sentiments, or, with humans, have the connection consciously explained, or not explained and so on.

Some idea of the possible relations that could be studied is provided systematically by the basic data relation matrix (Volume 1, p. 225). Reflexists did not study this, but they did, gradually, by taking steps to new combinations, ring appreciable changes on the original. However, as sometimes happens in the history of science, the pack of researchers settled down to a very stylized trail of inquiry, in this case, the repetition of experiments in CRI and $CRII$ paradigms. What has to be questioned is the notion that all relevant empirical laws and explanatory laws can be encompassed by and extracted from experiment confined to these paradigms. One can see immediately, for example, that discovery of the structure of ergs and sentiments could not be achieved by these bivariate paradigms, but only by experiment of a multivariate, structuring nature; and we can see that the acceptance of a paradigm as an empirical or even explanatory law would block the way to looking for more ultimate principles beyond CRI and $CRII$.

In the present Chapter 3 the writer purposes to open up the new concepts beyond present reflexology, though leaving their full development to the succeeding chapters. To make this exodus intelligible it is necessary first briefly to state and survey the paradigms as extensively investigated by reflexological learning experiment. Examining these from new angles we shall proceed to a statement of five laws that seem to meet the needs of both reflex and structured learning; the following chapters will examine the postulates and evidence for this theoretical position in the required greater detail.

Although psychology is today in a much more healthy and integrated condition than when it was subdivided, half a century ago, into a Babel of jingoistic "schools" with mutually incomprehensible languages, I am aware that the departure in structured learning is sufficiently basic to create "social" problems, of apparent disintegration. The student of a subject with growing pains needs orienting as much to these emotional forces as to the logical problems themselves. Any new development implies inadequacies in existing theory. For clarity I have referred above to a large part of existing learning theory as reflexological, which most correctly describes its central dependence on the reflex, S-R response. It is unfortunately probable that many reflexological writers will react to the present structured S-O-R development as a threat, or, worse, a demand to understand, in the richer new developments, a complex multivariate methodology and attendant statistics, such as factor analysis, that are not needed in mastering their segment of learning knowledge as it now stands. Let me preface any implied criticism with the sincere statement that I read the surveys and integrations of the principal writers in reflexological learning with pride, as a psychologist, in sharing one of the most impressive areas of psychological science. Amidst the welter of ill-conceived fashions and fads that wash across the legitimate domain of psychology, these writings stand as a rock and guide like a beacon. But from my first-published physiological-experimental and multivariate researches (1928, 1929, 1930, 1933) and especially since my participation in the Kentucky *Symposium on Learning and Personality* (1954), I have been grievously concerned by the lack of mutual interest between these rapidly growing subsciences of learning theory and personality theory. Individually, reflexology and personality constitute the two offspring of psychology having the greatest architectonic growth in the last 50 years and the finest scientific quality. Yet they continue to stand apart. And the few psychologists who have attempted seriously to unite them have, as often happens in science, suffered some degree of relegation to a no-man's land—as aliens, committed to the jargon of neither party. Yet in the end science always bridges its gaps, despite conservatives having difficulties with a new language—the language that expresses the integration.

It would be a worthwhile undertaking, but not one for the present book, for some able writer to high-light and examine the chief stumbling blocks to integration in present-day reflexology, on the one hand, and in personality study and psychometry on the other. Although space forbids us to do so comprehensively, we shall touch on the introduced changes of perspective in both as we proceed. In learning theory one suspects the readjustments have to do with (1) a shift from entirely peripheral and bivariate (*S* and *R*) concepts to an adequate study of multivariate empirical constructs (engrams, sentiments, factor loadings), (2) a due integration, in *human* learning, with cognitive studies, respecting the enormous capacity for symbol activity in man, and also with storage and other concepts from the computer, and (3) a complete shift from an abstract "reinforcement" action to one of reward in terms of dynamic calculus principles involving the impact of specific ergic goals and subgoals objectively defined and located.

Meanwhile, in an attempt at a really brief reminder, we summarize in Table 3-3 an essential statement of the present position regarding methods and concepts in reflexology, as our takeoff point in the enterprise of integration. (The takeoff point in personality theory has already been set out in the first volume of this book.) The concepts in Pavlovian condition, CRI, are sufficiently straightforward and well known to require no summary, and so Table 3-3 is largely confined to elaboration of the *CR*II, instrumental conditioning paradigms. It must be pointed out immediately that our later position will restructure concepts from these operations somewhat differently in sections 1 through 4 in Table 3-3, and decidedly differently in 5 and 6. In the latter we move to using the term *viscerogenic* and defining "appetitive," as in Chapter 2, in a more appropriate and also more technically precise way. At the same time we abandon the false antithesis of reward and punishment for what we argue is a truer division into reward and deprivation.

3-3. Possible Broader Approaches to Learning: Introduction to Concepts of Structured Learning Theory

As the reader looks today at the relatively cut-and-dried academic presentations of reflex learning theory, and wonders where the next growth will take place, he perceives possibilities of advance in several directions and is aware of investigators already setting off on some of them. However, we might consider first, the possibility that reflexological research in concentrating on only a few peripheral elements has not explored all the inherent relational possibilities of contiguity, succession, contingency of reward, and so forth. Second, there is the possibility that in gaining the good control offered in animal experiment, and in keeping within the narrow limits of ethical and practicable *manipulative* experiment with humans, reflexological research may have overlooked certain whole varieties of human learning. For example, has it dealt with the acquisition of a *general capacity* to inhibit impulses, such as we see in the growing child? Or with the human capacity to switch whole learning structures readily from one ergic or sentiment goal to another (as when one switches a skill in mathematics from chemistry to geography)? Or with the "spiritual learning," when such ergic goals as sex are, in their biological sense, given up altogether? Third, there is a possibility that research could work with relations among quite *different elements* from those peripheral *S* and *R* elements habitually used in reflexology: for example, connections between different feeling states, or between cognitive elements of sensory imagery, or between a sentiment structure and a response. At the moment there are dissident movements within reflexology itself (see general critique by Dulaney, 1968) one of which is instanced in a new concern with *cognitive* learning and meaning. In this we share, because it is highly important in human learning. Yet, like most revolutions, it is too much con-

TABLE 3-3. Measurements, Methods, and Concepts in Reflexology: Illustration in Instrumental Conditioning Paradigm: Basic Operation of Measurement, Designs, Covered, and Concepts Employed [a]

---

1. Response measures commonly used
    a.   Rate of responding
    b.   Latency of response
    c.   Speed of response
    d.   Choice or preference
    e.   Combinations of the above
2. Unitary versus choice situations
    a.   Unitary situations occur when a subject is given only a single response to make or a single manipulandum to operate.
    b.   Choice situations are those in which the subject is given two or more simultaneous options for response.
3. Discrete trial versus free operant situations
    a.   The discrete trial situation involves a time period between trials, in which the subject is either removed from the experimental situation, or prevented from responding, or the stimulus situation is changed to such a degree that responding is improbable.
    b.   The free operant situation allows continuous opportunity for responding on the part of the subject.
4. Simultaneous versus successive discrimination situations
    a.   In simultaneous discrimination situations the positive and negative stimuli are presented simultaneously, with responses to the positive stimulus being reinforced and responses to the negative stimulus being extinguished.

---

[a]The writer is indebted to Dr. John Sigurdson, in animal learning research, for drafting this, on the basis of Mackintosh's analysis (1974) and others, and it must be understood as representing in this book a resumé of *that* position, not the final position adopted in structural learning.

cerned with being a relatively narrow antithesis to a relatively narrow thesis, when true creativity might choose a number of different directions. Thus we would argue that the really new and most needed direction is not just cognitive learning but the shifting of all learning theory to a development on the basis of the dynamic calculus and its structural concepts. Even before attempting this theoretical restructuring, we would point out in Table 3-4 areas of empirical observation that are relatively neglected and would broaden the basis for our new start. The aim of Table 3-4 is to present a relatively unordered illustration of the sort of exploration that might be undertaken regarding (1) new paradigms and (2) new areas and forms of learning behavior.

Leaving this rough survey as an indication of possibilities we shall proceed in the next section to a concrete crystallization of five learning principles that we believe can be derived from wider examination of the area.

TABLE 3-3. *(continued)*

---

   b.   Successive discrimination usually takes place in a unitary situation where the positive and negative stimuli appear in succession with responses to the positive being reinforced and responses to the negative being extinguished.

5. Appetitive (positive) versus aversive (negative) reinforcement

      The distinction here is generally made on the hedonic value of the reinforcer to the subject. Both tend to increase responding, but appetitive reinforcers are those the subject will work to obtain whereas aversive reinforcers are those the subject will work to avoid.

      Exception: Negative reinforcement is sometimes used to describe the withdrawal of an aversive stimulus.

6. Positive versus negative contingencies between responses and outcomes

   a.   Positive contingencies occur in situations when a positive correlation exists between the occurrence of a response and the occurrence of a certain outcome.

   b.   Negative contingencies occur in situations when a negative correlation exists between the occurrence of a response and the occurrence of a certain outcome.

     (The orthogonal relationship between appetitive/aversive reinforcement and positive/negative contingencies)

		Reinforcement	
		Appetitive	Aversive
Contingency	+	Reward experiments (increase response)	Punishment experiments (decrease response)
	−	Omission experiments (decrease response)	Avoidance experiments (increase response)

In moving to this new position it will be helpful to be explicit about the departures we are making from traditional textbook reflexological learning theory, in four main respects, as follows:

1. As new "elements," additional to peripheral ones, structured learning theory introduces measurements on sentiments, M's, and ergs, E's. These can come into relation with S and R in the six ways existing among four things E, M, S, R. Note this innovation is an absolutely necessary step in moving from the S-R to the S-O-R model. In introducing E and M we actually introduce more than E and M scores, for they are accompanied by the behavioral coefficients of the specification equation, as elements in the learning relation model.

2. Recognizing that personality structures—M's, E's, P's (general personality traits), and A's (abilities)—are demonstrated realities in psychology, an addition is required to learning theory in which it addresses itself to *accounting for* these structures (in

TABLE 3-4.   Some Diversities of Learning Forms Recognizable in Common Observation

I.	Development of Performances That Are New, in the Sense of Involving Previously Nonexistent Connections

1. Evocation of cognitive activity, for example, recognition B by stimulus previously evoking cognitive activity A
2. Connection of behavior response A to stimulus B in place of stimulus A
3. Connection of behavioral response B to stimulus A in place of response A
4. Connection of behavioral response A to raised tension in ergic tension E, where connection did not previously exist
5. Connection of behavior response A to high excitation level of cognitive factor M, where connection previously did not exist
6. Acquisition of cognitive-emotional attentiveness to a stimulus situation previously neutral and ignored

II.   Development of Inhibition

1. Inhibition of response connections existing originally (innately) or through 1, 2, 3, and 4 above
2. Inhibition of innate or acquired responses toward an ergic goal A, triggered by ergic tension in A, by rise of behavior B from a different ergic tension B
3. Inhibition of path response A to ergic goal X by another path response B to the same ergic goal
4. Similar inhibition to 2, but between sentiment systems
5. Similar inhibition to 3, but between sentiment systems

III   Development of Integration, that is, of Maximization of Satisfaction Assessed over a Period of Time, in a Steady Environment

1. Acquisition of a different order or arrangement of stimulus-response, or ergic tension, or sentiment excitation responses already possessed
2. Application of any of the inhibition procedures in II above, resulting in greater over-all satisfaction

IV.   Modification of Ergic Goals Themselves

It is understood that, as in I(1) and others above, "evocation of response A" or "of A in place of B" describes not only an all-or-nothing event, but also an increase in duration or strength of a bond already weakly present.

ways that structured but not reflexological theory has in fact already had some success). Structure has been little experimented with in reflexological learning because (with the exception of a handful of studies, such as those of Tryon (1940), Cattell, Korth, and Bolz (1973), Cattell and Dielman (1974), Royce (1966), Scott and Fuller (1959)), the learning experimenters have drawn their conclusions largely from rats and pigeons, who are assumed to have no personality. Actually, even in the animal field as the above researches on individual differences for example in dogs, show, research would have been enlightened by taking temperament dimensions into account.

3. A third major departure is the innovation of studying the nature of *reward* and *reinforcement* (learning effect), for example, in *SS*, *CR*I, *CR*II, and other paradigms, in terms not merely of "bran mash," "electric shock," and so forth, but of vectors (patterns) of tension-reduction reward on a known, measurable, existing series of ergic tensions and sentiment activations.

The first innovative emphasis above requires no special explanatory comment here. The historical fact is that a precise and comprehensive edifice of checked ability (Cattell, 1972; Guilford, 1959. 1967; Hakstian & Cattell, 1974); general personality (Eysenck, 1960; Hundleby, Pawlik, & Cattell, 1965); and dynamic traits (Cattell & Child, 1975) has been available for some time to serve as an array of measurable vectors for experiment either on trait-structure acquisition or on understanding their effects on specific learning by including them in the specification equation. (Substantial learning predictions are instanced in Cattell & Butcher, 1968.)

Learning theory thus needs to recognize at this point that the above predictors should be taking their place with the *CR*I and *CR*II effects, assisting, interacting with, and modifying them in the prediction of learning. However, in recognizing the role of these traits abstracted from behavior—for they *are* abstractions—we may well wonder just how the welding can be achieved with the bare concrete observables of reflex theory—*S* and *R*—that generally do not go "under the skin" of the animal. We recognize that initially, that restriction to peripherals like much restriction in scientific steps was probably tactically sound. Deese and Hulse (1967, p. 108) stress that Hull (and, we might add, Pavlov) "wanted to emphasize an approach to learning where everything was to be explained in peripheralistic terms, like stimulus and response." The precision and consistency of the scheme and tradition of Hull is in this respect admirable, but its peripheralism adhered to by his successors in face of new structural concepts (*themselves* derived from behavior measures) has eventually stunted growth. What actually happened seems to have been due not only to such rigidity but to sheer unawareness, in the specialized reflexology area, of the advances in multivariate experimental personality research and the structural findings becoming available, at least for humans. The advance of personality theory, particularly of the dynamic calculus, has introduced broader concepts than existed in these stark peripheral entities, and greater precision than existed in broader concepts in older personality theory. Hull, it is true, made a cautious step to import the "organism" into the equation, though it was confined virtually to supposing something that possesses "drive." Mowrer (1939) and later Spence (1950), also vaguely unhappy with the deficiencies of a peripheral model, attempted to bring anxiety and fear into the picture, avoiding a shock to the users of standard *S-R* jargon by using only "stimulus" and "response" terms for these inner dynamic or emotional states.[1] None of these more adventurous thinkers could hope to break out of the framework in which they were locked, into a new conceptual domain, however, because reliable experimental structuring and measurement of personality and dynamics scarcely existed when they wrote, and the contemporary conjectures of psychoanalysis were not such as could be put into quantitatively testable form.

All this is now changed, as evidenced by Volume 1 of this book. Granted the possibility that personality structure research brings, of quantifying the internal equipment and states of the organism as accurately as the strength of an external stimulus or the magnitude of a reflex response have hitherto been quantified, new possibilities of conceptualization in learning are opened up. Let it be noted in this connection that the new approach is no less linked to "observables," that is, is no less behavioristic and operational, than the old. It merely abstracts concepts from the observables differently (especially adding internal structure) and over a wider foundation of observation. Some may consider sentiments and ergs as only "intermediate variables," in the sense of MacCorquodale and Meehl (1957), but because they do not arise from merely a bivariate relation they are actually better described as *empirical constructs* (though in later developments and interpretations here they become further enriched as *theoretical constructs*).

This enrichment, and the founding on a broader empirical base than the immediate *S*'s and *R*'s, whereby the M's and E's are largely independent of the particular *S*'s and *R*'s in a given prediction is possible because they are defined and measured from a foundation of multivariate research much broader in its observables than the particular *S* and *R* elements to which they are being related in a given experiment. Incidentally, in stating the pure reflex position one must recognize that some reflexist developments have not been as pure in adherence to observables as the theoretical position ideally requires. Thus Mowrer, Tolman, and others have used pattern concepts, for example, the cognitive map defining the *S* as an entire situational configuration instead of a focal stimulus. These speculative liberties needed but did not then have the definition of factors and patterns now possible by multivariate experiment.

In the sense that, in humans if not in animals, the reflexist has often conceived *traits*, the demand for readjustment is not onerous. But when we bring the structured specification equation to full action it will become evident that structured learning goes far beyond any vague concepts of traits. Indeed, it conceives of change not only in traits, such as E's, M's traits (D's and other T's), and state liabilities (L's), but also in the behavioral coefficients, p, r, i, and s (or, together, b). For example, soldiers whose fear erg, E_F, was formerly provoked by the sound of a shell only to the extent of the innate modulator coefficient s_k normal to violent sounds, may, after seeing the carnage caused by a shell, respond to the same ambient situation thereafter with an s_{k1} value that is much higher. This is not just a "conditioned reflex" but the growth of a sentiment structure modulating this erg and soon probably a number of others. *Any* learning, therefore, as will be developed in more detail in Section 3-6, can involve changes in E's, M's, T's, *and* the behavioral coefficients p, r, i, and s. In referring to the specification equation let us also note that S and R themselves take on a new symbolization in that the response is written in the dynamic calculus as an act or performance, a_{hijk} (generally of some complexity and time duration). And the "stimulus," S, is now analyzed into a focal stimulus, h, and an ambient situation, k.

By now, through the developments in Volume 1, and in Chapter 2 here, the reader will be assumed to be quite accustomed to the standard use of specification equation symbols such as h (for focal stimulus), i (for the individual concerned), j (for response pattern), and k (for ambient situation). For the present we shall interchangeably use the equivalents $S = h$ (some S uses will equal h *and* k), and $R = a_j$. The learning itself, as measured, will be incorporated in our behavioral specification terms, either as a change from a_{hijk} to a'_{hijk}, or from a_{hijk} to $a_{hij'k}$, the latter being appropriate where the response j alters not in quantity but in kind. Furthermore, innovation (1) above—essentially the shift from $S \rightarrow R$ to $S \rightarrow O \rightarrow R$—will require that the learning change in a_j be ultimately expressed in changes in all terms of the specification E_i, M_i, T_i, p_{hj}, r_{hj}, i_{hjk}, and s_{hk}. This brief statement concerning innovation (1) above will be clarified by expansion in Section 3-6.

Beyond the three relatively concrete and briefly and specifically definable innovations just discussed, that structured learning theory introduces beyond reflexology lies a fourth major change, (4) the resolution of the behavioral paradigms and relations in Tables 3-2, 3-3, and 3-4 into *five derived underlying learning* laws set out in Table 3-6 and to be discussed in Section 3-4.

In making these four innovations, structured learning theory must necessarily build hypotheses across some rather broad gaps in empirical findings, because most learning experiments have not yet oriented themselves to structured principles. It must rest its generalizations partly, therefore, on a massive, naturalistic survey of learning, extending beyond the laboratory to human culture and animal ethology, following in the spirit of the taxonomic surveys of Linnaeus and Darwin. As to experiment, it is realistic to recognize that structured learning theory inevitably requires more multivariate and complex experimental designs than the majority of students interested in the learning field have yet been given to learn.

Incidentally, one may note that the lack of observations now needed have arisen in the past through preoccupation with paradigms of learning new performance responses to old stimuli, or attaching new stimuli to old performances, whereas in human personality learning the teacher and clinician are much concerned with Category II in Table 3-4, the learning of inhibitions, controls, and postponements, and with III, the acquisition of courses of action that maximize *total* drive expression over a time span, over the full spectrum of ergs and in the full environment. These latter types of learning, incidentally, we shall call *confluent* and *integrative learning*, and shall give considerable study to them.

In a healthy reaction against much bogus, untestable theory in psychology, Skinner (1950) has expressed his opinion and, undoubtedly that of many of his colleagues, that the best progress is to be made without theory, simply seeking empirical laws among elements. Although the present writer has called (1966) for a very similar clearing of the jungle of untestable, "imported", data-unrelated theories in research in the personality field, yet we recognize that there *is* need for genuine theory. By this we mean clear models adjusted in their ambitions to the stage of development of the science. In both personality and learning this means more use of empirical than theoretical constructs, the former being easily definable in clear relationships among measurable variables. The reflexologist may ask why we do not always go the whole way to S and R elements if our structures are indeed based on behavior. The answer— over and above that which we have given about dependence on more remote behavior observations than in the immediate act—is that the higher order emergents are necessary to understanding. It is very possible that the truly illuminating lawful relations simply do not exist among single elements in nature's code any more than they do in some encoded message that some beginner in cryptanalysis tries to decipher. Everyone recognizes that the bivariate observation that, say, person A smiles at person B, is not susceptible to explanation unless we know whether they are rivals or lovers, or what the situation and the conversational subject is, and other such elements. The fatal limitation of bivariate reflexological models in attempting to proceed from paradigm findings to explanatory laws surely lies largely in this decapitation of the main body of evidence.

3-4. Initial Statement of Five Basic Laws of Learning Changes: 1. The Coexcitation Effect

Reflexology may have been tactically wise—especially in the chaotic state of psychology at the time—in confining itself at first to two or three paradigms of the form of CRI and $CRII$. But as stated the time has come to seek relations in higher levels of constructs and over broader fields of observation. In reviewing reflexology above, and showing the directions in which structured learning theory takes off therefrom, the mentioning of E and M, and of b, p, r, i, and s co-efficients has already given a glimpse of the theoretical model likely to emerge. But before proceeding further to that model we propose to state the basic learning principles that are needed for the model. In doing so we have moved from the above findings in terms of *paradigms*, like CRI, through *empirical laws* to what should have the status of underlying *principles*.

To state those principles certain contributory concepts must first be defined on an operational basis. One of the most important of these is the ergic goal.

The literature on dynamic goals has a variety of ambiguities on the meaning of goal. Is a goal an object in the physical world, such as a female, or a grade in a course? Is it the consummatory response behavior, say, sexual intercourse or the act of getting the answer to a mathematical problem? Is it an internal *state* in an organism, defined by a particular tension beforehand and a particular type of emotional satisfaction at the end? There is no contradiction in saying it is all of these, as different parts of the definition of a single concept, though the physical object is least vital. Thus the goal in a maze run can be defined (1) as bran mash; (2) as the consummatory behavior in chewing and swallowing it; and (3) as the internal state of satisfaction of hunger.

Process analysis (p. 323) is capable of identifying the goal as a repeating pattern of consummatory responses, wherein we recognize also the object associated therewith. The reader may be reminded that three very different statistical experimental approaches can be used as mutual checks here: (1) Factoring of attitudes leading to recognition of consummatory behaviors through their being most highly loaded on the factor; (2) Manipulative blocking of behavior. The end of a subsidiation change is reached when no further behavior can be found the blocking of which reduces the interest in the chain. (3) The recognition of chains of behavior process that repeat themselves from time to time in one person and from person to person. We suggested that this discovery be made by autocorrelation of behavior series, with changing lag. It happens that discovering a cipher in cryptanalysis meets almost exactly the same problem and Friedman's (1920) solution to it by his "index of coincidence" should be a boon to psychodynamic research. The method of this last discovery of the termination of a process is shown in Figure 3-1.

However, locating the consummatory situation, after which no immediate re-commencement of the process usually occurs, does not comprise the whole definition of the goal. For if there were no other existence of a goal than this we should have to suppose that later behavior causes earlier behavior—that is, we should relapse into teleology when we speak of a goal-"inducing" behavior. Instead we have to recognize that the nature of the intended consummatory behavior is represented by an internal equivalent—an ergic (emotional) state in the animal—of a kind particular to the given consummatory behavior, which arises into action long before the goal, and persists directively until dissolved by the consummation. If we wish to think in terms of homeostasis, then the goal is a return to physiological equilibrium. If we wish to explore the neurological and physiological

(a)   Continuous quantitative

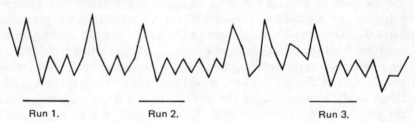

Run 1.   Run 2.   Run 3.

(b)   Qualitative variables

LPBRPPLXBOLBRPPLRPBPXOBXRBRPPLYX

Run 1.   Run 2.   Run 3.

Search procedure consists of programmed, stepwise, lead-and-lag correlation. Usually it would not be on a single variable as in (a), but on a matrix of several variables over time.

Figure 3-1. Calculation to recognize a repeating psychological process and locate an ergic goal or sub-goal.

substrate, it can probably be found in the hypothalamus and in the blood-sugar or hormone levels that affect the ergic drive centers. The point here is that an ergic goal (and the associated ergic process) needs to be found—in a psychology that is not either introspective or subjectively arbitrary—by first locating the consummatory activity situation. After having thus behavioristically located it one has to find its associate as an internal, physiological, conative and affective state, which is the real (not teleological) cause of the pursuit of the process.

A sentiment also is a goal—or in the lattice a sub-goal—which borrows its rewarding properties from its particular ergic-investment vector. Both by E's and by M's, structured learning theory has a precision of explanatory structure lacking in the reflexological use of "drive," "tension," and so forth. For the effect of an equivalent drive or ergic tension level is now recognized to be of a possibly different pattern for different ergs, and (no less important) the learning is considered tied, at least for the time being, to a specific ergic goal tension. Incidentally, the enormous conceptual and symbol-using capacity of humans, bringing great facility in switching "technical learning" acquired for goal A immediately to goal B, tends to mask this more fundamental tendency for learning to have some specificity in its goals.

The goals of ergs and sentiments are implied, therefore, when we introduce the term *means-end learning*, below. Incidentally, our preference for *means-end* over *operant conditioning* is not merely arbitrary, or an expression of a need for brief over ponderous and mandarin terminology. It is intended constantly to spotlight the essential feature: that a particular goal is always implicit in a "reward" (in the second use of the ambiguous term "reinforcement") and that it is asking for theoretical trouble if one forgets this.

With these concepts the first step we take in moving from paradigms to principles is to split the CRI paradigm, arguing that it embodies the action of *two* principles, not one. This is perhaps a disturbing assertion to make and it can be more fully justified only as we proceed through this and the next chapter. It claims that classical Pavlovian conditioning was so set up experimentally that it happened to involve both what we shall call the *coexcitation* (approximately, "contiguity") principle *and* the reward principle that is central in CRII—operant, instrumental, or means-end learning. The claim for reward is that there is a neural, physiological continuity in innate equipment between a simple reflex, a larger physiological reactive subsystem such as bladder emptying, and so on to a full-blown drive, and that, in fact, something that can be called "satisfaction" occurs across all, and therefore exists, even if not in conscious form, at the discharge of any reflex. (Satisfaction is here thus not defined merely on an introspective basis, but is a behavioral abstraction from certain qualities of associated behaviors.)

However, our conception of CRI is that excitation *as such* calls for discharge, that is that satisfaction is reduction of excitation. The additional excitation created by the conditioned stimulus adds to the satisfaction in the discharge of the excitation in the unconditioned reflex. Relative to the constant excitation produced (presumably in the hypothalamus) by the neural and hormone urges of a drive, the excitation from a passing stimulus is relatively brief. Consistently with this we have other evidence that the reward in CRI, in contrast to $CRII$, is brief, mainly that the paradigm for CRI operates successfully only with a very short time interval, and there is evidence even of "backward conditioning" (Barlow, 1956).

The Coexcitation Effect

Various approaches to viewing a reflex as a drive in itself, on a minor scale (or alternatively, concluding that a drive is commonly found back of the reflex, as an organizer) pop up in the literature, one of the most closely argued being that of Perkins (1968). However, most of these ideas of a reflex response as a reward make the *whole* of CRI a form of reward, like $CRII$, whereas we are going to argue for the CRI paradigm experiments having caught the action of *two* principles—coexcitation *and* reward. Letting further discussion of the nature and action of whatever dynamic satisfaction is claimed for the reflex and a briefly stimulated excitation be set aside for later discussion, let us concentrate on the other ingredient, *coexcitation*, which we shall call Principle 1. As will be seen more fully in the next chapter, much evidence points to mere contiguity or coexcitation (here symbolized CE) of stimuli acting as an engramming influence as does the reward in means-end learning ($CRII$). Nevertheless, as Hilgard and Bower (1966, p. 536) conclude, "Following some early dispute about the phenomenon there now seems abundant evidence from many sources that direct sensory-sensory conditioning of this sort occurs" (see also Seidel, 1959; Bandura, 1965). Some of the clearest support for this is of course in *sensory preconditioning* (see Mackintosh, 1974; Hilgard & Marquis, 1940) where the conditioning of a response to S_a automatically brings a conditioning thereof to S_b, when S_a and S_b have been linked by simultaneous presentation *on their own*.

Later we must ask more precisely, "coexcitation of outer

stimulus products or of inner experiences too?" but as a beginning we can let it rest on evidence of an effect from simultaneous action of two stimuli, S_a and S_b, such that some sensory, cognitive excitation resulting from one is henceforth capable of activating the sensory cognitive excitation that was produced by the other. However, if we may infer the existence of the sensory excitation in itself, as c_a (and c_b), the coexcitation principle can be stated *without* the limitations of the peripheral paradigm as:

$$c_a + c_b \rightarrow n_{c_a c_b} \tag{3-1}$$

where n is a bond or engram formed between c_a and c_b such that:

$$c_a \cdot n_{ca\ cb} \rightarrow c_b \tag{3-2a}$$

and

$$c_b \cdot n_{ca\ cb} \rightarrow c_a \tag{3-2b}$$

the dot here meaning "with." The possibilities here are summarized in Table 3-5.

Later, when the factor-analytically hierarchical structure of sentiments and their unrolling as a process are discussed (Chapter 4 and 5), we shall give a rationale for breaking down the hierarchy of partly independently excitable units within a sentiment into at least four sizes of units: M, the total sentiment structure; m, a sub-sentiment; t, a mental set; and c, a single idea, or cognitive-sensory perception. Here, at the reflex level of evidence we use the smallest

TABLE 3-5. Four Possible Forms of Fusion in Coexcitation (CE) Learning

	No directionality in bond	Directionality remaining in bond
Externally generated excitation	S_a (simultaneous) S_b → $c_a \ldots n_{ab} \ldots c_b$	S_1 excitation S_2 (temporal priority of S_1) → $c_1 \ldots n_{1\text{-}2} \ldots c_2$
Internally generated excitation	Education Logical relation Spontaneous appearance	Dynamic purpose Temporal priority Retrieval sequence Small-to-large excitation
	$c_a \ldots n_{ab} \ldots c_b$	$c_1 \ldots n_{1\text{-}2} \ldots c_2$

unit c, but later we shall evidence that the bond or engram, n, can arise at any level of size, for example, the coexcitation may link, for example, a c_a with m, or M, S_a with S_b (via c's), and any pair of cognitive elements, c_a and c_b. Incidentally a question that naturally arises in pursuing this notion of connections through Table 3-2, is whether that table should be extended to include a link of R_a and R_b. Presumably it is psychologically possible that if an organism is somehow induced to make two responses in very close contiguity, an association by coexcitation will be formed, such that making R_a is some incitement to making R_b, but no paradigm of experiment yet clearly shows this as a coexcitation effect.

By writing c's, as in equation (3-1) above and Figure 4-1 (p. 224), we have declined to limit the principle to ideas merely provoked by outer sensory stimuli, S_a and S_b. The reflexologist may ask, "If the c's are not so provoked, where else could they possibly come from?" Admittedly we tread on less firm evidential ground here, but our answer would be that (1) each might be the end of a chain of inner reflections from some long preceding external stimuli; (2) emotional states, as argued below, are capable of evoking cognitive ideas from past emotional associations; and (3) cognitive processes, notably Spearman's eduction of relations and correlates, are capable of internally creating new ideas, two of which creations might then be experienced together. (See also Egger and Miller (1963) on "reinforcement by information.") And in considering this coexcitation effect of inner ideas let us not overlook that the bulk of the discussions and memory experiments (Adams, 1967; Anderson, 1975) based on English associationism point to a need for such a coexcitation principle.

However, as Hilgard and Bower (1966) point out, there is relatively precise evidence in reflexology itself, despite such arguments as those of Morgan (1894), which seek alternative explanations, or Mowrer (1956), seeking to account for the whole of CRI effects in this coexcitation way (which would not fit the properties we wish to establish for CE here). The experimental results of Bitterman, Read, and Kubala (1953), in conditioning S_b to S_a by contiguous presentation and then S_b to an unconditioned response, as stated above, give the most solid evidence, though we might make some inference also from the general existence in CRI experiments of a slight degree of "backward conditioning" as argued by Barlow (1956), and Rescorla (1967a, 1967b)—with, however, some counter arguments to this basis of support by Razran (1956, 1957). Also contributory to the CE effect is the general evidence on which Tolman (1948) based his idea of the development of "cognitive maps" and the experimental evidence in the animal domain on the importance of frequency and familiarity relative to reward in *learning*, for example, in engramming, though somewhat confused in performance measures.

Among the objections to giving any *strong* role to a pure coexcitation effect are the following.

1. If engram bonds were easily established by contiguity, then virtually all ideas, turning over in consciousness, would sooner or later become memory bound with all others, thus producing associational anarchy. However, there are escapes from this conclusion studied below.

2. When slight temporal differences exist, the bond forms more readily from the earlier to the later object. Such a *sequence* effect suggest that a dynamic, goal-path-sequence "reward" quality, or some yet unknown sequence effect, also enters. It may thus be that in practice, as occurs regularly in using the CRI paradigm, reward can rarely be eliminated entirely from contaminating CE per se. The pure coexcitation effect might be an asymptote to all practical instances, and we may not have noticed that the asymptote is zero.

3. Particular connections might be favored, over and above any coexcitation, by what we define below as a *completion effect*, initially purely cognitive in nature but nevertheless something more than contiguity.[2]

These and other refinements and developments of conception of CE or "fusion" will be considered further in Section 4-1. Here it suffices to describe the CE effect; to indicate that its existence in CRI is indicated by the need to have S_1 and S_2 really close together (not needed in means-end reward), and, finally, to distinguish its role as an explanatory *principle* distinct from a paradigm, and beyond an empirical relation law. Regarding the last distinction, let us note that the coexcitation law differs from a mere contiguity "law" in that it posits that something we shall define later as "excitation" or "activation," which itself can be measured, is the real causal agent. That is to say, there is something more involved in the CE principle than in what psychologists mean who speak of a *temporal-contiguity* empirical law. Thus CE action may be finally stated: *If two existing engrams or new experiences are simultaneously brought to activation, there will be a tendency, proportional to the extent of the activations, for a new engram to be set up joining them, such that in the future activation of one will cause some activation of the other.* Although such Russian psychologists as Leontieff and Luria have been speaking of the whole Pavlovian paradigm rather than just the

CE component, they have attempted an explanation in physiological terms, that could be applied to pure CE, in supposing neural excitations in different areas to "run together." Reference is given below to the work of Guttman (1977), Walter (1964) (see also Nissen, 1977), and Irwin, Knott, and others (1966) on neural evidence of the presence of "ideas," which is necessary if we are to base the law (when external stimuli are *not* involved) on behavior rather than introspection. However, it is premature, we feel, to move from a law based on structures and states inferred from behavior and neural evidence to explanations purely in *physiological* terms, as in the Russian theories; but the parallelism of the physiological to the behavioristic coexcitation (CE) principle is noteworthy.

3-5. Further Laws of Learning Change: 2. Means-End; 3. Integration; 4. Ergic Goal Modification; 5. Energy Saving

In our introductory definition of five learning laws most space has first been given to CE because of the initial danger of confusing it with CRI and the initial need to substantiate its nature. All five are now set out in Table 3-6, and we shall now proceed in this section to the remainder, beginning first with the means-end (ME) law. This requires less discussion because it is identical with what has long been studied in the CRII paradigm, which, when labelled "*instrumental conditioning,*" in fact already implies the concept of *means to the end of a goal* by the word "instrumental." (Unfortunately the retention of "conditioning" implies, confusingly, a generic resemblance to CE that simply does not exist!) They are together only in the sense that they are learning laws, but are independent and radically different.

However, ME as a general law differs from CRII as the experimental paradigm around which so many generalizations have collected, for two important reasons. (1) The goal is explicitly part of the definition in ME, and (2) there is a change of scale in that the effect of the ME principle ranges from the "microscopic" reflex behavior to the macroscopic drive goal courses, for example, in attitudes in the human dynamic lattice as studied by the dynamic calculus.

Once again we must remind the reader that between the legitimate[3] use of "reflex," on the one hand, and the definition of an attitude course of action, on the other, there is a real gap. Qualitative differences may arise from the sheer change of scale. Our act, a_{hijk} in the behavioral equation, *can* be a highly specific and instant bit of behavior, as is an act on an objective personality test, such as pointing to a shape in a picture, or in *Q*-data, responding yes or no to a question. More frequently, when it is a criterion course of action being predicted, the behavior is an hour's performance, or a month's work on a job, or leading a group in a game, or answering an exam paper. In the dynamic lattice generally, it is the path representing a *course of action* expressing an attitude. It has been recognized that the transition from our macroscopic level of the reflex proceeds through hierarchical structures, extending through M, *m*, *t*, and *c* elements down to reflexes. One difficulty in generalizing from animal to human learning is that the relative frequency and prevalence of higher-order courses of action, M's and *m*'s, still correctly describable at different levels as "the response to a situation," is far greater in human cultural behavior. A detailed analysis of the hierarchical structure we assume typically to exist within a response as a broad course of action is undertaken in Chapter 5.

The central characteristic of the *CR*II paradigm, to the relation of which to *ME learning* we now turn, is the reinforcement of a response that happens to be made to (or in the presence of) some stimulus, in such a way that the response leads ultimately to a dynamic reward (reduction of tension of an ergic need) in contrast to other responses that do not. Thus that response is henceforth made to that stimulus. Let us again call to the reader's attention as we enter discussion on *CR*II that in the literature of reflexology the word reinforcement is constantly used ambiguously, sometimes meaning *reward*, sometimes a degree of *strengthening* of a connection ("This experience reinforces the connection"). Here we shall, as stated earlier, use *reward* for an ensuing satisfaction, and *reinforcement* for an increase in the probability of the stimulus-response engram connection becoming more strongly operative in future. (Incidentally, it is hard to discover what is wrong with the ordinary term "strengthened," that would avoid the ambiguous sense of reinforced. Perhaps it lacks the academic status of an unnecessary syllable!)

It will be seen that in Table 3-6 we have freely introduced the construct of an *ergic tension*, symbolized as E (having by implication a specific ergic goal). Further, the framework from the dynamic lattice has entered, and the symbols for the two aspects of the stimulus situation—k, the *ambient situation*, and h, the focal stimulus—as well as a_j, the response along a course of action. These would be in reflexological terms, S for $(h + k)$ and R for a_j.

With the above statement of the need to reformulate *CR*II in

Table 3-6. Five Hypothesized Underlying Learning Laws (Describing What Gets Connected and by What Mechanisms)

Law	Symbol	Description
(1)	*CE*	Coexcitation (Sometimes Called Cognitive Contiguity Learning)

Here we observe an experienced contiguity of cognitive experiences c_1 and c_2 or C and M,[a] which is often connected with simultaneous experience of two stimuli, S_1 or S_2. The establishment of connection such that thereafter c_1 tends to reinstate c_2, and c_2 to reinstate c_1 is partly inferred from responses following c_1 or c_2.

The basic effect, "explained" by saying that two simultaneous excitations tend mutually to connect, is a relatively weak one. It may be that secondary influences, such as directional preference when the simultaneous contiguity is not complete but allows succession, or the effect of meaning, by closure or eduction of perceived relations, or the intrusion of dynamic relevance, commonly strengthen the effect of the basic coexcitation mechanism. Classical conditioning (*CR*I) is considered a combination of (a), coexcitation (*CE*) with (b) means-end learning, *ME,* the latter generally predominating in the magnitude of effect.

| (2) | *ME* or *CR*II | Means-End Learning, Operant or Instrumental Conditioning |

The mechanism here is essentially the retroactive reinforcement of a connection between the ambient and focal stimuli (h and $k \equiv$ S) on the one hand and a response ($a_j \equiv$ R) on the other, which leads to goal gratification of an erg E. The relative roles of S, the external stimulus,

---

[a]At this point in the development of learning laws the reader should recognize that we are already in transition from dealing only with *S* and *R* peripheral symbols to incorporating structural terms, notably ergs, *E*'s, sentiments, *M*'s, subsentiments, *m*'s, and cognitive experiences, c's. In any case the response, *R*, is now always to be more fully defined as a measured and particularized course of action performance—a_{hijk}. In *CE* we use c's rather than *M*'s because at first we must cautiously assume that a stimulus *S* is likely to activate a more restricted internal cognitive element, or subgoal, a_c or, at most, a mental set, m—within the sentiment, rather than a whole sentiment, *M*.

structured learning theory, and to add, beyond it, three further laws, let us give fuller discussion as given above for *CE*, for all four further principles listed in Table 3-6, beyond *CE*.

Means-End (*ME*) Learning

The reader is reminded again that this is no *one-to-one* alignment of underlying principles with the paradigms that historically have been most intensively studied, although in this case we deal with generalized properties *very* close to those in *CR*II. *ME learning is learning that occurs to actions that prove contributory in the path*

TABLE 3–6. *(continued)*

Law	Symbol	Description

happening to be associated with the moment of response, of E, the ergic tension level, and of k, the ambient situation modulating E, will vary considerably, so that S may sometimes involve little more than a trivial stimulus, but made subsequently important by having initiated the response $(R \equiv a_j)$, which gratifies E.

(3) *N* Integration (Including Inhibition) Learning

This means acquiring a mode of response, when behaviors to two different ergic or sentiment goals from two different stimuli normally conflict, such that the total satisfaction of the organism is maximized. Learning the capacity to inhibit on a suitable occasion is part of this, as also is *confluence* learning, that is, discovering a new mode of response, a_{j3} different from the a_{j1} and a_{j2} in conflict, which gives sufficient satisfaction to the ergic goals involved in the specification equation of both a_{j1} and a_{j2}.

(4) *GM* Ergic Goal Modification

Laws (2) and (3), *ME* and *N,* involve changing response paths to a goal. *GM* involves accepting some change in the consummatory goal satisfactions themselves, as in sublimination, regression, and some forms of imprinting.

(5) *ES* Energy Saving

This principle states that of two response paths equally effective, as regards time and reward, in reaching a goal, the one will be learned that involves least expenditure of energy. If the rest-seeking erg proves sufficient to account for this behavior, then law (5) is superfluous, for it becomes only a special case of integration of diverse ergs for greatest total satisfaction, that is, it is sufficiently explained by principle N.

to a particular goal, brought about through the reward, having a specific innate quality, that ultimately occurs at the goal.

One important difference of this principle from the basic reflexological "explanation" given in *CR*II terms is that the latter, in most formulations, has no definite specification of what reward means. In others, as in Hull, it employs drive reduction but it is of a general unspecified drive term, *D.* The latter is a *scalar* quantity, whereas the usual goal in life behavior is some degree of satisfaction of *several* ergs, and this reward actually requires the richer definition of a *vector quantity*, specifying the amounts of the various ergic satisfactions incurred. A second difference is that the engramming that occurs becomes, in part and as determined by other principles, specific in quantity and in its operational associations to those particular ergic goals.

It may be desirable, until we know more, to represent the engramming of a response (R_j or a_j) to a stimulus (S_h or h), such as occurs in means-end learning (operant or instrumental conditioning) to another in CE learning, because, for all we know, they may behave differently. Consequently, the engram that accounts for the installation after learning of a steady S-R relation is written n. This n fades if not sustained by continued reward to the R, and it is not transferable, in full strength, to a different ergic goal vector; that is, in some degree it has the signature of the specific dynamic vector direction. Actually, several reflexological learning experiments in traditional frameworks witness to this specificity of attachment of learning to a particular E; for when the reward for a particular maze run is altered—say, from food to drink—there is a loss of performance, recouped only as the animal accepts the new reward. These further properties will be taken up in the more detailed examination of ME learning. The present purpose is simply to introduce and define the term. Except for the structured learning demand that it be considered, for completeness and ultimate correctness, in a framework of known dynamic structures, and in relation to distances from a goal, and allied parameters, it is so close to the familiar properties assigned to operant conditioning, CRII, that no further introduction is needed.

Integration Learning (N)

Two forms of integration learning can be recognized, corresponding to the two forms of conflict (Chapter 2), active and indurated. In the first form of integration learning the courses of action are situationally incompatible to the extent that one precludes the other, but there is no particular relation, compatible or incompatible, of their ergic vectors. What we have called *confluence learning* is the integrative answer here; namely, finding a third course of action that sufficiently achieves the ergic satisfaction of both. This, it has been suggested, can proceed by insight or trial and error, but it must frequently also require intervention of the control system (Chapter 2 and 6) to force an inhibitory pause of the two existing actions in favor of a new solution. In the second form, ego-planned integration, the learning process involves so much of the last (ego control) type of action that it is describable only after the structure and action of the ego controlling system are dealt with in Chapter 6. However, it can be stated that needs and actions first must be weighed, and then cues are evoked by the ego that modulate the various dynamic traits in such a way as to bring the subsequent action as close as possible to maximizing the total satisfaction, in terms of the specification equation for an indurated solution. Learning by gains from this source can in turn be augmented by learning *on the part of the ego structure itself* in both of the skills mentioned.

Two questions that arise about learning gains by integration (*N*), are (1) How can we measure it for experimental research purposes? and (2) Does it really require any new learning law beyond those of *CE* and *ME*, to the extent that we are called upon to call it a third principle? As to the first, nothing can be done unless we have conceptions (correct ones!) of dynamic structures (ergs and sentiments) and means for measuring them that are of established validity. The absence of these from existing reflexological research at present prevents its ordinary findings from being brought to bear, except very obliquely, upon the nature of integration learning. Even with taxonomic knowledge of different ergic tensions, such as structured learning can now call upon, one is faced with the technical problem of demonstrating the maximization of a sum of different ergic satisfactions, that is, of recording a gain in the sum across several ergs. The hope of a solution lies first in the psychometric employment of *real-base factor analysis* (Cattell, 1972), accepting inherently different strengths (variances) of the ergic tension factors, and, second, in the experimental verification of certain principles in the dynamic calculus (Cattell & Child, 1975) defining conflict and integration. Confluence learning and ego-planned integration may need separate study, the former with more relevance to education and the latter to clinical problems. As the aim of therapy is, centrally, one of achieving better integration, the development of experimental findings on this principle of integration learning is of great practical importance.

The second question about *N*, above, namely, whether *N* (integration learning) really requires a new principle or whether it is already sufficiently explained simply as certain combinations of the *CE* and *ME* principles, will be raised by conservative learning theorists. Unquestionably *CE* and *ME* continue to be at work in the engramming processes that go with integration learning, but we are going to take the position that it is highly probable that certain emergent effects will occur at this higher level not fully explicable by *CE* and *ME* laws as such. We believe the reaction of some reflexological learning theorists to integration learning as a superfluous concept, on the ground that it involves no new referents beyond *S* and *R* misses the importance in science of those concepts which we may call emergents, for example, that of nuclear fusion, which would not have been deduced from the valencies, atomic structures, and so forth, studied in lower atomic weights. Certainly the phenomena of N learning involves concepts of mutual inhibition operations by E and M forces that have not been encompassed by observations on CRI and CRII paradigms. At the very least there are going to be new *descriptive* laws here, having to do with summation of ergic rewards. It is equally possible that N involves a principle not yet known. Incidentally, we can point out here some oblique relation of N to Pavlov's primary concept of the tendency to respond being a function of $P(\epsilon - I)$, where ϵ is excitation and I is inhibition. We assign to inhibition an important role in integration learning, but Pavlov's inhibition, like inhibition in a neural refractory phase, was inherent in reflex behavior, that is, at the microscopic level, whereas the inhibition we shall consider in Chapters 5 and 6, as essential to integration learning, is of a higher level, deriving from personality *control structures.*

All of the first three of the principles, as above, might be referred to in terms familiar to the clinician as *dynamic* learning principles.

Ergic Goal Modification (*GM*)

All three principles above involve changes in behavior that lie on the path to consummation at a goal that does not itself change. But in *GM* we are no longer concerned with change in behavioral paths to a largely innate goal. Instead, we observe changes in the type of satisfaction *accepted at the innate goal itself.* Modifiable and innate may be logically contradictory, but the view that such change can occur was presented classically in the psychoanalytic concept of sublimation, specifically in relation to the sex drive, though, in principle, to any.

Experimental support for goal modification is not as clear as one would wish, and it lies largely in the field of imprinting, where it is not always certain whether the goal itself or some intermediate behavior close to it is being altered. The research in *imprinting* and critical learning periods, as in the work of Hess (1958), shows, for example, that a young duckling can be so deprived of the usual instinctive satisfaction of following the mother duck that it will eventually prefer to trail a human being. Among the several experiments showing powerful effects also of early deprivation on abilities (for example, Forgus, 1955), the data can be interpreted in part as evidence of a change of *interest* in normal instinctual goals. Obviously such goal modification of biologically individual-preserving ergs cannot proceed far without death of the individual, though race-preserving ergs, such as sex, gregarious, and parental ergs, permit wider experiment as far as the individual is concerned and seem correspondingly to be more susceptible to modification. Indeed, though perversion of the former—say, failure to eat, failure to avoid danger—must necessarily be fatal, perversions in the majority of discovered unitary ergs are scarcely dangerous to survival of self or society, and may even be socially adjustive, as in societies where childbearing is the task of some women but not others.

Any treatment of learning claiming to be comprehensive must recognize this phenomenon of modification of the consummatory goal itself, for indeed in minor degrees it may be far more prevalent than our means of observation have yet disclosed. We suspect it is most prevalent in sex, but also in seeking excitement rather than safety and in peculiar expressions of self-assertion. Incidentally, a hypothesis deserving research is that the sublimation of one drive may diverge into the domain of expression of another, as when a Christian devotee seems to convert sexuality into parental, protective, pitying behavior. Clinicians meet cases every day in which food has apparently been substituted for sex, as recognized in the folk saying that "A full stomach is the best remedy for an empty heart." Jungian writings in particular have argued that though there is specificity of energies resident in each erg, there is also access to a common pool, such that reduction of expression in one will inevitably lead to greater need for expression in others. Operationally this calls for the consummatory goal behavior of one drive becoming satisfying to another. The existence and nature of *GM* learning is thus tied up with questions of whether ergic tensions draw on a common pool. With the measurement of ergic tensions by objective motivation measurements, as in the MAT, experimental investigation of this question becomes possible, but has not yet been pursued.

The most substantial evidence for *GM* (goal-modification) learning still remains in the clinical and life-observation fields. A recent autobiographical study (Muktananda, 1974), showing how deliberate conscious denial of a drive, over a sufficient period, can lead to its eventual complete disappearance, as a goal, from emotional experience, suggests that sublimation is a relatively automatic readjustment with complete blocking. However, until search for all the new substitute behaviors is made, it may be uncertain whether sublimation or regression has occurred.

In goal modification we deal with a law that we would expect to be overlooked in reflexist research, conceived in peripheral *S-R* terms. For *GM* involves a framework of ergic goal concepts not precisely theoretically and practically handled before the dynamic calculus. Basically what we are hypothesizing in *GM* learning is that certain experiences, mainly of deprivation and frustration, especially in early years, will alter the absolute strength of a drive as such, that is of the $(C + H)$ term in equation (2-13).

The Energy-Saving or Rest-Seeking Principle (ES)

Finally, we encounter a little-discussed form of learning that constantly leads to modification of behavioral connections, through experience, in the interest of *energy saving*. There are countless instances in learning (some on a grand cultural scale, such as the dropping of gender and inflection from the English language, others in everyday personal habits) showing a tendency to drop from learned sequences elements that have no real value in reaching goals. There are also many clear instances in animal experiments, for example, Meehl and MacCorquodale's (1957) work on the elimination of blind entries, and experiments showing invariable ultimate preference for shorter (in "effort") rather than longer paths or procedures in mazes or Skinner boxes leading to the same goal. We can handle such consistent and widespread findings either by supposing a general dynamic principle of maintaining minimum energy expenditure that affects all ergs in all learning, or by recognizing, as seems likely, that there is a special erg, on a par with all other ergs, that has, ultimately, sleep, rest and energy saving as a goal and tiredness as its accompanying emotion (see discussion in Cattell & Child, 1975).

The action of this erg, in company with any other, would explain the goal of energy saving that appears to operate in deciding the final form of behavior learned in pursuit of any other ergic goal. This would lead us to subsume energy saving, principle 5 in Table 3-6, under integration, principle 3. We would favor this in the interests of theoretical parsimony, but it is a matter for experimental proof, and in order not to beg the question this fifth possibility is contingently maintained separately here.

Parenthetically, just as a rest-seeking erg demands economy of energy and withdrawal from stimuli, so a well-attested play erg (at least in mammals and species that modify behavior a good deal) by pre-adult learning, leads to seemingly unnecessary random expenditures of energy in the interests of trial-and-error learning. Thus the modifications under this fifth law would go either way according to the ergic tension levels of two opposing ergs—rest seeking or play—and it should be experimentally demonstrable that elisions of unnecessary acts increase in steady fashion with the rise of one (fatigue) and the fall of the other.

Support for the described natures and the independences of the above five principles must come from manipulative experiments with both animals and humans, as far as 1, 2, 3, and 5 are concerned. Integrative learning, 4, is probably more abundantly explorable in human learning. From this point, for most of this chapter and the next, we are going to clarify how learning gains of various kinds can be more accurately *described and measured*, as a preliminary to demonstrating the action of these five principles.

3-6. The Five-Vector Description of Learning Change

Although the full treatment of learning phenomena in terms of structured learning theory proceeds through Chapters 4 and 5, it is desirable not to postpone the reorientation from peripheral to structural concepts of learning change beyond this point. It has just been asserted that the five principles symbolized above as *CE, ME, N, GM* and *ES* (of which the first three will concern us) must be tested on more sophisticated concepts of learning gain, and these will involve the use of those intermediate concepts—ergic drives, E's, sentiments, M's, behavioral coefficients, b's (broken down into p's, r's, i's and s's) and the smaller engrams m's (linking c's with c's) and n's (linking c's with a's—that is, S's with R's)—that were recently described.

Again it is well before proceeding to remind the reader that (1) *learning gain* as *engram* change, that is, a change in the equipment of the organism and *performance change* are two different things, the former having to be inferred from the latter; and (2) unlike reflexology the *explanation* of the learning change by structured learning theory takes heed of other factors in the learning situation than the above 5 principles. Beyond, for example, coexcitation and reward per se, it considers the role of existing abilities, general personality temperament traits, and dynamic traits that affect the channels of use of the *CE, ME, N,* and other principles.

As far as the change in a particular *performance* between the beginning (1) and end (2) of a learning period, we may write it analytically as the change between two ordinary behavioral equations. But in what form shall we take the basic behavioral specification? In the past (p. 23, Vol. 1) we have written the behavioral specification equation in terms of *A*'s (abilities), *P*'s (personality-temperament traits), *M*'s (sentiments), and *E*'s (ergs)—sometimes throwing E's and

M's together as *D*'s, dynamic traits. To bring out the essentials of change comprehensively we will run all these person vectors together as *traits* (*T*'s) but retain the breakdown we made in Chapter 5, Volume 1 (and later) of the *loadings* (*b*'s, behavioral indices). The breakdown of *b*'s, up to this chapter, went as far as into *p*, perceptual, *e*, execution, and *s*, modulator, indices. When error of observer also needed to be taken into account we added *l*, so that the subscript for any behavior measure *a* included the subscripts, *hijko*, and the behavioral indices for any trait became $p_h e_{hj} s_k$ and l_o. The l_o we can drop from present discussion, since we are concerned only with the true scores. It will be remembered also that we considered the alternative of additive and product action for *p*, *e*, and *s*, but here again we shall for illustration express results in one only—the product (*p*, *e*, *s*), though the additive could also be used.

For full response to what is studied in learning, however, we propose to split *e* into two terms. At present p_{hx} defines the variance that trait T_x contributes to perceptual recognition of the stimulus; e_{hjx} the variance it contributes to the response *j* to the stimulus *k*, considered purely as effective execution of the performance *j*; and s_{kx} represents the modulation of the trait or state liability, L_x, by the ambient situation *k*. However, from this chapter onward we settle into a final five-vector breakdown of the specification equation in which the indices *p*, *r*, *i*, and *s* precede the *T*'s. The meaning and mode of calculation of *p*, *e*, and *s*, have been described. The breakdown of *e* into *r*, a motor proficiency, and *i*, a strength of interest or motivation in executing the behavior, is explained a little later in this chapter. In order to handle the learning formulation let us admit *r* and *i* for the time being this degree of definition as *motor* or other skill and strength of interest, respectively.

The *before* (a_1) and *after* learning (a_2) performances can now be set down to bring out the assumption that *all five vectors change* when there is a change in a specific piece of behavior a_{hijk}. For any individual in the group factored before and after, the change is that from equation (3-3a) to (3-3b). Thus we can present the before (a_1) and after (a_2) learning equations:

$$a_{hijk(1)} = p_{h(1)1} r_{j(1)1} i_{jk(1)1} s_{k(1)1} T_{1i(1)} + \cdots$$

$$p_{h(1)x} r_{j(1)x} i_{jk(1)x} s_{k(1)x} T_{xi(1)} \qquad (3\text{-}3a)$$

$$a_{hijk(2)} = p_{h(2)1} r_{j(2)1} i_{jk(2)1} s_{k(2)1} T_{1i(2)} + \cdots$$

$$p_{h(2)x} r_{j(2)x} i_{jk(2)x} s_{k(2)x} T_{xi(2)} \qquad (3\text{-}3b)$$

(The index *i* has been given a *j* and a *k* subscript because initally we must assume both the focal stimulus and the ambient situation may affect it.)

The step we take here in learning theory, whether it be right or wrong, is an extremely important one. It says that learning produces changes not only in endowment of the individual—in reflex or trait as an engram—but also in the way in which traits are combined and brought into joint action. In short, the learning has to be represented both by the trait (T) changes and by the changes in the behavioral indices (p, r, i, s). We have said "right or wrong"; but since at this stage the model is purely descriptive it cannot be wrong (except through, for example, linear approximation to nonlinear relations). The fact is that two separate factorings of the variables, before and after learning, *will* yield different T's and different b's (p, r, i, s) values. Since this is not a statistical text we shall not set out the technicalities of this calculation here, but a footnote (4, p. 216) will present a little more, and Cattell, 1978, will give the full factor analytic picture. But essentially this supposes that the group of people learning is factored separately on occasions (1) and (2), a_{hjk} being one of many variables, so that alterations in p, r, i, and s can be determined. It supposes also that the scoring system (real base) is such that changes in their trait scores (T's, comprising A's, P's, E's and M's) can be scored (see Cattell, 1973, 1978).

Besides this more radical concept of behavioral index as well as trait change being simultaneously required, this measurement by the specification equation emphasizes a relatively "routine" conclusion in multivariate research (still not common in learning theory) that any bit of learning (unless it happens to be *extremely* narrow) *affects in some degree the whole personality.* (Even the lowly rat learns not only the maze his experimenter has in mind, but also features of the room and the way to respond to the experimenter handling him.) However, in the midst of this emphasis on *all* terms changing we should note that the drive strength of ergs and the p, r, i, s values that belong to innate stimulators are exceptions in showing no change. However, ergic tension, $s_k E$, is not fixed, because s_k can change. Also, temperamental personality traits (P's among the above T's) probably change little.

Operationally, therefore, instead of measuring change only in a_{hijk} (R to the reflexologist) now with new subscripts h', i', j', and k', and plotting curves thereof or abstracting a learned engram increment therefrom, the structured learning theorist factors this behavior along with many others, and turns to consider the changes in the more analytical expression on the *right* of the equation. Among other things this amounts to recognizing that in learning experiments on a particular conditioned reflex the animal or human actually learns much more diversely than he supposedly is being taught. His "personality" is affected as well as the particular response the experimenter is thinking about.

At this point the difference between the classical learning approach, on the one hand, and structured learning theory on the other, opens like a fundamental chasm. In summary, structured learning theory differs from reflexological learning theory in maintaining the following.

1. It considers that even when change on only a specific reflex response is being aimed at by the learning experimenter, or change on a single symptom by the "behavior" therapist, there are also changes produced elsewhere that will be recognized only if one measures on all vectors of personality.

2. In the macroscopic situation of real persons in real everyday life situations, as distinct from measured laboratory situations, it changes in the main personality and ability factors (A's, P's, E's and M's)—and not just narrow bits of behavior—that teachers, industrial psychologists, and clinicians are most concerned about. It offers to these a sophisticated model and mode of measurement for researching on such change.

3. When we are concerned with more specific behaviors, the behavioral indices of the specification equation are capable of representing, in certain ways we have yet to discuss, learning missed in a mere change of level on the behavior performance itself. The changes in indices show learning in the way people "go about doing" something. *It can occur when their scores on the T's remain the same*, as will sometimes happen. The potential of structured learning theory here is evidenced by the fact that there are likely to be many instances of relatively trivial change in level of a_{hijk} (the response performance), when the analysis can yet show that there have been significant changes in p's, r's, i's, s's and T's, and that these constitute important statements regarding the acquisition of a new *style* of performance. This notion of learning being best expressed in "unobservables" has been well recognized by Sjöberg (1965) in a different context. The fact, say, that a child's school performance can show no significant change whereas the whole quality of his interest and motivation may have changed is important. By this approach unobservables become measurable, though as higher order abstractions. It is a commonplace of science in other fields that the most significant findings can lie in abstractions derived at several removes from the data.

To illustrate change of this type by proved psychological examples is not easy, because we stand only at the dawn of this and other research in structured learning, and the dawn may be slow because research of this kind requires combinations of skills that are not common. The initial evidence for significant changes occurring on the behavioral indices comes through most strongly in the work of Wherry (1941), Hempel and Fleishman (1955) and Fleishman (1967), for they showed that in the course of long training in a variety of motor skills the loadings continuously and significantly changed on factors such as, presumably, intelligence, visual perception, and motor dexterity. The need now is to extend these findings to measured strengths of attitudes and other dynamic-interest trait measurements, showing that in the course of learning to adjust emotionally the loading composition of attitude courses of action on various ergs will change. A beginning, giving support to the theory that ergic composition changes in the course of personality adjustment has been made, however, by Hendricks (1971) and by Laughlin (1974), comparing R-technique analyses before and after a learning period. Quite recently additional evidence of change in behavioral indices, on a symptom, has been provided by Birkett (see Birkett & Cattell, 1979) loading changes in the first and second half of a 100-day P-technique experiment on an alcoholic patient.

Research on learning changes in vectors of behavioral indices is a fairly complicated business, but that on changes in the vector of traits is not. It is therefore surely regrettable that in all the literature discussing personality change there is scarcely a small handful of studies recording measured changes on important primary personality factors. Somewhat more than a handful exists of sufficiently long or powerful influences but they are often vitiated by use of arbitrary variables rather than replicated unitary factor structures. One obvious reason for the dearth of researches showing real personality change is restriction of experiments to trivial laboratory influences. For ethical reasons such impacts cannot be made strong enough to produce results. In life, and notably in the clinic, where therapeutic results could be expected, few clinicians (with such exceptions as Birkett, Brunswik, Eber, Eysenck, Krug, and Rickels) have given the time to evaluating their therapeutic handiwork with personality measures, as Eysenck has several times brought to general notice. It must be confessed that yet another reason for the dearth of illustrations of change on a whole vector of traits has been the insensivity and concept invalidity of many personality scales used to reveal the lesser changes to be expected from, say, one semester, or even a couple of years, of a particular life experience. At this moment, however, there are just enough conclusive researches to show that both under therapy, and under the impact of certain everyday life experiences, significant and specific T changes *do* occur. In therapy the work of Hunt and others (1959) and of Cattell, Rickels and others (1966) show, for example, significant changes on anxiety (measured as QII and as UI(T)24), on ego strength, C, and on regression (UI(T)23), in the hypothesized directions.

As to changes through life experiences, a New Zealand study by the present writer, in which 1,000 high-school graduates were measured on the 16 PF at the age of 18 and again (with attrition) four years later, has shown a variety of significant personality changes definitely associated with intercurrent events such as getting married, being successful or unsuccessful at a job, suffering a long illness, being divorced. Results have been analyzed by Barton and Cattell (1972a, 1972b, 1975) and Barton, Cattell, and Vaughan (1973) and are under further analysis by Barton. Meanwhile further evidence by De Young and others (1973), Cattell, Kawash, and De Young (1972) extends to findings of environmentally produced changes recorded on dynamic traits. It is interesting to find that the vector (profile) of primary trait changes has a characteristic form for each type of intervening life experience.

The evidence therefore, though not ample, is sufficient to show that both the traits and the behavior indices change in the specification equation when learning occurs. The reader has already seen several occasions where we have handled the multiplicity of causal action which a multivariate theoretical model requires by resorting to matrix algebra. The latter is one of the chief aids that the mathematician can give us as psychology advances to its proper stature as a science, and the student will find it desirable from this point on to learn matrix skills, in such a clear introductory text as that of Hammer (1971) or the more complete text of Horst (1963). (Child has given a *very* simple introduction in Appendix II of Cattell & Child, 1975, as also has Gorsuch, 1974.)

Matrix representation is a considerable aid to bringing the propositions of structured learning theory to experimentally testable form, because the computer handles matrices with great facility and saves the experimenter the burdensome analysis calculations that he would otherwise have to do "by hand."

In the present model we have conceived no fewer than five kinds of vector that change in a learning experience. As some particular performance, a_{hijk}, changes there will be changes in the vector of p's, of r's, of i's, of s's and of T's. We can see now that the specification equation, with its $p_h r_{hj} i_{js_k} T_i$ terms even *before* any learning can, in a preparatory way, be set up in matrix form, as shown at the top of Table 3-7, algebraically and diagrammatically. The D's (diagonal matrices) are the five vectors of values put in diagonal matrix form, so that the five-element terms will be reproduced, and the I's (identity matrices) simply gather their sum into the single a_{hijk} end result. Part (b) of Table 3-7 shows how the subsequent learning increment is also expressed in matrix form.

An interesting inference from equation (3-5) and Table 3-7 is that it is impossible correctly to describe a learning increment on any performance without incorporating properties of the original position. That is to say that we are deceiving ourselves in the data for ordinary learning curves when a gain g from a position x is written down, and treated, as equal to a gain g from a position y because it is numerically equal. We are familiar, from the specification equation, with the fact that a given *absolute* performance can derive from an infinite number of possible combinations of trait strengths and behavioral indices. We now recognize, from the discussion above, that this is true also of a learning *increment*, and that, for example, changes in vector values can occur with zero gain on the given behavior. That fits our general position that learning gain is not adequately described by the usual scalar quantity. Furthermore, the gain cannot be calculated from the gains on the p, r, etc, values alone. (See Table 3-7, Part c.) (In this connection see Ross, 1964.)

To determine the p, r, i, s and T values above it would be necessary, of course, to include a sufficient sample of other behaviors of the subjects in a general factor analysis. If we wished to record the analytic changes of all at once it would be necessary to change (3-5) into the form of a super matrix. Not only does (3-5) remind us that the structure of the original behavior remains in the expression for the gain (as it does not with a scalar gain) but it brings out also that (a) the estimation of the factor score changes in the T's rests on changing weights from the p, r, i, and s values (b) one cannot learn in one area without affecting the mode of response in every other. For example, if the T's are changed by a series of learning experiences in a_{hijk} these will cause a change in the equation for another performance $a_{h'k'j'k'}$ that has not been touched by reflex learning.[4]

The novel learning analysis just described in this section is referred to henceforth and elsewhere as the *five-vector analytical description* of structural learning change. Note that it is so far a description, and, though analytical, it has yet to be brought into relation to the causal action of the learning laws and principle above. Such more explanatory hypotheses as to what particular experiences of repetition, insight, reward, and so forth, change these p's, r's, i's, s's, and T's are taken up in the next section and the next chapter.

Table 3-7. Comprehensive Statement of Structured Learning Change as a Five-Vector Outcome

Part (a)   Specification Equation for a Single Performance (Prior to Learning Change) Expressed in Matrix Form

$$a_{hijk} = I' D_p D_r D_i D_s D_t I \tag{3-4}$$

As matrix diagrams:

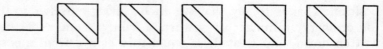

Part (b)   Change from Prelearning to Postlearning Performance,

$$a_{hijk}(2) - a_{hijk}(1) = a_{hijk}(I)$$

(Where I = Learning Increment) in Matrix Form

$$a_{hijk}(I) = I' D_{p2} D_{r2} D_{i2} D_{s2} D_{t2} I - I' D_{p1} D_{r1} D_{i1} D_{s1} D_{t1} I \tag{3-5a}$$

or, as a percentage change,

$$a_{hijk}(I) = \frac{I' D_{p2} D_{r2} D_{i2} D_{s2} D_{t2} I}{I' (D_{p1} D_{r1} D_{s1} D_{t1}) I} \times 100 \tag{3-5b}$$

Note these are restatements of equations (3-3a) and (3-3b) in matrix form. D_p is a diagonal matrix of the y values for the y factors concerned, and similarly for the proficiency and interest coefficients in D_r and D_i, the modulator values in D_s, and the trait values in D_t. The identity matrix I and its transpose I' are there only as part of the matrix mechanics, to collect the terms from the diagonal multiplications—$p_a r_a i_a s_a T_a + p_b r_b i_b s_b T_b + \ldots$, and so forth ($a$ and b being two traits)—into a single scalar, a_{hijk}.

Part (c)

Behavior Change:	$a_{hijk}(2\text{-}1)$
Perception Index Change:	$p(2) - p(1)$
Motor Proficiency Index Change:	$r(2) - r(1)$
Interest-Motivation Index Change:	$i(2) - i(1)$
Modulation Index Change:	$s(2) - s(1)$
Trait Change:	$T(2) - T(1)$

Descriptively, for various psychological analytic purposes, we can dissect the behavior change into changes in five vectors, of which one term in each is illustrated above. However, we cannot *predict or calculate* $a_{hijk}(2\text{-}1)$ from these differences of vectors (not knowing the original vectors), since in general the difference of two (or more) products cannot be resolved into the product of the differences of the elements.

3-7.   A Closer Look, Psychological and Statistical, at the Nature of Structured Learning

Even in ability performances it frequently happens that over a period of learning there is no reduction of time and errors such as learning experiments conventionally record, but only a sense of lesser effort, and perhaps of less demand, for example on conscious attention. These realities of learning are missed in most experiments on reflex learning and are lost information as far as the traditional plot of gains in a learning curve, but they are substantially caught by the five-vector structural learning analysis. However, it is in the dynamic field of "emotional learning" that the fuller illumination from this method becomes encouragingly apparent. Here we are frequently concerned not only with whether the attitude becomes stronger or weaker but with what changes in emotional subsidiation to it are occurring. The clinician's and the social psychologist's concern is with the change in emotional quality, and the changing role it plays in the individual's emotional satisfactions. Hendriks' (1971) experiment indicated, for example, that the attitude of beginners in first-year psychology, "I want to learn more about psychology," shifted by the end of the course from larger loading on the exploratory (curiosity) erg to larger loadings on the erg of self-assertion (competition over grades) and need for security (fear of failure). It scarcely needs to be pointed out that this method of analyzing learning change has tremendous possibilities not only in education but in the clinical monitoring of a patient's progress, as well as in social psychological study of the changes over time brought about by an individual's affiliating to an institution, as in marriage. It is central also to developmental psychology, where it offers means of more objective and precise statements of the changes in attachments and emotional attitudes, for example, during adolescence. In this connection the reader is reminded that p, r, i, s, and T changes if derived from R-technique will describe the *typical* group change, and if from P-technique, by contrast, the *individual* change, but that T changes are individual in both methods, though patterned as common traits in R and unique traits in P.

In referring to any concrete specific scalar gain ($a_{hijk(2)}$ – $a_{hijk(1)}$) we have been careful all along conceptually to distinguish between *performance* gain and *learning*, as engram change. It is now possible, in the structured context, to be more precise about this, beyond merely verbally defining one as performance and the other as an engram change in the organism. Reflexological formulation has approached this distinction by saying that the habit-strength gain must be considered relative to the drive strength at the time, that is, that one must discount the performance gain through due care to allow for change in the accompanying drive strength at the time, or to holding it experimentally constant across both occasions.

At this point we have to ask ourselves whether equation (3-5), expressing the difference of two specifications is intended to describe the learning gain, in terms of engramming, n, or of the behavior change. The answer is the latter, for we have *not* assumed that motivation is held constant. Let us therefore consider how we would "hold that motivation constant" and extract n's—the increments in various M's—from the a_{hijk} performance changes. Because our model (equation 2-4) now admits interaction of the dynamic, E, and engram, M, terms in the arousal of E by M and the activation of M by higher levels of need strength in the ergic investments of M, the disentanglement is not going to be easy.

It no longer suffices to suggest that in order to get at the M change, that is, at n, itself, the motivation level be held constant from the pre- to the postlearning occasion. For it is a part of learning that the original situation can now activate M and arouse E more strongly through changes in the modulators, the s_k's. Parenthetically, the reader should be reminded that the pure E term, being an innate need strength of the erg, is presumed not to be alterable, and the v and s terms for that E in itself apply only to the *innately* provoking elements of the environment. Our concern is therefore with the M, ME, and EM terms. If we may for the moment neglect the circular feed-back system between ME and EM, then since E in the second term is a need strength, which *can* be held constant, we need concern ourselves only with M and ME terms.

The problem of separating the engram change—the gain in M, which we have called n—from the behavior change becomes, psychometrically, essentially that of estimating a factor score on the second occasion and the first occasion from an array of performances on variables. To handle this assessment experimentally, an array of other variables beyond the a_{hijk} involved in the particular learning itself would be necessary, as mentioned above. Of course, if E can be *directly* measured by an ad hoc battery on the two occasions, then an estimate of the M increase could be made from a simple, single comparison of the performances before and after on one variable. But if this is impracticable, we are faced, in estimating M from many variables, with a new psychometric problem. The standard procedure for estimation of a factor from the factor estimation matrix of weights on variables, V_{fe}, needs to be modified when in addition to M we have the product term ME, but at this point the special mathematico-statistical procedures involved must be set aside for treatment elsewhere.

The five-vector analysis of learning change calls attention not only to the need to separate engram change from total performance change, but also to the need for increased conceptual definition of the behavioral indices p, r, i, and s in regard to learning change. The central conceptual problem is that in our model all sources of behavior *in the organism* have been reduced to E's and M's and their associated p's, r's, i's, and s's. All of these change in learning. The question now arises as we shift from a statistical to a psychological conceptualization: Where are the changes in the p's, r's, i's, and s's supposed to reside if not in the organism itself?" In dealing with this let us remember that the full roster of changeable traits (E's being set aside as unchanging) includes A's, abilities; P's, general personality-temperament traits; and M's, specific sentiments. The relation of behavior-index change to trait change we shall find easiest to follow in abilities.

Because A's and P's were for the moment left out of the specification equation (while we examined general properties closely), we did not explicitly remind the reader that engram changes affect them too. Especially in the case of abilities that belong to the species one calls skills, it is evident that substantial n increments will occur through learning. If we consider Thurstone's N factor of numerical ability, in a class of children simultaneously learning arithmetic, and, say, science, the loading of N on a science achievement measure (an a_{hjk} in the specification equation statement) might well increase (the science exam mean score remaining virtually unchanged) as the group moves to an arithmetic level at which examples in science that previously left all students "stumped" become readily solved by a good fraction of the group. The changing relation—b_{hjk}— between N and achievement is then seen to relate purely to a change in N, as far as the properties of the "organism" is concerned. In such examples, one recognizes that b is simply a *relation* between what is in the organism and what the environment is demanding. The change in b is not a change in some literal neural link in the organism but expresses a statistical relationship that has changed.

However, the conclusion that someone might draw—that if p's, r's, and so on are "relations" there is no ground for classifying them with "properties" of the organism, that is, that S, P, and M score changes suffice to describe what happens in the organisms, and that p, r, i, and s are, by contrast, superfluous terms in *describing the organism and its changes*—needs to be carefully examined. Epistemology and logic tell us that a relation and a property mutually involve each other. If a man is higher than the average, this, along with other relations, gives him the property of being a tall man. If the intelligence factor is related in magnitude to performance in an arithmetical reasoning test it must be (granted the direction of effect) that intelligence has a property of aiding a reasoning process. So here, in the five-vector description of learning, an increase through learning of p, r, i, and s, which are relations (indeed, simple derivations of correlations) implies, other things being equal, that the *properties*, that is the loading patterns of the M, A, or P traits to which they are attached have altered. "Other things being equal" is important, for we have accepted as part of reason for change in the loadings of Thurstone's N on science achievement that the variance on arithmetic ability had increased—a purely statistical effect. In short, there are *two* influences involved in changes in the p, r, i, and s relation values: first, a purely statistical effect of range of the trait and the criterion behavior which applies to a correlation from any source, and second, some real change in the *form* of the traits (at least in the A, P, and M traits) in the organism.

This latter is not a change, we have just said, in variance, nor is it simply a change in level. *It is a change in the very shape and quality of the trait.* It is just possible for the change to be one that shows itself only in the loading on a single performance. In that case the learning will only trivially have affected the score on, say, M or A, as a whole, as that score could well be derived, by the usual factor estimation summation, from 50 other variables. But it will have affected the way the trait "hitches on" to the specific variable response. For example, as the work of Horn (1970) and Undheim (1976) shows, the crystallized general intelligence factor g_c gives indication of climbing in its loading on vocabulary during the middle school years, which simply means that this ability structure extends itself by added engrams to include in the pattern verbal skills that were not included before. Similarly, in the realm of the dynamic calculus, a sentiment toward sport may come to encounter stimulation, in a given group, toward aquatic games not previously involved in the pattern, with result that encountering a swimming match may bring to bear an s_k modulation, not present before, now activating the whole sentiment, and due to the engram addition.

The enhanced values of the p, r, i, and s behavioral indices in these instances are thus not mere statistical effects, but arise from changes in the engram structure of the sentiment or ability itself, and presumably are concretely represented in physiological and neurological changes. These changes may well occur just for one variable, incorporating reactivity to that variable as a new element in the total pattern. However, as our preliminary study of the growth of sentiments (p. 85) has suggested, the engram increments on M are likely in many cases to result from simultaneous reinforcement on responses on many variables. Nevertheless, successive univariate increments, once a sentiment has some shape, may well produce significant changes in the meaning and score of the total trait. The question of how much univariate and multivariate learning normally contributes is a matter for experiment, now that the five-vector principle for analysis of learning is available.

It behooves us now to inspect in greater depth the nature of these five kinds of vector coefficient. The p value says how much a trait is involved in achieving perception of the stimulus, h, though experiment may show that it concerns also the global situation and requires a subscript, p_{hk}. On the other hand the skill of motor performance in r, though sometimes given only with subscript j, describing the executive performance itself, should probably have hj as subscript inasmuch as perception and motor action are seldom entirely separable. The value i, interest strength, is likely to be significant only in the dynamic traits. It should probably have both h and j subscripts because, granted the amount of arousal of the trait by s_k the extent to which it gets invested in the path j will depend partly on the prominence of h in the learning experience. According to our later analysis of learning mechanisms the arousal at an ambient situation k may be triggered into action by any one of a few focal stimuli, h's, that are present in the global situation. This will produce some partial correlation, across various variables of the magnitude of i_{hj} and s_k. Indeed, although p, r, i and s are in essence independent, there are reasons why some of their connections will yield positive, significant correlations. One is that just cited; another is that the skill in r_{hj} will tend to have some correlation with the past history of amount of interest, i_{hj}, invested in the hj outlet. Incidentally, though the separation of r and i values in experiment is possible because motivation can be held constant while skill levels are measured, in life data with in situ research the separation will have to be by the method we described of measuring different combination of skill and motivation strength. However, when measures of motivation strength as such are reliable it can be allowed for and taken out of the total performance directly.

As for the changes that occur through s_k, in the form of arousal (of E's) and activation (of M's) we shall argue later that most comes from the means-end principle. That is to say, when arousal in a certain ambient situation has been prone to lead to satisfaction, that particular k begins regularly to lead to arousal. The expression in an ensuing strength of behavior, determined by i_{hj}, will then, as indicated above, have some degree of proportionality to s_k. Some psychologists notably Mowrer (1956, 1960) and Staats (1975) have accounted for the attachment of arousal to a situation by CRI rather than CRII, means-end action, as we do here. For the time being we shall simply register doubts about the efficacy of *CRI* because it is considered by these writers to be a conditioning of an *emotional response* (affect), which is undoubtedly possible, but what is required here is the "conditioning" of an ergic tension (conation) which seems a doubtful possibility and less directly explanatory than the rewarding of an arousal response.

Another feature of the behavioral coefficients that needs to be noted is the likelihood that one class of coefficients will prove systematically to be high, for one modality of traits. The *p* and *r* coefficients, for example, might be expected to be largest with ability traits, *A*'s, and the *s*'s with dynamic traits, *E*'s and *M*'s.

Finally, let us pause to take note again that the product model for the behavioral indices is not necessarily better than the additive one. By the nature of the factor analytic equation *all* must multiply the trait score, but among themselves they can either add or multiply. With the two terms we can have either $(r + s)T$ or rsT. With the four we can have either $(p + r + i + s)T$ or $prisT$. Which psychology eventually settles upon will mostly depend on which gives the most constant values in a variety of contexts and transformations. In the general equation for learning gain (3-3) placed in matrix form in (3-4), the equivalent would be in the additive model

$$a_{hijk(2-1)} = I'(D_{p2} + D_{r2} + D_{i2} + D_{s2})D_{t2}I$$
$$- I'(D_{p1} + D_{r1} + D_{i1} + D_{s1})D_{t1}I \qquad (3\text{-}6)$$

where (2-1) is the learning gain in performance.

The caution should perhaps be repeated here that the coefficients and scores in these matrices are those derived from real-base factor analysis, so that factors may change size. These technicalities are important as we come to research and practice, but in a conceptual grasp can momentarily be set aside. We need *conceptual* progress in recognizing that learning that used to be measured only as a scalar increment can be analyzed into five vectors. These vectors already have precise and ample meaning, but we may anticipate that this meaning will become enriched as structured learning research proceeds. Meanwhile (Cattell, 1980) a partly different way of cutting the pie has been proposed whereby *p*, *r*, *i* and *s* correspond exactly operationally to loadings when the variance on the other three sets is eliminated.

3-8. Summary

1. All behavioral change over time must be partitioned into (a) learning; (b) volution (maturation and involution by an inner clock);

(c) somatic experience, in which behavior change occurs through direct somatic, neural, or hormonal influences; and (d) changes that involve no change of structure but in which behavior changes reversibly through inner state fluctuations and change from outer impinging situational stimuli, for example, level of drive arousal.

2. Reflexological learning theory has depended on two main *experimental paradigms* (ways of arranging an experiment): classical conditioning, CRI, and instrumental or operant conditioning, $CRII$. Well-executed research has developed dependable laws around these at the human reflex level and in laboratory behavior of lower animals; but we must examine critically various attempts to extend this from microscopic to macroscopic behavior patterns without invoking new concepts. The indispensable new knowledge for advance involves concepts concerning (a) the dynamic calculus; (b) the specific existing ability and personality structures in man; (c) laws to account for the rise of such structures; and (d) the methods of multivariate experiment and analysis. These additives are the hallmarks of structured learning theory.

3. A distinction is drawn among *paradigms, empirical data relation laws,* and *principles,* and it is pointed out that CRI and $CRII$, and the variants thereon, are experimental paradigms, based on restricted conditions of relation observation. One must consider that present reflexological research areas and conceptual repertoires have not exhausted the necessary empirical relations on which to base the extraction of ultimate learning laws.

4. From studying the relations found in the reflexological paradigm experiments, along with observations broadly though clinical and education psychology and ethological conclusions about animal behavior, it is concluded that five different basic principles are necessary to cover the true learning phenomena separated out above in (1) from other forms of behavioral change.

These abstracted principles are:

1. Coexcitation, CE, entering into contiguity and CRI paradigms
2. Means-end learning, ME, essentially one with $CRII$ but present also in CRI
3. Integration learning N
4. Change in ergic goal, consummatory behavior per se (imprinting; sublimation) GM
5. Energy-saving learning ES

These might be reduced; for example, energy saving could be a special case of integration learning, one involving the action of a rest-seeking erg. Integration learning may also be reducible in part to (1) and (2), although a new "emergent" effect is probably present and it needs more than peripheral *S-R* relations to define it. Classical conditioning, *CR*I, is thus regarded as a paradigm, not a principle, in which there is a combined operation of coexcitation (*CE*) and means-end (*ME*) principles.

5.   A systematic survey is made of the paradigms of reflexology in order to show more clearly just where the additions and changes of conceptual perspective occur through the development of structured learning. Reflexology is an internally consistent and experimentally clear *peripheral* system, concerned with all the possible combinations of S and R elements, the experimenter being free to arrange whatever contingencies he wishes—for example, to use a prescribed stimulus and response or to await stimuli from the environment, to measure immediate or delayed events, and so forth. *S* and *R* (as [*h* + *k*], and *j*) are also accepted elements in structured learning formulations, but other elements, as higher-order emergents are introduced, principally traits and states, ergic goals, the dynamic lattice, and behavioral indices (p, r, i and s). Structured learning theory is firmly behavioristic in basis, but on a broader foundation of observation than reflex learning theory, and using methods permitting discovery and use of pattern structures.

6.   The first principle, *coexcitation, CE*, states that the virtually simultaneous occurrence of two experiences leads to the establishment as a result of the common excitation of an engram bond, n, between them. It produces a weak effect compared to the *ME* principle. Its existence is supported mainly by observations on cognitive events, but also on behavior linked via cognitive events. It must be stated in most general terms are $c_a + c_b \rightarrow n_{c_a c_b}$, c being an idea (a symbol, perception, image, or other cognitive experience). Among instances of this general law the relation appearing between two external stimuli, S_a and S_b, is a special case, where c_a and c_b happen to be generated by peripheral stimuli, S_a and S_b. It is probable that the primary law of coexcitation involves secondary laws governing the intensity of its effect. These could be: the addition of an effect from experience of cognitive closure or of ideas appearing by eduction; a directional effect of flow from stronger to weaker, and from later to smaller and earlier excitations; and even some involvement of dynamic goal directions.

7.   The second principle is that a response to a stimulus that is followed beyond chance expectation (in repetitions) by a reward sets up an *S-R* engram. However, the term means-end, *ME*, is deliberately distinguished from the *CR*II term; "the operant conditioning" paradigm, which is a particular experimental way in which reward

comes about. Further in the ME principle the context of having a particular ergic tension is explicitly incorporated, making the essential concept one of learning behavior rewarded in relation to a defined and measured goal. It is suggested in this context that a distinction be regularly drawn between *rewarded* and *reinforced* (strengthened).

8.   The integration principle, N, operates when behavior becomes learned that maximizes simultaneously the reward to several goals. Like ME it is a concept involving recognition of distinct goals and requiring experimentally the use of dynamic calculus designs. It proceeds both by discovering confluent behaviors and by ego control, through inhibition, permitting new modulations and new path discoveries. Integration learning employs CE and ME action but is a new principle not to be explained by CE and ME alone.

The remaining laws—those of goal modification and energy economy—are stated but not discussed here.

The most frequent and important mechanism in human learning is judged to be an arrangement of coexcitation (CE) and means-end (CRII) linked in tandem, that is, S_2-S_1-R in peripheral terms, or c_2-c_1-R in more general terms. That is to say, a cognitive experience is typically first linked to a goal response by reward (ME) learning. Other cognitive experiences, such as c_2, are then linked by coexcitation to the first, perhaps in a series $c_n \ldots c_2c_1$. In the absence of human learning surveys we may conjecture that the building up of a cognitive network, $c_n \ldots c_2c_1$, by cognitive coexcitation precedes the formation of the c_1-R linkage, though this may be less frequent than the alternative order. In any case the tandem action of two principles, in what the reflexologist would call an S_2-S_1-R sequence, is central to structured learning. It implies that no stimulation of an erg can occur in learned behavior (as distinct from innate structures) without the formation of an engram linking cognitive stimulation with dynamic ergic action. An integrated collection of such n's becomes an M.

9.   In regard to the operations of *all* learning principles we must recognize in application to personality learning the effect of an enormous difference of ability to manipulate symbols and concepts existing between men and lower animals. This creates almost qualitative differences in learning calculations in animal and human learning. Nevertheless, the laws concerning actual establishing of engrams as a result of the learning connections (CE and ME) experiences proceed regardless of whether the new behavior connection is reached by a flash of insight or follows from prolonged blind trial and error. Thus the fact that a connection is reached by intelligent insight does not alter the fact that the new behavior, when ME learning is at work, has to produce reward sufficient to establish it. The difference

between insight and trial and error may, of course, do much to the acceleration of the obtained learning curve.

10. The most radical change and addition to reflexology, by structured learning theory, is the five-vector description of learning change. This is a "descriptive analysis" involving several new concepts, but still not yet interlocking with the base of explanatory principles (*CE*, *ME*, and so forth). It consists of mathematical models accounting for the change (in *T*'s, *p*'s, *s*'s, and so forth) on the basis of five-vector analysis. A minority of reflexological learning theorists have ventured toward "intermediate variables" but these have been derived only from bivariate peripheral data, whereas those in structured learning have the whole substance of research findings in personality and the dynamic calculus behind them and are of a different order of completeness of calculation.

The five-vector learning model of course rests in the last resort on the same evidence as reflexist models, that is on observations of stimuli, ambient situations and behavioral performances, except that it requires observations on *many* stimulus response events made in *many* situations in the organism's life, instead of one. Its observed variable—the unit, a_{hijk}—is the same as an extended *S-R* observation. By "extended" we mean that *S* is extended to a composite term, being more fully defined both by *h* (focal stimulus) and *k* (ambient situation). Similarly the *R*—the a_j—is likely to be a more prolonged "chain reflex" performance rather than a single reflex response.

The five-vector theorem states that the change between pre- and post-behavior (that is, the basis of an engram learning measure) is no longer represented by a single *scalar* quantity but by changes in the five *vectors*—*p*'s (perception indices); *r*'s (proficiency indices), *i*'s (interest strength indices); *s*'s (modulators); and *T*'s (traits, covering A, P, E, and M modalities). Both the behavioral indices and the traits remain abstractions from the same behavior as the reflexist observes, but as indicated above, pursued by multivariate experimental analysis of *many S-R*'s.

11. As the multivariate experimental approach is pursued, consistent with the multiple determination of all psychological events it becomes apparent that one of the first major mathematical aids needing to be incorporated is that offered by matrix algebra. Thus the specification equation, in the form of the five-vector determination, can be alternatively written, for certain calculations, as a tandem product of five diagonal matrices. And the learning gain can be expressed as the difference of two such matrix equations.

Among the important implications of the five-vector expression of learning, in either form, are: (a) that learning occurs and can be quantitatively described even when there is no change in the performance score itself; (b) that the same performance change can be reached in an infinity of different ways; and (c) that though a learning change as a scalar performance value can apparently be written without any content expressing the original score, a structured learning change statement always contains within it features of the original position (specification). (In other words, we *can* write five difference (change) vectors, each setting out the change through learning in that set, but the increment on the scalar performance value cannot be calculated from these alone.) The implication is that the scalar value is on a defective scale. In all calculations real-base factor analysis (and isopodic or equipotent factor score estimations) are necessary.

12. The breakdown of the original factor loading, b, into four terms—p, r, i, and s—required coordinated factor-analytic experiments. These have been described for s in Chapter 5 and for p and e in Chapter 6 of Volume 1. At this point e is further broken down once more into r, the proficiency, motor, or more cognitive skill involvements in *performing* in the given response path, and i, the intensity of interest generated by past learning reward in pursuing that response path. Means of separation experimentally are indicated. To avoid confusion of i and s it should be noted that i_j is the interest in the given path j per unit of ergic or sentiment strength, whereas s changes the magnitudes (number of units) of interest motivation offered by the ergs or sentiments themselves.

13. As regards the meaning of p, r, i, and s psychologically, Chapter 6, Volume 1, has pointed out that, having subscripts h, j, and k, for the environment and action, they are partly descriptions of *the psychological meaning of the environment* $(h + k)$ and of the *nature of the path of action, j*. But they also have in every case a subscript for a particular trait, and thus represent relations between the given trait and the performance-environment.

In approaching what p, r, i, and s mean, in their different contexts, it is necessary first to set aside purely statistical effects on their magnitudes, such as changes of variance of trait scores, which we consider averaged and held constant in dealing with the psychological meaning. The meaning resides in the trait and in the environment. The fact that crystallized intelligence, g_c, has a large loading on solving simultaneous equations and a small one on speed of reading is due to the relation of the intelligence property of "capacity to educe relations" respectively to a situation in which relations are everything and one in which symbol memory alone is mainly needed. Altering either the environment or the trait will alter the loading. In learning the environment is commonly held constant so the changes in p, r, i, and s must represent real changes in the engrams of the trait. For example, if subjects are trained in tricks of solving simultaneous equations the loading of intelligence will alter and it will alter because the structure of crystallized intelligence has changed, psychologically and neurologically, by the addition of an engram of new habits. Thus the unitary-trait engram structures, such as A and M terms, change through learning not only in total score level, but qualitatively, in the shape of their loading patterns. This change of loading on a specific variable implies in general (with constant environment) that an extra engram element (symbolized here as n) has been "hitched on" to the main trait associative network. The different characteristics of the p, r, i, and s indices covering perceptual, motor, interest reactivity, and modulation powers, respectively, imply structural additions to the traits that are of different kinds. The fact noted above that some types of index will reach significant loadings only on some modalities of traits will help differentiate the types of engram growth.

14. The above analyses are necessary to answer the question of how we can separate learning as such, defined as an engram change, from various observed changes in *performance*. The performance change is stated from the full specification equation, with four kinds of terms—E, ME, EM, and M (letting M be inclusive just here of ability and general personality terms, A's and P's). To reach the engram changes we need, by factor estimation or other methods, to evaluate the M terms (including abilities and personality traits) and their changes. According to the theory of their innate nature, the only terms in the specification equation not affected by the learning are the ergic drive need strengths—the E's—including the cognitive built-in innate connections to drive as such shown in b_e. Thus the changes in the M's (environment being constant) are the causes of changes in the p's, r's, i's, and s's. So although we describe learning in the specification equation by quantitative changes in all five vectors the same information would be contained in a statement of the changes of the factor patterns (plus change in levels). In a psychological and neurological sense the learning change is a change in engram pattern and levels.

15. In general perspective the extension from reflex to structured learning in this chapter says that the learning changes even in one term, such as a T or a p, can never be even roughly approximated by examining learning on a single variable, as in many classical experiments. Learning must be considered as change in a multidimensional organism responding to a multidimensional environmental situation. The central innovation here of expressing learning in regard to definable structures in the organism demands that we ask both how the existing structure *affects* new learning, and, conversely, how

learning principles have affected the rise of the prevailing patterns of structure. Thus the student of personality and learning theory must today step beyond the limitations of classical learning theory, accept a five-vector description of learning change, introduce equations for the effect of dynamic structures in learning, and understand the reciprocal effect of learning on the engrams of dynamic structure.

NOTES

[1] Again we must warn against the pseudo issues that result from confusing "stimulus" and "response" (both defined as external peripheral events) with the general terms, *cause* and *effect*, used in science generally, including a scientific psychology. Structured learning theory certainly treats "emotions" (ergic tension states), as causes, but it introduces a very different kind of term, with different properties from any outside stimulus as such, into the specification equation.

[2] Principally we are speaking of the major forward and minor backward associations in memorizing word series. The questions of reduction of learning with reduction of contiguity, of positional effects, and of cognitive perception of relation are secondary.

[3] The terminology, with a real precision of usage, began with Pavlov, and was quickly brought to confusion by Watson. A return to precision has defined the reflex as a very specific neural unit, with the recognition among careful experimentalists that one extends generalizations to "metaphorical" reflexes at one's peril.

In the drift from the precise work of reflexological researchers, such as Skinner (1958, 1969), Bitterman (1967), Grice (1942), Wickens and Wickens (1942), Kimble (1961), Mackintosh (1974), and Spence (1956) to the enthusiasms of looser writers (especially many behavior therapists) a confusing vagueness has arisen regarding the level at which the "response behavior" lies. In the precise work of Pavlov the reflex was definitely a neurological reality—a reflex—and the present writer, for one, has criticized several alleged developments of reflexology in personality for a somewhat insensitive imperialism, in which Pavlovian precision is overlooked and an attempt is made to take over the explanation of all kinds of more complex behavior. There seems no awareness by such writers that they have moved into a level requiring more respect for structure, and, still worse, they show a virtually complete absence of knowledge of the precise and extensive concepts that psychology has already established about that structure. Indeed these reflexological writings of the last decade have crashed roughshod over the carefully checked mosaics of personality structures and acquired no awareness of the methods of finding or using structural concepts. These generalizations of reflexology, without recognizing the need for new concepts, began, for example, to stake out claims to account for the integrated behavior of the total organism, using, quite unmodified, the principles that had been carefully verified only for the atomistic neurological reflex. The unfortunate result of this perhaps unconscious deception of the student was that it fooled the deceivers themselves into making no conceptual reforms essential to the new situation.

[4] As shown in the earlier part of this book, and elsewhere (Cattell, 1970, 1978), *ordinary* factor analysis applied to two successive (pre- and post-learning) score matrices will yield *either* a change in person's scores *or* a change in the behavioral indices applying to factors, but not both. If we measure N people on n variables, before and after learning, two alternative score matrices are possible. In one each person can be entered twice, his scores being those of the same person before and after. This gives a $2N \times n$ matrix. Alternatively, each variable is entered twice, the before measure being considered a different variable from the after measure. This gives an $N \times 2n$ score matrix.

Factoring the first will yield the same factors on which to rest the before and after scores, since the n's are the same, so persons can be given before scores and after scores. In permitting a change in the T vector to be measured, this forbids any learning on the behavioral indices, because the b's cannot change. The second analysis, on the other hand, will recognize different b's for the same performance before and after, but unless we confine factor-score estimates to n_1 and n_2 variable sets separately, it will give unchanged trait scores. Psychologically the change is to be expected in both, that is, a change in the indices, revealing, incidentally, a change in the *form* of the factors, and a change in the T-score *levels* of factors in individuals. The five-vector model recognizes this, and requires that both b's and T's be allowed to change. This result can only be achieved by (a) factoring the before-and-after matrices separately and (b) using the special principles of *isopodic* and *equipotent* scoring and analysis described elsewhere (Cattell, 1970) for making comparisons possible between before-and-after factor scores (see also Tucker, 1966). There are complexities to be faced and possibly some difficulties still to be overcome psychometrically, when we move on to real-base factoring, aiming to get changes in both indices and scores, and there may prove to be experimental difficulties in separating v into $p \times e$ as described in Chapter 6, Volume 1. However, we can be confident that multivariate experimentalists are likely to overcome these as they meet them.

CHAPTER 4

THE ACTION OF THE PRIMARY LEARNING LAWS
WITHIN A DYNAMIC STRUCTURE

4-1. *The interaction of fusion or coexcitation (CE) with cognitive relation eduction and dynamic purpose*

4-2. *A closer look at the laws within instrumental conditioning, or means-end (ME) learning*

4-3. *Requirements in the integration of CRI and CRII paradigm results in structured learning theory*

4-4. *Integration learning (N) as inhibition and resolution*

4-5. *Arousal and activation as solutions to the drive reduction paradox*

4-6. *The model relating engramming to activation-arousal, need strength, reverberation, and time*

4-7. *Means-end and coexcitation learning in the perspective of the general specification equation*

4-8. *The problem of retrieval and reinstatement of learned behavior*

4-9. *Summary*

4-1. The Interaction of Fusion or Coexcitation (CE) with Cognitive Relation Eduction and Dynamic Purpose

Sentiment structures, and, indeed, all traits but purely genetic ones, change through learning both in their patterns and in levels. (The level is a mean of elements, and, as an extreme case, could change through a single element.) This is the reality of the engram change, which is expressed alternatively in—and indeed first discovered as—a five-vector change in the behavior specification equation. If, by the stated learning laws, we can explain the engram change we shall have explained the five vector change and shall have bridged from the learning laws to the specification equation. That is to say, we shall place the testing of the learning principles upon a basis of operationally determinable specification equations for the real life behavior of human beings (and, also, for that matter, for experimental work with animals).

To begin with, we propose in this chapter to examine each principle at full-section length, both on classical learning evidence and as it is seen operating in the general ability, personality and dynamic structure of the individual. That *CE* learning should come first is appropriate because it forces us to keep in perspective from the beginning the enormous gap between human and animal learning, and stimulates the imagination we need to exercise in critically evaluating the bearing of studies with rats and pigeons on human learning.

Coexcitation deals with what happens when two ideas or perceptions that have not previously come together (or need not have) are contiguous in time in the individual's experience. This can occur from any one of three different causes: (1) the co-occurrence of two external stimuli, each evoking a perception; (2) a noegenetic act of eduction; (3) an act of retrieval, bringing what was absent into the presence of what was already present.

Classical learning, whether in the reflex framework or in learning of nonsense syllables or meaningful accociations, has given us abundant evidence of the first cause: the association of the perception of the stimulus S_1 with stimulus S_2, co-presented. For that reason there is little need here to do more than refer to a few salient studies, such as those from Ebbinghaus (1885) to Underwood (1966) in the human cognitive association area. We should note also Bogoslavsky (1937), Seidel (1959), Morrell (1961), and Sheffield (1961) and others repeating their work in the reflex setting. Finally we should consider the work of Bandura (1962, 1965) and related personality researchers in the area of human imitative behavior and the taking over of co-presented behaviors. In this area also is evidence indirectly from the fact that when S_1 and S_2 have been associated by contiguity, and S_1 is next made a conditioned stimulus to an R, S_2 will also show some weak conditioned connection to R.

Shifting to the second means by which two experiences come together we must consider noegenesis, which is internal, not external. In Spearman's fundamental contribution to cognitive psychology (*The nature of intelligence and the principles of cognition*, 1923) he distinguished the *noegenetic* and the *anoegenetic* process of producing new mental content. They correspond essentially to our second and third sources here, the anoegenetic being retrieval from memory according to associative principles we shall discuss.

It is the noegenetic act that alone produces truly *new* content (and that, as Spearman saw in *Creative Mind*, 1927, lies at the heart of real creativity). It derives from the capacity to perceive relations, and because this is the capacity that shows the greatest gulf between humans and lower animals (Köhler had to show much scientific ingenuity to bring out its presence in chimpanzees) it plays only a trivial part in the literature of animal learning as commonly given to the student. Spearman's perception is most readily indicated by considering the "analogy test" item: "Man is to child as cat is to _____?" With sufficient intelligence a subject educes the *relation* between the first two terms, "parent-to-offspring," and, applying this to cat, educes the *fundament* "kitten." This process is capable of creating content that does not exist in memory and can baffle us by our having no words or symbols to handle the educed item, as in H. G. Wells's invention beginning "Distance is to airplane as Time is to (Time Machine)."

Relation eduction regularly and frequently produces new *fundaments* (like the time machine above) or new relations such as Einstein perceived in a fourth dimension. These outstanding examples should not cause us to overlook the fact that everybody is perceiving, and often naming, new relations and new fundaments every day. Von Bertalanffy puts this succinctly when he says "Except for the immediate satisfaction of biological needs man lives not in a world of things but of symbols." A taxonomy of our symbols is in the dictionary. A taxonomy of *relations*, as such, showing the frequency with which we use them has apparently never been made, but it is easy to see that class (species)-to-class member, opposite, part-to-whole, identity, and causal antecedent, are very common. Whenever a psychologist defines learning as occurring through insight rather than trial and error he is talking about the eduction of relations or fundaments.

The third way by which experiences and ideas are brought together as a basis for an associating engram—beyond that of *contiguity* of ideas and stimulus-concurrence, and that of cognitive eduction—is retrieval from memory through association of a new idea with the idea already present. It may rightly be objected that this is not the preamble to establishing a new connection, for the second idea would not be retrievable unless there were *already* an engrammed connection with the first. However, (1) the connection may be very weak until successive recalls have established it by coexcitation, and (2) the possibility has to be considered of either random or emotionally, dynamically-determined appearance of an idea from memory storage, as in dreams.

The notion of "random" appearances of ideas or responses has been favorably received and tolerated by psychologists, yet it is a denial of all scientific determinism! Skinner's "operants"—random responses that happen to be around and become the raw material for important operant conditioning, come near to this conception of randomness. The apparent denial of scientific determinism need not bother us too much, for even physicists have had to accept that an atom will throw out an electron at random. But without resort to such a far excuse we can at any rate accept an *apparent* empirical randomness or spontaneity, leaving to more exact research the question of whether it is truly random.[1] Elsewhere we have pointed out the evidence at the physiological level for spontaneous, unstimulated firing of nerve cells. With the enormous number of cells in the human brain the possibility of a buildup of appreciable effects from trivial or remote stimuli (the α rhythm may be such, and the epileptic spike) is considerable. In short, the possibility that the immense volume of storage of memory in man may somehow introduce ideas with no previous connection with any in consciousness is not to be rejected.

However, it would seem that we do not have to lean very much on causes so trivial as to be called random, for there is plenty of evidence that new cognitive content can come from emotional action, as, indeed, we have hypothesized in the EM term in the specification equation. An emotional mood, in daydreams, for example, may readily evoke cognitive content. Thus an E term that happens to be high—through appetitive components in need, or stimulation by some other sentiment connection—will tend to activate the engrams of all sentiments in the ergic investment of which it plays a part.

Demonstration of some of the above processes depends in part on introspection, the use of which may seem to sacrifice our behavioristic position. However, this is a temporary crutch, for progress is rapidly being made in EEG, EMG patterns, GSR, and other signs, such as REMS or neural activity (see the recent work of Fahrenberg, 1977; Irwin, et al., 1966; Guttman, 1975; and McAdam, 1969) that should in time permit behavioral, or at least physiological, recognition of cognitive experience[2] such as we designate c in the equations for engram formation. Meanwhile, because restricting coexcitation only to instances when external stimuli operate would greatly shrink and bias the conclusions about human cognitive learning through the coexcitation principle, we must depend in part on introspective reports, at least in reconnaisance.

What we are here defining as the *coexcitation* principle has connections with what some investigators have called only the *contiguity* principle. This term may express legitimate conservatism, as these investigators may not wish to commit themselves to the concept of coexcitation as such, (which is certainly a positive hypothesis about neural action) but to stay with the barest description. Unfortunately, contiguity is a thinner statement even than it sounds, for contiguity is a necessary precondition for CRI, for SR action in $CRII$, and, indeed, the two things have to be there at the same time for virtually *any* scientific causal connection to take place!

Coexcitation implies definitely more than contiguity. It deals with a notion of cognitive activation (not to be confused with ergic arousal), and in Russian writers in the dialectic materialist tradition this is almost invariably taken as practically synonymous with cortical neural excitation. There is no objection to considering the coexcitation effect as mediated by neural physiology, but at present the physiology is not worked out sufficiently to count as an adequate explanation. Concerning the intrinsic nature of coexcitation, research is so scant that our position has to be largely one of theory building. As initially indicated in the last chapter, our hypothesis about the action itself is that any two simultaneous excitations in different parts of the cortex will tend to run together. Indeed, there would be no objection to calling the causal principle *fusion* instead of *coexcitation*, for coexcitation describes what the prior requirement is, whereas the law that we might call *fusion* explains what takes place when coexcitation occurs, namely, a running together. Unfortunately, fusion is also not physiologically documented. Fusion might indeed turn out to be the expression of a still more fundamental principle of unity of organismic action in organisms possessing a central nervous system. It would postulate that such nervous systems have so evolved that the maintenance of a unity of awareness and action must prevail over any influence tending to separation. Thus stimuli impinging on visual, auditory and other areas, and momentarily creating excitations in different parts of the nervous system, must tend to be brought into relation in a single executive or cognizing action. The CE law might thus be considered as an expression of a basic tendency for action in any neural network to maintain itself only so long as the excitations are not fragmented.

Meanwhile, reverting to an operational level, we are simply saying that the occurrence of two mental events at approximately the same time will tend to produce an engram, evidenced by the fact that the occurrence in future of one of them in the individual's attention will tend to retrieve the other from memory storage. Additionally, more speculatively, we hypothesize that one direction of association may be better developed than the other, and that this will be, in absolutely simultaneous excitation, from the lesser to the greater excitation, and, when there is succession (of a fraction of a second), from the earlier to the later.

Virtually all experimenters agree that the bond from a single coexcitation event is a very feeble one, sometimes hard to demonstrate. A general argument that this weakness must be characteristic and inherent is that, if it were *not*, all kinds of accidental connections would predominate in our mental life. The associational machinery would tend to be clogged by recent events and the situations of the organism would prevail over the organism's organization. A dictatorship of the recent and the accidental would make a purposeful and logical direction of thoughts and behavior impossible. (Perhaps what happens in schizophrenics, with their puns and bizarre logic, is a failure of strong purposeful learning connections to predominate over coexcitation effects.)

If the effect is typically very weak, however, how does it happen that quite an array of connections due to coexcitation are decidedly strong? First, we must recognize in these cases a very high *frequency* of repetition, especially in the connections that mirror the external world. We should relate here the models of Estes (1959) and Estes, Burke, Atkinson, and Frankmann (1957), which indicate that associations must reach outstanding frequencies relative to the average, chance frequencies, if effective engramming is to occur. There is no logical or purposeful reason why the sound we call that of a jet engine overhead should call up the words "jet plane," or why A should suggest B, or window should suggest house, except that the regularity of the external world ensures an extremely high frequency of experience of concurrence of these paired items. These come from external stimuli, but observation suggests that in inner-generated presentations, notably in the sets which cogitation binds together in sentiments—or even the tunes one repeats inwardly—equally unusual frequencies produce in the end powerful correlations from coexcitation of a purely internal kind.

Research needs to look for some ancillary principles (other than the dynamic ME, which, of course, acts with CE notably in CRI) in cognitive CE itself that will account for frequency not being enough, especially when some low frequency bonds are found to be strong. First we should consider the effect of cognitive structure as such. The early associationists such as Hume and Mill noted that recognition of words as synonymous produced stronger associations. Gestalt psychology documented the perception and memory value of an element completing a pattern. The Zeigarnik effect—remembering the intended parts of incompleted tasks—points the same way. The work of Spearman, Aveling and others on eduction of relations and correlates brought out still more clearly what the early associationists, the memory studies (prominence of beginning and end of a series), and Gestaltists have argued: that logical relations and cognitive meaning (as in noticing a synonym or opposite) make a coexcitation effect more powerful in the engramming of associations. The resurgence in the last decade of fresh experiments on cognitive aspects of emotional learning, and on meaning, are emphasizing this "cognitive structure effect" as one might generically call it, though there seems some tendency in some studies to confound it with a dynamic purpose (ME) effect.

It is tempting to look in coexcitation for a third determiner, beyond frequency and cognitive structuring that might be called cognitive intensity and in the case of outside stimulus could be simply the sensory intensity of a sound or visual stimulus. A notion that has been long entertained in reflexology, relevant to this and to directionality, is that of one stimulus being more "salient" than another, a notion derived from experiments on "overshadowing." This has relevance also to explaining the relative weakness found, for example, by Wynne and Brogden (1962) for the *CE* effect per se. (See "blocking" or "overshadowing" in Mackintosh, 1974.) The operational beginning of the overshadowing concept is that if a conditioned reflex $S_a R$ is set up and a second stimulus, S_b, is later invariably given with S_a (Figure 4-1), the amount of conditioning transferred to $S_b R$ is quite small. We might say that the complete coincidence on all the later conditioning occasions of S_b with S_a makes S_b a superfluous piece of information. In discussing the work of Konorski (1948), Egger and Miller (1962), and St. Claire Smith (1970), Mackintosh (1974) brings out in general terms that "the association between a stimulus and a reinforcer may be overshadowed or blocked if other more valid or more salient stimuli are presented simultaneously" (p. 219). Such findings, largely in the *CRI* paradigm, only indirectly support the tentative hypotheses we are making for a third modifier in *CE* action: that there is a quality of relative saliency (at least previous conditioning has occurred) affecting c's (or S's) and their engramming probabilities. This salience, which may be the same as excitation magnitude, affects, by our hypotheses above, both the magnitude and direction of the bond. It would seem that we must accept excitation magnitude as a third determiner in *CE* action, though it may prove a composite of sensory intensity of stimulus and some internal neural physiological condition, such that, for example, coexcitation might act more weakly under alcohol or in a sleepy state.

A summary of the inner and outer, with (3 and 4) and without (1 and 2) directionality possibilities in *CE* is given in Figure 4-1.

Other attempts to account for heightening of *CE* effects in particular situations use the notion of particularly strong attention; but this surely goes over into dynamic (ergic tension) reward, re-introducing the *ME* principle. In fact, our present conclusion on the undoubted directional effects in experiments investigating mainly *CE* is that they may be largely due to "contamination" by the *ME* (*CR*II) effect. We naturally assume that in all psychological experience the cognitive and dynamic effects cannot be purely separated (except conceptually and by analytic measurement), but always occur together in an experiment in some relative proportion. The fact that in research on the S_a-S_b paradigm (suggested by Thorndike, 1932; initiated by Brogden, 1939; summarized by D'Amato, 1970) there is commonly in such studies of close contiguity more association found one way than another, related to slight difference at time of impact (and possibly to magnitude of

1.   Contiguity, initially of *external* stimuli, S_a and S_b.

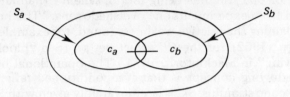

2.   Contiguity of *internal* cognitive excitations.

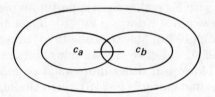

3.   Direction of association greater one way through temporal priority.

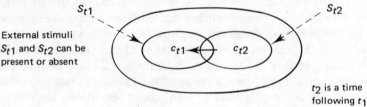

4.   Direction of association greater one way through greater excitation.

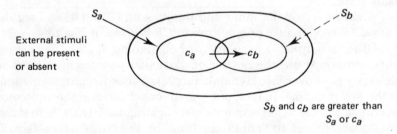

Figure 4-1.   Schema of possible mechanisms determining coexcitation (*CE*) Learning.

activation, as in Figure 4-1(4) and discussed below) suggests some dynamic reward quality has intruded; for *ME*, with its goal action, always has directionality in its engrams.

The possibility should indeed be considered that two of the three subsidiary CE laws (not frequency, but cognitive structure and intensity-salience) are in the last analysis dynamic. Contamination in our experiments could easily arise from the inability of our controls completely to exclude intrusion of motivation and purpose (see Wynne & Brogden, 1962; Mackintosh, 1974, p. 20). In the case of CRI, if we abide by our hypothesis that an innate reflex discharge is a satisfaction, when the unconditioned stimulus excitation is high, then the connection of the dynamic with the coexcitation action is part of the commonest paradigm in reflexology, namely CRI. The problem, experimentally, is to find enough examples of CE entirely free of dynamic intrusion to prove that the CE effect as such exists without dynamic aid. Equally needed are sufficiently ingenious experiments to separate the cognitive structure and intensity of excitation secondary law effects from the effects of dynamic purposes.

A directional property in CE almost certainly connotes the effect of purpose in some dynamic sequence. But if we could demonstrate more soundly what is now indicated in some experiments—that the directional effects gets less as the reward (ME) action decreases—we might find, by the nature of an asymptote, that if we could reach the theoretical limiting case of zero reward, the pure coexcitation association would still exist and be equidirectional. The alternative should nevertheless still be entertained that a nondynamic cognition—an idea without any ergic utility attached—simply does not exist, and that all cognition is the servant of purpose.

In these discussions on the CE principle we must raise the fundamental issue whether a law may need to be stated that *all* neural excitation seeks discharge (motor or into another cognitive area) and that this cognitive discharge need in the last resort is no different from what we call dynamic or ergic need. We have taken the position that the discharge of a reflex represents a mini-need. Any consideration of the continuum, from an eye-blink reflex to a scratch reflex to a bladder emptying, should surely suffice to indicate that the terms "satisfaction" and "reward" belong here as much as in a fully developed erg. The excitation created by a conditioned stimulus "needs" the satisfaction of discharge through the unconditioned reflex response. So far, we have considered coexcitation to be a cognitive and cortical phenomenon (as Russian psychologists also seem to do), distinct from the arousal of ergic tension, which belongs to the hypothalamus. A monist may be tempted to argue that in terms of need to discharge they are one, and that cortical activation is always a projection of hypothalamic arousal. Even so we would point out that cognitive excitation (activation) differs so much in degree as to be almost qualitatively different, and so deserves retention as a separate category from ME learning.

The position we finally take here, therefore, is that equidirectional coexcitation effects do exist, but are very weak without high frequencies of repetition or the addition of dynamic meaning. As regards the latter, the final view is that the *CE* connections are like a lightly dug irrigation system, the channels of which are selectively deepened when the flow of dynamic interests supervenes. This is another way of saying much that Tolman said under the concept of the "cognitive map."

The unity of a sentiment is indeed close to that of a cognitive map. The structure probably begins as a subgoal or node (m) in the dynamic lattice—an object or activity that signals opportunities for a variety of satisfactions. Encounters of the node object with various externally associated objects, and possibilities of action for satisfactions that are educed in reasonings giving insightful understanding of what will contribute to the sentiment satisfactions, then reinforce the response tendencies. Thus there is built up around m a cognitive network, initially growing by coexcitation. Where we have used the symbols M, m, and c for the structure around an object in a sentiment, in a subsentiment, and in a cognitive perception set or idea we have come to recognize that each is not only an object but an engram network around it. At the lowest level of such elements we may talk of them as sensations depicted as "points," joined by links (which we write as n's) based on learning experience, which produce a small unitary net c—a concept. The c's in turn can be joined by n's (from coexcitation) to form m's, and the m's may link up through farther acquired n connections to M's.

It is convenient to symbolize the coexcitation links as n's and the structural entities emerging as networks as M's, m's, and so forth, but all are engrams. The n's are the creeping tendrils of extension by which engram structures grow. This coexcitation extension makes subsequent dynamic effects possible because it *brings the new cognitive stimulus h into an effective role in using the dynamic resources (ergic investment) already in the sentiment.* In this way the network continues in a multivariate psychological structure what is recognized as a change from S_b to $(S_a + S_b)$ and $S_b \rightarrow R$ to $S_a \rightarrow S_b \rightarrow R$ (or simply the conditioned S_a-R to a Pavlovian) expressed in bivariate terms. Much of the latent learning discussed by Meehl and MacCorquodale (1949), MacCorquodale and Meehl (1951), and, by implication, Kendler and others (1950a, 1950b) may well be interpreted in man as due to such action of the *CE* principle, accentuated by the subprinciples of special relevance (cognitive structure) and high frequency of repetition of contiguity just mentioned.

Now the evidence of dR- and P-technique researches is that the pattern of attitudes that belong in a sentiment tends to become activated as a whole, its parts demonstrating a rise and fall together with daily stimulations and neglects. This consequence must follow initially from the unity of the cognitive network created by CE, probably further consolidated by dynamic purposes. It cannot arise from changing need strength of the ergs involved in the sentiment, for these are independent unities and would tend to strengthen only certain particular cognitive areas of a sentiment. It is true that according to our principle first mooted in equation (2-7), ergic tensions are considered (in EM) to activate sentiments; but if we were to come to scrutinizing this action more closely we should probably have to conclude that the process differs in at least speed and completeness of activation of the whole sentiment from that due to an external stimulus which by cognitive connections rapidly activates the whole network. For example, if self-assertive erg satisfaction is part of the patriotic sentiment an increase of self-assertion may bring the patriotic sentiment to a higher level of activation, but experiment may show that as regards activating the whole net, because of the cognitive connections, it still differentially activates certain parts.

In the converse direction of action, ME, presumably the activation of the net in M is relatively uniform and the arousal of the ergic investments correspondingly uniform. The ME term, of course (equation (2-6)) expands into $M(g_1E_1 + g_2E_2 + \ldots + g_pE_p)$, where there are p ergs involved, with weights in the investment pattern of g_1 to g_p. The engram properties of M which operate in the g's we shall call ergic *generators*. The cognitive net thus extends, to new cognitive perception and performances, the dynamic reward connection already existing for some given element. The great emphasis we have placed on eductive and other internal cognitive associative procedures in human learning permitting and augmenting coexcitation action is necessary because, although a kind of lip service is paid to it when animal experimenters try to apply CRI and CRII paradigms to human learning, the quantum leap is rarely sufficiently stressed or explained.

4-2. A Closer Look at the Laws within Instrumental Conditioning, or Means-End (*ME*) Learning

It is necessary now to study the foundation of evidence for means-end learning before we invoke it in the framework of structured learning theory. The most precise evidence lies in the almost endless experiments on instrumental conditioning, CRII, and to a lesser extent on the hybrid, CRI, if we regard even the reflex discharge as rewarding. However, a knowledgable recognition of "operant conditioning" in terms of the effect of reward and deprivation (punishment) on the learning of responses which precede them, is as old as history. It would be difficult to find in a textbook of reflexological learning anything not known, for example, to expert animal trainers in the last three hundred years. Nevertheless, more remains to be learned from experiment, though probably not so much as in the case of *CE*, where inability experimentally to determine strengths of cognitive activation as such leave certain matters speculative.

Although research in the *CR*II paradigm is voluminous surprisingly little of it goes beyond simple laws long known and into the phenomena the analysis of which would advance structured learning theory. The data yielded by past experiments are, for instance, largely confined to specific stimuli, neglect the unitariness of M's, and omit measures of the vectors defining the nature of the ergic goal satisfactions. Nevertheless, let us first pursue here what will be, for the learning student, simply a compact review of a familiar area. Our general plan of presentation is to overlap the old and the new terms for a time, until we shift most discussion to the new concepts.

Beginning with the more obvious and fundamental of reflexological and general learning findings, let us list what may be considered firm empirical laws. As we proceed to more complex findings, they necessarily become more entangled in the theoretical frameworks of those conducting the experiments, but we shall try to make clear when partial transitions from facts to explanatory principles occur.

Nine major reflexological and animal learning findings important to the understanding of means-end (*ME*) learning in personality can be gathered, as follows.

1. In a goal-seeking situation the more rewarded responses (by consummatory satisfaction) are reinstated on subsequent occasions more frequently than the less rewarded. This is Thorndike's empirical law of effect (1932), in which, let us note, the *particular* ergic goal in the reward has not hitherto been considered relevant. In a pure reflexological framework all reward is "reinforcement," unlike the more discriminating vector analysis of reinforcing reward in structured learning.

2. The higher the drive strength and the greater the reward ("incentive"), the more rapidly will a high performance be established with accumulated frequency of experience (Campbell & Kraeling, 1953; Crespi, 1942; Denny & King, 1955; Saltzman, 1949; Saltzman & Koch, 1948; Seward, 1956; Zeaman, 1949; and others). Whether this higher performance means stronger engramming or only higher performance because of higher motivation has not been answered in the literature to everyone's satisfaction. Hull (1951) considered the improvement as a result of what we are calling engramming, but others considered it to occur only in performance and related to persisting higher moti-

vation. We would argue from existing possible observations in structured learning that until (a) experiments involve *several* learning variables at once, and (b) the nature of a learning *measurement* itself is more defined (in such variables as performance, resistance to extinction, amount of revival after extinction, or time duration of learning) clear separation of motivation and engram effects will not be possible.

As to the relative power of the determiners (1) and (2), above, and (3), below, compared as measured ensuing *performance gain*, they might be put roughly in diminishing order of power (according to animal learning results) as follows: present motivation strength; past reward by the *CR*II (*ME*) principle; and frequency of contiguity by the coexcitation principle (*CE*). Findings on drive and reward-strength effects date back to Grindley (1929) and Wolfe and Kaplan (1941), and have been summarised in Logan (1960).

Research on human subjects seems to be less conclusive, however, the work of Spence (for example, 1956) in eyelid conditioning and *MAS* scores being among the comparatively few available results. Indeed, Mowrer (1960) even dismisses the *CR*II magnitude of reinforcement (reward) as a learning variable from first place, saying it has not usually been "very consequential." Other experimenters join him in arguing that ultimate consummatory gratification as such is not highly important in human learning and that the coexcitation effect of feedback of "knowledge of results" (Ammons, 1956) is more vital. The conclusion often drawn is thus that a small reinforcer (ensuing reward) serves as well as a large one in signaling the human subject that his performance has been correct, and any residual performance variance related to the magnitude of the reinforcer is too small to appear with any consistency. This assertion has received some support from the research of Dulaney (1968).

It might be best to assume that we do not yet have the experimental evidence for assessing the real importance of the *CR*II principle in man. Its role may often be virtually a cognitive one, revealing, at least for the human subject, *what* behavior is rewarded. The gain in performance thereafter is a function of the motivation strengths in the dynamic systems he consciously brings to bear. The uncertainty here offers one more instance of the risks of error in roughly applying reflex learning concepts from lower animals to man. These studies have had no techniques for studying ergic tensions in man, and have also perhaps not allowed enough for the enormous cognitive symbol- and relation-perceiving development in man in making coexcitation and reward connections unperceived by the experimenter.

3. The closer in time the reward is to the stimulus and response

(S-R connection) that ultimately leads to reward, the better established the memory connection (the engram) will become. In maze learning, by successive complete runs, this shows by the better learning revealed in steps nearer to the goal. But it is also argued that the goal distance and time-sequence relations permit no really simple generalization; for, in humans, "word-series" learning is better at the beginning *and* the end. The latter is a perceptual gestalt effect scarcely the same as goal distance, because for practical purposes beginning and end are equally remote (Grice, 1942; Kamin, 1957; Underwood, 1966). Even with true goal distance (in terms of time lapse and number of intervening sub-goals) taken into the calculation the conclusions are not unambiguous. Both the way animals are usually taught to run mazes, and in the natural-setting of the human learning of the dynamic lattice, the last courses (the goal-proximal courses) are learned first (and therefore with greater frequency and effect over the learning period. Incidentally, the tentative principle we stated for an isolated (tandem) chain of attitudes in the lattice would lead us to a conclusion contrary to that just stated, namely, to the expectation that learning would be essentially equal at all points in the chain, because interest (incentive) is equal throughout. However, this would apply only to the limiting "perfect" case, for, in practice, secondary principles, for example, the greater uncertainty of ultimate reward at earlier points in the chain, "friction," "leakage," and so forth, at points remote from the goal, become operative to make then less reinforced. But probably we can ascribe part of the effects here observed to the law we are now discussing, namely, that mistakes and correct responses early in the run have to wait longer for the punishments and rewards they bring about.

In controlled experiment the reduced effectiveness of delayed reward (as compared to immediate reward) in establishing and maintaining responses has been noted in animal research since Perin's early (1943) investigation. One interpretation of these findings is that incompatible responses occur in the delay interval that interfere with engramming the response under consideration (Carlton, cited in Spence, 1956), but alternative explanations have been offered (Logan & Wagner, 1965; Hilgard & Bower, 1966) and are considered in Section 4-7.

Mowrer (1960) discusses the issue in detail and—recognizing that in research on rats and pigeons "superstitious" behavior arises as a consequence of delayed reward or from incidental, or "noncontingent," reward (Skinner, 1948; Ferster, 1953)—concludes that the capacity of man for symbol manipulation, which enables him to "span the interval" between the "correct" response and perception of its reinforcement, has made it difficult in human research to demonstrate any diminished effectiveness of reward as the interval between the correct response and reinforcement increases. (See also Lorge & Thorndike, 1935;

Noble & Alcock, 1958 on this issue.) As far as insightful learning is concerned, which is prevalent in humans, the capacity to ascertain that a certain behavior today will bring reward a month hence could almost abolish the goal gradient effect, since the reward is, at least in considerable degree, today. But in blind trial and error learning, as in a maze, or making a golf stroke or socializing with another person, the human is subject to the same literal interpretation of the goal reward distance effect.

The work of Broadbent (1958) on short-term memory is also relevant here. Broadbent speculates that perceptual input is processed through the short-term memory process, as we suppose in Section 4-5, and that its temporary, "active storage" is of limited capacity. As in limited computer storage, the input of new information can occur only by displacing previous input. If reward is regarded as an "attention fixer," then we may further speculate that whatever is in short-term storage at the time of reinforcement will be prematurely "fixed" or transferred to long-term storage. The emphasis in Broadbent is that if the interval between the correct response and reinforcement increases, then engramming may shift from the correct response to whatever later behavior is occurring around the time of reinforcement, and a "superstitious" fixation consequently be formed. Our own "reverberatory" explanation for the preferential transfer of connections active in immediate memory to engramming in a "long-distance" memory storage is different. It supposes simply that gratification ultimately coming to a continuing activity in a reverberatory stage *after* immediate perception produces engramming, and so does not depend on Broadbent's immediate attention effects, operating merely in the short time that short-distance memory is active. However, there is no data suggesting that Broadbent's explanation is not also capable of operating.

Experiments, crucial to this issue, on delays of reward introduced after the goal box is reached, that is after activity has ceased, or after bar pressing (from three seconds to several minutes) show clearly that reward is diminishingly effective with longer delay periods. The effect (Hull, 1951; Harker, 1956; Fowler & Trapold, 1962) shows up not only in speed, error, intensity, and other such measures, but also in the increased *latency* with which the learned response is made to the stimulus.

4. There are extremely few natural learning situations in which the *CE* and *ME* principles do not interact. Cognitive links, begotten, for example, by running a maze without reward (except, perhaps, the reward to weak ergs like curiosity) are vital to *CR*II learning. As Blodgett demonstrated long ago (1929), exposure to a maze at virtually unrewarded levels leads to better performance on a subsequent re-

warded run than occurs in unexposed controls. The conslusion was that "responses are associated with their consequences rather than being "stamped in" (reward effect) by consequences." The learning laws as we have formulated them received support in two significant respects from the findings above. First, it supports the general position that *CE* learning through cognitive excitation can play a major role as a preliminary to the consolidating nature of *ME* learning. What is sometimes called "latent learning" is *CE*. The work of Bitterman, Reed, and Kubala (1953) on sensory preconditioning throws light on this while that of Meehl and MacCorquodale (1948), Rescorla and Solomon (1967), and others on latent learning clarifies it further. The most attractive theoretical integration seems to the present writer to be that of Tolman (1938) on "cognitive map" development, though the "map" concept has a vagueness that we must remove later here. A fine summary of the work on the coaction of reward learning (*ME*, *CR*II) and what we define as coexcitation (*CE*) is available in Mackintosh (1974), and we must point also to the coaction views of Staats (1975). The second issue on which light is thrown is our contention that learning always has some attachment to a particular ergic goal, such that when transferred to another there is initially some loss. This does not mean that appreciable transfer cannot be effected, as is obvious in the ease with which humans transfer their skills from one goal to another, but it implies that some quantitative loss in performance will be found when this is done, especially as more proximal courses in the lattice are involved.

5. A number of consistent relations have been found concerning effects of changes of strength and ergic quality of drive strength and incentive, which may be referred to as *drive shift* (quality) and *reward shift* (level) effects. Regarding reward strength shift, it has been shown that if one group learns at a high-reward motivation and another at a low, such that the *performance* of the former after the same number of repetitions is somewhat better than the latter, one or two new performances with both at the *same* motivation (reward or deprivation) strength will suffice to bring the performance of the latter up to the same level (Crespi, 1942; Zeaman, 1949). This seems to indicate that, at least in some performance consequences, that which we infer to be the cognitive engramming from coexcitation, *CE*, or from weak *ME* learning, is experimentally demonstrable to be as strong as from more rewarded *ME*. At any rate there are respects in which engramming is dependent to a higher degree on the number of repetitions (cognitive familiarization, as *CE*) than on the magnitude of reward.

Our introductory statement that *CE* learning is considered by most learning theorists as weaker than *ME* therefore has to be qualified by admitting that dynamic reward greatly enhances the *performance*, but that the connection itself can be a function of sheer cognitive exercise. Thus Thorndike was on the right track when (at a time when operant conditioning was the rage) he insisted (1932) on a *law of exercise* (essentially a paradigm of repeated S and R contiguity) being as important as the more dynamic principle—the *law of effect*. Unfortunately, the whole problem of (1) the modes of interaction of coexcitation (*CE*) and means-end learning (*ME*) (such as we have analyzed in *CR*I and in structural learning below), and (2) the extraction of an *engram concept and measure* from the observed *gain in performance*, has been somewhat neglected. Indeed, separating the performance gain from specific ergic tension investments, as we propose here (equation (2-4)), seems thereafter to have been (except for Hull) avoided or fumbled, as illustrated in the writings of Bitterman (1970) and others.

6. It has been proposed as a subprinciple above that there is some specificity of engramming to the particular ergic goal reward under which it originally occurred. This minor theme in the present *structured learning* was stumbled upon in animal experiment as a problematical issue, in the phenomena of *drive shift*. But the real nature of the law involved is not clearly formulatable in that framework, having essentially got lost in the acceptance of the concept of a "reinforcement" reward *in the abstract*, with ergic quality unspecified. When rats trained on hunger are shifted to thirst rewards for the same performance, there is at first a disruptive effect—marked loss of performance—followed by recovery in a new learning curve, as the researches of Tolman's laboratory conclusively show. The implication of this and other findings is that Thorndike's view of "reward in the abstract" and Hull's generalized drive, *D*, are inadequate, despite being patched up somewhat by Hull's "sensory carryover" effect, which apparently holds in the special case of mass trials.

We conclude that the structured-learning concept of means-end (*ME*) learning, with defined, particularized ends, is more realistic and in the end economical of theory than that of "operant conditioning," which speaks of undifferentiated "reinforcement" (using the ambiguous term reinforcement in this case to mean reward rather than the ensuing strengthening). These animal findings, and those in personality research, point to the need for concepts like Tolman's "expectation," Mowrer's "hope," or the notion that learning includes some approach to a general plan or cognitive map with a goal in it. It has been said by later animal experimenters that the animal learns not only *what* to do, but about *how* to approach a goal. These notions of goal-directed behavior are more precisely conceived in structured learning below.

The role of expectancy of a particular reward in learning is also shown in reward-strength shift (not to be confused with drive-goal shift, which involves a different goal, not merely a different magnitude of reward, although admittedly they are hard to separate). If high and low rewards on two learning groups are switched, as Crespi (1942) and others have shown, not only do the performances immediately switch levels, but they even "overshift." For instance, those previously at a low reward and performance level momentarily overshoot the performance of the upper group when shifted to the higher reward, as if by a contrast (gestalt) effect (and, conversely, the shift to lower reward causes an excessive drop).

On the other hand, evidence of relative ease of shifting an engram acquired under one drive to the service of another is abundant in human behavior. As one goes further distally in the lattice one reaches, for example, writing and arithmetic skills that have no steady attachment but can be shifted to the service of any erg. Some eminent eighteenth century contemporaries of Dr. Johnson report that they learned their polished sense of Latin and Greek grammar under fear of the birch, but they employed it later under the gentler motivation of esthetic goals.

The issues here have not been tackled in existing CRII researches in the structured learning framework of means-end learning sufficiently to clear several such questions. As regards the effect of differences of sheer motivation strength it would seem that they operate more at the time of behavior than at engramming, and, indeed, there are psychologists prepared to argue that at engramming CE is virtually everything and motivation beyond a minimum necessary to get attention is irrelevant. Means-end motivation would thus be concerned more with retrieval than engramming.

In spite of this general drift of the conclusions in existing animal learning we see enough evidence to advance hypotheses: (a) that certain properties of the engram over and above its sheer strength immediately, such as its persistence over time, and capacity to excite ergic tension, *do* depend closely on the strength of motivation during learning, and (b) that the qualitative nature of the erg involved, for example, whether it is sex, fear or hunger has some effect on the properties of the engram and slight effects on the ease with which it can be retrieved for different motivational, ergic ends.

7. A set of findings, many of them less expected on common-sense grounds than those above, has appeared in the domain of *inhibition*. Because these findings, since the time of Hull, have mixed actual data-relation statements with theoretical constructs (but at a level close to data), some clarifying discussion is needed. The main phenomena involved are those of (a) extinction; (b) habituation; and (c) reminiscence. The first—the tendency of a conditioned S-R connection to diminish without (in CRI) occasional reassociation with the unconditioned stimulus, or (in CRII) without some intermittent re-

ward, was well studied by Pavlov, as far as CRI is concerned. Whether we should stay with Pavlov's theoretical construct or follow the new principle here suggested (our principle 5, energy saving, in Table 3-6) is open to debate. Pavlov, it will be remembered, simply posited opposed excitatory and inhibitory tendencies (ϵ and I), explaining the level on any actual performance thus:

$$P = \epsilon - I \qquad (4\text{-}1)$$

where P is response performance.

The phenomena of extinction, habituation, and reminiscence may well be explained by interaction of two, or three, opposing influences. At present any adequate explanation of them is restricted by almost all exact findings having been cast in the paradigm of CRI (and occasionally $CRII$) conditioning. There is much to be said, however, for explaining them in dynamic terms by our principle 5 (or principle 2 if 5 is considered a subinstance of 2), that is, by supposing that rest-seeking or avoidance of energy expenditure is an ergic need. We see phenomena of extinction and spontaneous recovery, then, as outcomes in a simple ergic conflict between the erg being rewarded and the rest-seeking erg being punished (deprived), but with the latter showing more rapid temporal reduction of need strength than other ergs.

The second phenomenon, habituation, applies equally to an innate and an acquired response and says that a lot of stimulus repetitions, especially in a short time, result in diminished response. (Note that we can recognize this as happening also in extralaboratory ethological observations.) The third effect, reminiscence, covers results in paradigms that have been rather differently applied in animal and human learning fields. In the former, experimenters have dealt with the phenomenon of "spontaneous recovery" of a diminishing response after a rest; that is, the curve starts out at a new higher level after a rest. Conceptually it also covers the fact that reconditioning, after a zero point of extinction has been reached, occurs significantly faster than if previous conditioning had not occurred. Related to this is the finding that repeated conditionings and extinctions in a series will result in both procedures becoming quicker, as if "learning about learning" had occurred, or as if what we call the ambient situation, k, had become embodied in the learning.

The theoretical concepts to handle these findings are a different matter, and seem in some respects to have become redundant. They include *reactive inhibition* (Hull, 1951—the growth of an inhibitory factor to explain extinction, rather than simple loss of motivation—and *conditioned inhibition*, which supposes that the inhibitory tendency can itself be conditioned (Hull)—that it is rewarded and reinforced as part of the total response when reactive inhibition is building up. What seems to the present writer a much simpler explanation of most of these phenomena is the invocation of our fifth principle—of a rest-seeking erg which is stimulated by all repetitive activity.

In *human* reminiscence research, from Ballard (1920) to D'Amato (1970), the definition of reminiscence is somewhat different from that in animal learning. One encounters evidence of an activity continuing internally after active learning and after an initial *immediate* recall test. Items not recalled at immediate recall "pop up" an hour or a day later, so that although the *total* recall declines with time from the immediate postlearning test, certain parts of what is learned are actually better known later. We would suggest this is probably different from the animal "reminiscence effects" studies, in everything but name; but we shall embody it in later explanatory principles involving interaction of our five learning principles above.

8. It cannot be our aim here to cover exhaustively the lesser empirical generalizations that have emerged from the voluminous research with CRI and $CRII$ paradigms and which are excellently covered by such texts as those of Mackintosh (1974) and Hilgard & Bowers (1966). They consist of well-checked empirical laws concerning such matters as the effects of frequencies of learning trials, spacing of trials, regularity of trials, temporal regularity of rewards, effects of degrees of regularity of stimulus appearance, and all the permutations and combinations derivable within the framework of reflexological peripheral S and R terms. Much of this can be labeled under "schedules of reinforcement" in a taxonomy covering regular schedules, free-operant schedules, discreet trial reinforcement and its varieties, fixed interval, fixed ratios, and variable ratios, reward of different rates of responding, and so forth, which have been thoroughly worked out, especially by Skinner (1969) and his co-workers, by Herrnstein and Morse (1958), Herrnstein (1964), and others. A result of some theoretical prominence for human learning here is that with only intermittent reward it turns out that learning—in the sense of strength of engram established—is virtually as good as with continuous (regular) reward, and that it actually extinguishes more slowly. The main comment we would make on these intricate results is that they are entirely compatible with the concepts and equations of structured learning described later, though a whole book might be needed to present certain reformulations in detail.

9. A further set of interesting paradigm results are those well described by Mackintosh (1974), particularly under the labels of "overshadowing" and "blocking." These we have already briefly considered in evaluation (Section 4-1) of support for the coexcitation *(CE)* principle

4-3. Requirements in the Integration of *CR*I and *CR*II Paradigm Results in Structured Learning Theory

Following the above reminders of the contributions of reflex learning research, it is our aim to show what gains can be made by integrating them into structured learning theory. In the final formulations of structured learning we must, of course, go farther afield than reflex design experiments with animals—or humans—and take account of findings in school learning, as statistically examined by Cattell and Butcher (1968), Thorndike (1935), and many others; from personality change in therapy, as examined by Frenkel-Brunswik (1954), Eysenck (1972), Cattell, Rickels, et al. (1966), Rachman (1965), and many others in the recent trend to evaluate clinical results; from personality changes through life experiences, as analyzed by Barton and Cattell (1975), Cattell and Birkett (1977), Krug (1977), and others; as well as from less systematic approaches. From these domains we shall accept evidence only when it has the empirical firmness of that from reflexological experiment. In this section our concern is with some new perspectives on the *CE* and *ME* principles—mainly those within *CR*I and *CR*II paradigm findings in the last two sections.

To those who wisely seek illumination from considering any event in their own science in the wider perspective of the history of scientific development, it will be evident that reflexological and structural learning stand as a typical thesis and antithesis in a dialectical process, and that some of the social difficulties of a radical change are going to confuse the purely logical, conceptual difficulties. As such writers as Kuhn (1962), Beveridge (1951), Taylor and Barron (1963), and others have demonstrated, even when actual scientific progress is steady its progress in terms of social acceptance and support is often discontinuous, saltatory, and accompanied by the emotional problems caused by a turning inside out of treasured familiar ideas. Establishments duly develop, whose members would prefer to "creep up" on a new viewpoint by minor modifications rather than radically change their concepts. Any number of illustrations could be cited—the epicycles by which Tycho Brahe's astronomy attempted to avoid Copernicus' position; and the rationalizations using existing notions of spontaneous generation, and so forth, by which traditional medicine defended itself against Pasteur's germ theory of disease. In psychology such phases have been seen among the psychologists who pursued a continuous patching of ad hoc concepts of intelligence tests in the 1910-1930 period rather than comprehend Spearman's factor-analytic novelty. (It can be seen again in the same field today in the recent opposition to examining culture-fair intelligence tests based on the fluid intelligence factor). At a more trivial level, in the applied field the defense against any radically new concepts shows itself in the attempts to squeeze objective personality concepts out of ink blots or side-behavior in intelligence tests instead of boldly launching out with precise multivariate analytical methods on a broad new ocean of entirely objective, non-questionnaire, measures of diverse personality behaviors (see Chapter 3).

The signs noted by Kuhn and others that a method and some theoretical viewpoint are nearing the end of their usefulness—notably an increasing concentration of experiment on scattered, restricted local issues, an increasing incidence of useful discoveries coming as unforeseen by-products rather than answers to prevailing theories—have been seen and commented upon in reflexology in the last decade by learning experimenters themselves. An unmistakable restlessness and hunger for new theoretical vistas has appeared in current writings.[3] Among the more important vistas that have opened out in relation to learning theory, with a sufficiency of firm concepts are, as suggested here at the beginning, those of personality source trait structure and of the dynamic calculus. The direction of amalgamation that we have suggested here, and called structured learning theory, has so far incorporated concepts of ergs, ergic goals, sentiment structures, changing behavioral indices in the specification equation, and, as we shall see, the evidence for the organizing self. With these concepts goes the necessary capacity to provide an empirical foundation, for example, objectively to measure their magnitudes and modes of action.

In spite of the social problems in science which we have anticipated above, we propose now to write structured learning concepts with the findings of reflex learning. It will involve us perhaps in more speculative steps than some reflexologists will approve and in re-interpretation made in the gleanings offered by some rejected or neglected items lying on the harvest fields of reflexology. These excursions into reinterpretation must, however, be brief. They will turn mainly, for example, on: (1) the difficulties in reflex formulations in connection with concepts of frustration, punishment, and avoidance-aversive behavior; (2) the ambiguities and inconsistencies over "secondary drives"; (3) the unsatisfactory results, for example, in explaining "reward shift" and "expectation" effects, of using "general drive" instead of specifically located and measured ergic vectors; (4) the paradox in the basic *drive-reduction* explanations central to Hullian and post-Hullian explanations; (5) the failure to reach defensible constructs, which are dependable and meaningful, for measuring (a) drive strength and (b) learning gain as an engram increment, and (6) the inability to handle integration learning in CRI and $CRII$ paradigms as readily as by a natural extension of CE and ME principles as advocated here. A thorough review of the animal-experiment field by a progressive learning theorist would doubtless unearth other topics; but many current surveys, such as those of Bitterman (1967), merely encapsulate students more rigidly in an inadequate traditional system—that is, if the intention of psychology is to develop a learning theory effectively adjusted to human learning problems.

To be operational, in the sense of making certain that every concept is rooted in testable behavior, is admirable. But sometimes its essential purpose—to lock concepts into precise operations—gets frustrated in an academic pedantry that loses the real essence of the concept. Such a position is reached in reflexology in discussions of "aversive learning" when the meaning rests on a purely "geographical" statement of whether the individual physically approaches or withdraws from an object. No ethologist studying animal behavior in nature, no clinician interpreting human behavior, and, indeed, no commonsense man in the street, would single out for significance the accident of whether an organism approaches or recedes so many centimeters. Yet quite a number of reflexological articles are published annually in which the real complexities of patterns of ergic behavior, as in fear, sex, pugnacity and disgust are presumed to be more scientifically described if one uses such expressions and measures as approach-avoidance, approach-approach, and so forth. We recede from a stimulus for widely different ergic reasons—fear, fatigue, disgust—and we approach in love, in murderous fury, in curiosity, and so forth. To an understanding observer the important thing is the pattern of the total process and the goal, not just one arbitrary measurement feature among a thousand isolatable trivia of the total behavior pattern.

It is just possible there may be some use in categorizing so-called aversive drives. But actually they are more effectively brought into the processes of drive study if we recognize that they—and all other ergs—are goal-approaching drives! Fear seeks a goal of safety; disgust, a place where one is free from the noxious object; and rest-seeking, a quiet spot to sleep. Indeed, hostility is so far from being an aversive drive that it seeks to come to grips with its object! As ethologists and factor analysts converge in recognizing, the pattern of each goal-directed erg is a unique and complex process, and to attempt to handle goal-distance and the characters of emotions by the solemn pedantry of measuring inches of distance borders on the absurd. There is no substitute for factor analytically recognizing different ergs and, by process research isolating goals and subgoals, as on p. 347 below.

Tied up with such superficial taxonomy as that which speaks of aversive drives, is the adherence to a misleading semantics of rewards and punishments.

One can get into complicated confusions over the meaning of punishment through its having so many associations. For example, it has an aura of social guilt and expiation, which is irrelevant dynamically to pure structured learning concepts in terms of drive satisfaction and dissatisfaction. Then again, it is absentmindedly allowed to become identical with just *physical* punishment and with pain. Indeed, it is even "electric shock," that is used, with all its specificity, in 9 out of 10 animal experiments generalizing about "punishment."

To add to the confusion over these approach and aversive usages, "appetitive" has been used in much literature as the opposite of aversive. Appetitive is surely correctly used by its dictionary definition to apply to a viscerogenic drive in regard to its internal state change, that is, it refers to the quality of a viscerogenic erg dependent on a developing metabolic state. Thus, for example, fear and curiosity are presumably non-appetitive and non-viscerogenic, whereas hunger and sex *are* appetitive. From the above attempt to clear up certain verbal uses we come to recognize that both approach and aversive behavior are goal-directed. Appetitiveness is characteristic of either, if the drive happens to be viscerogenic. And if, finally, we define punishment as deprivation, it will be seen that certain fairly fashionable parts of the reflexological terminology, reported in Table 3-3, have created purely imaginary problems. They have produced misleading concepts because of the tortured attempts to couch them in immediate peripheral terms. These will be abandoned here, though our foundations will remain purely behavioristic.

They can be abandoned in favor of a simpler mode of explanation because of the possibility of using ergic goals and processes in the light of findings in Chapter 4, Volume 1, and Chapter 3 here. Reward and punishment can be comprehensively defined and related by using the perfectly general concept that *increase of satisfaction through perceived advance toward a goal is reward and increased deprivation is punishment.* The erg of fear (escape), for example, has the goal of being free of pain and danger. "Punishment" of the escape erg is *deprivation* of this freedom from pain, just as punishment of the hunger drive is deprivation of food. The conceptual gain here is that reward and punishment can become completely uniform in definition across both "withdrawal" drives, like fear, disgust, and rest-seeking, and "approach" ergs, like hunger, sex, pugnacity. A reflexologist may object that an electric shock is a much more concrete entity than the ergic goal of freedom from pain or danger (threat of pain). But the answer is, "Not when the study of ergs and the location and definition of their consummatory goals are taken seriously." *Any concept* is harder to handle for the beginning student than some *concrete event*; but the concept illuminates more phenomena and indeed constitutes science. Structured learning theory's orientation to goals as such, and to measurable degrees of goal deprivation, if accepted here and elsewhere, brings over-all gains in theoretical parsimony.

Consideration of behavior relative to the nature and strength of current ergic tensions means that the peripherally precisely defined sending of a child supperless to bed is no punishment if he is not hungry. It happens, it is true, that physical pain is always a punishment (except, let us note, to the masochist), and it is this social and experimental accident that we can "create a drive" by pain that seems to generate confusion to some students by suggesting a special class of "aversive" drives and, incidentally, makes peripheral definition *seem* adequate. To put a man on the rack, or give a rat an electric shock, is to create ergic tensions in the escape erg, which can be frustrated by denying its goal. When so eminent a theorist as Mowrer says (in Lindzey, 1974, p. 341), "in avoidance learning no reward (in Thorndike's sense) was involved" we see the pit of confusion into which the reflexological formulations can take leading researchers. The present writer, having researched with Thorndike, is reasonably certain that he would not have accepted aversion as an exception to his law of effect. The experimental *facts* are, as Mowrer states (op. cit., p. 341) that if "an initially neutral stimulus . . . is presented to an . . . animal and shortly followed by a (painful) stimulus (for example an electric shock) which can be terminated only by a specific response . . . the subject will be observed to leap into the air before the . . . (shock itself) occurs." But Mowrer's conclusion from this, as given immediately above, is not the only possible one, and, by the new structural concepts, is incorrect. If escape is considered as one with all other ergs (in defining which ergs we also carefully avoid the confusion of stimulus with goal), and we use a simple algebraic reflection of measured behavioral direction, the superfluous category of "aversive" disappears. The ordinary *ME* (means-end) learning principle, relative to a goal, suffices. It is true that (in later writings of Mowrer; in Rescorla & Solomon, 1967; and in Herrnstein, 1964) we see the capacity of fresh minds in an old field to climb out of the pit created by the jargon of that field, but many students today still seem to need some help in achieving the same emancipation.

We must not confuse this gain in unifying "punishment," "reward," "approach," "withdrawal," and so forth in learning into a simpler conceptual generalization with a certain oversimplifying reversion. We refer to reversion to that "drive in the abstract," *D*, with which many of Hull's followers have seemingly remained content. Structured learning theory recognizes on the one hand the unifying concept of drive patterns—ergs—across all drive phenomena, but on the other hand it stresses equally strongly that identifiable *specific* ergs exist and that *they have different goals and may have specific properties in their learning effects.* For example, appetitive ergs may have different properties in relation to learning extinction rates from nonappetitive, and the engramming action of fear may in various respects (for example, in permanence) be different from that of sex. Indeed, both clinical evidence on guilt and fear in the superego, and the demonstration by Solomon and Wynne (1954) that fear-learned behavior seems to extinguish less readily, indicate the need for experiment on possibly unique degrees of certain properties in the diverse ergic tensions.

As indicated above, *some* experimenters in the reflex framework have succeeded in stepping beyond the usual assumptions and given more attention to drive specificity. Angermeier, who points to such developments in Bolles (1972), Gantt (1965), Anokhin (1974), and others in the direct Pavlovian tradition, has himself (1960) added to evidence of the existence of a gregarious need in rats, operating in learning experiments that had previously been designed and interpreted on the assumption that no real drive is present when hunger and thirst are not arranged. Others have recognized that certain rat learnings designated "unrewarded" probably result from an erg of curiosity in the rat, and the whole question of what reward is involved in "reinforcement" has sometimes been given due attention, for example by investigators such as Premack (1959). Unfortunately in these cases this advance in hypothesis was not accompanied by the thorough application of those prior multivariate experiments in the animal field necessary actually to establish comprehensively and on a firm basis the nature and number of ergs present in that species.

In this same realm of drive some reconciliation of reflex and structural learning concepts is also called for in regard to what the latter considers the superfluous and erroneous notion of "secondary drives"—a notion seemingly taken for granted in the former. The fact that stimuli can *acquire* the property of evoking drives really does not need this concept and in most cases instanced in reflex literature the trouble arises simply from confusing a sentiment with an erg. A drive or erg is a demonstrated unitary character—a simple-structure factor—conspicuous in several behaviors connected with a simple goal-approaching process. There has never been any demonstration that true new *unitary* ergic structures are created when the action of secondary drives is claimed. Any motivations in humans that derive secondarily from primary ergs have only the unitary character of a cognitive sentiment network and operate, through the action of that sentiment, on the energy (reactivity) of a *diverse* collection of ergs. A second way in which the erroneous concept of secondary drive arose was seemingly due to the a priori belief that unless a concrete, physiological, viscerogenic basis could be discovered (as in hunger, thirst, sex) the pattern could not be innate and "primary." There is not the least ground for concluding that nonviscerogenic ergs, such as escape, curiosity, gregariousness, and pugnacity, are not innate. They may yet be demonstrable as physiological, in a neurological sense; for what cannot be shown in the soma can often be demonstrated as innate structure in the hypothalamus or mid-brain (Olds, 1956) and associated systems.

Turning to the relations of structured to reflexological learning concepts in instances when the new developments can build without prior demolitions, the structured learning theorist is intrigued by the above-mentioned exact experiments on drive shift and reward shift in their implications for means-end learning and the hypothesized differences of engram properties from different ergic satisfactions. From an early stage such experiments as those of Blodgett (1929), Crespi (1942), Rescorla (1967), and Elliot (1928) pointed to learning actually being "tied" to a particular *level* of drive, a particular *kind* of drive, and a particular *expectation* of reward. A recent overview of related work in the incentive area is found in Mackintosh (1974, Chapter 5), showing some of the difficulties in a purely *S-R* element and reflexological-law explanation, and other comments of the same kind will be found in Deese and Hulse (1967).

It should be repeated that structured theory does not suppose, in the *ME* principle, that an engramming that occurs in the path to a particular ergic goal remains available as a series of *S-R* connections retrievable from memory *only* in regard to that goal. Skills accumulate, for example, in unitary abilities and become an equipment available for *any* ergic goal. But it argues that there are degrees of entailment, and suggests that these need to be respected and researched. In summary, the evidence quoted above, which conflicts with the simple reflexological concept of reinforcement resulting from a *general* drive reduction, completely unrelated in properties to specific ergic goals consists of (1) the disruption in a learning curve when the ergic reward is changed in *nature* (drive shift) and (2) the effect of changes in deprivation *level* when the animal has experience of running at a particular level (reward shift). It is true that certain explanations of the former that do not accept an ergic goal have been offered in the conventional reflexological literature, but they seem unduly contrived. The changes seen in performance might arise, it is true, purely from the drive (E)-component change in our (M + E) formula and have nothing to do with the form of the engram laid down. Experiments are needed to check this, but at present a broader array of existing observations is better met, by the notion that there is some degree of dynamic, ergic specificity to any engram. The structured learning hypothesis is that this ergic quality affects the rate at which the engram is acquired, its degree of durability under time and circumstance, and the states of ergic tension under which it can be recalled or brought into action. Although a rat, having learned a section of a maze under erg A at strength X, is behaviorally upset when A and X are changed, and experiences delay in employing that skill for a different goal, humans, as far as one can see, achieve transfer more readily, perhaps as part of greater conceptual powers. Nevertheless, as every student knows, the early study of "transfer of training" by Thorndike and many others showed a far poorer transfer than educators had confidently assumed. A boy who had acquired orderly habits on his workbench, in the service of his interests in chemistry might show no order or tidiness in his English essay notebook or his bedroom. The fact seems to be that we have few concepts and fewer experiments handling the relative accessibility of skills and memories learned under different motivations, or the processes and time lags normal to their ergic transfer.

Parenthetically, the question concerns both action skills and retrieval of ideas from memory—tying a shoelace or recalling the past participle of a French verb. As far as present evidence goes, essentially the same form of specification equation applies to both, as is examined further here in Section 4-8 on retrieval. That specification equation contains, as has been referred to constantly and consistently above, an ME and an EM term, in addition to the E and M separately. It is the EM term—the contribution from the stimulation of an engram by an erg—that is at issue in regard to employing an engram on the service of different ergic goals. Are the weights very specific to the M's, or can any ergic tension bring, in some degree, any M into action? Obviously from common observation there is some freedom for the latter.

In stressing the importance of knowing which ergs have motivated the acquisition of which engrams we do so more in regard to the *general quality* of the engram, than its accessibility. More attention is needed regarding its rate of acquisition, its permanence, and so forth, because the question of erg and engram quality has been begged in virtually all existing research. The second way in which engrams might be so affected, namely as to retrievability by erg X when learned through erg Y *has* been investigated in animal work. Even in animals, after a brief upset, the skill becomes readily subsidiated to the new goal. And though we have mentioned Thorndike's surprising first results on transfer of training, yet when humans grasp what is needed to be transferred there is even less difficulty than with lower animals.

Nevertheless, the possibility of specific ergic associations with learned engrams, with respect to both properties *and* recall remains as a provocative question. To answer such questions experimentally the techniques for tying down the quantitative spectrum of ergic tensions in a particular organism at a particular time need to be substantially improved. It is curious that research on drives today stands in the unusual situation wherein specific ergs have been isolated more completely, and by far more systematic research, in *humans* than in any research yet applied to *animals*. As regards rats and mice, only five researches factoring spectra of behavior adequate to tie down structural, ergic patterns seem to exist, and the last of these is incomplete (Anderson, 1938, 1941; Anastasi and others, 1955; Haverland, 1954; Royce, 1966; and some as yet unfinished analyses of drive measures on 128 rats by Schneewind, Dielman, Rican, & Cattell). These studies show that distinct ergs *can* be located as factors in rats, with much the same precision as for humans (Cattell & Child, 1975).

One important inference from them, however, is that the widespread practice in animal experiment of basing a drive-strength estimate on a single variable, such as hours of food deprivation in the case of hunger, is open to doubt. The practice must have led to appreciable inaccuracy in quantified conclusions about relation of learning to drive strength. Furthermore, as the Cattell and Dielman (1974) factoring of a wide array of motivation strength measures in rats shows, both the drive strength (independent) and the learning measures (dependent variables) initially get confounded with measures of preexisting *abilities* in the animals. But recognition and separation are not easy, for although the researches of Anastasi and others (1955), Tryon's (1940), Royce's (1966), Cattell and Korth (1973), and Cattell and Dielman's (1974) show ability traits to be as real in rats and dogs as in humans, the separation of ergs from abilities and temperament traits is far less clear than that accomplished in studies on humans.

In this section's work of integrating reflex findings on *CR*I and *CR*II with structured learning, it seemed essential to begin with demolitions of a few superfluous or misleading concepts. But we are now emphasizing also that sheer absences of certain results and concepts from existing research require a new strategy of experiment in this classical learning area. The courtesy of scientific interaction urges us to say that this is not wanton criticism, but an examination of the weak and strong points, and a scouring of the interface, to ensure a better welding. Exept for psychometric ability and personality study no edifice has been erected with such dedication to existing scientific standards as that of reflex learning theory. The problem is that bridging to other fields has been slow. Progress requires learning theorists to master multivariate experiment, and personality theorists in turn to match the methodological precision and clarity of model visible in classical learning, in their study of personality and learning.

The omissions in reflex learning theory that we must attend to are, as already indicated, a neglect of ergic structure, including the restriction of experiment to three or four ergs—hunger, thirst, excape, and sometimes sex—out of a dozen possible. Probably the error, from this bias is at least no greater than that in psychoanalysis in Freud's generalizing about ergic structure from a small sample of urban, late-Victorian, middle-class Viennese.

In seeking to link up with dynamic-calculus concepts we find a deficiency not only in multivariate experiments to structure animal drives but also in the examination of the validity of drive-strength measurements. It has seemed likely that experiment might reveal in animals motivational components like those found in human drives. To progress from the uncertainties of such procedures as measuring the hunger drive by a single measure, for example, hours of food deprivation and measuring learning gain, by, say, number of responses persisting under unreinforced conditions, a factorial clarification of the structure among a large number of signs of drive strength and a representative set of measures of learning gain is needed. Regarding the latter, for instance, strategic coverage of a variety of learning-gain manifestations, wide and well chosen, such as change in speed, errors, rate of extinction, amount of transfer to other goals, rate of decay, (extinction without use), deprivation level in relation to frequency of trials, deprivation level in learning, reward, learning schedules, spaced and unspaced learning, has long been needed. It is hard to find as many as half a dozen studies in animal learning that have sought *correlation among as many as even two or three commonly used learning-gain variables*.

As far as can be discovered there is only one exeption to this dearth, and that is in the area of signs of motivation strength in rats, aimed to clarify motivation components, as described below and in Chapter 4, Volume 1. This study (Cattell & Dielman, 1974) measured 30 variables on 128 rats in five mazes, with results shown in Vol. 1, page 154. However, these measures were on *performances at the end* of extensive learning, and separation of abilities *per se* from the motivation components had to be made by secondary means. The results did show, however, a considerable resemblance to the results of research on human motivation components (see Table 4-6, Chapter 4, Volume 1). Tucker's (1966) method of dimensional analysis of learning curves seems also not yet to have been employed in animal learning.

The importance of putting animal-learning motivation measures on a basis of known motivational components is that without it the farther step of defining ergic structure (and possible animal equivalents to sentiments) is not on a safe, objective basis, and without knowledge of that dynamic structure the separation of engram gain measures from mere performance gain in learning cannot insightfully be made. An integration of animal experiment with dynamic calculus findings on humans, in the domain of the means-end principle (CRII paradigm) therefore still awaits systematic experiment.

4-4. Integration Learning (*N*) as Inhibition and Resolution

We have tentatively proposed above that integration learning, N, is not descriptively different from CE and ME (CRII) but may involve a new principle.

The definition of integration learning naturally involves the definition of integration. Two approaches have been made to this: in Chapter 2, on conflict among ergs and sentiments, we considered the role of the ego structure; and in Chapter 3 we briefly defined integration learning as maximizing the total ergic satisfaction experienced over some stipulated, appreciable, "foreseeable" period of time.

The concept of integration is one of the most difficult and elusive in personality study, especially as one comes to operationalize and measure it. Success in formulation is scarcely to be expected until more subtle experiment, based on the concepts we can presently reach, has been actualized. As Chapter 2 shows, experiment to this point has calculated total indurated conflict and shown it to be significantly positively related to psychosis and negatively related to ego strength, factor C scores. It has shown C to be positively related to internal logical-dynamic consistency of attitudes, negatively to instability of attitudes over short time intervals, and negatively to virtually all clinical pathology: the neuroses, addictions and psychoses. On that basis we have formulated a measure of integration, I, as $(1 - c)$, where c is overall conflict from $\Sigma n [b^2(-)]/n$ calculations. (Note regarding symbols, therefore, that C, ego strength, is virtually the opposite, conceptually, of c.)

Before pursuing this we need to analyze the notions of *adjustment* and *adaptation*, which give us an internal and an external behavioral evaluation to be brought into relation with the internal structural concept of integration just described. These two notions have often been used interchangeably, but a useful distinction can be drawn (Cattell, 1950).

Adjustment, by the majority of uses, comes close to our integration definition, though in general use emphasizing more perhaps happiness and sense of satisfaction than evidence of dynamic integration per se. However, it is clearly meant to be defined by *internal* measures: degree of conflict, happiness, freedom from anxiety, whereas *adaptation* is defined externally to the person, in sociobiological terms, by criteria of performing well, getting along with other people, and all that contributes to *surviving* sociobiologically. It is basically a Darwinian "fitness" concept, and often referred to nowadays as "capacity to cope."

Adjustment and adaptation can stand at different levels in the life of one individual, though doubtless they correlate positively across individuals and across time in the same individual. For example, it is even possible in the special case of some kinds of psychotics, to be adjusted, in the sense of low anxiety (as occurs typically in schizophrenics) and reduced internal conflict, but to fall far short of being adapted. Conversely, it is possible for a man to be adapted, performing his social-familial obligations and surviving as an individual better than others, but to be unadjusted in the sense of being unhappy, under tension, "worried to death." In the long run, full efficiency of adaptation may not be possible if the individual is conflict ridden, unhappy and unadjusted in meeting the adaptation requirements. Though full efficiency of adaptation may not in the last resort be possible without adjustment, the converse is readily possible, as in the happy psychopath.

The distinction of adaptation and adjustment may be helped by an image of two concentric circles, adjustment being a process taking place in the inner circle—the organism—and adaptation occurring between that and the outer circle of environment. The stresses on the inner circle will be partly those due to the outer ring and partly to inner deficiencies of structure upsetting the power to cope. Adjustment, which we continue to study here, may not be completely synonymous with dynamic integration, because there may be temperamental and ability components, but the correlation should be very high. Let us, with this perspective, ask how integration is learned.

An obstinate problem in regard to integration learning as defined in the last chapter is that it would suggest substantial correlation of existing integration measures (as made by C) with intelligence, yet the correlation of C, ego strength, or of the second-order anxiety factor, QII (inverted) with intelligence, has been negligible over most samples (Cattell, Eber, & Tatsuoka, 1970, p. 122). If integration is a matter of so arranging behavior, by insight or trial and error, that ways of behavior are found that will maximize the total ergic (and therefore sentiment) satisfaction, we would anticipate the intelligent and shrewd persons (high on B and N on the 16 PF) would tend to reach higher levels on C (actually C and N average an r of about +.12 over several populations but B and C remain with an almost zero r). Certainly, concerning the choice of a more or a less effective path to reach a *single* ergic goal, say, getting to meet an attractive member of the opposite sex, we can confidently expect intelligence and success to correlate, and in a primitive hunting society intelligence would surely correlate with greater satisfaction of hunger. However, by our definition, which seems correct in terms of clinical meaning and the elements in the dynamic calculus, integration is a maximization of satisfaction *over all ergic needs and over long periods* and perhaps this depends more on capacity to inhibit and restrain various immediate satisfactions than on intelligence.

The expectation that there should be a substantial correlation between intelligence and integration defined as discovery of a harmonious, nonconflicting set of paths of satisfaction for various ergs and sentiments probably overlooks three things: (1) that a higher intelligence may not only create better solutions, but also harder problems, through higher aspirations, that the individual is expected to solve; (2) that recognizing a good solution to an emotional conflict is different from following it, and most of the variance in handling emotional rather than intellectual problems lies in the latter behavior, which connoted ability to stand frustration and to inhibit; and (3) that the overall gain to the satisfaction of all ergs and sentiments springs much less from "cleverly" finding confluent forms of behavior, as the paradigm of an animal in a maze might suggest, than from evaluating one's needs and inhibiting a diversity of interfering behaviors, to allow a correct sequence or situational adjustment of expressions.

What the last mentioned involves will only gradually become clearer as we pursue the role of the ego structure (begun in Section 2-8) into confluent learning—the simultaneous satisfaction by discovered single paths satisfying two or more ergs or sentiments. Integration learning is measured by gain in total sentiment and ergic satisfaction over a substantial time period and some of it will be by trial-and-error learning, but we need to examine a more deliberate and planned process of adjusting successions of expression in relation to the realities of environmental situations. That planning is possible mainly through (1) recognition of true strength of experienced needs, (2) appraisal of outer situation and retrieval of past consequences of action, (3) capacity to inhibit impulse, defer need satisfactions, tolerate frustrations, and (4) the capacity ideationally to evoke ergs and sentiments to help control action optimal to ultimate satisfaction. The gaining of integration is essentially the provision of a "stop and go" system, enlightened by previous experience, either insightful or leaning on unconscious trial-and-error, of the consequences in relation to the real world.

The attempts to get this complex ego behavior into an experimental framework have met many difficulties. As pointed out the animal studies in the reflex framework on inhibition and on learning to defer satisfaction have used peripheral observations only. They have concerned themselves with conflict of stimuli and timed deferment capacity (Mackintosh, 1974). The early work of Warden (1931) in pitting one drive against another in animals was a promising beginning, but, again, translation to human integration learning is difficult because of the absence of those C, Q_3, and G sentiment structures so central in human action, or of any factorial evidence of some corresponding embryonic forms in rat or monkey.

The clinician, by contrast, formulates the problem with abundant observations, but does not pursue exact, quantitative, and replicable research. He sees the pitiful waste and frustration of human life through the insufficiency of insight, the slowness of trial and error learning, and the limits of restraint, but has not tried a quantitative model. Mowrer's (1938, 1960) attempts to translate clinical into animal behavior were most ingenious and promising, but again lacked the possibility of relating to human structure. The new objective measurement possibilities with humans, through such devices as the TAT, and better, the fully structured and objective MAT (Cattell & Child 1973) as well as the seven dimensions of conflict measurement referred to earlier (Cattell & Sweney, 1964) should now make instrumental, quantitative analysis of human clinical data possible.

As indicated in the *adjustment process analysis* chart (Figure 5-4, p. 307) we can be operational about the beginning of conflict, and therefore of integration by recognizing that the behavior begins with either (1) a complete or partial blocking of a familiarly used path, or (2) the clash of two situationally stimulated but incompatible courses of action, usually leading through different sentiment satisfactions to different ergic satisfactions. As far as this can be translated into peripheral terms we are saying there is a conflict between (1) a positive and an inhibitory response in the same domain of behavior, or, in (2) above, either two different responses to the same stimulus or two different responses to two stimuli simultaneously present. These S-R definitions must now be enriched in meaning by adding goal data as G_1 and G_2. If S_1-R_1 goes to G_1 and S_2-R_2 to G_2, then integration learning (Type (3) above) involves either inhibiting R_1 and R_2, in alternation, or inhibiting both while some new response is found to both S_1 and S_2 that will simultaneously lead to both G_1 and G_2. What we are saying in the last case, in terms of responses as attitude courses of action is that the new integrating attitude path must gain the degree and kind of satisfaction that is shown as an ergic vector in Figure 4-2.

Since the essence of drama is conflict there is an abundance of illustration in literature, and fortunately also in well documented biographical (non-fictional) cases of human experience. These dramas of frustration can be shown very typically to illustrate the above three phases of conflict, inhibition, and emergence of a new course of action. In terms of a whole life style being frustrated, and emerging later in a new integration, one thinks off-hand of Joseph Conrad's description of his transition from a Polish sea captain to a foremost British literary

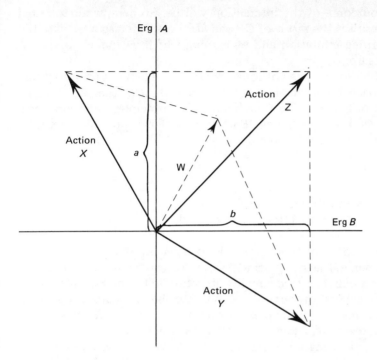

Figure 4-2. The vector evaluation of integration learning gain.

Course of attitude action *X* brings habitual satisfaction *a* on erg *A*; course of attitude action *Y* brings habitual satisfaction *b* on erg *B*. Because of some degree of indurated conflict between them, the total ergic gratification is only that represented by *W* and its projection on ergs *A* and *B*. A course of action *Z* would give the satisfaction of the ergs *A* and *B*, previously sought in behaviors *X* and *Y*, without loss. It would represent perfectly integrated action with respect to *A* and *B* and to the extent of the gratifications *a* and *b* originally required. The gain in integration in such a case is represented by the difference of the vectors W and Z.

figure, or in a religious framework of Loyola's pilgrimage from a "ladies' man" to a saint.

Our purpose at this stage has been only to define integration learning operationally and point out that it involves new laws. The argument tacitly accepted in most reflex learning tests that CRI and CRI paradigms (or CE and ME laws in terms of our analysis) are sufficient to explain integration learning in themselves seems to us highly questionable. The CE and ME laws are involved; but they are not sufficient. An analogy from another realm of science indicating similar insufficiency is found in the way that the laws and equations expressing the chemical affinities that permit a chemical reaction to proceed require the laws of mass action and the phase rule to define what the ultimate outcome of the interaction will be. So here, while the final learning result is the result of *CE* and *ME* laws, it is also a result of the laws governing inhibition and re-learning which we include under integrative learning.

At the present stage of research ignorance it is not proposed here to take space for discussion of more than the *CE*, the *ME*, and the present *N* principles. The fourth and fifth principles—goal modification, *GM* and energy saving, *ES*—we must leave with the degree of definition[4] given in Chapter 3.

4-5. Arousal and Activation as Solutions to the Drive Reduction Theory Paradox

Since the purpose of this chapter is to reach some understanding of basic and general learning principles, before watching their action in the full complexity of personality structure in Chapter 5, it is appropriate that we first probe more deeply into the mechanisms by which the above three main principles—coexcitation (fusion), *CE*, means-end, *ME*, and integrative, *N*, learning—exert their actions.

The underlying mechanism for the *CE* law has perhaps been discussed as much as is yet profitable, and we shall therefore begin by concentrating on *ME*. In leaving coexcitation let us summarize by saying its cause is virtually reduced to neural action, which supposes that any two excitations in the cortical neural network are brought together by some electro-physiological mechanism of fusion, establishing a slightly freer crossing thereafter of the synapses involved. A tendency to one way directionality, we have suspected, is due to secondary laws. These are, first, cognitive in nature, arising from the relative sizes and intensities of the excitations, and the experience of structural completion. Secondly they are, dynamic, that is, involving action of *ME* itself. Here we assume it operates not only in obvious fashion but through what look initially like cognitive satisfactions involving "gestalt completion" and "meaning."

In regard to the more powerful contributor, the *ME* law, psychology has encountered two problems, one perhaps a traditional misunderstanding the other more seriously inherent in the drive-reduction theory commonly associated with *CR*II. The first seems to bother only philosophers, and is concerned with the unacceptable conclusion that a satisfaction that *follows* an *S-R* event can be the *cause* of its acquiring strength. Both this and the fact that an animal "seems" to be drawn by the valency (Lewin) of a goal that lies ahead are at least correctly *described* by a teleological model. But no psychologist today, surely, accepts a teleological causal explanation. Our explanation is that "goal" has an internal equivalent—actually a cognitive-dynamic *condition* inside the animal before it begins to act—operating as we have already discussed. The second problem—the paradox of backward action in learning—can be dissolved by our reverberatory theory, now to be discussed.

The paradox whereby reward, by drive tension reduction at a goal at time, t_2, affects behavior at t_1, has evoked several ingenious explanations of mechanism, the need for decision among which seems today neglected, as if the problem were almost insoluble. What we commonly see in an animal or human learning a path to an ergic goal—at its clearest in viscerogenic drives—is (1) a mounting of need strength with time, which usually means with closer goal approach, and (2) an increase in the amount of external stimulation of the drive with approach to the goal, either through innately set cues, if the goal is innate, or, if this course has been run before, by learned cues. The paradox in the widely held theory that learning occurs when there is ultimately drive reduction (Hull, 1951; Miller, 1963; Young, 1961) is that the animal *should*, by this theory, in the first place decline to run from a lower to a higher tension situation. Secondly it should fail to learn all but the last step, since the preceding steps are each accompanied by higher tension (deprivation, punishment). To be exact in our postulates, this does not *necessarily* negate that drive reduction can produce learning, but if, logically, drive reduction is pleasant, then drive increase would be unpleasant, and the associations to the later stages, of, for example, a maze, would be so aversive that the animal would not endure the advances necessary to learning. (Note, incidentally, that our use of aversive does not contradict our rejection earlier of "aversive drive"; the *drive* here is positively goal directed: the behavior is aversive.) As to human experience of the aversiveness of high unsatisfied desire, we may turn to a thousand witnesses, of which we take, almost at random, lines from Edna St. Vincent Millay's sonnet on lost love.

> "There is a well into whose bottomless eye,
> Though I were flayed I dare not lean and look."

We must admit that the distinction, made in Section 2-5, between need strength and ergic tension, only hides, but does not abolish, the paradox. Need strength, by appetitive processes, expresses itself by a rise in stomach movements, the unease of reduced blood sugar, the impact of increase sex hormone, the autonomic disturbances of anxiety, and so forth, as well studied by Miller, Young, and others mentioned above. In our notation this ergic need strength is E, and it increases over time with the inevitable onward march of an internal clock. However, in most learning situations the approach to the goal is much faster and shorter than the progress of inner appetite per se, so that the increment in E during a learning session or maze run might typically be quite small. Incidentally, we do not actually have to confine the presence of this appetitive rise to viscerogenic drives, though it is less clear and documented in nonviscerogenic ergs. Probably in non-viscerogenic ergs it is quite small relative to stimulus-caused elevation.

Among the diverse attempts to handle the paradox mentioned above, some, like that of Hull, bring a signal of the ultimate reward back along the subgoals that lie on the way to the final tension reduction. But this could not operate (except among humans with insight) the first time a maze is run, and would operate even over the first few runs without much confidence. Yet learning occurs from the beginning. And in insightless learning, for example to ride a bicycle, unrewarded or punished behaviors get successfully eliminated. Another suggested device, which we call the saw-tooth-path theory, assumes a series of environmentally defined subgoals, in which, although stimulation of ergic tensions occurs on reaching each, the organism is willing to run the paths between because tension is lowered by some anticipatory sense of success on approaching such a near subgoal. On reaching it the elevation of tension that occurs from the stimulating situation presented by the familiar (or innate) subgoal is so sudden and unavoidable that the animal has no choice but to accept it. Thus, although each running section of the total path is downhill, the total trend is uphill, that is, toward augmented tension, by reason of the sawtooth vertical rises at each subgoal, as in (b) in Figure 4-3. This shifts the inevitability of rising tension from the inner clock to an external environment, built to be cooperative in this way either by innate "instinct"—ergic structure—triggerings or by past learning. A second model for which an argument can be made is a sawtooth in just the opposite sense (see Figure 4-3). Here we hypothesize that short-term increases in tension would be tolerated, and would not cause a reversal of movement (withdrawal) if quickly followed by reduction rewards at each of many closely successive subgoals. This simply puts the sawtooth upside down. The legitimate objection to both of these models is that by chopping a paradox into small pieces one does not necessarily make it more digestible. However, as mere mooted possibilities these alternatives are set out in Figure 4-3 along with the older, simpler hypothesis (Figure 4-3a) that ergic tension just goes on mounting to the goal.

(a)   "Classical" assumption of steadily increasing ergic tension in approach, with reduction at consummatory goal

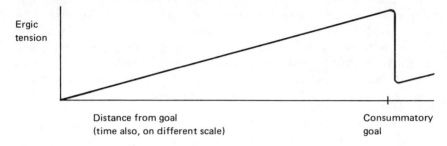

(b)   "Encouraging" reduction approaching each subgoal, but heightened anticipatory stimulation at subgoals

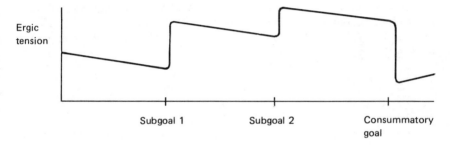

(c)   Intermediate sustaining of increased tensions with reward by reduction at subgoals

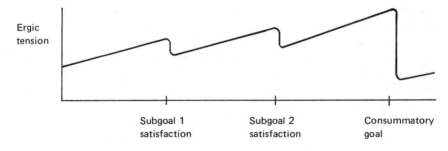

Figure 4-3. Some earlier drive reduction hypotheses regarding the course of ergic tension under inner and outer influences.

Reverting, in face of these difficulties to the models that somehow move part of the ultimate goal satisfaction backward in time, by a backward shift of reward along the subgoals, we encounter further difficulties. In the first place we should expect enormous differences in rates between, say, rats and humans, by reason of the greater capacity to anticipate and symbolize—a difference which scarcely actually exists between humans and rats learning mazes. And if we make it the main solution we run into another problem, that if the subgoal becomes more attractive than the goal, no learning of further steps will occur. The particular solution proposed here meets (a) the problem of why an organism advances through subgoals of increasing ergic tension, by recognizing two components in ergic tension—need strength and arousal—with different properties, and (b) the problem of backward action, by the concept of cognitive reverberation, as described below.

The first is not developed ad hoc for the present theoretical need, but already exists in the analysis of drive, need, and ergic tension strengths (Chapter 2, equation 2-13). This supposes that after stimulation of the need strength by s_k, the total previous strength remains still in action, as E, and adds thereto its derivative from s_k, which is arousal, E. Because the stimulus term is written in (2-13) (p. 115), as $(1 + s_k)$, equation (2-15) already expresses what is here being said, namely:

$$E = E + E \tag{4-2}$$

or "ergic tension equals need strength plus arousal." Here again there are models in physical science for this, as when the fission of uranium X_1 yields uranium X_2, producing a mixture, or when heating water yields a two-phase system of water and steam.

Parenthetically, it should now be pointed out in perspective that equations (2-11) and (2-12a) deal with the arousal of an *innate* ergic structure. But ergic arousal in connection with any typical learned behavior would go through an engram and require an M as well as an s_k, in the general form $E = s_{k\,m} ME$. For simpler setting out of the ergic-arousal relation we may use the earlier form, but as we approach the case where arousal cues are learned the $s_{k\,m} M$ will be regularly used to described the arousing connection.[5]

The model can be made to explain an organism's willingness to approach a goal through increasing unpleasant tension if we suppose that need strength E and ergic arousal, E , have different properties. The difference relevant here is that arousal is a pleasant excitement but need strength remains uncomfortable. As a conjecture we might suppose that the "pleasure center" in the hypothalamus studied by Olds (1956) and others is involved, via associative centers, in converting the need in some ergic center into the pleasurable arousal experience appearing with stimulation and excitement.

Whether the approach to what may prove an ergic consummatory goal will finally proceed, as an attractive experience, or be arrested, as unpleasurable, will depend on the balance in the mixture of E and E.

If it is to proceed it will require that the mixture be one in which the E component increases faster than the E component.[6] In the innately cued ergic behavior of a lower animal this will depend on whether it meets the innately prescribed cues in timely succession, for instance that the smell of prey be followed by the sight of it.

Let us consider next the "backward" causal action in learning. Classical learning theory has naturally concerned itself systematically with the problem of how intermediate subgoals on the way to consummatory goals acquire rewarding properties, as a glance at the index of any learning text will show. The models vary considerably, from Hull's "fractional anticipatory goal responses" to Tolman's "carrying back" of the "sensory properties" of the consummatory reward, and Mowrer's "hope" and "anticipation."[7] Almost all rest on cognitive effects, except perhaps "secondary conditioning" the properties of which are considered motivation-evoking.

The present theory is motivational in nature and brings the arousal effect into the framework of structured learning. It thus places emphasis not on any cognitive backward shift of the meaning of the goal, but upon it changing its emotional meaning as such through the s_k arousing an emotion at situation k that was not previously aroused there. The p, r, and i indices of the $(h + k)$ stimulus and situation (in the total situation) *may* also change, but except for what may be minor changes in p and r there would not be cognitive perception changes. The i change would be in the interest intensity with which action is pursued at the subgoal, for a fixed value of s_k and E, and is thus also motivational. However, in regard to this model we should recognize the admitted circular action of E and M, that is the E is aroused by s_{km} ME and also by innate elements in s_{ke} E, leading to effects on M in s_{ke} EM.

It is interesting to ask how the model agrees or disagrees with, extends or modifies the various theories we have briefly alluded to of fractional anticipatory responses, anticipation, hope, secondary conditioning, and so on. Staats (1975), in yet another variant, speaks of CRI as the transmitter of emotional meaning down the line from the goal to subgoals. Apart from the perhaps over-refined distinction we have made, from Staats' point of view, between emotion and motivation, Staat's model could be an alternative to our own. It would be an alternative in that he counts on cognitive contiguity to pass the emotional attachment down the line (each subgoal being near enough to the next—and actually contiguous in thought—to attach by CE (or by CRI as he would say) the emotion it excites to the goal preceding it. Our explanation on the other hand is that the power to arouse is passed back not by CE but by the ME mechanism. That is to say, if responding to subgoal X has proved to lead to consummatory goal Y, a motivational response of becoming aroused by X is "stamped in" (engrammed) like any other response at X that assists in leading to the goal. The precise mechanism in ME learning that is hypothesized to make this possible we shall soon discuss under the reverberation concept below.

If means-end (ME) learning can account for cognitive learning there is, incidentally, no difficulty in having it account for this arousal learning. It will be understood that the specification equation in its general dynamic form last discussed in (2-6) (p. 98) is carried forward in this book in evolutionary stages. At that point we had not added a systems theory mechanism: the activation of a sentiment through ergic levels represented the ergic arousal as $v_{hjx} \, s_{kx} \, E_x$ where s_{kx} is the *innate* arousal capacity of the situation k. However, in the next (2nd) term in the equation we see that E is aroused via learned elements of the sentiment, M, thus, $v_{hjy} \, s_{ky} \, M_y E_x$. It is this arousal and this only that we are speaking of in learning, for the $v_{hjx} \, s_{kx} \, E_x$ has an s_{kx} that is innately fixed and does not operate through any M. So we can set $v_{hjx} \, s_{kx} \, E_x$ aside from the present learning discussion, except for the v_{hjx}—the investment of this arousal in a given course of action—and the "side effect" in systems theory that $s_{kx} \, E_x$ will add to the ergic arousal in the third term to help activate M's. (That third term, with its due recognition of systems effects, will henceforth be $v_{hjx} \, s_{kx} \, E_x(f_{x1}M_1 + \ldots + f_{xq}M_q)$, where it is understood that s_{kx} is the arousal of E_x through both innate connections and the work of activated sentiments upon it.

The symmetry of the f's in the above expression with the g's, which we have called generators in $s_{ky} \, M_y(g_1E_1 + \ldots + g_pE_p)$ earlier (p. 99) raises an interesting question. The generators are numerical weights representing the engram branches of a sentiment capable of generating *arousal* in particular ergs. (The ergic investment vector for a given sentiment is thus $g_{y1}, g_{y2} \ldots, g_{yp}$). The *convokers*, as we shall call the reciprocal capacities of an erg E_x to call forth and activate the cognitive structures of various sentiments, also constitute a vector (of f's, at the end of the last paragraph). The symbol f, incidentally, has to be used for convokers, instead of c, because c is already in regular use for cognitive concept or image. A mnemonic to recall f is that it *fetches* cognitive content to fit the possibilities of satisfaction of the given ergic tension. Since the *generators*, g's, and the f's, *convokers* are engram links performing the same functional stimulation purpose but in opposite directions the question naturally arises whether they are the same two-way engram associative paths, and, therefore, of the same particular magnitudes, so that they could be respectively rows and columns in the same E x M matrix, regardless of dependent and independent variable status. One can conceive psychological directional forces that might make anything quite so simple unlikely; and with more space the question would deserve a pursuit we cannot take up here.

Meanwhile we shall focus a little more here on the generator relationship, and the distinction between learned M engram links and purely genetic (but cognitive) links to environment involved in generating arousal from primitive, archetypal stimuli in the E terms. Keeping to a single M and E for simplicity an aspect of the model needing to be clear is that the s_{ky} which *activates* the sentiment M_y is quite distinct from the immediately ensuing *generator* action of M_y on the erg E_x in the following contributor term to the behavioral equation:

$$a_{hjk} = v_{hj}s_{ky}\,M_y\,g_{yx}\,E_x$$
$$+ \text{(similar terms and reciprocal terms)} \qquad (4\text{-}3a)$$

From general psychological observation one may anticipate that this is approximate and will need later modifications in terms of (a) possible positive correlation of s_{ky} with the *average* of the g terms, since habitual high arousal and satisfaction will produce high values in both, and, (b) the g values possibly having some specificity to hjk.

In the converse direction, where the ergic tension convokes emotionally suitable cognitive implementers, the ergic tension will have been due, as explicitly brought out elsewhere, to influences other than activated M, so that the circular ME + EM action (as we have frequently described it) is indeed a circle but with an extra channel for an external input. The latter is (a) the innate environmental response, s_{kx}, effect and (b) the appetitive somatic condition. The physiological, appetitive state we have always considered in these equations to be *already* within the drive strength, E. The equivalent of (4-3a) is thus:

$$a_{hjk} = v_{hj}(s_{kx}\,E_x + s_{ky}\,M_y\,E_x)f_{xy}\,M_y$$
$$+ \text{(similar and reciprocal terms)} \qquad (4\text{-}3b)$$

Here both the E_x expression of ergic tension operate to activate the images, memories and directions to a course of action present in M_y. Jung was actually one of the few psychologists to make empirically based suggestions regarding the $s_{ke}E$ action, in his notion of archetypal responsiveness. Without necessarily embracing his associated embellishments we can accept the overlap with our concept *that every E has an "unengrammed engram,"* that is, a set of innate cognitive connections that are not acquired but otherwise have the properties of engrams. These: (a) cause ergic tension to be aroused by situations and stimuli in the "cultural" environment that happen also to be primitive, archetypal stimuli, such as the smell of food to the hunger erg; of excrement to the erg of disgust; a wildly running prey seeking to escape; a clap of thunder; a nude woman to the male sex erg; all diminutive and helpless things to the parental erg, and so on; (b) result in the raised ergic tension projecting itself in generating images, though we have to confess that research has no definite evidence of the nature of such non-acquired imagery.

That M should arouse E, as in (4-3a) has long been explained by *CE* and *ME* learning, for M is a repository of imaginal stimuli and of meaningful perceptions of external stimuli. But the converse relation, in the EM products of (4-3b) and the associated f terms requires fresh consideration. For clarity before proceeding let us remind the reader that we have rejected the reflexological theoretical slip of calling all causes "stimuli." An object seen, or an idea recalled can be a stimulus: but an emotion, a mood, an ergic tension or a hormone is not a stimulus. It is an internal condition which is a *cause*. Causes in psychology could doubtless be advantageously classified into perhaps four or five major varieties, but for our purposes it is enough to classify them into (a) stimuli and (b) other causes of behavior, generally internal tensions. (Roughly these would be respectively terms with h and k in the behavioral equation and all the other terms, such as states, traits and processes.) An ancillary definition would be that stimuli operate through cognitive elements—in perception or memory retrieval—while other causes contributing to behavior come through quite other channels. Or, in physiological terms, stimuli pass through the cortex, whereas other causes, such as ergic tensions, may originate in or act through the hypothalamus.

Now in (4-3b) we are saying that an ergic tension, aroused either by physiological processes registering in the hypothalamus (E_x) or by primitive "accidental" stimuli ($s_{kx}E_x$), is activating memories of stimuli, in various images (and, perhaps, if Jung is right, archetypal images). The awkward question here is "By what learning, *CE* or *ME*, could this have come about?" A rise in sex tension might cause a man to have images of a nude woman (which mechanism we will credit to Jung), and also to recall the telephone number of a rewarding woman. If we followed reflexology in calling the tension a stimulus, not just a cause, we would have to explain the latter as "operant conditioning," using the telephone number having happened by chance before when the "stimulus" was present and being reinforced. We would argue that the linkages we deal with here are more complex in origin than this alone. The telephone number (of this special meaning) probably originally produced some ergic arousal, the satisfaction of which made an $M_y E_x$ connection. We have therefore to posit a two way action—unlike anything supposed in operant *SR*—in the M engrams, though ordinary mean's end learning (operant conditioning) may add later to the effect. This principle of a two-way action (already mooted above) is a momentous issue for research. The proposition is not that such action necessarily occurs in ordinary cognitive-motor SR and SS; but that where a stimulus has become emotion (ergic tension) arousing, the tension will reciprocally become ideation arousing. (It cannot produce the external stimulus, but it can produce the image of it.) The likely corollary of this is that the relation of g and f values we discussed aboved would essentially prevail.

Some other possible implications of the above equations and the original (2-6) (p. 98) need to be briefly tidied. First, it does not follow that the activation of an M term necessarily and invariably produces conscious imagery. Perhaps we may be permitted to follow the clinicians in speaking of "unconscious imagery" which we would here define as directives to specific action without much conscious content. A second question that arises when one looks at the breakdown of an observed, measured ergic tension, in equation (2-13) (into C, H, G_p, etc., origins) discussed in Section 2-5, is whether any analogous breakdown into parts of a sentiment measure is called for. The answer is surely "no," for there are no drive strength and appetitive components except in the E's that M happens to command in its ergic investments. M is simply a cognitive network in being—a unitary sentiment structure acquired in the person's own life time. It becomes activated mainly by an external situation, k, and probably also a focal stimulus, h, as well as by internal ergic tensions, expressed in equation (2-8) as EM. The effective power of the term M is thus a combination of the actual degree of activation M at the time and the original engram strength, M, and can be strictly analogous to the ergic formulation only in

$$M = \text{M} + \text{M} \tag{4-4}$$

This formula is supported by the existence of parallel structural forms found on the one hand in R-technique, on the other in P- and dR-technique factorings of attitude strengths measured in objective devices. An erg reacts as a *whole* to a stimulus for arousal, as shown by the same ergic pattern of attitude reactivities appearing in dR- and P- as in R-technique. This finding has been well replicated (Cattell & Child, 1975) and is supported by other kinds of evidence such as diary associations (Kline & Grindley, 1974, Birkett & Cattell, 1978) and manipulations of stimuli and deprivations (Krug, 1977; DeYoung, Yoon, & Cattell, 1978; Cattell, DeYoung, & Barton, 1978). Thayer (1978) has raised the question of the dimensionality of this arousal. The more precise factoring will, according to the theory in equation (2-13) and the finding of seven primary motivation components, permit arousal (and also activation) to show up to seven "facets" of expression; but this does not deny the ergic unitariness across the content areas of ergic reactivity. The evident is equally clear that a sentiment structure found in *R*-technique preserves much the same form in the excitation pattern when it is activated, though theoretically we should expect the cognitive network of a sentiment to be less sharply bounded, and further research may also show some lag in spread of activation from one stimulated area to another.

The question that needs to be raised here concerns the relation of these factors of specific ergic arousal and specific sentiment activation to *general* states of arousal and activation in the whole personality. The two latter can be readily recognized among the eight "general mood" states (including anxiety, depression, regression, stress, etc.) so far isolated and made available in the eight state battery (Curran & Cattell, 1976). They have been extensively studied as to physiological associations and general expression by Malmo (1959), Duffy (1957), Cattell & Scheier (1961), Nesselroade (1960) and many others. But the evidence that activation and arousal appear as second order general factors among the primaries of, for example, the MAT is not clear, nor are the relations to *U* and *I* components (*U* should be arousal, *I* activation).

On general theoretical indications we nevertheless for the present stand by the hypothesis that general arousal will appear in some degree whenever specific ergic tensions are aroused, and that general activation will similarly be a by-product of most sentiment activations. This might call for the general states to be revealed as second orders among a dozen or more ergic tension primaries but the thin experimental evidence presently available on this matter (see Volume 1, Chapter 5, and Cattell 1957, 1979; Krug & A. K. S. Cattell, 1979) gives no clear conclusion. When these second orders are clarified it will still remain to test their correlations with the Curran (1968) general state measures indicated. Moreover, although the differentiation of the activation from the arousal state is clear in questionnaire data (Curran & Cattell, 1976) it is not so clear in objective tests (except in cortertia; Birkett, 1979).

Certainly such measures as direction of word association, information retrieval, and fluency (as output per minute) rise uniformly for the various attitudes representing a given sentiment, though by what mechanism this functional unity under stimulation is produced—other than by saying it is a cognitive network laid down by *CE* mechanisms—we do not yet know. Our hypothesis in fact is that a sentiment in an unactivated state consists of a reservoir of information connected by a network of engram links, *n*'s, constituting the major engram M. The activation state might be a generalized increase across M of speed and efficiency of retrieval. Grasping at straws of evidence, we are inclined to examine the evidence on fluency in the work of Studman

(1935), Cattell, (1971, p. 108), and especially Johnson, Johnson, and Mark (1951). The latter show clear evidence of a cognitive fluency output being regulated by the magnitude of storage, S, and a rate of retrieval, R, according to a formula:

$$f = S(1 - e^{-Rt})$$ (4-5)

(where f here is fluency output; t is time; and e is exponential e). Here R could conceivably be considered an index of the activation level M, through s_k operating on the M foundation. Fluency is one of the measures (as "availability," Cattell & Child, 1975, Table 1-2) of the α and γ factors which we have already interpreted (Chapter 2) as M activation respectively through ergic tension, E and environment, s_k. Whether these measures and others of α, γ (and of the integrated component) will appear more strongly (than U component) in sentiment *activation* directly measured remains to be seen. If the standing part of M exists purely as storage made, the M factor would show up in the factoring of actual behavior only to the extent that is shown in (2-3).

Basically, then, we posit that the activation of M's is a different kind of excitement—other than ergic—from the arousal in E's, and that distinct manifestations for measurement can be developed for each. Indeed a most promising hypothesis is that E is measured by the U component in motivation, and M by the I component. Under one label or another a number of psychologists have attempted distinction between *activation* and *arousal* principally on a neural basis, crediting arousal to the limbic system and activation to the ascending reticular system. Our distinction may well be consistent with this neural distinction, but operationally it says that the stimulation of a sentiment, which is the stimulation of many cognitive connections into a state of ready retrievability, as shown by word association, and so forth, is *activation*, whereas raising of the total tension level of an erg, as shown by lowered skin resistance, muscle tension, and autonomic phenomena, is *arousal*. The latter is consistent with neural explanation by the limbic system, which concerns stimulation of the hypothalamus by input from the forebrain and its perceptions.

Activation of the ascending reticular system is essential to virtually all heightening of consciousness, and sentiment activation can be considered as a regional emphasis in such cognitive activation. There is scope for fascinating experiment on the differences of the arousal and need components in ergs and the engram and activation components in sentiments. These differences are evident not only in everyman's introspection but already in the work on measured arousal by Barton, Krug, De Young, Kawash, Delhees, and others (see Cattell & Child, 1975).[8]

The formulation we have reached takes the usual position that cognition per se, as in sentiment activation, is not a driving force but that need and arousal are dynamic in quality. However, by the paradox in goal approach behavior discussed above we are compelled finally to hypothesize that need strength and arousal strength have different properties, the former being an unpleasant, restlessness-producing force and the latter a pleasant anticipatory arousal. In normal goal pursuit the latter, whether in innate processes or acquired ones, tends to mount much more rapidly than the need, and thus encourages the course of action to be followed despite higher need strength at later stages. However, as the following section explains, both need and arousal play a positive role in engramming.

4-6. The Model Relating Engramming to Activation-Arousal, Need Strength, Reverberation, and Time

With the above definitions of activation and arousal states in mind, let us turn to the mechanisms whereby learning produces the necessary engramming at subgoals along the way, necessary to reach the goal.

Our theory calls for both CE and ME laws to be involved, and it is hard to say that one is more important than the other, because they work in different areas. We have already contrasted this with an initial glance at the theory of Staats and some other reflexologists (especially in Russia) who would explain the whole chain of acquired motivation by CRI action. If S_1 originally arouses the consummatory excitement, R_1, then S_2, S_3, S_4, and so forth, each stepped back a little in time and place from S_1 and from one another, acquire that power by Pavlovian classical conditioning (CRI or CE). Two objections to this simple application of CRI in isolation have been raised in Chapter 3: The first is that the time limit for engram-producing overlap of S_1 and S_2 in CE or CRI is at most only a few seconds, and that thousands of such conditioning shifts would be necessary for setting up backward-acting long-term subsidiation tracts—say of an hour or so in length—in animals. The second difficulty is not so fundamental but deserves discussion. It brings up the distinction we made earlier between affect (emotion) which is an epiphenomenon to conation (drive). Though we admit that an emotional response can be conditioned by CRI like any other (motor) response it still raises the question whether a need strength can be so conditioned. The need strength is *not* a response to some (external) stimulus, so why should stimulus X appearing when the need strength is high be able effectively on another occasion to create need strength? Although we would still insist that ergic tension arousal is not emotion, and that existing experiments on conditioning of emotion do not directly prove conditioning of arousal, it seems not unreasonable to suppose that if S_1 causes arousal and S_2 occurs with it S_2 will generate arousal, S_1 and S_2 now being linked *by the CE principle.*

The main reason why we prefer the emphasis on the *ME* to the *CE* principle (as used by Skinner and Staats) for the backward passing of arousal properties remains, therefore, the impracticality in animal learning of stretching *CE* links over hour-long goal processes. Where conscious and insightful human learning is concerned this difficulty vanishes, because the cognitive elements in successive sub-goals can be linked by insights and eductions of relations.

But, admitting some *CE* learning in backward transfer of arousal, let us now turn to *ME* learning of arousal and reward at sub-goals, which we hypothesize carries a large part of the learning effects, especially when insight does not exist. The new principle we invoke here to supplement *ME* is called *reverberation fixation.*

In regard to this principle, it is immaterial, as is true of *ME* generally, whether satisfaction follows action by a long or a short interval (except as a matter of degree), with insight (as when a man notices his arthritic pains follow drinking) or without insight (as when a person is unaware that a certain style of participation in conversation increases his popularity or unpopularity). If we went into these secondary conditions we would probably recognize that the varieties of responses that are exposed to learning are either (1) random, or (2) imitative of some seemingly successful response by others, or (3) insightful of relation of action to reward as seen through relation eduction.

But the total circumstances of types of response, and so forth, are not our main concern, which is to present a basic *ME* explanation alternative to *CE* above for (1) the backward (goal-distal) shift of motivating subgoals, and (2) the engramming that takes place in responses leading to satisfaction. The first is a complete alternative to the *CRI* and Hullian explanations, the second, of course, accepts *CR*II (as *ME* learning) as a descriptive law but aims at a deeper explanation.

The approach can best be made through a diagram, as in Figure 4-4. We accept here the rising curve of need level to be the same as in Figure 4-3. But now we add to this curve, E, a curve of arousal, E, which unlike the other two curves is here measured from a baseline provided by E, so that its outline actually represents the level of ergic tension, E + E = E. The situation depicted is one in which we consider some learning of the path already to have taken place, in order to illustrate the acquired subgoal effects. That is to say there will be activation and arousal on top of need strength but the main illustration of new learning would not be affected by this more usual state of affairs.

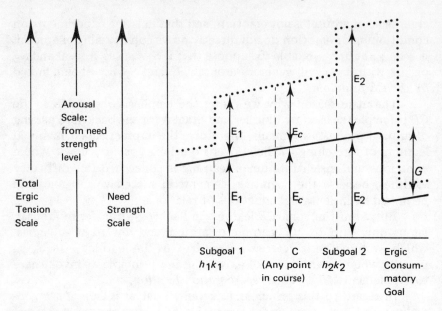

Key

——————— = Need strength curve: Plot of E

·········· = Arousal strength curve: Plot of E

Ergic tension = E = E + E

G = Reward (gratification) by fall of need strength tension at goal, G

Figure 4-4. Hypothetical course of ergic tension—as need strength and arousal—through subgoals to consummatory goal.

Need strength, E, will increase in the usual slow fashion, determined by the "inner clock" throughout the learning path to the goal. At subgoal 1 there is an elevation of arousal, E, due to the organism knowing from past experience that this is on the way to goal success. This will show itself also in ergic tension, E, which is a sum of E and E.

Now let us consider in Figure 4-5 a new stimulus-response event superimposed on the course of events in Figure 4-4. We suppose that at the point S-R a stimulus S causes a response R, which proves relative to past runs, to shorten the distance to the goal. (The horizontal scale would have run longer on the last run.) We now hypothesize that the S-R experience—the cognitive link of perception and response—persists into a *cognitive reverberation*—an "immediate memory" activity—which declines with time, as shown in the curves b_1 and b_2 (as broken lines) for two such events $S_1 R_1$ and $S_2 R_2$.

At the consummatory goal, G, there will be a comparatively

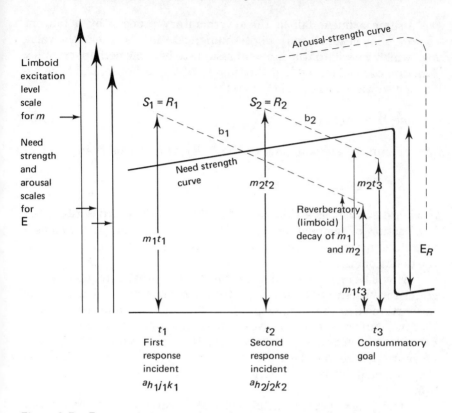

Figure 4-5. Engramming as a product of reverberatory trace and need reduction. Note $hk = S$, and $j = R$, in stimulus-response notation. m_1t_1 and m_2t_2 are the proto-engram activities immediately at the time of response, and m_1t_2 and m_2t_3 at time t_3 of the reward, E_R. The extent of final engramming (first response) is hypothesized to be the product $E_R m_1 t_3$.

sudden reduction in the need tension, E, indicated to be of a magnitude E_R. There is also at that point a decline in arousal, which may, however, take a little longer, as suggested by the curve. The residual of the cognitive excitation m_1 at t_1 has by t_3 fallen to a value $m_1 t_3$. At t_3 we have two main values to consider, the fall in ergic tension (the reward) which is E_R, and the magnitude of the reverberatory, residual action of the event at m_1, which now has a magnitude, $m_1 t_3$. The *reverberatory-fixation* theory is that *the amount of engramming that occurs is a function of the residual reverberatory activity* $m_1 t_3$ *at the time (t_3 here) that the consummatory reward occurs and of the magnitude of the need reduction*, E_R, *which then takes place at consummatory reward*.

Figure 4-5 depicts a second *S-R* event, numbered $S_2 R_2$ to illustrate how the reverberatory reward would differ for a later event. If we assume a linear fall in the reverberatory process, by a tangent (ignore conventional sign) whose numerical value is f, then the value m_1, which we will for the moment assume to be some perhaps complex function of need strength at the time t_1 of the response, will have become at reward a value $m_1 t_3$ such that:

$$m_1 t_3 = m_1 - (t_3 - t_1)f \qquad (4\text{-}6)$$

The amount of engramming, of the $S_1 R_1$ link will be then:

$$\hat{n} = E_R [m_1 - (t_3 - t_1)f] \qquad (4\text{-}7)$$

if we are content as a first guess to take a product as describing the joint action of remnant and reward. (The hat on n, indicating an estimate, distinguishes it from the n in (4-8) which contains the rest of the determiners.)

It will be recognized that this theory does what is required to account for "backward action," and for the engramming being inversely proportioned to the time elapsing between action and reward. However, we must now ask ourselves how satisfactory the evidence is from other sources for such reverberatory action, and secondly we need to be more precise about what goes into the measurement in the need strength (and arousal and activation area we have called m, in Figure 4-5.)

The general psychological evidence for this reverberatory activity can be found principally in some four areas of observation: (1) the varied and widespread evidence of *reminiscence* effects, showing activity going on after the immediate experience. This appears in many human committing to memory experiments; (2) the evidence of loss of expected engramming when severe shock occurs in the assumed reverberatory period; (3) the fact that responses closer to final reward are more quickly learned than those more remote (which may be due to the consolidation on the earlier being upset); (4) the evidence on the structure of memory, which shows, by factoring and other approaches, a *short-distance memory*, operating over some minutes, and a *long-distance memory* capacity—over, say, a year or more. These can stand at very different levels of functioning in different individuals, as factorial evidence shows, and have different properties (see evidence in the realm of individual differences in abilities: Hakstian & Cattell, 1976; Horn, 1972; Jensen, 1973; Kelley, 1954).

The function of short-distance memory has been intensively studied lately (Broadbent, 1967, Baddeley, 1971, 1976; Baddeley and Warrington, 1970, Gruenberg, 1976). It seems to be the retention of stimulus-produced cognitive or stimulus-response cognitive-motor activities persisting in some "reverberatory" form until they are sorted out as either unimportant (in most cases) or worthy of storage in long-distance memory by virtue of significant relation to either the cognitive systems (the M's) or to the dynamic satisfactions (of E's). These sorted links are passed on to become long-distance memory stimulus-response engrams. As few better analogies can be found for this than the medieval conception of a limbo where questionable souls await their transition to heaven or elsewhere, what reverberates might well be designated as *limboid activity* ("-oid" to avoid confusion with the neurological term limbic). This shorter term we have substituted for "reverberatory" in Figure 4-5 and later representations, with the added meaning that some "sorting" and reconnection goes on as well as a mere persistence of memories with steady diminution.

Foreshadowing of a concept of reverberation in models of committing to memory and of conditioning have repeatedly appeared in psychology. In experimental frameworks we have, for example, Walker's (Walker & Tarte, 1963) "action decrement"; and in virtually all recent models of *memorizing* (Broadbent, 1957; Adams, 1967; Wickelgren, 1973) some sort of short-term, temporary, and diminishing activity is envisaged in connection with perception of the sensory input and the sorting of data into what by contrast is designated a permanent storage. There have been studies on the length of this process, on the temporary inhibition of recall that may follow, and on the positive effect of greater excitation both at the occasion of initial engramming and the occasion of recall (see, for example C. F. Johnson, 1970).

We propose to carry the above discussion into a more formal precision of statement as follows, recognizing that the evidence links to the evidence on psychological states (Chapter 5, Volume 1) particularly those on activation and arousal. In the perspective of the whole process of engramming we are hypothesizing the following stages.

1. A sensory perception, occurring in a particular dynamic state of the subject definable by sentiment activation and a particular profile of ergic tensions. In the systems model this is "intake."

2. A persistence, with fading activity level, defined as "reverberation," of the cognitive perception. This activity can be evidenced by persistence, but with fading, of indices of recall, as well as by damage, as if to a process, by ulterior intervening, cognitive distractions. The encoding process in this short-term memory "limbo" is aimed at a search for apperceptive relevance, that is, connections with existing engrams, and consists of a "sorting" leading to connections both with cognitive frameworks and dynamic purposes. This frequently has been labeled the *consolidation* phase, but *reverberatory* is better because

consolidation is only one aspect of what happens. We have distinguished in measurable psychological states between activation, essentially cognitive, and arousal, which is entirely ergic. Reverberation is largely an activation phenomenon, though there is some suggestion of arousal effects too, as shown by relations of catecholamines to short-term memory.

3. A committing to storage, which follows in the last phases of the sorting process. The extent of this committing to storage—engramming—is dynamically determined. To a minor degree it is determined by the "interest" associations located in the sorting. It takes place to a major degree, however, if some ergic reward occurs while the perception and "operant" response to it are still in reverberatory cognitive activity. These three steps are the essence of our explanation of reward (means-end) learning, and are studied per se in equation (4-7) and what follows below.

4. There follows the phase of enduring storage, concerning the nature of which, as a process, little is yet known. There are indications of physiological effects upon it, for example, from brain damage, drugs, alcohol, and of the need of some persistence of dynamic relevance—that is, of continuing reward consequent on use of the engrams—to maintain the engrams. However, the separation of effects on final recall of the different phases has required such rarely achieved experimental control that there is uncertainty, for example, whether differences result entirely from committing, (3), and retrieval, (5) differences, or whether storage itself, (4), can be considered a continuing process subject to certain dynamic and physiological conditions.

5. Retrieval. The phenomena here range from deliberate, oriented retrieval, as in human memory experiments with given referents for the retrieval, (Adams, 1967) to animal experiments, when we simply ask whether some response appears to a given stimulus. Our model, expressed in our general equations, is that likelihood of retrieval is a function of *both* the *activation* of the M terms i.e. of M terms, and their separate elements, that is, of the relevant stimulus formerly associated with the cognitive element to be retrieved, and of the *arousal* of the ergic tension in connection with which the stimulus-response link was originally engrammed. Setting aside for a moment the qualitative, profile-indicated specificity of arousal, we find some evidence for the hypothesis that high arousal tends toward preferential retrieval of relatively easily available material (as judged by general order of appearance in other situations). Eysenck brings in individual difference evidence, moreover, suggesting extraverts use a wider "search" than inviants in retrieval processes. This exvia-invia difference was found also by the present writer (1933) in substantial correlations of total fluency with the surgency primary (in exvia) and in evidence of less

discriminating associations (Hundleby, Pawlik, & Cattell, 1965). However, the more important hypothesis here is that the effectiveness of retrieval of a given response (or idea) is a function, beyond the cognitive connections, of the similarity coefficient between the ergic tension profile (the vector of E values) at recall and that at the time of committing to storage. (See Bower, Monteiro, & Gilligan, 1978.)

The systems theory model of personality and learning in Chapter 5 will be seen to be consistent with, and a natural development of, the above model.

Let us consider next the question whether the consummatory reward is to be measured by reduction in need strength, E_R, alone or also by reduction in that ergic arousal produced by the stimulation of particular subgoals, en route, and expressed as s_{km} ME = E. In short is the E_R we enter in equation (4-7) to be E or E + E? There seem to be no guidelines at the moment either in everyday observation or animal learning to answer this. In a "logical" way one might argue that since E, arousal, is pleasurable and E, need strength, is not, it is only reduction of the latter that will have the potency to produce engramming. Actually we have not finished with the relations of E and E, for although arousal, E, is excitingly pleasant when E is large, it become unpleasant when E is small or zero, as when a hostess requires a man to eat who has just had a meal. Since E is thus a function of E as well as of s_k, as our equations indicate, the existence of a correlation of engramming with the level of E before consumption will in general produce a necessary correlation also with E, even though E should have no role in engramming.

As ongoing motivation component research gains still clearer separation operationally of E and E, (that is, of ME, from E) the question can be solved by partialling out E from the E correlation. In this obscurity our guess is that arousal *does* have an affect on engramming if only because it involves cognitive activation, M, and we would assign it a weight in any comprehensive model in equation form, leaving it to be reduced to zero if the data so indicates.

The possibility exists also of other influences needing to be respected in a comprehensive hypothesis. For example, we should consider also whether the limboid activity is also a function of some cognitive intensity of the stimulus S. At present it must be purely on a speculative theoretical basis, however, that we introduce, beyond need strength, the initial intensity of this cognitive activity, by adding a function of the cognitive stimulus intensity and of the arousal level.

The terms in equation (4-7) are those concerned with the fate of a particular S-R bond in regard to its engramming. The learning that goes on in any natural situation, however, needs to account for the general shortening of time and action in reaching the goal, by considering what happens to all the kinds of responses that, in trial and error, spread themselves over the subgoal path to the end goal, in a series of encounters of the individual with the overall situation. Obviously if some marked or appreciable learning effect (reinforcement) appeared for those less essential behaviors that preceded reward just once or twice in several runs, a tremendous variety of behaviors would tend to be reinstated. In the examination of frequencies from a statistical standpoint we would expect reinforcement to occur according to the degree of improbability of the actually occurring degree of (inward or external) repetition or combination. It is not our concern here to look into the technicalities of this aspect, but the general logic was well stated long ago by Guthrie (1952) and has been brought to refined formulation by Estes, Burke, and Atkinson (1957) and others.

Selective action then, must favor those stimulus-response connections that precede ultimate success, operate neutrally on those that can be present or absent with indifference to the outcome, and negatively on those that obstruct. We may suppose, as in a series of stimuli S_1, S_2, S_3, and so forth, to which the respective responses R_1, R_2, R_3, and so forth, are made, that there is some short persistence or trace of R_1 being made to S_1; R_2 to S_2; and so on. Although both early and late responses in the series might be equally necessary to achieve an end goal, the fact that reward comes only at the end goal, would cause the expected learning to be less on the earlier traces.

That trial and error learning is a relatively slow procedure even in a large-brained species is not surprising when one reflects on this need to get some differential reward between incidental and necessary behaviors, and the mishaps and irregularities which the environment can present. Sometimes the much needed response R_2 is given prematurely to S_1; sometimes, after S_1-R_1 begins to form, S_1 itself may not appear in the environment for a number of runs; and in any case the effective R_1, R_6, and R_8 (say) *combination* that brings success may have scattered within it responses R_2, R_3, R_4, and so forth, which may be substitute alternatives for success in some circumstances. Here we encounter also the complication that the "success" of a response cannot be considered as an atomistic element but is an effect of its pattern position in relation to others. It is not surprising that the average golfer seeks with exasperation for a conscious understanding of the particular stimulus-response combination that occurred when he pulled off an unusually fine drive, so conspicuously absent in other combinations! The thorough analysis of the basic propositions in probabilities we can leave to the works of Estes, Burke, and Atkinson (1957) and many other eminent workers in this field. Out of this complex action the main principle still emerges that the connection that is most *regularly* followed by the reward of success, among many that are not, tends to become engrammed.

To record this aspect, equation (4-7) needs to be supplemented by a term N for the number of repetitions of the run, the relation to which we will take to be linear over the main range as follows:

$$n_N = N(\mathrm{E}_R + d_r\mathrm{E}_R)[\mathrm{E}_1 + d_r s_{k1}\mathrm{M}_1\mathrm{E}_1 + d_m s_{k1}\mathrm{M}_1 - (t_2 - t_1)f]$$
$$(4\text{-}8)$$

where the first bracket is the reward and the second the amount of reverberation of the $S_1 R_1$ remaining at consummation. The reverberation is here counted *both ergic and cognitive*, but EM is not included and M subsumes m_1 in equation (4-6) and Figure 4-5. The f is a tangent as in (4-7), the d's are weights for arousal relative to need strength, and the M is the sentiment to which the n_N engram is adding itself. Incidentally, the change in n will appear operationally also as a change in the five vectors of the structural learning equation (M, p, r, i, and s), principally centered on the M term. And, in more complete views below, the full specification equation will operate in defining the gain n_N, with (4-8) adding the reinforcement from means-end reward that has not previously appeared in the specification.

4-7. Means-end and Coexcitation Learning in the Perspective of the General Specification Equation

Besides the question of backward referral of arousal there remains a miscellany of developments from the *reverberation-fixation* theory to be brought to some degree of completion in this section. A particularly important one is the joining of the ordinary specification equation with the reward equation (4-8) just analyzed; another is the sorting out of the action of EM and ME terms, and another concerns the combination of the n term with dynamic terms in retrieval, that is the reinstatement of courses of action (responses).

It will be noted that in terms of the new specification equation after learning there are changes (if we revert for a moment to the simpler *vs* representation of indices) in both the v's and the s's (besides, of course, the T's). After learning, the behavior at t_1 in Figure 4-5, in response to the global situation $h_1 k_1$ is altered in two respects: (1) the situation k_1 has come to arouse the ergic tension to a new level, via s_{km}ME, in which both s_{km} and M will have altered, and (2) the stimulus h_1 has acquired a new power of evoking the response j even in relation to an unchanging ergic tension. We have regarded both elements in this dual change—the raised response strength and the raised arousal—as contained in the engram increment n in equation (4-7). One could pursue the notion of a link, n_h, to the stimulus h, being separated from a link, n_k, to the ambient situation, k, though at this time we do not propose to do so and we recognize that both are in the built-on change in the engram structure of some sentiment, M. It should perhaps be pointed out here, however, regarding the v and s relation, that later (p. 332) we are going to argue that when the learning is at a subgoal node there are usually several h's waiting to stimulate further action on reaching the ambient situation, k. Assuming sometimes one and sometimes another is salient this would lead to a positive correlation of s with the sum of the v's. In the present context where we talk of *one* ambient situation and *one* ensuing behavior the extent to which the subject learns to be aroused by the situation k_1 will be an immediate function of the success with which the course of action, j_1, is repeatedly followed. The behavioral indices s and v would then be highly correlated (whether we take correlations within a person in P-technique or across persons in R-technique). For the present, therefore, we seem to lose little analytical value in considering n to define what happens both to v and s values.

Parenthetically we should remind the reader that in our concentration on a single E and M we have not lost sight of the fact that in any natural learning situation, and especially a human cultural one, the EM of equation (2-6) (p. 98) term will be $E(f_{ke1}M_1 + \ldots + f_{kep}M_q)$ and the ME term $M(g_{mk1}E_1 + \ldots + g_{kmq}E_p)$, i.e., each will affect all of the other series. This means, of course, that the reward by reduction of ergic tension for any attitude action leading to reward, will be specific to the particular independent E terms and the particular E terms weighted by g's in whatever sentiments are involved in the learning equation. This specificity of ergic reward is one of the several vital differences of structured learning from classical learning theory in its operant formulation. *Some* attention has occasionally been given in reflexology (see, for example, Glickman & Schiff, 1967; Rohner, 1949; Kimble, 1967; and Zeaman & Wegner, 1954) to the nature of drive reduction; but the model above is more precise and comprehensive on that issue. (Moreover, as pointed out elsewhere, the multivariate experimentalist would object to the bi-variate practice—Kimble 1951, Yamaguchi, 1951—of measuring ergic tension by a single need strength variable, in the light of Haverlands's finding on hunger, 1954.) The implication of using the term *means-end* (*ME*) learning, instead of *operant conditioning* (*CR*II), is that these further developments of reward into a vector of particular ergic satisfaction objectively measured can then be pursued.

The above discussion of *ME* learning must not obscure the fact that in the full learning equation *CE* learning also plays its part, and that it does so in alternations with *ME* learning. The work of Staats (1975), Staats & Warren (1974), Staats, Heard & Finley (1962), and learning theorists who have recently become interested in the cognitive, *CE*, elements in dynamic learning, enlarges on this action of symbols, words, and eduction of relations (not usually formulated as such) in forming cognitive networks to be increasingly established later by ergic reward (*ME* action).

Before incorporating *CE* along with *ME* action in the learning equation let us glance back to get perspective by remembering that ability, *A*, and temperament, *P* terms must go along with the reward term in the general learning specification equation, as in (4-9) below. This is another vital difference of structured learning from reflexology: that it brings the parameters of the organism into the prediction of learning gain. That the latter play a very prominent part in human learning is shown by Cattell & Butcher (1968) being able to predict at least two thirds of the variance in school learning without introducing any term for reward as such at all! However, it would make a better model (and probably prediction) to introduce interactions of reward with abilities, in particular. (The general finding is that reward motivation changes performance from *skills* considerably but *intelligence* test performances only trivially.) But at this stage a simple additive treatment is probably enough to guide research. One thus reaches:

$$n = \Sigma v_a s_a A + \Sigma v_p s_p P + v_d s_d D + (\mathrm{E}_R + d_r \mathrm{E}_R)$$
$$\times \ [\mathrm{E}_1 + d_r s_{k1} \mathrm{ME}_1 + d_m s_{k1} \mathrm{M}_1 - (t_2 - t_1)f] \tag{4-9}$$

(*i*'s omitted: *A* = ability factors; *P*'s = general personality.) The *D*'s (dynamic traits) here imply that the absolute level of various ergs and sentiments, as well as their changes in the reward term, may enter into the determining of the amount of engramming, though no particular hypothesis on parameters is proposed here.

Because the whole concentration here has been on the mechanism of the *ME* principle the role of *CE* has necessarily stayed in the background. But the strength of the bond *n* formed between the cognitive experience in m_1 at t_1 and the cognitive experience of reaching the reward at the goal *G* which we may call m_g, will further strengthen by contiguity to trace m_1 the response connection at t_1. This $m_1 m_g$ connection may have insightful contributions or be carried back by successive *CRI* actions, but will depend in the last resort on *CE* action, and the main parameter we need to put into it as far as we presently know is *N*, the number of times it has been reinstated. Thus the complete learning statement, granted we telescope all A's, P's and T's simply into T's, should be:

$$n = N\Sigma v_t s_t T + N(\mathrm{E}_R + d\mathrm{E}_R)[\mathrm{E}_1 + d_r s_{k1} \mathrm{M}_1 \mathrm{E}_1 + d_m s_{k1} \mathrm{M}_1 - (t_2 - t_1)f] + Ncm_1 m_g$$

$$(4\text{-}10)$$

where $m_1 m_g$ is the strength of occurrence of *coexcitation* of m_1 and the goal recognition, m_g, and c is a coefficient for other *CE* parameters.

The actual change in behavioral performance, that is, the observed difference between the original performance and that at recall, $(a_{hijkt2} - a_{hijkt1})$ through learning requires that the improved performance, a_{hijkt2}, be predicted from the role of dynamic and other traits at the time of retrieval as well as n. If n concerned only one particular sentiment we should have:

$$a_{hijkt2} = \Sigma vsA + \Sigma vsP + \Sigma vsE + \Sigma vs(\mathrm{M} + n) \qquad (4\text{-}11)$$

where the various subscripts on A, P, E, M, and n are omitted.

Finally, these equations should not be left without reference to specific factors which, as explained earlier, have been omitted from the majority of equations in this book as a statistical patch generally irrelevant. To suppose that there are no important small fragmentary structures such as might appear as lower order factors and specifics is probably correct for most abilities, like intelligence, or personality traits, like exvia, but since we have recognized that sentiments are hierarchies, having partially independent m's within them, and splintering finally into specific reflex conditionings and momentary mental sets, the latter will act as primary *factor* specifics not *variable* specifics in any dynamic specification equation. Incidentally one can reasonably doubt that E's have specifics. Still more can one doubt that they have personal *innate* uniquenesses of pattern. The conative unity of a drive would seem to preclude bits of autonomous specific behaviors unrelated in strength to the strength of the main erg, though the question must be answered by experiment with objective MAT measures. Unique traits are in general a reflection of the boundless variability of individual histories. The history of a species and a race averages all that, and, except for minor gene reshufflings, hunger, thirst, pugnacity, fear, and so forth, are likely to be felt and acted upon in much the same way by all members of a species. It is perhaps the tidying only of an academic matter, but we would shape the general behavioral specification equation with A, P, E, and M common traits but only M_j and perhaps A_j and P_j entering as specifics.

4-8. The Problem of Retrieval and Reinstatement of Learned Behavior

A learning theory is not complete without concern with what happens to an engram after it is formed and what influences enter its retrieval into action to engender responses. We can be certain that an engram does not remain *precisely* unchanging in storage, but is subject to change with, for example, the physiological history of the individual, as in aging. It is evident also that its preservation is enhanced by inter-current use, continuing the action of the *CE* principle that begot it in the first place. More obscure is the evidence of the effect on retention of dynamic influences after committing to memory. Obviously the *ME* law continues to operate insofar as actual use is made of the engram. But is it possible that retention itself is sustained by the engram being part of a persisting dynamic system even though that system does not happen to *use* the engram except very rarely?

Despite the light the computer model has thrown on sorting in the short-distance limboid memorizing phase, on retention, and on retrieval, it has perhaps blinded us, by its very neatness, to the fact that engrams are apparently not stored as completely unchanging entities, independent of upkeep, like points on a magnetic drum (O'Kelly & Heyer, 1951; Weiner, 1966). However, at present the nature of such effects, though suspected, is still in darkness, and as a first approximation we must proceed with the assumption that once an engram is in long-term memory storage it remains essentially intact.

So far we may follow a computer-like model, but when it comes to retrieval the human mind almost certainly diverges from the pro-cedure by which a programmed instruction goes to a "location." Indeed, psychology has been quite vague about the beginnings of re-trieval, at least in relation to the usual ongoing dynamic processes of everyday life. Retrieval from such a situation is surely quite different from that where the subject is instructed by the experimenter to re-call or recognize something like a cognitive presentation formally given. In fact the great bulk of research on memory and retrieval has pro-ceeded with the subject in a cage of controls and in isolation from the usual flow of action. In the everyday life action we deal with a flow which requires a systems theory model. And here we are perhaps surprised to find that "What will be retrieved?" is virtually synony-mous with "What will the person do next?" Indeed, not only does the problem of retrieval become synonymous with that of "which impulse to action shall next appear?" but it ramifies into that decision theory we have already begun to study and shall study again under the ego and systems theory.

Keeping to a_{hjk}, that is speaking in general and leaving individual values implicit for simplification of formulae, any person goes through the day on a chain course of action representable as:

$$a_{h_1 j_1 k_1} \rightarrow a_{h_1 j_1 k_2} \rightarrow a_{h_2 j_2 k_2} \rightarrow a_{h_3 j_3 k_3} \rightarrow \qquad (4\text{-}12)$$

That is to say he goes through a series of changing combinations of h's, j's, and k's. (Usually a given focal stimulus will go with a particular j, but the force of the j action will depend on the ambient situation k). As we shall see in studying the unfolding of a sentiment process the sequence is by no means a chance one. It usually follows a course followed before, and it has environmental expectations in it that are generally but not invariably met.

Let us take the simple instance of a man who, leaving his office and finding himself without cash, decides to stop at the bank, on his way to lunch at his favorite restaurant. A mental set, such as gives directions and continuity with suitably varied adaptation to circumstances is either an activated sentiment or an aroused erg, or both. In this case we consider first the sentiment which has to do with one's bank account. The first situation, k_1, is that of finding himself without cash, the natural link here is to the bank sentiment, which, activated, deals with questions of whether he has a balance, whether the bank will be open, and so on. It is possible he is surprised by the bank being closed, and in that case a new k arises activating new sentiments ("I'll call on a friend"). But, if not, the situation of being in the bank maintains appropriate sentiment activation to support and reinforce the responses to particular focal stimuli, such as cashier and checkbook. Incidentally this and other examples bring out what has been said before about the ambient situation concept: that it in part covers an external situation broader and more lasting than the various focal stimuli that appear within it, and in part certain reverberating cognitive elements from physical situations immediately before. In short it is experienced as a perception of global relations of the situation, the relations in which are both physical and temporal.

What now determines the appearance of the next a_{hjk} in the chain for this man? He has been getting all the while more hungry, so the E term, as need strength, has, independently of the external situations, hk, begun to throw more weight in the specification equation. The sight of the familiar restaurant down the street has activated now a sentiment about the restaurant which, by the term s_{km}ME has in turn raised the arousal level of E, hunger. Meanwhile, perhaps some more primitive, innate stimulus, such as the smell of fruit, has raised the ergic tension of E also, through s_{ke}E. The activation of the sentiment to the bank has now receded and is forgotten, and the big values in the equation are the v's and s's for the restaurant sentiment and the hunger erg, which now bring out the action of a different j—getting a table in the restaurant—from the previous series of j's.

In the course of this action the individual has "retrieved" from an engram store, the sentiments and ergic connections as surely as he retrieves the missing syllable in a purely cognitive experiment with paired nonsense syllables. The latter, though usually described in terms of a single engram link, involves the same total specification equation as here, though admittedly the role in that controlled situation of the various major ergs and sentiments—other than the self-sentiment which keeps the subject acting responsibly in the chair—is small. But it is this retrieval—which we recognize in its product as sentiment activation and ergic arousal—which decides the turning of the corner for the next course of action.

If we ask, therefore, what shifts to make the responses a_{h1j1k1}, a_{h2j2k2}, a_{h3j3k3}, and so on, different in the above chain the answer is:

1. Changes in h's, which are encountered as the action proceeds. These cause changes, through v's, either in the nature or the magnitude of the j behaviors.

2. Changes in k's, which are the keys deciding which M's and E's shall become excited and prominent in the specification.

3. Purely internal changes in the E's through appetitive effects, which, through the s_{ke}EM term partly decide also which M's shall be activated. These three influences, incidentally, are not only responsible for everyday life dynamic action, but also, though with different emphasis, for purely cognitive recall, as mentioned above in connection with laboratory experiment. The M terms—s_{km}M—would then be prominent, and the specifics at the bottom of the M hierarchy most of all.

It may reasonably be objected to the adequacy of the above three determiners of a_{hijk} sequences that they leave out the person himself! Supposing he finds the bank closed and his friend out. Does he quietly go back to face his afternoon's work on an empty stomach, or does he curse and swear, or does he steal a sandwich from some unwatched counter? What we have left out is the controlling triumvirate of ego, super ego and self sentiment. The operation of this controlling system upon the specification equation is still to be studied, but tentatively we have considered it (p. 131) as a higher order factor system which throws its weight, in the interest of more long term satisfaction, according to how it sees the behavioral indices (b's = v's and s's) tending to act on the rest of the sentiments and the ergs. Thus we must add that the behavioral shifts above are additionally determined by:

4. A manipulation of excitation levels of sentiments and ergs by the long term control system, which handles such things as curbing the momentum of excitations carried inappropriately into new situations, and the following of an a_{hjk} that would lead to disastrous long-term loss, as proven by post experience or present insight.

Thus in a broad view, the "retrievals" that determine total behavior direction and change of direction are partly externally determined, by h and k changes and partly internally by appetitive need changes and by re-adjustments of M and E excitations brought about by the controlling ego.

As a lemma on the above proposition it follows that the recall of an act or cognitive element will be best when the h and k of the external situation are creating v and s values closest to those at the time of learning, since not only the reward but the trait constellation at the time enters into the learning. This should hold, however, also for the internal situation—the pattern of ergic tension—since these additionally affect the activation of M's in the EM terms. Except for the work of Hernandez-Peon (1966) and Bower et al. (1978) there seems little work on the effect upon recall of the similarity of emotional and dynamic state at committing to memory and at recall. With provision of such objective motivation-strength measures at the MAT, directed to 10 unitary-factor dynamic traits, more systematic and precise experiment should now be possible on this lemma that dynamic similarity of mood state at committing to memory and at recall is a positive influence in recall.

Here we are encountering one more inference from the theoretical model of *engram-erg* (ME) and *erg-engram* (EM) interaction that can now be tested. Among the implications regarding the connection of an M to several E's and of an E to several M's in these middle terms is that which states that a cognitive or motor-action tool developed for one purpose can—with certain reductions of accessibility—be utilized by another. The added hypothesis of additional effectiveness of retrieval through similarity of *pattern* we can for future reference describe as the *dynamic isomorphism* principle of engram-forming and engram-retrieving specification equations.

4-9. Summary

1. Further conceptual clarification is made of the coexcitation or fusion principle, especially to avoid its casual identification with the CRI paradigm in which coexcitation is only *one* of two principles in-

volved. Most everyday-life learning is mixed coexcitation and instrumental (means-end) action, but in the limiting "pure coexcitation" case a cognitive link is formed between time-contiguous cognitive experiences, c_a and c_b, which may or may not be due to external stimuli S_a and S_b. The CRI paradigm is considered the coexcitation linking of c_a with a cognitive c_b, which already possesses (innately or by learning) a reward-generated connection with an R. The discharge of the conditioned stimulus *excitation* through the existing R is itself considered to have reward properties. It is assumed that the paucity of evidence for c_a-c_b (internal ideas) learning by the fusion law arises from insufficient experimental ingenuity in researching on behavioral-physiological manifestations for the presence and intensity of a conscious, *subjective* "idea."

2.   In the domain mainly of animal experiment a substantial body of precise evidence has been built around CRII, means-end (ME) learning. As far as possible "in a nutshell," the chief empirical laws reached are here summarized and listed as a basis for integration with structured learning theory. They include findings on the influence of reward magnitude, elapsed time to reward, and frequency of the learning behavior, in successive runs. These CRII findings extend themselves readily enough to the ME reformulations of CRII reached here. The ME principle absorbs for example, spacing, spontaneous recovery, generalization, partial reinforcement, latent inhibition, and higher-order conditioning.

3.   It is pointed out that a number of empirical findings in the framework of reflexological learning require, if kept in terms only of peripheral elements (S and R), some unduly elaborate subtheories to fit them into that rigidly maintained classical framework. This fact, and the fact that research in recent years in the reflex framework has tended to gravitate into limited local issues, suggests, from the perspective of scientific history, that the field is ripe for radical restructuring, transcending the initial reflexological principles. This is what structured learning theory offers.

Instances of more parsimonious interpretation by structured learning theory, availing itself of ability to recognize and measure specific ergic tensions directed to goals, are found in the simplification of "avoidance (aversive stimuli) learning," "approach-withdrawal conceptions," "punishment," "secondary drives," "drive shift" and "reward shift" effects—in all of which reflexology has to bring in what may be unnecessary "extra wheels." Punishment, for example, except for its purely social (group) connotations, is adequately subsumed uniformly under *ergic deprivation*—the opposite of satisfaction—for all ergs. Along with superfluities in traditional learning theory it evidences also gaps. A conspicuous hiatus is the absence of an acceptable structural model distinguishing *performance* gain from *learning*, which latter is handled in structured learning by the engram concept of learning. Another large gap in reflexological theory is its vagueness about what the specific drives are, and lack of technical development that would estimate the validity of various measures for their strengths. Another concerns the lack of systematic studies of the validity and structure of diverse measures of learning gain itself. The work of Anderson, Haverland, the present writer, Royce, and Dielman, on factoring the learning behavior of the rat, seems to have received no integration into reflexological concepts, where the motivation component and dynamic-structure findings could in fact provide substantial developments in the above areas.

4.   The development here leads to two basic principles, coexcitation, *CE* (*SS*) and means-ends, *ME* (*CR*II), learning. It then goes further, however, to recognize a third structural learning principle, *integration learning*, *N*. Though founded on *CE* and *ME* principles, in the sense of requiring *CE* and *ME* mechanisms for its own action, it seems to involve a new "emergent" principle. Integration learning works through (a) trial and error discovery of a confluent path and (b) the exercise of inhibition to build up a higher hierarchy of controlling habits. Integration learning has been more studied in ethology and personality-clinical fields, but *some* reflexological experiment has turned to it, though in a framework of peripheral terms that reduces the possibility of a more fruitful and effective theoretical model. An operational basis for recognizing what forms of integration learning may exist, and for scoring integration gain, is provided by the models of conflict measurement in the *dynamic calculus*. Trial and error both in response directions, as in *ME* (*CR*II), and in forms of inhibition (new to the *N* mechanism), are needed in the new integrative solutions. Further analysis of *N* is taken up in Section 5-2.

5.   A distinction is made between arousal, which occurs in ergs, and activation, which occurs in cognitive sentiment systems. Except for innate connection already tying certain stimulus situation to ergs, activation of learned sentiments is the source of arousal, so activation-arousal may *sometimes* parsimoniously be considered as a single phenomenon. However, their distinction as *general* states in *P*- and *dR*-analyses of questionnaires is very clear. (Incidentally the arousal pattern is so similar to extraversion as to suggest half the variance in alleged *trait* exvia could be state level of arousal.) The tie up of the general measures with the nature of excitation measures of individual ergs and sentiments (possibly as *U* and *I* components) is however not yet adequate.

6.   The concept of drive reduction as reward is probably most clear in such reflexological writers as Hull. If we equate the popular use of

drive strength with ergic tension, however, the concept has for some time been successfully hiding a paradox, namely, that in pursuing a goal an animal is moving *toward* less pleasant states of higher tension. Even admitting that part of this need increment is unavoidably tied up with passage of time, rather than goal approach, this has difficulties. The proposed solution is to recognize a qualitative difference between need strength and the arousal state (though they add together to ergic tension). *Need-strength*, as a component, then rises with physiological time, and arousal derives from the former through stimulation by (usually previously learned) goal-path subgoals. The former is uncomfortable, but so long as it is exceeded by the magnitude of the pleasant arousal, movement to the goal continues.

Many proposals have been made to account for the action of intermediate subgoals, as stimulus situations, in their being able to acquire capacity to reward (or, at any rate to reinforce) learning. Mostly the models have been in terms of passing back from the consummatory goal certain motor or sensory cognitive elements, the transfer commonly being assumed to arise by *CRI* conditioning. It is supposed here that the s_k modulating power of a subgoal, which gives it arousal properties, is acquired, like the v determining the strength of response tendency, by a principle of *reverberation-reward* described below, though it may be further transferred to other, earlier subgoals by insightful connection, especially in humans, thereby, permitting *CE* to operate. This modulating power, s_k, (along with changes in v, that is, p, r, and i indices) thus appears in any subgoal k, the attainment of and response to which have proved in the past to increase the probability of ultimate consummatory satisfaction.

7.   Any psychological event, such as an *S-R* experience, continues after the event to have some internal activity as a diminishing reverberatory activity, on the same time scale as—and appearing as part of the functioning of—short-distance memory. Short-distance reverberatory memory functions as a limbo for recent experiences in which sorting can occur. Its function is to reject irrelevant data and attach relevant and rewarded stimuli and response connections, as new engram extensions, to existing engrams such as sentiments.

It is hypothesized that the magnitude of the engramming of such a link is a function of (a) the magnitude of the residual reverberatory "limboid activity" at the time of reaching the consummatory goal, and (b) the magnitude of the need-strength reduction (reward) occurring at the goal. There are at least four sources of evidence (not repeated here) pointing to the existence of the reverberatory "limboid" activity after a psychological experience—that is, for $[m_1 - (t_2 - t_1)f]$ as in equation (4-7) or in the cognitive-dynamic expansion $[E_1 + d_r s_{k1m} M_1 E_1 + d_m s_{k1m} M_1 - (t_2 - t_1)f]$ in (4-8).

8. The learning specification equation parallels the ordinary behavioral equation, since the absolute levels of various traits are well known to determine the amount an individual learns, but it contains an extra part—that setting out the reward effect (*ME* learning) and the coexcitation effect (*CE* learning). This addition is written:

$$n = N[m_1 - (t_2 - t_1)f]\, \mathrm{E}_R + Nc_{m_1}\cdot m_g \qquad (4\text{-}13)$$

where m_1 is the cognitive experience at t_1, m_g is that at the goal and c is value for the degree of their cognitive connection (insightful or by *CE*).

Because there is no adequate experiment concerning whether the arousal part of the ergic tension amalgam and, the activation part of the sentiment have the same loadings on behavior—indeed, in *E* we definitely suppose that E, need strength, and ᴇ, arousal, behave differently—equation (4-8) presently directing research designs should keep different weights for them (by d's). This might lead to as many as 10 terms (with the specific *m*, and *its* modulation) covering total *E* and *M* effects in the specification equations. There are obviously problems in reconciling this with factor-analytic results, which at present produce only two series of factors, but more sophisticated factoring might, with ancillary experiments, fit this more complex model. In the learning equation also we do not know whether the amount of reduction of arousal and of need strength are equally potent in learning reward, so we have kept to a scaling weight, d, for arousal, ᴇ.

9. The specification equation for learning recognizes both *CE* and *ME* principles operating interactively, the latter often following and strengthening the bonds of the former. The results are shown, for the former, more in M terms and the *p*, *r*, and *i* behavioral indices; and, for the latter, more in *s* and *i* indices. Issues to which the theory points in research concern two questions: (a) Although reverberation-fixation accounts for both *S-R* connections (*n*'s and additions to M's in the engram notation) and the generation of arousal connections, *s*'s, to what extent are the formulae and weights different? (b) Our equation (4-10) has professed open-mindedly to assume that the absolute level of need, E, sentiment strength, M, activation, ᴍ, and arousal, ᴇ (wrapped together in T), play a systematic role in the learning equation, along with the reward and reverberation residual. Research needs next to ask what weights or exponentials indicate their relative roles.

10. Although the role of insight and conscious connection of events (including deliberate imitation) play a totally greater role in human learning than the trial-and-error learning of lower animals, this does not alter the dependence on the underlying *CE* and *ME* principles. The greater cognitive activity merely magnifies or speeds up their

action; an insightful cognitive connection has to depend on *CE* to engram it and on *ME* to consolidate it.

Nevertheless, more motor and social learning than is commonly admitted proceeds in humans by trial and error, actual or in imagination. Consequently some study must be given to the origins of what reflexology has called "random" or, rather, "endogenous" responses, which become available for reinforcement in trial-and-error *ME* learning. Endogenous carries the implication (a) that weak innate connections to certain stimuli in the culture that resemble primitive, archaically potent stimuli are partly responsible, and that, for the rest, (b) sheer ergic tension can generate responses to trivially small and indefinite stimuli.

11. The reverberatory-fixation principle has been stated in which the degree of engramming is multiplied simply by an *N* for frequency of repetition. However, for the ultimate quantification of the development of an engram, reference to the frequency spacing, regularity, and so forth of rewarding experiences will be necessary. Here, in the first place, we are indebted to Estes, Atkinson, and others, showing that in repeated runs those *S-R* links only followed by reward with "chance frequency" fade out in comparison with those consistently followed by reward. The gain, moreover, can be most consistent only when all links in the total, environmentally required *pattern* occur together. Other principles immediately applicable to *ME* learning repetition, of various kinds, are found in the extensive *CR*II experimentation. However, the plethora of animal-learning experiments must not cause us to overlook that in human learning attempted insightful connections, or internal "mental experiments" with imagery, can lead to what is virtually "one-trial learning." The reward principle, however, as stated in (10) above, remains the same no matter what the cognitive machinery—insightful or blind.

12. After accounting for engram formation by the above formulations it is necessary to ask (a) how engrams persist, and (b) what conditions govern retrieval. We argue here that psychological indications show the computer model somewhat misleading on (a) for it has no need for an engram (either a *c-c* or a *c-R* form of *n*) to require maintenance by exercise or by the continued existence of subsidiation to ultimate ergic satisfaction. These needs and their physiological bases are, it is true, not yet clarified for neural action, but it behooves us not to assume the mechanical perfection and immutability of storage present in the computer.

13. Learning has to concern itself with committing to memory, storage and retrieval. Their joint effects are commonly hidden in simple measures of learning performance gain. Our analysis here considers in the first place that the familiar controlled memory experiments on

retention and retrieval must, for comprehensive theory, be handled along with the wider, every day phenomena of "what a person does next." In the actual flow of behavior it is retrieval, of idea or impulse, that decides (after some control action) what is done next, and is experienced as decision. A sequence of a_{hjk} performances is decided by competition of their magnitudes, the magnitudes being in turn decided externally by the h's and k's encountered and internally by the appetitive E levels and the directing modulation of E and M strengths by the controlling ego.

Although an infinite number of different patterns of elements can be equivalent in the final values of a linear equation, it will tend to be true in human learning that retrieval of a particular course of action will be appreciably due to a similar pattern of E and M strengths, as produced by a particular pattern of s_k's. This theory of isomorphism of dynamic elements in learning retrieval would require more than a linear equation and could roughly be met by hypothesizing an addition to the usual a_{hijk}, which might be written:

$$a'_{hijk} = W_p \cdot r_{p(t_1 t_2)i} \tag{4-14}$$

where W_p is a weight given for similarity of pattern, and $r_{p(t_1 t_2)}$ is the pattern similarity of s_k's on dynamic traits in the learning situation at t_1 and the retrieval situation at t_2.

NOTES

[1] A very thorough treatment of random response is available in Hinde (1970), Chapter 14. Probably the least misleading term for this phenomenon is *endogenous* response, for although external stimulus is not absent its ratio to the endogenous source (in m's and E's—ergic conditions) in causing response is by definition very low. Hinde brings out some properties of random endogenous responses, showing that a certain random response to S_x, in absence of reward, reduces the likelihood of a repeat. He finds also that if the opposite (an increment in frequency) occurs one can usually associate it with some *general* effect, not specific to the stimulus. This ethological study leaves no doubt about the important role of "spontaneous" behavior in nature. We can only argue that in the human being, with a much larger cortex and vaster reservoir of engrams than is possible for animals, the role of "spontaneous" responses (R's) and ideas (m's) must be even greater. Humans also sustain longer periods of inhibition (we think of the mathematician Hamilton sitting meditating on a problem for four hours without pencil or paper). This surely encourages more accumulated "spontaneity" and more prolonged and far-reaching internal "reverberation" of chains of m's, producing a richer variety of responses available to be linked initially in CRI fashion to external stimuli.

Incidentally, in considering specific origins of "spontaneity" the chance resemblance of a stimulus situation to some *innately* potent stimulus must be recognized as important. In mentioning this we recognize that most ergless theories of learning systematically overlook the existence of innate predispositions (specific in action in lower animals, but less so in man) towards modes of action not only close to consummatory ergic goals but also in response to subgoals embedded in the primitive ergic process. This predisposition to relatively specific behaviors at subgoals has been well observed by the ethologists, and though they are vestigial in man they could yet account for "random" behavior appearing at points where no previous appreciable amount of learning could account for the nature of the response. As far as temperament factors in personality are concerned, factor M, autia, in the 16 PF, and factor UI(T)21, exuberance, in T-data (and the O-A Battery, Cattell & Schuerger, 1977) contribute substantially to individual differences in "spontaneous" productivity (fluency) and in the regard paid to internal by contrast to external stimuli.

[2] In humans we certainly cannot leave generalizations about c_a-c_b engramming solely to observations only from S_a-S_b experiments. If the properties of c_a and c_b have anything to do with the prediction of engramming then the uncertainty as to exactly *what c a given S produces in an individual mind* introduces error if we know only S. If the subject happens to be a Christian, a presentation of S as, say, De Ribera's "Calvary," can be assumed to evoke certain intense ideas of a specific kind that would be entirely absent in a member of some other culture.

[3] This is not an onlooker's comment but one made with increasing frequency inside reflexological academic circles. The pioneer days, extending from Pavlov and Thorndike, through the large issues raised by such as Blodgett, Crespi, Hilgard, Hull, Kimble, Miller, Mowrer, Skinner, Guthrie, and Tolman, to the 1950's (Estes, Spence, and others) seem to most observers to have simmered down to concentration on a variety of smaller "splinter topics."

[4] Goal modification, the fourth principle, must remain as an insufficiently explored and perhaps rarely occurring mechanism (except as degrees of imprinting, in H, in equation (2-11)). But the fifth principle we would easily finally bring under the second, as a form of reward learning operating through a general erg of *energy saving* or *rest seeking*—the basis of innate pleasure in sleep. The reason for setting this fifth principle temporarily on its own is that our factor-analytic studies have so far not located it. However, in the next decade we may expect psychologists to make both more extensive and more refined factor-analytic experiments in pursuit of ergic structure in man, primates, and mammals generally, and we are betting that the energy-saving goal pattern will then emerge. The third principle, integration, operates in its elements with principles 1 and 2 (*CE* and *ME*) and it is therefore *possible* to say in a sense that the greater part of learning is reduced to those two.

[5] The difference in form and manner of incidence between innate cues and learned cues is not so great as the different origin might suggest. Indeed the chief difference is that an acquired engram has to be entered in equations for the latter but we normally enter no engram for the former because the connection in the case of E is hidden in, and constantly fixed to, the E term itself, and represents an innately favored neurohormonal connection. It is interesting to note that the similarity of "model" springs from a strong formal similarity of the original racial acquisition of innate patterns by variation and natural selection in *evolution* to the process of trial and error variation in *learning*, as mentioned elsewhere here. Indeed the parallelism of model is so great that no thinking person would overlook the insights that one might bring to bear upon the other. There is initially

in most animals certainly no insight about the final goal to which given behavior is oriented, but obviously the "racially learned" behavior feels "right" in terms of a goal defined by the pattern of the ergic tension existing at each moment within the individual. Consistently with this we have recognized in (2-8) and (4-8) that as far as E terms are concerned the situation hk can have an innately prescribed arousal value s_{hke}. This innately cued behavior usually will not be very appropriate in man in a complex cultural situation but it provides the stuff of learning, as a marble block provides the indispensable stuff for a sculpture, and it still fits in well in behavior close to goal consummation (response to a table fork is not innate, but chewing is).

Skinner's useful term "operants" can be best applied to the subliminal stimuli provoking endogenous responses, with the proviso that it covers also some references to origins not in Skinner's concept. These behaviors, in short, are not really correctly described as "spontaneous" or "random" (except in relation to the current learning path envisaged by the experimenter), as we have said before. The addition to the concept here is that many of the operants have origins in internally developing (endogenous) ideas; in previous learning to somewhat similar stimuli, and in innate (endogenous) reactivities. The existence of the latter indicates an area of research toward discovering the innate reactivities that support learned responses, which give greater vitality for the same amount of learning for some responses than others. The pattern of civilized courtship, for example, is a learning embedded with fossils of primitive innateness, many not entirely restricted to consummatory behavior.

[6] An analogous case would be a person's decision whether to drink more of an insufficiently sweetened glass of lemonade, which could depend on the acid-sugar ratio. In regard to the rate of increase of arousal relative to need it will be seen that it depends on s_k in the multiplier $(1 + s_k)$ in equation (2-12).

When the modulator s_k is used in the above corrected rather than simple factor loading form (in which loadings over many k's would average zero), so that at 1.0 it means no external stimulation, then any value above 1.0 will mean an increase in the arousal component, the need-strength component staying at its original value. Thus if the s_k value is 1.4 it means that the ergic tension is 1.4E, where E is need strength, but that the quality of this ergic tension is compounded of one unit of need strength and 0.4 of arousal. (Parenthetically, some ergs such as fear may depend wholly on arousal for their ergic tension; and in the case of fear the arousal is that of a hope of escape.)

Tolman's (1948) notion of "expectations" and Mowrer's (1960a and b) of "hopes" give still further extraneous "fit" to this hypothesis that M's as such undergo a cognitive activation in the learning process. The difference of coexcitation from reward learning would also point to the buildup of two different types of organization to be excited—a purely cognitive M and a dynamic E with cognitive attachment.

In this area of arousal and activation-state patterns, recently clarified in psychological data, there is at the present moment, unfortunately, little linkage of the behavior-state measurement research (Barton, Curran, Nesselroade, and others) with the physiological research (Malmo, Lacey, Olds, and others). This deficiency of research integration arises through omission of clearly factored measures by the physiologists, and of use of physiological measures by psychometrists operating only with questionnaires. However, Cattell and Scheier (1961), Cattell and Bartlett (1971), and Van Egeren (1973, 1977) have now jointly factored psychological and physiological state measures with useful indications of unity and a joint pattern.

[7] However, these definitions of anticipation, expectation, and hope are not much more precise than those of the man in the street, and consequently are not much more welcome to the structural learning theorist than they have been to the reflexologist. The defects of such notions are the following. (a) They rest on no precise evidence of manifestations that would make them independent of the observed behavior they seek to explain. In this they contrast with the concepts located in multivariate experiment to measure the ergic patterns and the general states in man. (Incidentally, it is hard as yet to find a general state that could be called "hope" among the discovered state dimensions, thought it may well appear later.) (b) The expectation concept requires *a consciousness of goal*, in some ideational term, which is hard to believe exists in lower animals, as one goes down to the worm! and which even in humans is patently absent, for example, from much *motor* trial-and-error learning.

[8] The firmest presently available empirical research on the nature of such states, however, comes at first obliquely from work on *general* psychological states not states of particular individual dynamic traits. It is seen in the work of Barton, Birkett, De Young, Nesselroade, Cattell, Curran, Krug, Shotwell, Spielberger, and others using *P*- and *dR*-techniques, and from Berlyne, Duffy, Lacey, Olds, and others by physiological approaches connected with the reticular activation system. All indicate in the excitation-state factor (activation) a greater cognitive awareness and reactivity. The same researches demonstrate the clear existence of some eight dimensions of general state change among which we recognize this state of activation and a distinct one of arousal. The eight states are what we have just called *general*, that is, the excited response potentials do not follow the boundaries of action of some particular erg (as in arousal) or sentiment (as activation is here assumed to do), but the existence of specific ergic arousals and sentiment activations is well supported by *P*- and *dR*-technique experiments.

CHAPTER 5

MATRIX ANALYSIS (APA, PLA AND DPA)
OF THE LEARNING OF STRUCTURE AND PROCESS

5-1. *The attitude path as the culturally appropriate learning element in dynamic calculations*

5-2. *Path learning analysis (PLA), using a five vector description of learning*

5-3. *Concepts and methods for reaching learning laws through DPA and adjustment process analysis (APA)*

5-4. *The three unity-producing learning processes in the acquisition of sentiments*

5-5. *Expected patterns in the tripartite learning equation, expressing common schedule, inherent agency, and budding processes*

5-6. *The production by the inner structure of ergs and sentiments of an unfolding adaptive process*

5-7. *Experimentally checking the relay process structure in a sentiment and its acquisition by learning*

5-8. *Summary*

5-1. The Attitude Path as the Culturally Appropriate Learning Element in Dynamic Calculations

Theory construction to this point has led to five mechanisms by which learning change occurs, and to a five vector mode of description of learning gain in any particular stimulus-reponse performance. The changes of p, r, i, s and T in the latter express the effects of growth of one or more engrams. The growth of an engram is accounted for by a specification equation involving the existing traits plus terms involving the events in ME and CE learning experiences (as well as I, GM, and ES, if they occur).

The manner in which these formulations are to be checked, and the values for particular parameters therein found, has not been spelled out in detail. The trained experimentalist will perceive that much can be done by controlled experiment, handling, mostly one at a time, the number of repetitions, the level of ergic need strength, the level of development to which a measurable sentiment has been brought, the time lapse between action and reward, and so forth. Here we propose to develop instead certain multivariate experimental designs and, at the same time, to advance the precision of certain concepts, notably of the way in which sentiments arise as unitary structures, and of the way in which the structure of a sentiment leads to an unfolding process structure through *time*.

Here also we shall return to the representation of environment, which we showed to be indispensable in handling reactivity *in being* (Volume 1, Chapter 6) and which is no less important in calculations on learning. It is particularly important to the educator and clinician to have some standard taxonomy of learning environment whereby he can make less hazardous predictions than now of the effect on emotional learning of exposure to home, school, peer group, marriage, job success or failure, and so on.

The animal experimenter has little trouble with environment. Unlike the animal ethologist, the experimenter "fixes it" in the laboratory. Findings are built on mazes, Skinner boxes and, if learning is extended by the same methods to the human field, reflexes such as the eye blink to a standard puff of air. But if we are to make our learning law analyses in a complex culture, and, equally important, make them applicable in situ to everyday clinical and social predictions, then a taxonomy is necessary. If this is achieved we can come to grips with quantitative learning statements in the realm of personality, without, on the one hand, relapsing into the vague generalities characteristic of so much writing on personality learning or, on the other hand, retreating from the complexities of human behavior in the real world into the comfortable but artificial precision of much laboratory research literature.

The problem is one of defining both the stimulus situation and the response course of action. The reader is asked to switch back from the narrow lens of the microscopic view we used in our incursion into animal learning in the last chapter to that macroscopic view with which we have pursued the somewhat different data of human cultural concerns. In the typical human setting we have consistently analyzed the total situation into a focal stimulus, h, leading to a particular response, j, conditioned by an ambient situation, k, which is largely responsible for arousing motivation (via s_k) and setting the framework within which the response, j, can take place.

Our main answer to the problem of bringing cultural environment, and the responses therein, into a set of manageable behavioral elements analogous to the stimulus-response elements of the animal experiment, has been to adopt the *attitude* paradigm, defined initially in Chapter 4, Volume 1 (p. 130). The real relation of the course of action in the attitude to the analogous "reflex response," is that the former is actually a hierarchy of mental sets and short courses of action, ultimately fragmentable into a mosaic of "reflex-size" responses such as the animal psychologist or the Pavlovian deals with. But it has a natural dynamic unity which in ordinary terms might be described as that of an over-riding mental set, holding these more fragmentary behaviors to the purpose of a particular sub-goal in the individual's total goal and subgoal lattice. The course of action is not only determined by such a hierarchy but is also a *process*, as studied in Chapter 1, Volume 1, constituted by a whole series of responses to a whole series of stimuli. Its central mystery is what keeps it "on course" toward "doing this with that," that is, making a suitable total complex response to a large situation. This riddle we study in Section 5-4; for the present we shall only point to the ambient situation, k, and the reaction thereto, s_k, and rest on that mechanism as providing arousal and thus an over-all directive purpose. It must then be recognized that in the attitude course of action there is commonly not a single focal stimulus but a succession of h's appearing in the same k situation, and the j performance as designated and measured for the attitude as a whole is the summed result of many small j's. (This S_k might often be an S_{hk}.)

There can surely be little doubt from our discussion of a taxonomy of attitudes (Chapter 2) that the attitude course of action is the culturally most appropriate choice of a learning element. Unfortunately, the requisite taxonomic lists of life attitudes do not yet exist.[1] But in principle the same set as is used for the econetics of the *personality in being* (Chapter 6, Volume 1), would offer the basis for an econetics of *learning*. Illustratively, at a common-sense level, we can indicate as appropriate units for the study of learning the courses of action—or *paths*, as we may more briefly call them in relation to the lattice, that appear in common attitudes. In the standard verbal paradigm these would include such as:—"I want to get a high grade in this college course"; "I want to get promotion in my job"; "I want to play poker regularly with my companions"; "I want to get engaged to Sue"; "I want to put my son through college"; "I want to travel in Europe"; and so on. Admittedly the levels of dissection (though not the organic unity of the behavioral tracts concerned) are at first arbitrary, until factoring shall have established factor strata levels.

Defining the attitude course of action, a_{hjk}, includes of course defining the ambient situation, k, which brings the interest to maximum activation ("In these circumstances" in the attitude paradigm); the focal stimulus, h, for the action or set; the action itself, j ("(to do this) with that"); and the mode of measurement for this *response*, ("to do this") as measured by the scale value a. In the *test* situation the strength of desire for a given course of action—the "response potential"—is measured by objective devices in the U and I components, but it can equivalently be measured by some corresponding measure of strength and duration of *actual action* when it occurs in everyday life. Such a measurement would reside in the number of hours per week a student studies; the amount of money an art lover spends on *objets d'art*; the signs of affection bestowed on a fiancee; the number of times per month a music lover plays the piano; the fractions of his income deposited by a man who wants to increase his savings; and so on.

Basically our discussions will refer to the measures of actual life performance—the criterion. But there are advantages in keeping in mind the test measurement (as in the MAT) because this tells us about the U and I components in the interest, and, by inference about E and M contributions. The particular real-life *measures* one happens to include may be shown by experiment sometimes to involve more the dynamic and sometimes more the ability aspects of the performance among motivation component measures. Because ability is a well explained cognitive area of psychology, our analysis here dwells more on the measurement of learning as it concerns changes in the dynamic components; that is, in the strength and (vector) quality of the interest and the satisfactions associated with the attitude path.

Thus we shall assume for the present that psychologists will have no great difficulty in dissecting from the behavior of the average man and woman an array of attitude courses of action and the typical behavioral path followed in each. We will formulate both common and unique path processes, but, as usual, greater interest attaches to common paths—those similar in nature for the majority of people in a particular culture from birth to death, and frequently the result of learning from cultural institutions. As common traits they will be measurable in comparable ways across the members of the population.

5-2. Path Learning Analysis (PLA) Using a Five-Vector Description of Learning

Granted such paths, how do we propose to measure the learning change in strength of interest (response potential) in them, and how do we propose to analyze those measurements meaningfully? The measurements themselves, as we have said, can be either by objective motivation *test* devices, yielding U and I measures of response potential, or *real-life* measures of actual action. The latter may become more difficult and less reliable in circumstances where obstacles and internal inhibitions make real-life expression sporadic or devious. In those cases, incidentally, we may expect the U component in the test measure—the unexpressed and perhaps unconscious—to be high relative to the I motivational component.

As a result of increasing experience of a particular path, a certain pattern of learning will occur, and, as our five-vector representation indicates, changes would then be expected in the p, the r, the i, the s, and the T vectors. Demonstration of the breakdown change of the obtained loading vector of b's into changes of p, r, i, and s (or even v and s) vectors is still awaited. But indications that the b's as well as the T's do change has been given for ability factors by Wherry (1941) and confirmed by Fleishman (1967a), and extended tentatively for erg and sentiment factors by Hendriks (1971), Laughlin (1973), and (less directly) by Sweney (1969). Unfortunately, the repetition of measures after a sufficient learning interval, in R- and P-technique designs, needed to demonstrate this change in the behavioral indices, requires more technical skill than most research has demonstrated. Consequently, extension of present tentative findings may be delayed awhile. (See, however, Birkett, 1978.) But the results we now await are likely to be supremely enlightening for theories both of therapeutic action and of social change.

Let us consider the methodology and the problems of measuring the learning change on any particular path. In animal learning we would hold other experiences constant, provide for intensive learning in a maze (or whatever), and measure performance before and after. In human behavior such manipulation is not possible, and all kinds of learning-path experiences are going on simultaneously. The simple bivariate manipulative design is not possible. Consequently, as stated at the outset of this chapter we must consider the superior, but some-times more complex possibilities of multivariate experiment and matrix analysis.

The change measure will in any case be expressed first as a be-havior change—$(a_{hijk2} - a_{hijk1})$ or $d \cdot a_{hijk}/dt$ if we want to be re-minded of a differential and a time unit—which, however, we next can analyze as vector changes on the right hand side of the specification equation, affecting the terms v, s, and T (assuming we simplify p, r, and i to v). If we consider first the change in the trait vector of T's we recognize, of course, as psychometrists that in the measurements we operate with the state variance must be cut out of the real trait change variance, for example, by averaging measures.

Typically a person's traits would be undergoing a change from such life influences as were found by Barton and Cattell (1972, 1975), Cattell, Barton and Vaughan (1973) to produce significant changes in factorial source traits, such as (1) training to become an airline hostess; (2) getting married, (3) experiencing a family loss through the death of her mother, and so on through, let us suppose, e different learning paths ($\alpha_1, \alpha_2, \ldots, \alpha_e$ in Figure 5-1). To give properties to the results appropriate to the usual distributions of scores, and to permit common trait solutions, let us suppose scores are gathered for n people ($p_1, p_2, \ldots, p_n$) on the frequency or intensity with which they, as individuals, experience these paths. In Figure 5-1 the experimental results on actual magnitude of change during the year are supposed entered in the T matrix at the right, on personality factors A through Q_4 (we take the traits in the 16 PF test as concrete illustration).

Now what we may call the *elementary path learning analysis (PLA) theorem* supposes that experience of any given path will typically bring some change on all personality factors, as represented for the column for the path in L, the *learning path potency matrix*. It is called a learning potency or mean learning effect matrix because it states an empirical law about what that path, say, a first year of marriage, typically does to personality. For example, Barton & Cattell's (1972a; 1972b; 1975) results suggest that marriage reduces F, surgency, and Q_1, radicalism, and raises C, ego strength, and so on over various of the 16 factors.) If this learning path potency matrix, L, is multiplied by the experience matrix, E, which records how much (by frequency, intensity, etc.) each person is involved in each path, it will yield the empirically obtained matrix T. (The student unfamiliar with matrix calculations is advised to read as an elementary introduction Hammer, 1971, and for further developments sometimes met here Horst, 1962,

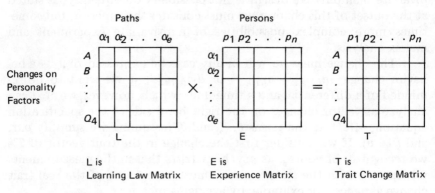

$\alpha_1, \alpha_2, \ldots \alpha_e$ represent, in L, path potency vectors, regarding path effects on traits. In E the α's as rows represent the frequencies (and/or intensities) with which people are exposed to the paths.

Figure 5-1. Path learning analysis (PLA) for trait vector changes, by matrix methods.

or other mathematical text. The simplest matrix procedure, as here, requires that the outcome of two influences—in this case the strength of an experience and the frequency with which it occurs—be treated as if it were a product, and that the effect of several different experiences be added. But this is a first approximated model which can be refined from the results of experiment to a more complex function giving a better fit, as required.

PLA principles can be employed in two ways: first, knowing the change matrix, T, and recording the degree of the persons's experience of paths in E, we can calculate L by the matrix procedure (Figure 5-1):

$$L = TE'(EE')^{-1} \tag{5-1}$$

(using the generalized inverse because E may not be a square matrix); and second, knowing L from previous research, and having recorded the experience matrix, E, we can estimate what the trait change would be for various people undergoing these experiences, as in Figure 5-1. In matrix algebra this is:

$$LE = T \tag{5-2}$$

The first use belongs more to basic research into the typical effects of life experiences, types of therapy, and so on, upon personality. The second is useful more in applied psychology in making estimates of outcome for individual cases. Incidentally, the path learning analysis calculation *can* be used for a single individual—a single vector column in E—but most research would do better to take a group of *n* persons. The importance of PLA is that it accepts the reality of *all* of a person's traits being affected by *all* the path experiences *simultaneously* occurring in his life. And as an experimental analytical instrument it is able to trace the fractions of that change occurring on each and all traits to their various sources.

As to the change in the v and s vectors one must remember that unless reached by a P-technique analysis they are properties of a group rather than of an individual. That is, if the path of, say, participating in group sports raises the s_k value of the elation state when k is a football match and the v_{hj} value of the gregarious erg (showing the ergic goal of avoiding loneliness to be increasingly reached by entering a group game, hj) then these figures are the average rate of translation of that state and that ergic need level into behavior. Incidentally, it is important to note that to reach these factorial values either in R- or P-technique, one must, in experiment, go beyond the particular piece of behavior to include *several* other behaviors. Indeed, it may be said that this is not only statistically necessary (because of the individual's simultaneous exposure to several paths) but necessary also to psychological understanding, for an increase in ergic investment in one attitude course of action may produce an otherwise unaccountable fall in investment in another. However, if one is to deal with PLA in regard to p, r, i, and s values, over and above T values, for one individual, a P-technique analysis before and after the learning experience will be ncessary.

Obtaining a trait-score vector change from such P- or R-technique experiments presents the slight difficulties pointed out in Chapter 7, Volume 1—that in the usual factor design alternatives one gives change of loadings without change of factor score and the other change of factor score without change of loadings. But the change-of-*loadings* design (factoring before and after performances, that is, two scores for each variable and therefore, beginning with n variables factoring $2n$ variables in all) can also yield a change of factor score by certain methods, notably the isopodic method for comparing trait scores (Cattell, 1970).

The obtaining of the changing values in the b (or v and s) vectors thus requires factor analysis, and a series of *groups* to factor, with different learning experiences (manipulative or life-produced), whereas mere direct measures of before and after trait scores in the individual, as in Figure 5-1, suffice to proceed to the *trait-learning* vector. It must be repeated that in order to use PLA as it explains *involvement and modulation vectors*, it is necessary to use groups. Of course, in P-technique, b, v and s changes *will* be obtainable for *one* person, across two time series. With such group data we then proceed to take *a single row from the factor-pattern matrix*, say for a_j, and set out, for group g_1, the change in the loadings on each trait—A, B, C, . . . , Q_4—between the pre- and postlearning factors. This, when repeated for other groups gives the behavior-index change vector, B, in Figure 5-2. The E matrix gives the differences in the *group* experiences of the learning paths. (For a P-technique change see Cattell and Birkett, 1980.)

These learning-frequency and intensity differences of groups, in any natural situation, will have to be the differences in group *means*—that is, means of members' experiences—for we cannot control or know what happens to individuals. L, as before, is the learning law matrix, setting out in this case the changes in the loadings (behavior indices) of traits on the behavior a_j as the result of a single experience of path α_1, α_2, and so forth. The two kinds of calculation here, in Figure 5-2, are knowing B to find L, and knowing L to find B, and are formally the same as for Figure 5-1 and equations (5-1) and (5-2).

It will be noted that whereas the T changes affect all other specifi-

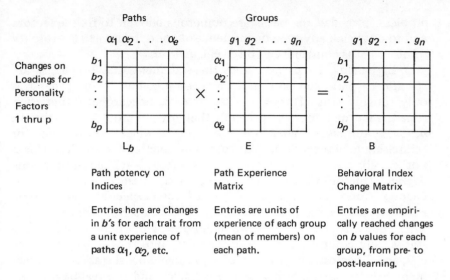

The solution for learning relation law matrix, L_b, is:

$$L_b = B \, E' \, (E \, E')^{-1}, \text{ as given in (5-1) in the text.}$$

Since obtaining behavioral indices requires a factor analysis we have either to compare *R*-technique results on groups, or *P*-technique results at different intervals of learning process progress in an individual. (These stages would replace g_1, g_2, etc., in E above.)

Figure 5-2. Path learning analysis (PLA) for behavioral index changes, expressed in matrices.

The calculation concerns the change in behavioral indices, *b*'s (or *p*'s, *e*'s, and *s*'s) for one particular performance, a_{hjk}.

---

cation equations and not just that of a_j, the behavior-index changes in a row in this kind of experiment affect only the behavior a_j. In a concrete psychological illustration a_j might be the ability to make a tactful reply in conversation, and the paths leading to such learning (among other things) might be α_1, having siblings, α_2, having a mother with more than a high-school education, α_3, studying arts more than sciences, and so on. The psychologist will in general wish to deal with changing behavioral indices for performance in a path as a whole rather than specific pieces of behavior, for the latter is too uneconomical of research time. The fact that the α's for these whole paths are now independent variables with respect to the learning influence and dependent variables (like a_j) for factor analysis should create no statistical problem, provided the paths are numerous enough to fix the factors and to outweigh any specific influence of one α_j relative to the totality of other paths contributing to the calculation.

In passing, let us note that the statement that b changes are specific to particular path performances, a_j's, but T's are general, is only roughly true. Throughout the five-vector learning formulation runs the mutually binding principle that any alteration in a b (that is, p, r, i, s) produces a change in the V_{fe} (the weights on variables for estimating a factor score), as discussed in Chapter 4. Moreover, this is not merely a statistical effect but arises from a real addition to the engram structure of the trait T, represented by the n links in the last chapter. Consequently, a change on a b value, specific to an attitude path course of action, a_j, necessarily connotes a real change, though small, in a T score. However, we shall not attempt here to go into the statistically complex question of the relation of those changes among v, s, and T vectors that are part of inevitable mutual statistical adjustments—differing somewhat in the ordinary and the real-base factor model. These are different from, and need to be allowed for in reaching, the true quantitative expression of the psychological change per se. For example, psychologically and statistically it is easy to recognize that the mean level of a trait in a sample could go up, through learning, without changing the role of increments in that factor in producing increments in behavior (the b or v values).

The alert reader may ask at this point if it is not likely that PLA is complicated by the fact that persons in the free daily-life situation who follow certain paths more frequently will be *initially* different in their personality compositions, in ways associated with their choosing or being pushed into the given path. There is every reason, for example in light of the diverse personality profiles found for different occupations (Cattell, Eber, & Tatsuoka, 1970), to expect such personality selection from choice. However, PLA deals with *trait change*, and if such change is a function also of the pre-path personality profile, this must be established by a calculation of the usual specification equation, regressing the *change* on factor X on persons's previous absolute score on all factors, and partialling out the effect before entering PLA calculations.

Our model has recognized (equation 4-2) that changes in involvement v, or modulation s, as an erg in a particular behavior and situation can come about, as we have just here reminded, only through change in an engram, n, m, or M. The v and s changes represent, though not in a one-to-one manner, structural change. And if we enter physiological psychology we may suppose this means a neural bond, within the subject. The p, r, i, and s values are, as we have stated, mathematico-statistical statements about the relation of an engram (in itself, a cognitive activity, as a mediator to ergic activity) to behavior. However, any change in a loading (other than statistical, through sample, etc.) as indicated above, connotes a change in structure of that engram. The action acquires, for example, new memory traces *extending* the sentiment, permitting the latter to act more on a certain behavior a_j than before. The b's (v's and s's) though separable by analysis from change in the level of a sentiment trait, express nevertheless the effect of changes in its structure and coverage.

5-3. Concepts and Methods in Reaching Learning Laws through DPA and Adjustment Process Analysis (APA)

We are dealing in this chapter with reaching the p, r, i, s, and T changes in a five vector description of learning. They can be reached only with relative inefficiency by bivariate methods, and our aim is, starting with PLA, to continue to develop multivariate experimental designs by which (a) basic principles can be uncovered and (b) applied psychology can handle the realities of prognosis in school, clinic and everyday life.

The question of relative efficiency will be answered if one reflects that in PLA above, if we took a single vector of path frequencies for one individual (a vertical column in E in Figure 5-1) instead of the full matrix, and then took a single row from L, instead of L as a whole, the product would be a single cell scalar in T. From this no solution would be possible of the frequency values in E or the learning potencies for various paths in L, since an infinity of combinations could produce the given T change value. For an adequate solution a whole matrix of learning gains (T), over an array of individuals at different paths experience levels (E)—say over a year—is necessary. (A single personality trait can however be investigated.)

As mentioned in introducing PLA, its great advantage is that broad personality learnings ("emotional learning" if one will) in true everyday life situations (not trivial artificial manipulatings) can be quantitatively investigated. From a basic research standpoint one reaches empirical laws about what the experience of a given common path typically produces, in increments or decreases, on personality source traits. From an applied psychology viewpoint one can take a vector of the life paths that an individual has, is, or will be experiencing, and the vector values in L which basic research has established, and readily calculate the change in all his personality source traits that have been, are, or will be due to those learning experiences. (Note we use the term "learning experiences" but, as the chart in Table 3-1 shows, the changes are inclusive of somatic and volutional change in the life situation, though the latter can be taken out as the common time element in all path changes.

Valuable though this broad answer must be to a scientific approach to clinical or social-psychological practice, from the standpoint of basic science it is yet not enough. It gives us a catalogue of important common paths and their properties as they affect the two vector values common in the specification equation, that is, b and T (or five—p, r, i, s, and T—if we accept the full breakdown.) But this L is like a seventeenth-century catalogue of common herbs that tells us (hopefully with empirical reliability) how each potion affects a variety of illnesses. By contrast, the modern pharmacologist wants to understand what pure chemicals are distributed in each herbal remedy and wishes to shift the prediction of effects from herbs to these pure chemical components. Just so adequate learning theory would wish to pass to a higher level of abstraction by proceeding from statements of the "teaching properties" of any given cultural path to an understanding of the *properties of ecometric and psychometric situational elements in that path that occur in different degrees in all path learning.* In short, paths, which are culturally innumerable, must be analyzed, by their action, into a more limited number of basic psychologically meaningful elements present in all.

The animal learning experiments accumulated by reflexologists have done a good job of passing from the properties of a particular maze or Skinner box to the properties of abstracted elements, such as length of path, drive (ergic tension) level, magnitude of reward, delay of reward, and so on. As we consider what we have called typical *human* paths, such as a year at college, the first year of marriage, a soldier's experience of two years of war and so on, it becomes evident that, at least in principle and to a rough degree, a vector description of a path *could* be reduced to constituent quantifiable elements meaningful in other paths also, though no one has yet done so. For example, a given path could be characterized by the number of subgoals to be learned, the level of cognitive difficulties, the kind of emotional frustrations at various points, the number and duration of inhibitions that have to be maintained, the amount of fatigue through sheer hours of work, the temporal delay between action and reward, the degree of uncertainty of reward, and so on. If we consider just ergic conditions alone we see that either the level of ergic tension at which the individual proceeds or the magnitude of rewards received or both (as in equation 4-13) would have to be expressed in a vector applying to about a dozen different ergs that could be in various degrees involved in any one path. When we consider the other ergic events that would need to be covered, it is evident that the roster of "teaching elements in a path," needs several vectors, each of appreciable length.

At this early dawn of multivariate, structured, learning theory we cannot hope to develop an essential list of elements, nor can we cope in the model with the usual objections that some relations will be complexly curvilinear, that contributory elements will be variously correlated, and that interaction effects will arise. Science has to walk before it can run, and special difficulties in a fundamentally correct approach are usually duly met by special later developments. Let us therefore consider in relatively abstract terms, that a vector of "teaching properties" of any path *could* be constructed, either by noting them by direct theoretical insights or by deriving them from other observations as significant elements as we derived L from the observations of T and E in Figure 5-1.

Again, we shall start with two matrices. For brevity we will call the "teaching" properties matrix D, a matrix of basic *determiners*. It describes the endowment of path a_x, and other paths, in the properties of determiners such as e_1, the tension level in erg E_1; r_1, the amount of reward to erg E_1; and so for other ergs. Further, it describes other parameters such as n, the number of subgoals to be learned; i, the amount (duration) of inhibition to be exercised; d, the delay in reward; and l, the length (time) in reaching the consummation of the path.

In Figure 5-3 we begin with a matrix, P, which tells what the potency of various determiners is in affecting a given trait (or, it could be, instead, a given behavioral index). For example, T_2 could be the dominance factor in the 16 PF and along its row, under r_1, which is reward, say, to the self-assertive erg, there would be a rather large value because we know that success under that achievement motivation raises dominance behavior. The other columns of P might be rewards to other ergs ($r_1 \ldots r_z$), effects of insight on learning, i, delay in reward, d, and other determining conditions, such as are studied in animal learning, and hypothetically considered the significant determiners in *any* learning path. Its specialization, however, is that it records their potencies for different traits, on the assumption—surely desirable—that a particular ergic reward, a particular delay in reward, or a particular complication in the cognitive area, will have different effects on the learning gain of some traits relative to others. The second matrix, D, as just explained, gives the endowment of each path in the determiners, that is, its "determiner properties."

Both this, and P, are, of course, for "people in general" and so therefore is their product L. But this latter is the same as L in Figure

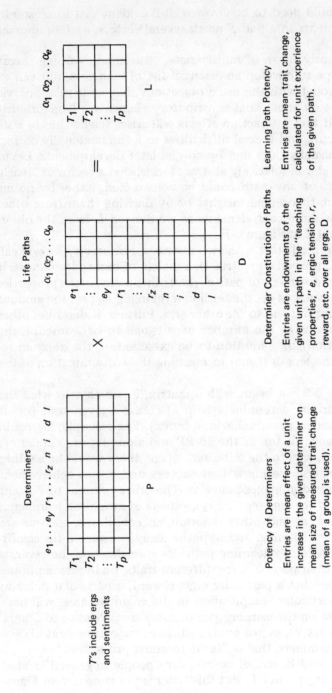

Figure 5-3. Determiner potency analysis (DPA). The discovery of potencies of constituent determiners in a path.

Determiners

T's include ergs and sentiments

P

Potency of Determiners

Entries are mean effect of a unit increase in the given determiner on mean size of measured trait change (mean of a group is used).

Life Paths

D

Determiner Constitution of Paths

Entries are endowments of the given unit path in the "teaching properties," e, ergic tension, r, reward, etc. over all ergs. D describes what one expects to meet.

L

Learning Path Potency

Entries are mean trait change, calculated for unit experience of the given path.

5-1 and so 5-1, and 5-3, can be placed in tandem, to proceed all the way from the known basic properties of the path to the estimated effects, in the fifth matrix, for given individuals with given exposures to the paths. The matrix equation for Figure 5-3 is:

$$PD = L \tag{5-3a}$$

But if we wish to go all the way through PLA (equation 5-2) it becomes:

$$PDLE = T \tag{5-3b}$$

while the backward calculation of the basic determiner laws in P when L and D are known becomes:

$$P = LD'(DD')^{-1} \tag{5-4}$$

This mode of calculation is necessary because D is not a square matrix (see Figure 5-3).

This serves the applied psychologist, but if he is to be able to do this the basic research which serves him must first have worked its way back from the fifth matrix of observed changes of trait in individuals to the third (L) matrix and so back to the P matrix which contains the more basic learning laws concerning the usual potencies of path properties such as magnitude of reward, complexity, delay in reward, etc. To do this researcher must have made an analysis of the path properties in matrix D. In doing this he is doing no differently from the animal experimenter who assigns properties to a maze run, such as number of choices, magnitude of reward, visual complexities, etc. That is to say, matrix D is a purely *ecometric* construction, based on dependable physical (and social) characteristics of the given path. These must, of course, be quantified, in terms relative to other paths. Thus a subscience of the ecometric description of life paths in terms of properties meaningful to basic learning theory has to develop here, probably as an enterprise for the social psychologist.

In this framework special attention needs now to be given to emotional learning, if only because it is the central concern of clinical psychology. With the exception of the vigorous pursuit of quantitative laws by Barton, Birkett, Cohen, Eysenck, Karson, Krug, Mahrer, Van Egeren, Wiggins, the Cartwrights (1971), and a few others, many clinicians have let themselves get bogged down in qualitative verbalities and failed to utilize the long published concepts of *adjustment process analysis* (APA) leading to quantitative steps such as can be incorporated in the above.

What we shall now describe in more detail as adjustment process analysis promises a scientific basis for quantitative testing procedures evaluating emotional learning propositions (Cattell & Scheier, 1961), for in all path learning analysis the most important class of determiners, concerning personality change is undoubtedly that dealing with the intensity and the nature of the frustration or reward occurring to all drives and sentiments. The first function of APA is systematically to focus and order the gamut of subsequent adjustment possibilities for humans, with respect to any one drive, when it is duly aroused at the beginning of some path toward satisfaction and in process of seeking satisfaction.

Figure 5-4, which has been extensively discussed elsewhere (Cartwright & Cartwright, 1971; Cattell & Scheier, 1961; Cattell, 1965; Cattell & Child, 1975; Cattell & Kline, 1978) needs little description here. It sets out in the light, initially, of both clinical and animal studies, the six choice points—*chiasms*, if we need a brief technical term—that can occur in the attempt to reach satisfaction, according to the situations that can be met in the path. This chart may seem to the unwary to suggest that all behavior ends in neurotic symptom formation, as this is the end of the chart. What percentages of human activities end at A_1, at C_3, and so on, we do not yet know reliably, and they probably change with the position of a culture on the cultural pressure dimension of cultures (Chapter 7, p. 470). But we can probably assume that only a minority of people are ultimately forced into the crooked paths beyond the E and F chiasms which head to neurosis and psychosis. Although animal frustration research will carry us with concrete evidence through C, the evidence for what is set out for humans in D, E, and F is bound at present to rest on clinical formulations.

What an APA chart offers as the next necessary adjunct to the PLA and DPA calculations is a basis for quantifying the fate of any and all drives in a given path experience *in terms of degree of expression, frustration, transformation to pugnacity, grief or anxiety, generation of defense mechanisms*, and so forth. Reflexology has been content, appropriately to its restricted and peripheral paradigms, to deal mainly in stimulus strength, drive strength, and reward strength in relation to responses made. But structured learning theory has to encompass the full possibilities of varied human experience in ergic events and the simultaneous occurrence of those events differentially on the various ergs and sentiments. The APA chart presents (1) a systematic comprehensive reminder of the adjustment possibilities, (2) an indexing notation system for exactly describing the adjustment reached by an individual in any particular clinical (or other) case (e.g., major weight on C_3 in the case of a delinquent; or F_4 for an anxiety neurotic), and (3) a means of quantifying (as well as symbolizing) the dynamic aspects of experience (as a path property) for a particular

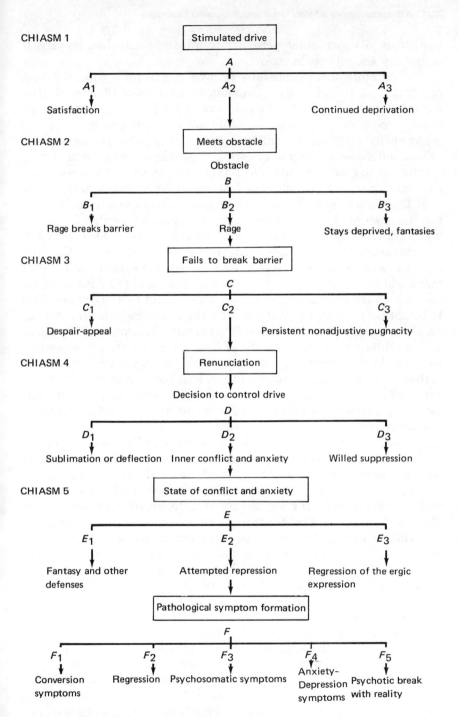

CHIASM 1 — Stimulated drive

A

A₁ Satisfaction A₂ A₃ Continued deprivation

CHIASM 2 — Meets obstacle

Obstacle

B

B₁ Rage breaks barrier B₂ Rage B₃ Stays deprived, fantasies

CHIASM 3 — Fails to break barrier

C

C₁ Despair-appeal C₂ C₃ Persistent nonadjustive pugnacity

CHIASM 4 — Renunciation

Decision to control drive

D

D₁ Sublimation or deflection D₂ Inner conflict and anxiety D₃ Willed suppression

CHIASM 5 — State of conflict and anxiety

E

E₁ Fantasy and other defenses E₂ Attempted repression E₃ Regression of the ergic expression

Pathological symptom formation

F

F₁ Conversion symptoms F₂ Regression F₃ Psychosomatic symptoms F₄ Anxiety–Depression symptoms F₅ Psychotic break with reality

Figure 5-4. The adjustment process analysis chart.

individual in a particular path. Its formulation can then be carried across any and all ergs in action.

If an individual successfully follows and learns a path, we must recognize, as we did in the discussion of conflict in Chapter 2, that for successive runs to continue to occur his *total* ergic satisfaction must be positive—otherwise he would not return to pursue it. But, as we know from indurated conflict, a given path may have *some* negative values, indicating inhibition of certain ergs. The list of determiners of learning in any path (Figure 5-3) is now seen, by the APA breakdown, to require rows not only for the features so far represented in matrix D of that figure, including each ergic tension level and reward, but also for the features that generate frustration, control, anxiety, fantasy, and various other defenses. It was recognized, of course, that the determiners listed in D, Figure 5-3, were given as a mere sample. Now that we scrutinize more closely we see that one systematic enlargement will be in terms of entries for the chiasms in the APA chart on which each erg and sentiment stands with respect to a given path. This information presumably will come to the recording observer, for example the clinician, with regard to particular ergs, and its effect may well be different in the potency of determiners matrix, P, according to what drive is involved. For example, repeated frustration of a viscerogenic drive such as hunger might well have different effects on personality traits from that of a nonviscerogenic one, such as self-assertion. (Perusal of a history of religious ascetics might give some research clues!)

The APA chart in its basic form, as set out in Figure 5-4, attempts to deal with the fate of *any* purpose—any erg or any sentiment in its dynamic aspect. Yet, as we have just admitted, the quantitative if not the qualitative consequences are probably different for different ergs, and almost certainly for sentiments of different strength and nature. The question arises whether this multiplicity is best dealt with by an appreciable increase in the rows of matrix D, through representing both the dynamic traits and their fates in the same matrix, or whether to carry the information of the APA chart into a separate matrix. The latter is probably cleaner and offers no great difficulty either to the matrix representation or the computer programmer of emotional learning calculations.

This advance is represented in Figure 5-5, where it is recognized that ideally the path determiners should take full account of the complexity of the dynamic structure and vary with the particular erg or sentiment involved. This requires a new matrix—D_d in Step 1 of Figure 5-5—in which separate determiner properties are entered for each erg or sentiment (column) according to what is discovered to be the *average* adjustment process "fate" of that drive in the one path. (Note that this *whole* matrix refers, however, to only one path, α_1, in this case.) In addition to the APA experiences for that dynamic structure, there would be added in a full diagram, other path properties, as in Figure 5-3, such as n, number of subgoals, d, delay in reward, and so on, but now *applying specifically to one dynamic structure, an E or M*. The result of multiplying what is essentially (but with the APA extensions) the same potency of determiners (D) matrix as in Figure 5-3 by this D_{d1} (sub-d for dynamic traits; ergs and sentiments) is to produce a matrix L_{d1}, which tells the trait change typically expected from the separate dynamic traits in path α_1. This is shown in Step 1 in Figure 5-5. Note that the Step 2 calculation is not psychological, but simply a matrix device to sum the effects of all dynamic traits on trait changes into a single total effect of path α_1. In Step 3 all columns of the kind produced by Steps 1 and 2 are brought together, again merely as a matrix device, to produce an L-matrix—learning path potency—relating trait changes to unit transit of each path, as in (5-2).

One would wish in this presentation not to perplex the general reader with complexities of matrix calculation, even though they must ultimately be faced by the researcher and by those computer services that the expert clinical psychologist will eventually need to use. However, we are handling at this point the crux of a difficult problem, and though the reader at first reading may do well to skip certain details, the *logic* of the general model should be faced. For example, it should be understood that what we have just covered in terms of changes in traits can be extended to calculating changes in the behavioral indices, as was worked out in the simpler learning specification earlier, with a transition from comparing individuals to comparing groups (Figure 5-2). It will be noted that without this the PLA, DPA, and APA models would not take account of the existing personality in its effects on change. But when p, r, i, and s, values are included in the change description it does.

In short we finish in the case of either traits or indices with an L-matrix that can be determined from the further data implicit in Figures 5-1 and 5-2 by equation (5-1). However, if we consider the aim of basic research, which has been to work back to P and now is to work back to matrix P_d—the general psychological principles telling how the APA experiences of success, frustration, anxiety, sublimation, and other properties of any path and any dynamic trait affect personality change—we encounter a problem. The problem is that of reversing Step 2 to arrive at the separate dynamic trait effects in L_{d1}. Ways around this are complex and yet to be set out. But in principle, if we have L_{d1} and the motivation strength (MAT) and conflict measures to reach the values for each erg needed to describe the APA results needed in D_{d1}, it is possible to calculate back and reach basic

The analysis is for a single life[1] path.

Step 1 in Calculation: Trait Change from Each Dynamic Trait's Fate

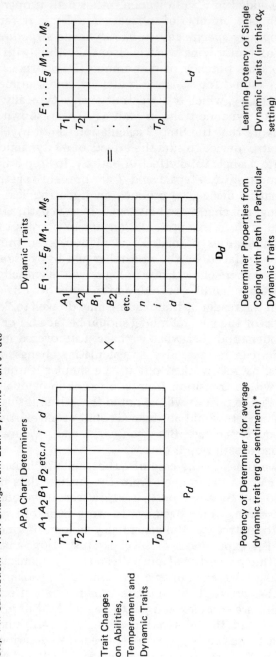

Trait Changes on Abilities, Temperament and Dynamic Traits

P_d

APA Chart Determiners

A_1 A_2 B_1 B_2 etc.n i d l

$\times$

Dynamic Traits

$E_1 \ldots E_g M_1 \ldots M_s$

D_d

$=$

$E_1 \ldots E_g M_1 \ldots M_s$

L_d

Potency of Determiner (for average dynamic trait erg or sentiment)*

Determiner Properties from Coping with Path in Particular Dynamic Traits

Learning Potency of Single Dynamic Traits (in this α_x setting)

*It may prove desirable to average separately for ergs and sentiments, in which case D would have only one class of entry, E's or M's.

[1]It is important here to distinguish between the life paths which are α's here, and the APA chart incidents which are things happening in the course of life paths as analyzed in APA terms. Thus rather than think of a path itself producing effects on traits we refer now to

310

Step 2 in Calculation. Total Trait Change for Path α_x

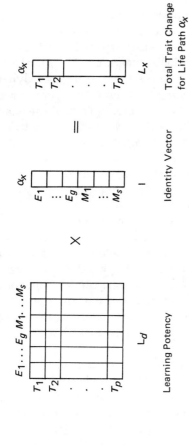

L_d

Learning Potency

by Dynamic Traits in Path α_x

$\times$

α_x

E_1
$\cdots E_g$
M_1
$\cdots M_s$

I

Identity Vector

$=$

α_x

T_1
T_2
$\cdot$
$\cdot$
T_p

L_x

Total Trait Change
for Life Path α_x

Step 3 in Calculation: Assembling Results in Terms of e life paths

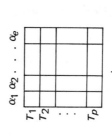

$\alpha_1 \; \alpha_2 \cdot \cdot \cdot \alpha_e$

T_1
T_2
$\cdot \cdot \cdot$
T_p

L

Learning Path Potency, as in Figure 5-3

Figure 5-5. Determiner potency analysis with assumption of specificity to dynamic traits (DPA·DS)

311

laws about the potency of learning determiners that reside in matrix P_d. In fact, this repeats the forms of equation (5-1) or (5-4) with the new entries, thus:

$$P_{d1} = L_{d1} D_{d1} (D_{d1} D'_{d1})^{-1} \tag{5-5}$$

(Subscript $d1$ here denotes one particular dynamic trait.)

5-4. The Three Unity-Producing Learning Processes in the Acquisition of Sentiments

Path learning analysis (PLA), determiner potency analysis (DPA), and determiner potency analysis with values specific to a dynamic trait (*DPA·D*) can now be seen in perspective as three steps from the simplest to the most refined analysis of personality learning. The scope of the processes covers both general personality-ability traits and dynamic traits, but in the later developments applies more to dynamic traits, namely sentiments. The perspective to keep in mind is that the analysis leads both to laws regarding *trait* change, if we deal with individuals in one group, and to *behavioral index* changes, if we compare factor-analytic structures across several groups.

In PLA we begin with relations between particular life path experiences and resulting personality or index changes, solved by experiments designed for matrix calculations. The relations sought in PLA are nothing more than the products of path indices and path frequencies leading to personality change, such as may suffice for guidance in many applied situations such as counseling, clinical, and political science predictions. In DPA, on the other hand, we analyze the paths as to their determiners in terms of learning theory concepts, so that eventually the learning laws of reward, *ME*, and of coexcitation, *CE*, can be brought in, inasmuch as the reward and other determiners of that kind can be introduced into matrix P in Figure 5-3 and P_d in Figure 5-5.

However, to make use of the precise *reverberation-fixation* model for action of reward, arousal, need strength, time lapses, and so on, as set out in Chapter 4, matrices and calculations auxiliary to those in equations (5-1) through (5-5) will be necessary. We have not entered into these here because the mathematico-statistical digression would be disproportionate in the overall purpose of this book. Nor have we pursued further the ways in which the codified experiences in adaptation process analysis are best to be handled in determiner potency analysis. Experiment needs to catch up more closely to existing theory before these additions to the model can be made felicitously.

Assuming that trait and behavioral index changes in learning can ultimately be lawfully connected with basic learning determiners by experiments designed on the above models, we plan now to investigate the learning of those dynamic trait structures that are acquired, namely, the sentiments. What follows will rest first on the evidence for dynamic structures in Volume 1, Chapter 3, and secondly on the discussion of the three mechanisms of sentiment growth in Section 2-3 here. Indeed what we purpose is a repetition of the examination of those three mechanisms in the broader context we have since reached.

Before proceeding let us remind the reader that the growth changes in a sentiment structure M itself, recorded in a trait change vector are systematically connected with the behavioral index changes. These changes are actually *expression of new engrams, n's* or "bonds" in the Thorndikian sense. They link the total sentiment with the particular expression, j, with which one happens to be concerned. Thus r, the *response proficiency* index, expresses some part (or even the whole) of sentiment M, as it mediates between a stimulus h and a response j. Reflex learning theory would simply leave this as an abstract hyphen in S-R. Structured learning, on the other hand, regards the r index as one expression of a substantial neuropsychological entity— an engram, n or M—which is responsible for the response j appearing when the focal stimulus h is met. Similarly, p expresses a part of M that is responsible for the perception that h is meaningful. Again, s must be some engram link in M that causes it to be activated as a cognitive system in the broad ambient situation k, while i (the index, not the individual) is a cognitive-dynamic bond in M that leads to its calling in the ergic investments it possesses, thus determining the intensity of interest in the course of action j.

From these considerations we realize that the engram structure in M is multifaceted in its connections. Indeed, if we wish to enter neurological speculation we can suppose that p corresponds to connections of the central, activated M pattern to sensory areas, r to connections to motor areas, i and s to connections to hypothalamic drive areas, and so on.

The learning of a sentiment will be experimentally evident as we have seen, by data changes in p, r, i, and s, in relation to particular performances, j's, in particular total situations $(h + k)$'s, and also in the resultant change in the total M (or other T) score. What structured learning theory has to account for is the factor-analytic evidence that the sentiments themselves have decided unity of structure, of growth and of action. This is shown in R and dR results in important major instances (though perhaps of a vaguer, more straggling pattern in others), and indicates also some hierarchical form. In Section 2-3 above, we concluded that there are three kinds of learning process accounting for this unity: (1) *common learning schedule* of elements, (2) *inherent common growth agency*, and (3) *budding*, from an existing sentiment. We shall briefly polish and review these concepts.

1. *The common learning schedule* could be—indeed is in essence—a mechanical process producing simultaneity or equality of reward and of frequency in a certain collection of attitude courses of action. These attitudes *need* have no logical or organic connection and may not be perceived by the individual as part of a conscious functional whole, though commonly they will be. For example, what Skinner aptly defined as "superstitious learning" in animals—picking up a response to some accidentally present *h* stimulus irrelevant to the system—could be an element of this kind. An extreme example in humans might be that, if people study classics at College X, they are acquiring (along with the unified pattern of classics knowledge acquired as a result of coexcitation), through contiguity and repetition, a motor skill in weaving through the labyrinth of back streets to get to College X. The factor-analytic M we call a sentiment to classics would (for *that* population sample) contain the *m*'s for the labyrinth as definitely as the grammatical and philological elements we would expect to find in a factor delineating a sentiment to classics.

2. *The inherent growth agency* source of unity, on the other hand, has logical dependency, psychological transfer, and often full consciousness of the sentiment as the essential source of the M unity. What reflexology has called stimulus generalization doubtless puts some of the mortar between the bricks of such an edifice. But in our broader analysis of the human learning laws we would ascribe far greater importance in acquiring unity to the human capacity to perceive relations, educe correlates, and understand personally the organic and causal connections in some sentiment purpose. Thus when a person is acquiring a sentiment to a foreign literature, or to a home of which he is proud, or to a political party he is, unlike the case of the common schedule, aware that the parts hang together logically and in regard to necessary outer world subsidiations. Thus the same degree of reward (in *ME* mechanisms) is diffused over all the behaviors, and the coexcitation (*CE*) connections are made by the frequent common recall of the sentiment elements in consciousness. It may be that the main contributor is coexcitation, but subsequent *ME* effects operating upon what is cognitively brought together must also be considered.

3. *Budding* is the rise of an ancillary sentiment in the service of one already well established (or occasionally more than one, when two sentiments happen consistently to demand the same service, as when both the job and the home sentiments demand interest in keeping a car in good condition). What brings the several attitudes and behavioral elements in the new sentiment along at the same rate, so that they

intercorrelate positively in magnitude to yield an M factor pattern, is that the ergic investment of the main pre-existing sentiment puts equal motivation into all of them.

From the results of Sweney and Cattell (1961), Butcher (1963), and others it appears likely that children have more fragmentary sentiments than adults, that is, more smaller and fewer larger structures. (Note, however, that the popular view that children will have more numerous temperament (general personality) factors, such as A, B, C, D, E, etc. in the 16 PF, seems definitely *not* to be true.) Child development researchers have neglected precision factoring on the age changes in children's sentiment structures, but it seems very likely that the growth of the larger sentiments occurs by subsidiation and "clotting" of smaller sentiments. For example, a child's sentiments to mother and to father would be initially very distinct, but as the cognitive concept of the family develops, around the reality of whatever unity of authority, finance, and home structure is perceived, say, by adolescence, a single super-ordinate sentiment to the family would appear. This is not simple budding, since it partakes also of the dynamically unifying effect of a cognitive agency—the concept of the family—but it involves, in part, mutual subsidiations, through mother being a transmitter of rewards from father, and vice versa.

The last point has value in bringing out that though we can recognize three distinct sources of the unification which produces correlaton among the elements of attitude reactivity in a sentiment, yet any given sentiment *is likely to be the product of all three*. What their relative importance is must remain to be revealed by experiment, but in non-laboratory, everyday life examples we must accept that these mechanisms will overlap and collaborate in the genesis of the unity of a sentiment.

The budding mechanism inevitably brings us to consider the relation of abilities to sentiments, for we frequently see what we would normally call abilities branching off as subsidiaries to sentiments. Indeed, therein we encounter again the concepts in Chapter 1 concerning the simultaneous dependence of the level of aptitudes and skills on innate capacities, on the one hand, and, on the other, on interests in sentiments.

Traits—the *T*'s in the various matrices—are treated by nearly all psychologists as falling into three modalities: (1) *abilities*, (2) *temperament* (or general personality) traits, and (3) *dynamic* traits concerned with attitudes and interests. The precise operational meanings given[2] to these categories (which formerly have rested on intuition or such ad hoc rules as that ability measures have right and wrong answers and temperament tests do not) needs careful consideration. At the conclusion of the survey in Volume 1, Chapter 2, of source traits derived from the complete personality sphere we pointed out that (although distinguishable by such rough rules as above, and such bases as media of observation, degree of hereditary determination, etc.) the attempt, by an operational definition, objectively to separate traits by modality has only recently been made (Cattell & Warburton, 1967). When source traits appear simply as factors, from a wide array of behaviors, traits of different modalities naturally can crop up side by side, unordered in the factor series. Indeed, it was only when structural research began to deal with motivation measures that assured (Volume 1, Chapter 4) recognition of dynamic structures among the more familiar ability and temperament traits appeared. As was theoretically expected, it then turned out that at least two factors found in general behavior variables in the media, L and Q, namely, Q_3, self-sentiment, and G, superego, were actually dynamic factors. It is interesting to note, however, that the probable reason for these, and C, ego strength, being found in "general personality traits" is that they are dynamic factors of a peculiarly *general* kind. They are not specific ergs, or sentiments to school, hobby, home, and so on, as are most dynamic traits, but are concerned with modes of handling, in conflict and integration action, *all* kinds of subsidiary dynamic traits.

Abilities, on the other flank of the dynamic trait realm, can also be understood in some cases as if they were special forms and aspects of what we commonly consider a dynamic sentiment structure. A sentiment is, after all, an acquired organization for the effective satisfaction of ergs in a cultural environment. Some abilities could be seen as standing to sentiments in the way that a sentiment stands to an erg. Especially in the budding growth of a unity we can conceive a unitary primary ability as a subsentiment acquired for the effective workings of a sentiment. This concept of certain abilities developing their form as dynamic effector patterns, isomorphic with interests, is dealt with more thoroughly elsewhere (Cattell, 1971, p. 321). It is particularly obvious in occupational sentiments, when, for example, the cluster of skills of a secretary or a doctor is clearly fashioned around the dynamic sentiment to the job. The ability pattern that could doubtless be extracted as a common factor in such populations is to some degree part of the common sentiment pattern creating it.[3] However, such abilities cease to be servants merely to one sentiment and can be subsidiated, usually, to any and all, as a man who learns to shoot as part of a sentiment to hunting might transfer it to a military sentiment developed in war.

This detachability of an ability from the sentiment or sentiments for which it was created makes abilities something almost, but not entirely, categorically different from sentiments. At the least, abilities evidence the property of a sentiment in growing in a pattern of simultaneously learned habit elements subsidiated to some reward. However, a major sentiment can scarcely be detached, without breakage from its ergic goals, but abilities switch to *any* sentiment or ergic goal. The difference is probably that abilities are more distal structures in the lattice, subsidiating to several sentiments (and also under immediate ego control), whereas sentiments, less distal, subsidiate only to several ergs. The essential conclusion for present purposes, therefore, is that abilities are engrammings of skills similar in structural learning origin to sentiments (especially by budding) but more purely cognitive in nature, more distal in the lattice, and of less strong and definite ergic investment. Chapter 2 has indicated that sentiments are hierarchies, with smaller subsentiments, m's, within the large M factor we have called the sentiment, and still smaller engrams we might call sets, or t's, within the m's, and so down to S-R units. Ability and skill factors develop in the lower hierarchy.

Let us next begin to look at those social psychological aspects mainly considered in Chapter 7. Obviously by any method of learning, but particularly the first, the *form* of sentiment or acquired aptitude-ability growth will depend entirely and intimately on a person's position in life. This begins with his national culture (Republicans and Democrats are manufactured in the United States and Communists in Russia), class, family, religious associations, rustic or city life, proximity to the recreations of mountain or sea, and so on. Thus, when we say a sentiment is often the impress on the individual's learning of an institutional pattern in society, the term "institution" must be stretched to include geographical and mechanical features of the environment. Nowhere in psychology are we in greater need than we are here of that comprehensive econetic study and mapping of ecometric-psychometric alignments discussed in Volume 1, Chapter 6 (and including personality-culture isomorphisms).

5-5. Expected Patterns in the Tripartite Learning Equation, Expressing Common Schedule, Inherent Agency, and Budding Processes

One may reasonably expect that the distinctive action of the three modes of sentiment learning will be evident in the differences in the comprehensive learning equation (4-9) (p. 275). The experimental examination of the characteristics of those equations for all of a set of attitudes observed to be apparently growing together in a unity should, indeed, be a main way of checking on the above three hypotheses about sentiment growth.

What we are saying is that if a subset of attitudes finish up by being highly correlated over people, thus evidencing a sentiment structure—their rates of growth must also be correlated, and this should be evident in the learning equations for those attitudes being more similar than for attitudes at random. In P-technique the waxing and waning of a state can give correlation, but in R-technique we must look for common variation in the non-individual features of the most comprehensive learning equation (4-9) above. Attitudes could there have common variation in their rate of learning either because the behavioral indices on the traits that help learning are similar, or because the repetition and the reward terms (involving E_R, goal distance, etc.) are similar. If we keep to the simpler, more easily supported form of the behavioral indices, splitting b's only into v's (involvements) and s's (modulations) by ambient situations this means similarity of the attitude learning specification in four ways (1) the v's, (2) the s's, (3) the repetition, affecting CE learning, and (4) the reward, etc., affecting ME learning. As regards the two first the psychometrist will recognize that the correlation of two performances is highest (if their communality is the same) when the profile of loadings is most similar. (This finding is commonly encountered in restoring the correlation of two (row) variables by taking their "inner product" in the factor matrix.)

Few empirical research results yet exist that could reveal to us the relative magnitude respectively of the roles of (1) the behavioral index similarities (of v's and s's), (2) the common frequency of coexcitation, and (3) the common reward effects, in producing that common learning which brings a set of attitudes into the same sentiment. However, the case of fluid and crystallized intelligence in the ability domain has been reasonably well explored, and though it is in the ability modality it is sufficiently close to the present sentiment growth phenomena to justify extrapolation. In this case the performance increments that build up the sub-skill in the crystallized intelligence pattern are all uniformly highly loaded on just one factor in the equivalent of equation (4-9), namely g_f, fluid intelligence (see Horn, 1977). People higher in g_f therefore tend to pick up in higher degree the main performances that constitute g_c (crystallized intelligence). Although we have spoken of similarity of loading profile over the whole specification equation as characterizing two attitudes or skills that grew together, the similarity in many instances, as in g_c's skills may rest on a single large loading on one trait. The g_f-g_c example also illustrates the two other features of the learning equation, namely, frequency of joint coexcitation, and a common strength of reward. For covariance of skills in the crystallized intelligence pattern arises also from some children being longer than others in school, and from some having greater incentive to learn the judgmental and scholastic skills involved in g_c.

The "budding" principle in sentiment acquisition is also in part illustrated by this concrete example, for crystallized intelligence buds from fluid intelligence, though not in the dynamic sense in which a pre-existing sentiment leads to uniformly greater learning in the elements of some new sentiment structure that is totally subsidiated to it. The high loading of the new attitudes on the old sentiment will cause their correlation, and it is probable that, from the subsidiation similarity they will also experience common coexcitation and a similarity of reward. In introducing the budding conception we used the example of a person with a powerful sentiment toward a science deciding to learn a language, say German, in which the scientific output in his field is high. Such attitude courses as attending a language course, listening to radio in that language, paying visits to the country, reading journals in the language, and so on, will all have a similarity of motivation strength that will bring about a high correlation among them. The foreign language interest sentiment will thus appear as a new sentiment pattern, though subsidiating (as least initially) so closely to the science sentiment that the two factors would be expected to be highly correlated and perhaps even difficult to separate. One suspects, however, that because of differences in frequency of reward, age of formation, and other such differences, some autonomy and clear separation will characterize the budded sentiment.

Note that this budding form of growth best fits our basic representation of a sentiment as a subgoal structure in the dynamic lattice. An interesting historical instance would be George Washington's translation from a country gentleman to a general. In him and his fellow patriots a preexisting sentiment of attachment to the new country produced, according to its varying strength, levels of reward for previously undeveloped military attitudes and skills. The growth of the latter would be similar in a given person for all of them. This common reward—and new subgoal in the lattice distal to the existing sentiment—thus produced a military interest sentiment—which not all were so willing to relinquish after the war as was Washington!

In discussing the dynamic lattice we have stressed the fact that reward in a sentiment does not entirely reside in the main *goal* of the courses of action alone, but also in the side satisfactions in the action itself. This latter is evident also in our example of a sailing hobby sentiment. The obscure ergic satisfactions in the surge of a boat before the wind, and the like may puzzle us considerably as to the ergic roots of such satisfactions. But there is no doubt they exist, and in some ergic factor loading patterns such rather strange loadings have already appeared, for example, in the oral sexual satisfaction of cigarette smoking loading the sex erg. Incidentally, it is these more subtle satisfactions that cluster around obviously goal directed behaviors, that enabled Allport to bring plausible evidence for functional autonomy. In the dynamic lattice they would have to be represented as tendrils leaving the main stems—the subgoal to subgoal paths—and probably going directly to ergic goals as responses probably to innate cues. The tripartite learning equation in (4-10), p. 276, expresses the existing personality, the *ME* principle contribution, and the *CE* learning principle contribution, as they enter into a single attitude. To the extent that two or more attitude courses of action are the same in N, E_R, m, m_g, etc., they will wax at the same rate and thus eventually yield such correlations among themselves as are revealed when we find a sentiment factor, by R-technique. From the formulae we should expect this kind of congruence to arise particularly in sentiments generated by common schedules and by budding. In both, but particularly the latter, the attitudes will also tend to share the same ergic investment vector.

However, the full extent of the *CE* effect is not seen simply in helping two attitudes to grow at the same rate. It also forms links between the inner effects of the stimuli (h's) and ambient situations (k's) that trigger two (or more) attitudes, and so far this has not been expressed by (4-10) alone, which describes a single attitude.

To encompass this we have to recognize an engram built up between h_1 and h_2, and k_1 and k_2, and, for the moment throwing h and k together we have:

$$n_{h_1 k_1 \cdot h_2 k_2} = N m_{h_1 k_1} \cdot m_{h_2 k_2} \qquad (5\text{-}6)$$

where N is the number of times $h_1 k_1$ and $h_2 k_2$ (or their inner effects, m_{h1k1} and m_{h2k2}) have occurred together. This engram becomes a part of the growing sentiment concerned, M, and thus brings similarity of learning rate, and of ultimate strength to a_{h1j1k1} and a_{h2j2k2}, and other attitudes in M.

We have not immediately assumed that the R-technique correlation of attitudes from common schedule influences will produce more than what might be called a "hollow" structure, that is one in which the members of the set all stand high together or low together but have no *functional* connections. But the fact that all sentiments so far investigated appear as dR- as well as R-technique factors, suggests that generally the other growth effects come in, especially, *CE*, and, probably secondarily in relation to common schedule, to produce functional, dynamic connections manifested in common arousal and activation.

The phrase "cumulative learning" is fairly frequently used in reflexological attempts at explaining such aspects of human learning as we have just examined. As far as one can tell it might be more precisely called "cumulative common schedule learning," but the reflexological notions have never been pursued to any such sharpness of concept as in our tripartite equation (4-10) and equation (5-5). What we can certainly agree on is the need for action to be cumulative (N above) and for there to be "teaching schedules" or cultural frameworks in the structure of the culture or the ecology. As suggested above, the advance of research on sentiment acquisition needs to be coordinated with a thorough study of the environmental frameworks that provide the schedules. Only when such a matching of the sentiment structures with a sociological inventory of cultural-ecological schedule structures has been made are we likely to understand the whole process of sentiment learning.

In regard to the development of the functional aspect, as shown by arousal and activation spreading through the whole set of attitudes in the sentiment, much must be ascribed to the capacity for relational perception operating in humans. These perceived relations produce greater frequency of contiguity than occurs in contiguity by actual simultaneous external events, and more powerfully extends the cognitive network or map of any sentiment. The interaction of CE and ME in establishing the unity of a sentiment is probably substantial though virtually uninvestigated. On the one hand, the dynamic purposes of the sentiment will invoke with greater frequency, via the ME term, those cognitive associations, for CE action, that are relevant to the dynamics. For example, a sailor in a race may notice that a competitor has special jamming cleats. The throught of a main sheet will thereafter suggest jamming cleats. A small engram, an n addition, initiated by dynamically directed relation eduction, has been made to the cognitive structure of the sentiment to sailing. Not only is the eduction of the relation of cleats to speed begun through dynamic interests, but, further, the cognitive addition is allowed at once to share the dynamic resources—the ergic investment—possessed by the sentiment as a whole. The whole investment of the sailor in his sailing sentiment demands that he get jamming cleats, and a mention of the latter is now one more stimulus avenue toward evoking his whole interest (E, arousal, in the ME term) in the subject of sailing.

In hypothesizing that ME, the means-end principle, (CRII), is most active in the multiple-learning processes we have called common schedule and budding, and the CE principle, on the other hand, in the inherent growth agency process, we are of course not hypothesizing that each form of sentiment growth is due *exclusively* to one mechanism. We have seen a cooperation of two processes in forming a single factor pattern of crystallized intelligence, g_c, and it would seem that in the formation of sentiments the *ME* and *CE* principles will interact in a far more closely interwoven fashion than in this example. A thorough, quantitative research study of their interaction in the natural history of growth of even one or two prominent human sentiments would be of inestimable value in illuminating our concepts on such interaction.

5-6. The Production by the Inner Structure of Ergs and Sentiments of an Unfolding Adaptive Process

So far the unitary character of a sentiment has been that recognized in *R*-, *dR*- and *P*-technique "clustering of attitudes" with indications also of a hierarchical form extending from the central major engram to engram subsets. We have discussed three main hypotheses for the learning origin of the unity, but have scrutinized relatively little the mechanism for the unitary *activation*.

We purpose now to examine this activation as a process, and in doing so the model involved in the learning of a sentiment will be further extended. However, let us note at the outset that except that one is learned and one is acquired by "racial learning" the sentiment and the erg are very similar in their activation and guidance of unfolding action. Some fine work has been done by ethologists on the arousal of ergs and their subsystems in adaptive processes responding to successions of natural stimuli. From their observations we would argue that, with minor adjustments, the "process" mechanisms and equations we here set out for sentiments could be employed for ergic processes.

To grasp that a sentiment is both a *structure* and a *process*, let us recognize, at a level of taxonomic principles, that much to which in everyday life we give a "thing" label is also realized to be a fleeting process. Language uses nouns for both, as for summer, waterfall, adolescence, fever, and so forth. We must, of course, view this with a little suspicion, because common language is the chief seducer of the scientist from the independent thinking required in any discipline. That is why in Chapter 1, Volume 1, for example, we split simple ideas of a "pattern" into *surface* and *source* traits, *types* and *processes*. These entities need to be given not only distinct names, as in the verbal concepts which have attached to them for centuries, but mathematical description as *patterns* from statistical analysis of data. It is only recently that (see Harris, 1963; Harris & Lemke, 1974; and Miller, Galanter, & Pribram, 1960) processes, as unfolding plans, have begun to receive, in *P*-technique and elsewhere means of recognition by more than words.

A trait has been classed apart from a process as a pattern in *R*-technique (Chapter 1, Volume 1). We now have to recognize, however, that a psychological structure may manifest itself simultaneously in both kinds of relationship. The *trait* (*R*-technique) and the *process* (*P*- or *dR*-technique) may prove, both in the elements that are salient in them and in their psychological nature, to be two aspects of the same thing. The present discussion will make clear that this is so in the case of the sentiment structure. Nevertheless let us begin by reminding the reader that M's were first discovered, usually, by *R*-technique, as *traits* consisting of a set of attitudes, varying in strength *together*, *across people*. But such an engram structure, when it meets the right stimulus situations in the environment, is also a design for response actions to be released in a suitable succession, and having the character of being directed to achieve a certain goal. The structure, in short, is more than an *R*-technique pattern and has the capability of producing a behavior pattern unfolding as a *process*.

As a side glance we may note that traits that are not dynamic in nature, as sentiments and ergs are, will be less likely to have a process character, but *may* do so. The warmth an affectic temperament (*A*+ factor) person has for those he meets in a group may unfold in a particular way; a surgent (*F*+ factor) individual frequently has an overpowering conversational gambit; a groom with an occupational ability trait of ability to manage a horse has particular sequences in his actions built in as part of that ability, and so on. The clearer psychologists can become on this trait-process relation and the sharper their recognition of structural process concepts in the technical forms of psychometric behavioral measures per se, the less confusion psychology will have in subsequent theoretical discussions.

In studying this "process character" of sentiments we shall note the complication that, in humans at least, the process, as a descriptive "narrative," may be held up by intermittent *internal* control inhibitions dictated by other sentiments, as well as by unexpected outer circumstances (notably missing stimuli)—a difficulty which animals also encounter. But this does not deny our use of a concept of an essentially unitary and typical process character, which manifests itself successfully provided the environment does not vary too far.

In looking at the process and inner structure we propose to discuss simultaneously the *learning* of the structure, although the nature of the structure and its final action when "in being" is our main topic. Its "in being" could be illustrated by the sentiment to a car, where, across a set of people more or less involved with cars, the factor will load knowledge of engine parts, steering skills, responses to traffic signals, knowledge of oil and gasoline prices, and so forth. In the process aspect of the sentiment, however, we recognize also the presence of certain sequences. A person with such a sentiment well developed will have certain response sequences: trying to start the engine; looking at the "choke" if it does not start; checking the brakes when it does; looking at the gas level, etc. There will be correlated individual differences in these just as there are in the knowledge variables and cross-sectionally measured skills. How did the mechanisms for these sequences arise by learning?

To discuss this we shall take three instances, each representable by what we may call a *tract* in the dynamic lattice. A tract is a collection of functionally related, commonly subsidiating attitude courses of action in some part of the lattice. The above example of a car happens to do with immediate sequences, but in that sentiment, as an attitude tract, days or even weeks may separate one phase of the action from the next. It is the essence of a process that alternative response reactivities exist in the individual to permit him to reach the desired end goal despite change in stimuli and obstructions in the environment. The tract therefore typically has parallel possible paths, as shown in Figure 5-6. The broken lines mark a particular tract, ending at subgoal 3 ($SG3$), in its setting in a broader lattice. The attitudes will be in part parallel, but with all ending at the same ergic goal or major subgoal, as shown. Let us take, for example, a career sentiment in which an individual is concerned to reach the subgoal of becoming a qualified air force pilot (we choose this because we have substantial experimental data (see Cattell & Child, 1975), on the attitudes loaded in such a sentiment). For diversity, let us take also a recreational sentiment, say one of interest in owning and sailing a small sailboat. For comparison, and to bring out the rather remarkable similarity between an ergic goal tract, *innately* laid down, and an *acquired* sentiment, let us also take the imaginary case of a hungry lion, about whose ergic sequences the ethologists have given us some ideas.

The problem confronting a psychologist who would describe a model capable of guiding a dynamic process, innate or acquired, is essentially to account for persistence toward a more or less remote goal, with varied response effort adjusted to the uncertain incidence of various situations and stimuli. The model should also admit that with changes of ergic need levels, or of situations, beyond certain limits, predictable *new* goals and goal paths departing from the original intention, will appear.

What up to this point we have been content simply to call a subgoal and to represent as a node in the lattice must now be scrutinized more closely. It is not only the satisfying goal of a course of action, bearing a reward of ergic tension reduction, such as we have designated by E_R in the last chapter; but also a situation k, generating arousal, by s_k, and carrying an environmental-determined probability, of meet-

Tract as in Figure 5-8

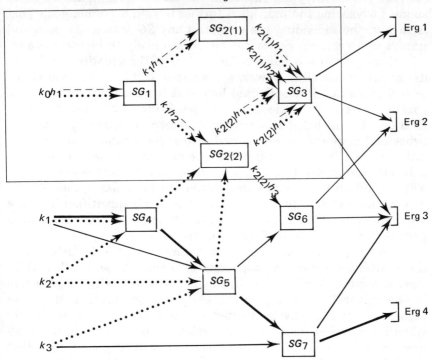

Three kinds of abstractions are illustrated in this dynamic lattice. (1) A simple tandem *chain* from k_1 to Erg 4, by the heavy line ——————— (2) A *sentiment* structure with the goal, subgoal SG_3, running from k_0, k_1, k_2, and k_3 the courses in which are shown by •••••• arrows (3). A *tract* beginning at k_0 and ending at SG_3, shown by — — — — — lines. the remaining courses, e.g., those ending in the four ergs, are in simple lines.

The sequences are shown in detail only in the tract. The subgoals are there numbered in order 1, 2, and 3, and the ambient situation k created by each is similarly numbered. At ambient situations k_1 and k_2 there are in each case two stimuli, h_1 and h_2, one of which will be paramount on any one occasion.

Figure 5-6. Sentiment, tract, and chain structures illustrated in the dynamic lattice.

ing two or three new stimuli h_1, h_2, and h_3, each of which, though with different convenience, can provoke a response capable of leading on to the goal. To compress this meaning of the probabilities of meeting suitable stimuli at a subgoal we might call the node a *subgoal-stimulus-probability-situation*. The implication of the name is simply that reaching a given subgoal will create a probability of certain further environmental stimuli appearing, any one of which, by past learning (or past evolutionary experience in the case of an erg), has led to responses advancing the individual further toward his or her goal. That is to say, the individual has a tryst at any SG with a situation and stimuli that past experience has taught are likely to be there as a result of the previous behavior. The feature of the situation producing its present modulating power, s_k, we shall call k, and it will be attached to an SG. It is supposed here that the attainment of any subgoal in a tract (or the lattice generally) has in the past, by reverberatory fixation, shown that it is appropriate to react by arousal to k and by behavioral response to any one of several *focal stimuli* immediately following the SG. They will stand, of course, among several to which it is *not* appropriate to react. The choice among the relevant stimuli will depend on the environment making them available, their prominence, and on their dynamic appeal. The last is quantified in v, the involvement in the stimulus, which is a function of the reward from past response to the given focal stimulus.

To bring out more clearly the nature of an SG, let us contrast this ambient situation, k, appearing at a subgoal, and followed by diverse possible focal stimuli, h_1, h_2, and so forth, with the elements in the classical reflexological stimulus-response chain, as shown in Figure 5-7. If it is strictly treated as it is defined—involving simply stimuli, h's, rather than our dual mechanism of k's and h's, which allows arousal by k and direction of response by h—it is easy to see that the reflex series of h's is capable of explaining a *chain*, but not a *tract*. But it is the tract behavior that most human and animal patterns of "persistence with varied effort" demands to have explained. The persistence to a more remote subgoal, with varied response courses, is essentially accounted for by a combined action of s_k, from the ambient situation at subgoal, k and, and a set of v_{hj}'s from alternate h's which present themselves there. In Chapter 4, on the learning acquisition of s_k's and h's, it was hypothesized that the arousal due to s_k (namely $s_k ME$) would be fixed by the extent to which behavior at SG_k had led to reward, but that since this is also represented in the v_{hj} values for the h's at SG there would necessarily be some proportionality of s_k to the mean v_{hj} value for the h's (focal stimuli) at SG. This needs to be more intensively examined in relation to the reverberation-fixation model of Figure 4-5, where the s_k and the v are tentatively assumed to acquire their values separately as engrams from the reward occurring at time $(t_2 - t_1)$ later. However, even in that case we should expect them to correlate in magnitude to the extent that they have a common elapsed time to the reward, and other similarities. Further analysis of the extent of s_k and v correlation will be set aside for the present.

Meanwhile it may help to consider what we have defined and represented as a *tract* (cut out of a total lattice with other features) in

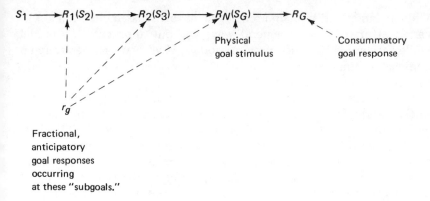

Fractional,
anticipatory
goal responses
occurring
at these "subgoals."

Figure 5-7. The classical reflexological formulation of a stimulus-response chain, with hypothesis of stimulation at subgoals.

Figure 5-6 above, in more concrete psychological terms. One can do this a little more colorfully if one steps aside into the parallel case of an ergic tract process, which is formally identical. For this let us take out again our lion. Let us suppose that through internal physiology he has reached a level of hunger at which he roams restlessly. From this he is moved by the sight of a thicket to respond by hiding therein close to a drinking hole where previous experience says food is to be found. In the thicket by the drinking hole, which is the first subgoal, k_1, he experiences a specific new arousal, by an s_{k1} modulation. (In the human this might be "expectation," if fully consciously representable.) This inner response to the ambient situation raises his susceptibility to the focal stimuli characteristically likely to appear at this point, h_1 (a gazelle), h_2 (a wildebeest), and so on. The appearance of a succulent gazelle, h_1, triggers a course of action, a_{h1j1k1} (h_1j_1 being specific to the gazelle), an approach, stalking the animal. When the lion, unobserved, gets close to the gazelle, it has reached the next subgoal, a new ambient situation, k_2, consisting of close proximity to the animal, and scenting it. This arouses, by s_{k2}, an attention to and susceptibility to respond to, a new set of focal stimuli. The responses to the behavior of the prey, constituting stimuli h_{21}, h_{22}, h_{23}, etc. will be j_{21}, a fast run, j_{22}, a long leap, or j_{23}, a cat-like crawl. (The subscript 2 here indexes them as the h's at subgoal SG_2.) According to which h is most prominent and which absent, a path will be followed which, because of the functionality of the acquired structure, is capable of leading to a further subgoal, SG_3, which is the object of the tract.

Since writers with a broadly, encompassing view of behavior, like

William James and William McDougall, have discussed persistence with varied effort only in a general way, without approach to a model, while reflexologists, with precise models, have never successfully encompassed the behavior, the model here deserves to be critically examined at greater length.

The next step in developing the model requires us to take account of the various structures that become activated or aroused by the focal and ambient situations recognized in the tract. Here we shall begin to use the world "field" as in a magnetic field, but with a precise operational meaning. For it is necessary to recognize that the more specific s_k and v_h impulsions are embedded in a broader directing field, which is provided by the general activation of the sentiment M concerned or the general arousal of the erg E. In the former case there is nevertheless also ergic arousal because of the usual engram-erg interaction term $s_{kx}M_xg_{xy}E_y$, where g_{xy} measures the extent of the particular sentiment's capacity to arouse the particular erg. (Eq. 2-8a,   p. 99.) The strength of motivation to act at each SG thus has finally to be recognized, as far as sentiment effects are concerned, as due to both the s_km, where m is the strength of the subsentiment at SG in the hierarchy of m's in M and the $s_{k0}M$ from the initial stimulation $s_{k0}M$ of the sentiment as a whole. In factor-analytic terms we have supposed M a factor that is a higher order to the m's. (On the question of whether there are hierarchies of e's in an E we have stated earlier that it is a probability, but unsupported as yet by any evidence.)

The model of an ambient situation k at each subgoal, immediately accompanied by an array of alternative h's leading to alternative response paths, may at first appear too mechanical to account for the flexibility which common observation recognizes—at least in human behavior in contrast to insect behavior. Before proceeding to precision the model a brief discussion on its setting is therefore desirable. One must recognize that though we speak of an internal sentiment structure it is not completely rigid, but subject to modification by internal forces from changing ergic tensions and by control forces of the ego not yet discussed. For simplicity of initial illustration of the model we set aside these influences which account for much observed unpredictability. The reader needs also to recognize that human environments are in the main more stable than we are inclined to think. The house preserves its pattern such that a fuss may arise even if the furniture is put in unusal positions. The numerous persons one encounters preserve their personalities (sometimes unfortunately!) and the parents, bank cashiers, policemen and doctors reliably maintain their roles in most cases. A learned, complex internal sentiment structure, fitted to these expectations, is therefore quite capable of functioning in a successful process by the model mechanism we have described. At the moment it is not easy to point to a concrete instance of a machine so constructed that will do this. A pianola piano or phonograph record is more like a simple chain reflex: the servo mechanism which puts a plane back on course when deflected by a gust of wind, is nearer, but still not a response to different options, and one would probably have to go to modern computer programs for the precise analogy.

A claim is not made that this sentiment process model infallibly leads to attainment of goals under *all* circumstances. Such a claim would invalidate the model; for the fact is that "the best laid plans of mice and men gang aft agley," and many a process halts, temporarily or finally, because the present learnings and the present outer situation do not mesh. What happens in a faltering process—especially when the environment is another person, as in courtship—is worthy of special study—but not here. What we have to recognize here is that our basic model of M's and m's in the person, and k's and h's in the external environment is the simplest case, overlaid in most human behavior by the individual's capacity to inhibit a sentiment by higher control systems, by his capacity to conjure new stimuli from memory, and by appetitive changes affecting the ergic resources of the sentiment. We recognize also that attaining certain subgoals can be postponed, or even transposed, and that secondary effects may come in from the need to "warm up" and so on. In the hunting lion it happens that we have described a continuously unfolding process in an uninterrupted stretch of time. The tract in the lattice that is part of the career sentiment of our officer candidate will, by contrast, cause him to pursue his reading on airplane engines even with many interruptions, and his exercises in landing a plane perhaps only at weekly intervals. The typical lattice sequence "I do this in order to reach subgoal 1, which I do in order to be able to do what is necessary to reach subgoal 2" is not an unbroken temporal sequence, but requires inhibition and storage. For often the different subgoals can be reached only by degrees and at different times, so that the subject may work intermittently and shift irregularly between later and earlier stages of the tract.

This is what we complain of as "the complication of life." Repairing a tear in the jib before entering a regatta may be the best order for a sailboat hobbyist; a functioning jib is a necessity, subsidiating to good sailing. Yet circumstances may demand that he do these in reverse order—reach the starter mark and then repair the jib—on some occasions. The sequences in the dynamic lattice structure are thus recorded as necessary *dynamic* subsidiations but need not correspond *invariably* in their *temporal* sequence. (Animal maze learning may lead us to forget this.) This irregularity must not hide from us that we are still dealing in general with a structure unfolding in a process. However, in research on process and sentiment structure the episodic absence of a number of situations and stimuli, or the interruption by a more important job, or some requirement of prudence, will tend to hide the connections and will call for greater technical resourcefulness in our investigation of the model. With these interruptions of temporal sequence will arise secondary mechanisms: reminders ("stimulus control"), re-warming up, and need for prolonged maintenance of arousal or sentiment activation.

A tract corresponding to a sentiment process has been presented first in Figure 5-6 in topological form as part of a dynamic lattice. Further pursuit of the model is, however, perhaps better conducted in algebraic terms, without an immediate spatial representation, such as fits closer to the form of a computer program. The tract in Figure 5-6 is accordingly abstracted, and enlarged to a four step (four subgoal) form in Figure 5-8, introducing at the same time a systematic scheme for representing the changing values of the path motivations in specification equation form. We propose to trace the action from an initial stimulus situation activation, $s_{k_0}M$, through alternative adaptive paths, to the ending of behavior in a goal that is its consummation as far as that tract is concerned, SG_3. In the course of so doing we shall ask why, under the impact of diverse h's and s_k's the individual is not more easily shunted off to stray *completely outside* the tract, as could happen for example at subgoal $SG_{2(2)}$ in Figure 5-6, by going to SG_6. An equally essential question concerns how much we must allow for the discharge or non-discharge of arousal at earlier phases in the process as affecting the choice at later choice points (subgoals).

Figure 5-8 sets out attitude action courses proceeding from the initial ambient situation k_0 through k_1 and k_2, passing through subgoals SG_1 and SG_{21} or SG_{22} to a goal SG_3 which is a subgoal as far as the whole lattice is concerned, and subsidiates to various ergic goals, but a final goal in the sentiment tract. After each subgoal two or three h's, *focal stimuli*, are shown. They have acquired by past experience the capacity to release corresponding courses of action, which are proven alternatives to anyone who has reached the subgoal concerned. The choice among them will depend on which is present, or present in greatest strength, as the individual is aroused at the given ambient situation. Incidentally, a fully adequate notation for the dynamic lattice for systematic use, and which one hopes will eventually be constructed, could be quite complicated and would bristle with many subscripts. At this introductory stage, however, we have compromised in the interest of simplicity in the immediate example. The subgoals are numbered here in order of subsidiation SG_1, SG_2, and SG_3, with their ambient situations, k_1, k_2, and k_3 (the last not continued on the figure) corresponding. The simplicity here is that this could not be done over a whole lattice, for the order of a goal from one starting

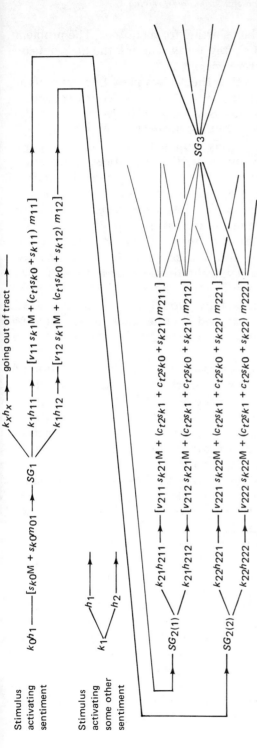

The subgoals, SG's, ambient situations, k's, and stimuli, h's, are numbered and in the same positions as in the lattice in Figure 5-6. What is newly introduced here relative to Figure 5-6 is a more detailed treatment of the paths in the form of (a) specification equation (dynamic part only) for the path, (b) extended subscripts to separate terms, e.g., the h_1's, more than was needed in Figure 5-6, and (c) terms, e.g., $c_{t1}s_{k0}$, to state the hypothesis about persisting motivations from earlier paths in the process. Central in these are the stimulation $s_k M$ of the overall sentiment and $s_{km} m$ of the engram particular to the given subgoal path, as is usual. Additionally, however, the hypothesis is here entertained that a cumulative reverberation, c, is continued into later action from the degree of stimulation reached by the previous m. This is shown by both of the alternative paths at the next subgoal. Thus $c_{t1}s_{k0}$ is the first reverberation of $s_{k0}m_0$, and $c_{t2}s_{k0}$ is the amount persisting into the second, (SG_2) k_2, ambient situation response. There is inevitably some complication of the subscripts to recognize the different phases in the chain, and, indeed, if the representation were carried to the full logical implications of the model there would be more. In any case the expression in brackets is set out to represent the total motivation strength (response potential) in the given attitude course—or, on a smaller scale, mental set. That is to say, the bracket expressions correspond to the specification equation for a_{hjk}.

Note (1) that there are still more alternative stimuli and paths at the end of the four last courses for reaching subgoal SG_3, and, of course, since SG_3 is in a larger lattice, some stimulus paths (four here) after SG_3. (2) The subscripts here are particularized one figure further than in Figure 5-6.

Figure 5-8. Mechanisms determining response potentials to provide adaptive behavior in a trait process.

point is different from that when starting from another. The problem is met in Figures 5-6 and 5-8 simply by numbering the SG's outside the tract in a convenient arbitrary way.

The attitude courses of action themselves need two symbols as subscripts—a k and an h—for their s's and v's. The two courses of action at, for example, $SG_{2(1)}$ in Figure 5-8, are assisted by the arousal of the same subgoal post-situation, k_{21}, but are started by focal stimuli, h_{211} and h_{212}, which set off, respectively, course of action $a_{h\,211j211k21}$ and $a_{h\,212j212k\,21}$. These are represented, in specification equation form, but without j's, in brackets after $SG_{2(1)}$ in the end branches of the process shown in Figure 5-8 (lower extension). Thus, as that figure shows, the unfolding sentiment behavior process can lead to the desired subgoal, SG_3, through alternative subgoals, $SG_{2(1)}$ and $SG_{2(2)}$, and alternative courses of action started according to which of the learned responses to stimuli are activated by the stimuli of greater environmental salience. Typically there would not just be two subgoals or two alternative stimuli after them, but several of each. The same general pattern, incidentally, would apply to pursuit of an ergic goal; but in that case an aroused E rather than an activated M would tend to keep every response course safely on the path to the goal.

Our theoretical model supposes that it is the initial activation of a sentiment as a whole, M, that keeps behavior to the tract, and which continues to appear in all paths to the sentiment goal SG_3, as $s_{k\,0}M$, $s_{k\,1}M$, etc., but not in any outside the goal paths. This tends to direct all behavior to SG_3. Parenthetically, among the 15 courses of action leading off through further ramifications at the end of the map in Figure 5-8 *some* (5 shown) will not go to SG_3, but to other goals in the lattice because of subsidiations to other sentiments typically shared by any action course. As at $SG_{2(2)}$ in Figure 5-6 a switch to a goal like SG_6 may be occur through temporary unusual ergic tension patterns and unusual external stimuli.

Whether we should assume that the sentiment M initially gets activated by a single k_0 ambient situation, as shown, or whether by some group of ambient situations, variously activated by the existing environment and spreading excitation among them from previous co-excitation learning, is a secondary matter for research. But in any case our assumption is that through the various n engram interconnections the M is activated *as a whole*, and, as Figure 5-8 now suggests, in more detail than 5-6, $s_{k\,0}$ M is a main contributor to the first course of action and to maintaining pre-potency of others later.

In passing we should note what is meant by this action of M "as a whole." It is something independent of the action of the more local substructures in M, which we have called m_c in equation 5-7, and m_{01},

m_{211}, etc., in Figures 5-8, and a still more local "set" specific to one attitude or mental set and indexed as t_j. For we have accepted that sentiment structure is hierarchical and that *SUD* factoring (Cattell 1978) would place the M's, m's and t's as successively smaller, related factors. But the three levels of engrams will be encountered together when the situations that evoke an s_{kc} or an s_{kt} are met. Thus in the specification equation the total *sentiment, subsentiment,* and *set* action on any specific attitude course a_{hjk} is normally:

$$a_{hjk} = (f)v_{hjx}s_{kx}M_x + (f)v_{hjc}s_{kc}m_c + (f)v_{hj}s_{kj}t_j \qquad (5\text{-}7)$$

The term (f) for "function of" is added here with cautious regard for some later modifiers of the mode of action that might be needed, and to remind us that the interaction with E's in the full specification is omitted here for simplicity. Incidentally it will be recognized that all three engram terms, M_x, m_c, and t_j, in diminishing breadth, will be present in both a *trait* and an activated *state* form, for $s_{kx}M_x = (1 + s'_{kx})M_x = M_x + {}_M x$, where M_x is the trait score and ${}_M x$, as usual, the activated state condition.

The argument that a sentiment M_x and its activation addition ${}_M x$ will continue to act throughout the attitude tract as a unitary whole is of course based on the finding of a unitary M factor in R and dR experiments, and has been hypothesized to arise from a combination of *CE* action (including the usual contiguity association and also that mediated by relation eduction, and conscious envisaging of the meaning of the sentiment) and of *ME* learning fixation. Descriptively, it means that M in Figure 5-8 is preset to bring in its activation effect at all subgoals, SG_1, SG_2, and so forth, and therefore to augment the response at k_1h_{11}, k_1h_{12}, $k_{21}h_{211}$, $k_{21}h_{212}$, $k_{22}h_{221}$, and $k_{22}h_{222}$. Thus the weight of the whole cognitive sentiment structure M as well as its ergic investment, ME, is, according to this theory thrown into the courses of action $a_{h11j11k1}$, $a_{h12j12k1}$, $a_{h211j211k21}$, and so forth, each represented in the bracket terms in Figure 5-7.

Incidentally, in order to illustrate a single action more clearly, in Figure 5-6 there is supposed to be only a single focal stimulus, h_1 (in k_0h_1) and therefore only one possible course of action at the outset, whereas at SG_1, in Figure 5-8, more typically, there are three and at SG_2 there are four. As Figure 5-8 at SG_1 shows, however, a new engram m_{01}, corresponding to the goal SG_1, brings in its influence in the hierarchy here, so that the combined activation (and therefore arousal, through the E in the ME term (not shown) is $s_{k1}M + c_{t1}s_{k0}m_{11} + s_{k1}m_{11}$, as shown in the total strength of this attitude course indicated in brackets to the right of goal SG_1 in Figure 5-8. The individual E_i's and M_i's that these behavioral indices would multiply, in the equation for a particular person, are of course not shown here, because we are concerned only with the common structure.

A first function of the M is thus seen in augmenting the strength of any attitude element falling within its structure, as indicated by $s_{k0}M$ in the various attitude specification equations (behavioral indices only) written on the attitude courses of action in Figure 5-8. But a second and more important service it offers in our model is its capacity to keep the sequences of attitude actions from "running off the rails." If we had a model with no M's, the choice of action at each subgoal would be determined purely by local conditions, largely the strength of the local m and especially of the strength and availability of each of the alternative k stimuli present immediately after the subgoal. In that case there would be nothing to stop the behavior running through the lattice in what would be an irregular and irrelevant set of courses as far as the given sentiment is concerned, ending up at any of several ergic goals. For example, at $SG_{2(2)}$ in Figure 5-6 the course to SG_3 could be supported and sustained by the main sentiment in the tract, so that even if h_3 were a more prominent stimulus than h_1 or h_2 the action would not necessarily go off to SG_6.

We need to remind ourselves, in passing, that the courses of action at the subgoals and h's will have their strengths determined partly by the need strengths of various E's which we know enter into every behavior specification (equations 2-8, 4-11). Consequently, in the absence of a powerful effect from the given M over the paths in this tract, an accidental high need strength in some erg to which, say, SG_6 subsidiates could swing the choice of action toward SG_6. In general the appetitive or other component in an erg can re-direct the courses at some subgoal to an h response particularly affected by that erg, which would carry action right outside the courses subsidiating in the tract to the given sentiment goal.

The vital theoretical element in accounting for the important type of behavior we set out to explain—persistence with varied effort and alternative behaviors toward a common goal—is thus the unity of the sentiment structure (or of the erg in a purely ergic animal). When aroused, it suffices at each choice point to turn the action, despite local conditions (up to certain limits set by the dual determination by local and general E and M forces) toward those response courses that serve the purposes of the sentiment. It is possible that closer scrutiny of the action of the specification equation will suggest that in the initial action, as at k_0 in Figure 5-6, the initial activation weight, s_{k0} (for M) should not be only that of the situation k_0, but (through the earlier coexcitation we have discussed) should be a broader term representing k_0, k_1, k_{21}, and k_{22}, and perhaps written $s_{k0\ldots2}$. This concerns the question of how a sentiment comes to be activated as a whole in the first place—by a single stimulus situation or an accumulation of situations. In a fully integrated sentiment the "situation" may be some symbol, verbal or otherwise (for example, "What are you planning about your career?"). In another event, say sailing, it may be a smell of pitch and the taste of spray. In the present diagram we have allowed a single ambient situation, k_0, to set off the activation of the whole sentiment, but as indicated, the diagram or program might need to enter an accumulation of k's. For example, a contemplation of k_1, k_2, and k_3 in Figure 5-6 might more commonly set off the sentiment.

Note that the activation or arousal (the s value) of any given situation is actually a composite result of activations that occurred earlier in the process. Thus (in the lower part of Figure 5-8.) at $SG_{2(1)}K_{21}$ there is $s_{k21}M + c_{t2}s_{k1}m_{211} + c_{t2}s_{k0}m_{211} + s_{k21}m_{211}$ which contains the carry over of the previous upper line from SG_1. The c_{t2} before $s_{k0}m_{211}$ indicates that some change, c_{t2}, commonly an augmentation but sometimes a decline of m_{11}'s activation level, has occurred from what it was one step earlier, and is likely to change the persisting $s_{k0}m_{211}$ value. In shaping the most probable model we have to make a choice here between accepting a declining arousal in M as the process proceeds due to the reverberation, as in learning effects, as expressed in the preceding sentence, or of supposing that through the stimulating power of further associated situations in the process the original M retains or even increases its activation. The effect may well apply to the more local m but not to the broad M. The formula actually used here admits, by the c term, (Figure 5-8) the likelihood of a change in the m activation level as time proceeds, but not in M, so long as the overall M unfolding is in action.

Let us next look more closely at the mechanism of choice at a subgoal, and consider in that connection also the vexed question of whether the lack of earlier discharge of a normally required course at the appropriate point interferes with the inner dynamics as well as perhaps wrecking the integration of the process with environmental requirements. The latter is virtually certain—one cannot, for example, give a paper at a scientific meeting without having the paper ready— but discussion of the former mechanism plunges us in matters not experimentally explored. In time, if step x is dropped and y pursued, without any resulting failure to reach the goal, we know that step x will fall out of the habit system; but what is the *immediate* effect? The absence of stimuli h_{11}, or h_{12}, despite the ambient activation by k_1 ((after SG_1 in) Figure 5-8) would bring the process to a halt. But supposing the individual is nevertheless by some environment "fluke" physically brought to the environmental subgoal SG_2, will the persisting activation of m_{11} by s_{k1} from subgoal SG_1 interfere with the normal response to SG_2? This probably occurs relatively infrequently in everyday life—a person does not often find his car engine already running after he has unlocked the door—but experimental investigation of processes "interrupted" in this and other ways might help check the model.

As indicated, some uncertainty also enters regarding whether a single ambient situation will simultaneously (or, at least, with comparative completeness) fire a whole sentiment, and whether the encountering of the lesser, local stimulus situations as the process unfolds have a specific action to increase (as in the warming up of an interest) the major M activation, which is presumably weak when set in action by the first attitude connected with the sentiment (and presumably relatively distal in the sentiment tract from the sentiment goal),

Our model supposes both of these actions, but the first—the tendency of cognitive excitation to spread easily throughout the unitary cognitive network of the sentiment; but not beyond it (except to an altogether lesser degree)—may justifiably strike some psychologists as deserving more experimental investigation than it has yet had. The evidence at present is broadly in two different methodological areas. First there is the factor analytic evidence from both dR and P-technique experiments (see, for example, Cross, Williams and others in Cattell & Child, 1975, and the recent study of Birkett & Cattell, 1978) showing that the attitudes that load the R-technique sentiment factor also come out with much the same pattern in change measures. In some cases the stimulus situations which caused these changes can be recognized. Secondly, there are manipulative experiments, admittedly mainly in verbal material, and primarily designed for semantics (Rips, Shoben, & Smith, 1973; Collins & Quillian, 1972; Smith, Shoben, & Rips, 1974) which explore semantic distance in terms of associated meaning and retrieval time (Collins & Quillian, 1969) with operational relations that would fit our expectations of spreading activation. However, a cognitive structuring as seen by these investigators was not conceived as a sentiment network, and work in this area therefore needs checking for present purposes within the cognitive-dynamic unities established by attitude factoring. An important check of this kind, concerning (a) the effect of stimulating one attitude in a sentiment upon the cognitive activation and motivational arousal of other attitudes factorially defined as in its area, and (b) the relative role of U and I motivational components in producing the unity of sentiment change (as viscerogenic arousal and cognitive activation measures, respectively), is currently being made by J. Campbell. Experimental designs for investigating these and other aspects of the process model are touched on again in the next section.

In terms of everyday life observations we are asking "Does an overheard conversation about planes excite the young air force officer's interest in *all* the attitudes defining an air force career sentiment pattern (see Volume 1, Chapter 4)?" And does the sight of animals at a drinking hole stimulate the lion's level of appetite as a unitary whole? One must remember, of course, that in humans the triggering of a sentiment activation does not necessarily begin with an ambient situation for *one* attitude in it. Instead the whole cognitive-dynamic network of a sentiment can be conscious and effectively represented and activated by a single verbal symbol. We say, "My friends and I have agreed to go sailing today," or "Unless I do better in mathematics I shall be dropped from aviation school." A verbal concept thus seems sufficient to activate all the cognitive dynamic elements of the sailing or career sentiments concerned.

One must consider also the immediate effect of the cognitive activation upon dynamic structures, by the ME term. The fact that each sentiment has its own pattern of ergic investments lead us to expect that each would have some introspectible emotional quality defined by that sentiment pattern. As a corollary on the concept of distinct ergic investment patterns (vectors) one would certainly expect such composite affect qualities to exist. There may be no systematic data from the pre-behavioristic, introspective stage of psychology—from Kulpe, Meinong, Ach, Titchener, and others—available to support this. But common experience seems to indicate that thoughts of a career examination or a day's sailing have immediately distinctive emotional atmospheres and affective meanings, again witnessing to prior activation of the cognitive sentiment as a whole and its ergic investment.

From this concept of the persistence of unitary cognitive and ergic action through the network of an ordinary sentiment, certain inferences follow for experimental checking. One approach would be by correlational studies of attitudes as studied in the next chapter. The second would be investigation of cross-stimulation effects on retrieval as just mentioned. Another would be to test that such effects for sentiments should be more limited and fragmentary in young children and far more so in lower animals possessing no concepts (in the true sense) and no symbols for abstractions. Again, our theory of growth of sentiments would require that the degree of unity might differ according to whether the given sentiment arose by common schedule, budding, or other sources. In that connection, what the clinicians call "complexes" should prove to have recognizably peculiar patterns, showing ergic arousal produced by cognitive elements completely detached from the main cognitive network. And we might also check experimentally the expectation that, in this growth of sentiments the attachment of new, limited engrams, some difference of readiness of flow through the main sentiment excitation would arise between older and newer elements.

Let us turn finally to a closer scrutiny of the full specification equation (whose source is in Figure 5-6 and 5-8), in connection with the choice (not necessarily conscious) that occurs among the h's after attainment of a given subgoal. But for the present let us assume the model that the sentiment action will neither increase nor decline in the course of the action through the tract. Inasmuch as a subsentiment, (m_{211}, m_{212}, m_{221} or m_{222}) connected with SG_2, and activated by k_{21} or k_{22} (Figure 5-8) is a part of the extended M sentiment, the sentiment is nevertheless stronger in its action as the process proceeds successfully. A more complex model might in fact recognize this by some effect of k_{21} and k_{22} directly on M.

The whole model is thus one of a relay system, in which older excitations are carried forward into fresh environmental stimulation contacts. The relaying of activation of M has to be at a substantial level, if the execution of the sentiment responses is to keep to the theme of the sentiment and not be side tracked. But the relaying of the local goal effects—for instance (Figure 5-8) of the $s_{k11}m_{11}$ drive from SG_1 beyond SG_2—has to be temporary; for otherwise its effect would be to "overload the past" and get in the way of later equally local adjustments to the new environmental circumstances. Consequently a coefficient c, less than one, is attached to these relays (Figure 5-8) and phases them out, though permitting the success of the action up to that point to add to the strength of the approach to new stimuli. The v's would be outside the bracket which covers (M, csm, and sm) indicating that the course of action, say, at k_{21}, is sustained by all of them, so that csm is at any rate not an old course of action, but only an old impetus.

To bring out the above relations clearly Figures 5-6 and 5-8 have dealt only with the activation of engrams. But the specification for the courses of action in fact contain also E terms, and, indeed, also terms from the ability and temperament modalities. Though it would be satisfying to complete this section with a truly comprehensive statement of what fully accounts for behavior in any path of the sentiment process, the introduction of the E's is sufficiently complex without adding the A's and P's, and is more to the point.

The complexity lies in the fact that where we have an M or m term in Figure 5-8 the full dynamic specification would require us to have an E, an M, an ME, and an EM term. Let us consider the individual's choice of action between $a_{h211k21}$ and $a_{h212k21}$ immediately after SG_{21} and confine ourselves to M_1 and m_2 alone, leaving out also the straight M term and confining to those with E, namely, E, EM and EM. We then have for the first action, and, *mututis mutandem*, the second:

$$a_{h\,211k\,21} = v_{2211}s_{k\,0}M_1(g_{m\,1}E_1 + \ldots + g_{p\,1}E_p)$$
$$+ v_{2211}s_{k\,0e}E(f_1M_1 + \ldots + f_qM_q)$$
$$+ v_{2211}s_{k\,21}m_{21}(g_{m\,211}E_1 + \ldots + g_{m\,21p}E_p)$$
$$+ v_{2211}Efm_{21} \tag{5-8}$$

Here E in the second and last terms would actually be a whole series of E's. The g's and f's here, are, of course, the generator and influence terms defined in Chapter 2.

The v_{211}'s have four different values because each of these sources of motivation may have contributed differently in the past to reaching the goal satisfaction at SG_3. The ergic arousal and satisfaction in the first term, as shown by the gE's in the bracket will be the same for any path in the sentiment tract, though the v_{211} before it will depend on the path. The satisfaction in the special course of action at the subgoal, as initiated by h_{211} and expressed in the bracket of $g_{m\,1}E_1$, etc., will be in some degree different from that for the main sentiment, because, as Figure 5-6 reminds us, the courses of action after SG_{31} and SG_{32} can branch off in the lattice to ergic and sentiment goals outside the given sentiment tract. The path $a_{h\,211k\,21}$ will differ from the above principally in the third term, which has to do with the satisfactions and SG_3, being different, in subsequent extra-tract possibilities.

In seeking to understand why certain paths in the lattice are taken up at any given time in the unfolding process we recognize the basic theorem set out earlier in decision theory that the a_{hijk} will be followed which has the larger value. If we look at subgoal $SG_{2(2)}$ in Figure 5-6 the first choice is between going out of the tract altogether by the path stimulated by $k_{2(2)}h_3$ and following either path in the tract leading to SG_3. The reason the tract is normally followed is that (turning now to the more detailed lay-out in Figure 5-8) the M term reinforces $a_{h\,221k\,22}$ and $a_{h\,222k\,22}$, but not this new path.

To assist the student in coordinating Figures 5-6 and 5-8, it should be pointed out that though they represent the same they do so with a change of scale, which requires more expanded subscripts in 5-8. Also, whereas 5-6 represents the goal path only by arrows, 5-8 inserts the specification equation for each path, in the "boxes," each of which would evaluate the a_{hjk} for that path, as far *as the engram parts* of the dynamic equation are concerned. (Note also that the subscript for a particular individual is omitted, for a less entangled view.)

Thus if we look at the lower right two rows of Figure 5-8, we can examine the choice between courses of action $a_{h\,221j\,221k\,22}$ and $a_{h\,222j\,222k\,22}$, (now adding j's for courses) which follow subgoal

$SG_{2(2)}$, with its k_{22} ambient situation, and the respective focal stimuli, h_{221} and h_{222}. The past-activated interest is the same in both, namely $s_{k22}M$ and $c_{t2}s_{k1}$, but the local engrams to be excited are different, namely m_{221} and m_{222}, and involvement indexes are different, namely v_{221} and v_{222}. It is by the strength of these, in their *products*, that the choice between $a_{h221j221k22}$ and $a_{h222j222k22}$ will be made. "Product" is italicized to remind us that the action from within as from ergic tensions at the time, when the expanded specification equation with E's, $(g_{m221\cdot1}E_1 + \ldots + g_{m221\cdot p}E_p)$, etc., is finally used, will also determine the choice of response course.

Thus the choice of attitude action courses within the tract will be decided partly by the activation at subgoals, partly by the prominence of stimuli, partly by relayed motivations, and partly by the overall emotional tension pattern of the individual at the time. And the chief causes of going completely out of the sentiment tract will be (1) a failure to encounter expected stimulus situation objects, (2) initial weakness of the s_{k0} activation and the sentiment M itself, and (3) sufficient change in the ergic tension vector ($E_1 \ldots E_p$) to carry the individual at some choice point into a course with a goal possessing a larger ergic tension satisfaction vector.

5-7. Experimentally Checking the Relay Process Structure in a Sentiment and Its Acquisition by Learning

The model for a sentiment as a process has reached a challenging level of complexity, but if we would understand behavior in realistic scientific fashion such complexities have to be faced. (The calculations are probably less forbidding than those of putting a satellite around Mars!) Actually the last section has not fully expressed in a final equation system all the interactions indicated in the test to be necessary features. More space and specialized reasoning is needed for that than is appropriate here.

It remains to indicate—alas, in terms of what can be done in a cramped space—how the above model can be experimentally investigated, and, also, how we hypothesize that its structure can be brought about by learning.

Investigation so far has been limited (1) to cross sectional R-technique, showing that response potentials of courses of action about a sentiment object, at a given moment, are positively correlated and indeed separate out clearly as a factor of individual difference strengths in sentiments and ergs and (2) to longitudinal dR and P-technique studies showing that the same set of response potentials wax and wane together with environmental stimulation and internal condition. To proceed to the kinds of experimental design that are needed to reveal these structures it is best to begin with consideration of a notion that has been central in the minds of clinical psychologists, and is at the moment a bone of contention between reflexological and dynamic clinicians, namely, the existence of alternative dynamic equivalent behaviors, i.e. alternative expressions of the same need (clinically as alternative symptoms). In our model (Figure 5-8) we can consider for illustration, at the bottom, four such alternatives to reach the satisfaction of SG_3, namely, $a_{h\,211j211\,k\,21}$, $a_{h\,212j212k\,21}$, $a_{h\,221j221\,k\,22}$, and $a_{h\,222j222\,k\,22}$. (These are not written in 5-8, but their provokers and specifications for the course are.)

In an R-technique analysis of a sentiment, such dynamic equivalents in attitudes tend to be positively correlated. If flying a single- or two-engine plane is the option for members of a flying club, sentiment M, representing attachment to the flying club, taken over a sample of people who do and who do not belong, will load positively both behaviors, for flying club members are accustomed to both, and non-members to neither. But, if we use P-technique, the two plane interests will tend to be negatively correlated in a flying club member, for on the days she uses one she cannot use the other. And similarly in clinical observation of a patient who substitutes at times one dynamic symptom expression of an underlying maladjustment for the other, the two will be negatively correlated, in P-technique and dR-technique.

The first reaction of some psychometrists and clinicians to a negative correlation between two symptoms has been to apply thinking familiar in the ability field and say that two negatively correlated or uncorrelated behaviors cannot be part of the same structure. A more sophisticated multivariate experimenter will not make this mistake of taking a correlation matrix at its face value, and will pursue the problem by the comparative correlational and factor analytic analysis of cross sectional and sequential measurement. At a first reading of this chapter, the reader unaccustomed to CORAN statistics might be well to by-pass the rest of this section, taking the conclusion for granted, but if he does so now he should return to concentrate on it, particularly if other research on clinical dynamics is contemplated.

In cross sectional analyses, such as might follow if we took measures across the four behaviors to the right end of Figure 5-8 we are dealing among other novelties with what has now been formally studied by psychometrists in terms of *ipsative score* psychometry, though not all ipsative score problems are dynamic, as here. Note first that to get a score matrix in the dynamic field for an R-technique study we need to take, say, 100 people and have each go through, say, 20 runs of the tract, so that score from 0 to 20 is possible for frequency of each of the four. As a concrete illustration let us take the behavior habits in commuting each day to one's place of business. Let us suppose each person is free to take a subway or a car to work. An R-technique correlation of a_{j1} and a_{j2} over N people, each score being the responses summed over, say, 50 occasions, will here *tend* to be -1.0, because they are mutually exclusive behaviors. Consequently, our first naive expectation is that R-technique factoring will produce a factor loading for a_{j1} of +1.0 and for a_{j2} of -1.0. However, we notice next that people have different eagerness for work and could differ considerably in the number of days they turn up at the office at all. This second influence will give a *tendency* toward a positive correlation of a_{j1} and a_{j2}, and could produce a "desire to work" factor loading both positively. The final correlation of a_{j1} and a_{j2} with two or more factors could thus even end up positive.

Wherever we have a set of variables whose total summed for any one person is necessarily the same as that for another person we are dealing with *ipsative* scoring and the problems of correlating and factoring such scores.

Ipsative scores are generally forced upon psychologists by circumstances (for no one likes their awkwardness in calculation), and, before psychometrists had an explicit term for them they were often handled, for example, in inventories of job interests, in ignorance, with essentially absurd results. Scores would be ipsative if, for example, we scored some 20 interests by the fraction (or percent) of 24 hours the person spends on each, or if we paired 20 objects in every possible combination among them (190) and get preference scores for each object. (The sum total of all preferences will be 190 for any person, but the sigmas will in this case be different.) Some features of correlating ipsative scores, i.e. scores wherever there is some limit of energy, time or whatever, the same for everyone, have been discussed by Cattell, 1935, 1966, 1978, Clemans 1966, and Tucker, 1956. Apart from any influence of a real psychological or other structure, it will be found that a negative correlation of $1/(n-1)$ will arise among all variables. With a large N this admittedly is small, but still enough to obscure the existence of a real positive general factor if it exists in the psychological structure as such. What actually appears in the r's in our dynamic variable case will depend on the relative variance contribution of (1) the positive factor common to the alternatives $a_{h\,211\,j211\,k\,21}$ etc., and so on. For example, if we took say, 100 people over 200 work days, scoring them on whether they worked on the first or second shift, a positive general factor would still appear in the data if there was a good range of absenteeism across the workers. The relative size of general factor and bi-polar factor of equivalence would similarly be decided here by the relative variances of the common M and m in the present dynamic models) and (2) the number of alternatives—h's and k's here—

that are in competition. A simple illustration of the action is given in Table 5-1, first, in Part I, with the simple case of two attitudes illustrating the effect on the correlation matrix of two different factor variance contributions. Part II, continues the illustration with four alternative attitude courses (h_j's).

Part I shows two intermediate possibilities for a two-choice equivalent, first with half the variance coming from the dynamic ("variation in going to work") factor and the second with more than half (specifics being allowed in both) for that factor. In (a) we observe a zero correlation, and unless we had the indicated hypothesis to test, we would drop it, assuming no relations. In the second case a positive correlation, .31, appears, suggesting a dynamic connection of the two behaviors. In Part I(a), with a zero correlation actually observed between alternatives, we assume the common positive variance from the common sentiment and the inverse variance from the path alternatives to be equally strong. In example (b), which is probably more common in life, we assume that the common variance is stronger than what we might call the circumstantial factors, so the observed correlations remain positive.

Part II of Table 5-1 extends to the general case where there are more than two alternative equivalent behaviors. In general psychometric terms, we are dealing in all ecometric factors with results based on ipsative scoring (Clemans, 1966). As stated this rests on the condition that the sum total of an individual's scores on n alternatives must always be 1.0. Unless any other factors intervene, this will produce a correlation matrix in which all values are negative. Typically, ecometric factors will then appear in a factor matrix having larger, L, and smaller, S, terms patterned as in Part II(b). As shown in II(a), such a set of ecometric factors, *along with a larger dynamic factor*, can nevertheless produce an entirely positive matrix. Note that we would not actually extract five factors from four variables, as seems in this illustration. There would actually be other variables than these, sharing the sentiment factor, number 1.

Part II thus considers the more frequent situation in real life, with at least four (commonly more) alternative path variables (hj's). Here the factor structure will probably admit two alternative solutions, though there is as yet insufficient experience of ipsative factoring to judge which will have better properties. One solution—that represented in II(a)—will offer as many "choice" factors as variables; another, in II(b), *may* represent the four alternatives and the main sentiment in fewer factors.

In the general introduction to process analysis in Volume 1 (Chapters 1 and 5) we pointed out that there are broadly two models for investigating and representing a process. The first, which may be

TABLE 5-1. The Correlational and Factor Structure to Be Expected from Psychological Subgoal Structure

I.   Simplified to Two Attitudes

(a)

	Factor Matrix, V_0				Observed correlation matrix, R_v	
	Factor 1	Factor 2	μ_1	μ_2	1	2
Attitude 1	.6	.6	.53		1 (.72)	0
Attitude 2	.6	-.6		.53	2 0	(.72)

(b)

	Factor 1	Factor 2	μ_1	μ_2	1	2
Attitude 1	.8	.5	.33		1 (.89)	.31
Attitude 2	.7	-.5		.51	2 .31	(.89)

Note: The communalities, h_2, instead of r's, have been put in the diagonals of the R_v.

II.   More Typically with Several Attitudes

		Factor matrix, V_0					Observed correlation matrix, R_v			
		1	2	3	4	5	1	2	3	4
(a)	Attitude 1	.8	.3	-.2	-.2	-.2	.85	.52	.60	.36
	Attitude 2	.7	-.2	.3	-.2	-.2	.52	.70	.52	.31
	Attitude 3	.8	-.2	-.2	.3	-.2	.60	.52	.85	.36
	Attitude 4	.5	-.2	-.2	-.2	.3	.36	.31	.36	.46
(b)	Attitude 1	L	-S	-S	-S					
	Attitude 2	-S	L	-S	-S					
	Attitude 3	-S	-S	L	-S					
	Attitude 4	-S	-S	-S	L					

Part I shows two representative possibilities for a two-choice equivalent, first (a), with half the common variance coming from the environmental choice factor, and the second, (b), with less than half coming from the latter. The zero *r* of the two attitudes in the former might hide from a superficial inspection their dynamic relatedness.

Part II supposes four mutually possible alternative attitudes choices. Incidentally, since 5 factors could not be taken from 4 variables, we must suppose the latter embedded in a larger matrix. But each attitude would have a corresponding factor. The correlation matrix that would be observed when there are several attitudes is all positive and even at a glance does not hide their common dynamic origin. In (b) a general statement is made. (*L* = large; *S* = small *r*.) Each attitude factor has a large positive loading on its own attitude and small negatives on the others.

called a *quantified process matrix* gives quantities for the presence or strength of each of a set of variables—stimuli and responses—on each of a succession of occasions. The second, the *stochastic* model, represents the *probabilities* of certain events occurring at series of points in time when the incidence rate of certain previous events, at certain earlier intervals in time, is known.

The quantitative model is most apt to the dynamic sentiment or ergic process and we shall give it greater consideration. One begins, as the table in Volume 1, Section 5-6, shows, with a score matrix containing both psychometric and ecometric measures, that is covering both the behaviors and stimulus situations that typically occur in the process. The score matrix runs over perhaps a hundred occasions and the entries can be either for one person, as in *P*-technique or an average for all people, as in *common P-technique.*[4] However, a special development is needed here called *cumulative P-technique.* For a single run will give only all-or-nothing scores on any path (the stimuli being fixed). Cumulative P-technique, distinguished from ordinary and common mentioned above, takes several experimental runs for the person on the identical set of occasion-situations, spaced as usual on each run—but with some changes possible in the stimulus strengths. The entry in each response-occasion score cell is then the sum for that cell over the various runs. Incidentally the fact that a choice point an "all-or'nothing" choice of one or the other has to be made does not restrict us to a frequency score, since the chosen attitude course can also be quantitatively scored, making scores "intensity-frequency" in nature.

In the introduction of the quantitative process model (Volume 1, Section 5-6) a set of behavioral and econetic (stimulus magnitude, situational press, etc.) variables were put at the top of the descriptive score matrix, and measured over rows of temporal occasions. The psychological dimensions and meaning of the descriptive "score" matrix was then found by factoring. In the present setting the behavioral measures would be made on the strength of all courses of action (say the 7 that appear in Figure 5-8), along with ecometric measures of the variables (k's and h's) hypothesized to be associated. For an individual it would be a cumulative score matrix summed over, say, 20 occasions. The factoring would then give a specification equation for the variables and scores on the factors for the occasions. Both are useful, but our concern here is to check on the existence of the M_1, m_1, m_2, etc. factors and their behavioral indices for the courses of action. An obvious weakness of the unmodified common *P*-technique approach here described is that for a substantial proportion of the occasions there might be zero scores for certain behavior.

A concrete illustration of such a cumulative P-technique matrix is given in Table 5-2. According to the model in Figures 5-6 and 5-8 one would expect the M, m, and e (ecometric) factors to appear much as shown. The e's—here corresponding to just a pair of stimuli, h_1 and h_2—would have h's respectively showing positive and negative loadings on a single factor. A correspondence of e factors would be expected with distributions of h's and k's (SG's).

Turning now to the question of how such a sentiment factor structure as M, m_1, m_2 and an econetic structure of e's could arise along the lines just discussed, we find little need for further discussion beyond what has already been said about CE and ME principles in the three mechanisms (common schedule, etc.) of sentiment production. The e's, of course, belong to the environment, and can be set aside, though it would be true to say that the subject often arranges these, as when he arranges for people to meet him at certain times in carrying out transactions.

As with most learning, of which the maze is an epitome, we generally learn beginning at the proximal and ending at the distal end of the lattice. If SG_3 is an agreed desirable, we learn the path from SG_2 to SG_3 and, later, one from SG_1 to SG_2. When there are different available, practicable ways to reach SG_3, as there are in Figure 5-8 both ($SG_{2(1)}$ and $SG_{2(2)}$) will start acquired paths. The learning itself can be, in cognitive aspects, insightful or trial and error, but in either case what we have to account for is the rise of an activation and arousal potential of the type s_k ME at the subgoal situation SG_1 (Figure 5-8) and of a triggering of actual behavior by one of the stimuli immediately following the subgoal, h_{11}, h_{12}, etc., as represented by an involvement of the s_k ME to the extent v_{11}, v_{12}, etc.

While we have admitted some aid from the CE principle here, the main weight in the generation of the s_k value, such as $s_{k\,21}$ which operates on m_{211} after SG_2 in Figure 5-8, is ascribed to the ME principle. That is to say, the fact that getting into the situation at this subgoal has repeatedly been followed by more ultimate satisfaction *directly* produces an arousal capacity in the subgoal, subject to the laws of reverberation and time lapse studied earlier.

Our model postulates that normally the ambient situation, k, does not itself provoke particular actions but possesses a set of h's— focal stimuli "nested" in it—and that these have provoked operant responses, in some cases leading to the next goal. This tends to bring about a relation between the summed v_h values for the separate effective h's at the subgoal and the s_k for the whole ambient situation, the existence and magnitude of which we have discussed and suggested should now be experimentally checked. Indeed, as stated elsewhere, experiment may show that h should join k in the subscript of the modulator s.

TABLE 5-2. Factor Structure of M's (Sentiments), m's (Subsentiments) and e's (Environmental Circumstantial Factors), Expected from Process Factoring

	M_a	M_d	m_2	e_{21}	e_{22}	m_{31}	e_{31}	e_{32}	m_{32}	e_{31}	e_{32}
Initial stimulus h_1, act a_1											
Subgoal 2	b										
a_{21}	b		b	$-b$	b						
a_{22}	b		b	b	$-b$						
Subgoal 3_1											
$a_{31(1)}$	b					b	$-b$	b			
$a_{31(2)}$	b					b	b	$-b$			
Subgoal 3_2											
$a_{32(1)}$	b								b	$-b$	b
$a_{32(2)}$	b								b	b	$-b$
Initial stimulus h_2, act d_2		b									
d_{21}		b									
d_{22}		b									
$d_{31(1)}$		b									
$d_{31(2)}$		b									
$d_{32(1)}$		b									
$d_{32(2)}$		b									

Similar general form for d's to that of a's, but extended beyond matrix at the right,

The a's are the actions from h_1 in Figure 5-8, the d's from h_2, which are not shown there. The b's (loadings) here take any nonzero values; that is *they are not all the same quantity.* The blank spaces are zeros; e's are environmental stimulus situation factors. The latter express the fact that the subject is presented with an inevitable choice of responding to stimulus k_1 or k_2 by courses of action (see matrix) $a_{31(1)}$ or $a_{31(2)}$. Note that m_1 in Figure 5-8 would be a specific and not appear here as a common factor.

In this connection research is also needed on the proposition that the sentiment factors, M's, that we have found are actually higher order factors, first among m's and then among t's, as one proceeds to base of factoring resting on more numerous, narrow bits of behavior. The m's we can fix at the level of subgoals, and the t's as the engrams which permit response to individual h's. Unless the factor analysis proceeds to the full SUD factoring model (Cattell 1978), the t's will at present be included in the m scores and m's in the M. However, in Figure 5-8 we have recognized the breakdown of M into more specific, local, lower-order factors as far as the m's (but not as far as the t's of equation 5-7). If we keep to our model of m's and M's as engrams being bundles of what reflexology treats (when adhering consistently to atomic S-R's) as S-R connections, then we must recognize m as a special subset of S-R engramming extending M at a particular point. The SUD factor model (Cattell, 1978a) will, as in (5-7) contain here the contributory term $v_{hjc}s_{kc}m_c$, though an addition for something still more specific to h, namely $v_{hjt}s_{jt}t_j$ could be further added by this model. Presumably, however, in whatever neurological form engram storage occurs, m and t are joined, as engrams, hierarchically to M.

Just as the magnitude and frequency of reward to the situation-contained (k-associated) and immediately ensuing h's in part determines the value of the subgoal, as represented by s_k, so the activation value of the grand M must depend in part on the strength of activation potentials of the m's which follow it. The engram magnitude itself of M will, as in any second order factor, depend on the engram values of the lower order factors, and, structurally, M is simply a collection of m's with the necessary interconnections among them. Those interconnections are complex and deserving of more attention than can be given here. It will happen in everyday life that there will be occasions when, say, an $SG_{2(1)}$ is reached and $k_{21}m_{211}$ activation occurs (Figure 5-8), but none of the expected h's happens to be present. An adaptive act would then be to backtrack from that situation to what has been experienced as an alternative subgoal. Presumably, this can only be done through the maintenance throughout the process of such a degree of activation of M as will, after a moment, lead to the activation of a new m, i.e., to M + m_2 exceeding M + m_1 (m_1 being the abortive path). The modulator s_{k0} (Figure 5-8) for M itself must therefore be a powerful one, in some way symbolizing or reflecting the activations learned at *all* the SG's. And connecting mechanisms of special kinds in the cognitive network of the M are indicated for the above substitution of subgoals in face of environmental undependabilities. The question may arise at this point whether the above account of the learning of the sentiment *process* requires anything more than has been described in the three modes of production of a sentiment *structure*. What has just been described is probably the main mechanism in what we have there described in less detail as the "budding" mode. For there a fixed goal, such as SG_3 in Figure 5-8, is set, and the paths of interest, action, and skill that lead to it have to be found by learning successive subsidiations of smaller subgoals.

In broader, and more methodological context one has to note that the psychometric study of process patterns has been quite neglected by most psychologists, relative to the central importance of understanding processes by clear models. Propositions have, however, been made, for example, by Carroll (1976), Messick (1973), Royce (1957) and the present writer (1966) which have not "caught fire," probably because of the mathematical and statistical complexities inherent in the problem. Even at a simpler, more empirical level the notion that personality needs to be measured by observed processes (rather than instantaneous responses as in ink-blots or questionnaires) has been only slowly perceived, despite the processes in numerous concrete testing designs (Hundleby, Pawlik, & Cattell, 1965; Cattell & Warburton, 1967). In the ability field, the distinction, in the triadic theory, among *capacities, powers,* and *agencies,* explicitly used a continuing process to account for the genesis of the factor pattern and its unfolding expression (Cattell, 1971), and equations were set out to express this. At that time concrete research did not permit closer alignment of factor structure findings, with the three *process* domains, describing 12 parameters, in ADAC (*ability dimension analysis chart,* Cattell 1971, p. 67), but a more concrete attack has since been made by Carroll (1976) and by Messick (1973). Indeed, the whole issue has come alive recently in such writings as those of Gagné (1967) on learning, Nesselroade (1967) with Bartsch (1977) on successions of states, and Royce (1957) on genetic, volutional processes. Royce's recent exhortation (1977) to psychometrists to consider factors also as processes is very timely. However, this new field calls less for comprehensive theorizing than for a step by step exploration of diverse important processes in relation to structures, by tentative models, such as the above, aimed at adaptation to the psychological nature of the process.

5-8. Summary

1. Restricting learning to units truly describable as reflexes can build up a consistent, tightly organized body of experimental generalization, particularly applicable to animal research, as in the more conservative reflexological learning studies. But for handling human emotional and general learning in situ in our culture, multivariate methods and decidedly larger "course of action" measures, as response units, are

needed. Consequently, it is important to define these attitude course of action units more explicitly than has been done in the almost clandestine attempts to extend reflexology to all kinds of human behavior that in fact it only fits "metaphorically." The basis of the needed real-life behavior units, discussed earlier as *attitudes* (potential courses of defined response action in a given life situation), is more explicitly considered here in relation to the cultural form of the dynamic lattice common to most people. The hierarchical structure within each attitude course, down through *sets* to *reflexes*, is emphasized in formulating for experiment the nature of attitude units that we really have to measure and encompass in social theory.

2.   The learning laws of reflexology apply to co-excitation (CE) and to the acquisition of motor responses to specific stimuli while receiving (in CRII or ME experiments) particular concrete rewards. However, by suitable summation, or application of an integral calculus, it is in principle possible to switch to an attitude unit and to relate the *determiners* (reward, contiguity repetition, delay, and so on) to learning gains over the larger unit constituted by the whole attitude course of action. In the extreme case this extends to a whole tract in the lattice, such as centers on the subgoal marking a sentiment. In short, the lattice can be cut into attitude courses, or even whole tracts, in which the *learning gain* (scored for total course performance), on the one hand, and the total reward, repetition, given to the attitude that determine it, on the other, can now be quantitatively related just as formerly for a single reflex unit, though with regard now to the master *pattern* in the reflex elements.

3.   For humans it is not possible, as in animal learning, to control learning in all other attitude paths than that concerned, and subject the individual *solely* to so many trials and rewards in a given path. Nor is averaging out of this unavoidable diversity of other experiences a very efficient mode of investigation both because the "error" variance is likely to be very large, and because the design is inherently less efficient than a new matrix approach. The multivariate (nonmanipulative) experimental answer to this dilemma (namely, that the typical individual in our culture in his daily life is simultaneously following several paths) is the design called *path learning analysis* (PLA). In this method, using number of individuals and knowing the particular frequencies and intensities of path transits for each, we can calculate back to a "learning path potency matrix" that tells us the typical *vector* of trait changes constituting the quite particular average learning effect on an individual of a unit experience of one given path (assuming the end result in an individual is a *product* of this mean effect and frequency-intensity of the experience). PLA can yield empirical laws also on the relation of learning change on the behavioral index vectors (p, r, i, s) to path experience thus completing a five vector de-

scription of learning change. Obtaining p, r, i, and s values requires a different design of experiment—comparing values across several *groups* with different exposures to experience, instead of across several individuals.

4. Since PLA (Figure 5-2) leads only to a vector statement of the personality changes or behavior index changes to be expected from transit of a *particular life path*, for example, a first year of marriage, getting through college, or similar culturally-defined experiences, a second phase of analysis is necessary to connect learning to determiners of a more basic, universal, analytic, and interchangeable nature that exist in all learning paths. These more basic determiners, occurring with varying frequency in all concrete life paths, are frustration, magnitude of reward, social group approval, delay of reward, frequency of experience at various chiasms in the Adjustment Process Analysis (APA) Chart, and the various basic vicissitudes of living. (See Hamlet's soliloquy!) The most promising avenue for categorizing and quantifying the emotional experience elements in concrete life paths is the schematization of countless clinical observations in the Adjustment Process Analysis Chart. It permits precise encoding of the equilibrium point reached by an individual in respect to the expression of any particular erg or sentiment—and hence, with suitable summation, for the whole dynamic structure.

Granted progress in quantifying this APA vector of dynamic events, and using it along with other determiners of the effect of a given path, it is possible to move beyond the PLA calculations specific to empirically determined path values and to proceed with analytical insight to apply general principles to determine the path values.

This is possible by invoking *determiner potency analysis* (DPA). Therein (Figure 5-3) we proceed by matrix algebra from the vector of potencies for particular cultural paths to a further vector expressing the potencies of the above elemental learning determiners, common, in different degrees, to all paths. (The assumption is initially made in DPA that all dynamic traits react to frustration, reward, and other features of APA vectors, in the same way. However, this assumption can be avoided if necessary by having different D matrices.) The scoring of the determiners must be initially for a particular erg or other dynamic system, and it will include in the vector of determiner strengths also broader nondynamic features of the given life path, for example, difficulty in terms of intelligence demand, time length of path, degree of involvement of primary abilities.

5. Using the additional perspectives gained in structured learning regarding coexcitation (*CE*) and means-end (*ME*) principles, a summary is made of the learning processes that are capable of leading to the rise of factorially *unitary sentiments* or other broad engram structures. It is concluded that the causes of observed unity are essentially of

three kinds: (a) *Common schedule*. Here we recognize a common magnitude and frequency of reward to the members of the set of attitude courses found in the sentiment, for each individual—but, of course, difference in the common intensity from individual to individual. Instances of common schedule learning action are generally rooted in some particular institutional impress in the socio-culture environment, but can also come from differing length of exposure to some sentiment object. (b) The single *inherent agency* effect. There are several kinds of possible agency, each tending to spread the learning initially occurring in some narrow area to a wider set of elements. Probably cognitive coexcitation (*CE*) and stimulus generalization, the former leaning on relation-eduction, are the must important. A special case is the extension of a once-successful problem-solving method, as seen by Piaget in the ability field. Another is the conscious shaping of a sentiment around a particular symbol. The inherent action of reasoning and imagining, far more active in humans than in lower animals, results primarily in a cognitive network (ultimately resting on and matured by the action of coexcitation), which is strengthened by ensuing means-end learning. (c) A *budding* process, in which the single force (ergic investment) of an existing sentiment is *uniformly* applied to developing several different needed features of a new sentiment, ancillary to and subsidiating to the first, and attached to the goal by either trial and error or insightful discovery of reward.

6.   An inevitable effect, particularly of the first mode of learning, is to produce that isomorphism of the common human internal engram structure with the form of external environmental and cultural properties that we noted in Chapter 6, Volume 1. Incidentally, on a broader biological perspective, we note that a similar isomorphism of neuropsychological structure and the environment—but now for the environment sometimes of a million years—exists also for the dynamic elements of *ergic* factors. For example, the innate patterns of ability built into a bird's brain to govern flight reflect the aerodynamic properties of the atmosphere. The difference is that the ergic structure has a high degree of temporal rigidity, constrained to the probabilities over hundreds of generations, whereas the sentiment structure is open to extinction and relearning as the regular reward expectations offered by the individual's environment change.

7.   The differences among the three processes of learning that lead to unitary engram structures (sentiments) should show in various features of the structures. For example, the common activation of all elements, as shown in dR analyses would be expected to be less evident in sentiments from common schedule. When budding takes place from a pre-formed sentiment, with an already characteristic ergic invest-

ment pattern (vector) one would expect all the attitude paths in the new sentiment to be more highly similar in their ergic vectors (in their specification equations) than for sentiments not of that mode of origin. The differences also show in the relative emphasis of the three parts of the learning equation for a typical attitude in the given kinds of sentiment.

8.   The general point is made that most traits are also processes, short or long, with in-built sequences related to environmental probabilities. Although Cattell and Warburton (1968) illustrated this in many objective personality tests, relatively few psychologists, notably Messick (1972) and Royce (1977) have explicitly recognized the research task of locating traits as reactive process patterns. Process has been discussed for some time, on the one hand, in the reflexological chain reflex, which is scientifically sound but does not account for persistence to a goal with varied mechanisms, and, on the other, by writers like McDougall and Lewin, who correctly recognized the problem, but strayed outside scientific positivism with notions of valency "pull" and teleological causation. Actually it would have been difficult to develop a scientific model before experimental work had clarified the existence and nature of dynamic structures.

9.   The trait operating also as a process is most clearly seen in sentiment structures. The model here hypothesizes that a sentiment structure is stimulated as a whole. It is this activation of M which keeps behavior, despite alternative subgoal paths in the dynamic lattice, able to converge ultimately on the final goal of the sentiment. That the attitudes found loaded on a sentiment change level together is experimentally well supported, and recent experiments in cognition suggest that this is due to ready spread of excitation across a preformed cognitive network, favoring easier retrieval.

An analogous directing process occurs in a primitive, untutored ergic process, but with a single kind of ergic tension being the coordinator. However, "mood states" (ergically compound) generated at each subgoal by the s_k's are also the motivational part of the directors in sentiments. Thus, according to our theory, because of the term $s_{kx} M_x (g_{x1}E_1 + \ldots + g_{xp}E_p)$ the unitary cognitive activation is accompanied by an ergic arousal of a particular emotional quality, $(g_{x1}E_1 + \ldots + g_{xp}E_p)$. Indeed, the dR demonstrations of unity in sentiment activation refer also to an ergic arousal component which is part of the usual objective measures of an attitude. Another inference from the model is that if the capacity of an attitude to aid and be aided by the activation of a sentiment is proportional to its loading on the sentiment factor (particularly in dR analysis) the initial activation of M by attitudes distal from the sentiment goal would be expected to be weak. However, empirically it is not so evident as in ergs that the more distal attitudes are more weakly loaded. If they are then the model must emphasize the as yet little stressed mechanism whereby M becomes more activated, and its ergic endowment more aroused, as the various subgoals in the sentiment are successfully passed. This means that until thus "warmed up" the sentiment is in danger of "running off the rails" of the tract.

The hierarchical elements in the sentiment process, giving and receiving power from M, but accounting for the handling of varied situations are (1) subgoals at which some degree of ergic reward occurs (2) action of the attained subgoal as an ambient situation, k to increase arousal for the succeeding action, of a local engram, m (3) the appearance of environmental stimuli, $h_1 h_2$, etc. any one of which has been learned as evoking action that will carry the subject further toward the goal of the tract. The motivation state of the subject is a result of earlier activations, mainly of M, relayed on, and of the activation and associated arousal at the present k and h of M and m. The adaptability of the process arises from a readiness at k to respond to that one of the stimuli that is most apt and forcefully present; but at the same time to keep to the main tract of the sentiment, because the motivation weight of the activated sentiment M (with associated arousal) and other relays of earlier tract activations override, at choice points, the prominence of other stimuli that might call for courses of behavior outside the tract.

10.   A process in general (Chapter 5, Volume 1) can be descriptively represented in immediate behavior either by a *quantitative multiple series* or by a *stochastic series*. The latter is a system of probabilities linking earlier behaviors with the appearance of later behaviors. The former is more apt to our whole model development and begins with a score matrix of variables (measures of courses of action, strength and frequency in this case) at the top and temporal occasions down the side, as in P-technique. However it differs in that the actions are often alternatives, and not followed every run, so it has to be represented as a cumulative score matrix over several runs, for an individual or as a group average. It also contains variables for environmental stimulus appearances and strengths, so that when factored as in P-technique it can yield both the internal dynamic structures of the person(s) and the ecometric factors which describe the environment's structured contribution to the process.

11.   Clinicians, in the main, have been sceptical of the capacity of objective multivariate experimental methods to reveal the dynamic symptom connections which they perceive intuitively. The facts are, however, that the methods are logically sound, and empirically more

dependable, as shown by the mutual disagreement of intuitive solutions and by both the better consistency and better therapeutic outcome by *P*-technique diagnosis (Birkett & Cattell, 1978). The explicit misundt standing of some clinicians arises from their argument that symptom alternatives should be positively correlated if one is to argue that the substitute symptoms come from the same source, whereas in fact they do and should tend to show zero or negative correlation. It is shown here, by factor matrix models, that the clinical argument does not heed the real complexities, and that in fact longitudinal factoring of cumulative scores should reveal the M, *m* (and *t*) factors and sub-factors commanding a process, as well as *e* factors for the econetic structure that presents the subject with alternatives.

12. The learning of a sentiment can be by any one of the three modes, but budding gives clearest scope for illustrating process learning. It begins at the proximal sentiment goal in the lattice, and picks up, insightfully or by trial and error, paths which lead thereto from particular ambient situations and stimuli. A major role is assigned to the *ME* (means-end, operant) principle in developing *v* values for stimuli, and activating *s* values for the subgoal situation in which the stimuli are "nested." A consequence of the association of new stimuli with the attainment of a subgoal (*SG* in the lattice) is that a positive correlation would be expected between the total of *v* values of *h*'s at the subgoals, and the *s* values for the ambient situations themselves. The engram, *m*, developed at the subgoal is assumed, consistently with this, to contain the bonds also for the responses, *j*'s, linked to the *k*'s. The model thus supposes that the subgoals, as ambient situations, offer (1) reward for the preceding course, (2) activation-arousal strength for the succeeding actions, and (3) a setting for encountering the new *h*'s. The *m* engram there developed should arise as a sum of the *v*'s of the alternative courses of action from the various *h*'s placed there and also, in regard to its *s* properties, of reverberatory action, in relation to its nearness to the final goal.

The above relay model describes the origin of sentiment structures, and their unfolding in processes, as responsible for most human action in a cultural setting. However, it will be perceived that the model does not immediately fit the totality of behavior, because it is confined to single sentiments, and still requires concern for the action of higher control mechanisms, as discussed in the next chapter. For in man the process does not generally run in simple temporal sequence, but is subject to halts, intervening runs of a different interrupting sentiment or erg, and even inversions of order. The final action requires dynamic concepts analogous to physical momentum and especially a study of the controlling nature of the ego, self-sentiment, and other structures yet to be fully discussed.

NOTES

[1] It is surprising that an adequate taxonomy of perhaps a hundred or so principal "paths" or courses of action constituting the warp and weft of lives in our culture has not yet been made, even by sociologists (see, however, regard for the principles here by the political scientist, Rummel, 1977, 1978). However, a deliberately culturally wide range of attitude courses was taken under measurement by Cattell, Horn, Radcliffe, Sweney, and others, and we can be reasonably sure that the presently accumulated research has covered much of the main fabric of human interests, as a sampling of the dynamic lattice. That work has also begun the depiction of the strata, separating attitudes from sentiments. But a wise strategy of human learning research would consolidate an extensive map of common cultural "paths" as soon as possible, and attempt more completely to cover our equipment both in sentiments and ergs.

[2] The operational distinction discussed in more detail elsewhere by the present writer (Cattell & Warburton, 1967, p. 80) has two stages, the first locating features of the environment, the second distinguishing traits in terms of their relation to these features. The first stage analyzes all ecometrically designatable and measurable features of environment into two kinds: (a) incentives and (b) complexities. Their separation is achieved by first discovering incentives. This requires longitudinal process study, correlating stretches of behavior to discover block patterns that repeat themselves, always ending at a certain goal—the period to the repeating sentence in the code. (As noted above, formally the same problem of locating a self contained process has been met by the great cryptanalysts, and a solution for finding such "runs" has been offered by Friedman 1923.) The strength of activation and consummatory behavior at this discovered goal defines the incentive and its strength. All ecometric measures that are not of *incentives* define, by exclusion, what are *complexities*. Turning next to individual differences in behavior we define as ability traits those involved in performances the scores on which alter most (as to mean and sigma) with change in the discovered ecometric, *difficulty-complexity* features of environment. We define as dynamic traits, on the other hand, those whose scores change most with change in ecometric *incentive* strength measures. Then, by exclusion, we define as temperament traits those that change minimally with either complexity *or* incentive change. It will be clear from Chapter 1, which recognizes *all* traits as having a genetic component, that the slipshod alternative definition of temperament as "a completely inherited trait" is unacceptable. Some abilities are highly inherited.

Doubts have sometimes been expressed about defining temperament measures as above by exclusion. However, both by test and by the subjective and intuitive basis that psychologists have hitherto been prone to accept for modality divisions, it turns out that most temperament measures are ratio or oscillation measures in some performance which maintain much the same level despite appreciable changes of complexity and incentive, that is, the latter modalities are cancelled out. That is to say, speed of warming up to, for instance, a cancellation task, with complexity and incentive held constant, varies from person to person, and is largely independent of changes in complexity or incentive. And spontaneous oscillation of interest strength is a characteristic largely independent of the absolute interest levels. Such observations on temperament traits are encouraging for acceptance of the above postulate that what we call temperament is separable as something independent of complexity and incentive in the environment. However, we may still wonder whether there are fixed features of environment of some third kind, the response to which would *directly* measure temperament. For example, some measure could be derived to express the repetitive monotony of a course of action, and two people would differ in total performance according to a temperamental capacity to tolerate such monotony. We could, however, perhaps argue that this capacity to tolerate monotony is already shown in the performance ratio and oscillation measures themselves which we have used for locating temperament. For the present we should keep open the possibility that there are features of a path itself—in the repetitions and ratios of complexities and incentives—that are temperament-measuring.

[3] It is well to remember that the agency concept comes from the study of ability structures, which are sometimes the cognitive skill aspect peeled off a sentiment structure. The agency concept (Cattell, 1971) is actually double. It covers (a) an inherent connectedness that promotes transfer of training, or stimulus generalization, as a man who acquires a sentiment of kindness to dogs may "logically" extend it to embrace all animals, and (b) the "aid" role in agency formation, in which the constant use of certain alternative paths (analogous to Piagetian devices in solving cognitive problems) to meet a preexisting need binds them in a common frequency and strength of measurement. Actually, this second form of "agency" growth should be brought alongside our third principle of "budding," which is dynamic in nature.

[4] *Common P-Technique* is not the same as *chain P-technique*. The latter yields a common factor state response pattern across whatever number of people is included in the chain experiment. This typically ignores the stimulus situations involved because the subjects' responses do not usually occur to corresponding stimuli. In common P-technique, on the other hand, we have an experimental setup such that all in the sample are going through the same process, meeting the same econetic environmental variables at the same points, and being scored at those points. In that case, among those who reach, say, $SG_{2(1)}$, in Figures 5-6 and 5-8, some will perhaps never respond to h_{211} and others never to h_{212}, so that, over the group, and using frequencies of intensities as scores, averaged at each point for the group, we finish with a P-technique-like score matrix (as for one person), but, unlike that of a single person, containing scores for all channel points.

CHAPTER **6**

THE ACQUISITION OF INTEGRATING STRUCTURES AND THEIR ACTION IN A SYSTEMS THEORY OF PERSONALITY

6-1. *Controlling structures: The acquisition of the superego (G or SE)*
6-2. *The acquisition of the self-sentiment (Q₃ or SS)*
6-3. *Further analysis of the Function of the ego structure (C) and CET action*
6-4. *The acquisition of the ego structure (C)*
6-5. *The nature of general states and their relation to dynamic traits: The action of anxiety*
6-6. *The integrative action of the ego in the field of the general states*
6-7. *The advance to a systems theory of personality: Additions to the VIDA model*
6-8. *The VIDAS seven component systems model and hypotheses on its manner of growth in the individual*
6-9. *Sustaining the structure-based systems model in current personality research*
6-10. *Summary*

6-1. Controlling Structures: The Acquisition of the Superego (*G* or *SE*)

Volume 1 has dealt with the structure of personality, in trait, state and process, while Volume 2 to this point has asked how motivation and learning produce those structures. But the treatment of traits has accepted them on factorial and other evidence, as if they were all of the same status (except for strata relations) and as if all sentiments were of one class. In this chapter we look to the further evidence which tells us that the conductor is different from the rest of the structured orchestra, and thereby we aim to explain the mystery of integration and control. The systems theory necessary to encompass this action is among the most complex in psychology, and the learning theory necessary to account for its rise is still more intricate.

Let us begin, however, simply with more intensive attention to the trait structures themselves that have controlling functions—the ego, the superego and the self sentiment. The evidence for these we have so far given only along with the L, Q, and T media observations on other trait structures in the lists in Chapters 2 through 5 of Volume 1 and in the discussion on integration in Sections 2-7 and 2-8 of this volume. In this last, it is true we have already gone a long way to explain the roles of the triumvirate—ego, superego, and self-sentiment—but not with regard to the learning which produces them, or their action within a total systems theory. The foundation on which the present discussion rests will only be sketched in here with what may seem sometimes unsupported brevity; but the reader has the earlier chapters just mentioned to fall back on.

Correlationally, and in developmental evidence, the relations of the three source traits with obvious controlling properties beyond those of ordinary sentiments—namely, C, G and Q_3 in Q—data and SE (superego) and SS (self-sentiment) in objective motivation measures (T-data)—are now fairly clear. G and Q_3 are (1) cooperative, in loading more than a chance number of behaviors and attitudes in common, and (2) correlated in development as shown by their common emergence in the second order factor QVIII, Control. The former effect is interpreted[1] as due to G injecting some moral values into the self sentiment, which is otherwise concerned with manners more than morals, and mainly with gaining esteem and ensuring survival in the social group. It points to probable dynamic subsidiation of Q_3 to G (among other structures). The correlation of Q_3 and G would support the same conclusion, though it may also indicate the effect of good home and school education in control, *simultaneously* affecting growth of G, Q_3, and the restraint of surgency (since $F-$ also consistently appears in QVIII).

Although the longitudinal study by Barton and Cattell (1975) on 1,000 18 year olds over their next 4 years gave the first objective—though scant—evidence of changes of G under life education, and although there is now abundant evidence through the 16 PF, HSPQ, CAQ and MAT of the relation of G to occupations, educational performance and clinical events, the experimentalist is at this moment reluctantly compelled to depend on non-quantitative clinical evidence more than he would wish for outlines of how the superego develops. There is no doubt (see Vol. 1, Chap. 2) about the correctness of identifying what the most careful clinical observers have described as the superego with the behavioral factor pattern that we have described and defined as G in Q and L data and as SE in the MAT. The doubts reside only in the clinical speculations about its mode of emergence in the first few years of life. Meanwhile, to complete the statement of interrelations in the source trait trio, the experimental report is that C, the ego strength factor, is in most normal groups virtually uncorrelated with G and Q_3, though in some samples it has shown a slight but significant entry, positively, into the second stratum QVIII control pattern. C and Q_3 cooperate, however, in jointly entering, strongly negatively, into the second stratum anxiety factor, QII. Moreover, as clinical findings show, low C is the most universal characteristic of all pathologies: neurosis, psychosis, addictions, chronic conflicts and instabilities (as measured in repeat measures on attitudes).

Because we have to depend a good deal on clinical evidence regarding the growth of G—experiment on factor-analytically checked measures being so sparse—it would be wise to recognize that many clinical practitioners, if not theorists, can be suspected of taking a jaundiced view of this factor's real nature. Practitioners have seen it in neurotics as a primary cause of conflict, anxiety, and damage to ego development, and in therapy have usually whittled away at it, sometimes converting neurotics into sociopaths! They have stressed its "unintelligent" rigidity (confounding their concept of compulsiveness" with superego) and its anachronistic inappropriateness in a changing world. The fact is, however, that in the vast normal population range there is a substantial *negative* correlation between SE strength and anxiety (Horn, 1961: Gorsuch and Cattell, 1977) and also of anxiety (QII) with the second-order control factor (QVIII—UI(T)17 in T-data), so that the psychiatrist's allergy to the superego, which began in Freud's Viennese consulting room, and was joyously welcomed by the general public, has to be wisely discounted as an occupational disease. Certainly in some vulnerable, particularly pre-neurotic, personality patterns superego growth damages ego development and favors anxiety and neurosis, but the balance of effects in normal samples can empirically be shown to be a reduction of anxiety where there is stronger superego growth.

Although in extreme instances, such as the saint or martyr or honest man among thieves, SE (G) may work against ergic satisfactions; yet, inasmuch as its pattern of injunctions contains the wisdom of the ages, the injunctions of this structure provide an individual with ready-made courses of action that are likely to help maximize *long-term ergic satisfaction* and reduce anxiety. The various criterion correlations that have been established for G (Cattell, Eber, & Tatsuoka, 1970) show, furthermore, its powerful role not only in moral but in *persevering* behavior (as the rating patterns for G in Chapter 2 show). Thus significant statistical relations of G scores have been shown to election to leadership in small groups; high regard for parents and absence of criticism by them; working longer hours as a student; effectiveness ratings as office candidates; taking on social responsibilities (including marriage) earlier; and higher academic performance. Regarding the last, the consensus of research (Cattell & Butcher, 1968) is that next to intelligence, G is the best achievement predictor. Thus the clinician has tended to stress the inhibiting functions of the super-ego, which may indeed predominate, but a cross sample of behavior brings out strong positive as well as negative control action as seen in perseverance, support for honesty and other ideals, and achievement (Cattell, Eber, & Tatsuoka, 1970). G scores are consistently significantly below normal in psychopaths, criminals, and gang delinquents, and somewhat low in neurotics and attempted suicides. Occupationally, it is above average in airline pilots, policemen, priests, executives, and accountants.

The expansion of meaning of G, beyond our introduction in Chapter 2, may be followed further elsewhere (Cattell, 1973; Cattell, Eber, & Tatsuoka, 1970; Horn, 1966; Gorsuch & Cattell, 1977) as our main concern is with growth and learning. Here research on the well-defined, measurable unitary factor of G in a developmental framework has only just begun, and we must depend more on the psychoanalytic view or on a number of scattered bivariate studies using ad hoc scales that cannot be confidently equated exactly with a G factor. Paren-thetically, it is a considerable reproach to what aspires to be a socially recognized science that it has done virtually nothing over the last de-cade to design researches of 2, 3, 4, or more years duration relating learning changes on well-defined personality factor measurements, including G, to measures of the usual cultural molding influences, as proposed in the previous chapter.

Beginning at the beginning, however, we now know that G has a significant small genetic root (estimated at a heritability of about 0.3), as also shown clinically by studies of psychopaths, and we know that the age curve of development shows (with some fluctuations in adolescence) a steady rise from the earliest measures (taken around eight years) on to 40 years and later (Cattell, 1973). This would suggest some continuing reinforcement from society and experience of whatever is inculcated by parental influences in the earlier years.

The studies beginning to use adequate G measures, in relation to learning (Bartsch, Barton & Cattell, 1973; Barton, Dielman, & Cattell, 1972; Cattell & Butcher, 1968; and Barton et al., 1975, Karson & O'Dell, 1976), show G increased by experience of early social responsi-bilities, by belonging to a church or idealistic institution; by experienc-ing bereavement of a close relative (mostly a parent); by being married; by warmth and affection in the early parental relationship; by absence of use by parents of trivial restrictions or of specific detailed rewards and punishments (a result contrary to some reflexological theories); and by more years of education of the parents, particularly of the father.

The psychoanalytic picture is consistent with the above, but fills in on the role of the earlier years, on which we have little quantitative data. At risk of some oversimplification in condensation, clinical theory states that superego implantation occurs before age three and is largely complete by five to six years. The essential concept is that the child "introjects" the values and style of the parent, and that the main motivation in doing so is fear of loss of parental affection and support (which some have called "fear of nonsurvival"). The child is presumed to recognize emotionally, if not explicitly, that its survival depends on parental affection ("Honor thy father and thy mother, that thy days may be long in the land"), and that a terrifying chaos would ensue without the parent. As one defense and escape from this separation anxiety the child adopts the parental injunctions, and this incorporation may satisfy also some self-assertive need, as when a child punishes himself by a slap on the hand, proudly imitating the parent's authority. The fact that greater superego growth is found with stronger early parental affection, is presumably due to the greater punishment capacity through deprivation when approval is withheld. The writer's own clinical experience could cite several striking instances of completely aborted superego development where the mother (and sometimes the father) was, for ulterior reasons, hostile to the child from birth.

The two questions that dynamic calculus research most seeks to answer are, first, since we identify G as a sentiment, what are the major ergs rewarded by the superego—that is, what is the ergic investment profile? The superego is perhaps as odd among the general run of sentiments as is the sentiment to the mother, in having an unusually early development, reaching a substantial early strength. As Kohlberg (1973) has attempted to show, there ensues considerable cognitive development, concerning to whom the moral responsibility holds. Unfortunately Kohlberg's work is marred and rendered questionable in interpretation by the failure to analyze the assumed unitariness of the measures used, or to relate to the dimension of the G factor as well fixed among other personality factors by multidimensional simple structure. It ignores also the question raised here of coordinating the changes in the cognitively stated values in the sentiment with *objectively assessed* ergic investments which sustain them.

A clinical estimate of the ergs involved in early life would be that they are initially fear (of loss of affection), and a double play of initial self-abasement and later self-assertion through the authority as introjected. From ethology there can be no doubt of a self-abasement erg in primates, which becomes an ingredient in admiration, awe, reverence, and especially imitation, all of which favor introjection. Results with the 16 PF on neurotics show significantly lower mean dominance scores among obsessional compulsive types, suggesting that more introjection of authority's commands as in the expiatory behavior of the compulsive is in fact aided by the action of the self-abasement erg. Unfortunately, at this point in ergic research a clear factorial separation of the self-abasement erg from what has merely been treated as the self-assertive erg in reverse has not yet been obtained. All we can recognize at the moment is a single factor which would restrict us to the psychological interpretation of a bipolar factor, with self-abasement and self-assertion at opposite ends. We prefer the ethological evidence here of distinct ergs, thus rejecting the present factor analytic findings as technically insufficiently developed.

We may suspect that the gregariousness erg is also involved in these midchildhood continuing developments of the superego connected with peer action ("It isn't done"). That is to say, the peer group, in adolescent, sets a second and differently motivated G pattern, which only later normally becomes integrated with the developing parental inplantation we have discussed. Thus what is clinically constantly labelled as a specific "emotion of guilt" is almost certainly a secondary, derived, composite emotion of fear, loneliness (gregarious need deprivation), and self-abasement. This is very close to what is described by subjects in the O factor of the 16 PF, CAQ, etc., labelled "guilt proneness." However, the O and G factors always emerge as distinct in factoring and what one might call the positive aspects of the superego such as perseverance, and setting of moral standards, and which seem to involve self-assertion and even pugnacity (moral indignation), better fit the G pattern.

A check on the above should readily be possible by factoring an appropriate span of erg-representing attitudes, preferably at several age levels, and examining the ergic investment. The available experiment (Cattell & Child, 1975, Table 2.10, p. 38) was not specifically designed for this purpose, but it does support an excess of negative loadings (-.68, and -.27, versus .19, and .19) on self-assertion—which implies positive self-abasement and some negative narcism (but so far not fear, on the evidence of that particular matrix) in the superego attitudes. Freedom from fear, attachment to parental home, and strength of career sentiments also have been associated elsewhere with G. There is thus a strongly indicated research need to pursue developmental study of the superego, with as much regard for the ergic subsidiations as the conscious cognitive associations. This would involve cross sectional factorings at regular age intervals. There is also a strong need to separate ecogenic and epogenic effects (Cattell, 1973) in this source trait, for there is unpublished evidence of appreciable change in content of the patterns and its level over the last 20 years. One suspects it will prove a marked case of changing motivational structure and social content, when cross cultural and cross-epoch measures are taken.

Although we recognize that G has the peculiarity among senti-ments (other than those to parents and siblings) of beginning very early, the psychoanalytic emphasis should not lead us to overlook the fact that measured development goes on through life, as the age curves indicate. In some of this the early forms of motivation may continue, as in the surprising finding that adult prisoners in concen-tration camps seem unconsciously to introject the values of authority and order, though alien, to which they are subjected. It is probable that a major new ergic investment in G occurs at adolescence in that hormone-tied rise of altruistic feelings that Stanley Hall so strongly emphasized as aiding "conscience." Presumably in this concern for others we are seeing the enhancement of the parental protective "pity-ing" erg and the sublimation of the sex erg, both occurring at ado-lescence and partly hormonally determined. (The distinction of two consciences—the angry Jehovah of the Old Testament and the emphasis on love for one's neighbor in the New Testament, which historians and theologians have discussed at length, are not just cultural, logical entities but need to be related to hormonal and social contributions to superego at two different life stages in the individual.)

The later ergic investment change that thus undoubtedly occurs in this sentiment structure we call the superego, expressed largely through the agape of the parental erg and sexual sublimation, may nevertheless be slight, as psychoanalysts assert, compared to the pri-mary guilt form of investments built up early, around three years of age. What needs investigation in regard to these earlier components, however, in relation to our second question above, is how the senti-ment retains its motivating power when the primal causative parental situation no longer exists.

Although the superego is a primary example of this persistence of rewarding qualities from an object that no longer exists, except as a memory, the phenomenon runs through all dynamics and calls for a slight digression at this point on the general principle involved. It was first noted most clearly by Allport (1961) and given the name of *functional autonomy*. As stated earlier, we have felt it necessary to reject this concept as anything more than roughly descriptive, because evidence does not support as a general principle *pure autonomy* defined as behavior persisting with the goal removed. Consequently we have accepted that *ergic determinism* is basic: that is, that any continuing habit or attitude must continue to have subsidiation paths to a reward-ing ergic goal. In stating this we have explained apparent functional autonomy by secondary principles, which may produce the appearance of abrogation of this law. First we must recognize a class of *ideational rewarders*, which generally have been and remain subgoals in the dynamic lattice on the way to ergic reward. The parent *image* remains a bestower of affection and security. This may seem to imply an absolute functional autonomy to the parent image as a subgoal in the superego sentiment. The existence of something close to functional autonomy certainly has to be explained here. We have also recognized that an activity itself may acquire "side-rewards" as when a man who walks to work through pleasant surroundings may continue to walk there when he retires. One must recognize effects also from goal modification (*GM*) learning, p. 192, in which the goal is not absent, but has itself become modified. In the superego, though the parents are gone (in the case of the older individual) there is a strong persistence that comes close, descriptively to functional autonomy. Explanation by side effects, and goal modification, and substitution of the approval of an adult society, scarcely seems enough to account for the behavior of martyrs, in which, as conspicuously in, say, Savonarola, the approval of existing society is entirely rejected. Probably we must account for the persistence of superego motivation by the following:

1.   In the power of early imprinting to produce effects close to functional autonomy, especially with certain ergs, such as fear.

2.   In general by the fact that the search for *new* goals by fresh trial and error is slight once a system is in equilibrium.

3.   In some cases—and *G* may be one—by recognizing the reality of repression causing ideational rewarders (and threateners!) to become inaccessible thereafter to conscious reasoning and experience. The person cannot reason that the satisfaction could be obtained in other ways since the earlier subgoal path is lost to conscious intervention.

4.   In the fact that the environment often no longer offers ergic satisfactions equivalent to those available in childhood. This could well be the case in the superego, in regard to which no one offers such complete security and affection as the parent offered to the infant. Consistent with this theory is all that has been written about the systematic connection of the superego with religion and with the need that creates belief in a benevolent God. In short, inner rewards suffice.

5.   As a fuller development of (1) above, which states that we would expect a substantial relation of the degree of persistence of a ergic-cognitive connection to the earliness of life at which it was established, let us consider the possibility of other concomitants of earliness being involved. The potency of imprinting could spring, as is usually implied, from the maturational freshness of a drive (at adolescence "the first love is the best love"). But absence of encumbrance of the drive with previous investments could also be a factor. If we argue that all ergs in infancy have this quality, but not simply because

of age, then further definition of "freshness" in terms of a dynamic strength (declining with age), unencumbrance, and so forth, must eventually be pursued. Whether the imprinting effect is from sheer "freshness" of a drive, as we have assumed in (1) above, or from an "economic" principle of the drive being unencumbered by existing investments ("mandates" to use our technical expression in the last chapter) it surely must be given credit for the unusual persistence, in compared to other sentiment action, of the superego.

6. In connection with our earlier hypothesis (Chapter 3) that learning laws may be considerably different (in parameters, not in principles) according to which erg is involved, we should consider here the hypothesis that nonviscerogenic ergs, such as fear, gregariousness, curiosity, stand at a different level, quantitatively, from viscerogenic ergs, in relation to rate of extinction. The appetitive oscillations of viscerogenic ergs may well render them more open to reattachments. Indeed, as the results of Mowrer's, and many others', reflex results with electric shock in animal learning show, the attachment of a fear response to a stimulus is very hard to bring to extinction, especially in conditions of ineffective response. If fear of nonsurvival and chaos is as central in the infant's early acceptance of parental values as psychoanalytic observations suggest, this ergic quality may contribute to the persistence of such powerful rewards (avoidance of fear, and so on) as the superego seems able to continue to offer.

Apart from the above peculiarities, the superego seems to follow those styles of learning acquisition we have studied for the whole class of sentiment structures to which it essentially belongs. The growth of adult ethical values, which in most people today occurs with some rational argument and personal awareness, is an example of "budding" and "agency" action, although the childhood acquisition is more a "common schedule" phenomenon. As regards "budding" and "agency," the original desire of the individual to do good, to link on to something greater than himself, and to escape guilt leads to building onto this basic desire more specific values and actions that reason shows to be compatible, in the newer, later, cultural situation. The psychopath who, through a combination of genetic insensitivity and absence of early parental attachment and instruction, has escaped the creation of this desire is still incapable of growing further with new cultural ethical values.

The superego structure begins as a guilt and aspiration structure in the infant and ends in the philosopher as a system of values. That Haeckel and many other rationalists have finished with a trinity of Truth, Goodness, and Beauty suggests an esthetic element in the developed superego that psychology has not probed. In the next section we shall look at such values, for, although they begin in the superego, their integration, we argue, takes place in the self-sentiment.

6-2. The Acquisition of the Self-Sentiment (Q_3 or SS)

What multivariate experimental psychology defines and measures as the self-sentiment has been unknown to clinical theory except by McDougall, in his *Outline of Abnormal Psychology*, and a few others who did not take the ego-id-superego trinity as the whole gospel. Elusive though it may have been in the consulting room, it stands out very clearly in L, Q, and T-data factorings (the T-data being in objective motivation measures, where it has been indexed SS).

There is no need to assemble again and repeat here the evidence in Chapters 2 and 4, Volume 1, and the criterion relations found for 16 PF, CAQ, HSPQ, MAT and SMAT test measures. The self-sentiment, in which the self-concept is the focus of several strong attitudes, is a dynamic structure concerned with maintaining self-respect and the respect of others, with self-control standards, with health, with self-knowledge, and with excellence in job, and maintaining social aspiration levels.

The fairly marked cooperative loading pattern with the superego is immediately evident and suggests that the self-sentiment subsidiates to, among other sentiments, the superego.

Because its structure recognizes that the social and functional integrity of the self is a precondition for almost all other sentiment and ergic satisfactions, we would infer (it is not yet tested) that the SS (Q_3) structure lies distally in the lattice to other sentiments, or is circularly involved with them, i.e., it subsidiates to most of them.

The explanation of higher strata structure shows that it appears in a well-defined second-order factor, QVIII (and, in T-data, UI(T)17, Wardell & Yeudall, 1976), called *inhibitory control*, along with G. It also enters into the second stratum anxiety factor, QII, as a reducer of anxiety. The appearance of Q_3 in QVIII we have hypothesized to be due to better home backgrounds, morally teaching in a way simultaneously to foster G and Q_3 (and somewhat to reduce F). This suggests Q_3 is to an appreciable degree a learned pattern. Its appearance in QII can be explained as due to better control and a better integrated self-sentiment reducing the incidence of conflict anxiety. Indeed, over large normal samples (totalling 1652) the correlation of Q_3 with anxiety stays at about -.54.

Among life criteria it is significantly positively related to school success, freedom from accidents, following the more exact professions (pilot, scientist, electrician, administrator); and negatively related to delinquency and neurosis.

Finally the evidence on its nature by behavior genetic research shows it to have a moderate but significant hereditary component and a life curve showing an upset (dip) in adolescence, followed by a steady increase into the 40 to 50-year-old range.

In the 1950s and 1960s much research concentrated on the self-concept as a cognitive entity without recognizing its position as an anchor and expression of the dynamic self-sentiment. We can see that without objective motivation-strength measures the largely cognitive experimental comparisons scarcely permitted dynamic and broader interpretations. However, it was repeatedly shown that anxiety was greater with a greater cognitive discrepancy between the ideal and the real self-concept. This omits at least two relations necessary for perspective: a stronger interest in the self-concept is significantly negatively related to anxiety; and, over a normal sample, there is always a substantial positive correlation of the perceived and the ideal self, and, so far as methods of real (observer-measured) self are dependable, of *both* of these selves with the real self (Cattell, Pierson, & Finkbeiner, 1976). Consequently we remain uncertain whether part or all of this correlation with discrepancy is due simply to the correlation, just mentioned above, with an absolute low level of self-sentiment development.

In this connection, before handling learning principles and the self-sentiment, let us note that any discrepancy of the perceived and the real self (leaving the ideal self out of the picture) is likely to be punishing. A little boy who thinks he can jump a six-foot stream and a young lady of mediocre voice who goes into opera are in for trouble. But the rewards of realism are obviously not all on the side of excessive modesty, and error is distributed plus and minus, though perhaps skewed in distribution (at least in youth) toward the optimistic side. An interestingly explicit example of reward and control by the *SS* is Ben Franklin's chart of 13 virtues, whereon he checked each day that he had manifested one or more of them. A central feature of psychosis, mainly but by no means only in paranoia, is the large discrepancy of the true and the conceived self, resulting from a breakdown of reality-testing under heavy emotional pressure or through brain damage, as in general paresis of the insane. The adjustment of the *SS* to personal realities, and therefore of ego action partly directed by it, is consequently a learning theme of the greatest importance.

Some of the earliest writings, notably those of James (1890), Jung (1911), and McDougall (1932), remain the best in sensitivity and subtlety of perception of the issues in the self-concept, although they did not follow the difficult paths into operational, experimental testing that the moderns are attempting (often, alas, without reading back 50 years). Most of the early writers in psychology, like the novelists we quoted in Chapter 2 stressed the importance of "modeling" on admired characters (and inverting the model of unadmired characters!) But though the importance of modeling and the forms it takes have been well analyzed in literature back to Plutarch, Herodotus and others, and we shall give extended attention to in the more recent work of Bandura and others in this field, it would be a mistake to overlook the probably equal role of other mechanisms.

Briefly, the other self-sentiment shaping mechanisms are:

1.   The individual's gradual experiential discovery of his departures from the average in various natural aptitudes and temperamental tendencies. The individual discovering, perhaps accidentally, that he has some advantageous capacities, for example, to run 100 meters or quickly learn foreign languages, to a deviant degree from the general population, will naturally incorporate these (like his somatic characters) in his peculiarly individual self-image, and he will probably go out to develop them more.

2.   Favorable and unfavorable comment by family and society. Such comment is likely to produce attempted changes in self and self-image.

3.   The usual processes in sentiment formation apply also to the self-sentiment. *Common schedule* action will alter the sentiment structure as such, and self-image will adjust to it. *Agency* action will produce inner spread of values and interests, perhaps more directly entering the self-concept. *Budding* must be constantly in action to shape the self-sentiment to sentiments independently developed, because the SS subsidiates and assists in making possible, the satisfaction of major job, hobby and home sentiments. Thus, if association with a friend has led to a development of an interest in, say, skating or photography, the self concept comes to include these extensions of interest ("myself as a photographer") determining attitudes and actions in the self-sentiment.

Especially important in this growth of the SS by budding action—that is, by its subsidiation to existing dynamic structures—is its subsidiation to the superego, G. There is no reason to suppose that in general dynamic action this subsidiation to G is different from the self-sentiment's shaping to the demands of ergs, or of other sentiments doing the same. But in quantity it represents a special emphasis, as is shown by the number of attitudes in the self-sentiment that are simply taken over from, or modified from, the demands of the superego.

Most self-sentiment patterns, in short, are concerned not only to do the right thing by the self and its social effectiveness, for example in relation to the peer society, but also by the categorical right and wrong of the superego (see attitude lists in references in Cattell & Child, 1975). One must remember also that the superego is itself peculiar among sentiments in the earliness and rigidity of its ergic investment so that it operates with a stability of demand close to that of an erg.

We owe to a few investigators otherwise in the classical learning tradition a recognition that the animal studies in that tradition are not adequate for human personality learning. They are well represented today by Bandura, 1962; Bandura and Walters, 1963; Inhelder and Piaget, 1958; Loevinger, 1969; Staats, 1975; and Vigotsky, 1962. In these currently labelled "cognitive approaches" to personality learning there is a growing recognition of the importance of insight (relation eduction), of means-end learning through symbols, and of the importance of cognitive controls essentially (Ellis, 1962) in what we have called integration learning. They contribute to understanding the true role of modelling. This modelling theory was explicitly defined and concretely illustrated in the present writer's personality development theory (1950) but took another decade to stimulate suitable research. The especial recognition in experimental form is that *vicarious observational* learning and modelling play a major role for humans. Not that vicarious learning (Bandura, 1965) is unknown in animal learning. As Angemeier (1960) has demonstrated, the reflexologist can find clear instances thereof if he steps free of his paradigms. The capacity of humans and higher mammals to watch certain actions successfully leading to reward and then to imitate them, or even store the knowledge away in a "cognitive map" for use when dynamic need demands, has now been shown very clearly in Bandura's laboratory by several others using quantifiable experimental approaches.

Here we propose to use the term *personality modeling* to represent a special subdivision of *vicarious learning* concerned with formation of the self-sentiment. One must distinguish this from subjective *mental experiment*, in which a person or animal goes through a possible solution in imagination. For this latter is self-planned. But vicarious learning and mental experiment are likely to get interwoven.

What is not studied so easily in the manipulative experimental situation as in personality measurement in the life situation is the effect of degree of admiration or related emotional attitudes toward the person imitated (although the adage "imitation is the sincerest form of flattery" shows such connection was realized before the first Ph.D. in psychology). The English public schools selected their housemasters more for modeling purposes than for academic distinction (a goal too distant for schoolboys anyway); but the brighter, and also the rebels, in those schools were apt to disdain the immediate models[2] for those they read about. As Bolitho (1950) sums up, "Self-realization by imitation of heroes and heroines, found in books, legends, dramas—the self-direction by the help of fiction, very widespread, or unprovably universal—we will call Imitatio Herois, saving the name Quixotism for the special case, when the model is most obviously ridiculous, and when the devotion is extreme, illogical, or saintlike." He proceeds convincingly to bring out the quixotic insanity of Charles XII of Sweden, with his models of omnipotent warriors, which well illustrates our point above, that any serious discrepancy of the adopted self-image and reality is on the road to psychosis. (The discrepancy, naturally, could act both as cause and consequence. Damage to the reality-testing function from enduring a poor fit could be followed by an impaired capacity to reject a still poorer fit.) In connection with *Imitatio Herois*, the tremendous concern of Maoism in providing in China, over recent decades, "desirable models" for all, is worthy of study; and there is, of course 3,000 years of historical illustration in religion (for example, *The Imitation of Christ* of Thomas à Kempis, 1530) of the social-psychological effects of this modeling. However, from a personality standpoint, all we need conclude is that modeling is one of the more powerful of three or four methods by which the self-sentiment grows.

As to the antecedent and family environmental conditions shown to accompany better learning of the self-sentiment, we find (Barton, Dielman, & Cattell, 1972; Cattell 1973, p. 176) in those of high Q_3: more demonstration of affection by parents; a more harmonious family; reasoning used more than crude punishment in upbringing, little temper or acting out in school; a preference for science and mathematics; more participation in discussions; and not rated a hinderer in group activities. The Barton-Cattell studies of personality changes from events in the 18 to 22-year-old period showed that Q_3 increases more with those who experience a college education; who obtain more steady employment; who experience an unhappy love affair or a parental illness, or a bereavement. Q_3 declines with excessive drinking. Consistent with the finding of the adolescent dip in the age curve for Q_3 (Cattell, 1973) there is much evidence, for example, in Stanley Hall's classic *Adolescence*, that the self-image acquires some stability in preadolescence and is then reshuffled—with temporary loss of level of total investment score and quality of integration within the pattern—in adolescence. As one perceptive novelist has neatly said, "One must excuse [the adolescent's] behaving like a Greek actor, with many masks; he has to put on several to see which best fits." The evidence is ample that the loss of fit of the mask that sufficed earlier in what analysts dub the "latency period"—say 8-12 years—arises both from internal change (sex and altrustic ergs hormonally determined, that now have to find expression) and external demand changes: the challenge of adult responsibilities and freedoms.

Observations on the relation of Q_3 to G are plentiful and have been summarized above, but the relations to the third member of the control team, C, cannot be so readily focused at this stage of research. What is certain—in spite of confusion in clinical theories—is that C and Q_3 are distinct factors, which nevertheless have special interaction. The correlation of C and Q_3 is regularly significantly positive in the general population, but virtually all of the correlation is due to the second-order anxiety factor, QII. This can be interpreted to mean that anxiety is deleterious to both self-sentiment and ego-strength growth, or, conversely, that higher C and Q_3 act in positive fashion to reduce anxiety. The existence of QII as a second stratum "influence" inclines one to argue against the usual third alternative in causally interpreting a correlation, namely that growth of Q_3 helps growth of C or vice versa. Nevertheless one can readily conceive that the emotional stability of C would make the construction of a definite self-sentiment easier, and a consistent and realistic set of attitudes in the self-sentiment would make the decisions of C easier and more realistic.

To get perspective on this, and also to understand how the environmental influences affecting Q_3, as discovered above, operate by the ME (operant) learning principle, it is necessary to ask what particular ergs enter into the ergic investment vector for this sentiment. What, in short, are the ergs that get their satisfaction largely through this sentiment and build up its engram strength? Only three or four experiments, two of them using P-technique and on few attitudes, exist to guide us (Cattell & Child, 1975; Birkett & Cattell, 1978). They indicate some of the largest positive loadings are on the security erg (fear), the superego, narcism, and, rather curiously, sex. In some samples the self-assertive and gregarious ergs also play an appreciable part. That the SS would subsidiate to the superego was predicted and has already been discussed, but the other indications of its ergic investment are new.

The large role of an interest in security in the learning of self-sentiment attitudes likewise fits our hypothesis that the intactness of the self-sentiment is viewed as an indispensable precondition for the satisfaction of all other sentiments—indeed, for the continued social existence of the individual. That self-assertion and gregariousness should have some slighter positive role is also to be expected in view of the competitive and group-standing-oriented attitudes fairly prominent in the pattern. What was not in the original hypothesis, and requires some reconstruction is the satisfaction the SS attitudes seem to give to sex and narcism. The loadings of the SS on the sex attitudes, such as "I want to have normal sexual relations in my life" suggests that sex relations in young adults in our present culture have become part of self-regard. The unexpectedly significant involvement of the narcistic erg in the self-sentiment is intriguing and requires new concepts. The narcistic erg is typically substantially negatively correlated with the superego strength, so that the fact that both it and G support the self-sentiment demands some special inquiry. What is becoming increasingly evident from clinical uses of the MAT is that narcism expands for many people into forms of expression through the self-sentiment. Its self-indulgence and overvaluing of the self (egotism) accommodate to the superego demands in the self-sentiment by aiming at a compromise of social respectability, self-importance, and self-care which is readily recognizable in life and literature.

As the end of discussion of the superego above we pointed out that that structure is commonly thought of as the repository of values—meaning thereby ethical and religious values. However, in the recent interest in research on values some mystery and a good deal of confusion springs from psychology's inheritance of special semantic and philosophical associations and some diverse popular usages of the term. We recognize as a plague in many debates that one participant is using the most general possible meaning—including art and food values—and the other a purely ethical or purely political sense. In the *general* use, as "valence" in Lewin's sense, we talk as if hunger, for example, gives beefsteak the "value" of being delicious, and thunder has the "value" of being frightful. Our concern in personality control systems is with the precise and more usefully restricted sense of *moral* (and to some extent of esthetic and social) values. A value of this kind is typically a belief such as that "I and everyone else should be honest." From the structural positions of discovered attitude loadings for such value beliefs, it seems that they get their dynamic investment almost entirely as part of the self-sentiment, and, less consciously, and at one remove, from the superego. That is to say, the original dynamic force for interest in moral values resides in the superego, and continues, to some extent in all people, and in martyrs and saints to a high degree, to reside there. But the broader amalgam of conscious cognitive, ethical, social and esthetic values commonly explicitly thought of as *life values* (not, however, the boundless "values" that are merely projected desires and "valences" as discussed above) seems, according to surveys of attitude correlations, to be mostly in the self-sentiment structure. This SS location of values arises also because the self-sentiment coordinates other sentiments by requiring their compatibility, mutually and with the self-sentiment. Thus it is not just that "Painting interests me," as a sentiment, but that "I am a painter." And if, for the person concerned, being an artist is incompatible with, say, earn-ing a living, the self-sentiment has somehow to bring peace between the conflicting sentiments by reference to some self-constructed central personal values, e.g. "I believe in being interested in art."

To assign importance to values, however, is not to accept the position of some psychologists and philosopers that values are in some way extra, free-floating forces external to the biologically rooted personality dynamics. They draw their capacity to exert dynamic effects on behavior ultimately from the same ergic forces as do the other sentiments, namely, the innate ergs. The self-sentiment tells the individual, say, "I should not be happy if I lie or steal or am regarded as a lazy parasite." The fact is that by learning experience these behaviors have come to be recognized as frustrating the self-sentiment and, at one remove, the superego, the security erg, and the gregarious erg to which the self-sentiment subsidiates. It is a further step of intellectual abstraction from these accepted behaviors to conclude as a "value judgment" that "I hate dishonesty." Often the person stating a value would be hard put to define exactly what he means by dishonesty and what its boundaries are, which alone throws doubt on the independent existence of a value per se. What he actually means (unless he is a philosopher) is more realistically psychologically expressed as an attitude, "I want to be honest myself and I want everyone else to be honest." And the meaning of the strength of a value is the strength of this attitude, as it stands and is reinforced (in the ordinary "strengthened" sense of that term) by the self-sentiment. In considering certain dynamic attitudes (as response potentials) as the operational meaning and motivational reality of a value, we must not overlook the capacity of some human beings to attain great precision in handling abstractions and to succeed in attaching emotional responses to symbols for them. We are saying only, then, that abstract concepts—such as the self-concept—can acquire ergic investment, but that it is psychologically a mistake to consider "values" as having motivation apart from their position in the self-sentiment and superego ergic investments, into the structure of which they fit.

6-3. Further Analysis of Functions of the Ego Structure (C) and CET Action

Penetrating the nature of the controlling action which is commonly referred to as the area of expression of "the ego" brings psychologists to face what is unquestionaly the most subtle and complex of psychological concepts. That this fact is also recognized by scientists in other fields is shown by the fact that when he turned his thoughts to constructing a cosmic language for interstellar communication, Hogben, apropos of his "Astraglossa" wrote "The last topic about which we could hope to achieve [inter-stellar] understanding . . . would be the concept of the ego. . . ."

Since there is an almost ineradicable tendency for readers to assume that "ego" connotes all the trailing meanings of a plethora of psychoanalytic writers it must be made clear—if it is not already so from Volume 1 and Chapter 2 here—that what we are studying as the ego here is a structure evident in a pattern of behavior functions factor analytically established as a unity. The serious student who prefers to get down to operational definitions will find them, therefore, in the behaviors reported in the Q and L loading patterns in Volume 1, Chapter 3, and in Chapter 2 here, for the C factor, and in objective test, T-data patterns for UI(T)16, 17, 23, and 31. (The fact that the choice in the T-data area is left to further research and discussion is a concession to the psychoanalysts' previous use of the label. These source trait factors are real, uniquely definable, and measurable, and seem to us to be the core of what psychoanalysts have talked about. But it rests with the psychoanalyst to decide whether he wishes more precisely to anchor his terms on the statistically established personality factor patterns—and, incidentally, to make it possible for all analysts to talk about the same thing when they use the same term.)

On this basis we proceed in this section to analyze the ego structure per se and, in the next, the manner in which it is learned and the role it plays in integration learning. The reader may wish to keep a finger in the earlier chapters, so that when we generalize briefly here about properties he can refer to the concrete form of the evidence. The T data identification of the ego, as defined in C, L, and Q data needs, for reasons Pawlik (1968) has well stated ("inherent theory in language"), is urgently in need of research to establish cross media correlations, with UI(T)16, 17, 23, and 31. But in L and Q data the meaning is very clear as emotional stability and adjustment, frustration and deferment tolerance, absence of evasion of realities, comparative absence of defense mechanisms, a good record of managing one's affairs (intelligence partialled out) and capacity to act well under psychological stress.

The further developments here rest solidly upon the data and analysis of Chapter 2 of which for convenience the following brief reminder is given:

1. C, G, and Q_3 have ample replicated factor analytic definition in Q and L media, and G and Q_3 in objective tests (Horn 1961). In T-data there is still a challenge of deciding among alternate identifications with UI(T)16, 17, 23, and the second orders; TII, Expressive

Ego, which adds UI(T)19, and *TV*, Restraint, which adds UI(T)31. One may reasonably surmise that *C* has not yet appeared among sentiments factored from attitudes because the choices of attitudes have not included those expressing the high generality of the ego's aims ("I want to maximize my satisfactions by control").

2. Ample criterion relations support the ego concept as being realized in the unique *C* factor definition and measurement in *L* and *Q* data.

3. *C* has the general purpose of maximizing long term ergic (and therefore sentiment) satisfaction, and is essentially a "clearing house" and a decision mechanism.

4. *C* measures prove to be related positively to measures of integration, inversely to measures of conflict, inversely to measures of attitude inconstancy, and strongly inversely to psychopathology.

Before proceeding to theoretical analysis two more empirical observations need to be thrown in: (1) Concerning age curves: the C curve, with a possible drop in early adolescence, definitely goes on climbing through the main life period (2) Concerning a genetic component we have definite evidence, though with some quantitative uncertainty as yet, of significant genetic contribution.

As we have seen in Chapter 1, *all* psychological trait endowments, when measured, prove to have some degree of genetic determination, and good reasons are known in behavior genetics and sociobiology for this being sometimes high and sometimes low. It is a sad comment on the persistence, into this age of behavior genetic precisions, of a naive reflexological environmentalism that still today we can find such comments on ego control as "It is assumed that self-control does not emerge from any innate potential within the individual but is acquired through experience" (Goldfried & Merbaum 1973, p. 13). As the wide vision of William James (1960) saw, the control of instincts, like instincts themselves, must have been subject to evolution through natural selection. Neurological-hormonal structures must have emerged, such as modern neurological function research localizes in the limbic system, concretizing the advantages in adaptation (and adjustment, related thereto as defined on p. 247) which led to superior survival rates. (Incidentally it is enlightening to perceive the analogy to this neural coordination function in the control exerted on the hormone system by the pituitary, also evolved by the survival advantages of such coordination.) Any product of an immense age of evolutionary action is likely to stand at different levels in biologically different individuals, so it is not surprising to find that measured ego strength, *C*, like measured intelligence, has an appreciable heritability coefficient. That coefficient, as presently determined is, as Chapter 1 records, decidedly lower than for intelligence, being, at a rough estimate about $H = .41$. We discuss below which aspects of the C factor may more directly expresses this origin (Cattell, Schuerger, & Klein, 1980).

In Chapter 2 the conception has already been briefly introduced that the action of the ego, like any more typical sentiment, unfolds in a process and that this process has four panels of action: that is four activities which to a psychological analysis seem appreciably different. We shall now pursue this analysis further under the following headings:

1. *The inner evaluative actions on dynamic needs and conditions.* This means sensing the real strength of the ergs and sentiments competitively demanding expression, by devices (a) direct awareness and (b) evocation (*CET*) described below.

2. *Evaluating the external situation directly and in relation to past consequences of action.* This involves (a) emotional realism and perceptual capacity, and (b) retrieval from memory of relevant experiences from the past.

3. *Decision.* This includes (a) control long enough to inhibit impulse for deliberation and (b) final effecting of a cognitive decision for a particular action in spite of conflicting impulses. It involves in (b) the weighting of information from 1 and 2 and the formulation of a best action. (a) is the first in order of all C action.

4. *Effective Implementation of the Decision.* Here we see in subsequent theory two "effectors": (a) The weight of the dynamic investment of the ego itself, operating like any other sentiment, and (b) What we are calling *CET* (cue evocation of traits) action: the importation of cues (external or internal) to modulate dynamic traits to assist in the implementations. This process can also appear in 1.

Parenthetically, let us point out that there is noticeable in the later writings of Freud (1949) a willingness to ascribe importance to the *outward* evaluative tasks of the ego (2 above) beyond the first *internal* struggles (3 and 4 above) ascribed to it with regard to id and superego in earlier writings.

About the first of these panels we know very little experimentally, but it seems that having words to label experienced emotions and ergic tensions improves control, as Schacter and Singer's (1962) work obliquely shows. It could be that a substantial part of whatever improvement of control occurs from psychoanalytic treatment in the neurotic comes from creating a greater sensitivity to borderline conscious ergic tensions and a recognition of what they mean in terms of portended action. Of course, the greater claim of psychoanalysis to improving function in this panel has been that it removes repressions and resistances normally existing to such recognition. In T-data research an apparent temperament factor, UI(T)30, has also been located, called Dissofrustance, because it favors handling frustration by cognitive dissociation. This would be the chief impediment to the present action. As would be expected from present theory UI(T)30 shows in its criterion and second order associations a pathological contribution (Tatro, 1968).

Our theory as to the mechanisms whereby the first panel of the ego action achieves its ends is that two related processes act together. First (a) there is a direct sensing of the ergic tensions, as direct as when we say we are hungry or tired. But since there would be uncertainty about the strength of possible competing but latent unactivated ergs and sentiments the ego must regularly call up a stratified sample of stimuli, acting as "agents provocateurs" for latent needs. The first panel process as a whole is thus one we may call *balloting* (of ergs and sentiments) (a) directly and (b) by evocation. Just as a real life act, a_{hjk}, has behavioral indices marked by h's and k's, invoking ergs and sentiments, so here an *imaginal* call up of an array of h's and k's reveals the potential of the associated dynamic traits. As suggested above differences in ego strength could arise from differences in efficiency of sensing of needs, of organization of cues to test them, and of degrees of action of past repression and dissociation upsetting contact with the needs.

As important as this internal sensing is in the subsequent effectiveness of ego action to maximize long term satisfaction, yet direct soundness of judgment about external realities is no less so. Apart from inherent weakness of perception which we would think at first to come from inadequate intelligence, and insufficient or poorly preserved experience, defective emotional habits could operate here, such as autistic evasions of reality, disorders of thought process, and repression of unpleasant memories. The second panel activity is one both of (a) scrutinizing the existing external situation and (b) of retrieving relevant memories concerning the long term result of past actions of the kind presently contemplated.

Process 3, below, may in a sense be out of order, since control—the holding of a moratorium over all action—is a pre-requisite for the success of all three of the other processes. The hypothetical extreme individual who reacts to the present stimulus with immediate impulse would be unable to (1) size up the total internal situation, (2) size up the external situation or (4) assemble the dynamic traits necessary to implement the decision. This we can discuss under 3, noting here in 2 that it is already in action.

Since we wish at all points to show empirical bases for the hypotheses, we naturally turn in 2 to evidence on the nature of perceptual abilities. There can be no question that intelligence—Spearman's g, as g_f and g_c in more refined analysis—enters largely here. A more correct appraisal of the external situation and the solving of the problem of getting dynamic satisfaction therein depends on the perception of relations (the operational definition of g_f), but, of course, even this perception depends also on stored skills, g_c. Part (b), the retrieval of relevant memories of past conditions, rewards and punishments, depends however substantially on the goodness of memory, which the work of Thurstone (1937), Hakstian & Cattell (1977), Kelley (1954) and others shows to be a factor independent of g.

From these analyses we would expect the soundness of ego functioning, that is, the strength of the C measure, to correlate positively both with intelligence and with the memory factor. As regards retrieval, however, we recognize, as above, that ability is not the whole story and that specific dynamic repressions, as well as the general personality factors UI(T)21, exuberance, UI(T)22, cortertia and UI(T)30 dissofrustance (Tatro, 1963; Cattell & Schuerger, 1978) would be expected to show correlation with C (respectively +, + and -). Primarily we are saying that C factor should be assisted by richness of experience, as in the long distance memory factor and by an orderliness of storage (in relation to inner control needs and tactics for the external world) facilitating retrieval. As far as outer reference is concerned there is an appreciable body of discussion (Ellis, 1962) and some experiment, for example, Weir, 1964, on the tactics the ego needs. But surprisingly little experiment yet exists to investigate the notion that C scores receive an increment from such learning. However, support with some intervening assumptions can be seen in the climbing of the C factor with age into middle age in a manner paralleling the age trend of judgmental skills in crystallized intelligence (Baltes & Schaie, 1976, Horn & Cattell, 1966). That a large and retrievable reservoir of past experiences of action contributes to ego strength is implied by the older person's condoning impulsive action in the young with the adage "You cannot put old heads on young shoulders."

It would be natural for a psychometrist, aware of the very wide action of general intelligence, and specifically of its role above in C perceptions, to conclude next that there should be an appreciable positive correlation of C with g (indexed B in the 16 PF, HSPQ, etc.). The quite astonishing fact (see summaries in Cattell, Eber, & Tatsuoka, 1970) is that over many different normal samples and a fair range of age, the average correlation, though positive, is very close to zero. (Birkett's recent (1979) thorough study checks with +.10 and QVII with QVIII, Control and Moral Upbringing, is even slightly negative.) One would naturally expect that the more intelligent individual would be more successful also in the emotional realms in finally finding realistically effective outlets for his needs (Process 4). On the other hand, we must admit that everyday life offers no particular evidence that saints are more intelligent than criminals, or that professors have more character and frustration tolerance than ditch diggers.

Possible solutions are:

1.   That although the ego operates through the most extensive and complex cognitive network in the personality, linking the present outer situation, the present inner situation, and the memories of situations past, much of the linkage is trial-and-error rather than insight-based. Of course, we do not yet have the *whole* story of correlation of B and C: as usual the r's are mostly based on 18 to 25 year old students, and when derived from earlier ages and more extended ranges a positive correlation could emerge. But until those relations are explored we suggest the following further hypotheses to explain the strange finding of an essentially zero correlation (in the common 14- to 50-year range) in direct experimental attacks.

2.   We may argue that the capacity to *perceive* (B and g) ways to satisfaction when an erg is blocked is a small part of C's variance relative to that which comes from the *capacity to control*, for future satisfaction, ergic needs and aspirations. Only in a primitive society or one at borderline subsistence, by this argument, would the more intelligent manage a more complete satisfaction of needs.

3.   Contrary to the present arguments, and Freud's later writings, the management of the external world to maximize ergic satisfaction may contribute only minor variance in relation to the problem of emotional dissatisfactions. The bulk of the variance in emotional frustration may derive from problems that are intellectually simple but badly handled through uncontrolled impulse. Shall I give up a good job in order to marry Mr. A? is not a complex intellectual question, but one requiring dependable balloting of inner needs, and there is no reason to believe that intelligence plays much part in balloting (1 above).

4.   If ego strength is actually gained by experience of frustrations and deprivations, as many wise writers—mainly religious perhaps—have maintained down the ages, the less intelligence would be expected to have greater ego strength than the bright person to whom success has always come easy! (Hence Kipling's "brittle intellectuals who crack beneath a strain" and who are certainly not conspicuous for emotional balance.) The exception to this would be the neurotic in whom the adjustment to frustration has gone awry—but there is no reason to repeat the sampling error made by Freud in psychoanalysis, or the logical error of supposing that since many people die in bed, beds are dangerous.

5.   The probability that the more intelligent set themselves, in the same environment, *higher* goals and thus are subject to *more* frustration. As Shakespeare reminds us in *Troilus and Cressida* (Act 1, Scene 3) "Checks and disasters grow in the veins of actions highest reared." This supposes, as we have done all along, that C gathers strength by success in solving frustrations, not by merely encountering more frustrations. Certainly top executives and generals face more urgent complex problems than unskilled workers and army privates. And though the former may have twice the mental age, the level of complexity in decisions at the top of our culture increases boundlessly, so that solving problems there would *need* 10 times the mental age required in lower everyday decisions. The frustrations and real inadequacies of the more intelligent, by the standards they have set themselves, may therefore be greater.

A seemingly opposite and yet tenable hypothesis is that the less intelligent, through being less able to manipulate the external world for their *basic* needs, will encounter greater total *ergic* (not sentiment) frustration. The cross-cultural data on anxiety levels (Lynn, 1977; Cattell & Woliver, 1979; Cattell, Eber, & Tatsuoka, 1970) seem to show more anxiety, and inferentially lower C, where the physical basis of life is poor. But from a general learning standpoint one might argue that if ego strength is a capacity to make dynamic compromises a greater experience of having to make emotional compromises—over a measurable range and without the pathological onset of repression and defense mechanisms—should *increase* ego strength. And it is the individual who is not clever enough to solve all the obstructions of external circumstance who will get most practise in compromise and emotional control. The upshot of these considerations is the conclusion that since intelligence enters into only one of the four main processes we might expect it to be associated with roughly only a fourth of the variance in C. If the suggestion above that frustration is greatest at the extremes of intelligence is true, the resulting curvilinear relation could well register a virtually zero linear correlation. As for the relation to crystallized intelligence, g_c, of developed talents and judgmental skills we may take a hint from Goethe's remark that character and talent need different growth environments, and note that the need to make instant decisions develops what we define here as ego strength. The job data that the airline pilot, soldier, or politician develops more ego strength than the intellectual in an ivory tower is not offered as an argument for an inverse relation of C and intelligence, for the former may be intelligent enough. But at least the absence of a positive correlation might be due to the fact that within the general population range the more intelligent perceive more complications and avoid many decisions as far as possible, whereas the man of action, to act instantly, insists on simplified stereotypes. (We are reminded of President Truman, famed for "the buck stops here," and his recorded remark about a leading "egg-head" rival that "He could not even decide when he wanted to go to the bathroom.")

These digressions on the unexpected indications of a zero *B-C* correlation are made to suggest hypotheses for experiment on the general relations of *C*, *G*, and Q_3 to intelligence and to one another. The outcome is crucial to the question of how much the perception and management of *outer* circumstances is an important part of ego function, relative to the other panels we are discussing; since it is impossible to believe that intelligence is not appreciably related to success in solving *outer* world problems.

Turning to the third and fourth panels of ego action—control, and implementing decision—we find ample evidence that higher *C* score is associated with capacity to control emotional impulse, decide action, and direct thought processes. Various developmental observations (McFarlane, 1965; Argyle & Little, 1972) point this way. In looking at the social aspects of this control the reader needs to remind himself of the properties of the *SE* or (*G*) and *SS* or (Q_3) traits dealt with in Chapter 2. The ego is not, in the normal person, "crushed between the superego and the id," and it is not concerned with social and ethical conformity except in so far as its subsidiations to *G* and Q_3, among all other sentiments and ergs, throw some weight in that direction.

Probably *G* and Q_3 will throw their weight positively with the ego in the specification equation more often than not, because they are repositories of cultural wisdom concerning control, but many times they will conflict. Then the ego has the problem of balancing the satisfaction of urgent impulses against the shame, guilt and anxiety which *G* and Q_3 threaten.

In Chapter 2 it has been suggested that there are two models in which the controlling action of *C* may be conceived and represented in the behavioral equation. In the first, shown in equation (6-1), *C* simply acts with forces of its own, like any other sentiment, and along with other sentiments, which may help it or overpower it. However, if it is habitually to control adequately;

$$a_{hijk} = \sum_{x=m} v_{hjx} s_{kx} E_{xi} + \sum_{y=n} v_{hjy} s_{ky} M_{yi} + v_{hjq} s_{kq} Q_{3i} + v_{hjg} s_{kg} G_i + v_{hjc} s_{kc} C_i \qquad (6\text{-}1)$$

its forces must outweigh those of most other dynamic structures, which means in the ordinary factor model that it must have many big behavioral indices (b's or vs's) and be a factor of large variance. In the second model, as shown in equation (6-4) (p. 390) it effects its aim by changing the weights on other dynamic structures, that is by invoking and suppressing the forces of others, in their contribution to the augmentation or reduction of the disputed course of action.

This concept of the second, CET, mechanism—maintaining control through stimulating the strength of "allies" among the other dynamic traits (both sentiments and ergs)—is novel in the dynamic calculus, at least in any precise statement and in relation to the usual form of the behavioral equation. Consequently we must pause to give it more intensive discussion, which will, also, bring out more clearly the mechanism in the *direct* control. Incidentally, a familiar illustration of this pattern of control is available at the group behavior level in such an organization as the United Nations, where the Security Council has no forces of its own, but seeks to direct what is agreed upon as desirable action by the invoking of various military contributions from many nations.

We are supposing here that ego action is at that stage in the ego action process where the internal appraisal of needs and the external (but memory directed) evaluation of consequences, has led to a decision, at stage 3 above (p. 378) and that this needs to be implemented. Our hypotheses regarding this implementation concerns both psychological processes as such and the way in which the model as so far developed has to be advanced to account for their action.

We need to recognize at this point the basic similarity, indeed the common generic quality, of recalling an image or concept (c in our symbols) and recalling an action (a in our symbols). In the unfolding of a sentiment process the appearance of a given response (attitude course of action) was seen to be dictated by the usual behavioral equation of b's, h's, k's, E's, M's, etc. The unfolding of any half conscious habit is the same: a behavioral act is "remembered" and retrieved from the memory storage just like any idea. The only difference is that in matters at the level of consciousness there is opportunity for willed interference by the ego between the idea and the act. But there is an appreciable function of behavior in which recall of idea and of action are generically the same, as we argued in analyzing the sentiment process. For instance, the recognition of an old friend and the accompanying smile and handshake are one, and the seasoned chess player recognizing a certain gambit in his opponent's attack, at once moves a pawn to queen's fourth.

Consequently, while recognizing that ego action *may* step between an idea and a response, the actual generation of the idea can be described in just the same behavioral equation as an act, thus:

$$c_{hjk} = \Sigma v_{hj}s_k A + \Sigma v_{hj}s_k P + \Sigma v_{hj}s_k E + \Sigma v_{hj}s_k M$$
$$+ \Sigma v_{hj}s_k EM + \Sigma v_{hj}s_k ME + v_{hj}s_k m \qquad (6\text{-}2)$$

where "understood" subscripts (the individual and the specificities of the hj's and k's to the traits) are omitted to let essentials stand out clearly. This being its first statement it is given for perspective in "full dress," with abilities, A's, temperament traits, P's, and the dynamic traits separated into the E, EM, ME, and M contribution. Moreover, a specific or narrow term, representing an engram m especially active in c, has been preserved, since we have accepted a sentiment as a hierarchy or network with lower order factors possessing some degrees of autonomy in their liability to cognitive activation.

Although the retrieval and the action equations are similar in form they will be different in emphasis. The retrieval of a memory, c_j, will depend on the activation power of the given stimulus situation k, represented in s_k, or the identity of the focal stimulus (or previous idea), h, and the strength of its previous experimental associations, v_{hj}, and on the various trait magnitudes. But now especially large weights will be given to an ability, A_m, which may correspond to Kelley's, Hakstian's and Horn's second order memory-efficiency factor, and to a particular sentiment structure M_y, representing (with the aid of m) the amount of actual cognitive storage in the area in which c_j occurs. This emphasis does not overlook that besides the purely cognitive M term the help to retrieval through the dynamic, emotional term EM also exists, and, if the "memory" is in the primitive, innate (Jungian archetypal) class, also through E.

The recognition of the multiple determination of memory retrieval in (6-1) opens the way to a broader multivariate experimental attack on retrieval phenomena, that could isolate and give due weight to the combination of dynamic and cognitive structures in both cognitive learning and retrieval. (As regards learning, one might expect *CE* processes to account appreciably for the buildup of the M network and *ME* processes for the ME and EM terms.) However, here the foundation in (6-1) has been laid in order better to understand ego control processes.

All action, with the exception of that small fraction through the usE term (innately triggered), is mediated by cognitive engrams (by ME and M; for even EM is only contributory to the M activation in ME). Therefore, ego control—and indeed the power of any sentiment—is achieved by command of cognitive elements. Action controlling systems in the mind operate by capturing ideas. Even the direct action of the ego in (6-1) must depend on the ego's possessing the cognitive associations, of past success and failure in maximizing the total satisfaction, permitting it to draw upon an ergic investment. (Representable in a vector $(g_{ci}E_i + \cdots + g_{cp}E_p)$ as in any other sentiment.) But in the indirect, CET action we are now analyzing it calls upon cognitive material calculated to affect the vs values for *other* sentiments and for ergs that could come to its aid in implementing the "best" decision. Here we are supposing that any vs before an M or E is augmented (or reduced) by invoking an image or concept c_j which is so largely in control of associations by the ego that we can virtually write (6-2) with only the ego term, C, thus:

$$c_{hjk} = v_{hj}s_k C_i \tag{6-3}$$

Before we deal with what may prove a complex mechanism for representation in a mathematical model, let us consider these basic propositions (a) that memory control is dynamic control and (b) that the ego operates by adjusting cognitive influences on other dynamic traits in ways the ego has learned to be effective for total satisfaction. The first proposition makes repression (concerning which clinicians may reasonably object that our theories have to this point given insufficient attention) a special and extreme case of what we would represent in (6-3) as a matter of degree in the general ego action of accentuation and reduction of memories. In the representation and measurement of conflict (Chapter 2) we have recognized that a dynamic term may have a negative behavioral index (b or vs) for a given course of action. The term itself can never go negative, but only range from zero to some positive value, but its strength can oppose some particular action. Consequently the elimination of conflict, when conflict itself rather than the course of action becomes a painful problem, is only to be achieved by reducing vs; since in regard to that course of action it can, by the nature of the dynamic trait and life, never be made positive. (For example, if the parent erg (compassion) is opposed to the act of murdering a child, there is no cognitive stimulus the ego can offer to the parental erg that will bring it to contribute in a positive way to that action.) The avoidance of conflict equation (Chapter 2) is therefore only to be achieved by the ego by removing any stimulus whatever to the negatively loaded dynamic trait.

The conclusion we come to here is that the ego's manipulation of behavior by heightening and reducing contact with stimuli to dynamic traits—in relation to either memory or the external world—extends to complete blotting out of memories or complete avoidance of certain situations in the external world. In the Cattell and Sweney (1964) factoring of the principal manifestations of conflict the first large factor (Chapter 2, p. 129) was one of willed suppression with cognitive distortion, and the second one of avoidance of stimuli. The first involved, as experimentally seen, misperceptions and failures of attention, and the second restriction of what was perceived as relevant, and rejection of humor on the topic. In the first "the mind goes blank," and more speculatively, we would hypothesize that in any ego conflict with a major sentiment the latter exerts a destructive or reductive influence on the necessary cognitive associations for the ego's ergic resources as much as the ego does on those of the sentiment or erg, the former winning out only because its ergic investment is larger. Clinically similar behavior is described as an emptiness, of consciousness, a lack of confidence in current ego decisions, and a rise in anxiety.

That a rise in anxiety, or a high anxiety, is accompanied by reduction of memory, mainly as recall capacity, has been known for several years from the several studies of Cattell and Scheier (1961), in Geer (1966) and in the three or more factor analytic studies collated by Hundleby, Pawlik, and Cattell (1965) showing lesser fluency in recall of personal characteristics (tests MI 473 and 763) and lower accuracy in checking numbers (MI 674). On the experimental evidence it would be uncertain whether cognitive suppression causes anxiety or anxiety causes cognitive loss. Incidentally, one could employ this theory of conflict and cognitive blackout to explain the major relation in schizophrenia, assuming that the conflict is now on so many fronts, and so evenly matched with the strength of the given ego, that a major impairment occurs both of the cognitive action and of ego control. With an initially different temperament—highly extravert and dissofrustant—the split personality and hysteric responses occur, in which the conflict is resolved by clean separation of the cognitive memory systems. Conflict over cognitive access, as it concerns the action of the ego, and its growth, deserves more investigation with objective personality and motivation measures.

The discovery of the U and I motivational strength components adds further support to the theoretical model here. The nature of the unintegrated component gives tangible shape to some descriptions of the Freudian unconscious; for in clinical work with the MAT the U measures exceed the I measures in those dynamic systems where a psychoanalyst sees conflict with unconscious needs. The measures which load on U (Volume 1, Chapter 4) are projection, GSR and physiological indicators, fantasy, and so forth, and those on I, the integrated component, are information, word-association and others rich in cognitive content. Thus command by cognitive connections of ergic tensions, as we hypothesize in the ego, characterizes integrated motivation, while unintegrated motivation (U score) is that which has mainly physiological, emotional expressions that have either never found cognitive connections or have lost them through conflict, suppression and repression. However, our approach would suppose not that there is a dichotomy as psychoanalysis taught, but a continuum from high to zero cognitive affiliations, though probably with a bimodal distribution. The effect of the unintegrated, largely unconscious ergic tensions upon behavior is, however, substantial enough, as shown by U loadings on typical courses of action being apparently not *much* less in magnitude than I loadings. (Cattell & Butcher, 1967; Cattell & Child, 1975). However, if we look at the psychological character of the U trait we see that the effect is "oblique," making less sense than the nature of the I loadings, presumably through U being irrationally attached to idiosyncratic symbols, and by its inflating ergic tensions that would otherwise have a more moderate loading on a particular course of action. (An interesting puzzle here is that in 6th and 7th grades reading achievement is significantly correlated with strength of integrated pugnacity positively and unintegrated equally negatively (Cattell & Child, 1975, p. 190).

Let us now consider the above model in terms of how it should appear in the behavioral correlations, and how it should be experimentally checked. At first we might think that the CET action of the ego, operating as a contributor to all other terms, should cause it to appear as a second order factor. However, the intrusion on each sentiment is that of a special loading, which, besides being unique to the sentiment, is *peculiar to the situation and response (hjk)* as well as to C itself, so as shown in equation (6-4) below, the solution for C and the special loadings induced by it becomes more complex. In either hypothesized mode of C action it will change its loadings with the situation-response it seeks to control, but in the first kind of action, in (6-1) it does so just like any other sentiment. Consequently, if the direct action model holds, C's loadings and personal score level can be simply factorially ascertained. So also can its power in terms of ergic investments $(g_{c1}, g_{c2} \ldots, g_{cp})$.

However, from psychological considerations a predominance of the second, that is, the CET, action is surely to expected. It will be recognized that CET action is hypothesized to act in slightly different ways at two points in the ego control process. First it adds to the accuracy of direct sensing of internal needs by what we likened to "agent provocateur" action, that is, giving a slight stimulus provocation to each dynamic trait to make sure of its potential demand strength. At the stage of implementing action that we are now discussing, however, CET means deliberately "harping on" a certain cognitive stimulus (or diminishing it) for each dynamic trait to bring that trait into action in a direction to support and ensure ego-planned action for maximum long-term satisfaction.

The illustration that may help here is that of a conductor, with an encouraging nod or a steadying inhibition by his baton, inducing a desired emphasis from the different parts of the orchestra. In the ego the required invocation is by cues, that is, by the ego's engineering a retrieval from memory of internal stimuli, imaginary, or symbolic (or sometimes by focusing attention on external stimuli of known potency) to arouse various ergs or activate various sentiments. For clarity it would probably be best to call this *CET* action "trait orchestration"—to distinguish it from the cue ballot or cue trial in the *CET* sensing process. For *CET* orchestration now uses a presumably learned and organized set of cues to bring action from the required dynamic traits, whereas in cue balloting the aim is only to reconnoiter the strength of the ergs and sentiments.

As stated the evidence for this *CET* orchestration has not yet been derived from multivariate experiments demonstrating a fit to the equation (6-4a and b) below. One must in fact at the moment depend on general observation and certain clinical observations of strengthening of the ego (or, at least, clinical advance) through deliberate teaching of stimulus-manipulating skills. This experience of control through arousing images calculated to represent certain ambient situations and cause arousal or reduction is, however, surely well known to every intelligent self observer. From the early Christian anchorites to Shakespeare and beyond men have sought to control sexual impulse by imaging that women had certain unpleasant aspects, while medical students have been aided in restraint by specimens of venereal disease. And someone hesitating to go to a dentist may be enabled to act by constantly imagining the peace of being without the toothache.

The nature of *CET* control, as well as the preceding ego processes of sensing, and, especially, "sizing up" the prospects of satisfaction in the complex external world, call for a conception of an altogether more *cognitive* function in the ego than the relatively purely dynamic concept that has reached us from the clinic. The ego is now seen as, above all, a clearing house, connecting and resolving highly diverse sources of information. We have already discussed the perhaps naive expectation that this would require C to be substantially correlated with intelligence. We now see that *numerous* relations may nevertheless not mean highly *complex*, intelligence-demanding relations. (A person does not need to understand the theory of relativity in order to manage his everyday business.) But effective C action, by our hypothesis of structure, does seem to demand a large storage of tactical skills and an efficient retrieval process. The correlation that might be expected of retrieval efficiency with C has never been investigated, though the unquestioned decline of C in alcoholism and some forms of brain damage gives indications. And as for the size of the memory store for problem solving and adjustive devices, the discovery that the age plot of C shows a steady rise through most of life (Volume 1, Chapter 2) is supportive, indicating effects of accumulation.

Let us now state the CET form of ego action in a more exact model. Equation (6-3) expresses the degree to which a particular ego strength in a particular action situation will beget an image, concept, verbal message or other internal stimulus capable of affecting the participation of an erg or sentiment in the given course of action. We can translate this c_{hjk} into a $v_{hj}s_k$ expressing its arousing and directing properties. It seems appropriate to suppose that a dynamic trait already has a "natural" reactivity in that situation, such as would exist if the intervention of ego control did not occur, and this would be written as usual $v_{hj}s_kD_i$. Consequently this particular bit of equal control action, which we could call a_{hjkc} would be:

$$a_{hijkc} = (v_{hjc}s_{kc}C_i)(v_{hjd}s_{kd}D_i) \tag{6-4a}$$

It might be acceptable—though psychology suggests a product relation—to approximate this by a sum.

$$a_{hjkc} = v_{hjc}s_{kc}C_i + v_{hjd}s_{kd}D_i \tag{6-4b}$$

This (6-4b) type of equation could be collapsed ($\bar{v}_{hjc}\bar{s}_{kc} = \Sigma\ v_{hjc}s_{kc}/n$ over all n D's) to give essentially the equation (6-1), which is soluble by ordinary factor methods, and might hold over small ranges. The total equation of ego action by expanding (6-4a) need not be set out: it expresses a_{hijk} as the sum of terms as in (6-4a) over all the traits involved.

No multivariate experiment studying the above model yet exists, but one can assemble some general evidence in psychology not incompatible with (6-1) and (6-4a). If these are correct C should be a pervasive factor across much behavior, and it should show relatively strong loadings in behavior recognized as requiring self control. Factoring questionnaire items generally shows C with fewer items in the hyperplane than most factors, and, incidentally, peculiarly difficult to separate clearly from O and Q_4. On its relative loadings on decision behaviors conclusions are not yet possible (see, however, Birkett, 1979), but its subnormal value for persons with all kinds of pathological behaviors (Volume 1, Chapter 2) is so dependable that we may conclude impaired C is systematically associated with poor decisions.

Support of a different kind comes, curiously, from the introspective phase of psychology, if we are prepared, as behaviorists, nevertheless, to give introspection some role. In the studies, for example, of Ach (1905), Aveling (1931), and Cattell (1930) on the introspective experience of decision the evidence was at least based on large numbers of protocols, under experimental control and quantitatively analyzed. They reported first on the fluctuating awareness of the self, and the experience of a "subjectivity" which sometimes attenuated the boundary between the perceiving subject—the ego—and the perceived object. They showed that the highest awareness of the acting self (which we recognize here as the ego structure in action) occurred either at moments of decision or when conation (dynamic action) was high. When conation was low, as would be seen in today's transcendental meditation, both consciousness of the self as such and of the object-subject distinction tended to fade. But there emerges, at least, definite evidence that moments of high decision bring heightened awareness of C action, that is, of the introspected self.

Elsewhere, and in quite recent experiment, there is reasonably neat evidence of what we have called CET action, and of the manner in which it gets learned. Unfortunately, none of this bivariate experiment carries factor markers for the ego structure itself. Much of this experiment springs from Skinner's (1969) notion of "stimulus control of behavior," which also occurs under "self-directed stimulus control" and the therapist's current "environmental stimulus control" expressions. By the peripheralist (S and R outwardly observed) nature of the reflexist model, the explanation of control has been attempted predominantly in terms of external stimuli, or by "cue-producing responses," which propel the individual up against some suitable external stimulus. If we approach the control problem without having to neglect internal structural measures, however, the whole emphasis in human beings is seen to be in reality upon internal controls, and these realities require more sophistication of principles and models than the external "stimulus control" defined by the reflexologists. Indeed, for the sake of genuine perspective on whether psychology is or is not advancing,[3] we must point out that the recent jargon in behavior therapy on "discriminative stimulus control" (cue control) is a thousandth case in our bogged-down science of making progress by offering new and polysyllabic names for very old ideas. For external "stimulus control" is close to 2,000 years old as seen in the Lord's Prayer. "Lead us not into temptation."

At a clinical level we certainly see widespread evidence of internally conjuring up cue situations (k's) as images, thoughts, and symbolic entities known to be capable of modulating dynamic traits. If, for example, Miss X is given to overeating, is fighting obesity, and is tempted by the refrigerator door, the alert ego may call up images of the weighing scales, of the disparaging remarks of Mrs. Y, of some loss of respect from her friends, and of a dismayed self-sentiment when Miss X gets into her party dress on the weekend. Such invoked cues are directed by a retrieval of consequences of the course of action as such that is, of a_{hjk}. We have supposed above that by past learning of rewards and punishments the invoked cues are there to operate at the same time on the dynamic traits getting satisfaction through that course of action. Thus in the above invoked cues the disparaging remarks of Mrs. Y. punish the self-assertive erg, the loss of regard by friends deprives the gregarious need, and the thought of bulging out of her dress is a frustration of the self-sentiment. Thus C in (6-4) would modulate +, +, + on these interests. We should note in passing that the cues need by no means always be inhibitory. Frequently the ego will be required, instead, to arouse and activate dynamic traits, notably the self-sentiment and superego.

This field of experiment is at the moment trapped in terminologies that are cumbersome, jejune, and likely to mislead design. Basically there are internal and external stimuli (the former cognitive, and not to be confused with such causal influences as ergic tensions, which are not stimuli), and there are positive stimulus cues and inhibitory or negative stimulus cues. But, if the argument above is correct, the positive and negative apply to the effect of dynamic traits on the action in dispute, not to the stimulus effect on the dynamic trait. The latter ranges from some positive value to zero and the most the ego control can do is to reduce the stimulation to zero. The signs belong to the direction of action of the aroused trait on the particular response. And "punishment" of a dynamic trait is simply removal of its satisfaction, for example, denying the fear erg its goal of escape from pain.

Among the several recent experiments on cues, bearing more or less on the ego control behavior, an interesting example is Johnston's (1962) demonstration, at least at the clinical level, that if what we call inner cues are concretized as verbal reminders of rewards and punishments, and, further, effectively brought into repetitious action (as in our "common schedule" principle), by use of printed cards as reminders, noticable gain in ego control results. There are indications, however, as would be expected, that verbal self-production of cues becomes ineffective below the age of 3 or so (Luria, 1961). Johnson's result is supported at higher ages (grade school) by Meichenbaum & Goodman (1971).

The experimental evidence is therefore still thin. More substantial progress in the area of this extremely important third panel of ego action, that is, *execution of action the ego has decided upon*, may surely be expected when multivariate methods are employed[4] and valid psychometric measures of unitary structures are brought into experiment.

More substantial progress in this extremely important area of ego action can be made only if manipulative experiment is closely linked with valid psychometric measures of distinct structures. And here unfortunately the *T*-data identifications remain obscure in relation to the readily understandable and highly replicable *Q-L* media. Since ego action can be recognized psychologically as falling into four panels one naturally asks whether the unity of the *C* factor perhaps admits of recognizing it as a second order factor based on 4 well correlated primaries. The fact is, as stated introductorily, that at least 3 and probably 4 well defined *T*-data factors—UI(T)16, UI(T)17, UI(T)23 and UI(T)29—admit of possible interpretation as ego action. For lack of studies correlating these separate measures, and especially because experimental evidence for control by *CET* action is limited one can perhaps lean on general evidence, such as that in motor action the cerebellum seems constantly to send out minor muscle stimuli to get responses concerning the position and muscle tension in limbs before it acts to move those limbs.

As regards experimental checking on the model, as in equation (6-4), the complexity of the required multivariate design is such that many pages would be necessary. Meanwhile, more partial approaches are possible through further analysis of the objective test patterns in UI(T)16, 17, and 23; through examining changes in various performances with age and life experience; through dynamic trait measures monitoring therapy; and through comparisons of decisions under various emotional situations. Most of these, to control the effects of other traits, will be manipulative *and* multivariate. In considering earlier the claims of UI(T)23, UI(T)17, and UI(T)16 in *T*-data personality factoring to be the ego pattern in *T*, we were struck by the presence in UI(T)23, capacity to mobilize, of several features such as we have just encountered in the ego concept, such as capacity to control motor-perceptual rigidity, ability to coordinate simultaneous tasks, reduction of attitude fluctuation, low suggestibility to others, and ability to hurry without losing control of errors.

A thorough recent study by Birkett (1979) has cleared up the larger obscurities in the relation of these *T*-data (*O-A*) factors to the ego. It is now evident that the ego is a broader structure than are the former and it accounts for a considerable part of the variance of a second order factor among them, formerly indexed (Cattell & Schuerger, 1978) as *TVI*, and roughly named "Narcistic self-expression." *TVI* has shown, over independent studies, significant loadings on UI(T)16+, 17-, 19-, 20-, 23+, 26-, 27+, and 34+. Incidentally, despite the ego's divergence in growth from UI(T)17 thus shown, it aids (loads) UI(T)1 markers for orderly execution of inhibitory performance (loadings 0.3). But otherwise, as the correlations with UI(T)19- and 34+ show, the ego opposes compulsive conformity defences. The loadings on UI(T)16 and 23 support for TVI and the ego the concept of decisiveness and "grasp," while that on UI(T)26 adds an indication that self expression is central.

One speculates on the logical possibility that each of these T-data factors represents one of the four panels of ego expression defined on page 378. Thus inner evaluation would come from UI(T)20-; evaluation of the situation and implementation from "capacity to mobilize, in UI(T)23 and UI(T)19, and decisiveness from UI(T)26, and UI(T)16. While the alignments (see O-A subtests in Cattell & Schuerger, 1978) may not be immediately convincing they point to a promising avenue of research.

Some support for the action in (6-4)—though no easy approach to finding the actual values—comes from the relation of C to low attitude fluctuation (which we have already noted in the work of Das, 1953; Cattell, 1943; and others). If a particular strength of response on a particular attitude a_{hjk} is considered most realistic in terms of adaptation and adjustment, then C needs to exert itself through such C values as will check the natural $v_{hjx}s_{kx}E_x$ effect and various M effects to bring about that magnitude of strength. Ergic need strengths (and some sentiments) we know vary from day to day from inner and from some circumstantial causes. The extent to which C will keep the resulting variations in a_{hijk} down will be mathematically a function of the strength of C and its loadings relative to the ergs and sentiments in the given individual. In a series of measures of the attitude a_{hjk} for individual i over n occasions, we can calculate the strength variance as:

$$\sigma^2_{a_{hijk}} = \frac{\sum\limits^{x=n}(a_{hijk\cdot x} - \bar{a}_{hijk})^2}{n} \tag{6-5}$$

where a_{hijk} is the mean value of a_{hijk} over several days. Our theory would require that C show itself as an inverse function of this value, thus:

$$C = (f)\frac{b}{\sigma^2_{a_{hijk}}} \tag{6-6}$$

where b is some scaling value and the function f could be more complex than a linear one. The significant correlations by Cattell (1943) and by Das (1953) support this 6-6 relation, but it deserves more subtle experimental investigation, for example, with emotional manipulations of subjects' attitudes and with inclusion of the above UI factors as referents.

If we grant that most citizens—other than those in mental hospitals and prisons—reach tolerable levels of impulse control in relation to our culture, it must follow that in general the ego-strength factor (and probably Q_3 and G) acquires, after early childhood (see age curve), a larger weight in most behavioral equations than most other personality factors, ergs, and sentiments. One approach to checking this theory that needs to be made is an analysis of a wide range of attitude decision situations using real base factor analysis capable of recognizing absolute difference in size of factors.

It has been accepted above that C is a sentiment structure, though of a unique kind, and that like any sentiment it will be also in broadest terms a process. If we look at the four panels or kinds of action recognized above as parts of C action, but now look at their *temporal order* as a process, the latter would be as follows:

1.   Inhibition of impulse while a dynamic sensing is made.

2.   A sensing of ergic and sentiment needs immediately and by cue sounding.

3.   Examination of the external situation, with retrieval from memory of outcomes of past responses satisfying various tensions. This may be not fully conscious, and its success will also be a function of freedom from defenses.

4.   An implementing of the decision on best action by CET (cue evocation of traits) and direct C action, in the behavior specification equation, in which C acts both simply as a sentiment and in a new and unique index-modifying manner.

6-4. The Acquisition of the Ego Structure (C)

To begin at the beginning we should ask about the maturational-genetic influences. It is obvious that animal species differ innately considerably in their capacities to control impulse in the light of possible longer term satisfaction, and the heritability quotient for C of about 0.4 shows appreciable differences exist within the human species. Somewhere an innate component operates.

That difference, we hypothesize, is partly in adjuncts at later stages of the C process, for example, in determining the memory capacity, but mainly in the initial control of emotional impulse. In his extensive study of young delinquents in London, Burt (1923) gave appreciable quantitative value to what he defined as *general emotionality*—the demand for "instant satisfaction"—a trait characterizing all ergic impulses equally. Numerous biographies observe the presence or absence of a trait of this kind. At Pericles, Socrates, and Newton, for instance, their biographers stand amazed, perceiving levels of equanimity maintained under all kinds of emotional provocation. On the other hand Boswell well describes the emotional outbursts of a probably equally intelligent man, Dr. Johnson, while Rousseau has vividly described the sea of emotionality on which his life was constantly tossed into inconsistencies. Terman and others have noted higher emotionality in the early lives of artists and writers than in their scientific coevals of no higher intelligence. Ruggles Gates (1946) records genealogical studies pointing strongly to appreciable inheritance of violent temper and general emotionality. One wonders whether the inheritance is of some special ardour of emotions as such, which might rest on the structure of the hypothalamus and midbrain, or of defective equipment in the limbic neural connections between the hypothalamus and the controlling frontal lobes. The unmistakable rise in general emotionality and impulsiveness following destruction of the frontal lobes suggests the latter, and indeed it is harder to think of much variation in properties so fundamental to life as the ergic strengths themselves, as the first hypothesis would require.

The growth of the ego is to be considered here in the light of general models for all kinds of personality growth (Nesselroade & Reese, 1973; Buss, 1974; Labouvie, 1975) and particularly our models for *phasic* and *direct* growth in sentiments. Our hypothesis is that the growth of C is phasic, for as a necessary preliminary to the evaluative and organizing action there must be some degree of immediate control of impulse. The notion of the ego simply as the highest order factor in some hierarchy of personality factors, explicit in Royce (1966) and implicit in other writing (Amarel, 1962; Weiss, 1971) is logically pretty but very questionable. Nor do we have to suppose that atomistic, specific operant conditionings—ME learning—over many situations need in some way add up to the *generalized* control capacity, C, which we find to exist. We know that C has a quite appreciable genetic component, which we hypothesize appears in this capacity for initial inhibition of impulse. It is the same behavior as has been studied in animals as tolerance for delayed reward (MacIntosh, 1974; Garcia, Ervic & Koelling, 1966) and in which big hereditary differences are demonstrated among different species. In humans this can most probably be identified with $UI(T)17$ (QVIII in questionnaires). That this is more subject to maturation than learning would explain the trauma in childhood when teaching of control exceeds the innate control capacity of the given individual.

Granted the maturational phase has reached a certain level the teaching of control does not proceed merely by the summation of blind, atomistic conditionings, as already suggested. Over the years of childhood every human culture is replete with parental and school injunctions generalized in words to "Control yourself." And smackings for displays of temper or other excessive emotionality are accompanied by exhortations to pursue this *general* ideal. (Doubtless there are cultural differences, and the older European cultures, as in England and France, are more exacting, earlier, than, say, Hawaiian or African cultures.) It is true that nature itself is fairly uniform in punishing uncontrol,[5] as when the over-hungry child takes scalding porridge, the over-curious puts his hand in a wasp's nest or the over-assertive jumps too wide a brook; but the human being with normal intelligence surely learns emotional control as an explicit, *generalized* goal of behavior, rewarded so frequently by *ME* learning as to reach in most cases almost a "physiological" neural limit in most cultures.

The contribution of psychoanalysis has been to recognize the deviations from a simple "learning curve" that can occur through early events in this learning, mainly demands and threats beyond the developing individual's current capacity to control rationally. The concept is an old one. Francis Bacon around 1598 observed "He that seeketh victory over his nature, let him not set himself too great nor too small tasks, for the first will make him dejected by often failing, and the second will make him a small proceder. And at first let him practise with helps, as swimmers do with bladders or rushes, but after a time let him practise with disadvantages, as dancers do with thick shoes." (This fully anticipates behavior modification discoveries today, but is less rich in concepts—right or wrong—than, say, Anna Freud on the defense mechanisms.) The reader will note, incidentally, that one of our theories for the absence of correlation of intelligence and C hinges on the "thick shoes": that the disadvantages in gaining ergic satisfactions suffered by the less intelligent ultimately strengthen ego control—sufficiently to balance the otherwise positive correlations.

Regarding the second panel of C action—that of sensing inner needs—it is reasonable to assume that much learning can occur, and that civilized man gains greatly in having words for various inner states. Probably (except for comparing C growth in societies significantly differing in such equipment) this relation to C will be demonstrable only by comparing age groups, and, for example, those with large readings in introspective novels and drama and those without. Almost certainly literature and drama offer a vicarious learning experience here, both in "sensing" emotions and in knowing common devices for adaptive reactions. This vicarious emotional education should produce decidedly more growth of C (and self-sentiment, Q_3) than in the illiterate.

Regarding the third panel of action—the evaluation of the outside circumstances and the retrieval from storage of an array of usual consequences of alternative action one would expect, at least in this phase, some correlation of learning with intelligence, and certainly with time and experience. At certain ages, for example, adolescence, the magnitude of this storage would often be a critically limiting value. The success of retrieval as such may not be much changed by learning—except as it depends on initial orderly storage—and may depend more on physiological condition (consider delirium tremens) and the absence of dynamic repressions. The level reached in equipping oneself with the stored information on reward and punishment per se is surely a matter of cumulative personal experience and of the above vicarious experience. If this is true a willingness to venture and gain experience should show a relation to C, and indeed we do find (Cattell, Eber, & Tatsuoka, 1970) significant correlations of C with H factor (adventurousness) of .34 for women and .38 for men. A number of enterprising researchers have begun recently to study the learning of these cue evocation strategies and tactics for emotional control that most people pick up by personal experience. But we are still far from even a descriptive taxonomy of the main devices used and must be content in the following pages with a thin sampling. Part of the learning for C is thus building a store of equipment covering strategies and tactics for managing oneself in such a way as to reap maximum long term total satisfaction in recognized environmental circumstances. These environments are sufficiently universal and the required behavior sufficiently generalizable for this clearing house activity to become a unitary personality trait—as C is—stable across environments.

Finally, we have to examine the acquisition of the control behavior itself: the action of the fourth panel. Our model, in equation (6-4), supposes that C comes into controlling (inhibiting and enhancing) action in two ways. It acts directly, of its own strength, like any sentiment, and it acts indirectly by manipulating, through its $v_{hjc}s_{kc}$ influences the various other sentiments and ergs. The acquisition of these two kinds of capacity seems to follow sufficiently different paths to raise the question of whether a *single* unitary C factor would, statistically, be expected.

The acquisition of the indirect action could well be more consciously achieved and more sophisticated in manner than that of direct control, and we shall look at some detailed experimental illuminations below. Let us continue to distinguish the two control processes, even if later we find they correlate highly, namely the *indirect, evocative C* control, and the *direct sentiment C action*. In equation (6-4) we have explicitly hypothesized that the sources of these two actions ultimately become the same structure and are therefore given the same symbol, C, though the former (6-4a) acts by evoking aid from other dynamic structures and the latter (6-4b) simply "throws its weight" into the specification equation as one more dynamic structure.

The first problem in explaining the rise of the directly acting sentiment C, itself, as a *unitary* trait is that we assume that much learning—especially the earlier and the non-social—will lack the teaching generalization to "control yourself." It will be blind trial and error learning, just as in, say, learning to ride a bicycle, producing many *specific* control behaviors. In general, the more rewarded behaviors will be those in which, first, a control of impulse, followed by deliberation, and by thowing in the weight of the nascent ego sentiment, has successfully occurred. But will not these rewards merely lead to strengthening the *specific* habits and sentiments invoked, that is, a particular control rather than such a generalized behavior as ego control per se.[6] If we consider two sentiments, M_1 and M_2 in conflict (actions j and $\bar{j}$) and C coming in in favor of M_2, in one case too weakly to outweigh M_1 and in the other strongly enough to do so, we have:

$$a_{hjk} = b_{hjk1}M_1 - b_{hjk2}M_2 - b_{hjk}C \qquad (6\text{-}7\text{a})$$

$$a_{h\bar{j}k} = -b_{h\bar{j}k1}M_1 + b_{h\bar{j}k2}M_2 + b_{h\bar{j}k}C \qquad (6\text{-}7\text{b})$$

Let us suppose the b weights are such that overt action j is followed in (6-7a) but that with the larger weight of C in (6-7b) the balance is tipped and the reverse (alternative) action $\bar{j}$ is followed. If $a_{h\bar{j}k}$ leads to ultimate long term reward and a_{hjk} does not, the learning result will be not only a change in specific sentiments (reduction of M_1 and strengthening of M_2) but also a strengthening of C. Over many different acts, M_1 and M_2 will be sometimes on one side and sometimes on the other in terms of ultimately rewarded behavior, and will reach sizes appropriate to the balance of reward commonly existing for some sentiment with general positive usefulness. But C, to the extent that its vision (via the clearing house) of long term satisfaction is correct, will be constantly rewarded, suffering reduction only in the fewer instances where its control attempt is defeated. The reasons that growth in C is not as rapid as the above algebra would suggest are probably (1) that its successful action depends on a correct sequential pattern of the several panels—forcing a deliberate pause by control of immediate impulse, retrieving from memory consequences of previous related action, and so forth, and (2) that its rewards are by definition of its purpose—*long term* satisfaction—more remote than of the ergs and sentiments with which it may conflict. The tired businessman who forces himself to go jogging before supper instead of sitting down to a Martini, may not get his C reward until he experiences a more sprightly feeling the next morning—or next week.

If we consider that the above calculations, as well as the necessary verbalization and realization of control as a rewarding goal, from childhood on, can account for the rise of a C sentiment as a unitary trait with a relatively abstract goal, then there remains a second problem in our hypothesis. It is a problem of feed-back and limits of growth in such a structure. Failure, in a sufficient number of instances (as 6-7a and b suggest) to command long term satisfaction should weaken the ego. Mistakes early in the adjustment learning history should tend, by weakening of the ego and deterioration also of the external situation, to increase the probability of larger mistakes, in still more deteriorated circumstances. The experiments and analyses of Kanfer and Phillips (1970) for example, though externally directed only to bivariate specificities, show how essentially unadjustive response courses (as far as long term satisfaction is concerned) get replaced. They bring out first the importance of the learning opportunity, created by the controlled pause, to deliberate, and secondly the vital need to introduce the self controlled, inhibitory action *early* in any action series that has risks of going "off the rails." If, in ego control "nothing succeeds like success" and "nothing fails like failure," we are dealing with a positive feedback system leading to utter success or utter failure, and so to an expectation of a bi-modal distribution of C scores, with perfect control at one end and complete degradation of control at the other. Since this C distribution has so far not been observed the riddle remains that some additional unknown regulatory principle must be at work.

This regulatory addition may occur through the importation of defense mechanisms (such as repression, projection, reaction formation, fantasy, etc.) so well known through Freud and Anna Freud (1937) as to need no digression here. These may be the stop-gaps that prevent the downward spiral to catastrophic loss of ego strength, but at the cost of loss of flexibility and of venturesomeness of the ego in further learning. As indicated above, the psychoanalytic treatment of these responses to failure of normal ego growth is so clear as to require no repetition here, though we would point out two experimental extensions: first the demonstration by Cattell & Wenig (1952) in perceptual responses, that the number and nature of unitary defense processes found factor analytically essentially supports the Freudian description, and secondly that the discovery (Hundleby, Pawlik & Cattell, 1965) of personality factor UI(T)28 in objective behavioral measures, points to generalized effect of too early an imposition of ego and superego demands, weakening the ego. (UI(T)28 is above normal in depressives, neurotics and some psychotics, and below normal in delinquents, addicts and sociopaths (Cattell, Schmidt & Bjersted, 1972; Cattell, 1964, 1978b).) That the correlational evidence points to ego growth being proportional to the successful long term expression of ergic need is evident, and Rapoport (1974) has neatly expressed this in "the autonomy of the ego is guaranteed by the drives." The expectation that C will not be normally distributed when the right scaling units are found, but will be skewed to the lower end, deserves attention from experimenters, in terms of finding the sources of regulation of the positive feedback, we have inferred. But meanwhile, the principles of growth of *C* as a direct-acting sentiment are reasonably clear.

By contrast to *C* acting directly, and developing by trial and error learning, one may surely suppose that the indirect, evocative *C* growth has appreciable conscious, insightful learning origins. Indeed, although not enriched by structural concepts, there is much experiment now available on behavioral control by evocation of both internal and external stimuli. The former is well illustrated in Ashem and Poser's (1973) work, while Skinner's "self-directed stimulus control" belongs in the second category. This, of course, is not only a device for inhibition of undesirable action, but also for encouragement of desirable, positive action, in that an individual can use the tactic of exposing himself to stimuli (including external stimuli) that increase the probability of the response decided to be desirable.

However, to preserve perspective one must, in evaluating behavior therapy's claims to the efficacy of stimulus control, beware of overlooking the effect of the *initial agreement of the client* not to encounter the stimuli that normally lead to the undesirable satisfactions. For this shows that the balance of dynamic forces in such selected individuals already outweighs the strength of the symptom. Skinner's "environmental support systems" have real effects, but in the too dramatic instances of behavior therapy texts they have contributed only by reinforcing a "fait accompli" in the subject's self-control. As Francis Bacon observed in 1610 (edition of 1948), "If a man have the fortitude and resolution to enfranchise himself at once of a bad habit that is the best." In his words, more exactly:

Optimus ille animi vindex laedentia pectus
Vincula qui rupit, dedoluitque semel.[7]

In modern dress this is Guthrie's recipe for breaking a habit "by getting a new response established to an old stimulus," except that Bacon is not caught believing that a peripheralist system can accomplish it alone and implicitly recognizes that it needs the total personality structure to bring the break about. In many experiments when the effect has been ascribed to stimulus control we would argue that four-fifths of the gain is actually from the inner rewards that begin the decision, and which we have described as resulting from *cue evocation*—notably the cues that arouse the self-sentiment ergic rewards. And in several cases such as the above these operate before stimulus control purely in an *environmental* support system ever comes into the picture.

Fortunately the enhancement of ego control, by introduction of inner verbal and symbolic stimuli—cue evocation—rewarding either inhibition or stronger action (according to which is required), can be considered established by several experiments (Ayllon & Azrin, 1965; Mischel & Liebent—see Mischel, 1973). But the evidence is that it is decidedly greater when *followed up* by real (external) rewards, especially when these are presented with consistency. Once again we are shown that "functional autonomy" is temporary, though we have argued that to some extent in all subgoals and sentiments, and to a very high degree in some, such as the self-sentiment and the superego, reward can continue to emanate from them in symbolic representations almost indefinitely (especially in non-viscerogenic ergs).

Frequently, in the daily life of the average person the individuals who have served as models in the vicarious learning, such as Bandura has studied, stay around in the life of the subject after the self-sentiment concepts that help reward ego action have been formed. Situational props and the continuation of stimuli to the self-sentiment and ego have an appreciable contribution to observed levels of control. Just how much, in general, the assistance to ego control in everyday life springs from continuing actual situations and models and how much from ego-invoked, earlier-engrammed, internal stimuli representing the self-sentiment is a rather subtle question for experiment. We must further take account, as in the work of Bandura and Kupers (1964) and Bandura and Perloff (1967), of the fact that the imitator imitates the degree of approval (satisfaction) that the admired model shows of *his* own action. It is interesting to find from these researches also that adults continue to be, over most years of imitation, more strongly reinforcing models than the child's peers (Bandura & Kupers, 1964).

Before asking more definitely in what manner the ego is itself rewarded and taught for arranging the right rewarding cues for the ergs and sentiments that it coordinates, it will help if we turn from the necessarily weak motivations and uncertain degrees of permanence of findings in miniature situations in the laboratory, (as in much of the above study of evocative action) to the broader experiments in everyday life. Unfortunately, as the section on the C factor in Chapter 2 points out although we have much solid data on life behavior and absolute C measures the analyses of *changes* of C measures under life impacts are all too few! However, if we may summarize from Section 2-8, we have firm evidence that the C factor normally increases with age and experience; deteriorates in neurosis and psychosis; is elevated by general psychotherapy (no evidence yet on behavior therapy); in 20-year-olds grows more in a group that marries than in a control group; is below normal with chronic illness; but is strengthened by experience of a bereavement of a valued person and (less clearly) by other challenging experiences; is higher in occupations demanding decisions in action situations; is lower in partners in unstable than stable marriages; is stronger in a group retaining jobs relative to a control group undergoing many job changes; is very low in chronically unemployed; is higher in psychiatric technicians who can handle patients wisely on a mental hospital ward than in those who cannot; grows more in a group of subjects joining a church or other morale-building institution than in controls who do not, and so on.

Evidence for growth of C factor through success in control of impulse came from a new angle in a by-product result of an experiment by Rickels, Cattell, et al. (1966), which like many by-products may turn out to be more important than the main hypothesis tested. It showed, in effect, a significant rise in neurotics in measured ego strength (16 PF) proceeding steadily over some weeks of administration of a tranquilizer. The hypothesis, which of course urgently calls for further checking, is that under the tranquilizer these subjects experienced reduced general emotionality and therefore fewer disturbing upsets of their emotional control. At the miniature situation level Davison and Valens (1969) have shown an interesting positive growth effect from individuals experiencing apparent success in control, even though it was, unknown to themselves, actually engineered for them.

The above evidences of the causes and manner of ego growth by learning are based on a total C measurement, so that it is presently not possible to conclude whether the effect is only on one C process or all four. As discussed earlier, the nature of the behaviors in the objective test factors UI(T)16, 17, 19, 20, 23, 26, 29, and 34 is such that each could be concerned as one aspect of ego strength and the factor evidence at present begins definitely to place C as the second order among them. Relatively straightforward research designs could clear this up, and if it should prove that UI(T)16 and UI(T)17 as *ego standards*, and *inhibitory control* correspond to direct ego action and UI(T)23, *capacity* to mobilize, to cue evocative capacity, the tools would exist to explore the cooperation of the two actions in equation (6-4). Reverting to our hydraulic model the direct C action in phase four is the analogue of the stopping of a flow by shutting off the tap (a never fully efficient tap, however) at the outflow, and the indirect C action in phase four is the analogue of operating various taps further back to lessen the need for direct action at the leaky faucet. One might surely expect that the cue evocation action (CET) would begin to be learned later than the direct action both because one must first discover that direct action is strenuous, risky and incomplete, and also because CET involves more self-conscious and complicated learning.

The problem in CET learning is that the weights that C applies to each sentiment and erg need to be different, as a total pattern, in each control situation. Let us put the magnifying glass on this by taking out of equation (6-4a) (p. 390) just the *CET* part and let us simplify it (beyond using just D's for dynamic traits) by using b for the v's and s's expressing the normal involvement of D in a_{hjk} and $\bar{b}$ for the modification of that usual action that C brings about. Then (neglecting i subscripts) and considering p dynamic traits, we have:

$$a_{hjk} = \bar{b}_{hjkc1}C \cdot b_{hjk1}D_1 + \cdots + b_{hjkcp}C \cdot b_{hjkp}D_p \qquad (6\text{-}8)$$

If C brings to bear the $\bar{b}$ weights that produce the desired increase or reduction of a_{hjk}, to maximize ultimate long term satisfaction of the total organism, b and C will tend to grow in strength, by the ME learning principle, just as in the learning of direct C action. If the ego's aim is the reduction of this behavior, then the b values should be negative, and if the C action succeeds in fact in inhibiting a_{hjk} there is more reward for the negatively loaded C. However, the reward to C, since it involves the total balance of satisfaction to *all* ergs, must come also through increases of general satisfaction in many other a_{hjk}'s than that in the immediate case. Thus the "success" of immediate behavior has to register as a reward partly to later behavior of a different kind.

There are, indeed, one or two weaknesses in the model unless and until later research shall show that certain mechanisms that now seem somewhat improbable can in fact operate. The first is that we have just seen: C can grow, by the ME principle, if the reduction of behavior in (6-8) is rewarded; but can this reward amount to much if it comes hours or days later to actions which the inhibition of the response today has made possible? Since, with humans, it is possible for the individual to look back days later and say, "Yes, I made the right decision" perhaps we need not be too worried about this delay in the positive reward to C. Secondly, the "good" *CET* pattern of restraint and appeal on D's is different for every particular hjk, which calls for a very great repertoire memory for C. Furthermore, each of these patterns has to be coordinated in the best relationship to other action patterns, in regard to effects in the external world. The learning in the typical sentiment is, as we have seen, in the form of additions to its structure, which we have called m's (when involving some larger subgoal formation) and n's (when more specific). These are the engrams whereby the sentiment becomes able to respond to the situation hk by j and they are expressed by a b_{hjk} attached to M in the specification equation. It might seem that it is no greater task for C to store all its associations peculiar to hjk's than for any other sentiment to do so. But we must notice that the $\bar{b}$ coefficient in (6-8) and its associated n, is a three cornered affair, linking C, D, and hjk with a value peculiar to both D and hjk, so that there is slower learning and more to keep in storage.

Our concept of ego strength is now enriched by this perception of it, at least in its controlling action, and in the CET "government by proxy" part of that action. It is a structure systematically linking an array of external situational responses, hjk's, with an array of internal D's (or, indeed, in lesser degree, of all T's). It is not surprising that in such complex learning the $\bar{b}$ values (with their $\bar{n}$'s, as we may distinguish the three-cornered) should sometimes be rough and ill-adjusted, and incidentally, liable to get out of date. Much of psychotherapy is an attempt to change $\bar{b}$'s that have stood inapt but uncorrected from childhood. Since trial and error—even as insightful "mental experiment" carried out in images—is part and parcel of most ego learning, the estimate of $\bar{b}$'s the ego makes on the very first encounter with a difficult emotional choice situation could be poor even for an effectively developed ego. It becomes evident as one recognizes above (1) the distance of the learned behavior from the reward to the ego, and (2) the great variety of weighting patterns to be learned, that our earlier concern about positive feedback (ego strength begetting ego strength, by more complete satisfaction of ergs) leading to a runaway maximization and perfection of C action was premature. The regulating mechanism on that feedback is the sheer increase of complexity of learning as the ego attempts ever closer approximation to maximal long term satisfaction.

In summary then the learning of the ego structure is hypothesized to take place at each of four stages in a process (the three last each having two successive related phases), but with such interaction of reward to these different stages that a unitary structure emerges. It is hypothesized that research on UI factors in the OA battery may demonstrate some factors corresponding to stages and linked in a second order C factor. Thus we can reach now a fuller statement of the four panels initially hypothesized:

1.   A control of immediate impulses, to permit deliberation and evaluation. It improves by trial and error learning and by society's explicit repetition of approval of control. It is here that the genetic component in $C-$, innate general emotionality or "impulsivity," probably contributes most of the genetic variance, as a resisting limit to acquiring control capacity.

2.   A sensing of the strength of internal needs, which becomes improved by language terms for introspectible experience ("ability to talk to oneself") and by using provoking cues to sound real strengths (CET action).

3. (a)   An examination of the realities of the external world

and perception of possible solutions for obtaining ergic satisfaction. It is in this phase that one would expect intelligence, education and experience to play an appreciable role.

(b)   A scanning of memory storage and retrieval of relevant records of rewards and punishments for some of the contemplated alternatives. It is here that magnitude of storage (length of experience) and efficiency of retrieval would be expected to correlate with C. The action of C (a) directly as a sentiment and (b) as an indirect coordinator, by cues, of the "proxy" action of other dynamic trait strengths, begin to diverge at this point. The memory operations could be conscious for (b) but would be those in any unconscious trial and error learning for (a). Along with (2) and (3) this leads to a decision on a course of action (or more or less of various courses of action) being finally made.

4.   The implementation of the decided course of action, leading to a still more clear separation of (a) and (b) action. In direct sentiment action C simply throws its weight (as would any M, with a given ergic investment) into the specification equation as much as is necessary to overcome opposition and ensure that action in a_{hjk} that will permit maximum later satisfaction of all a_{hjk}'s. This weight is learned by trial and error. In indirect action C conjures up cues necessary to bring other dynamic traits to its aid to implement the considered course of action.[8] This involves the learning of a whole pattern of $\bar{b}$ *modifiers* (different from b, modulators) for each of all major courses of action in the lattice. Such learning may be hastened by psychological insights. The patterns of modifiers have an optimum mutual relationship: a pattern among patterns.

It is the increasing complexity of the learning acquisition of the three-cornered links (C, D, hjk) that provides a negative feedback bringing the operation of the positive feedback inherent in ego learning growth to a halt—at limits for different people determined by the genetic and learning parameters above. It might be argued that a limit to ego growth also exists in the limit to the ability of a person to bring about his satisfactions in a difficult external world. Some psychotherapists have made much of the importance of the part of the fourth function of the ego to which we have given little emphasis, namely, the acquisition of skills, for example, social skills, in achieving ergic expressions. This perception of the best act to increase satisfaction we have given due role to in 3(a). Patients may be operating below their real capacity to get real satisfactions, but no one can hope to go beyond a certain limit in commanding the world to his wants, and so we hypothesize that the greater part of the individual differences in ego strength does not lie therein.

6-5. The Nature of General States and Their Relation to Dynamic Traits: The Action of Anxiety

The learning of personality structures, especially of the controlling structures, is more tied up with the action of the *general states*—anxiety, depression, arousal, regression, fatigue, stress and so forth—than psychological texts have yet realized. Let us focus what is known about these states before proceeding. The methodology of recognizing and uniquely measuring state changes has been thoroughly handled in Volume 1, Chapters 5 and 7, through coordinated *P*- and *dR*-techniques. The reader might well refresh his memory there at this point, regarding the number and nature of the dimensions so far found. Taxonomically one can recognize, in *Q*- and *T*-data, some four classes: (1) Slow changes in general personality and ability source traits in which the *P*- and *dR*-pattern conforms so closely to that of the trait itself that we best call these *trait change* factors. (2) Patterns in dynamic strength measures which clearly correspond to ergic tension changes and represent the action of the primary ergs under stimulation (3) Allied to (2) there are some evidences, in introspective *Q*-data, of the emotional experiences—primary emotions—which are the epiphenomena around the primary drive strength levels in (2). (4) The general or derived[9] emotions, such as anxiety, depression, which appear in *Q*- and *L*-data, and less reliably in *T*-data. Parenthetically we may say, as pointed out elsewhere, that excessive importance in theory, and insufficient substantiation in research, has been given to class (3) in the writings of James, Lange, Wundt, Woodworth, Royce, and others. Whereas (1), (2), and (4) are based on analyses of behavior (3) is a hangover from the introspective phase of psychology, and unfortunately, writings in that area, describing emotion as "drive" and dynamics, though rooted in the past, have not gone far enough in their attachment to the past to recognize the difference clearly drawn by the Scholastics, and, indeed, Aristotle, between *affect* and *conation*. Actually, the difference is clear in modern experimental work (for example, Cattell, 1929) where it was shown that GSR response (like other measures of dynamic action) is strong in conation but negligible in passively experienced emotional states. We would not neglect the introspective evidence of distinct primary emotions, but would say that since these primary emotions have a one-to-one identification with primary ergs, as epi-phenomena occurring only to sustain awareness through delays or frustrations, they are sufficiently covered for most purposes by studies of the primary *ergic tensions* themselves, as in the MAT, SMAT, and in the laboratory measures described in their handbooks.

The central problem in the class (4)—general states and moods phenomena with which we are here concerned is their relation to the ergic tensions, and to the control thereof in the adjustment process. Our first theory here, implied by the use of the term *derivative* above, is that the discovered general states are generated from the impact of events on the primary ergic tensions (as measured, for example, on the MAT) and are nonspecific to them. In fact, as the APA (Adjustment Process Analysis) Chart (p. 307) indicates, the various crossroad (chiasm) events will generate anxiety, depression, arousal, and so on, from *any* ergic tension, or a combination of any such specific drives.

The most important of the derivative emotional states, in terms of variance contribution and relevance to dynamics, are probably anxiety, elation-depression, general excitement, arousal, regression, guilt, and stress (Curran, 1968); whereas fatigue has more relevance to performance levels. The role of one of these, anxiety, has already been stressed by Freud as of a dynamic intermediary, and experimentalists like Spence have taken anxiety literally as a dynamic trait, motivating behavior just like the ergs. Our thesis here is that all of them have dynamic-trait-related properties, though none of them, including anxiety, is properly regarded simply as a dynamic, ergic trait. Those properties are mainly (a) operating as a temporary storage for ergic energy, with certain changes of properties through the transformation, and (b) creating a field—in a field theory sense—in which the controlling ego, and perhaps other controllers, operate differently according to the state of the field. Much of our evidence must deal with the anxiety state because when Freud said that "anxiety is the central problem in the neuroses" the pack of clinical writers proceeded to give it highest status in the motivational scheme of things, and its unquestioned predominance as a distress symptom in patients has caused it to retain this somewhat disproportionate apparent importance, in relation to the action of other general states, ever since. As far as present research evidence is concerned, however, it would be more realistic and open minded to recognize that depression, effort stress, arousal, and regression may have equally important psychological associations and consequences.

Anxiety, unlike, say, depression, which can be cleft into no fewer than seven primary factors, proves to be factorially relatively simple; much of the variance in the countless manifestations that psychologists have named as anxiety fall into one general trait and one general state factor (Chapters 3 and 5). What *some* psychiatrists call "bound anxiety" can also be recognized as a factor (Cattell & Scheier, 1961; Rickels & Cattell, 1968), but when this factor is seen in all its manifestations its nature proves so different as to make the psychiatrist's generic use of the term anxiety for it appreciably misleading.

Systematic researches between 1950 and 1960 by Cattell and Scheier (1961) gave factorial definition to anxiety as a state and as a trait, in Q- and L-data, in physiological associations, and in recorded frequencies of symptom associations. This work also discovered the marker variables distinguishing it from stress and arousal. It is to researches strictly confined to this instrument-transcending unitary trait and state concept, and their validated measurements, that we give primary regard in discussion on the following theory. The basic patterns of behavioral measurement of anxiety have been set out in Spielberger (1966) and Cattell and Scheier (1961), and in children by Sarason (1966). Physiologically, anxiety can be defined as a pattern of *total* autonomic excitation, the sympathetic and parasympathetic patterns being distinguishable from this general factor as distinct subfactors (Cattell, 1950, based on measurements by Wenger, 1940).

A theory that the generation of anxiety springs essentially from three and only three mechanisms has been put forward by the present writer, in Spielberger (1972), as follows.

1. *Situational uncertainty in relation to fear of deprivation.* From Freud's early discussions on *angst* and *furcht*, debate has persisted as to what distinguishes anxiety and fear. Some argue that the cause of fear can be pointed to by the subject, whereas that of anxiety cannot. Our position is that anxiety is a diluted fear response, chronically continued from inner stimuli, and that the above distinction (an unconscious cause) is *sometimes* also present because the subject *may* be unable to contact consciously the real inner stimuli, a condition common in the neurotic but not in the normal.

Recognition of this source requires realization (a) that fear need not be of an object but is frequently *fear of ergic deprivation*, that is, of punishment as we have defined punishment. Just as pugnacity is a general first reaction to frustration of any erg, and is proportional to the frustration, so fear concerns possible frustration of any erg and is proportional to the magnitude of the risk of contemplated deprivation, and (b) that every contemplated future satisfaction has a cognitively appreciated risk, expressible in a "probability of deprivation" statement. If we call this source of anxiety a_e (e for environmental risk of ergic deprivation), an individual's level of anxiety may be expressed:

$$a_{ei} = (f)(E_{xi} + M_{yi}E_{xi})U_d(E_{fi} - H_i) \tag{6-9}$$

Here (f) is "a function of," as in our previous instances when we did not want necessarily to be committed to a product relation; E_x is the erg under consideration, which appears both "free" as E_{xi}, ergic tension, and as part of the ergic investment in a sentiment, M_y, which is also involved in the contemplated satisfaction. The first expression in parens is thus the size of the dynamic system involved. The U_d is a value combining the risk or uncertainty, U, with the fractional magnitude of $(E_x + M_y E_x)$ that may be subject to deprivation (for example, a 20% risk of a 50% deprivation). All terms are here given an i subscript for the individual and the last term in parentheses introduces the effect of the individual's personality in determining the anxiety effect of a specified deprivation risk. E_{fi} is the magnitude of the individual's personality endowment in f the fear erg; H is the temperament factor (in the 16 PF, HSPQ, and so on) of boldness versus threctia, which modifies all fear responses, so that $E_{fi} - H_i$ is a first statement of individual susceptibility to fear-anxiety. The reader will note that the activation of a sentiment, M_y, appears in (6-9) and (6-10). This keeps track of the fact that it is not ergs alone that operate in transformations to anxiety. Sentiments have their ergic investments and if cognitive contact with a sentiment is interfered with for example, by repression, all the ergs involved in it are in a position to enter anxiety transactions. What a clinician may see, for example, is a man unable to recognize a hostile sentiment to his wife's relatives, leaving a discharge of hostility into anxiety.

2. *Anxiety through fear of loss of control.* This we symbolize as a_c. Freud first recognized this as a source of anxiety, beginning with the transference neuroses in which excessive, undischarged sexual libido seemed to be transformed into anxiety. Such a theory of transformation is not unreasonable, in view of our recognition of the anxiety factor as autonomic excitation, but, as various analysts have since argued, the quality of fear in this anxiety needs to be accounted for by the inner experience of threat to the ego. That is to say, we hypothesize that a suppressed ergic need strong enough to threaten loss of control evokes fear of this catastrophe in terms of severe past punishment for loss of control, and perhaps through some primal fear of chaos. The present findings in the dynamic calculus of course spread the reference from psychoanalytic sex libido to *all* ergic tensions, though in our culture sex and pugnacity may be the strongest rebels.

According to this view of the transference or transformation component, a_e, the anxiety should be less in proportion to the excess of ego strength over the ergic tension and greater in proportion to the ergic demand, so that it might be represented as:

$$a_{ci} = (f)\frac{w(E_{xi} + M_{yi}E_{xi})}{(C + Q_3) - v(E_{xi} + M_{yi}E_{xi})} \tag{6-10}$$

Here w and v are just scaling weights, but Q_3, self-sentiment strength, has been added to C because in this situation of control in the interest of social values it is likely to be fully allied with C. On the other hand, the present writer's earlier (1972) formula probably mistakenly included G (superego) with Q_3; for the objection holds that a strong superego might, as psychoanalysis argues, add to the severity of conflict.

The strong association, in the domain of ratings (Cattell, 1946) and self-ratings, of "worrying" and "fearful" with low C may well express this "eruptive" component in anxiety fixed in magnitude substantially by low C alone, though uncertainty, U_d, in a_e naturally acts too.

3. *Anxiety from sheer and certain deprivation.* The existence of anxiety from deprivation, when no uncertainty exists about the deprivation, has properly been questioned. It may be argued that if a man knows for certain that he will go foodless tomorrow or have a tooth out he will not be anxious. (There is humanistic, literary psychological support from the famous or infamous remark of Dr. Johnson that "If a man knows he is going to be hanged tomorrow it settles his mind wonderfully.") The arguments for certainty being incompatible with anxiety may be logical, but are empirically dubious. In fact the most substantial evidence for the contrary argument is the present writer's finding (supported by further data of Lynn, 1971) that over nine countries the average anxiety score on the Cattell-Scheier scale comes close to being completely inversely related to the economic level. True, to live at a low level of economic satisfaction is perhaps not only to be deprived of satisfactions but to have some uncertainty over the satisfactions. However, some of the highest scores were in countries with a highly dependable support of the individual in a low standard of living. If uncertainty were the sole source of anxiety it might be expected to be higher in countries with a wide economic range, where the better off have farther to fall. It seems reasonable therefore to interpret the situation of low economic level as a constant anticipation of general ergic deprivation, and to consider the "certainty" a generator of anxiety.

Ergic dissatisfaction as "free-floating," unassuaged need, empirically observed by psychoanalysts, seemed to convert drive directly to anxiety, and though we would explain much of that conversion as fear of loss of control, as in a_e, yet the neurological and physiological similarity of anxiety to ergic tension leads us to hypothesize, in a_p below, that there can also be some *direct* transformation of ergic need long held without satisfaction, into anxiety. Common speech certainly draws no sharp line between ergic tension and anxiety, saying "I am anxious to do so and so," and although we criticize below the simple acceptance of "anxiety as motive" by various psychologists, yet we shall accept that one form of tension can so readily switch into the other that this subtle form of transformation may get overlooked:

$$a_{pi} = (f)(E_{xi} + M_y E_{xi}) - E_{xri} \qquad (6\text{-}11)$$

where a_p is anxiety from punishment (deprivation); E_{xr} is current ergic reduction, that is, gratification rate and E_x is need level.

We have accepted above that there are many variables in common to the ergic-tension, motivation-component measures, and to anxiety. Empirically they seem to be (Cattell & Scheier, 1961) raised pulse rate, raised metabolic rate, raised systolic blood pressure, increased keto-steroid output, and the other signs of a general anatomic overactivity, with some emphasis on the sympathetic system. When we recall also that Cannon and Rosenblueth's studies of pugnacity and escape be-havior (Cannon, 1929), as well as the studies of Freeman and Katzoff (1942), point to the major ergs expressing their arousal by physiological readinesses that overlap with those of anxiety, it is reasonable at first to hypothesize that anxiety can act as a "garbage pail" for simple, excess, undischarged drive. However, we anticipate that more refined factor-analytic research will leave us with still more distinction of the main ergic patterns for drive from the well-defined anxiety pattern. In any case, we must use this "garbage" metaphor rather than "reser-voir" because various results show that (1) the anxiety "energy" is no longer wholly returnable to a simple ergic drive fuctionality, and (2) there are already many indications that the anxiety pattern repre-sents a deteriorated form of drive, with several disorganizing and dis-ruptive features such as reduction of recall, increased errors in calcu-lation, and diminished physical endurance. Clinicians are as familiar with those as experimenters, and, indeed, have questioned the libido-into-anxiety theory on the ground that problems of sexual perform-ance in males are often associated with high anxiety, and the disruption property of anxiety better explains this.

Nevertheless, in certain formulations, notably of reflexological experiments (see Mowrer, 1939; Spence, 1958), anxiety has been somewhat uncritically accepted as a measure directly equatable with drive strength. Although anxiety may appear to act simply as an ergic tension does, the present writer has from the beginning raised ob-jection to conclusions from experiment in which anxiety is considered the equivalent of unadultered drive, rather than a degenerative pro-duct of ergic tension. The objections to all drive being anxiety should surely begin with the broad common-sense observation that it is a dreary philosophy that would described all human motivation as arising from anxiety rather than from more lusty, positive ergs! But there are more technical objections to the role of anxiety as motive. First there are the ambiguous results in ME (CRII) types of learning, where higher anxiety sometimes improves but generally reduces learning performance. It will be found that most instances of uniformly increased learning with measured anxiety occur in CRI, coexcitation learning, and even then largely in *autonomic* system conditioning, which suggests that sheer rise of excitement, as a function of anxiety, in the coexcitation experience, is really responsible.

By contrast, in all kinds of cognitive achievement, especially over long terms, as in school (Cattell & Butcher, 1968) and in learning motor performances, anxiety is significantly and substantially *negatively* related to learning. Sarason and Eysenck have attempted to patch up the inconsistencies by invoking what seems a scarcely appropriate generalization of the Yerkes-Dodson law. The generalization that a little is good and a lot bad has a vague fit to data, because the notion of a curvilinear rise of performance with increased anxiety, followed by a drop, can be made to fit almost any data, with suitably manipulated scaling, and because the authors have not confirmed the purity of the anxiety measures in these experiments. As regards the latter, if two distinct components were confounded in their anxiety measures (or in the criterion performance measures), as seems likely, it would be possible to explain the apparent curvilinearity as a linearly increasing curve over one range, due to the first, truly *ergic* constituent, confounded with a linearly decreasing curve, over a later range, from the *anxiety* constituent. Thus, if such different entities as activation or ergic tension were confounded with anxiety in the "anxiety" scale, the performance might rise over the range of the former, but eventually drop as an expression of the increasing drop of performance with increasing anxiety. Indeed, that is precisely what we successfully fitted to results elsewhere, namely, that achievement increased to a plateau with ergic tension and general activation over the earlier range, while declining steadily over the whole range with increased anxiety.

With these comments on what we judge to be digressions from sound concepts on anxiety—anxiety being in fact a distracting by-product of motivation—let us return to the main theory. Our theory is that a single "pool" of anxiety, as measured, results from the sum of contributions from three sources, as described above, thus:

$$a_i = a_{ei} + a_{ci} + a_{pi} \qquad\qquad (6\text{-}12)$$

If we look at what this would mean as a summation of formulas (6-9), (6-10), and (6-11)—which we will not do literally because of the uncertainties of the weighting functions—it will be seen that, in terms of individual differences, anxiety would be expected to be greater for persons lower on C, lower on H, lower on Q_3, and higher on the fear erg and total ergic tension (as measured on the MAT). There is only 16PF data on the last, but both D. R. May (1971) and J. M. May and Sweney (1965) have noted in high anxiety cases higher ergic tension scores on fear in the MAT, especially on the U component. Supporting the rest of the hypothesis is the fact that the second-order Q-data factor, QII, shown by Cattell and Scheier (1961), and many since, to operate as anxiety, is outstandingly negatively loaded on C, H, and Q_3 and positively on Q_4, which last is close to general ergic tension.

The aim of our study in this, and the next section, of the *general* derived emotions (as distinct from primary emotions and ergic tensions) is to bring out their role in the personality control system. It has seemed desirable to take what is by far the most researched instance—anxiety—into intensive study as representative of all eight of the secondaries so far located (Curran, 1968; Curran & Cattell, 1976), but about the associations of which experiment is still scant. At least as regards anxiety, the connections with ergic tension terms has been clearly brought out. And although the personality terms, C, H, Q_3, and Q_4 concern individual differences, if we consider these differences to be reached by processes, then the general functional connection is again supported that anxiety is a product of frustration and deprivation of ergs (beyond remedy by pugnacity and passing to the third chiasm in the APA Chart). Anxiety is thus in the broadest sense a transmutation of ergic tension, but it is transformation into a derived product that interferes with performance, and that further study may show is not to be exchanged back again for ergic tension except with restrictions and a discount. Nevertheless. as entertained in the next section, the possibility exists that though it is inimical to cognitive learning, reasoning, and recall processes it yet may aid long-term emotional integration learning.

6-6. The Integrative Action of the Ego in the Field of the General States

In the last decade much progress has been made in locating and defining, by the necessary P- and dR-technique experiments, the major primary *ergic states* and the *general* state factors which we believe are secondaries. In Q-data, at a second-stratum level, the general states amount to eight—anxiety, depression, fatigue, activation-apathy (also called exvia-invia), stress, regression, arousal and guilt. (In the Curran-Cattell battery stress response has been included despite its *possibly* final *first*-order status.) As the discussions in Chapters 5 and 7 of Volume 1 remind us, the picture of *strata* of states is not yet fully illuminated. For instance, although the eight primary depression factors in Q-data (defined in the CAQ) yield the general second-stratum depression factor as measured in the Curran Battery, they also yield two lesser second order depressions. Should the Curran second order general state survey have included these? Krug argues "No," because they seem to be traits rather than states. Secondly, there are areas to be cleared up in the alignment of states in T-data with the states of the Q-data secondaries. UI(T)24 aligns excellently with QII, anxiety; UI(T)32 with QI, exvia (or activation) in the Curran Battery; while UI(T)22 cortertia aligns tolerably with cortertia measured as QIII. However, in depression state factors *three* exist in T-data, confirmed by their association with clinical depressions (Cattell, Price & Patrick (1979). Since, as seen above, there are three in the second-order Q-data medium, in QIV, QXI and QXII, a Q-T alignment is expected though still insufficiently established.

The theoretical position taken here has to consider the notion sometimes mooted (both for these derivative affects and for the primary emotions) that the depression factors are dynamic factors, in the precise sense used here (Wessman & Ricks, 1966). This we reject, even in any ordinary sense, by the same kinds of arguments as used above against so considering anxiety. On the other hand, we offer the theory that they and anxiety are what will be defined as *ancillary motivation* state structures, with a particular relation to the dynamics of control, adaption, and integration-learning processes now to be discussed.

Some of the general states—notably fatigue, activation, and arousal—can be considered simply expressions of the condition of the *sum total of ergs*, augmenting and reducing ergic reactivity both directly and in the sentiment involvements of ergs. We have supposed that dynamic traits can show activation individually (cognitive excitation), as in sentiments, and can show arousal, as in ergs, and, probably, fatigue, restricted to a single dynamic trait. (In the last case by exercise to the point of inhibition.) The relation of the *general* states to these *single* trait conditions is assumed to be that they consist of an average expression of these dynamic state properties at a given time across all the dynamic traits.

Anxiety, depression, regression, and stress, also represent the average condition of all dynamic traits but in relation to their fate in the steps in adjustment process analysis, not to arousal and fatigue as above. Guilt, the eighth state (Curran & Cattell, 1976), may be peculiar in largely expressing the dynamic situations for a single structure, the superego. The analysis of the higher orders among the eight scales (themselves, however, secondaries in the questionnaire primaries) of the Curran 8 state battery, is at present beset with some uncertainties. However, at a purely descriptive level it is clear that this third order presents a factor of anxiety, invia and fatigue, and another on which arousal is positive and depression negative (Cattell, 1973, p. 218; Wedding, 1977; Brennan & Cattell, 1979). The objective test battery (Nesselroade, 1960) adds effort stress and adrenal response to the negative (low anxiety) end of the first factor, and cholesterol and pulse rate rise to what is presumably the arousal end of the second. (Cattell, 1960). The first factor is interpretable as situational (Cattell, 1973), namely, attacking a problem, with stress, versus retreating from it with anxiety. This choice and sequence evidently applies to all ergic goals, (as recognized in the APA chart at crossroads C) as also does what is probably the next dimension of possible change—into depression—as mapped on the APA chart (Chapter 5) at F. Thus what we call the *general mood states* are possible derivatives of all ergs, and all sentiment action involving the ergic investment therein.

The ergic nonspecificity of anxiety has already been stressed, and the point made that it is not 100% functionally useful. The general point has to be made here that although most organic processes have utility, as the raised temperature in a fever may be therapeutic, yet some may be neutral by-products, like the accompanying headache or delirium. From a biological standpoint it is improbable that anxiety is wholly the somewhat degenerative and deleterious by-product of frustration or ergic tension that we have seen it *in part* to be. Similarly, the view implicit or explicit in the items and associations for depression in the work of Beck (1974) and Weckowitz et al. (1971) but clarified in Van Egeren (1963) that depression is a purely pathological reaction needs to be questioned here. If one goes outside the clinical field the correlations among normals tell a rather different story. In fact they suggest that we must examine anxiety, depression and guilt particularly for possibly useful adjustive functions.

That anxiety is to be treated simply as a drive on the same footing as any ergic motivation (Spence & Taylor, 1951) we have repeatedly questioned (See Spielberger, 1966, 1973), citing, for example, the experiment of Tsushima (1957) showing it as a product of the destruction of drive. The unpleasantness of the diffuse autonomic disturbance which we call anxiety, appearing, as we have seen, from internal conflict following external frustration, nevertheless has the useful function of exerting pressure for *a resolution of conflict*, as soon as possible. In other words, anxiety may play no part—or only a poor and questionable part—in motivating ordinary performances, but justifies itself by motivating *attempts at integration*; that is to say, when solution by manipulating the external situation is a fading

possibility it presses for an inner solution to conflict and scouts possibilities for the goal of integration, just as ergic tension presses for
external action to give drive reduction. It remains to be seen whether
field theory in an exact sense can be applied to the actions we are
about to consider, but let us initially recognize that metaphorically
the ego pursues its integrative functions in a field of anxiety, and, according to its position in that field, becomes moved to learn those
acts that reduce anxiety.

It has been less readily or explicitly recognized in clinical psychology that depression may have as positive a function as anxiety, and
that neither is to be regarded as *merely* an unfortunate symptomatic
by-product. Anger, anxiety, and depression appear in the APA Chart
from the *B* chiasm onwards and in that sequence, and depression ultimately may be followed by ergic regression and apathy at chiasm *E*.
The extent and degree of irreversibility of frustration by the time depression appears are far advanced, and a more basic readjustment of
goals is required than is probably called for when only anger or anxiety
is produced. By creating a longer "pause for deliberation" than that
which naturally occurs by acts of will at earlier stages of adaptation,
depression seems to function effectively to promote that major readjustment (as the religious mystics recognized in the phrase "dark night
of the soul," or as appeared in such complete reorganization of personality as occurred in Loyola, Gauthama Buddha, and St. Francis). That
is to say, the arrest of impulse and the enforced deliberative pause
which we have seen to be a first vital function of the ego in obtaining
the best integrative decision in some immediate conflict situation is
repeated by the state of depression on a larger scale because the
smaller scale will no longer work. On the smaller stage of the willed
pause a compromise solution tolerably satisfying to the ergs concerned
is almost sure to be reached. But by chiasm *D* on the APA Chart that
hope has been left behind and no solution can appear except by
abnegation in relation to existing ergic attachments and the discovery
of relatively remote new paths of possible satisfaction. An act of will
by the ego controls the existing satisfaction habits temporarily, but
depression virtually dissolves the desires themselves, producing a state
of abulia and life-weariness, the greater length of which permits an altogether more fundamental redirection of dynamics. It may be objected that this useful function is scarcely to be claimed for *reactive*
depression, as occurs at a simple but profound and irremediable
object loss; but even here it may be the best solvent of existing ergic
structures, most potent in de-cathecting the previous object satisfactions. Depression should thus have a relation to speed of reflexological extinction that could be experimentally checked.

Turning to the next general state, regression (as defined in the

Curran 8 state battery and in UI(T)23 in the O-A battery kit) we see it expressed as retraction of interest from more developed expressions, without necessarily any *strong* depressive affect. It shows itself in a weakness of ability to mobilize, in rigidity and error proneness, and in Q-data as listlessness and various symptoms that used to be thrown into the ragbag of "neurasthenia." It may have physiological, for example, low adrenalin resource, associations. Though it conduces to poor external adaptation it is possible that, like depression, it arises from the generalized frustration situation, and has some useful function in favoring complete changes, as in *GM* learning (Table 3-6) expressed in sublimation or perversion.

By contrast with anxiety, depression, and regression, the states of stress and fatigue seem to belong with the simple, cross-ergic properties which we have noted in the arousal-activation states. Various studies suggest that fatigue is not merely a simple statement of exhaustion but also has a protective function against possible damage from over use. In all general states in which physiological associations of the introspective Q item patterns have been studied, they have been found to be substantial; for example, protein breakdown in anxiety, keto-steroid excretion in stress, low skin resistance in activation, adrenal output in arousal, and the various physiological changes, from lactic acid increase in muscle onward, in fatigue. The general conclusion is that each general state expresses some inwardly coordinated, unitary, autonomic neural, hormonal, or other physiological response in its own particular pattern.

The question we raised earlier, therefore, as to whether these general states are to be regarded as motivational, depends on the nature of broader and narrower definitions of motivation. We have preferred to keep "motivational" strictly for the ergic tensions and to call those of the discovered eight general states that have interaction with ergs the *derived*, or *adaptation*, states. The theory put forward here is that the directing dynamic traits—mainly the ego, but also the *SS* and *SE*—operate in their interaction with ergs in what is at least best *described* as a *field* of conditions created by these adaptation states, so they might be called "motivational adjuncts" in the domain of motivational re-adjustment.

As far as the depression-elation state axis is concerned, for example, it seems that, if all is going well with the basic ergic adjustment, what may be required is only improved ways of reaching agreed goals. Then a state of elation, producing more venturesome, varied, "hypomanic" trial and error, accompanied by greater imaginal fluency, is appropriate. On the other hand, if the direction of striving is more radically wrong, a condition of depression may better guide the ego in its attempt at a new integration. The theory, in short, suggests that depression has a more functional role than that of a clinical and social nuisance.[10]

The chief difference between anxiety and depression, as recognized in the APA Chart is that anxiety persists as long as there is future-directed hope of the desired ergic satisfaction through channels then contemplated. The extension of such life-embedded *P*-technique studies as those of Lebo and Nesselroade (1978) with pregnant women, and Birkett and Cattell (1978) with the struggles of an alcoholic, into relations of the state scores to diary-reported situations and behavior can alone give clear answers here. In this area we would raise a question about a_p component in equation (6-12) above, in as much as *certain* deprivation to-morrow *may* evoke depression rather than anxiety. But because almost all life situations—even a sentence to be shot at dawn—have a glimmer of hope of escape from deprivation, we would expect, as we find, that these two general state responses, anxiety and depression, play hide and seek across the boundary between hope and absolutely certain loss.

This is almost certainly the reason that all existing research (Brennan & Cattell, 1979; Curran, 1968; Kameoka, 1979; Laughlin, 1973; Wedding, 1978) show decided state correlations between even the most factorially pure measures of anxiety and of depression.[11] However, anxiety can scarcely be regarded as offering a similar assistance to readjustment as depression, for the evidence is that if its pressure for a solution exceeds some moderate optimum it (1) weakens the ego, (2) generates defenses of high rigidity, and (3) impairs the cognitive functions involved in the ego's decisions. Positive functions of anxiety as we have suggested, also exist, namely, first to act as a temporary storehouse for ergic purposes stalled in satisfaction in situations where the postponement may frequently be temporary, and, second to bring *some* degree of pressure on the ego for a solution of conflict. In this formulation we come close to using a concept of "psychological energy," but a more explicit attack on the formulation of such a concept must be postponed to the next section.

Once again, in this chapter concerned with the highest levels of personality learning—those of integration—we have to recognize that the gap between the theoretical model and the methods of testing it is a perplexing one to many researchers. However, it promises to be bridgeable if advances continue in the precision and purity of measurement of particular general states and differentiated ergic tensions, as well as in defining behaviorally the particular adjustment stage ($A2$, $B1$, $C3$, etc.) at which various ergs stand at any given time in the APA Chart. Granted such measurements, research can concern itself with the significance of relations between each general state level in the individual and certain individual and averaged measures of the dynamic traits. For example, measures of the frustration and conflict level for each erg on the MAT should, when averaged, show a high correlation with the general anxiety state. When re-measured after a longer interval, with respect to duration and degree of irremediableness of frustration, and with weighting for magnitude of ergs, the averaged ergic values should correlate substantially with the depression scale measures. A variety of significant relations, in short, would be expected to exist between the dynamic structure (MAT) and general state battery measures, and some are already supported by experiment.

These issues will be pursued further in the next section, where a systems theory model is proposed in which the controlling ego operates in the field of modifying influences offered by the general states.

6-7. The Advance to a Systems Theory of Personality: Additions to the VIDA Model.

Although the theoretical development so far has made some new demands on the psychometrist, in such matters as adding states to the behavioral equation, recognizing new varieties of behavioral indices, and admitting trait product terms, and on the classical learning theorist in introducing ergic and other structures, it has not departed from what might be called an analytical and elementist treatment. That is to say it has analyzed behavior into elements of structure and process, and put the individual and his environment together again in initially linear equations seeking to account for behavior at a particular place and time.

We now approach a decidedly more demanding attempt to fit a model to the full complexity of the living personality, through incorporating what has developed in the last thirty years, by researchers yet to be mentioned, under the rubric of *systems theory*. A systems model is more demanding in that the algebraic treatments we have so far made will have to advance into the differential and integral calculus. And in psychological systems we must contemplate mathematical forms which systems theory has at present incompletely worked out.

A first step toward a systems treatment has been made in our model of the sentiment as a unfolding process. Therein adjustments occurred according to situations encountered, and past excitations continued on, summing their contribution with new excitations. The position we reached prior to these systems theory developments has sometimes been called the VIDA model (Cattell & Dreger, 1977), the V standing for vector representation, the ID for the elements—ids—in the dimensions of the data box, and the A for analysis.[12] The full behavioral specification equation as we last reached it (equation 7-11, Volume 1, p. 321) has terms defined by each *id* in the coordinates of the data box—the stimulus, *h*, the ambient situation, *k*, the individual, *i*, the response performance, *j*, and the observer *l*—and when *analysis* has been performed the pattern of *each* of these can appear as a *vector* of scores on the factor dimensions by which that species of id is characterized.

This VIDA model is clearly adequate to deal with and abstract from data the nature and development of traits, states, processes, and situations and to predict behavior outcomes when the trait, state, and so forth, values are known immediately before the behavior. It handles the interaction of the elements (additive and product) in the immediate, static description of what will happen, but lacks the potent extensions which a systems model brings to follow the kinetic adjustments[13] between one set of equations and the next.

The VIDA model as it stands to this point has actually already included the *beginnings* of system theory, and has incidentally handled—but in measurable and calculable form—what gestalt psychology "sang hymns about" (to use Allport's perceptive phrase!). It has handled the latter by dealing with *patterns as such*, for example in trait and state loading patterns; by vectors that express most of what Wertheimer (1959) was asking for in face of Watsonian atomicity; and by the control triumvirate of ego, self-sentiment and superego for most of what Smuts (1926) demanded in the philosophy of wholism.

The beginning of the systems theory by which the VIDA model ultimately grows into VIDAS—the *VIDA systems* model—are seen in the model of a sentiment as a process; in the field theory which states that ego action must be understood as involving the ego properties in relation to the general states; in the adaptation process analysis chart; including the transformation of ergic tensions into anxiety; and most clearly in the discovery that the usual behavioral specification equation is not enough to handle the interactions of E's and M's. In the last we saw that immediately after we enter the value ME the E value in EM becomes changed, and thus also the M value in ME (equation 2-6). Unless the system happens to be kept in equilibrium by other forces, these reciprocal feedbacks will require changes in the behavioral equation from instant to instant. In general, as Willard Gibbs and modern physicists recognized (and as we were forced to recognize in the realistic measurement of learning change; see equation 5-5) prediction of the outcome of existing moments and velocities, (in the case of physics) is possible only by including the previous state of the whole system.

A sufficient statement of the historical development of systems theory and its many aspects is obviously not possible in this space.

Like most concepts it had a history of partial perceptions before the full formulation. When the physiologist Claude Bernard, over a hundred years ago, wrote, "All vital functions . . . have only one end—to preserve constant the conditions of life in the *internal environment*." he began to describe systems theory. And the notion of such coordinated, balanced action in the organism was given further substance and a suitable name—homeostasis—by Cannon, early in this century. The recent brilliant growth and mathematical formulation of the general notions of organismic control, cybernetic direction of interactions, and positive and negative feedback systems are to be found in a widely ranging literature by von Foerster, Gerard, Klir, McCulloch, Laszlo, Mackay, Rashevsky, Shannon, Von Neuman, and Wiener. Most of these discussions being enriched by reference to computers and electrical networks, which are central and precise models, especially in the writings of Buerle, von Foerster, George Lucas, and von Neumann. The more concrete biological and physiological applications are found in Eccles, Gerardin, McCulloch, Olds, Platt, and Verbeck. Finally we get close to psychology and "artificial intelligence" in Ashley, von Bertalanffy (1967, 1969) Feigenbaum and Feldman (1964), George, Hebb, Jackson (1974), Miller (1978), Pribram, Rapaport (1973), Royce (1973), Sayre and Crossen (1963), Royce and Buss (1976), and Scriven, and these we bring into our bibliography.

Since there has been some tendency in recent discussion to set up the VIDA approach and the systems models as rival, monopolistic concepts, let us pause to be clear why this is not so. The VIDA model constitutes a necessary statement of the firm ground of psychometrically and experimentally checkable concepts needed before taking off into systems theory; for at this moment there is precious little quantitative data in psychology for bringing systems theory as such to the tribunal of scientific evaluation. That it is growing very naturally however into a systems model, which we have designated the VIDAS model, is shown in the intrinsic growth we have just mentioned and which deserve fuller listing, as in: the sentiment as a process; the EM and ME feedbacks; the spiral action theory of emergence of the second-order factors (Chapter 7, Volume 1) QI (exvia) and QII (anxiety); the field action of general states on the control structures; the demonstration that description of a learning gain must include a statement of the full prior state of the system; and the specific hypotheses—involving reservoir, channel and feedback concepts—for individual personality factors such as surgency (F), ego strength (C), exuberance $(UI(T)21)$, cortertia $(UI(T)22)$, and several others.

Those limitations of classical learning theory (and, we might add, classical psychometry!) that led Von Bertalannfy to call it "robot psychology" have certainly long been transcended in the later VIDA developments as so far brought together in this book. The reader who is familiar with such developments of systems formulations as are surveyed, say, by Miller (1973, 1978), may appropriately be reminded at this point of the main conceptual repertoire by the sheer listing of such terms as: "bits" (of information), cybernetics, control, decision theory, game theory, feedback stabilization, closed and open systems, information flow, channels, decoders and encoders, message, networks, noise, compensators, filters, positive and negative feedback, plasticity (or flexibility), reverberating loops, storage, effectors, self-organizing parameters, time scanning, and transformation.

In applied illustrations the cybernetic aspect of systems theory is most associated with the physics and engineering of servomechanisms, now increasingly operative in homes and industry as self-directing pieces of machinery. They usually—but not necessarily—have homeostasis—a steady state—as their goal and negative feedback as their mechanism. Like the adjusting human organism, they find out the result of their initial response and, observing the amount of error relative to an intended goal, check and modify the next response. (A standard home instance is the thermostat; a familiar laboratory instance is the subject's behavior in a track tracer experiment.) By negative feedback the restoring force is opposite to the error or divergence. But the action of positive feedback, with added conditions that do not allow it to get out of hand, is also often demanded by our psychological models, for example, in accounting for shifting from one level of homeostasis to another. Much of the construction in getting multivariate, self-organizing, self-maintaining, goal-directed behavior system models to work centers on the invention in the model of suitable positive and negative loop connections between perception and storage units appropriately defined in their properties. Here experimental machine construction, as in Gray Walter's famous "turtles" and other automata, and in many uses of the computer, as by Loehlin, 1970, as well as the observations of organismic psycho-physiology have given much perspective and mutual aid between the limited complexity of artificial models and the complex realities of living organisms (Wiener, 1948).

The simplest of organismic systems models to do with psychology has frequently been represented as in Figure 6-1.

Here the essential systems concept is the feedback of perception of the response to affect the continuing response, as when one misses the keyhole with the first poke. The memory storage is not necessary to the basic model, and for that reason is set apart in Figure 6-1, but it is normally so important a part (the person remembers that he often

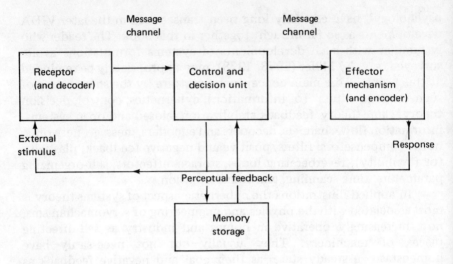

Figure 6-1. Behavioral systems model.

does not notice that the key is upside down) of cybernetic behavior, in conjunction with perceptual feedback, that we have added it as most typically present.

In considering the best form for a psychological systems model, as in VIDAS, we need to note that the concepts of systems theory that can be common to biological organisms, machine design, group behavior, economics, and other areas where such theory is developing are fewer than broad theorists like to think. An awareness of emerging effective common features is important, but so also is an empirical sensitivity to what a particular science most needs. The definition of a system to which most would subscribe is "a set of elements, some better called subsystems, in continual interaction in such a way as (within limits) to reach a certain goal state for the whole system." The expression "within limits" is necessary because it is always possible to strain the system beyond its adjustive capacity, and the point of breakdown is a function of the parameters of the elements and the nature of the message channels between parts.

As mentioned above, the goal is not always homeostasis—the return to a desirable equilibrium, and it may instead be maximum growth, or maximum handling of information from the environment, or maximum absorption of energy from the environment, and so on. This mention of environment brings us to a further basic definition, in that we must recognize two kinds of systems—open and closed—and in psychology we deal with an open system as far as the organism is concerned, and a closed system when organism and environment are included in a single predictive system. A closed system, in the well-defined instances of physics, is inevitably subject to running down—the maximization of entropy—but a living organism, which is an open system when considered on its own, may have interactions with the environment, such as digesting it, that permit it to restore itself and avoid running down. If physics is correct the closed system will *always* run down.

The most vital difference between VIDAS and other systems theories, on the one hand, and the classical *S-R* reflex theory (Bertalannfy's "robot psychology") on the other is that the stimulus is no longer regarded as triggering a response in an organism that acts as a mere transmitter. Instead the latter—the "black box," which many reflexologists are content to leave empty—becomes very much inhabited. The stimulus is considered to set in motion a whole set of interactions within the subsystems (components, elements) of the total organism system, which, governed by laws operating on the parameters listed above (reservoirs, channel rates, feedback paths) end in a response assumed to obey laws very different from those developed to be consistent with a fixed one-to-one relation of response to stimulus. Indeed, the center of interest shifts appreciably from the organism's external re-actions to the re-arrangements that go on within it to permit it to make the best external adaptive responses. Those "re-arrangements" consist of communications among the parts of information and energy.

For psychology the parts and exchanges that the VIDAS model finds essential are:

1.   The conception of *reservoirs* of information and energy, each characterized by a type of content and usually by some limit of size. The limits will vary, psychometrically, from subsystem to subsystem, time to time, and person to person.

2.   The conception of varying carrying capacities of channels with respect to information and energy messages between subsystems.

3.   The existence of channels (loops) serving positive and negative feedback transactions among subsystems.

4.   The existence of reversible and irreversible transformations.

5.   A hierarchical structure whereby some subsystems are so endowed, with greater resources and richer communications, as to outweigh, in controlling cybernetic action, the other subsystems.

6.   The existence of the decoding and encoding units, mainly for transformations between the ecometric, outer world, of stimuli and material to be manipulated in responses, and the organism's in-

ternal symbolic and signal (sign) understanding and storage activities. (The term transducers is sometimes used for elements performing these functions.)

Central in this development of the concepts of VIDAS, beyond the VIDA model is the question, "What is the nature of the "information" or "energy" that is passed along channels, stored, retrieved, encoded, and so on?" Systems theory generally deals with three "substances"—matter, energy, and information. If we were considering the organism biologically, as, say, the doctor sees it, we should be much concerned with the transmission of *matter* between subsystems, as in blood circulation, the hormone system, and so on. If we were considering computer-simulated behavior models, we should be concerned with transmission purely of information. And if we were concerned with engines and engineering, our concern would be largely with transmitting energy. It is probably correct to say that precise systems theory, from Shannon and von Neumann on, has been expressed in terms of transfer of *information* rather than energy. (Indeed, cybernetics writers have been prone to speak of energy-producing machines as belonging to an earlier era than their new information-processing generation of machines. Energy, of course, can undergo exchanges in a system through transmission of information to release energy from this or that reservoir, as checks circulate among banks, but in the last resort this has limits, and energy itself must be moved, like gold bullion among banks.

Information, in some scorable form of cognitive "bits," presents no problem to the psychologist, but energy as a concept shatters his peace of mind. He cannot use the physicist's $\frac{1}{2}mv^2$ nor show the elegant transformations into chemical, electrical, etc. energy equivalents (and, since Einstein, into a mass equivalent) which make energy in physics so robust and vital a concept. Nevertheless, McDougall in his *Energies of Men*, Freud, James, Jung, Spearman (in the cognitive field), and virtually every clinician today have continued to use the concept. Of a psychologist and the energy concept, it must be said as of a certain type of man with his wife, that he cannot live with her and cannot live without her. Only the reflexologists have stood by the cold logic of the situation: that if psychic energy cannot be operationally defined it should not be used. But even in behavior therapy a careful reader will find numerous surreptitious uses of "energy." And, incidentally, it makes no sense to retreat to *physiological* energy, by putting the individual's head in a calorimeter, though doubtless when mental energy is ultimately behaviorally defined it will show some moderate secondary correlations with neural calory output.

At a number of theoretical crossroads, mainly concerning interest and motivation, the present writer (1935, 1950, and with Child, 1975) has struggled, with what degree of success critics must decide, to find an adequate operational basis for psychological energy. It begins on a common sense footing through recognizing that from the normal person, through the schizophrenic, the depressed, the sick, and so to the dead, the basic feature that declines is reactivity: responsiveness to stimuli. It faces the fact, however, that the noisy adolescent at a party is not really showing more mental energy than, say, a mathematician like Hamilton, with his habit of solving a problem by thinking for hours without even a pencil in his hand.

The investigatory proposition made here, hitched to a theory, is that individual differences in mental energy might be assessed from (1) the number of objects or symbols to which the person proves able to make a meaningful response (2) the amount of "interest" he is able to show in each. For a safe individual difference score, problems of stratified sampling of areas, essentially no different from those with crystallized intelligence, as discussed below, have to be heeded. It is in the second area—measuring the equivalence in interest of the physicist's work (energy), that truly novel conceptions have to be introduced. (For if one merely counted objects to which *some* reaction occurred one would be measuring nothing very different from memory content or capacity to retrieve from storage.)

Here the solution surely lies in measuring (by the devices in Volume 1, Chapter 4) the motivation strength components. Since these have the quality of force rather than work, it is necessary to find an equivalent to the physicist's distance through which a force acts against some resistance. Experimentally, it would be necessary to arrange a situation in which the individual can pursue the interest without any need for internal inhibition by his own dynamic forces (themselves being of unknown strength and useless for a standard). The most universal common resistance outside a dynamic system is that of fatigue. The number of repetitions of the response (or time as the equivalent of the physicist's distance) suggests itself. Accordingly, one might take the recall, word association, autism, GSR, attention, blood pressure and other measures as used in the MAT as a measure of *force* of the interest and set them either against the fatigue resistance in short time repetitions of demands for response, or against some more substantial resistance such as, say, learning to express the interest in words of some new foreign language, or performing long arithmetic computations connected with the interest.

In either case we may confidently anticipate a declining curve of response over, say, an hour's performance. It will be noted that this phenomenon has relation both to the systematic studies of fatigue, a generation ago, and to the curves for extinction of a conditioned response. The latter has been carefully experimentally analyzed in a reflexological framework by Leonard & Capaldi (1971), Tombaugh (1967) and many others in regard to reward, repetition, spacing, etc., and in relation to theories that two or three different principles apply to extinction phenomena. Our dynamic calculus formulation does not doubt these ancillary effects, but puts the main extinction process down to a relation between the dynamic strength (E and M functions) of the response a_{hjk} and what is, in everyday terms, fatigue, or in our principles, the energy-saving principle. Conceivably, what has been experimented upon in "spontaneous recovery" would also relate experimentally, if tried with humans and the objective measures of attitude strength in a_{hjk}, to the above measure of work.

From the numerous experimental extinction curves available, for example, those represented in Mackintosh (1974, p. 430 and 464) one may reasonably choose as a first approximation to the equation for the curve that of a hyperbola as shown in Figure 6-2. Assuming the successive repetitions of the response, j, to the stimulus, h, and situation, k, are optimally arranged, the value we need for work accomplished is the area under the curve as shown. (Let us suppose that for experimental practicality a response size $a_{hjk \cdot n}$ is fixed, arbitrarily or on a statistical basis, which is considered of insignificant magnitude, so that the curve need not be pursued further.) The equation for such a curve would be, when $a_{hjk \cdot r}$ is any response size at the rth repetition, and a_{hjk1} is the initial size

$$a_{hjk} = \frac{a_{hjk \cdot 1}}{1 + (r/c)} \tag{6-13a}$$

where c is a given constant and r is the number of repetitions (along the base in Figure 6-2). (a_{hjk} reaches infinity only at $r = -c$, considering the r scale projected backwards in the units we use for the actual repetitions, and it goes to zero when $r = \infty$)

For a single individual, which is what we have so far alone considered, (and therefore have not put a distinguishing i subscript) the integration necessary to get the area which equals the work done to the point $r = n$ can be made as;—

$$W_{hjk \cdot n} = \int_0^n \frac{a_{hjk \cdot 1}}{1 + (r/c)} \cdot dr = ca_{hjk \cdot 1} \int_0^n \frac{(1/c)\, dr}{1 + (r/c)}$$

$$= ca_{hjk \cdot 1} \int_0^{1 + (n/c)} \frac{du}{u} \tag{6-13b}$$

where $u = 1 + (r/c)$

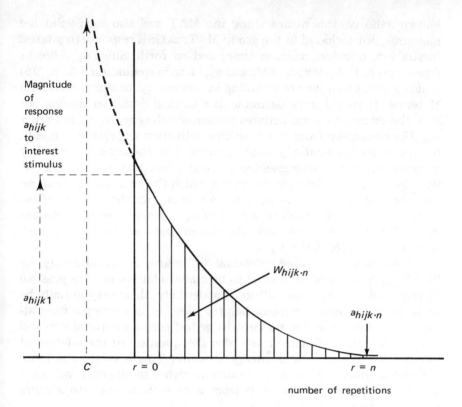

Figure 6-2. Estimation of work done on a particular interest by a particular individual.

Thus when we come to sum not only over the repetitions for a single psychological interest, but across the stratified sample of p interests, we have a comparative value for the individual i (now inserting i as a subscript) as follows, e being the total energy.

$$e_i = \sum_{hjk=0}^{hjk=p} ca_{hijk \cdot 1} \ln [1 + (n/c)] \qquad (6\text{-}13c)$$

(ln = natural logarithm)

Regarding experimental conditions one would need to look closely into what measures are most appropriate for the strength (force) score in a_{hjk}. Pending further relations found for the e_i score, for example, its clinical relations, and relations to physiological energy measures on brain action, it would seem best to add the U and I components (or all seven primary m.c.'s). In terms of devices of presently known validity, this means using the MAT and also such validated measures, not included in the group MAT, as GSR response to interest frustration, decision reaction time, and so forth. Since a_{hjk} breaks down into $b_e E$, $b_m ME$, $b_{e'} EM$, and $b_m M$ terms (equation 2-6, p. 98) it also appears that we are summing in this energy measure both E and M terms. It would seem desirable as a tactical design in finding out how the energy measure behaves to measure the ergic force in $(b_e E + b_m ME)$ separately from the cognitive activation in $(b_{e'} EM + b_m M)$, for the latter is essentially nothing more than the activated memory capacity which we have rejected as insufficient to equate to energy. But the former is the ergic energy on which the cognitive system can call, and will appear more in some m.c. measures than others. However, the degree of sustained action of a_{hjk}, which is to be measured in (6-13b), *may* prove also to be directly proportional to the sentiment activation term $(b_{e'} EM + b_m M)$.

Naturally, for scoring individual differences in mental energy the list of a_{hjk}'s measured will need to be made as fair a sample as possible of the total a_{hjk}'s in the culture. Incidentally, there may initially be some invidious and egregious failures here, as in corresponding attempts to develop a general knowledge test across a culturally mixed population. This reference raises also the question of the relation of intelligence to the mental energy measure. This is surely one more cultural sampling problem, inasmuch as higher intelligence will shift the domain of relevant stimuli from a more concrete into a more symbolic and abstract life space.

The energy concept, defined as above, is obviously at present largely empirically uninvestigated, though the existing MAT would provide a measure on a somewhat inadequate sampling of cultural domains if one added scores across the ten factors only on the *un*ipsatized tests. The standardization in the MAT for the *total personal interest* score essentially already provides such a measure. Ipsatized scores, as in "preference tests" cannot give such a measure because every person finishes with the same total scores, his interests being essentially ranked within him. To get a good measure more nonipsatized subtests, for example, rate of learning in the area, need to be added in to the MAT. Meanwhile there is a reasonable probability that the T-data source trait UI(T)21, exuberance, will prove substantially related to the general energy measure as defined above.

With this attack on the problem of measuring the energy concept, with which, as we have seen, most psychologists rightly decline to dispense, we can return to the systems theory model in which both information and energy units are considered to be transmitted. It has been supposed above that here, as in other systems, the transmission of energy from one subsystem to another may be done by information transmission releasing from local reservoirs, as in our analogy of transferring money between banks. But also there will be direct stimulations and use of energy directly, as in the $b_e E$ (more fully $v_{hje}s_{ke}E$) innate response term in the behavioral equation. In passing, the comment needs to be made that in the existing attempts at computer simulation of personality it is the lack of an analogue to ergic tension in the computer that creates inadequacy. Programs for human *cognitive* operations do well, but until an analogue for dynamic needs is built into the program the computer does not approach a personality model.

6-8. The VIDAS Seven-Component Systems Model and Hypotheses on Its Manner of Growth in the Individual

Let us now proceed to develop those nascent features of a systems model in VIDA—states, processes, E and M interactions—and bring it to a full systems growth in VIDAS. References have already been given to the general development of systems theory *per se*, and we now focus more on the designs defined by Bertalannfy (1967), MacKay (1956), and Laszlo (1969). As Figure 6-1 (p. 424) has indicated the central features of these existing models include an *environment*, a *receptor*, a *control or decision-making unit*, and an *effector apparatus*.

The development made here (Figure 6-3) has essentially four such parts but fits in the psychologically more advanced and substantiated features of the VIDA model and leads to seven definable subsystems. The system deals with the concepts we have defined as processes, reservoirs, channels, transmissions, capacities, apparatuses for particular procedures, for example decisions, and capacities representing fixed personality features represented until now as ability and temperament traits. The last remind us that we are making no rejection or elimination of elements of the VIDA model, that is, of those concepts and structures that have entered so far into the behavioral equation. We are only building new predictive relations thereon, and these enter principally into the dynamic structures—the E and M terms.

Let us first define the subsystems and the symbols used for them:

1.   P is the *Perception or Input Handling* subsystem. This has been a feature of all organism system models, especially when put in computer program forms, and is often broken down, for example in Royce and Buss's model (1976) into an input transducer; an internal transducer (both concerned with going from environmental terms to those of the system—for example, from a decimal to a binary number system), a channel; and net, and a decoder. These more cognitive de-

tails are of less concern here and are condensed into this first single subsystem. (Similarly, in the interests of a more appropriate perspective, we have condensed at the output end by bringing the encoder and the output transducer together in an *action* (response) shaping appendage, A—closely following but separate from the Control or *decision unit*, D.)

In Figure 6-3 we have divided the "box" of a subsystem by an interrupted line wherever (in three subsystems) a part of the subsystem has some relatively specialized function. Here in P we have a subsection PD which looks at the environmental feedback S_2, from the response to S_1, to ascertain the amount of reward or punishment—success or failure from making the response R_1. Its ensuing connections are immediately with the learning section of the M's and the E's (assuming E's sometimes directly affected) through channels (5) and (6). P occurs in the specification equation as the behavior index (the perceptual index part) p attached to various traits, as recognized by channels (2), (5) and (6) for E's and M's and (4) to non-dynamic traits, T's.

2.   E is the *Ergic Need subsystem.* It has a section E storing the aroused product of ergic need stimulation, and has both give and take channels (8) and (9) with M. Its other channels are: from P (No. 5); to the learning apparatus LM (No. 8); to and from the general states, GS (Nos. 13, 14, and 18); to the controlling ego, D (15 and 16); and to non-dynamic traits (17).

3.   M, *the Engram Storage.* This has two closely tied sections, M the storage position of activated engrams, and LM the apparatus for adjusting engram growth as reaction to reward and punishment. In addition to its channels already mentioned, it has channels (10), (11), and (12) respectively feeding engram strength information to the control D, receiving sensing stimuli from it and receiving cue stimuli in the interests of control. Since memory storage looms large in many computer based models it should be pointed out the M is essentially all memory storage, since all factual and emotional memory clusters around the structure of the sentiments. Channel (10) providing the ego structure with information on the general success of past sentiment action is therefore especially important.

4.   GS contains the *General States.* These respond by channels (7), (8), and (18) to perception of success and failure, by (15) to ergic levels and by (18) to ego control. In turn the general states affect ego decisions by channel (19), and the arousal of ergs (as in depression anxiety) by channel (14) through (18).

5.   T is the *Trait Properties of the Organism*, other than dynamic. It imports the properties of the non-dynamic states—the individual's levels on ability and temperament traits. These enter first, into the

controlling ego's estimations of what will give most long term satis-faction (Channel (22) for sensing and (23) for input); and secondly into the manner and competence with which dynamic behavior decisions issue in action, by channel (24).

6. D, *the control system.* Fitting our evidence of the ego as coordinating E's, M's general states and non-dynamic traits, the channels by which D is connected (twelve in all) are more numerous than those of any other subsystem. Three are concerned with sensing strength and gratification of the ergs and cue controlling (*CET* action) them. Three are concerned correspondingly with the sentiments, one of which is re-trieving the sentiment records of success of previous actions. Two are involved with the general states. Two take account of cue control and response to the non-dynamic traits, and one (No. 20) passes on the considered dynamic impulse for a course of action to the executive subsystem, A.

7. A is *Machinery for Execution of Response.* Equivalents for this in some systems are simply labelled "motor action." However, this scarcely does credit to the complexity of speech, intellectual activity, and so forth that characterize much human response. Al-though our model supposes that the force and direction of the dynamic intention as such have been settled in the ego control apparatus inter-actions (that is the whole dynamic part of the behavioral equation is covered) there remains scope in determining this behavior for oper-ation of the ability and temperament traits. With the end of the action within the open system of the organism a response course of action completes Figure 6-3, as R_1. Certain changes then occur from R_1 within the environmental system which present the organism with S_2— or h_2k_2 in our VIDA symbols—and, from this, fresh adjustments are made within the organism, as illustrated in our analysis of a single sentiment as a process. These environmental changes, which complete a closed system need not concern us here, being either physical situ-ations or the provoked social reactions we study in the next chapter.

The subsystems above are empirically supported as to their exist-ence and nature by the personality structure investigations which have indicated the roll call of traits—A's, E's, M's, and P's, including the control traits in D—and states, including M's, E's, anxiety, depression, arousal etc. The perceptual apparatus (P in Figure 6-3) is substantially supported by the abilities, for example, the primaries of Thurstone and Hakstian.

The channels—which, incidentally, in number amount to a sub-stantial fraction of the logically mathematically *possible* linkages of the subsystems—must now come in for more study. However, before proceeding, a word is necessary on features of certain subsystems only lightly touched on in the above main description. For example, it will

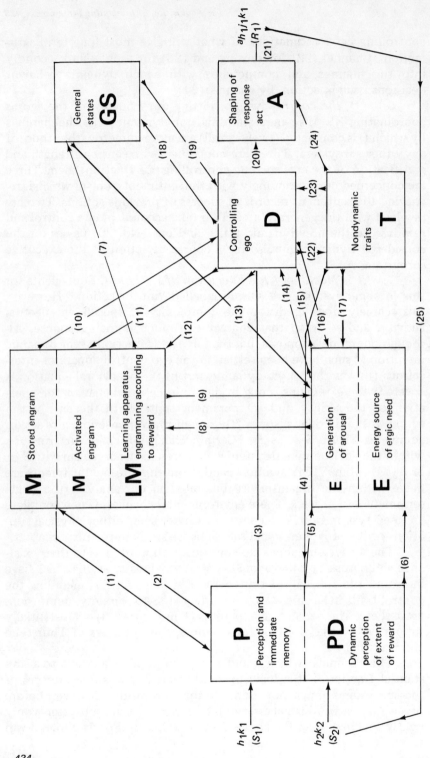

(1) Apperception information contributed

(2) Referral to memory bank

(3) Direct information on result of simple motor action

(4) Trait effects on perception

(5) Direct innate stimulation of ergs

(6) Information on reward

(7) Information on reward

(8) Reciprocal action of ergic tension on M activation

(9) Stimulation of ergs by sentiment

(10) Cognitive feedback on final responses and results of earlier experience

(11) Referral to sentiment "committee"

(12) Invocation of controlling cues

(13) Tempering effects of general states on ergs

(14) Action urged by ergic demands

(15) Information on degree of ergic gratification occurring

(16) Invocation of controlling cues

(17) Temperament limitations to arousal

(18) Effect of ego decisions on general states

(19) Effect of general states on ego decisions

(20) Dynamic goal decisions sent for executive action

(21) Emergence of response to stimulus S_1

(22) Sensing fitness of action to ability and temperament traits

(23) Call on abilities to help decision

(24) Temperament-ability endowments shaping effectiveness of response

(25) Response success or failure as new stimulus (S_2) input

Figure 6-3. VIDAS systems theory model of total personality process in adjustive action

be noted the content of what is broadly labelled M extends beyond the straight engram (memory) storage to include a "holding" also of *activated* M, that is M, and it also contains whatever apparatus, LM, is involved in continually producing the learnings—the m and n additions—M as a result of the impact of ergic rewards (channels 8, and 12). These subsections of M could, if one wished to be microscopic, be entirely separated from M, with separate channels to them but to keep the diagram of the system in proportion we have recognized that they are such close derivatives of M as to be in one subsystem.

Similarly the E subsystem, includes both unaroused need strength and arousal tension—indeed all that goes into the $(s + c)\ [C + H + x(P - G_p) + y(B - G_p)]$ term in equation (2-13). If we accept a possible operational definition of energy then this subsystem is the power house of the whole system, and though messages come into it as information they go out as energy. The only source of direct energy outside it is in the ego, in so far as it acts as a sentiment with power of its own, in the D subsystem.

The only subsystem that may seem anomalous in terms of our recognition of a one-to-one relation of subsystems with discovered personality structures, is the perceptual system P. It is true we have referred to Thurstone's (1944) perceptual ability factors, and to the primary ability and memorizing factors of Hakstian & Cattell (1974), Kelley (1954) and others agreeing on a factor, distinct from long distance meaningful memory, aptly called short distance processing. But the whole of M is also involved in this perception of each situation, and if some especially high level of channel traffic could be represented by thicker arrows then channels (1) and (2) would so represent the particularly close association of P with M.

It is perhaps questionable whether a separate section PD should be demarcated from P, to be concerned with reward. Its perceptions, however, are not of the immediate situation S_1 or $h_1 k_1$, but of a comparison of S_1 and R_1 with S_2 $(h_2 k_2)$ that is of an extent to which the response R_1 or a_{hjk}, has successfully modified the situation. At any rate this PD has connections with ergic arousal (channel 5) and sentiment modification (channels 6 and 8) which P as such does not have.

The role of the reservoir of general states, GS needs no amplification. They originate according to the adjustment process analysis chart from perceptions of the external situation (channel 7) and the state of satisfaction or dissatisfaction of the ergic reservoir (by channel 15-18) and they have modifying feedback effects on the ergs (channel 13) and create a field for the decision processes in D (by channel 19). They are in turn affected by these control decisions (channel 18).

Attention needs more specially to be given to D in regard to the less traditionally recognized channels (3), (15), (16), (18), (19), (20), and (22). Balancing and in competition with the cognitive messages of (10) and (12), the ergic tension source E (E + E) delivers to the control system, D, messages on the urgency of the need and aroused tension (resulting from the M interactions, and so forth), via channel (15) and (14), which, if Figure 6-3 expressed differences of channel traffic by thickness, would be recognized as heavy-duty channels concerned with actual energy transferral. It is thus through channels (3), (9), (10), and (15) that the ego is made aware of the success of its operations and is rewarded, to bring about its learning.

It may be that the systems machinery we have stated at this point, in connection with D, is not as complex as it really needs to be. Nevertheless we have aimed to represent here the outcome of our discussion on the ego's invocation of symbols and images both to sound out, by the experience of the degree of activation and arousal resulting (cue balloting), the extent of the M and E requirements, and to control by the modulating effect (cue orchestration) of these invoked symbols, the subsequent action. For this purpose we have let channels (10) and (12) represent the sounding and control of sentiment activation and (15) and (16) operate for the same actions with respect to E. The controlling D action on E proceeds indirectly through action of M and E, channel (12) to (9), because we must assume that all but innately cued E action is guided by acquired cognitive engram signals. But interaction of D with ergic tension occurs directly through (16) and also indirectly in that it proceeds through the mediation of the general states subsystem, GS, by channels (18) to (13).

Finally, a brief amplification is called for on the action of T in the lower right of Figure 6-3. This represents in the behavior specification equation the contribution from nondynamic traits, there represented by A's for abilities and P's for general personality-temperament factors. They determine such effects as level of relation eduction, motor skill, rate of warming up, style of persistence in action, degree of irrepressibility (ardor), rate of onset of fatigue, and diverse qualities modifying the way in which a dynamic commitment to a certain goal or subgoal can be expressed. These trait endowments contribute by channel (17) to certain features, e.g., general susceptibility to arousal, in the ergic subsystem, before reaching action expression; they affect control, in D, through channel (23) as such traits as UI(T)17 or exvia-invia, UI(T)32, typically do, and as abilities, they enter substantially through channel (24) into the successful shaping of the response in A. They also naturally have a role, as shown by channel (4), in the operation of the perception unit.

As regards the relation of learning to this model it will be seen that the learning gains must exist both in the reservoirs and the channels. Virtually all learning—for example that in perception and in the learned arousal of ergs—will center on the engram deposits in M. However, D is also a repository of learned skills and tactics of the ego. And there will be change with experience in all the traits in T and in the executive machinery in A. If we accept the general verdict of the nature of change in systems as they mutually adapt (as open systems within a larger closed system) an equally important change will be in the flow capacities of channels. For example, the information on reward (channel 6) could be more, or less rapidly and completely transmitted to LM, or the effect of general states on the controlling ego could be transmitted more or less sensitively.

Parenthetically, physiological psychologists will naturally speculate whether the above systems analysis can be translated to neural and hormonal terms. A translation must certainly be possible, but the history of psychology tells us that there is danger of prematurely adapting the system to physiological conceptions before it has firmly stood on its own feet as derived from behavioral experiment and analysis. With one eye on this caveat we can nevertheless see good reasons for expecting the action of E to locate in the midbrain and hypothalamus and associated hormone secretions; for the control system D, to locate in the frontal lobes and limbic projections; for M to locate in the cortex generally, and so on. But for the trade with neuroanatomy to be profitable the psychologist must first operationalize the systems concepts in measurable behavior, a problem to which we now turn.

6-9. Sustaining the Structure-based Systems Model in Current Personality Research

As far as the VIDAS systems model is concerned personality research[14] is at a tantalizing stage where solid support can be given to important features, but where development of uncommon multivariate research skills and imaginative new approaches are urgently needed for further advance. What we seek to establish regarding the varieties of transmission channels is reasonably clear: the inner nature of the subsystems has been less established. In general they might be classified either as reservoirs in the sense of repositories of "data" (information, energy) at levels differing from person to person, age to age, and so forth, or as organs for special "machinery," also showing individual differences in development. M, E, GS and T can be taken as examples of the former, representing "banks" respectively of cognitive networks, ergic reactivity, existing mood states and of capacities in the form of abilities and temperament limits on behavior. P, D, and A represent the loci of kinds of machinery for particular process; respectively, perceptual sorting, dynamic decision making and motor executions. The channels also have two varieties; those concerned with information transmission, like (1), (2), (10), (11), and (21), and those which transmit power to react, like (8), (15), (19), and (22).

Inasmuch as the internal system in Figure 6-3 represents what goes on between the outcome of calculations on the internal system must fit the specification equations of the VIDA model. In asserting that the elements in this internal system are properly based on the structures in VIDA we take a stand on the principle that whatever unitary conceptual entities exist will covary in their parts from person to person and moment to moment, and be susceptible to recognition and isolation as factors in the final output from the internal system. However, the VIDAS model will permit predictions beyond the VIDA model, particularly in estimating the state of the system at a later point in time from an earlier point.

As regards the derivation of the structures in the structure-based VIDAS from the VIDA researches of the last forty years, it is time to make some of the above assumptions in the system's structure more explicit. The basis of the separate E and M reservoirs rests, of course, on the findings of separate E and M factors in the dynamic calculus, and, more closely inspected each will be multiple, that is, the E reservoir will contain the arousal capacities of each of p ergs, and the M the activation potential of each of g distinct sentiments. T needs no comment except to point to the long familiar ability and temperament source traits. The GS subsystem, a reasonably extensive sampling of state behavior is known to cover the general states of anxiety, depression, regression, etc. In the D subsystem is primarily the factor isolated ego structure, C, but the superego and self sentiment structures each checked as unitary factors across three media, also have influence there. The multiple character of the E reservoir incidentally raises the question of whether the E's do or do not draw upon a single total energy. But even if the former should be true the relations in channels (8), (9), and (14) are those of specific ergs with specific sentiments.

Apparently then both what we might consider reservoirs of definable amount (E, M, T, and so forth) and machineries of definable processing capacity (P, LM, D, and so forth) should and do appear as S-R factors, from analyzing ultimate a_{hjk} magnitudes. But what research designs go farther and reveal the nature of the channels and the topology of their connections? For so far these have not been recognized in specification equation form. Different behaviors (a_{hjk}'s) will naturally involve different participations of the various subsystems which will necessarily be reflected in different degrees of activity of the channels, and these different activity levels should contain terms for the capacities, flow rates, and so forth of the channels. We tentatively suggested earlier that these inner system channel properties would appear in the behavioral indices; p, r, i, and s, since each different action by a person possessed of fixed subsystem scores would have different p, r, i, and s values. Thus a large flow in channels (10) and (15) must mean large p, r, i, and s loadings on E and ME terms in the behavioral equation.

These relations of indices to internal flows in channels, however, are bound to be quite complex, and there is not even a glimpse yet available of the mathematico-statistical analyses that would lead from one to the other. Path coefficients, however, indicate the type of analysis we perhaps need to begin with (Blalock, 1971, Rao, Morton & Yee, 1976). If in subsystems A, B, C, and D linked by channels, we find correlation r_{ab}, r_{bc}, and r_{cd}, then if the variance of all is the same, the input of A will figure in the variance of D to the extent given by the correlation:

$$r_{ad} = r_{ab} \cdot r_{bc} \cdot r_{cd} \tag{6-14}$$

(This applies, however, only if no other channels flow in at B, C, and D.)

The calculation can be carried somewhat further, with certain allowances for new contributory channels, bifurcations of the path, for resistances in channels and sizes of reservoirs. But at present advances along these lines have to proceed by fitting the outcome of various intermediate hypothetical values to the final outcomes in the magnitude of the final response in relation to initial stimulus input. The direct translation from values in a behavioral equation, based on factoring many a_{hijk} values, to the systems values is still not worked out. This we realized already when we introduced into equations (2-5), (2-7), and (2-8) the expressions for the internal interactions between E and M, namely, the functional weights (f's) of an E_x in activating q possible M's, and the generators (g's) of an M_y in calling into action its ergic investment, repeated in simplified form in (6-14), thus:

$$E_x(f_{x1}M_1 + \cdots + f_{xq}M_q)$$

and $\tag{6-15}$

$$M_y(g_{y1}E_1 + \cdots + g_{yp}E_p)$$

among p ergs.

Although it is possible that eventually means will be found for inferring the internal interactions in the system from the a_{hjk}'s, that is, observations that concern only the stimulus and the ultimate response behavior, we should at least quite specifically recognize that the movement from our VIDA behavioral equations to our VIDAS systems treatment demands elucidation of the internal exchanges, by *some* means. These exchanges include: (1) discovery of the equations which handle the purely *internal* adjustments and interactions, over and above our familiar VIDA equations relating final behavior to structural entities (traits and states) and their gross, final interaction expressions, and (2) discovery of the equations which handle *sequential change*, from one internal state and behavior of the system to another. These involve terms for reservoir magnitudes, processing capacities of "machinery," the topology of channels and feedback loops, and all that goes with following a process rather than an instant structure responding to an instant environment.

Just as we have taken the veriest glimpse at an equation (6-14) that could start exploration of the first problem, so we may take a token illustration of the approach needed in the second. Here the typical parameters will be the size of a reservoir, for example, of the energy in a drive or the cognitive memory resources activated in a sentiment, the time rate of release, and various parameters of a curve of transmitted information or energy. The suggestion of Johnson, Johnson, and Mark (1951) explaining the fluency factor in abilities (or in such a temperament trait as exuberance, UI(T)21), measured as output for a given time, has been mentioned in another connection, but illustrates well here the dependence of a total transfer upon reservoir size and time and transmission parameters, as follows:

$$F_i = s_i \left(1 - e^{-r_i t} \right) \qquad\qquad (6\text{-}16)$$

where F_i is any individual i's fluency score in output after the agreed time interval, t; s_i is the reservoir size, for example, his memory store of words or amount of aroused ergic tension, E, and r_i is the rate at which the individual i's retrieval channels can operate on the reservoir. Because in the case of fluency we can point to a factor, it seems likely that other empirical instances will appear in which factors will initially be isolated that on closer examination will prove to be functions both of reservoir sizes and channel capacities. Some possibilities of experimental separation of values are discussed below.

It should be recognized that in going from the "static" or cross sectional VIDA model to the VIDAS system model we have not impugned the essential correctness of the former as an "instantaneous" description and calculation. The trait scores and the behavioral index values we attach to them in the behavioral equation are expressing the overall outcome of a stimulus input in terms of a response performance output, but without a detailed statement of the intervening machine. In so far as the equation represents a weighted interaction of the subsystems—ergs, sentiments, ego, general states—in the system it *does* heed the system structure, but only in terms of a total outcome. Consequently it is likely that, being only an approximate description of the real complexity of the interaction it will, even as an instantaneous photograph, not predict *as much* of the response variance as would the full VIDAS systems calculation.

A practically-oriented applied psychologist might at this point ask what the concrete advantages of the systems treatment really are. First, let us note that though we can predict by VIDA the behavior a_{hijk} at time t_1 and again at time t_2 when the ergic tensions, states, etc. of the individual are different, we cannot handle the transition from t_1 to t_2. We have to measure the individual afresh at t_2 to get his trait and state values. By VIDAS, if we progress experimentally to determining equations of the type (6-14) and (6-16) as above, we can hope to derive the values at t_2 from those at t_1 (with limits, in terms of knowing pre-t_1 values, and environmental changes). Moreover, even in the "single moment" prediction by VIDA we recognize that stimulus and response are not actually simultaneous. A general is fed all available information about disposition of enemy forces: the orders for disposition of his own forces may be given hours or days later. Even in the simplest response, as to "What time do you want to dine?" the cue soundings and decision process roll through fairly complex sequences. Even if there were no advance in accuracy from the VIDA specification equation in knowing exactly what these interactions are, scientific curiosity—the completion of science as such—would urge us to try to understand the intervening systems events. Even in practical values, it is likely, as suggested, we would achieve a higher accuracy of prediction by surpassing the approximations in the linear, additive VIDA equation.

The experimental elucidation of the realities of the VIDAS model is something on which only a couple of pages speculation can be offered here. One can safely predict that it will keep the best minds in the next two generations of psychologists challenged and, hopefully, productive of solutions.[15] First the model—or, rather models, since many modifications even within the seven element system—needs to be stated in full mathematical detail. Then it will be for experiment to ascertain the goodness of fit to that model and its modifications.

It seems very probable that *P*-technique, with repeated measurement at short intervals, will be one important avenue of investigation. The specification equation in *P*-technique for various behaviors changes from occasion to occasion. We have argued above that the behavioral indices *p*, *r*, *i*, and *s* will represent mainly the action of channels between the subsystems, and that learning in the systems model will take the form (along with m additions to M) of changes in the capacities of channels.[16]

In systems theory in other fields (for example, electrical and hydraulic), a refined mathematical representation of channel flow has been developed for speed and volume ("bits" per second), viscosity, pressure, cross-section magnitude, effect of duration of flow, and so on. We can imagine that the information flow from M to E in Figure 6-3, determining the number and kind of ergic energy units released in E, could be determined by the pressure from the intensity of P's stimulation of M, by the duration of the stimulation, by the degree of conflict among different stimulated sentiments, by the degree of reward in the past (as represented by s_{km}), and so on. But this degree of refinement is not possible in psychology yet.[17]

Already in the VIDA model we introduced in the interaction of E's and M's (eqs. 2-5, 2-6, pp. 96–98) a vector of generator values, g's, defining a sentiment's generation of particular ergic tensions, and a vector of *convoking* capacities, f's, defining an erg's capacity to "fetch" cognitive memories toward retrieval. These and the other channel parameters ultimately issue in p, r, i, and s values in the specification equation, and must therefore be hidden in them. It seems probable that if suitably related a_{hijk}'s are measured experimentally, and analyzed into the specification values, the latter could be used as simultaneous equations to solve for the more abstract f, g, and other internal system values on which they depend.

In due perspective one must not forget that finding the individual properties of channels cannot proceed except on a hypothesis of the *actual topology* of paths and feedbacks, such as we have proposed in Figure 6-3. The solution of equations will be specific to each model, and goodness of fit will indicate which model is best. In deciding among these hypothetical topologies of networks some general conceptions of the goal of the system and its general characters is helpful.

An important instance where some further development of the equations is called for is that of escalating positive feedback effect where (neglecting other terms) ME and EM appear in the behavioral equation (pp. 98-100) thus:

$$a_{hjk_1} = v_{hjm}(s_{km}M_1E_1) + v_{hje}(s_{ke}E_1M_1) \qquad (6\text{-}17)$$

A one is given as subscript here to indicate values at a first moment. In the next moment E_1 will have become E_2 with the value:

$$E_2 = s_{km}M_1E_1 \qquad (6\text{-}18)$$

and M_2 will be:

$$M_2 = s_{ke} E_1 M_1 \qquad (6\text{-}19)$$

(v_{hje} is not involved in the amplification). Whence, repeating (6-16), but with E_2's and M_2's each substituted, by (6-17) and (6-18) respectively:

$$a_{hjk \cdot 2} = v_{hjm} s_{km} s_{ke} E_1 M_1 s_{km} M_1 E_1$$
$$+ v_{hje} s_{ke} s_{km} M_1 E_1 s_{ke} E_1 M_1 \qquad (6\text{-}20)$$

Not only is this a complex expression, but it is also a runaway one, for if the s_k's exceed unity, as they often would the positive feedback would bring a_{hjk} after a few repetitions to enormous values. Normally, and with viscerogenic ergs, psychological observation makes clear that this does not occur, though a case could be made for its occurring up to a point with non-viscerogenic ergs such as fear or self-assertion, which are sometimes described as feeding on themselves, respectively in panic and in manic episodes. A nervous person alone in a house at night may hear tappings that evoke fear. The rise in ergic tension in fear may activate cognitive images that are more stimulating than the original tappings, and an hysterical crescendo may either happen or tend to happen. Similarly, a person angered by some slight insult may next recall many other cognitive (engram) causes for anger toward the offender, and burst into rage. McDougall's *Abnormal Psychology* casebook instances how stimulation of self-assertion can lead (success feeding success, as perceived) to manic behavior.

If we look at (6-20) we see that it requires only one of the terms, E or M, to be denied movement beyond a limit for the whole expression to flatten out at a limit. It seems most likely that self limiting term would be the ergic tension, E, where physiological homeostatic mechanisms, in blood pressure, hormone resources, and so forth, would put a limit to arousal levels. This might be represented in Figure 6-3 by a negative loop within the E subsystem from E to E.

A second source of balance in the whole system is, of course, the control from the ego or D subsystem external to the possibly self accelerating ME + EM subsystem. Actual channels for this inhibitory action on M and E by D are shown in Figure 6-3 as "Invocation of controlling cues" by channels (12) for M and (16) for E.

The conception of some subsystems as reservoirs, subject to emptying and filling by channels, as well as from physiological sources (underlying for example, E, GS, and D in Figure 6-3) also affects homeostatic and other functions of the system, as equation (6-16) would remind us. These subsystems—at least E and D—along with M and T (general ability and temperament traits) remain stable enough to be picked up as R-technique factors, though the E's and M's show decidedly more fluctuation than ability and temperament factors, with different results where they are involved. It is GS—the condition of the general states such as anxiety, depression, and excitement—that contributes the most instability to the system, over and above the imbalances among ergs, which are closely connected with these GS values.

Although we have suggested that psychologists should build up their conceptions of the VIDAS or other systems from a purely behavioral basis before seeking physiological supports, this does not mean that the role of physiological influences in determining "reservoirs" and temperament traits should be ignored in seeking closer definition of the system. Several instances could probably already be cited with confidence where limits and constants in the system reside in physiology. For example, the ability trait recognized factorially as fluid intelligence, g_f (Cattell, 1971; Horn, 1977) can be inferred from the writings of Spearman, Hebb and Lashley to be some simple function of the total number of functioning cortical neurons in the individual brain. Again the correlations of g_c, crystallized intelligence, and UI(T)23, capacity to mobilize, with g_f, along with other observations, suggest that UI(T)23 and g_c might be different derivations from the same quantitative g_f capacity. An instance of a different kind, cortertia, UI(T)22, suggests that the trait level is a "reservoir" in equilibrium between excitatory flow, from the midbrain tract, and some source of cortical inhibition.

The structure-based systems model has to account, of course, not only for the ordinary functioning of personality but also for cognitive and emotional learning—mainly the acquisition of sentiments and of the control system—which has been described above. The M gains and shapings are adequately accounted for by the connections of the LM apparatus in Figure 6-3 with the perception mechanism PD and with E. The more complex learning of the ego, in the control system D, has been described as depending on reward and punishment with regard to the undertaking of maximizing reward to all E's and ME's. The direction of reward to the D system requires that it have contributions from two sources, the perceptual unit, P, to keep in close touch with environmental reality and the success of its decisions therein, and the ergic reward occurring in E. We have just recognized this by supposing the ergic reward occurring in E for a given course of action must not only go through the learning unit LM to strengthen an engram in M but must reward the ego structure in D—which has engram structures itself. Contingently we have supposed D (the location of the ego structure, C) to be rewarded through the channel

(5-15). But we have supposed a perception of the success of the response to pass directly from P to D by channel (3). However, a cognitively perceived reward is not the same as a "gut level" experience of reward, which requires activation of E (5) and the use of channel (15).

In summary, whereas the VIDA behavioral equation approximates the interaction of subsystems by a linear additive equation, yielding the best estimate we know of the response performance at a given moment, with predictors measured at the given moment, the VIDAS model adds, further, the *internal* interaction of the subsystems and does so with respect to sequential processes, regard for which could ultimately permit prediction from time 1 to time 2. Prior to the VIDAS model the VIDA model had already recognized the nature and importance of some of these interactions, notably of the f and the g vectors in the mutual interactions of E's and M's. But the VIDAS model goes much beyond this regard for richer representation of internal exchanges into the recognition of flow within a system. It connotes that a state at t_2 cannot be predicted from t_1 without knowledge both of the *position* and the *momentum* at t_1, as in physical systems. (Analogous also to our discovery, p. 202, that a measured learning gain of X units does not uniquely define the amount of learning broadly conceived without information about the parameters of the initial position.)

The VIDAS model promises at last an understanding of personality as a living and constantly moving entity. But the mathematical treatment, requiring networks, and integral and differential calculus, belongs to a multivariate psychometrics of which we can only catch a glimpse at this stage of research. Doubtless computer simulation of such models as in Figure 6-3 will help guide investigators to the most apt equations for a true mathematical representation. The purely structural depiction, in VIDA, needed as a foundation, is, however, still incomplete, especially in the subleties of theory and accuracies of experiment needed in objective motivational measurement of states at a given moment. But hopefully a concerted attack, with MAT and SMAT measures as a factor reference core, will soon firm up this psychometrically relatively obvious need.

6-10. Summary

1.   The comparatively firm identification of the clinical notion of superego with an established unitary factor G (in L-, Q-, and T-data) by numerous criterion and other associations, permits us to lean for initial hypothesis about the learning of G on earlier clinical obser-

vations. However, *experimental and statistical* data on its clinical, occupational, and life criterion relations, as well as the discovered age curve, and the evidences on change of G with life events, already permit some inferences on its mode of acquisition in and beyond infancy. Nevertheless, the evidence is strong that the bulk of the learning takes place in infancy, by introjection of parental values, under the fear of loss of the parent, and the operation of such ergs as self-abasement and self-assertion. Existing measures of the ergic investments of G support this to a point, but are too recent and rough to lean on. In explaining the persistence of guilt-producing power after the original rewarding object has gone, much weight must be given to the mnemonic potency of earliness of imprinting, to special qualities of the security-seeking erg, and to certain subtle mechanisms of reward here discussed. The irruption of sexual needs (insofar as they get sublimated) and of the protective (succorant) erg at adolescence produce a typical modification of G toward altruism, in the continual learning that goes on around the original G structure.

2.   The self-sentiment pattern, Q_3 or SS, also appears as a factor expressed in and aligned across L-, Q-, and T-data. The numerous clinical, educational, and life criteria associations; the age curve; Q_3's changes under life impacts, its negative relation to anxiety, and other empirical associations, throw appreciable light on its development. It subsidiates partly to the superego and partly (as a device for maintaining "good standing") to the satisfaction of most sentiments. The cognitive self-concept, which is its core object, is a compromise of the ideal and the real self, the gap between the two when wide being a source of anxiety. The sentiment is rewarded when the individual brings the action attitudes as far as possible into line with his accepted self attitudes.

Much of the learning of the concept is by trial and error designed to adjust the image to the individual's real abilities and emotional capacities. To this trial and error trimming, generally from too idealistic a picture, are added vicarious learning experiences, for example in literature, and modelling on admired personalities. The actual operation of learning laws in building the self-sentiment takes place through the usual three processes contributing to *any* sentiment formation. An extreme failure of alignment of the self-concept with the realities of capacities and needs occurs in psychosis, by the breaking of reality testing of all kinds. Appreciable experimental data have been gained on development of Q_3 in late adolescence, greater growth being significantly related to experience of higher parental affection, success in employment, the challenge of a bereavement, and the effect of continuing education.

3.   Ego strength, C, recognized in Q- and L- but not yet unambiguously in T-data factoring (in which there are competing UI patterns), is

amply interpretable from its many significant clinical, educational, and life criteria associations. It has significant genetic determination, which could represent endowment in frontal lobe resources for control of emotional impulsivity.

Descriptively, the ego has four functions which are often successive stages in a process: (1) Control of immediate impulses in a conflict situation: the deliberative pause. (2) A sensing of strengths of internal needs, (a) simply and directly and (b) additionally by cue evocation of trait strengths (CET). (3) An evaluation of the external situation, with regard especially to maximizing long term satisfactions, (a) by perception of relations (intelligence) (b) by scouring of memory with retrieval of previous records of reward and punishment concerning behaviors contemplated. (4) The processes in (2) and (3) lead to a decision on the best course of action, which is implemented, in face of opposing impulsivity, by (a) the weight in the behavioral equation of the ego as a sentiment, with broad ergic investments and (b) CET action by the ego which now has a different function and strength from (2) above. There it evoked dynamic traits by internal or external stimuli to sense their strength: here it does so to enlist their "proxy" in support of the action approved by the governing ego.

The steady rise of C with age; its reduction by traumatic conflict; and its enhancement by success in control, suggest that like other dynamic traits it grows especially through the means-end (ME) learning principle. Its end goal is the maximization of satisfaction, over a foreseeable time period, of the needs of all ergs, occurring from both innately provided stimulus connections and (more extensively) through sentiment investments. Although all dynamic traits are basically on an equally privileged footing as far as this balancing of satisfactions among them by the ego is concerned, yet because sentiments generally, and the self-sentiment and superego especially, are by their nature oriented to more future-satisfaction and stable order their indices are more likely to be of the same algebraic sign as the ego in a majority of conflict decisions. Consequently, in control in a cultural environment, it is appropriate to consider control as the work of a triumvirate of superego, self-sentiment, and ego in cooperative inhibitory and stimulating action. A well stored repertoire of cues, easily retrievable, to weight dynamic traits appropriately in CET action is a major asset from integration learning (N) in personality, probably playing a larger role than mere confluence learning by trial and error. Experiment has begun to substantiate the occurrence of learning of such stimulus control, by both internal and external cues, and of the arranging of responses to bring the right stimulus contacts. But much of this has been by bi-variate designs only and has lacked the measures on unitary structures that would give the whole picture. As far as we yet know the growth of the ego by learning occurs through success either in rewarding direct control action or in reward to the CET activity, and it is damaged especially by traumatic failures of attempted control.

5. The two different modes of attempted control hypothesized for C require two radically different uses of behavioral indices. In direct control of each action C has only to discover and engram v and s values particular to itself, in relation to the given situation-response and to the usual indices to be expected in the other traits contending in the decision. It acquires the ordinary appendage engrams necessary for it so to respond in the situation. In the CET control it has to learn more, namely, how to respond to the situation to produce the image or concept cue that will modify the behavior index of every other operating trait. This is a three-cornered engram, associating (1), C, (2), a dynamic trait, and (3), a situation-response. Note that with q sentiment traits and n life situation-responses (a_{hjk}'s) there would be nq specific engram learnings for C, instead of simply n as with any ordinary sentiment. This expanding burden may be the negative feedback to growth that we have sought to explain why the positive feedback of ME (CRII) learning does not lead to run-away growth. Research designs to check the direct action and the CET model of ego action are mooted, in terms of multivariate equations. Meanwhile experiments on stimulus control of behavior give general support to the CET model of C action.

6. The study of ego action brings out still more clearly the principle that dynamic control is achieved by control of cognitive elements involving memory retrieval potency. The ego, as the most central clearing house of cognitive relations is able to manipulate cues better than any other dynamic trait. The earlier factoring of conflict manifestations gave major role to phenomena of cue misperceptions, attention blanks, and avoidance of conflicting stimuli. It is argued that what has been perceived psychoanalytically as repression is an extreme of what is really a continuum of emphasis and de-emphasis of memory cues by the ego. (It appears that the same blocking of memory cues is a general tactic used between all conflicting dynamic traits, and the ego itself may suffer losses in conflict with the more powerful sentiments and complexes.) The findings on U and I motivational components, in which the information and association measures fall in the integrated, I, component, and the unintegrated and unconscious component affects behavior only obliquely and through poor and irrational associations supports this.

7. State research has shown, beyond ergic tension factors and the associated epiphenomena of their introspectible primary emotions, a set of some seven or eight broad states or moods called *derived emotions* because they derive from the interaction of dynamic traits

with adjustment situations, as in anxiety, depression, and so forth. Taking anxiety as one of the most discussed derived states we set out a theory of three sources of anxiety: situational uncertainty or fear of privation; fear of loss of control, and sheer absolute degrees of ergic deprivation. It is shown that experimental findings, and especially those placing $C-$, $H-$, and Q_3- in the second order anxiety factor, QII, support these hypotheses. Anxiety, a *general* autonomic excitation factor, is thus a reservoir for temporarily frustrated ergic tension, transformed. Dynamically it is as much a "disease process" as an adjustment, because the transformation is not easily reversible and anxiety has disorganizing as well as merely amplifying effects on performance.

8.   The general derived states, however, in most instances have other and useful functions that offset their less happy by-products. Though anxiety is not an efficient motive behind much ordinary behavior, or a necessary one in a well-adjusted person, it functions usefully by exerting a pressure on the ego for solution of conflict. Similarly, depression operates in many instances to dampen motivations in their existing outlets, helping to bring about a radical dissolution and reintegration in a better total adjustment. (In this its action resembles on a larger scale the deliberative pause in ego action.) A field theory action is suggested, in which the controlling forces of ego, self-sentiment, and superego, as well as the counter actions of the ergs and sentiments they control, operate within the mood field of elation-depression, high and low anxiety, arousal, regression, fatigue, and so forth. These secondary general emotions derived from the ergic primaries carry into the adjustment machinery information about the *general* state of adjustment of the dynamic system and aid appropriate action of the controlling trait triumvirate as such. The cooperation of the control traits and the derived states occurs both in any immediate action and in the learning. What we have called integration learning (N) is, for example, aided, when the advance is mainly on the right track, by a mood of elation which, by inducing higher fluency, provides richer suggestions for trial-and-error solution search. When on essentially an impossible path, with massive frustration, the mood of depression assists the ego in inhibiting present needs, and retracting in favor of a radically different search for satisfaction.

9. Personality theory as developed from 1930 by the present writer and research colleagues has had an emphasis best indicated by calling it the VIDA model, VIDA being an acronym for vector-id-analysis. That is to say it begins with the five id coordinates—responses, stimuli, people, ambient situations and observers—of the basic behavioral data relation matrix (Cattell, 1946, 1966) and analyzes the unitary structures in each type, representing individual ids (people, situations) by

vector quantities. The unitary concepts measured in the vectors are traits, states, processes, etc., and use values combined in linear additive equations.

The VIDA model thus constructs intermediate constructs and concepts from *S-R* behavior directly, though *S* and *R* are more broadly defined and measured than, say, in reflexology. Though the VIDA model has substantial theoretical and practical success, it has been developed in recent years into the VIDAS model, which extends into a systems theory.

10. The VIDAS model is synonymous with a *Structure-based Systems Theory* of personality, developing as a systems model on the basis of the structural and relational findings in the VIDA model. The main difference is that the VIDA model, even though it operates with relations among internal structures as well as between them and the environment, can deal only with values as provided at a given moment. The systems model, on the other hand, takes account of continuous interactions among the internal structures—interactions, incidentally, that are more varied than the linear, additive relations of the VIDA behavioral equation.

11. In the VIDAS model person and environment constitute a closed system, with the person as an open system set to maximize long term dynamic satisfactions, which include survival. In the person system the ergic subsystem, as the prime energizer, essentially has the other elements subservient to it.

The evidence of the structural base has called for seven major parts (elements, subsystems, organs) in the system, with flow channels among them for units of information and energy. The subsystems are (1) P, a perceptual apparatus, or input encoder, with action also of the kind assigned to a short-distance memory activity; (2) M, a storage memory for engrams, that is cognitive-dynamic links and cognitive records generally; (3) E, a reservoir of ergic need energy, residing in recognizably distinct ergs; (4) D, a decision or control unit; (5), a "decoder" for putting decisions into a repertoire of appropriate executive, motor actions; (6) *GS*, a general states developer and reservoir; (7) T, a behavior-modifying unit of nondynamic traits (abilities and temperament traits) contributing to the shaping of both perception and response, beyond the contribution of the dynamic traits. Some of these subsystem units, notably E, M and probably *GS*, have the essential systems character of reservoirs (as already suggested in some instances) that is, they are raised by input and lowered by outflow. Others, such as P, D, and A represent "machinery" (probably with internal channels and sub-organs) which process an input to produce a different kind of output. Sub-system 7, the ability and temperament traits element, T, is scarcely to be described as either a reservoir or a piece of machinery, though it is nearer to the latter in that it shapes limits, for example by intelligence and temperamental tolerances, to perceptual input and behavioral output.

Some 25 channels conduct exchanges among the 7 subsystems, with varying carrying capacities, leading to a hierarchy of cybernetic potencies among the subsystems. The action of the whole is determined by the parameters of the subsystems and the channels, and the topological (network) form, notably regarding positive and negative feedback loops.

12.   The kind of mathematical treatment needed for the VIDAS model is illustrated first by two simpler equations already in use. One shows how we may estimate by path coefficients the role of the flow magnitude of an earlier channel in a chain upon the flow outcome in a more remote one, when reservoir and channel sizes are known. Another shows how the integral calculus may be used for the general problem of assessing total reservoir transfers, proceeding with changing rates, for a given time.

The VIDA model will give substantial estimates of behavior at t_1 and t_2 when we know the trait, state and behavioral index values obtaining at those particular moments, but it will not allow us, as the VIDAS model theoretically will, to reach the t_2 equation from the levels and the momenta at t_1. The last is important, for in saying we can, if we know the system, "deduce t_2 from t_1" we have to recognize that, as in physical systems, we must know not only the static values at t_1 but also the momentum of the system. Even when the subsystem and channel topography is established by research the calculations are likely to have high complexity (of the order of those in astronautics), involving both network equations and the differential and integral calculus. But only thus can we approach understanding and prediction regarding the living personality in an historically changing environment.

13.   The research methods for discovering the system structure can only be tentatively sketched today. A variety of definite models, like that in Figure 6-3, will need to be used in trial and error fashion, checking against measured results. Here computer simulation can postpone, as far as practical estimations are concerned, the need for too complex a mathematical analysis. Multivariate experiment, especially with advanced factor analytic methods as in the reticular design (Cattell, 1978), should help, however, to narrow the choice of specific parameters in models.

Although the more likely path to determining the properties of the system within the individual is to cut into the internal processes by some mode of direct observation, the theoretical possibility is raised here that with sufficient mathematico-experimental ingenuity the structures, channels and flow rates could be inferred from purely peripheral observations on stimuli and responses. One is encouraged in this hope by the success in mapping the structural basis of the VIDAS model in the VIDA model, operating purely with peripheral *S-R* evidence. It is suggested that this purely peripheral approach to the VIDAS solutions would require no longer the simple multivariate approach but a solution of simultaneous (behavioral) equations gathered in specified experimental sequences, in *R-*, *dR*, and *P*-technique approaches, and with experimental manipulations, for example, of ergic tensions, physiologically. Therein the experimentally determinable *p*, *r*, *i*, *s*, and *T* value would have substituted for them, in auxiliary equations, the reservoir sizes, flow rates, and so forth in the VIDAS system hypothesized to determine the behavior index and trait values.

NOTES

[1] It is desirable to be explicit here about what certain empirical correlations among dynamic traits do and do not mean. It is possible for two factors to be cooperative, that is, to have similar loading patterns (Cattell 1978)—in this case on attitude variables—without correlating *at all* in their true scores (they will spuriously correlate in their *estimated* scores). The fact that Q_3 and G are cooperative on value attitudes (or that any other two dynamic structures are) is thus most likely to mean that one is *subsidiated* to the other in the dynamic lattice, as we believe Q_3 to be to G. The further fact that Q_3 and G positively correlate as factors, through the second-stratum factor $QVIII$, we hypothesize to arise from good upbringing tending environmentally to generate both. But ego strength has virtually zero (just slightly positive) correlation with either. Consequently, if, as we argue, C will tend to have the same loading sign (allied action) in many behavioral equations as Q_3 and G, this does not mean that people's scores on them need be correlated (except spuriously in estimates wrongly based largely on such common variables) with C.

[2] What happens in the case of the young man inclined to literature should not be allowed to distort our view of what counts in modelling the self in the case of his less expressive, less read, and more average brothers. These look to the man of action in the everyday world and to local models. The basic fact is that in early years and for most people the models are parents, big brothers, or other immediate characters. Of his youth Jefferson wrote, "I had the good fortune to become acquainted early with social characters of very high standing, and to feel the incessant wish that I could even become what they were" (Letter, November 24, 1808). An equally explicit English-American instance of modeling is found in Captain John Smith of Virginia, who averred that he "admired and imitated Sir Francis Drake above all men." The captain's subsequent performance and life style show the power of that modeling.

However, it is important to note also that in all these modelings, concrete or literary, the secondary process of *trimming to capacities and needs* noted above constantly proceeds. The adjustment moves both ways; we recognize that a man with a naturally strong appetite will tend to incorporate gourmet (or gourmand) values in his self-image, and that a person with a lusty sex drive will have difficulty in accepting self-sentiment or superego values of saintly chastity. The dynamic reward system thus is one geared to reaching an equilibrium between the motivation of the budding self-sentiment, in relation to which the assertion, fear, narcism, and other ergic needs in the ergic investment are rewarded in proportion to the approach of actual behavior to the model. They are also punished if the self-image is stretched to goals beyond their capacities for satisfaction or for enduring suppression. Thus the attitudes around the self-concept, constituting what was often studied as "aspiration level" do not depart, except in the psychotic, by any glaring discrepancy from the actual self that such a person would record for example in the 16 PF or other questionnaire test. (Parenthetically, the development of abnormal discrepancy appears to show first in UI(T)28 and later as loss of reality contact in such personality measures in the T-data realm as UI(T)25 (−) and, less strongly, in UI(T)19−, UI(T)21−, and UI(T)23−.)

Because of these adjustive processes the self-sentiment tends to be more complex, more far reaching, and more explicitly and constantly conscious than other sentiments. Further, like any sentiment with an abstract entity at its cognitive core, it would not be expected to appear in correlational studies in lower animals and only fragmentarily in young children, as Sweney and Cattell (1961) found.

[3] We suspect that the historian of this period of incursion of researchers with simplistic reflexist concepts into personality will sum up much as a famous historian summed up the brief restoration activities of the Bourbons—"That they had learned nothing and forgotten nothing." The simple reflexologist learned nothing in that he approached personality learning with no demonstrable awareness of the growth in this generation of a substantial field of precise human personality and dynamic structure findings, unknown in animal psychology, and he forgot nothing in that he continued to seek to apply in an inappropriate field a jargon barbarously stretched beyond its original field of appropriateness. One has to mention also the continuation of such prejudices (inessential to reflexology but common in its followers) as that individual differences are entirely products of environmental experience. It is hard to say whether the lack of awareness of personality research or the rigidity of clinging to paradigms from a simpler world has caused the greater obstacle to the necessary transition.

[4] The psychologist's impotence in attempting conclusions in these complex behavioral areas by bivariate methods alone could be illustrated in hundreds of published studies. Not because it is a severe case, but because it offers a simple illustration, we may take Schacter's (1959; Schachter & Singer, 1962) experiment comparing the suggestion pressure of small groups of American and Japanese subjects upon the constituent individuals making decisions on line lengths. The hypothesis was that individual Americans show to a greater degree the trait of being "group independent" (what in fact a personality student would recognize as Q_2 in L- and Q-data). By the single performance—change of line length judgments—which these experimenters thought fit to represent the broad trait (Q_2 as we now see) the hypothesis could not be demonstrated. The multivariate experimenter would have pointed out that it is impossible to equate a concept like "independence of mind" (or anxiety, or ego strength, or anything else) to any single variable like judging line length (except in the advanced stage of factorial research when particular variables have been demonstrated to have significant loadings

and even then one would need to depend on a whole battery to gain sufficient factor concept validity). This highly prevalent type of attempt to short cut logic in design concerns an ordinary trait (Q_2: self sufficiency versus group dependence) in this case, but much experiment now beginning on the far more complex trait structure we call the ego is likely to be vitiated if experimenters experiment on ego strength and "control" capacity with single bits of behavior. The results will mostly be null, or, if significant uninterpretable, or, if interpretable, conceptually complex. The classical learning theorist experimenting in this area would be far more effective if he acquired newer methodological perspectives deliberately employing the now available measures of unitary broad personality concepts, for example, in the O-A Battery.

One of the most vital areas of experiment for the immediate future is investigating the *CET* action of the ego in executing decisions. This cannot be carried to sufficiently definite conclusions by bivariate experiment on "internal" stimulus control. In so far as a complex design can be indicated in a footnote experiment will need to take instances where changes in the real world call for substantial change in the strength of an attitude or even its reversal. The aim is to study how the ego brings about a successful execution of this decision. To investigate this we need to determine the behavioral indices in the group for the attitude in its original adjusted and largely conflictless state, and then again after people have been compelled by circumstances to decide to, say, reverse the attitude. The comparison of the two factorings will not immediately yield the *evocation weights* exerted by the stimuli brought to bear by the ego, as the complexity of equations (6-4) and (6-18) show, and further calculations will be necessary. Comparison of two subgroups at the second factoring, one instructed on the best evocation stimuli and a control unistructed, as well as relation of success in reversing a_{hjk} to existing individual ego strength could be made in the same experiment. What one would basically like to know from experiments of this kind is whether cue action directly on the dynamic traits is the normal mode of operation, and how effective the tactic of rehearsing with a suitable given set of cues can be. If we do not rule out introspection it would also be interesting to see whether the learners in the first situation find themselves invoking cues referring entirely to the outcome of the response a_{hijk}, or whether humans already have generally learned by life experience to apply the cues to the "sensed" component dynamic traits.

[5] A reader of the manuscript has offered the criticism here that "control" by the ego smacks of the authoritarian and moral concept of the superego, and confuses superego with ego action and growth. If so, the point above (p. 377) needs to be repeated that the superego is only one of several dynamic traits—indeed including the whole spectrum of ergs—to the satisfaction of which the ego subsidiates its courses of action. At any rate, as regards the self-sentiment, we have tangible, significant loading values for attitudes of moral control in the superego, which then clearly repeat themselves (as typically in a cooperative factor) in the self-sentiment. But both the self-sentiment and the ego embrace control itself, the latter without any ethical overtones, as a desirable goal. On the teaching side, too, we must remember that parent and school teach physical and social reality as well as moral injunction. "Behave yourself" may mean "Don't get into difficulties," or "Don't upset so and so who is ill," or some similar simple ego purpose, rather than "Do nothing morally wrong." A child is punished for crossing the street dangerously in front of traffic, and countless other vicarious, more rapid and less painful acquisitions of reality tactics for the ego are inculcated vicariously by what we broadly call education. Such learning may still be without insight as when a child accepts parental disapproval of smoking without knowing about

lung cancer, but it is scarcely ordinary trial and error learning, and as research proceeds we may be startled by findings of the relative proportions of trial and error to educational learning of ego function being in certain areas decidedly different from our assumptions.

[6] The student of learning needs to be as alert to the problem of unitariness in functioning as the personality theorist. The begetting of a unitary nature for the ego structure presumably requires no more than the three principles of growth we studied for sentiments generally. It is important, therefore, to ask the student to study critically what reflexology has apparently claimed as an alternative explanation, namely, stimulus generalization. When closely examined this will be seen as another instance of improperly carrying microscopic to macroscopic, and of cognitive to dynamic to which we objected when complex courses of action are treated as reflexes. Stimulus generalization will properly account for a person taught to react to a blue light reacting to a bluish green light—until further conditioning produces stimulus discriminatory learning—but scarcely handles the development of the cognitive network in a sentiment.

What happens in the unitary growth of a sentiment, or when control acquired in one ego action shows some contribution to ego control generally, evidences, indeed, quite a different principle, and one needed also to illuminate discussion of certain important kinds of transfer of training. A habit of, say, writing out a problem fully before attempting to solve it does not transfer, say, from a mathematics course to a course in psychology either because (a) the person has not recognized it as the same behavior or (b) (without recognition) it has not been rewarded in the second situation as it was in the first. (The second (agency) sentiment learning principle is denied in (a), and the first and third in (b).) In the agency principle we suppose that CE (coexcitation) learning has entered cognitively to tie up this instance of control with that, so that the reward existing for the second flows into and is at the disposal of the first. In the common schedule and budding actions the behaviors become tied and of equal magnitude through two senses of common reward. Becoming knit by any of these three ways in a common reward system is quite different from mistaking one stimulus for another cognitively as in the stimulus generalization in reflex conditioning. Insofar as cognitive linkage of what were first considered two different stimuli, occurring in coexcitation in sentiment growth is concerned, we have pointed out earlier that in man it is rarely as a sensory stimuli experience. Rather the coexcitation fuses, for retrieval purposes, complex ideas brought together by reasoning, mainly involving Spearman's principle of noegenesis, that is relation and fundament eduction. This is indeed a far cry from stimulus generalization operating on simple sensory colors and tones.

[7] Roughly translated, "He liberates his mind most effectively [that is, acquires a new response in place of the old] who breaks the chains by force of will and is freed of further worry." In reference to this discussion, the emphasis in Bacon's observation is on the invoking of an existing dynamic structure of CET's rather than an arrangement of "environmental support systems."

[8] We are at this time very much in the dark as far as experiment is concerned on even the more basic parts of this action. How far, in the typical adult, does the "partly insightful" realization extend regarding the dynamic traits involved? That is to say, how far do people sense their b values in the specification for the given behavior? (Another way of asking this is, "How accurately does any man know his dynamic lattice?") And, if he has some insight on this, does he nevertheless apply all control cues to the action a_{hjk} or does he analytically ask about

and apply cues to the various dynamic traits, asking "How much will this satisfy my sentiment of self-regard? How much my need for security?" and so on?

[9] The use of the terms "derivative" and "secondary" we have settled on here is somewhat different from that of some other writers on emotion (for example, McDougall), but we believe more logical. (Secondary is used here for emotions such as awe, gratitude, or hate, which are mixtures of the primary (ergic) emotions (anger, lust, curiosity, fear), just as secondary colors are obtained as mixtures of three primaries. *Derived*, on the other hand, applies to the general mood states now studied, which derive from the events in the dynamics of the ergs created by encountering the APA situations. They are "derived" because they are no longer simple mixtures of primaries, as in secondaries, but something generically new.

[10] The argument that depression can be an effect preliminary to a relatively radical restructuring of dynamic trait attachments may indirectly be supported by the discovery of the success of electric shock therapy in this situation. It may be that its capacity to break up persisting memory and habit systems comes as an effective aid to the existing slower action of depression naturally proceeding. May's (1964) finding of a significant increase in the self-sentiment measure (on the MAT) following ECT suggests a move toward successful reintegration.

[11] As mentioned in connection with states, the rather high correlation arises not only between anxiety and depression, for which a good reason can be given, but also between all derived emotions, though sometimes positive and sometimes negative. The meaning of these high state interrelations has not yet been clarified, the alternatives being (a) that a broad *trait* expression (of proneness to anxiety, depression, regression, fatigue, low arousal, and so on) is mixed with the state measures, and (b) that one or possibly two second-order *state* factors subtend these primaries. Possible support for (a) exists in the T-data source trait UI(T)22 matched with Q-data second-order QIII, *cortertia-versus-pathemia*, which Jung perhaps saw as "feeling introversion." Central in this trait is a greater willingness, at the pathemic pole (UI(T)22−), to entertain various secondary states, like anxiety, elation, or depression, as opposed to the dry, cognitive, practical, cortically-alert condition of cortertia. It would be interesting to see if more fundamental emotional readjustments can occur in pathemic persons.

[12] It should be noted that the designation VIDA connotes a generality not specific to a psychological theory, yet excluding a substantial fraction of what texts often call psychological theories. Essentially it considers the world made of designatable objects (*ID*'s: people, stimuli, response patterns—or, outside psychology, cabbages and kings), the properties of any specimen of which can be represented as a vector (V) of quantities on discovered dimensions. Analysis (the A in VIDA) refers to finding the multivariate relations interconnecting the various vector values. To this point, though VIDA is a static model giving "predictions", instant in time, it is dealing with kinetic data. To handle the same concepts in motion it has to become a systems theory, S; hence VIDAS as a brief acronym for the essentials of the total model.

[13] It is desirable that we avoid some current confusions of the terms *kinetic* and *dynamic*. Physics has long presented to psychologists a reasonable model of tidiness of concepts. Kinetic, from the Greek for motion, has to do with change over time, per se. Dynamics has to do with the additional concept of force (and its derivatives of work done (energy) and power (energy per minute). In physics, mass is involved in the further inferences about dynamic phenomena from kinetic observations, but although psychology is scarcely yet prepared (see below) to

handle with logical precision the concept of energy, at least it seems pragmatically able to give to the word *dynamic* a meaning of force, or goal-directed motivation, as capacity to work, which is something more than mere process, or growth, or state sequence, which latter can be adequately described (if not explained) in purely kinetic terms.

[14] The best single expression for the present writer's personality theory development is *Structure-based Systems Theory*. The term "systems" is clear enough from this and the preceding chapter. There are, however, many possible types of personality systems models quite different in bases and forms from the present, as illustrated for example by Royce and Buss (1976). The specific character of the present system is given by the term *structure-based*, which connotes that it takes its foundation on confirmed multivariate structural findings about the functional unities in personality and society. That is to say, the system is not based on remote analogies or subjective concepts from the thin air of philosophy, but on the findings of factor analysis and the working concepts of the dynamic calculus. These are the "elements" that the systems theory can work with, and that require to be fitted into and developed by the systems superstructure.

The matter of a correct brief label is important because students can be sadly misled, as in instances of surveys of half a dozen "types" of personality theory in which this has been pigeonholed as a "trait theory." Regardless of justice to the present author's theoretical developments this is an absurd title for any scientific theory. All sciences have first to develop their taxonomies. Chemistry has its traits of compounds and elements; physics and astronomy measure traits of stars, spectra, and various electro-magnetic rays; biology became a science with the botanical trait system of Linnaeus and the zoological traits on which Darwin based his evolutionary analysis. An equally strange idea of what constitutes a scientific theory is apparent in those textbook writers who have presented this theory to students as a factor analytic, or correlational or quantitative type of personality theory. What would a student in chemistry, physiology, physics, engineering or modern medicine think of a text that divided theories into those that use arithmetic and those that do not?

[15] The appeal for checking of theoretical advance has been made in this book more to the small dedicated band of experimentalists than to the far larger group of applied psychologists. The obvious reason is that the latter are distracted by other objectives than scientific advances and that even those who are not are likely to operate without adequate objective measures. Nevertheless, in science generally, and certainly in the domain of personality structure in Volume 1 of this book, the "pay off" in the applied field can reflect back some extremely valuable checks on basis research. Those from industrial, social, educational and clinical experience with life criteria were extremely valuable in Volume 1.

We could afford no space in Volume 2 to show the implications of structured learning theory for the current debates—naturally largely in the clinical field—among Freudian, Jungian, behavior-therapeutic, and other positions. However, consistently with our position on the inadequacy of reflexology as covering basic learning theory, we shall maintain that behavior theory is not the answer to the scientist's prayer in the domain of psychotherapy that many suppose it to be. We infer this at the empirical level from the presentations of such writers as Eysenck and Rachman (1965), Eysenck and Wilson (1973), Rachman and Teasdale (1969) on the one hand, and Craighead and Kazdin (1976) and some of the more experimental psychoanalytic attacks on the other. The future to us seems to lie neither in moving into the cul-de-sac of a superficial reflexology, nor in falling backward into the pre-experimental subjectivities of psychoanalytic and related theories. Potent practice will come in a new direction, from structured learning theory. At least we must give thorough trial to the diagnostic and therapeutic developments that Birkett and the present writer (1979), and others, have aimed to show are the logical consequences from this theoretical model.

[16] Discussion of the relation of the specification equation factors to the systems theory model is likely to provoke also the question of the relation of the latter to the dynamic lattice, because certainly such relations must exist. The lattice is of course a statement about the subsidiation relations among the factors in the M, E, and D subsystems—the purely dynamic systems—in the VIDAS model. Consequently there will be some correspondence between its paths and the flow in channels among M, E, and D. When sentiment M_x subsidiates a certain amount to ergic goal E_y in the lattice, there will be some equivalent flow in Channels (8) and (9) in Figure 6-3, but lattice and systems models deal with two different modes of analysis that will not be parallel in a *simple* fashion.

[17] Wiener (1948a and b) dwells on another interesting aspect of such chains of communications, the calculation of amount of *error* (probability of failure) in the final outcome from the probabilities of error in the successive channels of the chain or network. In a factor approach this would be represented by the size of error factors, and we should expect these to load more the variables of a complex kind hypothetically having more successive channel links between P and A.

CHAPTER 7

THE SYSTEMS THEORY OF PERSONALITY, SOCIETY, AND CULTURE

7-1. Scope and central concerns of the social psychology of personality
7-2. Three panels of group description: Syntality, structure, and population
7-3. Synergy and the laws relating it to individual attitudes
7-4. The kinds of group organization with which the individual deals
7-5. The elements of group internal structure: Roles, ties, and communication networks
7-6. Systems action among subgroups: Supply-demand equilibria; social status movement
7-7. Personality-syntality transactions: Synergy isomorphisms, educational transmission, acculturation, and group conflict
7-8. Group learning and personality change
7-9. The individual in relation to other types of social change: Evolution and revolution
7-10. Systems theory, the life of groups, and the philosophy of science
7-11. Summary

7-1. Scope and Central Concerns of the Social Psychology of Personality

It would be hard to complain that the personality model developed here has failed to keep environmental determiners in constant focus and properly incorporate them. It has done so in the very definition of a trait, in recognizing the interaction of heredity and environment in the production of structure, and, above all, in structured learning theory. The social environment of personality, however, is important above all environments and deserves special analysis, and in the two-way sense that personality is shaped by the culture and in turn expresses itself in molding culture.

As we pass from individual to social psychology the major new concept to be focused is that of the group, and the main new technical areas we shall encounter are those of the social sciences—sociology, anthropology, economics, and political science. These sciences deal with the interaction of men, but since first they have to understand *a* man, social *psychology* is the center of the more restricted and specialized aspects of behavior with which they severally deal. One can logically assert that the study of exchange behavior in economics, of group control in political science, and of traditional habits in cultural anthropology will become sciences in proportion to their incorporation of psychology—of ergic dynamics, learning theory, the distributions and genetics of human ability and temperament, and much else that social psychology is now attempting to encompass.[1]

By the nature of its central position in the social sciences, social psychology is forced to abstract from the elaborate and specialized detail of, say, sociology and anthropology, which are initially descriptive sciences. There are millions of forms of groups, for example, the Mexican village family, the Samurai cults of Japan, that sociology and anthropology need to describe in detail. But social psychology has to abstract to the psychological dynamics of *any* group as such, and similarly with the laws governing status, role, population distributions and communication networks. This condensation the student must expect to find, in abstractions in the present chapter, in its dealing with person-group and group-group relations.

Our point of takeoff from the individual study followed so far is the recognition that the typical individual grows up among people, in structured groups formed by those people, and in a cultural matrix of ideas, attitudes, roles, ideals, and moral sanctions that is the product of history to that point. Our principal groups for consideration will be the family, the peer group, the professional organization, and the nation. These will involve us with such concepts as the dimensions of culture, the relational networks among people, group learning, and the relation of the individual to the flow of history.

Let us begin, therefore, by defining and investigating the essential group. From this we can pass on to communication networks, ties, status positions, roles, supply and demand equilibria, cultural transmission, and other vital constructs. A group may seem a simple idea, but its diverse meanings in mathematics, political science, biology, and psychology call for our proceeding early to a precise psychological usage. Mathematically and logically, a group can be made of all people definable by some common operation, for example, all born before January 1, 1970 or all wearing sandals. These are logical but psychologically superficial bases, and a more functional use can be seen in biology, where a group, say, a species, can be set aside by a degree of mutual resemblance compared to the degree of pattern resemblance to others judged "outside" (as in the operation of our taxonome program (Volume 1, p. 35), or, by some biologically vital single trait such as mutual fertility within the species. Finally in psychology there is a kind of group defined by the frequencies of relations in a communication network of people, and this important concept we shall attend to. But the most fundamental definition, valuable over most predictions in which the concept of psychological group is involved, is a dynamic one, as follows.

A psychological group is a set of people whose behaviors are so interrelated that most members contribute positively to satisfactions of other members, who stay in the group because of those satisfactions. This is a dynamic definition, distinguishing a group as a functional entity from a mere aggregate. It will be noted that it makes the group an *instrument* of the individual—a means to an initially individual end—in his search for ergic satisfactions. A group thus falls into the system of the individual's dynamic lattice. This subsidiation through the group as a subgoal to ergic satisfactions explains why individuals desire to belong to groups. Even an individual "coerced" into belonging is satisfying the need to escape punishment (deprivation of safety), and thus gets satisfaction in belonging. But in general the satisfactions are not uni-ergic, but rest on broad and diverse ergic goals—food seeking, self-assertion, sex, security, and so forth. We must glance at Hobbes' *Great Leviathan*, or suffer personally a few weeks as a Robinson Crusoe, to realize fully how little the isolated person can achieve relative to the satisfactions gained through group affiliations, even though he may have ambivalence toward such groups.

This definition of a group can quickly be operationalized in dynamic calculus terms both as regards the group and the individual. The individual's desire to belong to the group is an attitude "In these circumstances I want so much to belong to this group," and like any attitude defined by this paradigm (see Chapter 4) its magnitude and dynamic strength can be expressed by an ergic vector. As usual this vector says nothing, for example, about whether the individual is wholly conscious or partly unconscious of his or her gains and of the group identity (its boundaries), on the one hand, or whether each or all are conscious of who constitutes the group membership and what the group objectives are. A dog is a member of the family group, held by certain satisfactions, but might be a little vague as to what they are or whether Aunt Jemima belongs. (Parenthetically, this illustrates that in the symbiotic dynamics of the group the members may even be of different species.) On this essential, dynamic, symbiotic basis, further properties such as different degrees of awareness of membership, or conscious loyalty to a named group; or the nature of particular satisfactions; or roles and duties, can be erected. However, in fact, most groups we deal with here will have higher degrees of awareness than sponges or a flock of sheep, as well as a role structure in the form of organized leadership.

Stripped to essentials—and everything in a chapter-length account of so vast a field must be so stripped to essentials—social psychology deals with the relations (1) of individuals to individuals; (2) between individuals and groups; and (3) between groups and groups. We shall be least concerned with the last—the area of political science—though, as we shall see the conflicts and liaisons of groups have unavoidable counterparts in the breasts of individuals tied by sentiments to those groups.

Much "beating about the bush" that occurs in social psychology would be eliminated if we recognized methodologically at the outset that social psychology faces essentially the same tasks as we have faced in individual psychology, namely (1) to *describe* any group initially, in static, instantaneous cross-section (that is, at a given moment) by determining the most meaningful attributes (that is, unitary trait dimensions) for a vector quantification; (2) to discover the genetic and learning sources that account for the character of the group at a given moment; (3) to understand the processes of change, and the flow of interaction, which here are called *history*. And finally, raising the technical demands still more, it has (4) to deal with relative motion—encompassing the interaction of a life-course-developing individual with a historically changing society. Clearly, if we are to cover models for these essentials systematically, we shall have little time to linger esthetically over colorful concrete illustrations.

7-2. Three Panels of Group Description: Syntality, Structure, and Population

Bewildering and endless as the topics in the journals of sociology, social anthropology, and social psychology may appear, they yet turn on comparatively few basic concepts. One of them, if a wise methodology is followed, is the character, description, and therefore measurement, of any particular group. This is a necessary prelude to all the others. The necessity of such measurement is part of the scientific demand for a taxonomy of groups. And the history of personality research unfortunately repeats itself here by the same slowness of social psychologists to develop methodology and data for quantitatively defining a given group at a given moment.

A taxonomy of groups operating with adequate group dimensions needs to begin with an array of variables based on the same naturalistic observation of groups as was applied to individuals in mapping the *personality sphere*. If we are going to speak meaning-fully and with a practicable degree of economy of, say, the differences among 100 football teams, it is no use talking any longer in terms applicable only to behavior of individuals, nor must we when truly looking at the group, lose ourselves in 100,000 variables possibly applicable to groups. We must look at a new field of significant, functionally unitary emergent behaviors, such as enthusiastic teams, quarrelsome teams, capable teams, of higher and lower integration, teams of steady and unsteady morale, and so on. And, if teams thus possess any characteristics at all, the only rational and economical way to begin to map them is to factor a very *comprehensively* surveyed population of group behaviors. Because groups have traits, which appear in patterns of various specific behaviors, as all obser-vation—from national history to betting on football teams—proves that they do, we may hope ultimately to measure independent unitary meaningful traits of groups just as we have succeeded in doing with individuals.

There are, however, two facts about groups that give a different emphasis in method relative to personality factoring.

1. *Whereas individual humanity shows at most some limited splintering into subtypes—classes, sexes, clinical types, occupational types—the subtypes of groups are enormously diverse, for example, in size, purpose, and structure.* We have to recognize in the taxonomy of groups that what we have called (Chapter 7, Volume 1) the inter-type factor dimensions are much more varied and prominent than the intratype dimensions, by comparison with their roles in people. For example, as to group size, there are two-person groups, as in tennis or marriage, 11- and 15-person groups as in football, and groups peopled by many millions as in nations. As to structures and goals, there are commercial groups such as banks; groups bound by sentiments and ideals, such as churches; recreational groups, universities and so forth. Each and every one of these has be be treated as a distinct species, with its own within-type dimensions.

2. *Groups have intergroup connections of an entirely new kind for which there is no parallel in interpersonal relations. This is most obvious in that they can overlap and share members.* It is true that there are certain *ultimate* groups, like married couples, religious communities, and nations, in regard to which a person may, like the Vicar of Bray or John Paul Jones, belong to two or more in succession but may not without serious trouble belong to two at the same time. But the majority of groups, which we may call nonultimate groups, *do* have membership overlap. One and the same person belongs to a

sailing club, a university, a family, a psychological society, a religion, and a country. This produces special laws of dynamic interrelations unknown in ultimate-membership, discrete, non-overlapping groups or in interacting but independent human personalities.

The term *syntality*, suggested some time ago for the analogue in groups to *personality* in an individual, seems to have been a widely adopted as well as a useful concept for referring to the characteristics of a group. Within the whole gamut of traits that define a syntality, separation of some under the term *synergy* has been useful for referring to the group's purely *dynamic strength* dimensions (interests, needs, and so forth). In harking back to personality study we note, curiously, that it lacks any parallel special term for the area covering the E and M factors in the total personality, and there we speak rather clumsily of "the dynamic aspects of a personality.")

Progress in determining group syntality dimensions has been regrettably slow since its inception in 1950, but fortunately it has been strategically advanced by concentrating on two diverse representative levels in group size and structure, namely, small, "neonate" groups and the ancient cultures of nations. Less systematic work has also been done on families and other special groups.

With reference to groups, neonate means newborn; where people who have never met before are put together to perform as a group for the first time. The rules necessary to make such a new set into a group are such that an individual's reward can come only through the group performance. Of course the groups are not entirely "newborn", inasmuch as the members of a neonate group unavoidably carry with them their personal histories containing the traditions of the larger society to which they have belonged. But at least it is true that the new group of, say, 10 persons, starts with no explicit traditions, values, or roles defined as its own, while meeting the basic requirement of the group being an instrument of reward to all. Work by Borgatta and Cottrell (1956); Cattell, Saunders, and Stice (1953); Cattell and Stice (1953); Cattell and Wispe (1948); Gibb (1949); Haythorne (1953); Hemphill and Weste (1950); Roby (1957); and Stogdill (1950, 1952) has established, in the last generation, many basic findings in regard to the taxonomy of these and other kinds of small groups. But it is experimentally and statistically exacting work, which has consequently not moved so rapidly since the post-World War II explosion of interest in group dynamics. As empirical support for this theoretical concept of definable *group* "source traits," however, the work on neonate groups did establish (1) that groups, after an initial "shaking down" period, are reliably persistent in their characteristics, (2) that factor analytically the dimensions of small group behavior are fairly numerous—about a dozen to twenty, as in personality, (3) that the factors make good social psychological sense, (4) that they have statistically significant relations to the mean personality scores of the members and to size, structure, leadership rules, and so on. Two examples must suffice, as given in Table 7-1, and because of the wide interest in group morale the traits that would be generally considered as morale are taken for illustration.

Very stable group dimension patterns have also been found in studies by Cattell, Breul, and Hartman (1952); Cattell (1950); Gibb (1956); Rummell (1963, 1972); Cattell, Graham, and Woliver (1978) and others, for 80 to 120 nations on a wide spectrum of economic, social, vital, demographic, and psychological variables, as shown in Table 7-2.

The mixture of syntality and population character variables (which are regarded as theoretically distinct in equation 7-1) appearing in these findings illustrates one of the research dilemmas encountered: whether to work *entirely* with *group action* variables or include *population* (individuals averaged) behaviors, too, on the assumption that they must be mutually dependent. The clearer analysis calls for syntality concepts to be based entirely on variables that represent the *actions of the group as a group*, through its organized government channels. Thus number of treaties negotiated or the passing of a welfare law would be group action, whereas average stature, or IQ, or family size would be population characteristics. However, on closer consideration, such "population characteristics" as length of time spent in school or typhoid fever cases per 100,000 turn out to be dependent in part on group organization, group political values, and so on. The basic theorem that has been propounded on this (Cattell, 1950) is that syntality factor scores are emergents from the given characteristics of the population, P, and the role structure and cultural habits of the group, R, thus:

$$S = f(RP) \tag{7-1}$$

This f (for "function of") admittedly holds half of social psychology hidden—indeed as yet unknown—within its simple symbol. But it states clearly that syntality (S) is a function both of the characters of the people (P) *apart from their belonging to that group*, and of the structure (R) of the group, which covers mode of government, traditions, subgroup structure, and roles. In the case of our experimental work with neonate groups the P values separated out clearly, as the persons were measured *before* they entered the groups. But in living, traditional groups obtaining a P vector that is

TABLE 7-1. Factors Illustrating Dimensions of Small Neonate Groups

Primary Morale Dimensions; Good Leadership[a]

	Session 1	Session 2	Session 3
High satisfaction with leader[b]		82	78
High group unity[b]	82	55	81
High influences of formal leader[b]		60	70
High morale following dynamometer[b,c]		29	54
High feeling of freedom to participate[b]	-35	-29	-43
High degree of interdependence[d]	30	10	-02
Construction: Most planning done for early trial	03	-49	07
Small number of negative effectors[b]	02	-03	-52
Low "population" mean on affectothymia (A)[e]	-04	-42	-12

[a]The three columns of factor loadings on the right are given as they stand, for three experiments, without averaging, to show the degree of consistency reached. Note, however, that this consistency includes some 30 or 40 other variables being consistently zero (nonsignificant) on this pattern across the three experiments, but not shown here.
[b]These are mean values of ratings over several group task performances made by all members of the group.
[c]A tug of war on an unpleasantly electrified rope—a situation which tended to break down morale and cause drop-outs.
[d]Observer's ratings.
[e]Meaning that members are by nature unsentimental, forthright, self-sufficient, tending to aloofness.

experimentally independent of S and R is impossible because the syntality has had time to mold the personality. In neonate groups, however, statistically significant relations were found between the performances of a group—its syntality—and the average level of its members, a population value, on such personality measures as ego strength, surgency, superego strength, intelligence, and so forth. These relations must have been due to the personalities affecting the syntality characteristics of the group, not the converse. As for R—structure—if we have two groups each of three members, both groups averaging an IQ of 90, but where one group has three persons with IQ's of 90 and the other has two 80's and one 110, it is probable that if the last member is chosen leader the structural effect will cause the syntality performances of the second group to be decidedly better than the first. Structure, in terms of leadership forms, class strata and communication networks is probably highly important in accounting for syntality.

Thus, to summarize, *three* panels of observation and measurement are needed in group behavior research: the actions of the group as a group, defining its *syntality* (including synergy); the way in

TABLE 7-1. *(continued)*

Second Morale Dimension; Congeniality, Company, or Mutual Respect in Membership[a]

	Session 1	Session 2	Session 3
High degree of group organization[b]	42	61	66
High degree of leadership[b]	68	52	73
High degree of interdependence[b]	31	53	58
High degree of we-feeling[b]	50	66	51
High orderliness of procedure[b]	53	46	49
High mean on intelligence *(B)*	24	31	46
Much explicit concern with procedure[b]	25	56	68
Low group mean personality test measure on Protension *(L)*[c]	-85	-05	-13
Low degree of frustration[b]	-53	01	-04
High strength of motivation[b]	46	71	33
High freedom of group atmosphere[b]	08	48	04
Dynamometer: High level of non-shock pull	40	64	
High group mean personality test measure on emotional stability *(C)*[d]	47	23	-06

[a]The three columns of factor loadings on the right are given as they stand, for three experiments, without averaging to show the degree of consistency reached, Note, however, that this consistency includes some 30 to 40 other variables being consistently zero (non-significant) on this pattern across the three experiments.
[b]These are ratings across divers task situations averages for a set of observers behind a one-way screen taking notes on the group oerformances.
[c]In popular psychiatric terms this means that the individuals in the group are possessed of less than average paranoid, jealous, suspicious tendencies; a contribution to morale.
[d]This means that groups composed of individuals of higher than average emotional stability (*C*, Ego strength) develop better morale than those inherently, emotionally unstable and neurotic. Note also the higher average intelligence.

which people habitually interact—its *structure*; and the average make-up of the individual people in the group—its *population characteristics.*[2]

At this point we shall make no serious attempt at deep interpretation of dimensions of syntality given for neonates and nations above, but a brief indication of some discovered R and P connections may be given. Although we shall argue in the next section the first factor in Table 7-1 is largely of structural origin, yet it *is* related to the mean population score, being lower for groups with higher neuroticism scores and certain introvert traits. At the level of national groups Lynn (1976, 1978) gives several instances showing syntality-population correlation, as also do Cattell (1949), Cattell, Graham, and Woliver (1978), and Cattell and Woliver (In press). The last

TABLE 7-2. Factors Illustrating Syntality Dimensions of National Groups
National Groups

The Cultural Pressure Dimension of Syntality in Modern Nations[a]

Variable

High ratio of tertiary to primary occupations
High frequency of political clashes with other countries
High frequency of cities over 20,000 (per 1,000,000 inhabitants)
High number of Nobel prizes in science, literature, peace (per 1,000,000 inhabitants)
High frequency of participants in wars (1837-1937)
High frequency of treaties and negotiations with other countries
High expansiveness (gain in area and resources)
Many ministries maintained by government
High creativity in science and philosophy
(High emotional complexity of life)
High musical creativity
High death rate from suicide
High incidence of mental disease (especially schizophrenia)
High horsepower available per worker
High percentage of population in urban areas
High cancer death rate
High divorce rate
More severe industrial depression in world depression
High total foreign trade per capita
Numerous patents for inventions per capita
Higher number of women employed out of home
More riots
Lower illegitimate birth rate

---

[a]Variables are here arranged in declining order of loading, averaged over two or more
researches, but for actual numerical loadings the original researches must be consulted.
Thus the first listed variables are more closely connected with the action or genesis of
cultural pressure than the last.

found 6 correlations between national population means on the 16
PF and national syntality measures significant at the $P < .01$ level.
The "intelligent affluence" dimension of syntality was related to
high population means on polite, restrained, somewhat introverted
and little—environmentally—stressed personality; the syntality
dimension labelled "careless, unintegrated culture" was positively
correlated with exvia, surgency and dominance in the population,
and the syntality dimension described as political-cultural alertness
relates to higher population means on dominance (E), affectia (A),
and high superego (G). There are also less definite grounds (Lynn,
1978; Cattell and Woliver, in press) for the hypothesis that the
affluence factor in nations is related to the intelligence level of the

TABLE 7-2. *(continued)*

The Intelligent Affluence Dimension of Syntality[a]

Loading	Variable
(0.50)[b]	(High level of technological skill)
−0.73	Low death rate from tuberculosis (tuberculosis a disease of poverty)
0.70	Large gross area (contribution of large trade area)
0.67	High expenditure of tourists abroad
0.55	High real standard of living (judged by expenditures)
0.51	High real income per head
0.42	High expenditure (all sources) on education (high level of intelligence)
0.40	High musical creativity (index of cultural interest)
	(More books read per person per year)
0.37	High sugar consumption per head (index of luxury expenditures)
−0.36	Low degree of government censorship of the press (liberality of education)
−0.27	Low suicide rate
−0.25	Low death rate
0.23	High ratio of exports to imports

[a]Variables are here arranged in declining order of loading, averaged over two or more researches. Thus the first listed variables are more closely connected with the action or genesis of intelligent affluence than the last.
[b]Estimate from separate study.

population, as a pristine variable—though still more to its educational level.

The researches so far have only reached the level of exploring correlations, and equation (7-1) remains still bare of more precise development. Meanwhile there is no doubt that in groups as in individuals we must ultimately come to a systems model. At a gross level the subsystems are the population characteristics and the social structures by which the syntality of the group, in its interactions with other groups, feeds back modifying influence. But even studies of such a simple three fold system are for the future, though Rummel's recent work (1975) on field theory and national dimensions stimulates promising ideas for a systems analysis.

Although equation (7-1) proposes in neonate groups set up experimentally as described above to recognize dependencies only in one direction—to derive the syntality from the structure and from the average personalities of the group members—we recognize that in general the system has two-way dependencies. In short, the mathematical relations found to predict any one panel from the other two represent, in general, two-way causal action. For example, in the national culture dimension that we have called *cultural pressure*

(Table 7-2), the syntality shows loadings on more international action, by treaties, trade, and war; the structure shows a higher ratio of tertiary to primary occupations; and the adjustive personality population mean shows more creativity, more neurosis, lower self sentiment (Q_3), and more suicides. Here we seem to have a dimension of rather rapidly and stressfully enforced adaptation to culture complexities, notable in rapid urbanization, which produces conflict, anxiety, damage to the self sentiment but also, as in the APA chart, sublimation of ergic frustrations into higher cultural creativity, along with the direct expression of frustration in violence, revolt, and war.

It is necessary to stress this two-way causality among S, R, and P because psychologists (educational and clinical in particular) have been almost exclusively viewing connections in terms of what society does to the individual, omitting what the individual does to society. This was perhaps inevitable in Freudian psychology, where all the data comes to the observer from the individual. Freud heard about the individual's unfortunate parental repression and Margaret Mead dealt with cultures that necessarily preceded, by decades or centuries, the appearance of the individual. Nevertheless even there we see instances (Caesar, Christ, Napoleon, Hitler, Stalin, and also some leading physical scientists) where an individual, or small group, powerfully changes society for better or worse. But in our experimental neonate groups we were able definitely to show that in regard to society the clinical view of the neurotic or the criminal as the victim, is very one sided; for the more neurotics we added to a group the poorer became its morale and its performance on various dimensions of syntality!

7-3. Synergy and the Laws Relating It to Individual Attitudes

The synergy dimensions of the total syntality are those that are concerned with what is roughly called psychological energy and expressed in interest and motivation. We shall study this next both because it is an important aspect of syntality and because it is one of the first areas in which the relations of groups to individuals can, at least theoretically, be expressed in some precise and rational propositions. We shall continue, as stated in the last chapter, to treat the concept of psychological energy gingerly, as something that cannot yet be operationally defined to everyone's satisfaction, yet is too useful in general prediction to be abandoned. We proposed earlier that the energy in a given dynamic system, such as an attitude, is the amount of work the individual will do to obtain the gratifications habitually reached by that course of action. Under certain economic conditions, and making allowance for the amount of money the individual has, that energy can probably be equated to what the individual would be prepared to spend, if money were made the only way to achieve the given satisfaction. Here we encounter one of several links in this chapter where transactions can begin between social psychology and economics.

It is a matter of common observation (assuming we take the same N individuals simultaneously belonging to g groups) that the psychological investment of interest and energy available to different societies varies enormously. Most men would take disbarment from their tennis club with little upset, their excommunication from their church with more, and the breakup of their family relations with a sense of frustration and anguish requiring major efforts at adjustment. Naturally these group investments—synergy vectors, as we shall presently define them—alter with culture and time. One cannot, in historical comparisons, treat them as permanent values for given groups. The emperor came in sackcloth to Canossa because in medieval Europe the church community had greater investment from the population generally than did the national units. But when Napoleon's attacks stimulated the rise of modern national mass affiliations he was able to take the crown out of the hands of the Pope and crown himself.

The individual's attitude strength in the attitude course: "In these circumstances I want to belong to this group," can represent as a vector the amount and kind of satisfaction he obtains and therefore the energy he is prepared to donate. Actually this "attitude" is properly a sentiment (Chapter 4), for although it can be condensed into the above it covers all the attitude actions and satisfactions the individual gets through *all the attitude courses of action he enjoys because of the group's existence.* That satisfaction quantity and its quality can be represented in terms of our usual dynamic specification equation as in (7-2). This equation takes from the usual four terms only the two in which E is the ultimate product, and it sums over p ergs and q sentiments:

$$I_{gi} = \sum^{x=p} v_{gx} s_{gx} E_{xi} + \sum^{y=q} \sum^{x=p} v_{gy} M_{yi} E_{xi} \tag{7-2}$$

The interest strength, I, of individual i here has a g subscript for "group interest."

The reader should be alerted, from this point on, to a policy in setting out these equations that may best be designated schematic, and that obviously has been applied to some degree in some earlier equations. The most schematic use, as in (7-1) above, hides all the machinery in an "*f*"—"function of." But in other cases we are in command of the relations that go into the equation and omit them as "understood," as when we omit ability and personality terms from (7-2), or we omit understood subscripts to avoid cluttering the equation. Since in this chapter we have to cover and condense events on the broader stage of sociology, economics and history, resort to schematic equation forms must be more frequent. As any student of mathematical statistics realizes, all kinds of particular conditions and explicit assumptions—for example on distributions, scoring units, and so forth—are necessary to any precise and literal use of a particular formula. But the discussion of these even for one formula could take a whole section. For example, in (7-3) we propose to sum certain psychological values assigned to individuals across a group of people instead of within one individual. We alert the reader to the fact that this summation sign has a new sense, but we have no space to develop a branch of psychometry to handle the cross-person scale-unit problems. Psychologists habitually work out mean IQ's; but we may be on less accepted ground when we add and average interest strength units.

To proceed: if we accept (7-2) as a statement of any one individual's satisfaction in, and his corresponding energy contribution to, his group, *g*, *if we sum these attitude specifications for all people belonging to the group, we have a measure of the total energy of the group:* that is, of the energy it can call on for its purposes as a group. This may be called *synergy law No. 1*, expressed in the equation:

$$S_{eg} = \sum^{i=N} \sum^{e=p} v_{ge}s_{ge}E_{ei} + \sum^{i=N} \sum^{m=q} \sum^{x=p} v_{gm}s_{gm}M_{mi}E_{xi} \qquad (7\text{-}3)$$

Here S_{eg} is the synergy of group *g*. This contains the unusual feature of summing across people (N) as well as across different ergs (p) and sentiments (q). Note that the equation is consistent with the earlier statement that the satisfactions obtained by *different individuals* belonging to one and the *same* group may be qualitatively and quantitatively different. The addition also accepts that the ergic tensions of people are different and takes the loading ($b = vs$) as the measure of how much those ergic tensions operate. We could divide (7-3) by N and get a *characteristic* (mean) member's satisfaction (and energy contribution) to the given group. Equation (7-3) is thus saying (among more recondite things) that, other things being equal, the synergy of a group will be greater with more members, with larger loadings on E's and M's per person and, indeed, with larger E and M scores per person, which different populations, e.g. by age, might have. It also states that there exists a characteristic ergic composition (a vector) describing the synergy—the average "emotional" services it renders—for society. Thus one group, as is visible from its synergy vector, satisfies needs for security (an insurance company), another for sex, gregariousness, security (the family), another self-assertion (an honor society), and so on. For some purposes we may not want the spectrum of the full vector, in which case we can condense it from a vector to a scalar quantity (calling it I_{gi} instead of S_{eg}). One important operational link of social psychology to economics may lie in the mutual exchange rates among ergic satisfactions that go on through money. If a man will pay \$10 for so much security, so much food, so much satisfaction of vanity (self-assertion) then we have a ready-made scale for the conversion of different ergic satisfactions, and thus for adding the ergic tensions in a specification equation to a single scalar quantity. The proposal admittedly quickly becomes entangled in market questions of scarcity and marginal utility, but these relate price realistically to the average person's deprivation level, which enters appropriately into the evaluation of ergic tensions. These are extraneous features to be removed from the relations, but, basically, economics and the dynamic calculus blend.

If any difficulties that arise in the addition of ergic tension values across people can be psychometrically handled, as seems probable, then the calculation of the total synergy of a group as in (7-3) is a realistic and basically important step in group dynamics. The next step—the evaluation of the ergic quality of that satisfaction as a vector of ergic and sentiment numbers—opens the door to a remarkable array of possible calculations.

At a common sense level one can see that these vectors will be very different for different groups. To a husband and wife the family offers sexual and parental protective ergic stimuli and satisfactions not provided or providable by, say, a football team or a book club. This points out to us from a different angle our basic proposition that the existence of a given group is an *instrument* for the satisfaction of its members, and that the latter cease to belong when those satisfactions fall to zero. However, we must not fall into the error of supposing that this typical vector of the group is the same for all members. To anticipate the discussion below on roles, let us note that though there will be a *characteristic* vector profile of total synergy for each group, and though the majority of members may approach the central tendency, there can be considerable variation among the vectors of "I want to belong" of different people, according to their role positions. The treasurer of a football club may know nothing of the pleasure of taking the ball successfully down the field, and the children in a family draw ergically very different satisfactions from the family's instrumentality than those obtained by their parents. Not only do individuals tie their interests to a given group in very different styles, but the patterns are seen in a different functional setting by the group and by its members. A person and a group are alike organisms, seeking to survive. Hobbes, Rousseau, and many more modern writers (Ardrey is a valuable unacademic contributor) have considered this relation in the light of a "social contract," and lawyers have codified it, but hitherto there has been little analysis of it in a precise group dynamics model. From the individual's standpoint it is a matter of shopping around to find a collection of groups the ergic vectors of belonging to which will sum to round out the needs of his adjustment. From the converse standpoint of the survival of a group it is vital that enough human interest, of the right kind, be invested in it. The contracts, which represent the compromise between the group's requirements and those of individuals, aim to satisfy both to a viable extent.

Since the sum total of members' *belonging attitudes*—the satisfactions habitually gathered from their activities in the group—gives the limits of the synergy that the group can call upon, a number of lawful relations exist in the model that can be empirically tested and offer new domains of prediction. They concern all three possible relational systems: individuals to groups; individuals to individuals, and groups to group. First let us consider the proposition that in a *population of N individuals belonging to z organizations the sum total of the individuals' energies (assuming all are expressed in some way through groups) must equal the sum of the synergies of the z groups.* The assumption in this statement, unfortunately for simplicity, is not completely correct. People invest their interests also in inanimate objects for example a house, or objects incorporated in no groups, for example a horse. Our initial proposition speaks of a closed system that is not a closed system and to make it correct let us close it with a term W to represent the total of all non-social interests. It is probable that when psychologists get to quantifying the world of interests they will be surprised how little the amount of interest is that falls outside any group connection. A man's car, for example, has investments that spring from his job, his family, his insurance company, and so on. Consequently, W may be relatively small and, small or large, we can hold it constant in the following propositions.

This second law of synergy derives first from equation (7-4), stating that this constant total, T_e, holds initially erg by erg (and sentiment by sentiment, for T_m)—assuming that transmutation of ergic satisfaction (from one erg to another) is impossible. The total ergic energy T_{eN} of N people belonging to z groups will be (if we illustrate by one erg and one sentiment):

$$T_{eN} = \sum_{}^{g=z} \sum_{}^{i=N} v_{gx} s_{gx} E_{xi} + \sum_{}^{g=z} \sum_{}^{i=N} v_{gy} s_{gy} M_{yi} E_{xi} + W \qquad (7\text{-}4)$$

(W could also be expressed in vector form but we have no need to do so). If we now consider this energy from the standpoint of groups we can write an expression (7-5) for the *total* synergy of z groups, N persons, over all p ergs, and q sentiments. This assumes the ergic tensions of different ergs can be added, as indeed is done in any specification equation. By the above proposition $T_{eN} - W$ will equal the total of group synergies, which can be broken down:

$$T_{eN} - W = \sum_{}^{g=z} S_{eg} = \sum_{}^{g=z} \sum_{}^{x=p} \sum_{}^{i=N} v_{gx} s_{gx} E_{xi}$$
$$+ \sum_{}^{g=z} \sum_{}^{y=q} \sum_{}^{i=N} \sum_{}^{x=p} v_{gy} s_{gy} M_{yi} E_{xi} \qquad (7\text{-}5)$$

where S_{eg} is synergy and E and M have the usual meanings. It is conceivable on further research that the activation values for sentiments should be included as such, but in an introductory statement we have couched the whole proposition in terms of ergic tension as energy. This includes the M values, of course, to the extent that they arouse the E values in the ME term.

Thus we have a true systems theory statement of the principles of adjustments among groups: that the totality of group synergies must satisfy the totality of individually stimulated need, at least erg by erg as in (7-4). The total need of erg E_x can be distributed in any way across the groups that are instrumental to satisfaction, but for the totality of groups the ergic tension must reach a constant, at least to the extent that the life situation maintains a constant stimulation of the erg in the general population. From the viewpoint of economics, the important point is that this puts a fixed value, T_{eN} to the total ergic resources—the energy or economic output—of the total society, for a given population (production methods being constant). This says that because every individual belongs to several groups, if we take a universe of g groups known to N individuals (and no others), then it follows that the sum of all synergies of the g groups (as shown in expression 7-5) will add to the same total as that of the energies of all N individuals. Further, if we assume that the energy of any erg is locked within itself, that is, that no amount of extra food satisfaction can make up for a lack, of say, sex or security. then not only the total energy (a scalar) but the actual *pattern* of the vector of sums of group synergies must be identical with that of the vector pattern of the sum of individual ergic energies. Actually this *principle of nontransmutation* of ergic reactivity may, according to clinical observation, not hold entirely, but it probably holds nearly enough for most purposes. If it does, then (7-5), the second law of synergy, must be expressed as a vector, not a scalar sum, and might be renamed the *law of vector conservation of total group synergy*.

As a first corollary on the above, it follows that if any one group alters the pattern of synergy to which it gives stimulation and satisfaction then some other group (or groups) must alter its vector in compensating fashion. This is concretely seen most clearly in the present generation by the change in the synergy functions of the family brought about by the rise of groups outside the family offering services previously provided by the family. The general principles in (7-4) and (7-5) thus lead to a second statement (law or corollary) that a change in the demands and satisfactions of one society, caused mainly perhaps by events internal to the group, tends to require readjustment of the synergies of other societies.

It follows also from the above that the ergic quality of the total synergy that goes into groups must bear a definite relationship to the largely biological fixed ergic needs of the population as a whole. There is a certain quota of needs of hunger, security, sex, and other innate ergs—under fixed situational stimulation—that must be met by the aggregate of groups (societies). This is illustrated by the beautiful mathematical treatment of aggression by Richardson (1960) showing that, in times of war, other forms of pugnacity—civil murders and suicides (aggression against the self)—decline systematically. Evidence along the same lines, though with less precision of data analysis, exists in our theory about the cultural pressure dimension, where the ergic investment seems to sublimate into cultural productivity in proportion to the degree of frustration.

It has been suggested above that the calculations of synergy will prove to be one of the important bridges by which economics will find its way back to being a branch of social psychology. Economics is the branch of social psychology that is largely concerned with exchange behavior (the market), the value judgements that follow therefrom, and the interaction of resulting payments for a product and of rewards for producing it. The question of marginal utility, for example, which enters so centrally into prices, is a matter of calculating need strengths and therefore rests on our understanding of ergs and sentiments and the decision and conflict calculations in Chapter 5. The particular decision in economics is to buy or not to buy.

Further aspects of synergy in relation to the individual "belonging" attitudes will be brought out with regard to types of group and forms of satisfaction, in Sections 7-4 and 7-5.

7-4. The Kinds of Group Organization with Which the Individual Deals

Because this chapter deals with personality in relation to the group, the nature of groups as such must be still further pursued if that relation is to be correctly handled. We cannot, for example, pursue calculations on syntality and synergy until we know the species of a group; for each set of syntality dimensions is peculiar to a given species of groups.

The immense variety of groups can itself be focused, like that of individuals, in terms of either dimensions or types. The reader in areas of sociology, economics, and cultural anthropology that deal with groups will, unfortunately, find that the same confusion about types and traits—such as we have sought to dispel in personality—also exists abundantly in this domain. In short, students have come to grief in the perennial confusion of variables, dimensions, and types. If there is any lack of methodological perspective here the student should return to Chapter 1, Volume I. Nevertheless, as to species, despite the advance in method, one still has to depend on an arbitrariness in the lists of types of group appearing in sociological textbooks. There happens to be one exception which can be briefly described as an illustration of the truly objective allocation of instances to type classes, by measured profiles and the taxonome program. This concerns the grouping of modern nations by their syntality dimensions. On syntality score profiles on data over the first part of this century the taxonome program grouped 80 nations (Cattell, 1950, 1968) into some 12 species types. (This has recently been repeated by Cattell, Woliver, & Graham, in press, on 1970 data.) A dozen syntality dimensions were initially employed, but Table 7-3 shows the central tendency of some discovered types on the more widely known 6 of these.

It is striking that the groupings coincide quite well with Toynbee's (1947) "civilizations" based on the more intuitive and developmental approach of a leading historian. There is also good general agreement of the dimensions and profiles with Rummel (1972). With this firmness of quantified patterns we may feel the stage is set for some effective theorizing on the dynamics which yield such types.

Although this demonstrates that the same basic analytical methods are needed, and can be effective, in typing groups as in reaching an individual descriptive taxonomy, provided an objective basis is used (as in the Taxonome program), the task is nevertheless more complex in groups, for a variety of reasons. For instance, it has

TABLE 7-3. Objectively Located Types of National Culture

Cultural Dimensions, Measured as Factors

Factor 1: Size
Factor 2: Cultural pressure versus direct ergic expression
Factor 3: Enlightened affluence versus narrow poverty
Factor 4: Conservative patriarchal solidarity versus ferment of release
Factor 5: Emancipated urban rationalism versus unsophisticated stability
Factor 6: Thoughtful industriousness versus emotionality
Factor 7: Vigorous, self-willed order versus unadapted perseveration
Factor *8: Bourgeois Philistinism versus reckless bohemianism
Factor 9: Residual or peaceful progressiveness
Factor 10: Fastidiousness versus forcefulness
Factor 11: Buddhism-Mongolism
Factor 12: Poor cultural integration and morale versus good internal morality

Patterns Found by Taxonome Program for Numbers 1, 2, 3, 4, 7, and 12 above;
Individual Profiles on Six Cultural Dimensions

High magnitude	High cultural pressure	High affluence	High conservative patriarchalism	High order and control	High cultural integration and morale
					Mean for all countries
Low magnitude	Low cultural pressure	Low affluence	Low conservative patriarchalism	Low order and control	Low cultural integration and morale

TYPE 1
KEY: Australia_ _ _ _Britain.........U.S.A._____

High magnitude	High cultural pressure	High affluence	High conservative patriarchalism	High order and control	High cultural integration and morale
					Mean for all countries
Low magnitude	Low cultural pressure	Low affluence	Low conservative patriarchalism	Low order and control	Low cultural integration and morale

TYPE 2
KEY: China_____India...........Liberia _ _ _ _

TABLE 7-3. *(continued)*

Contrast of Central Tendencies in Three Culture Patterns[a]

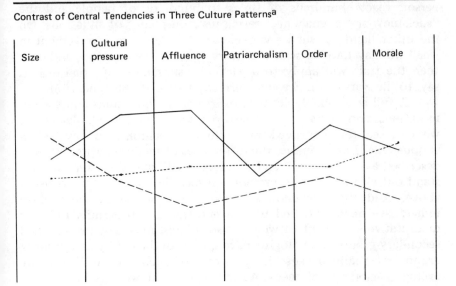

Size	Cultural pressure	Affluence	Patriarchalism	Order	Morale

KEY: _____ The American-British-Australian Pattern

_ _ _ _ _ _ The China-India-Liberia Pattern

.... The Russia-Argentina-Arabia Pattern

[a]The vertical scale is in standard score units for each factor, but is not set out numerically.

already been pointed out that groups extend on many variables for which there is no equivalent or analogue in individuals. Thus an important variable (but possibly not a dimension) is the extent to which a group shares its membership with other groups. This is readily illustrated in a school, which has members simultaneously belonging to different families, ethnic groups, religions, athletic teams, and so on. In a factor analysis we should probably find this mean number of groups to which members of any group X belong marking a first-order factor of "complexity of life" fairly highly. The score on such a first-order factor could be defined as the size of the fraction of the individual's total satisfaction that the group takes care of.

Again, we use such variables as "sociable" and "pugnacious" in describing individuals. But when we come to groups the number of historical behavioral instances from which such "traits" can be estimated becomes very small. Rummel's "dyadic analysis" gets to a concrete basis by taking the number of alliances of one nation with others, or the number of acts of war. Essentially this differs from our rating or measuring of individuals only as a sampling problem. A person reacts hundreds of times to hundreds of people and the "sociable" or "pugnacious" rating rests on plenty of situations. On the other hand for such a variable as "frequency of involvement in war" we may have to wait a century to get a score scatter, and even then the trait will apply to a particular subsample of situations, as say, to the wars of France and Germany between 1855 and 1955.

A full and reliable account of syntality dimensions and species in nations, and many other groups remains to be gained. Meanwhile we can see the improved methodology beginning to pay off in various area. For example, the differences of modern nations loosely described as "developed" and "undeveloped" and the "third world" stand out clearly and interpretably on specific syntality factors listed above. And the discussion above on the fraction of the average individual's needs satisfied by this and that group permits a clearer quantitative statement of what the sociologist means by primary and secondary groups. Sociologists have spoken of the family as a *primary* group, essentially because it takes care of such a large slice of the average person's total needs. Again, the measure we have just spoken of as the number of groups simultaneously joined by members of a given population is likely to be positively loaded on a complexity of life factor. Societies where the sociologist sees mainly primary groups would probably score low on that complexity factor.

From the standpoint of complexity affecting individual personality structure, the score of any population on the primary or monopolistic dimension of its groups is important. We have recognized that the major sentiments developed in individuals will tend to reflect the patterns of such major, primary group institutions as family, school, or church. If we are permitted to count the various ergs as equally important, so that we can sum the loadings on them, across all ergs, then an index of completeness of a group's "monopoly" or "predominance" can be suggested as follows:

$$\text{Group predominance index} = \frac{\Sigma b_g^2}{\Sigma b_t^2} \tag{7-6}$$

where the b_g's are the behavioral indices from the ergic terms in the specification equation for "I want to belong" to this *particular group* and the b_t's are from the totality of specifications for *all* groups to which its members belong.

Other variables or dimensions that a social psychologist might theoretically expect to be important either in an initial interspecies factoring to locate species types, or for intraspecies profiles of individual groups are: (1) membership size; (2) average size of the contact network (average number of ties per person in the group, with ties defined below); (3) uniformity of that network in terms of the fraction of members involved in total contacts, as contrasted with members being shut in segregated subnetworks; (4) degee of explicitness of leadership; (5) presence (or numerousness) of sub-castes in a hierarchy; (6) frequency of various *modes* of interaction among members; (7) existence of free or closed entry to the group; and so on. These are arbitrary variables anyone might choose, but there is some likelihood that they would also appear as factors, that is, as more primary *dimensions.*

Correlational and factor-analytic structuring across groups of the almost innumerable variables of interest to psychologists and sociologists still largely remains to be done. But meanwhile sociologists and anthropologists have by naturalistic observation made primary and secondary groups their main division, when using "types."

A fairly widely taught typology of groups is that of Sorokin (1937) (recently somewhat modified by Boulding, 1970), which classified according to the "common motives"—a concept more precisely defined here as a synergy vector. The grosser approach has also somewhat confused the classification by "common motives" by not distinguishing between motives in exchanges within the group and motives that hold the group together, as we have done in the *maintenance* and *effective* synergies, below. At any rate on this basis some sociologists have made a rather gross division into three types (as contrasted with a dozen on empirical syntality profiles discussed above). Although the writings are independent one cannot help tracing some continuity from Plato's *oligarchy, democracy* and *tyranny,* through Sorokin and, later, Boulding.

The first type of group is held together by the motive of in-security (the fear erg?). This is called *threat* response by Boulding, but *compulsory organization* by Sorokin. Here the group and its organization hang together principally by a need for security; and the members are willing to substitute limited fear of an autocratic leader for boundless fear of diverse outer threats. Such a society is perhaps partly created and exploited by a class, as in the feudal system, but the psychologist will see it as arising primarily from external threats.

The second type is called an *exchange* society (*contractual* in Sorokin). A free exchange of services develops among interacting individuals, which holds the group together; belonging to the group brings the benefits of what games theory calls a "positive-sum game."

The third is called the *familistic* or integrative society. Here (according to Boulding) "Love, affection, status and respect" are the motives and the cement of the group. This last, the sociologists suggest, requires a greater development of role and institutional structure.

The psychologist will be inclined to recognize that these are types that could be much more fully and objectively defined and refined, when dimensions have been clarified, as types in profiles of syntality and synergy. Furthermore, there is surely likely to be a greater number than three such points of high density in the syntality space of national groups at least as our empirical research (Table 7-3) already shows. However, because no research has been done except on national groups, it would be premature to name the number of generally possible points of equilibrium in the factor space. What we do know consists of a number of dimensions, such as cultural pressure, affluence, degree of "bourgeois structuration," and so forth, in nations, and two dimensions of morale connected respectively with leadership and congeniality in small, neonate, face-to-face groups. The meanings of the former, and the types of civilization (Toynbee, 1947) into which they throw modern nations are set out and discussed a little more fully by Cattell, Graham, and Woliver (1978).

Out of the contradictory and inadequate systems of classification, however, there come glimpses of a few clear propositions, again, as in the equations above, in the domain of synergy. Looking across the varieties of groups, we can see some—a manufacturing organization, a church missionary society—with purposes beyond themselves. Others, such as a bridge club or a sociable set in a pub, seem to have the sole object of mutual entertainment of members without any purpose outside the group. From the above equations (7-4) and (7-5) it is clear that synergy can be examined as input and output. As input it is the sum of "I want to belong . . ." attitudes, based on some incentives common to all members and some idiosyncratic, such as special office-holding satisfactions. The human energy thus stimulated by the existence of the group can be used as output in the work of maintaining the group by suitable circulars, elections, committee decisions, and so forth, and also in some group production, as in a school, factory or missionary society.

In groups of the type that have only internal activity, that is, no purpose beyond their gregarious satisfactions, what we define as *maintenance synergy* alone uses up the income of synergy. Contrasted with this we can define as *effective synergy* the energy the group expends in producing results outside itself and in interacting with other groups. From this analysis we would conclude that the energy income (the synergy) must equal the sum of maintenance and effective synergy. The economist will view this in the income of a corporation applied to running costs and production costs, by cost-accounting analysis. The translation of synergy into economic terms is legitimate and useful, but not simple. As indicated before, it needs further analysis.

The fact that synergy is initially not a scalar, like money, but a vector quantity, with particular ergic quality is probably not a main obstacle since it can be reduced to a scalar if we accept equality of energy—or a fixed exchange—among ergs. We see in the APA chart several such transformations, for instance, through frustrations, of sex to anxiety, and love to hate. So also in groups the synergy may undergo a transformation, with some regard for quantitative laws. Thus a society built on a maintenance synergy of mutual love among individuals, as was the medieval Christian society, may have its synergy issue in fact in hate, as in the crusades. In terms of our proposition that the group synergy is the sum of individual invest-ments this presents problems needing later discussion, though if all members are well informed of the frustration of the group *their* own investments will also individually make the transformation into pugnacity, and no failure of the simple equality proposition then occurs.

As to maintenance and effective synergy it may be doubted whether *any* organization can be totally without effective synergy, for groups are forced to interact, and even the members of a bridge club may develop an effective synergy if a brass band decides to occupy the next room. However, the ratio of effective to maintenance synergy is an important dimension in describing types of groups and the ultimate relation of groups to the sentiment systems of individuals.

In seeking to understand groups and types of groups, psycholo-gists and philosophers have often made some advance through using the theoretical model of a biological organism. But this must be modified in a rather radical way by the recognition above that groups—except in the limiting case of an all-embracing totalitarian national group—have overlapping memberships. More compatible with the organism model is the behavior of primary groups, which, from a basis of independence, do indeed mutually interact just as self contained organisms interact in the behavior expressions we encompass in syntality. One has thus finally to recognize that the interactions of groups are of two kinds: (1) those that arise from shared membership and are of a new order of complexity, due to the synergy relations we have discussed, and (2) those that arise as part of the study of independent interacting organisms, such as we have just encountered.

In the latter relations groups act as individual organisms. They conflict, form alliances, compete, and form dynamically subsidiating and exchanging structures, just as individuals do. Often groups exist to serve other groups, for which purpose they are often created by the other groups. Such studies as those of Guetzkow (1955) and Simmel (1969) have begun to investigate these mutual service and subsidiation effects.

The whole of history reflects such conflict and subsidiation effects as well as the vast subject of more multifarious types of inter-action among groups. What happened when Athens set out to form the Athenian league is a good example of the diversity of exchanges—from protecting to terrorizing—that can exist in psychological terms. However, if precision and new methods are to be used in studying dimensions and species of groups, we have to leave much of cultural anthropology and history as merely suggestive and turn to such quantitative methods of analyzing existing groups as have recently been developed by Rummel (1968, 1969, 1972, 1977), Sawyer (1967), and the present writer (1948, 1949) and colleagues Breul, Hartman (1952) and Woliver (1980). From these quantifyings of the psychological dimensions of groups as such, the student and researchers generally can move on to such refined methods of studying intergroup relations as are now being developed by Brams (1966), Chadwick (1971), Deutsch (1968), Rummell (1967), Singer (1968), and others.

7-5. The Elements of Group Internal Structure: Roles, Ties, and Communication Networks

Syntality and synergy have been dealt with up to this point as the final over-all outcome of the characteristic population and structure panels. As between the two last somewhat more attention has been given, because of our interest in personality, to the population para-meters, which we average over people. The time has come, however, to look at structure: at leaders and followers, interaction networks, classes and castes, synbiosis between subgroups, roles, and the traditions by which the structure and mores are handed on. In this nutshell we can deal at all adequately only with those that readily link with work on personality: roles and status effects. If an apothegm helps, let us capture the essence by saying that structure is defined by roles and goals. In synergy we have already said something about goals, and in Section 7-6 we shall consider how the traditions and group goals that are also part of structure are handed down through individuals; here our concern is structure per se.

We have distinguished the anthropologist's conception of role as a social expectation in the onlookers, from the psychologist's as a learned psychological structure in the individual (Chapter 6). A third approach, that of the sociologist, defines role as a place in a particular network of communication with other members of the group. The form of a network has also been invoked by the sociologist as a definition of a group. What is more natural, one may ask, than to define a group as a set of people who are in constant mutual interaction? The communication net is a valuable empirical construct, and a systems theorist, like Wiener (1948a, 1961) would base most structure on information paths. Though we shall study such networks as vital to structural definition, let us assert straightway that *it is not the most basic definition of a group*, though seemingly an attractive one. For, in a war between groups, for example, interaction is high with people outside the group. Conversely, interaction can be low within a group, a stoker on a liner may never meet the captain, yet both are indispensable elements in the group as an organization for common satisfaction and their fate will be to sink or swim together.

Just as a group cannot be defined primarily by a communication pattern, but requires a definition based on dynamic utilities, so is it inadequate to define a role simply by mapping the persons with whom a person in a given role has contacts. As we have seen, role has many facets—social expectation in the minds of other members; a contact network; a dynamic sentiment structure acquired in an individual; and some other features. Naturally these aspects will be interrelated by isomorphisms. To perceive those isomorphisms better, let us look in more detail at the four characteristics of a role that seem most important for definition.

1. A role can be recognized as a set of behavior ties of an individual occurring with particular frequencies to particular objects and people in the group. This is the emphasis in sociology.

2. It can be seen as a set of expectations (sentiments) in the minds of the group members, for example, that a person will act as a husband or a policeman, and so-and-so in the tribe will perform what is expected of a medicine man. This has been the special emphasis of cultural anthropologists, comparing roles in different societies.

3. It can be seen as a dynamic structure, falling into the class of sentiments, in the personality of an individual, causing him or her

to react powerfully to particular social stimulus situations. This is the natural approach for structural psychologists.

4. Finally, it can be seen as an important part of the group structure, recognizable in necessary effects to be produced in the group syntality. This social psychological functional aspect can be made operational only through the recent work on measuring group syntality.

Let us deal with each in order, and with their relationships. Concerning precise, quantitative methodological procedures, we must unfortunately face the fact that the first people in the field—mainly cultural anthropologists—could see roles so clearly (or believed they could) that no concepts and methods for discovering (and exactly defining) particular roles were thought out. Some roles—a chieftain, a soldier, a shaman, a mailman—are so clearly marked out, with explicit labels, prescribed behavior, and even regalia, that search methods are indeed superfluous. But the psychologist sees a considerable variety of more subtle, though behaviorally equally definite, roles, which are highly important but commonly unnamed and unrecognized. The person himself may not be fully conscious of them and society is inexplicit about its expectations and the area of behavior. The "unconscious" roles can nevertheless be very important.

The psychologist need not intuit these, for multivariate experimental methods are capable of recognizing such patterns. The initial location of a role is, as indicated in (3) above, as a *factor in dynamic attitude variables*—a factor that shows peculiarities capable of distinguishing it from ordinary personality factors (Chapter 6, Volume 1, p. 257). We suspect that many or even most role factors will also show a peculiarity of score distribution, in that the histogram or distribution curve among members of the group for the behaviors concerned will tend to be bimodal. Indeed, in many occupational roles and some domestic roles, there is no continuity of distribution and one is either "in" the role or "out" of it. In general, especially if it is found that more than one factor is needed to define a role, we are searching not only for a sentiment-like factor structure but also for a species type (by such programs as Taxonome), to be located by distributions.

Turning back from facet (3) to (1)—the sociologists' pursuit of role discovery by ties—we reach a score matrix, as shown in Table 7-4, that gives a count of the ties of an individual recorded as contacts as he performs in the given role. The patterns could equally well be shown, as in some sociology texts, by arrows between people, in one and two directions, with thicknesses proportional to frequency. These figures may be considered likely values in concrete instances.

TABLE 7-4. Recognizing and Defining Roles
by the Tie Count Patterns

Ties, as One or More Contacts Per Week with the Stated Number of Persons or Objects, of the Following Character	Sea Captain	School Teacher	City Policeman
Children of 6–18 years	4	60	15
Parents of school children	1	32	10
Ship owners	2	0	0
Sailors	30	0	2
Criminals	1	0	25
Auto accidents	0	1	30
Books	2	12	2
Restaurant keepers	0	1	5
Own home	0	16	12

The score for the ties could be either by contact counts as here
or by objective measures of strength of attitudes or sentiments.
The values here are not empirical, but are intended as likely
illustrations of the mean scores that would be empirically
obtained.

They illustrate numerically what is put in general algebraic form in
Figure 7-1. (Note that the matrix at upper right of Figure 7-1 is
transposed in Table 7-4, for convenience of reading.) The role matrix
in Figure 7-1 can be considered the first supplement to the very
different kind of role matrix in Table 6-5, Volume 1, which gives the
patterns of behavior *performance* implementation. It will be noted
also that these two matrices—that of ties, as in Table 7-4 and Figure
7-1, and that of behavior "trait" structure (Table 6-5)—together
cover the definition of a role as a set of expectations in the popular
mores, for they imply what a perceptive member of the population
would see, directly but not quantitatively, as the expected predominance of certain ties and modes of behavior. (What the average
person *actually* sees is a matter for questionnaire research to supplement role description.)

What we must first broadly call a "tie", however, can be many
things. In sociology a tie is commonly evaluated in a communication
network as a *frequency of contact* or *count of delivery of messages*
score. However, because we can now assign an ergic and sentiment
specification equation and a vector to any attitude, we recognize that
ties also can differ greatly in psychological nature so that counts of
sheer contacts only leave out vital information. We realize then that
the fine new development of the mathematics of communication

nets, by Kleinrock (1964), Kendall (1953), Shannon and Weaver (1949), Wiener (1948), and Riordan (1961), as stochastic, Markov processes, needs to be augmented by reference to the *qualitative dynamic nature* of the ties.

Of course, when an experimenter or theorist counts traffic in any kind of channel, he has set up the qualitative nature of the units beforehand. They are usually defined as "bits" of some particular kind of information, for example, on temperature. In everyday life social interaction, however, counting the "bits" or number of daily contacts is to go through the formalities but not the stuff of science. Richer aspects of the data must be preserved. But if we are to condense to a point at which social science is something more than a deluge of detail, several steps of abstraction must generally separate concrete data from effective concept. The concept we have found highly useful elsewhere, and that is desirable to use here for consistency of social and personality findings and predictions is again the *attitude* as a dynamic vector. Thus we propose to link people in a network and to describe their role and other interactions primarily, but not solely, in attitudes, measurable as ergic and sentiment vectors. The tie of person A to person B is to be defined as a vector stating what ergs and sentiments in A are habitually satisfied in the transactions with B—and, of course, vice versa, for the reciprocal ties are not the same, for example, in teacher and student.

Although the dynamic transactions are in many ways the most important, they are not the sole ones, as just indicated. Human networks transfer information, money (and its equivalents), moods, and even germs. And within "information" there are numbers, facts, orders, requests, and so forth. These systems probably can be pursued by methods analogous to those for attitude action networks, of which they are part; but this aspect need not be followed further here. Classifications for scoring interpersonal behavioral exchanges have been suggested by Bales (1950) and by Cattell and Stice (1953).

For some purposes knowing the particular ergic elements in the dynamic vector of the role tie, that is, the *nature* of the motivation, will be important. But for other more general purposes it suffices to know what the *total strength* of the tie is—from a *scalar* value simply summing the b_eE and b_mM terms in the vector. Parenthetically, the interaction of individuals in groups admits of various kinds of simplifying abstractions, and it is important to be alert to what information is being parcelled, and what applications of the indices are legitimate. At this point we are considering the recognition of roles by the patterns of sheer strength of ties to various people and institutions; p_1, p_2, . . ., in Figure 7-1. A sociologist might measure these by frequency of contacts, but we are using the usual a_{hijk}

strength of an attitude tie, since this will permit calculations in regard to several other kinds of personality dynamics.

The *tie strength treatment of roles* in Figure 7-1 has first the object of representing any given role by a vector of tie strengths, and secondly of calculating the probable vector for a given individual in the light of information about the way individual personality factors affect the tendency to develop particular ties. For instance, high surgency, $F+$ factor, might cause a man in a father role to have stronger ties with his children, and low H factor (threctia, shyness) might cause a policeman to chat less with taxi drivers on the stand than would an $H+$ policeman.

In (a), the upper part of Figure 7-1, we see centrally a $(q \times o)$ *personality-tie role expression* matrix, R_J, which contains what experiment has found about the tendency of each of q personality factors to cause deviations on each of o ties from the central tendency for the role *in role J*. Pre-multiplying by the individual i's personality trait scores on the q traits we obtain on the right his tie deviations from the role means on those tie intensities.

In (b), the lower part of Figure 7-1, the result from (a) is set out at the left in vector rows for each of n people and each is added to the mean known tie scores for role $\overline{R_{JP}}$ in the central matrix to yield on the right the estimates of what the tie behaviors of those n people will actually be role R_J in terms of tie strengths.

The empirical determination of these matrices, through personality measures, for example, on the 16 PF traits, to get the individual and the typical role tie values should offer no difficulties in experimental design.

The exploration of tie networks, by frequency of contact, but especially strength of attitude of person A to person B and vice versa, representing the extent of mutual service and dependence, is the basis for more than role recognition. It is a necessary basis for mapping organizational structures, social classes, and other features of the big R we have called structure. For example, such ties, though not often quantitatively defined as vectors as we would recommend here (but rather on contact counts) have been studied in defining hierarchical and management structures in industrial, military, and other groups, by Bavelas (1953), Borgatta and Cottrell (1956, 1958), Borgatta and Meyer (1956), Stogdill (1952), Fredericksen (1972), and many since. Some of these studies also bring out the relevance of strength and breadth of such networks to morale "atmosphere"—or syntality dimensions, as we should conceive them.

Our approach has thus covered the first three aspects of role above—the acquired dynamic structure in the individual, the tie pattern, and the social expectations. The fourth and last—and most

(a) Calculation of individual role action deviation matrix

Personality factor traits

	T_1	T_2	$\cdots$	T_q
Person P_i in role R_J				

P_i

Individual personality matrix

This is one row (one person P_i in role R_J) from the population matrix P (which is $n \times K$)

$\times$

Ties

	p_1	p_2	$\cdots$	p_o
T_1				
T_2				
$\cdots$				
T_q				

R_j

Personality role expression matrix

(Weights of traits, for people in general in increasing role tie expressions in role R_{ji})

$$P_i \quad \times \quad R_j \quad = \quad R_jP_i$$
$$(1 \times q) \quad (q \times o) \quad (1 \times o)$$

$=$

Ties

	p_{1z}	p_{2z}	$\cdots$	p_{oz}
Person P_i in role R_J				

R_jP_i

Individual role tie action deviation matrix

Note: The causal direction in the text assumes a trait causes increase in particular tie behavior. The actual matrix model above would fit also the causal action of a tie experience, conversely increasing a trait or state.

492

(b) Summations for the final individual role action vectors

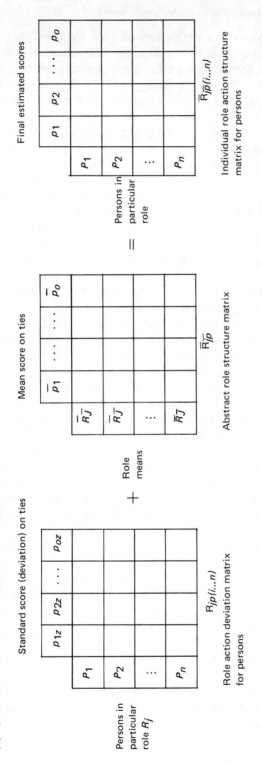

The theory in these two matrix models is that there is a definite role trait, fixed by a central tendency found characteristically in those in the role, and expressed by a pattern of frequencies in ties (p's) to people and things, which can be written as a row in the abstract role structure matrix, $\overline{R_{j\bar{p}}}$.

The general personality traits (T_1, T_2, and so forth) of an individual, P, however, cause him to deviate in these p tie expressions from the average way of expressing the role. This personal deviation is calculated from his personality endowments, in the calculation (a) and is then added to the central average role matrix in calculation (b) to yield his specific tie behaviors when in the role. This model is entirely consistent with the specification equation in Chapter 6, combining weighted personality and role traits in estimating any specific behavior.

Figure 7-1. Role patterns, individual and general, recognized by scores on ties.

493

recently investigatable—is the definition of role by the function it performs in the group syntality. If a stranger to mechanics wished to know what function the brakes or headlight switch or distributor play in the functioning of a car, one way to find out is to see what is different when each is removed. Removing *some* parts, especially from an organic whole, may stop the whole performance. But in many organisms and social groups this is not true and a partial loss of function occurs. The introduction of *practical syntality measurement* makes this independent approach to roles—which we may call the *successive abstraction* method—a present experimental possibility.

Results of the present writer's study of 100 neonate 10-man groups operating with and without leaders unfortunately have never been published. (See Cattell & Stice, 1953, for the experimental setting.) But they showed a definite increment in most instances, in group syntality performance in groups that incorporated the role of a leader. Other investigators have compared leaderless and leader groups, with interesting and largely similar findings, though syntality as such was not generally measured. The more central experimental design in our groups concerned the relation of group performance (syntality) to *different personality qualities* in the leader, and the discovery of the personality qualities (profiles) of different *types* of leader. Some personality associations found are shown in Table 7-5. Many interesting psychological theories have been and could be given explaining the action of these trait combinations. Having seen in Table 7-1 that there is a synergy dimension of morale-through-leadership, we can proceed to analyze its roots in the leader's personality. Thus we understand in the above high average extraversion discovered in leaders that it is the means to get across easily to his followers the ways in which the group's existence can serve its members' needs, and other messages. His higher than average level of Integrity (G, Q_3) guarantees the sense of fair play and justice which all followers demand, while the higher score of leaders on emotional stability, or ego strength (C), is necessary to withstand the buffetings of public life.

Table 7-5, and several others that could be given for various social positions (see Cattell, Eber, & Tatsuoka, 1971), show that role positions in society exercise the significant selection for general personality factors that we would expect. Consequently, the personality structure model of a role as a single sentiment must take account also of the accompanying pattern of deviation on general personality factors, as indeed we argued in Chapter 6, Volume 1.

However, at this point our concern is with the fourth avenue of approach to role characteristics—the effect of a role on the syntality vector of the group. Considering this in relation to the leader

TABLE 7-5. The Personality Profiles of Different Types of Leader Roles

STENS: 10 9 8 7 6 Mean 5 4 3

Profiles

Source Trait	A	B	C	E	F	G	H	I	L	M	N	O	Q1	Q2	Q3	Q4	QI	QII	QIII	QIV
	N																			
Elected leaders	92 M	6.0	7.3	5.7	5.8	7.1	6.3	6.7	5.2	5.2	4.8	5.7	3.9	4.9	4.9	6.4	4.9	6.8	4.6	5.9	5.6
Effective leaders	43 M	4.7	7.8	6.2	5.9	5.5	6.1	7.0	5.0	5.0	5.1	5.9	5.0	5.6	6.2	6.5	3.8	5.8	4.2	6.4	6.2
Technical leaders	90 M	5.8	9.0	6.0	6.1	6.2	6.1	6.9	5.0	5.3	5.0	6.0	3.9	6.0	5.1	6.6	4.5	6.5	4.2	6.0	6.2

Sten Weights*

	A	B	C	E	F	G	H	I	L	M	N	O	Q1	Q2	Q3	Q4	Constant
Elected leaders	-.14	.62	-.97	.00	.39	.26	.09	.04	-.06	.06	.03	-.99	-.44	-.07	.26	.02	10.45
Effective leaders	-.33	.68	-.52	.10	-.05	.07	.65	.01	.05	-.16	.00	.64	-.31	.18	.14	-1.01	4.73
Technical leaders	-.05	.93	-.69	.07	-.10	.20	.21	.01	.12	-.03	-.05	-.55	-.18	-.19	.32	-.11	6.11

*The values here are taken from the study by Cattell and Stice (1954) of one hundred groups of 10 men each. The profiles are in stens (standard tens: see Cattell, Eber, and Tatsuoka, 1972) and the weights are those of the specification equation found for good leadership of the type indicated. (To be applied directly to an individual's sten scores.)

495

example, we find it brings clarity to debates on how to locate and define the pattern of a positive leader. The experimental answer indicated by this approach to roles is to take out each member in turn from the group and remeasure its syntality at each change. The person whose removal causes the biggest syntality change is, operationally, the leader (for good or ill), no matter whether he is thought to occupy that position or not. This is an objective way of locating the leader, and then of finding the structural and personality qualities that go with that role. Of course it is possible, a priori, that if the syntality change magnitudes for the removal in turn of all members were plotted, as to distribution, in a histogram, we should find only a continuous normal distribution, offering no really sharp break between the leader and the rest. Our general theory, however, suggests that in most groups one or two individuals would scatter far to the high end in their syntality effects, producing a bimodal distribution with a small but modal frequency at the leader and leader associate level, separated from a general large distribution of followers.

7-6. Systems Action among Subgroups: Supply-Demand Equilibria; Social Status Movement

Within some larger group, such as a nation or a worldwide religious community, many smaller groups live as special subgroups in a state varying from symbiosis to conflict, the whole assembly usually being in a tolerable equilibrium. A frequent form of relationship among them is service, in which one group employs another, which subsidiates to its purposes. When examined closely such relations generally show a utility that is mutual, with some kind of psychological exchange. A manufacturing business may channel some of its synergy—its subscriptions from stockholders—into a subsidiary or independent business, which produces for it, say, some particular metal supply, and this in turn develops a subsidiary, or an exchange with an independent business, which mines metal ore. The group acts as a coordinator, taking the dynamic (psychological interest and money) investments of many individuals' attitudes to the group and creating a single synergy. This synergy—in business corporations transformed into monetary equivalents of psychological "energy"— becomes distributed in dealings among groups as such, leading to relational structures remote from any individual member's primary interest as an individual, or even from his knowledge, as illustrated by the typical shareholder's ignorance of what his company is actually doing technically.

There are certain principles in the exchange of services and in barter and monetary exchange that are central to economics but which, as we have confessed, have never been worked out in terms of vectors of ergic and sentiment satisfaction familiar in personality and clinical psychology. Space forbids us to do more than sketch the nature of the problem here. The relationships between individuals in this domain are no different in primary principles from those between groups. An individual leader, *or* a group, can effect its purposes through a chain of individuals or groups, passing along a purpose from group to group as between individuals in a marathon race. However, psychodynamically we would recognize that although quantities of satisfaction must be the same along the chain, the *quality*, that is the ergic and sentiment vector, is often very different in individuals or groups forming the links. This group satisfied hunger in that group, and its members are in turn satisfied by, say, prestige from a third group that wishes it to gratify hunger in the first.

A lattice-like diagram could therefore be constructed showing group dynamic exchanges (which should not be confused with the individual dynamic lattice discussed earlier, from which it is very different). This group-interaction lattice would be constituted not by subgoal structures but by group entities, the channels between showing the degree and kind of the symbiotic exchange. Furthermore, as we have seen, the difference from the subsidiation paths of the dynamic lattice lies in the action of what might be called the "equivalence of dynamic diversity," in that the exchanges must have some equivalence in energy or desirability, but, as suggested, can be dynamically diverse. If we look at what happens at the interindividual level (the reaction between groups being strictly the same, however), consideration of just a pair of people will suffice to demonstrate that the satisfactions in mutual services can be entirely different psychologically, as ergic vectors. The man who repairs a television for Mr. X gives Mr. X, say, the gregarious satisfactions of watching television, but the money he gets for it may represent to him, say, satisfaction of a need for security. We may suppose that some quantitative equivalent passes along and is constant in a closed chain of people, as in a closed tandem series of acts and subgoals in an ordinary dynamic lattice. But in the latter the ergic vector quality of reward is transmitted unchanged, whereas in the chain of people it goes through countless metamorphoses. Since money is the main vehicle of exchange of potential satisfactions, the lattice structures of interchange of individuals and groups encompass the science of economics, and it is here that the bridge from the dynamic calculus to economics has to be built.

Group interaction in everyday life has to do with interaction of nations, classes, political parties, families, regional governments, and so on. Most of these involve the complication of common, cross-group membership as defined above. The interaction of nations has understandably, by its dramatic quality, engrossed the attention of historians, journalists, and finally social scientists, and, except for cross-national religions, it is relatively free of the "common-members-with-other groups" complication. Apart from the application of factor analysis and systems theory being made with military secrecy in the intelligence departments of governments, substantial progress has also been made in the public domain in the last decade, notably by Rummel (1975, 1977). Essentially, Rummel has investigated, checked and operated with the dimensions of nations on our Tables 7-2 and 7-3 above, and then related them to dimensions of *diadic* analysis, that is, dimensions from measures of *interaction* variables of nations taken in pairs. Just as in personality, the interactions are in fact functions of the source trait scores of the two national syntalities interacting, and partly of the *situational field* in which they find themselves. The situational field of nations is far more idiosyncratic than that of individuals and more permanent (consider Germany, Russia and France, tied to geographical contiguities) and consequently makes the prediction of particular behaviors often depend more on situational indices (v's and s's) than on syntality traits (T's), which makes replicable syntality dimensions (beyond 7 or 8) difficult to establish.

Returning to the interaction of individuals within groups, we recognize that a large part of the interaction is economic, just as between groups. A central principle since Adam Smith and Ricardo has been recognition of the balance of the forces of supply and demand determing the "marginal utility" value of goods. The relationship can be summarized by a combination of positive and negative feedbacks in a system, as shown in Figure 7-2.

This diagram leaves out the nature of the ergic and sentiment motivations involved in the attraction of profits and the individual's felt need for various goods, and is consequently like a black-and-white photograph compared to the dynamically colored photograph the psychologist must ultimately produce. Because the links of psychology and economics are still weak, and it is a major task to improve them, we shall pursue them no further here, except in one area where psychology is particularly relevant, the exchange of human services in employment.

Ever since Ricardo (1817) had the clarity and courage to treat

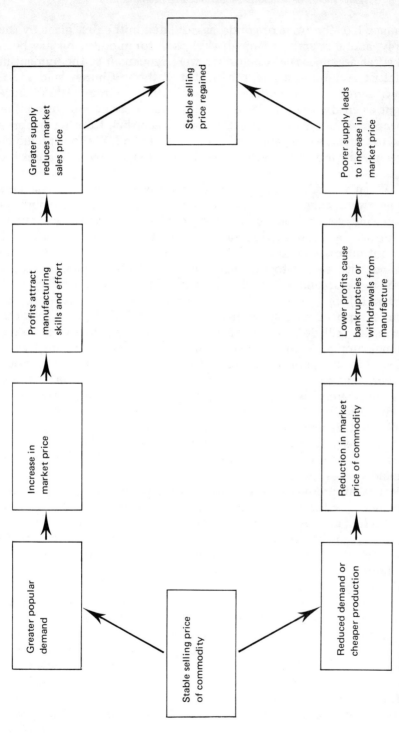

Figure 7-2. Positive and negative feedbacks on a social variable: equilibria in price of goods.

earnings, like the price of goods, as regulated in the first place by the supply and demand of human skill as a commodity, he has been looked at askance. His conclusions were repugnant to the humanism of leftist communism and the rightist Catholic Church, and social scientists too (for example, Boulding, 1970; Hardin, 1963), have sought scientific reasons for avoiding the unpleasant conclusion that if people should be paid (on this basis) according to other people's need for them, some people will not be paid at all. Without prejudice to secondary modifying values, let us consider the basic relationship itself.

When we talk of supply and demand in a society as it concerns people, we recognize that production of "the adult in being" in varied kinds and proportions in the population is partly determined genetically by reproduction rates and partly by environment, as a distribution of education. If there is any dislocation of supply and demand with regard to different types of "adults in being" supply could therefore be adjusted through either or both of these—or, alternately, by stopping free social evolution and dictating the cultural form of society so that the proportions of jobs of various degrees of skill demand are made to fit the reproductive and educational supply. At the moment, concerning supply by the birth rate, society has not gone beyond concern about mere total population numbers and their fit to the food and energy supply. But the real issue, ultimately, is balancing the distribution of skills in people to the distribution of skill demands in the culture, so that the law of supply and demand does not unfairly produce miserable support at certain levels. Individual or government initiative in education to ensure that enough people acquire skills at the levels where a higher demand makes reward higher, may seem enough. For example, in a society that produces its food by scientific farming with complex machinery, and spends leisure on plays on television, the demand for the ditch digger is reduced and that for persons who understand machinery and electronics is increased. Changes in education can do much to adjust supply to this new distribution of demand. But a psychologist who knows behavior genetics, and recognizes, for example, the substantial genetic component in intelligence, sees that the adjustment has to begin further back, in appropriate birth rates for the given culture at different intelligence levels (Chaper 1).

Clear discussion of this issue need not get bogged down in disputes on the relative potency of hereditary and environmental influences that we studied in Chapter 1, provided we assume a reasonable attainment in society of the ideal of adjusting the intensity of education to gifts, so that, across individuals they are simply proportional. In that case let us begin in Figure 7-3(a) with an adjusted state of society in which the normal modes of genetic and educational supply of educated intelligences on the one hand, and the normal course of cultural demand, on the other, fit very well. In (b) we depict a dislocation of this equilibrium, either through the culture becoming more complex or through a higher birthrate of the less intelligent. This can only be partly adjusted by society spending more on education. Whereas in (a) the earnings would theoretically be the same at all levels, the excess of demand at higher levels and of supply at lower levels in (b) will now produce a relation of income to intelligence as in (c) and a resultant distribution of incomes (through supply-demand ratios) roughly as in (d). Incidentally, since an attenuated form of this distribution has held throughout history we may assume that cultural demands have always found too few people at, say, the top quarter of the population, to cope with them.

The *ability supply and demand theory* in Figure 7-3 actually offers explanations not only of the existing income distribution, but also of a permanent unemployment pool, of inflation (at least of one factor therein), and of business cycles. As regards the last, if we suppose the slightest pendulum movement has begun, then in boom periods industry can employ more at lower competence levels on the distribution curve and the mean competence level of the work force falls. It falls also because, at the same time, management loses (through their achieving affluence and leisure) those who work and plan in the most intelligence-demanding positions. The over-all reduction of competence (by action at both ends of the distribution) of those employed in production must result in reduced efficiency of production and in increased cost of the product. The increased cost of the product, with earnings remaining as before, will result in decreased buying and the economy will move out of a boom into a depression phase of the cycle. This should result (assuming industry is at all effective in sifting out for steady employment the more competent employees) in more unemployment at the lower level and more return to work at the upper level of those whose savings no longer permit them leisure. Many more superficial sources than this enter into determining the cycle, but the ability supply and demand theory (in more detail in Cattell, 1937, 1971) is one for social psychological economists to study.

As in individual psychology so in social psychology, the study of energy and power, proceeding to systems theory, needs to begin with a complete overview of structure. We have considered the essential features of a group as such, the appearance of roles, the form of interaction networks, and the patterns of inter-group subsidiations. It remains, under structure, to look at the pervasive present of status—in large societies mainly as class status—in most societies.

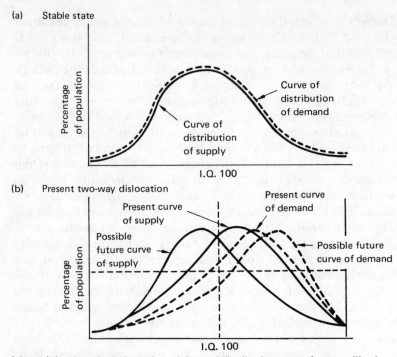

(a)   Stable state

(b)   Present two-way dislocation

(a) and (b): Hypothetical supply and demand distribution curves for crystallized intelligence, g_c (fluid intelligence, g_c, with education proportional) in (a) a stable, unchanging society, and (b) a society with various possible directions of change occurring.)

Figure 7-3.   Supply and demand and earnings.

Sociologists having long made us familiar with studies of class status in relation to such phenomena as social mobility, marriage, value attitudes, and political activities. The possibility exists that they have fallen into the error, which factor analysts disinter in many fields, of assuming that a single term is matched in nature by a single dimension. It happens to be true in this case that when correlation and factor-analytic methods were first applied (Cattell, 1942) to such status indicators as salary, size and locality of home, years of education, and other commonly accepted signs of status, most variance fell into a single factor. However, just as more refined research on "social desirability" (Edwards, 1957; Wiggins, 1972) has shown that there are two dimensions involved (Cattell, Pierson, and Finkbeiner, 1974; Cattell and Vogelmann, 1976), that is, toward high standing

(c)   Ratio of demand to supply: price

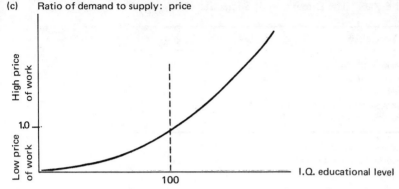

(c): Ratio of demand to supply to be expected with greater skewing of curves in opposite directions, as in (b) above.

(d)   Distribution of earnings to be expected from natural adjustment to curves in (b).

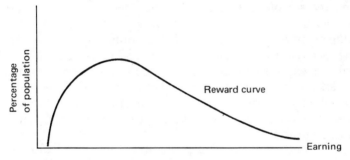

(Reprinted from Cattell, R. B. *Abilities: Their structure, growth and action.* Boston: Houghton Mifflin, 1971, with the permission of the publisher).

and respectability as defined by the "establishment," and toward a "good-fellow" popularity in terms of being liked by the peer group, so here *could* be more dimensions in social status in some cultures. (Thus in the rather unusual culture of native Hawaiians, the peer-pleasing rank is primary, and competition for establishment goals "bad form," as in some public schools of the 19th century and also in the "hippie" cultures of the 1950's and 1960's.)

Very thorough factor analytic studies vital to the whole concept of social status have recently been made by Stricker (1978a; 1978b) on a range of variables that embraces most previous important discussion, such as that of Chapin, Duncan, and Artis, Hollingshead, Marx, and Engels, Warner and Weber. He obtained, on black and on white samples, approximately 18 primary factors, 6 secondary, one

TABLE 7-6. The Dimension of Social Status

Social Variables[a]	Loading on General Factor
1. Prestige rating	.98
2. Mean IQ of occupation	.97
3. Mean annual income	.93
4. Years of education required	.87
5. Practice of family planning[b]	.85

[a]Scored for *occupations,* as entries in the correlation series.
[b]As recorded in 1940; the greater spread of birth control
may have altered this. Data from Cattell (1942).

or two tertiary. He notes that 3 seem to match previous factors. His results certainly show that many of the previous arbitrary definitions by sociologists are awry, but leave doubt whether a third order factor can be found corresponding to the general factor of "intelligence-prestige", and so forth found by the present writer among occupations. Evidently there are quite a number (18?) of specialized expressions of social status that are going to have to be taken into account in future "positioning" of a person on social dimensionality in exact work. Meanwhile, in this we must concentrate here, with relation to personality as our main concern, on the single largest dimension.

In Western culture (and probably in India and China) the fact seems to be that if one correlates social variables, using *occupations* as entries, the central feature in the social-status factor, that is, the highest in loading, as in Table 7-6 turns out to be *prestige*. It is thus a psychological variable, rather than the material measures—earnings, size of house, cost of education—on which sociologists have typically based their social status estimates, that should direct us to interpreting the meaning, satisfactions, and effects of status.

To climb in social status is doubtless to bring greater freedom from the restrictions of poverty and other problems, so that, especially in nonwelfare societies, the ergic gain is broad, including satisfaction of the erg of security seeking. But in terms of the attitudes of onlookers to the social status of others it would seem that satisfaction of the self assertive erg must play a larger part than hunger or even the need for security. Since no one has yet experimentally analyzed with the MAT or other objective measure of ergic tensions what goes into the ergic and sentiment composition of the attitude "I want to elevate my social status," a more precise statement cannot be made. But attitudes close to this, such as "I want to be proficient in my career" and "I want to maintain a good social reputation", show their loadings mainly on the self-sentiment and on the ergs of self-assertion, need for security, and narcism (Cattell & Child, 1975, p. 84).

That these psychological motives in the social status field are real forces—though sometimes offensive to our ethical values—is strongly indicated by the test which psychology always needs to apply—namely an extrapolation to human from primate behavior, which is useful in understanding society as well as the individual. Ethologists have given us in recent years many analogues of human social status, from the dominance order in extended primate families, to the pecking order in hens. In short a social hierarchy in animal societies akin to human social status is widely observable, as in the work of Wilson (1975), Carpenter (1952), Maslow (1935, 1936), Ardrey (1966). The primary drive that brings the hierarchy about seems to be self-assertion of a dominant individual, though sex also plays a part. The pattern of ergic motivation may thus have some interesting difference from that in humans. What these observers bring out is a useful functionality, not previously recognized, in that exercise of the dominance motive leads to a stability in animal societies favorable to their survival, reducing, for example, the incidence of conflict and disorder. Those societies are in general characterized by a dominant male, a harem of subservient females, children and a set of young bachelors, living on the fringe of these families or roaming as gangs in peer groups.

Although these animal societies show us some underlying fundamental patterns akin to the human hierarchies in motivation—as when kings were the guarantors of social order, as Hobbes (1651) claimed—it would be as big a mistake to suppose that this dynamic system is the whole buttress of modern human hierarchies as to ignore the Ardrey position with abhorrence as some authority-allergic writers do. The fact is that evolution of mammalian groups has found it necessary to generate an erg of satisfaction in submission[3]—an erg active in worship of the great and in religious awe. For a group of individuals who knew no social satisfaction of ergs but that of the erg of self-assertion would create a turbulent and self-destroying society. Parenthetically, McDougall (1932) had an interesting observation that a lesser endowment in the self-submissive drive has been responsible, in Greece and Iceland and Britain, for the appearance of democratic forms of government, rather than stable submission to kings. However, in general, the biological development of a satisfaction in devotion to another makes it possible for all members to draw ergic satisfaction where otherwise there would be such massive dissatisfaction of the self-assertive erg that the group would fall to pieces. Of course, in the period before the "pecking order" is established one should hesitate to condemn two assertive individuals fighting for power as "group disorder," for what they are doing is to establish that order by which groups live. And this form of order is still in the skeletal structure of modern societies, nicely managed by polling and by acquiescence of the defeated in the program of the winner.

Although social psychologists have not yet widely and carefully used such measures as the MAT (Motivational Analysis Test) to determine the vector composition of important status, supply-demand, and intergroup social attitudes with precision, enough of such attitudes have been analyzed in studying ordinary personality dynamics to show that simple "dominance" is not sufficient explanation of motives for social climbing. Nor does social order seem to require, as Hobbes argued, a simple hierarchy rather than a system of checks and balances among symbiotic subgroups. As regard motivations in the individual, Cattell and Butcher (1968) found, in studying striving for position in the school system, that loadings for achievement success appeared mainly on the self-sentiment (Q_3), superego (G), and self-sufficiency (Q_2) source traits, with varying values on dominance, self-assertion and self-submissiveness, according to the form of achievement. Indeed, it is noteworthy that submissiveness (as $E-$ on the HSPQ and 16 PF) is strongly positively related to ordinary classroom academic progress (as might be expected from the Latin root of "docility"). But self-assertiveness ($E+$) is positively related to creativity and unconventional achievement later.

The fact is (as shown by high self-assertive scores in both creative scientists and criminals) that self-assertion as such is involved both in climbing on the status axis and in defying society. The motivational source that is *most* closely tied to status-seeking in human societies seems to be the self-sentiment, with its aim of receiving approval from the established society and of shaping oneself to its values. The superego also has slight positive status correlations, but, as we know, it addresses itself to more permanent values than those of a transient society. By whatever combinations of ergs and sentiments the average person or a particular individual is motivated in his social attachments, it seems that there is one axis of differentiation in society—the socioeconomic dimension—that confers status more universally and powerfully than any other. On that axis all roles and status positions have a definable position, and in that field human beings attempt to move like charged bodies in an electric field.

This last comment turns our attention from the structure of social status to its functions—or, at least, what it does to society, for better or worse. The tendency for everyone to move in much the same direction in the "field of force" created by the polarization along the status axis has three or four major consequences worthy of study. First, in a democracy (as contrasted, say, with the feudal system) where promotion and social mobility are not impeded by any deliberate obstructions, the system is bound to develop class status differences in psychological qualities, innate and acquired, even if categorical, *labelled* classes do not exist. Already psychologists have accumulated much evidence on systematic relations of personality and ability traits, as well as attitudes, to social status. Naturally the statistical magnitudes reported are of different orders according to whether individuals or groups—say, occupational group means—are entries, and, if dealing with individuals, whether the individual's status or that of his parents is entered. Social status gradients are found in intelligence (about .3 for traditional intelligence tests, .20 for culture-fair "fluid" intelligence measures), and in several personality factors. Ego strength, C, dominance, E, surgency, F, superego, G (in some age groups), self-sufficiency, Q_2, and self-sentiment, Q_3, tend to be higher in upper social status groups.

One might expect that after all the bureacratic reports on mental hospital populations and clinics our knowledge would be firm on the distribution of mental disorders, but most statements presently available still obviously need allowances and qualifications. There is clear evidence that schizophrenia is more prevalent with lower social status, and manic-depressive disorder relatively more frequent with upper status. In the neuroses, obsessional compulsive neurosis has been found more with upper status and anxiety neurosis and conversion hysteria more at lower levels. Lynn (1970) shows more anxiety also in *countries* at lower economic levels, but again there are other factors at work. There are promising theories as to the two-way causal actions which produce these social position associations.

It is not the purpose of this book to make extensive evaluations of surveys, but rather to develop theories and models capable of expressing the main relations, and sufficiently precise to be tested. As far as the social status dimension is concerned we might say briefly that up to the social level of a really adequate economic basis, at least, the *motivation* for upward mobility is as we have seen, the forces of self-assertion, security, narcism, the self-sentiment, and the superego. Some of this motivation to climb is good, as in the superego aim toward maximum utilization of one's gifts. Beyond the broad middle range some of the motivation is "bad," in that one suspects a narcism component with its goal of luxury and Veblen's "conspicuous expenditure." Similarly, in the resulting class segregation of trait levels we can perceive, as Fisher did, that the existence in a society of "fair" climbing conditions produces more good qualities in the upper half, and the absence of control of unfair and antisocial means leads to the segregation of some selfish and undesirable qualities at the top. However, by almost any value standard of *capability*, the upper half of the status distribution shows, presumably by climbing selection, higher levels, of, for example, intelligence, emotional stability, self-sentiment dependability, freedom from schizophrenia and other maladjustments and pathologies, and so on. What prolonged possession of a privileged position does to personality is another matter.

In regard to measured *dynamic* traits Lawlis (1968, 1971) and Sweney (1969) have shown a pattern that Sweney has called "the loser syndrome," which is most prevalent in those at lower status levels, for example, the chronically unemployed. As Figure 7-4 profiles show, the low score on assertiveness and self-sentiment and the high score on insecurity (fear) match what has been indicated in other social status correlations, but the lows on sex and attachment to spouse call for further analysis. A further significant finding in these E and M profiles is the high conflict score at the lowest social status on career, superego, and (less definitely) spouse, this score being the excess of unintegrated over integrated, realistic interest behavior. Clearly, the status dimension in social structures, especially when we reach the chronically unemployed, has important associations in the personality and motivation structure of individuals.

Although of vague and arbitrary outline in a democracy, classes will yet operate to some degree as functional groups, though the evaluation of whether the functions are good or bad is another matter. Obviously, however, they help determine, notably in the professional societies and trade unions, the outline of networks of social interaction in self-interest groups. Among other things, these groups, by affecting intermarriage, produce genetic associations, as pointed out by Fisher (1930) and by Darlington (1969). As the latter shows, although these genetic links are of slower formation than the learned cultural tradition links with which sociologists have exclusively concerned themselves, they are historically potent. Thus R. A. Fisher (1930) points out that characteristics such as intelligence and ego strength, mainly good but sometimes bad, that help individuals in social promotion will, as far as they operate with two distinct genetic components, tend to become associated with greater than chance frequency in an upper social group. That is, both will tend to be high with upper status and both low together in lower status persons.

A secondary consequence of any degree of emergence of social status psychological differences is to be expected not only in effects on general social interaction in classes, but also on the assortiveness of mating in family formation as mentioned in connection with the analysis of Fisher (1930) and Darlington (1969). It is unnecessary to repeat here the evidence that substantial positive correlations of husband and wife exists in stature, physical type, education (Kelly, 1937; Cattell & Nesselroade, 1967), intelligence, and virtually all personality traits in the span of the 16 PF test. Greater resemblance, is, moreover, associated with greater marital stability (Cattell & Nesselroade, 1967). If social status segregations facilitate assortive mating, they therefore make some contribution to marital harmony. Sociologists have mooted the question widely over the last 20 years whether mating habits and values are becoming less assortive, though breakdown of class diversities and segregations. Superficial impressions would seem to support both cause and consequence, but there is no sound evidence of such a change, and possibly the greater interest of the general public in popular psychological writings has in fact led to *more* assortiveness in mate selection. (See Vandenberg, 1970.)

A little recognized, and perhaps more important social result in the long run, than effects on marital harmony, is the genetic consequence of any reduction of assortiveness. A positive correlation of husband and wife on cultural and genetic bases of traits will increase the population range on such traits in the children. As will be recognized from the principles of behavior genetics in Chapter 1, assortive mating can produce substantial increases in the *genetic variance* within a society. Thus if the correlation of the genetic components in intelligence for husbands and wives is about .6, as it may be in Europe and America, the genetic part of the range after 1 generation of assortive mating at .6 would be $V_p[1 + (r/2)]$ where V_p is the genetically additive variance in the parental generation, and $r = .6$, that is, it would be $1.3V_p$ (Cavalhi-Sforza & Bodmer, 1971, p. 543). If we consider environment constant, the standard deviation of IQ in the population, even with a modest genetic similarity of .4, a 20% increase would occur, that is a rise from 16 to 19.2 points. A reversion to random mating, from the .4 value now presumably partly maintained by social stratification (and the coeducational college) would thus reduce the percentage of IQ's *above* 130 and *below* 70 from 5.9% to 3.01%, that is it would halve IQ's above 130. The reduction below 70 might be welcome but since cultural historians have estimated that most of the growth of science, and its consequences in real wealth in the community as a whole since about 1400 A.D. is due to about 500 people in the high IQ range, it is likely that changes in social habits producing even a slight increase or decrease of assortiveness of marriage could have profound consequences in society.

The segregation by social status levels, like that in political and

Sten mean U	Sten mean I	Dynamic areas	1	2	3	4	5	6	7	8	9	10	Centile rank U	Centile rank I
							Standard ten score (sten)							
7	4	Career sentiment	.	.	.	.	.	.	.	.	.	.	77.3	22.7
5	4	Home-parental sentiment	.	.	.	.	.	.	.	.	.	.	40.1	22.7
6	7	Fear erg	.	.	.	.	.	.	.	.	.	.	59.9	77.3
5	5	Narcism-comfort erg	.	.	.	.	.	.	.	.	.	.	40.1	40.1
7	4	Superego sentiment	.	.	.	.	.	.	.	.	.	.	77.3	22.7
6	4	Self-sentiment	.	.	.	.	.	.	.	.	.	.	59.9	22.7
5	5	Mating erg	.	.	.	.	.	.	.	.	.	.	40.1	40.1
5	5	Pugnacity-sadism erg	.	.	.	.	.	.	.	.	.	.	40.1	40.1
4	4	Assertiveness erg	.	.	.	.	.	.	.	.	.	.	22.7	22.7
5	4	Sweetheart-spouse sentiment	.	.	.	.	.	.	.	.	.	.	40.1	22.7

Unintegrated sten mean ——————— Integrated sten mean − − − − − − − − − −

		Standard ten score (sten)											Centile rank U	Centile rank I
Sten mean Conflict	Sten mean Total motivation	Dynamic areas	1	2	3	4	5	6	7	8	9	10		
9	5	Career sentiment											96.0	40.1
7	4	Home-parental sentiment											77.3	22.7
5	8	Fear erg											40.1	89.4
6	4	Narcism-comfort erg											59.9	22.7
9	5	Superego sentiment											96.0	40.1
8	5	Self-sentiment											89.4	40.1
6	4	Mating erg											59.9	22.7
6	4	Pugnacity-sadism erg											59.9	22.7
6	2	Assertiveness erg											59.9	4.0
7	3	Sweetheart-spouse sentiment											77.3	10.6

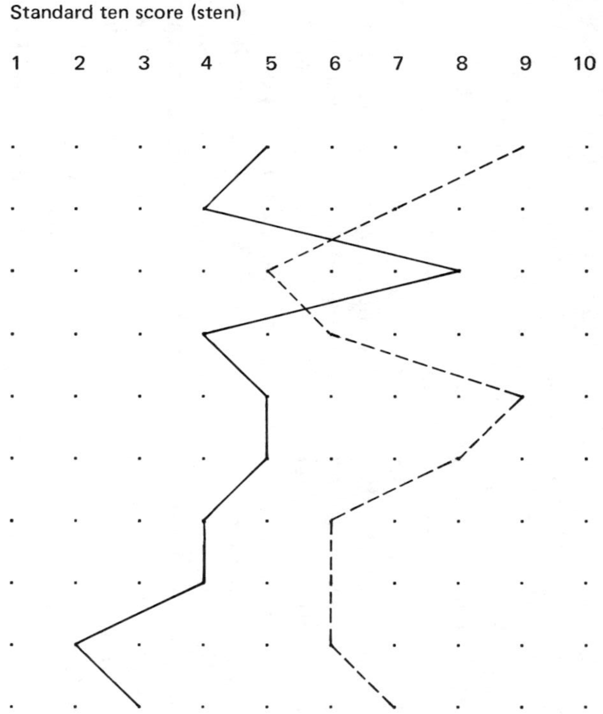

Total motivation sten mean ——————   Conflict sten mean – – – – – –

Figure 7-4. Dynamic adjustment on the MAT: Factors in chronically unemployed. (F. Lawlis, 1967.) $N = 75$.

511

religious views (between which there are loose but statistically significant associations) may have another effect. This is the possibility that containing much of the individual's activity within a social subgroup, rather than the whole society, may reduce the demand for emotional adjustment. (The extreme adjustive subgroup might be that in a monastery.) The result might not be good for emotionally robust individuals, but could reduce breakdowns in others less endowed. The argument that social classes may both provide such "asylums" and assist in fuller personality development in special ways has been given more explicitly elsewhere (Cattell, 1942). Kipling, on the other hand, held it up as a strenuous ideal for the self to "walk with Kings—nor lose the common touch"; but Kipling died of a stomach ulcer, which might suggest the stressfulness of that view! What might be good for the individual, however, might not be good for society. A society like India, with over 500 language groups and almost as many cultures, seems to have difficulty in matching a more homogeneous society in organized progress. On the other hand, diverse subcultures may offer limited " laboratory experiments" for the trial of consequences of diverse life styles. This presupposes that, first, recognition of success, and then imitation, will follow. In this connection the social status axis has commonly operated as an upward direction of imitation—"keeping up with the Joneses" in values and life styles if not always in economics—though in times of revolution or loss of morale instances of the converse direction of imitation can be found.

In summary, in the structure within groups per se we have to consider the equilibria of subgroups in symbiotic, subsidiating relations; the streams of population supply and demand adjustments in a systems framework, particularly in social mobility about the status axis; the existence of roles and status positions, and the effects on personality of certain degrees of segregation from the totality of social influences. Some idea of the magnitude of personality formation from these influences, relative to those within the family can be gained from the σ^2_{wt} and σ^2_{bt} values in Chapter 1, which suggest very roughly about an equal potency.

7-7. Personality-Syntality Transactions: Synergy Isomorphisms, Educational Transmission, Acculturation, and Group Conflict

With this cameo of the features of group structure as such, let us consider next the dynamic bonds through which the individual personality interacts with that structure. So far we have spoken of a single sentiment vector describing the total ergic and sentiment satisfactions a given individual gets from belonging to a given group. But now, recognizing in more detail the sub-structures within the social group, we want to know how the dynamic structures in the individual operate in relation to a complex hierarchy of such sub-groups.

First, let us look at the nature of the vector "I want to belong to this group" in relation to the activities of a single group. The varieties of satisfaction are usually considerable. The member of a select tennis club gains satisfaction from proudly telling other friends that he belongs, from the games themselves, from the club dances, possibly with amorous aspects, from the status of being the treasurer, from the gregariousness of congenial friends, from the relaxation the club gives from the cares of his profession, and so on. A wide spectrum of ergs is satisfied in the belonging vector as well as in such associated ancillary sentiments as political sentiments (for a Republican, the fact that many members are good Republicans) and his own self-sentiment, which demands for him personally a high standard of physical fitness.

The group analyst needs at this point something less detailed and more general than the highly varied particular activities which any specific group has, and the following 5-panel analysis has been suggested for usefully classifying the varieties of stimulation and dynamic satisfaction *an individual* can experience in any group.

1. *Effect of the perceived purpose of the group beyond itself (The individual's equivalent of group goal synergy).* It has been stated that the *effective synergy* of a group is the fraction of its synergy that it bestows on some activity beyond that of merely keeping the group together. A church in its missionary activity, a factory in its production, and a university in its teaching and research output have such synergy. Individuals will vary in the extent to which their pleasure in belonging derives from participation in the expressed ultra-group purposes—the ideals and activities for which the group exists—and from group life as such. Half the members of a yacht club may go there only to drink. There will be some, but not full correlation between the sum of members' interests in this purpose and what synergy the group sets aside for effective synergy.

2. *Intrinsic group "company" synergy.* This covers the satisfactions the individual gets from the person-contact activities (mainly gregarious in large groups or sexual in the family couple), regardless of any orientation to a further purpose as in (1). For these satisfactions it is necessary only that the group continue to exist as a group of people with whom one may spend one's time. It will be

noted that the total synergy resulting from these individual satisfactions in "company" per se seems to factor out as a distinct morale
factor of congeniality as shown in Table 7-1. Correspondingly, (1)
above also produces it own morale factor—"morale of leadership"
as we have called it, as a distinct factor, supporting the theoretical
division we have made into group goal interests and company satisfaction synergies.

   In passing, let us note that several currently accepted definitions of total *morale* describe something that would be readily
explicable as total *synergy*, and would result in total morale being
defined, not unsuitably, also by the term "cohesiveness." Group
cohesiveness is variously defined by its users of a decade ago but we
would operationally define and measure it as a specific operational
variable: the ultimate resistance of the group to attempts to dissolve
or annihilate it. Note that as so defined it is not to be identified with
morale of congeniality, or what we have here defined as intrinsic
synergy, which is the satisfaction that people get from each other as
people, apart from the specific purposes and investments in the
effective synergy goals. Cohesiveness is hypothesized to be the sum
of all five sources of satisfaction—the total synergy from all group
members in all domains. All individuals satisfactions in the group are
conditional on the group being held in being, so that resistance to its
dispersal is simply proportional to the total synergy the group can
command.

   3. *Status synergy.* This is the satisfaction an individual gets
from his particular role status activities in the group. Not only could
this occur largely without regard to the particular quality and nature
of group purposes (a foreman might be as proud and happy regarding his directive job role in a carpet factory as in a shipyard), but also
independently of enjoying all the people as people in (2). The
summed status synergy across individuals will have some proportionality to the group's maintenance synergy since it is concerned with
keeping the structure of the group. We would hypothesize that the
ergic character of satisfaction in status positions is appreciably that
of self-assertion and the self-sentiment.

   4. *Personal activity synergy.* We are speaking now of activities
specific to a particular society—of tennis in a tennis club, welding in
a car factory, the activities of being a hostess on a plane, playing
bridge in a bridge club, and so on. The activity satisfaction can be
separated from the status satisfaction, for often the person obtaining
this satisfaction has no status other than that of being an ordinary
member. When the activity is social it will be difficult to separate the
parts connected with this activity from intrinsic synergy.

   As noted in the dynamic lattice, we are at present very ignorant of the nature of the ergic goal satisfactions in many simple activities, for example, drawing, water skiing, reading a newspaper, gardening, or enjoying esthetic surroundings. But obscurity of specific ergic sources does not mean that, in many occupations and group activities, the activity in the work and its situation themselves do not have substantial immediate satisfactions. The notion that modern industrial activities, as contrasted with those of the craftsmen, lack this satisfaction was a common belief in writers so diverse as Karl Marx and William Morris.

5. *Extraneous reward synergy.* A contribution is made to the energy of a group, especially in a complex society, by individuals who have none of the above satisfactions in its activities but who are simply paid to perform. In this way a teetotaler might be paid as manager of a brewery, or a worker in an occupied country might manufacture arms to defend his conquerors. We may call this a personal intragroup satisfaction or extraneous reward (although (1) to (4) are also in a sense personal). Indeed, both (4) and (5) can exist without a group being involved, and although (3) cannot do so, it may not always serve group purposes. It should be said that this does not work out as a *contribution* to the group, because there is only an exchange. The group must give out funds to pay the individual and the individual puts in synergy proportionally. However, our five categories are looking at the group from the standpoint of where the individual finds *his* satisfaction in the group, and the paid worker is a member inasmuch as these satisfactions cause him to want the group to continue. In immediate balance on (5) he is contributing no more than he takes; but the relations bring, usually, other contributions to group survival and synergy.

In a very general way we have stated the proposition that there will be appreciable isomorphism between the institutional structure of society and the dynamic sentiment structures found in individuals. The discovery of factorially unitary sentiments for religion, games, family, and job gives massive support to this.

In passing one notes that psychologists encountering these dynamic calculus results (Chapter 2 here and Chapter 5 in Volume 1) and the isomorphism proposition sometime ask "If there is parallelism of institutions with sentiments, may not there also be with ergs?" Jung made many original observations, unpopular at the time, that suggested a shaping of at least fragments of social institutions to his "archetypal ideas" (essentially perceptual proneness aspects of ergs) and sociobiologists have today (Wilson 1975) offered substantial support for such molding of social institutions by innate predispositions. (Cultural anthropologists, for that matter, regularly *analyze* cultures in terms of how they handle the basic needs for food, sex, security and so forth). Our theory here is no denial of the essential correctness of Jung and incorrectness of Watson. When in apparent opposition to "the organism—its genetics—molds society" we repeat the saw "Social institutions mold the organism's sentiments" we are not denying the truth of the former but only recognizing that the psychometric reality is more complex than either oversimplified slogan. The sentiments are investments of the ergs, and therefore, if one wishes so to say it, are "products of the innate makeup of man." But culture and genetics have therein come to a compromise, such that a sentiment is rarely largely the expression of just one erg, and is forced to express several, as the vector values show, and as the unsystematic overlap of ergic and sentiment factor patterns shows. (This permits, incidentally, a readier separation of factors than might have been anticipated.) The family, for example, is not a sex institution, but involves several ergic satisfactions. One must not, however, entirely dismiss the Jungian, Ardreyan, and sociobiological argument that *some* innate tendency may exist to patterning these ergs together, as shown in the last mentioned writer's claiming that the kibbutz style of living often tends to fall away into a more deeply satisfying primal family unit pattern.

Without prejudice to these issues let us consider further the undoubted fact that the factoring of objectively measured motivation strength in a wide sample of life attitudes yields sentiment structures (as well as ergs) and that only the former clearly correspond to the institutional structure of society. Because any one institution requires, and rewards, a fair span of types of roles, however, the isomorphism is not as uncomplicated as the initial broad recognition thereof might suggest. Clearly the group gains synergy—energy to hold it together and to perform its goal tasks—from the various member individuals, and the individuals put energy (work) into the group according to the satisfactions they get out of it. The above five aspects remind us, however, to expect possible differences of structural form among different individuals in the components of their sentiment to the group. They may be distinct to the extent, for example that he says "I like the objectives of this group (Investment (1) above), but I don't much like the type of person in it" (Investment (2) above). In the first case the attitude vector for belonging, and the individual's desire for the group to continue will have a larger loading on superego, and in the second—if company is what he wants—on the gregarious erg.

Psychometrically considered, it is probable, therefore, that the common pattern we obtain by R-technique, being the overlap of many moderately divergent individual interest patterns, tends to underestimate the magnitude of the sentiment variance, as always happens in R-technique when the common pattern tends to vary. The unique pattern obtained through P-technique would almost certainly give more substantial variance to sentiment factors. This presents a practical scoring problem in comparing, say, the church sentiment strength of a Methodist and a Presbyterian, of a deacon and an acolyte.

Despite these differences in sentiment structure, largely associated with differences of status and role, the isomorphism principle is a sound one, and it extends still more obviously to the pseudosentiments (largely cognitive and dynamically freely attachable) that we call abilities. The patterns found in *aptitudes and skills* (though not those found in primary *abilities* by Thurstone, 1935, or Cattell & Hakstian, 1974, 1976), clearly classify themselves by social institutions, largely occupations, as seen in the shoemaker, the parson, the farmer and the doctor.

What happens to this general isomorphism, however, when there are complex subsidiations among social institutions, as when the trade union to which a person belongs subsidiates to (is controlled by) a political party to which the worker may or may not belong; or when the chemical factory in which a pacificist works supplies a munitions manufacturer? Leibnitz imagined a "pre-established harmony" to account for the relations of his monads to another reality; but the psychologist has to realize that the conflicts of the larger society become represented obliquely within the dynamic system of the individual. There is a legend that Margaret Mead drew a whole culture from examining its last living member—a drunken Indian. Isomorphism would admit that by examining the microcosm of the individual one should be able to sketch the macrocasm of the culture, but whether alcoholism in this case represented cultural or personal conflicts is open to doubt!

We can probably take as fact that even the average educated person is only vaguely aware of the political and economic interrelations of groups to which he belongs. He may not know the subsidiaries of a company in which he has stock, or he may not (as a student) know how much his alma mater is support by federal, state, and private funds. And he may belong to a society for eliminating public smoking without realizing that some of the taxes he pays goes to support tobacco producers. In short, the sentiment pattern in the individual is isomorphic with the immediate groups to which he belongs, but may represent very little of the complex interactions and dependencies that we have called symbioses and conflicts among those groups.

This state of affairs can produce a special kind of malintegration in society and conflict in the individual. These may exist unconsciously, as when the person simultaneously belongs to a Taxpayer's Protest Society and votes for a party that switches government funds to an insolvent welfare service. In other cases, as when the country a citizen has adopted goes to war with the country of his birth, the group conflict may propagate itself as a more overt conflict in an individual.

To understand the conflict effects we need to note that group conflicts cover two very different types of action: (1) conflict in their purposes as groups, and (2) conflict over membership. These will often become related. Isomorphism therefore indicates that some, but not all, overt conflicts among groups will tend ultimately to produce corresponding conflicts and cognitive dissonances in individuals. No one knows what proportion these bear in the emotional conflicts studied by clinicians, but if we speak of what the anthropologists call primary groups, the individual effect of group conflict would be considerable, and anyone who has studied immigrants who have switched national cultures after, say, 30 years of age, realizes that cultural conflict can produce emotional disturbances of no lesser magnitude than those of a personal neurosis.

The second form of conflict among groups—that of mutual competition for synergy and membership—is often less publicly realized and *can* exist quite powerfully without overt conflict between the groups as such. It is nevertheless conflict for survival and is necessitated by equations (7-4) and (7-5) above, which state that the sum of group synergies equals the sum of individual energies. The more an individual gives to one group, the less he can give to another. An empirical instance when actual motivation strength measures were made occurs in an unpublished study by Cattell, Scheier, and Howard of 200 doctors, in whom the strength of affiliation to their active professional societies on the one hand and to their families on the other (as measured by the MAT) yielded a significant negative correlation. (A well-known scientific society that chose to meet during the two days following Christmas had to give up that plan because of family protests!) Groups are indeed well aware of this competition, as shown, for example, in the demand for celibacy in some priesthoods, and the perennial inquiries in Congress about conflict of interests. Groups are justly mutually jealous, and mutually suspicious of the ultimate danger of infiltration into group A of members with a more primary interest in the goals of group B.

Many valuable, shrewed observations on the interaction of groups with one another and with individuals are part of the professional know-how of politicians and business men, and need to be gathered into the more explicit models and calculations that psychologists can at least begin to develop to apply quantitatively. But certain generalizations already emerge. As Boulding (1970) observes "The more developed the society the more roles are likely to be combined in a single person." It is equally probable that a more developed society will have more roles in all the society and also symbiotic subgroups. If so, this spells a greater dynamic complexity within each individual and accounts in part for the pattern of the *cultural pressure* factor (Table 7-2) with its signs of greater conflict, frustration, sublimation and regression, which we shall study further. Regarding the last it remains to be checked whether more alcoholism and drug addiction also belong to the loading pattern. The empirical evidence for more sentiment factors with more developed societies is, however, not yet provided. Cattell & Sweney (1964) found, surprisingly, that there seemed more sentiment factors in children than in adults, but, if confirmed, it points only to sentiments being more fragmentary. For example, children seem to have sentiments to a particular food rather than to food; to mother and to father separately rather than to the family, and so on—before later integration occurs. But this is not necessarily in disagreement with the greater complexity of sentiments in more complex cultures. A theory for investigating personality-cultural relations, by quantitative, dynamic calculus advances will need to distinguish between the psychological burden of sheer numerical increase in complexity, on the one hand, and emotional incompatibilities on the other, as in the instances above, or where society forbids murder in general but enjoins it in war. So far clinicians have thought of the early family constellation sources of neuroses as being decidedly more important than a clash of cultural sentiments. But it may be they are right in this only because conflicts at an early age register by imprinting more than later.

It was said here earlier that social psychology has to deal with the relativity of a developing personality and a developing society. With the degree of isomorphism we have recognized one can see that the rate of change of cultural traditions is fixed partly by the rate of intergroup impacts and internal inventions that produce social change and partly by the rate at which individuals can learn and change in their own sentiment structures. That rate must be to some extent fixed by the psychological and even physiological properties of the human mind, and Toffler in *Future Shock* suggests that in this century the properties of the individual (and therefore of the population, P in equation 7-1) are all on the side of slowing the change rate independently generated by group events. As we shall point out in studying population measurements (p. 525) there is evidence of development factors being tied to population traits, and one would like to see evidence on relation to the radicalism-conservatism factor, Q_1, to the age of the population, and the extent to which anxiety has produced rigidity.

Before continuing the above into the study of evolution and revolution in Section 7-9, let us look more closely at the mechanisms which account for the primary stability and continuity. Every society has cultural mores, traditions, and constitutional values, partly set in writing partly conveyed more subtly, partly deliberately conveyed in school, churches and mass media, partly unconsciously "taught" in family and peer groups. Psychologists' attacks on the initial problem of finding out the relative magnitudes of their effects in sentiment formation and character building have shown some inconsistency, partly through being scattered over forty years of social change, and different classes, and partly through too much methodological dependence on questionnaires, polling and the like, which lack the validity and the discrimination of dynamic calculus methods. The *majority* of findings (but depending on epoch and country) suggest that a 25 year old has taken more of his or her values from the parental home than from school or from the peer group. Himmelweit, and some researchers on mass media, give more weight to press and TV than do students of the home. As to peers, it must be noted, however, that the effect at 20 can look superficially and immediately large, because it fits the adolescent's need to revolt and redefine himself. But with what psychoanalysis has called "the return of the repressed" it can be hypothesized that in a statistical examination of values and sentiments at 35 and after, the subject's parental home would be found predominant again. In the U.S., by common consent and constitution, state education is secular, and character building in any deliberate or intensive sense of an integrated set of particular values is secondary to cognitive learning. But in other schools, such as the (private) British residential public schools, and religious parochial schools, it is possible that emotional learning will be shown to be as potent and pervasive as in the family.

The difficulties of any group seeking to impose inhibitory and complex learning and still retain the individual in the group are notoriously greatest in the school, but also appear in the military, the reformatory prison and the family, from all of which there is a sufficient percentage of drop-outs, truants, AWOL's and run-aways to indicate that in these cases we are rather near the limit where the totality of reward in belonging to the group drops for some individuals to zero. In a well integrated society one group can lend its synergy to another. School attendance in most countries is compulsory, which almost always means that the schools depend on the synergy of the child to his family to get him to school—at least initially; the primary group thus acts as a lever to get the individual to adopt the second group—producing a sentiment growth by budding.

A whole chapter could easily be given to the structural learning processes in individual personality formation associated with this machinery for transmitting the culture pattern. For example, studies have been made from time to time of classroom resistances (conscious and unconscious) to learning. The makers of such surveys comment on task avoidance by rationalization, distractions, projection, and various defense mechanisms familiar to the clinician—and, alas, to the teacher. The synergy of schools, as far as the average child is concerned, is not (or was not) very high. Studies of dropouts (not to mention reminiscences by the many authors who ran away to sea!) make any summary here unnecessary. Incidentally, recent studies of college dropouts by the 16 PF indicate that we should beware of thinking of dropouts from school as failures, since the personality characteristics associated are often of a positive kind (Cattell, Eber, & Tatsuoka, 1970). We are dealing rather more with a motivational than a personality failure, in which the group synergy incentives are probably inadequate.

Granted that our basic analysis of the nature of a group demands the primary dynamic condition that the group must give more positive than negative ergic end satisfactions to every individual member, it behooves us to look a little more closely at the negative satisfaction that necessary control and inhibition by the group imposes, like a tax, on individuals' positive satisfactions. The issues in moral and political control, in police forces, tax collectors, and schools, etc., are fairly obvious, and have been assessed from time to time, though so far only in the verbal, polling type of attitude survey. Let us give space here, therefore, to the more subtle and pervasive controls in public opinion e.g. peer group, family and friends, which have a common character that we have characterized by the term *coercion to the bio-social norm*. Both in persons in particular roles and in members generally there are numerous situations where it is to the immediate advantage of the group to have behavior approach a stereotype. Bees and ants form remarkably efficient and persistent groups and it is only in sophisticated human societies that the advantages to society of a certain degree of individual deviation are perceived. Even there, however, stable expectations of what is correct behavior cause a central tendency to be preferred in most roles, including that of basic membership.

In discussing coercion to the biosocial mean in behavior genetics (Chapter 1) we noted that every individual is likely to deviate appreciably, in the genetic components of one or more personality and dynamic traits, from the biological average of his group. Similarly he deviates from the levels aimed at by education in his cultural group. In some variables, such as intelligence and superego strength, the ideal happens not to be the central tendency. Most people are likely in this second case to fall to the lower side of the stereotype, so that socioeducation pressure is all in one direction. In quite a lot of traits, however, one sees a measurable, socially exerted pressure toward the mode or mean, for example, to a decent but not excessive modesty (an average E score) or a talkativeness that sustains but does not hog the conversation (a middling F, surgency) or a moderate but not excessive emotional sensitivity (an average level in premsia; Chapter 2). However, in a first attack on the principle, we may subsume "ideal" and "mean" under "norm," since one or the other is the desired norm.

These and other observations were formulated by the present writer (1950) in terms of the *law of coercion to the biosocial norm* although some have objected to the expression "coercion," and *possibly* the term "impulsion" is better. The statistical evidence for it lies in an observed decreasing standard deviation in some traits over the period of education, greater signs of maladjustment in those who are initially merely statistically deviant, for example, the left handed, and especially, in *negative correlation of genetic and threptic contributions*, as found by the MAVA method (Chapter 1). "Biosocial" is used because the target is probably as much set by biological as social norms, as when dieting aims at what a given society considers neither too fat nor too thin.

Regardless of whether coercion is toward some presently socially desired control mode or some ideal envisioned above humanity and roughly opposite in direction to the ape, the stress of adjustment to cultural coercion is one of the main problems for study in the personality-culture area. That stress could almost certainly be factored into more than one direction of pressure upon our present biologically given human nature. Adjustment to sheer cognitive complexity is one, and we seek to alleviate this by occupational and other specialization. A few men at the Renaissance kept in touch, as did da Vinci, with virtually all culture, but few indeed today could at once mend a TV and a car, understand the action of what is picked up at the pharmacist, make a sculpture in marble, state the legal fine points of the U.S. constitution, and navigate a plane. Both human intelligence and the magnitude of our memory storages fall short of the full cultural demands. If we turn from the obvious cognitive harrassments to the demands on emotional learning we encounter the demands on the ego for weighting decisions with respect to an increasing roster of different engrammed sentiments and ergic investments. With this effect we move into the area of *deflection strain*, *long circuiting* and the *dynamic complexity of a culture*, which we have defined elsewhere.

These concepts we shall now study in greater depth and bring to fuller precision. We need to study them both in this section, in relation to acculturation of the individual, and in the next two sections in relation to group learning and evolutionary-revolutionary social change. Naturally we begin with acculturation to a steady culture and proceed to adjustment to a changing culture. In these domains of psychological interaction of individual and culture we need on the one hand such equipment as the above concepts of parameters of individual dynamic adjustment, and, on the other, a closer description of those dimensions of modern cultural syntalities (nations' data) that are of a dynamic nature. If we consider long circuiting, and so forth, as the independent variable in these associations, then in addition to looking at syntality consequences we shall look at population consequences, namely into population personality measures having to do with the clinical effects to be expected from the individual's attempts to cope with the dynamic complexity. But personality effects on syntality are also to be studied.

The ways in which the properties of a cultural affect the dynamics of the acculturation process are many. The cognitive demands on intelligence and memory capacities we shall discuss later. The demands on the dynamic make-up will obviously be grossly related to the amount of ergic frustration the average citizen has to tolerate. Starvation, overcrowding (population pressure), epidemic, disease, denial of freedoms, constant threats of war, denial of social mobility by compartmentalized classes with absolute barriers, excessive labor relative to reward, and other deprivations put a demand on frustration tolerance over a wide spectrum of ergs such as hunger, need security, self-assertion, sex, and gregariousness. Constant new adjustments emerge to the pressures, as the "slave religion" of early Christianity made tolerable and self respecting, by humility and denial of pugnacity, the adjustment of a down-trodden class already with but little choice but to express these virtues; or as the brutal chaos of the Middle Ages made men willing to sacrifice much for feudal security.

The over-all level of ergic satisfaction in a culture is surely the first determiner of the adjustment problems in acculturation. But the rate and manner in which demands for rewarding long-circuitings and complexities are applied come next. One would guess with some confidence that the level of sheer ergic satisfaction is higher in present day society than ever it has been; but this has been achieved by an adaptive increase in inhibitions and complexities.

In senses most meaningful to individual dynamics we have defined, on p. 531, the concepts of *ergic deflection strain, long-circuiting* and *dynamic complexity of expression* and have set out formulae whereby they can be more precisely defined and measured. To remind the reader: the first is the remoteness of both the executive *S-R* elements on the path to the goal, and the consummatory behavior itself (in some cases) from those built into the organism by countless generations of shaping of the innate ergs. The second is the distance, in terms of number of subgoals, in the lattice, between initial action toward an ergic goal and the goal itself. The last, which we hypothesize would be positively correlated with the second, is the extent to which the average attitude course of action in the lattice is ergically complex.

Many qualitative observations have been made by cultural anthropologists and historians on the psychological demands of various cultures. Among the best of these one can mention Margaret Mead's *Coming of Age in Samoa* (1949), Gibbon (1910), Winwood Read (1949) and on through a very large bibliography that provides the social psychologist with rich material for re-formulation in psychological terms. A recent hypothesis by a perceptive biologist (Huxley, 1953, in *Africa View*) is that the impact of Western culture on tribal life in Africa produced an increase in schizophrenia.

In the last twenty years a rapid but methodologically shakey growth of cross cultural psychological research has occurred. Before such personality measures as the 16 PF were checked to demonstrate what traits held up factorially across cultures (see Cattell, Eber, & Tatsuoka, 1972) comparisons commonly used hurriedly produced, ad hoc measures, making subsequent interpretation difficult. The supplementary approach by measured frequencies of mental disorders, suicides, murders, and so forth encounters considerable difficulties because of non-equivalence of record keeping. World data in psychological epidemiology is at present very poorly provided. Especially, as mentioned, there are doubts in crosscultural scoring about the conceptual equivalence of the pathological categories. As Marsella (1974) and others have pointed out the percentage of schizophrenics differs, from diagnostic reasons, even in different federal and state hospitals in the U.S.A., and there is a tendency for differences in percentage of diagnosed cases to reflect different thoroughness of diagnostic sources, or even hospital beds available, as much as actual differences. Nevertheless, on scanty data, various speculations about causal relations have appeared in the last decade by Arsenian, Fried, Leighton, Marsella and Parker and Klein.

Although very substantial research efforts will be required we believe the basic methodological approach requires (a) the consolidation of present evidence on the syntality dimensions of nations and the scoring of the 100 (approx.) available for comparisons on these dimensions, (b) the measurement of population samples on the verified crossculturally applicable concepts of individual personality and adjustment parameters, as in the 16 PF, MAT, and primary ability batteries. Although the evidence in this area is (except for syntality traits) recent and scanty indeed (only 17 countries on the 16 PF) we shall venture some hypotheses of the effect of syntality traits on acculturation on these population measures, confining ourselves to syntality traits that have been replicated (Woliver & Cattell 1979) and that appear dynamic in nature. Examples of these syntality dimensions have been given in Table 7-2, but we shall now look at them more interpretively.

Vigorous Development is the main factor separating developed from "undeveloped" countries. Its highest loadings are on *high degree of industrialization, restriction of birth rate, high per capita consumption of energy, high proportion of tertiary occupations*, and so forth. (Cattell, Breul, & Hartmann, 1952; Cattell, Graham, & Woliver, 1978; Rummel, 1972). The population scores associated with this are sizia (*A-* factor), which betokens an emotional self discipline (absence of undependable sentimentality), *forthrightness* (*N-*) (both r = .45 or above) and, at a significance level only of indications (remember this is on only 17 nations), *introversion, desurgency*, and *low narcism*. It is evident that these are qualities which might be covered in more popular terms as a self-disciplined, controlled, but energetic temperament, adjusted to decided ergic long-circuiting. As Myrdal (1968) by social survey methods was seemingly reluctantly compelled at length to admit the problem of aiding undeveloped countries to develop is more than economics and involves some basic changes in personality values.

Intelligence affluence (see Table 7-2, Intelligent affluence) correlates with *educational level, low ergic tension* (Q_4-), *low dominance* (*E-*), *introversion* (*QII-*) and *desurgency* (restraint) (*F-*). Whether these qualities of "calm and gentlemanly" restraint are products or contributors to the real wealth of a society can be debated. The highest correlation—that with low ergic tension, Q_4, which is a measure of degree of unsatisfied drive—indicates that acculturation to a society combining more education, with technically derived affluence, involves substantially less sheer ergic frustration. The introversion and desurgency can be understood as the result of teaching toward higher dynamic complexity of cultural attitudes.

Careless, unintegrated society is a syntality dimension loading *high incidence of typhoid, fewer deaths by heart disease and suicide, high gross birth rate, very few Nobel prizes per million*, and *many people per dwelling.* The significant population associates are high surgency (F) and high premsia (I), and other traits with a happy-go-lucky and reality-ignoring character, which could be cause or consequence.

Cultural Pressure. In the latest research (Cattell, Graham & Woliver 1978) it is recognized that this previously much discussed dimension splits into two factors, one being a reaction of pugnacity against the pressure and the other representing, perhaps at a later stage, a cultural sublimation. The former—the intolerant reaction against cultural pressure, expressed in *riots, strikes and* wars, and high urbanization correlates with personality traits in the population of low guilt proneness $(O-$ factor$)$, surgency (F) and low self-sentiment development (Q_3-). One can see readily in these traits an inability $(F$ has substantial genetic determination$)$ or unwillingness (non-incorporation in the self sentiment) to inhibit or to accept *deflection strain* and *long circuiting* that the growing urbanization, population density and technical complication bring about as a by-product.

Cultural Pressure with Sublimation which correlates with and resembles in technical complication *(gross national product, industrial invention)* the above syntality dimension differs in its population associations. The reaction to deflection strain and long circuiting in the first factor (above) is aggression to frustration (wars, riots—and inward aggression in suicide). In the second, which may be a culture at a later phase where pugnacity has exhausted itself (see the APA chart, p. 307), the denied direct ergic expression now takes the path of sublimation, and the loadings are on *cultural productivity, Nobel prizes per million, musical compositions per year, higher education of women* and *number of patents for inventions.* The population characters significantly related are *greater susceptibility to inhibition* $(H-)$, and higher anxiety $(QII+)$. Whether this means an impact of cultural pressure on a naturally more inhibited racial strain, or on a population that has passed through pugnacity to anxiety, as in the APA sequence, is uncertain, but perhaps the latter is more probable.

Morality-morale shown in such variables as *fewer murders, less venereal disease, low % unemployed, low gross death rate, high ratio of agricultural to other workers, fewer calories per day per capita, fewer deaths by heart disease.* It is still a less confirmed syntality-factor but relates at below significance $(r = .39$ and $.38)$ to guilt proneness (O), and anxiety QII.

Both restricted space and scientific caution dictate that we do not pursue farther many interesting speculations on these syntality-population relations. The methodology and concepts constitute a break from those of the qualitative observations of Benedict, Keyserling, Mead, and others, not to mention the speculations of psychoanalysts. Though new, and as yet confined to distinctly small samples it has yielded (a) consistency in syntality dimension patterns across experiments at different times (b) statistically significant relations of syntality to population dimensions, of a kind that readily fit our psychological hypotheses. More work is needed on cross cultural personality comparisons, as in Cattell, 1973, Cattell, Eber, and Tatsuoka 1970, and Tsujioka and Cattell 1965 on Q-data factors, and Cattell, Schmidt and Pawlik (1973), Undheim (1976), and Vandenberg (1959, 1967) on objective test structures. What is most needed is a tightening of the score comparisons,[4] an extension of samples and inclusion of dynamic (MAT) measures in the population scores. Some temporal sequence measures are desirable too, to explore the direction of causal action in $S = f(P.R)$.

Although ability differences are of less importance to our theory than dynamic trait relations, let us give them a side glance. It is strange that this area of testing, consolidated earlier than others, actually has been less explored as to group differences than have personality measures. It could be that this is due to the tardiness of many practising psychologists to recognize both the theoretical foundation and the practical demonstration of the possiblity of essentially culture fair intelligence tests (see discussion, Cattell, 1979).

The demonstration that culture-fair tests reliably repeat their loading patterns on "g_f" in different countries and can yield the same mean scores (from an *identical* test form) in cultures so different as the U.S.A. and Taiwan, has too often been ignored. So also have the basic experiments (Cattell, 1971; Vandenberg, 1978) pointing to the theory that g is a universal factor of capacity to perceive complex relations, no matter what the fundaments and cultural matrix in which the relations appear. At a common sense level the meaningfulness of both the culture fair measures of fluid intelligence and the traditional, culturally local measure of crystallized intelligence in revealing group differences can be readily seen. For the latter will give significant geographical area differences in a nation e.g. Britain with a tightly knit culture; while a culture fair test will give complete equality of mean scores in culturally quite diverse nations, while yielding significant differences among people in the same culture. Thus Thorndike and Woodyard (1942) in the U.S.A. and Lynn (1978), and Saville (1975) and the present writer (1937) in Britain have shown certain typical significant differences, for example, in rural levels being exceeded by urban norms, and among various regional populations. Lynn (1978), for example, shows higher mean in Yorkshire and the South East of Britain than elsewhere, and a decline in the mean in Scotland over 50 years. He also brings evidence of a higher mean IQ in Japan than in the U.S.A. (1971) (though with translated English tests rather than culture-fair tests), ascribing it to a comparatively recent but thorough impact of family planning in Japan.

Such differences of various racial-mixture populations with time (Maxwell, 1969) and place are to be expected from migration (MacKay, 1969) and birth rate differentials (Cattell, 1937). A theoretical analysis of how cultural syntality dimensions might be expected to change with mean IQ has been presented (Cattell, 1938), but until the above pioneer data by Lynn and by Maxwell appeared, no support was available. Correlating over 13 regions, Lynn found a first component among community indices as in Table 7-7.

Lynn infers that intelligence is the primary determiner of the pattern, though this would be more highly defensible if culture-fair tests had been available for his survey. However, on indirect inference his position is far more defensible than that of a recent U.S. report investigating the downturn in school standards over the last six years, ascribing it to school and parent morale and teaching methods (which doubtless play a part), while blandly ignoring the evidence on intelligence and birth rates, such as is set out in Figure 7-6.

In our comparisons above of national syntality dimensions with population characters reliable IQ means were not available for sufficient countries but since available evidence points to small but significant differences of IQ among various populations we can look for syntality dimensions that might express the effect of such population differences. A likely one is surely that which we have called *intelligent affluence* (Table 7-2) for although we had no actual intelligence measure on that study the syntality pattern resembles Lynn's in Table 7-7 which does contain that measure. Actually, in the intelligent affluence factor the variables related to high living standard represent education rather than intelligence, and of course we have mooted the alternatives that (a) educated intelligence raises the standard of living and (b) money to spare goes into more education. As a limit to the former one recognizes the accidents of natural resources, presently apparent to Americans in the matter of gasoline. But there are countless historical examples of intelligent and educated societies making resources out of thin air. (A literal example was Fritz Haber's response to the blockade of nitrates from Germany in World War I, when he and his fellow chemists made nitrates from air. Hopefully the ingenuity of the U.S. and non-OPEC countries will similarly master new sources of energy.) Incidentally, one needs, in seeking the correlations of affluence and the level of

TABLE 7-7. Regional Associations of Measured Mean
Community IQ (after Lynn)

	Loadings on First Component
Population mean IQ	.94
% Frequency of Fellows of the Royal Society	.96
% Frequency of first-class honors university degrees	.70
Mean (per capita) income	.87
% Of unemployed	-.87
Infant mortality	-.87

the national currency unit with intelligence to consider not only the mean but the distribution of intelligence, for the size of a broad elite in the upper range of the distributions might be more decisive than the mere mean in determining the affluence dimension.

Let it be repeated that theory does not expect any one-to-one relation between syntality and population dimensions. In the two-directional causality the interaction of *several* personality population characters might contribute—as exemplified above—to one syntality dimension, and vice versa. Thus intelligence should surely be a contributor to the *sublimated cultural pressure* syntality trait which shows itself in Nobel prizes per million, invention rate, and other contributors to civilization. Conversely, it is not supposed that the affluence pattern is solely derived from intelligence. As the evidence below shows (Cattell & Woliver, 1978), the measures of population means on the F factor shows highly educated affluent countries also significantly lower on surgency, that is, they tend to be desurgent, inhibited, controlled. (The contrast of Switzerland and Southern Italy is illustrative.)

In accordance with our general systems model, which goes beyond equation (7-1) and assumes that genetic and threptic population characteristics affect syntality and syntality characteristics feed back on threptic qualities, and, eventually, also on genetic population characteristics, the relationships of syntality and population measures *should* be complex. We must take into account also the population *structure* term (R in equation 7-1), which has much to do with the information networks and exchanges.

An illustration of the role of the structural term, R in regard to communication network effects can be given in the present area of discussion—that of intelligence, where much work has been done. Among the hypotheses proposed for study are: (1) the concept of a *percolation range* (Cattell, 1938) *for ideas* in relation to the total population whereby certain complexities of reasoning will have specific possibilities (measured in speed of propagation perhaps) in different IQ strata; (2) the concept of *emergents*, whereby small mean differences in the IQ of groups will result in comparatively great differences of syntality in cultural level (in the narrower intellectual sense); (3) the related notion of *coercion of individual communication style toward a mean*, so that a person of IQ 110 could not operate so intelligently in a group averaging 100 as in one averaging 120; (4) that (2) may be aided by a small percentage rise in the mean bringing a large percentage rise in IQ above, say, 130 (distribution being preserved).

A model can be worked out for (2) if we suppose that, say, each 10-point rise in IQ enables the individual to grasp *p* new, more complex, social ideas than one ten points lower in IQ. Let us suppose that to get intelligent democratic action on more complex ideas each person must be able to interact with every other on them to produce group understanding and that action ensues when two thirds of such dyadic discussions lead to assent. If we consider the resulting action a measure of the intelligence of the group, then we can enunciate a *law of emergence; that the intelligence of the performances of a society has an increase proportional to the square of the increase of the mean IQ of the population.* For the increase of the dyadic assents to the more complex solution $[dA/d(IQ)]$ will be 2/3 times *np*, $(np - 1)/2 = n^2 p^2 /3 - np/3$.

It remains to give that more precise definition of the meaning of *deflection strain, long circuiting* and *dynamic complexity* which we gave only in clinical or general descriptive terms before. Incidentally, in earlier writing "deflection strain" has also been used as a generic term for all three; but for this broader meaning we will now use "deflection stress." To *deflection strain* we now wish to give a specific operational definition. We have distinguished in the dynamic specification equation between the loading on an erg, b_e, which represents the *S-R* connection due to *innately* meaningful aspects of the situation, and b_m which loads the acquired sentiment action on an erg.[5] The following thus expresses the ergic tension component.

$$a_{hj} = b_{hje} E + b_{hjm y} M_y E \tag{7-7a}$$

From this it should not be impossible empirically to reach a deflection strain index, *ds*, thus, concerning erg E above:

$$ds = \overset{hj=n}{\underset{}{\Sigma}} \overset{y=q}{\underset{}{\Sigma}} b_{hjm y} - \overset{hj=n}{\underset{}{\Sigma}} b_{hje} \tag{7-7b}$$

The summation would have to be over a time sampled set of *n* behaviors (*hj*'s) in each of the cultures compared and might with a *small* attitude sample best involve also the E and M strengths. The index *ds* is then a measure of ergic activity motivated by cultural stimuli minus that which comes from primitive situations.

Long circuiting is, of course, the *distance*, either in time or the number of intermediate sub-goals, between the typical stimuli encountered and the ergic, consummatory goals. The argument is fairly obvious and convincing that the time between stimulation of an attitude and the individual's reaching of ergic goals would be so closely proportional to the number of subgoals that the correlation of long-circuiting and complexity would be high. Nevertheless, it deserves separate measurement, though we shall not attempt here the quite complex expression that might be necessary on account of the time lag to different goals involved in the attitude being disparate.

Dynamic complexity can be defined, in keeping with the meanings of the dynamic calculus and the lattice, as the extent to which many final ergic consummatory satisfactions, rather than a few are involved in a typical attitude. As a measurement of a culture it needs to be gathered, like the others, from an adequate stratified sample of attitudes. The complexity, as a "spread" of loadings, is readily expressed by counting the number (out of *p* ergs) that reach significant loadings on each of the suitable stratified sample of *n* adult attitudes in the daily life of the culture. This long circuiting, or dynamic complexity, c_d, index for a culture would thus be:

$$c_{de} = \sum^{x=n} \frac{c_x}{n} \tag{7-8}$$

where c_x is the number of significant loadings on the *p* ergs in a given attitude action *x*, and *n* attitudes are covered. An argument might be made for including major sentiments as well as ergs in this count. A corresponding long-circuiting index by count of sentiment subgoals involved would then be:

$$c_{dm} = \sum^{x=n} \frac{m_x}{n} \tag{7-9}$$

where m_x is the number of sentiment subgoals significantly loaded in the specification equation for *x*. However c_{dm} may prove to have some different associations from c_{de}, and, indeed, though these four different measures (above) of what might generally be called deflection stress will correlate they should have interestingly different special properties. In regard to (a) the personality characteristics in the individual which enable him to tolerate deflection stress in the culture, and (b) those which deflection stress may produce in individuals of average tolerance, we have to consider cognitive abilities as well as personality traits. Obviously, as the mirror of the culture in school education shows, individuals of higher IQ and better memory will experience less stress. Presumably the personality traits known to have weights on school adjustment, such as C, G, $O(-)$, Q_2 and Q_3 (Cattell & Butcher, 1968), offer our best available indication of tolerance also of cultural stress in adult life. Presumably also capacity to build up more extensive sentiment systems, which is involved in meeting high values in the equations such as (7-12) above, is partly dependent on general memory capacity and intelligence.

These cognitive abilities are presumably themselves little affected by the cultural stress. Indeed when we turn to consider the culture-to-personality direction of action it is the personality and dynamic traits that will be most influenced. From what is known about clinical and occupational effects on primary and secondary personality factors we would hypothesize (but without space for the detailed arguments) that deflection stress would tend to produce desurgency $(F-)$, threctia $(H-)$, sizia $(A-)$, guilt proneness (O) and sophistication (N). These primaries would mean, in secondaries, introversion $(QI-)$ and anxiety (QII). More deflection-stress-producing cultures might also be expected to affect G, superego, and Q_3, self-sentiment, inasmuch as the latter (additional to geographical, economic and technical demands) would tend, through its association with sublimation, to accompany the growth of a culture in complexity.

The above hypothesized connections can be examined in the recent Cattell and Woliver data (1979), and one hopes, soon in more extensive data from other investigators. The association of cultural deflection level—if we consider it represented in the syntality traits of *cultural pressure as sublimation, vigorous development, intelligent affluence* and *industriousness*—is found to be with personality traits $H(-)$, O, N, and QII, but the Q_3 and superego, G, associations are not at all evident. Thus on the whole these expectations are met but there are intriguing anomalies, too. The relation will be further pursued in relation to group change and revolution, below.

7-8. Group Learning and Personality Change

Having looked at the essentials of group and individual interrelations as far as present data justify, we are as prepared as we may reasonably expect to be at present to look at group learning, that is, the learning change in a group's behavior. As before, our central concern is still in understanding personality, but its relations to the group and group change are an essential extension of that understanding. Thus a brief digression to study the learning of groups *as groups* is indispensable. Any functioning group, like an individual, is an organism, and the laws operating in it can be understood only by considering it as an organism and an acting system, rather than statically as a mere aggregate. Nevertheless, although we ultimately come, in this chapter, to a systems theory of the group, we are not denying that the best research strategy is that which succeeded for personality; namely, a cross-sectional study of structure, to be *followed* by the kinetic study of the changing specification equations.

As with individual learning, so with group learning; it behooves the careful investigator to put learning in perspective among other varieties of change by clean definitions. Although there are resemblances to the three forms of individual change: *learning, volution* (genetically effected change), and *somatic* change, the ultimate variety of forms of change is actually greater.

The first three in the following forms of group change are matchable with the individual forms just mentioned; the remainder are new.

1. True, group learning, with subvarieties discussed below.

2. Effects of volution in individuals if the average population age changes.

3. "Somatic" changes caused by famine, disease, crowding, climatic change and so on.

4. Genetic change through natural selection and migration.

5. Change in group membership by in-and-out-migration.

6. Change in synergy through the energies of members changing in relation to "coactive" groups to which they belong. (We shall continue to use "coactive" for groups that share the interests of some or all of the same common population of members.)

Some sociologists have thrust (4) and (5) out of discussion, sometimes for extrascientific reasons and with the rationalization that cultural change is of so different an order of speed from genetic change that the latter can be ignored. The recent work of Lynn (1977), however, pointing to about a three-point fall in IQ in Scotland within a century, probably resulting from emigration, indicates that group changes from these biological causes can be real enough. In any case, over the longer perspective of history, as Darlington (1969) shows, changes in group syntality from causes (4) and (5) play a noticeable role.

The main concentration here must be on category (1) learning, with brief asides on (5) and (6), and two other sources of group change. Clearly, the branch of psychology we are here studying is nothing less than history. But social psychology is more advanced in its statistical methodology and more committed to systematic theory about human personality, than other academic specialties in this area. History and political science have, until the last century, been so completely deprived of measurement and statistical analysis, that social psychology has difficulty in meshing with historical method as used by any but a relatively few recent researchers in these disciplines (Rummel, Chadwick, Deutsch, Alker, Singer and others). But at least the reference to the drama of history should remind any social psychology student with narrow conceptions of learning as "gain" that we do not necessarily mean improvement only, any more than we did with individuals, for when "learning" occurs it can be in a maladjustive direction. In short trends in history can be good or bad, just as individual learning in the APA chart can end in adjustment or neurosis. Should we need reminding of the latter possibility, let us note that Oscar Wilde once defined history as "an account of things that should never have happened!"

Just as investigation of a group arrested at an instant of static experimental inspection deals with syntality, S, structure, R, and population, P, so also learning investigation must be prepared to deal with *change* in the features and measures analyzed in S, R, and P. An enormous amount of research has been lavished on population change because measuring changes of attitude, or polling results, or achievement in the classroom, makes few methodological demands beyond those in individual research, and the research labor is far less when dealing say, with 200 people, than with 200 groups. On the population variables *as such* some of the most systematic work has been done on children in classroom groups, for example, by Gage (1963), Cronbach (1964), MacLeish, Matheson, and Park (1973), and many others. But we shall not pursue it here because the learning of groups, *as* groups, requires that they should be free continuously to change *structure*, which can scarcely happen in the teacher-classroom unit, dealing with *average individual* learning.

So recent are the experimental studies with living groups, using the concepts of syntality, synergy, and structure (using multivariate definitions of roles, and so on), that concrete evidence is very limited (except for 2 or 3 successive measures of nations at few-years interval in the work of Rummel (1968, 1969, 1972, 1975) and Cattell and Woliver (1977). However, the P-technique studies of Adelson (1952), Cattell (1953), Gibb (1956), and a few others extend over most of a century. Good psychometrics requires that *change* measures be based on *absolute* measures that are unusually accurate and so the sheer reliability of the syntality profile must now come up for scrutiny.

The two main questions that arise are (1) Is the loading pattern of a syntality trait sufficiently constant over a reasonable historical period (say 20 to 80 years) to permit us to compare measurements on it using the same weighting of submeasures? and (2) As in personality is the absolute level constant enough for the dimension to be considered a *trait* or do we have only *state* dimensions in syntality, to which no steady growth or trend can reasonably be assigned? The answer to the first is given by the Woliver and Cattell (1979) study of Rummel's, Breul and Hartman's and Cattell's results showing significant and adequate congruence coefficients over at least eight dimensional patterns over 25 years. The answer to the second is given in cross-national calculations of the dependability and stability coefficients (defined for example, in Cronbach, Gleser, Nanda, & Rajaratnam, 1972; Cattell, 1973; and Nunnally, 1967) over 10- and 50-year intervals which show (Cattell, 1949, 1950; Rummel, 1972; Woliver & Cattell 1979) that nations are surprisingly stable. In fact the stability coefficients over most syntality variables are at the same level as for personality variables in individuals.

Because historians discuss dramatic change, they are likely to overlook the criterion of the psychometrist, that an organismic continuity of the society itself be demonstrated. For example, a great change, from the usual historical viewpoint, came over Russia in 1917–1918 but perceptive intellectuals (like Joseph Conrad, who, as a Pole, had an alert eye on the behavior of this big neighbor) declared it had changed relatively little and many statesmen have now come to the same conclusion. And the psychologists' indices of syntality, although showing sharp changes in some variables, manifested surprising persistence of certain traits from the Czarist to the Stalinist period. A nation is a complex organic system, with momentum in its organic parts that on closer and deeper scrutiny manifests something more constant than the merely conscious ideational and political changes. What is still more surprising is that, at the opposite range of size, 10-man neonate groups (with a leader) show group performances stability coefficients (Cattell & Wispe, 1948; Penman, 1951) that are very significant, though not as high as in large groups with their perpetuated traditions.

The beginning of an empirically based learning study can therefore safely begin with measured syntality change from stable syntalities. Alas, we must still wait for repeat studies of the work of Cattell, Breul, and Hartmann (1947); Rummel (1972, 1977), Woliver and Cattell (1979) and others to supply enough points on the curves for syntality dimensions for nations generally to permit any generalizations. However the longitudinal *P*-technique studies done on Australia (Gibb, 1956), Britain (Cattell, 1953), and the United States (Cattell & Adelson, 1953) have given us some substantial indications, notably in regard to the cultural pressure dimension. Any skeptic of the mathematical approach to history who asserts, as some do, that syntality factors are non-organic mathematical abstractions can see in Figure 7-5 that each factor very definitely shows a unique developmental life of its own. The rise and final "hesitation" in [1], the cultural pressure factor, advance seems to have been premonitory of what has been more obvious in recent years.

With this comment on the empirical basis of learning curves in syntality (and also, of course, in structure and population parameters), let us consider sequentially the above six forms of group change or learning. Every one of these forms (despite the fact that several do not *begin* in the individual) involves *changes in the individual's attitudes* and skills. Although change is seen in the group as a group it is thus correct to recognize that all group learning—as syntality and synergy change—is ultimately locked into and dependent upon changes of the individual nervous systems of the population. But this is certainly not to say that the changes in individual attitudes bring about changes in syntality. Causality acts in both directions. Nor does it assume any simple relation between changes in the group and changes in the individual—in either direction of causality.

As regard sentiments alone we have recognized that there *is* a relatively simple isomorphism between sentiment structure in the individual and institutional structure in the group, but syntality is dependent on more than the dynamic modality of personality traits—as both the small group and the national correlations show. Still more important in bringing about this non-conformity is the basic fact that syntality is a product of population characters and group structure. If we switched the dining room steward with the chief navigator on a liner, the population characteristics, in total skills, and so forth, would stay the same, but the behavior of the inhabitants of the liner might be drastically different. In considering revolutionary change, below, we shall see that this re-shuffling of structure means that syntality change and population trait change need have no simple relation, though a close dependency still exists in terms of more complex formulations.

As far as the *population* learning of a group is concerned there is no need to suppose that any more or any different principles operate from the five we have basically posited in individual learning. That is to say, if laws of learning of groups as such were formulated, say by the intensive study of groups by historians, there should be ways of reducing these to the five psychological learning laws *plus* additional principles deriving from the domain of structural re-arrangements in groups. (Just as our third law—integration learning—in individual learning, derives from *CE* and *ME* (*CR*I and *CR*II)—plus derivatives coming from the change of structure personality.)

In various fields of science we are familiar with what (since Lloyd Morgan) have commonly been called *emergents*. These are concepts and effects which could not have been predicted from knowledge only of the *elements* in patterns and composities, for example, the taste of salt from the properties of sodium and chlorine. One has to investigate the higher structures before being able to understand fully what the familar lower elements can do. All we can say with confidence at present in social psychology is that the emergents are extremely important. The difference in performance between two groups normally distributed as to intelligence and equal in sigma but differing in mean by 5 points of IQ may be a far greater difference of performance than we associate with a 5 point difference in two individuals. But more than the non-additive results of popu-lation traits is the transforming effect on emergents of group structure and roles. The mutineers and non-mutineers on the *Bounty* were, as far as we know, not particularly different in traits and background, but the leadership structure of the latter gave them survival against heavy odds, whereas the former, with every advantage, degenerated into rapine, murder, and virtual extinction.

Group learning as such probably employs most largely the *ME* (*CR*II) principle. Groups like individuals, are commonly forced to trial and error learning, and the structural and population changes which accompany the gain of a group reward tend to become established. The new technical problem we face in group learning is explaining how this group learning comes about—through changes in roles, status positions, and communication networks—by transform-ing group reward into that reward of individuals which is necessary for learning to come about in the minds of individual men, by *CR*II principles.

The models that will help us understand the transformation of group learning into individual learning are going to be of an awesome but fascinating complexity, and we can only glance at the nature of them here. They will differ for different types of group,[6] so that the need for experimental attack branches out in all directions. Small group research, with its ready manipulation, is a strategic point to begin, and the work of Guetzkow (1955, 1959), Asch (1952), and others shows how experiment with communication networks of different types can be profitably pursued to clear conclusions. Our

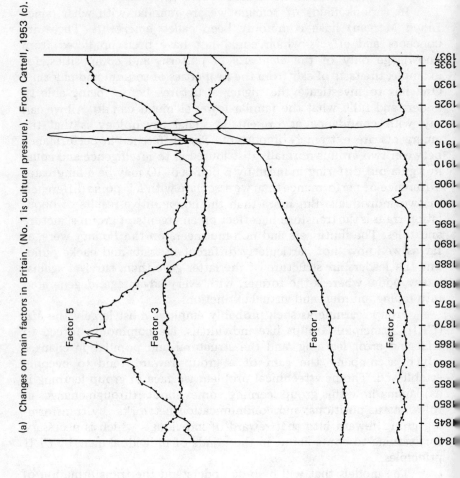

(a) Changes on main factors in Britain. (No. 1 is cultural pressure). From Cattell, 1953 (c).

Factor 5

Factor 3

Factor 1

Factor 2

1840 1845 1850 1855 1860 1865 1870 1875 1880 1885 1890 1895 1900 1905 1910 1915 1920 1925 1930 1935 1937

538

(b) Courses of cultural pressure factor measure in three Western cultures

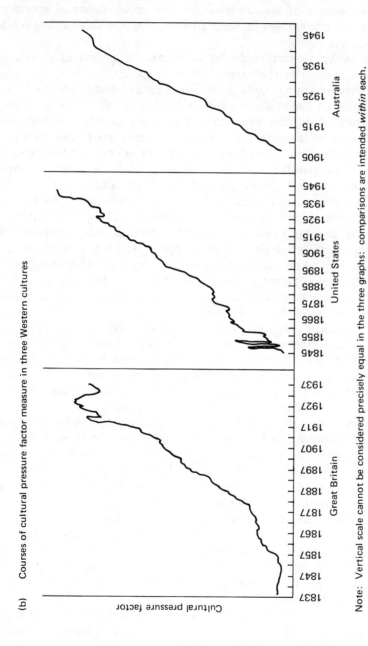

Great Britain

United States

Australia

Note: Vertical scale cannot be considered precisely equal in the three graphs: comparisons are intended *within* each.

Figure 7-5. Syntality dimension changes in Britain (1838–1938) and other countries.

own work (Cattell & Stice, 1967) on small groups concerning the increment in syntality from leaderless to leader groups, and on the relative capacities of leaders to satisfy the group needs of members and to increase members investment in synergy, nibbles at the initial edge of such analysis.

The many alternative forms of restructuring and of change of interaction networks that are possible in groups in the process of trial-and-error learning make group learning proceed at an altogether slower order of speed than individual learning. For each trial-and-error learning of the correct response by the group there are hundreds of trial-and-error learnings by individuals which must come out in a particular pattern of result for the group to respond correctly and be rewarded. The painful, hesitant, relapsing path of social progress through recorded history supports this analysis. And whereas insightful learning plays a major role with intelligent individuals, there is no single integrated consciousness in a group—unless it is under a dictator or an able committee member who is also persuasive—in which the flash of insight that brings a sudden change in the analogous individual learning curve can appear. The dangers of dictatorship and tyranny must not blind us to that fact that although a dictatorial leader's decision may be wrong, and would often benefit from group debate, yet a decision by a single leader permits a group to respond with life-saving speed in certain types of situation. The lengthy discussion by a committee may lead to a group insight, and, further, is likely to be more balanced, but human experience has commonly recommended reversion to the single leader in time of war, in ships at sea, in a surgical team, and wherever the highest coordination in a short time is required.

On the other hand, as R. L. Thorndike (1938) and others have shown, the accuracy of certain types of group decisions increases (at least over smaller numbers) with the number of (essentially) equal-intelligence persons involved. Indeed the accuracy seems neatly to follow the same Spearman-Brown law as applies to the effect of increase of number of items in determining test reliability. Even when the best insightful or trial and error decision for the group has been made, a second decision has to be made on how to modify the internal structure to bring about or facilitate the group act. This was well recognized by the U.S. government, for example, upon the decision to enter World War II. Countless new roles and communication networks were set up, and numerous education courses created, to effectuate the desired syntal action by structure changes. (The same occurred in peace, and in grimmer fashion, in Stalin's reshaping of Russia to a power posture.)

Group learning (by which, we should perhaps re-emphasize, we mean the learning of groups, not the far more familiar and simple learning of *individuals* in groups, as in the classroom) is of such a high complexity and so little investigated on a clear model that at present we grasp at straws of evidence. For example, as regards the effect of existing structures on learning, a first firm law, beyond the well known effects of existence of a leader structure as such, has been made in Fiedler's findings (1958) about the potency of the *relationship* of leader and "lieutenant", in the insights around "powers behind the throne" by Gibb (1949); and by the experiments of Guetzkow (1955) and Simmel (1969) on effects of communication networks.

As regards leadership and learning it is surely abundantly evident from history that a machinery which selects efficiently from the group resources of intelligence and character the most capable will cause the group that embodies this in its structure to make more effective adjustive learning. But, at least in a democratic setting, there are results modifying this basic generalization to the extent that too large a gap in intelligence between leader and led will not produce the best progress.

A model for analyzing leadership relations in modern national cultures, utilizing presently maturing methods of personality measurement and dynamic measurement in networks, has not yet been proposed. We can, however, get some insights from small group experiment of the kind reported in Table 7-1. The greater success when leaders are high in superego strength, G, on ego strength, C, and on some primaries in the extravert second order (A, F, H) points to the structural effectiveness respectively of assurance of approved moral values in the leader, of his capacity in ego strength to stand firm in the pull and push of particular interests, and of a high capacity to communicate by extravert expressiveness. Here it *may* be that qualities useful in *any* member get magnified effect in the leader, for better performance is found with higher *mean* endowment of the group itself on a sub-set of these qualities. That morale growth (the second dimension in Table 7-1), which comes from a structure of mutual trust among members, we see to be aided by higher mean on ego strength $(C\text{-})$, low ergic tension (low frustration) $(Q_4\text{-})$, and high parmia $(H\text{+})$. We hope that this general personality factor evidence will soon be extended by evidence directly on dynamic investments by such measures as the MAT, through which an attack on the relationship of group learning to changes in the structure or flow of ergic reward channels to various subgroups and roles can be made.

Six types of group change have been defined above. So far we have discussed the first and most important—true learning. This covers population, structure, syntality and synergy changes. Certain synergy changes from a different source, along with genetic and migratory selection changes remain to be discussed. In closing this brief analysis of the first form of group change we would suggest that the research developments most needed are in communication (interaction) networks and the application of systems theory. However, as we suggested in static analysis, so here in the analysis of learning change, we would stress the importance of (1) expressing the interpersonal ties not only in terms of (a) information exchanges, but also of (b) the dynamic vector satisfactions in the attitude reciprocities—which include economic, monetary exchange as a special case, and (2) of taking heed of the personality-ability trait profiles of individuals. As we said in the static treatment of the group, so here in the learning situation, the psychologist cannot accept either the philosophical, Leibnitzian treatment of individual minds as equal monads or the sociologists' and economists' counting of heads, all entirely plastic and of equal potential. It may be objected that science cannot hope to handle the full particularity of an infinite number of objects, and must calculate with abstractions. This is quite true, but we are only asking that the abstractions heed the qualities of people that have to be averaged, examined for distributions, correlated, and so forth.

This brings us to consider, in group action and group learning, what we might call the *social distribution properties and* laws. Perhaps the best introduction to these is in what we have called the *percolation range of ideas* in a society (Cattell 1938, 1953). Anthropologists have set out one or two laws regarding the kind and rate of *cultural diffusion* among societies, and mass media advertisement research has possibly turned up a few others; but in both cases the effect of measured psychological traits has not been included. The cognitive ability effect instanced in the percolation range law is a useful introduction to the more general statement. From the early studies of mental age levels of items in the Binet, to the more sophisticated study of Spearman's relational hierarchies it has been evident that we can affix an IQ level below which a given idea cannot be understood. (There are degrees of being able to act appropriately on an idea, so precise work will recognize a penumbra beyond the black-out point.) Thus, knowing a population's distribution on IQ an "action fraction" can be used to say what fraction of that population can act on any idea defined as to its cognitive complexity. (For unless an idea can be understood it cannot be acted upon even when the dynamics is appropriate.)

It is not quite so easy to get obvious examples showing that a percolation range and action fraction exist also with respect to each unitary personality and dynamic source trait. The present writer once showed for an advertiser that interest in a particularly vivid lipstick became higher with the extraversion score of the buyers. An implication for the corporation concerned was that since the British population is half a standard deviation more introverted than the American, this product would not "go" there, and this proved to be the case. Data of this kind positively demonstrating resistances and limits to acceptance of practices and ideas from temperamental factors is yet rare, though Eysenck (1954) has made a good case for the importance of personality factors in the adoption of political ideas.

The source trait of Premsia (I in the 16 PF, where premsia is an acronym for over*p*rotected *em*otional *s*ensitivity) has particularly been shown (Cattell, Eber, & Tatsuoka, 1970, also as Eysenck's "sensitivity" scale) to relate to acceptance of socio-political values, (negatively to capital punishment, expenditure on armaments) as also have A, affectia, G, superego, Q_1 radicalism and Q_2 self-sufficiency. Knowing that the understanding and acceptance ratios for a particular idea are significant on just three traits, T_1, T_2, and T_3, and that the action fractions are ½, ¾, and ½ we would conclude that ³⁄₁₆ths of the population would be prepared to act on that idea. In more general terms, if the action fractions for idea x are (in positive action directions) a_{x1}, a_{x2}, and a_{xp}, for traits 1, 2, and p, then:

$$a_x = a_{x1} \times a_{x2} \times \cdots \times a_{xp} \qquad (7\text{-}10)$$

The actual distribution of strengths of readiness for the act a_x would be a more complex derivative of the specification equation for the ability, personality and dynamic traits involved, since we can suppose that each of the p traits has its contribution to acting on the stimulus idea. The percolation or diffusion range concept applies in its diverse ways to information networks, and the plans for circulation of cultural propaganda by newspapers, and magazines of various qualities; while television presentations are implicitly guided by this concept. Distributions in terms of psychological traits are thus a useful beginning of the study of social structure; but far more complex role and other relationships must ultimately be studied in calculating actual diffusion rates.

7-9. The Individual in Relation to Other Types of Social Change: Evolution and Revolution

The five remaining types of group change (p. 533) are not learning in the strict sense, but in the complex group-to-individual give and take these group changes nevertheless affect individuals and are affected by them.

Volution change (No. 2 in the list above) concerns mainly the effect of change of age distribution in the population. Since a marked shift toward a relative bulge in upper age groups is occurring in this generation the effects on public discussion have been considerable, though mainly on economic and political outcomes. Age change in intelligence has long been recognized to be substantial (in units of within-year sigmas) and debate now centers on whether they are downward in fluid (g_f) but not crystallized (g_c) intelligence factors (Cattell 1971, Horn and Cattell 1978, Baltes & Schaie, 1976). Even though no change of level occurs until extreme old age in g_c, its pattern of expression in skills may belong to an earlier epoch. The age curves of primary abilities are also well known (p. 164, Cattell 1971). Evidence essentially as reliable as that for abilities is now available for personality factors in Q-data (Cattell, Eber, & Tatsuoka, 1970) and in T-data (Cattell & Schuerger, 1978) and again the mean age score plots show magnitudes that are likely to be socially important. For example, the sober and cautious behavior of desurgency $(F-)$ increasing greatly from 17 to 70, could modify toward soberness and caution a culture that increases the longevity of its population.

No checked data is yet available, however, on the typical age curves for the ergs and sentiments (even for the 10 factors in the MAT). But though we lack evidence on the central motivational structures, there is a lot of scattered evidence on age change in particular cultural interests. In any case, even where there is empirical age trend evidence on ability, temperament, and motivation traits available to-day, it invariably confounds what are called *epogenic* and *ecogenic* sources of change. The analysis of results due to epoch from those due to general volution is postponed until the next section. Although no exact empirical findings relating volution changes to group syntality changes are yet available one surely cannot doubt from the magnitude of the age changes, that differences in age of populations would definitely affect syntality.

The third type of change, equivalent to somatic change (somatic change *not* age correlated) in the individual, is represented in groups by changes in nutrition (extreme in famine), disease (consider the effects of plague in Europe), population density, and climatic improvement or deterioration. Such effects are certainly not trivial, but the reader will simply be referred to a major inspired source; Huntington's fine synthesis (1927, 1964) and to recent models for "the study of natural catastrophes." Population density changes are so dramatic in effect that we consider them below, under revolution.

The fourth source of cultural change—by genetic change—is so completely neglected by the last generation of sociologists that one wonders whether they are uninterested in long-term change or whether other inhibitions prevail. Actually, if Darlington (1969) and Lynn (1977, 1978), for example, are substantiated, the changes may not be so slow, since Lynn's measures on Scotland suggest a change in a substantially genetic trait within two or three generations. Genetic change may be either through differential survival (birth and death rates) or migration, or both. It must be freely recognized that since both heredity and elements of culture are passed on through the family the effects are not going to be easily separable except by the special methods, such as MAVA (p. 15, Chapter 1). Consequently increase in proportion in a group, by birth and survival rates, of genetic type X_g is likely to be associated (not permanently however) with increase in basic family values (because schools are relatively ineffective in that value area) of cultural type X_c which happens to be initially historically tied to X_g. (For example, the large families of middle-class Victorians contributed to the growth in Britain of Victorian values, and the small families of professors today may contribute to a reduction in size of community groups interested largely in intellectual values.)

Although genetic selection must be going on in human societies on genetic bases of virtually all psychological traits, and occasionally we run into firm indications thereof, for example desurgents appear to have a somewhat higher marriage rate, the only really substantial investigations of differential reproduction concern the trait of intelligence. Quite a number of studies (Finch, 1946, Tuddenham, 1948; Maxwell, 1969; Lynn, 1978; and Cattell, 1950) have compared scores with the same or highly similar tests on the same age community population after the lapse of years, to test possible consequences of differential survival rates. Studies examining the possible *causes* of change, for example the differential birth rate, however, are few (Burt, 1950; Cattell, 1937, 1950; Lentz, 1927; Sutherland & Thomson, 1927; Higgins Reed, & Reed, 1962: see survey in Cattell, 1974). Concerning demonstrable changes themselves the results are conflicting and are best resolved by distinguishing crystallized, g_c, from fluid, g_f, intelligence and recognizing that the latter, in the societies tested, has definitely increased by several points over the period 1910-1950, whereas fluid intelligence has stayed essentially unchanged (Cattell, 1974). In the second area—causes of change—only one study above used culture fair tests and without this technical aid the traditional intelligence tests are merely measuring more expenditure on teaching children the particular skills they learn in school and which appear in the cultural g_c pattern.

The present writer calculated that from the differential birth

(a) Rates

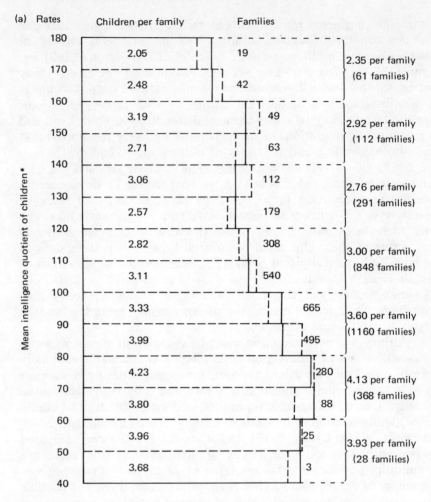

Mean size of family in urban area: 3.36

*Note the standard deviation of IQ in culture fair tests is 24, not 16 as in Binet, etc.

Figure 7-6. Intelligence and size of family.

rate in itself (see Figure 7-6a) there would be a fall, in fluid intelligence mean level of close to one point per decade. However, he recognized that the influence of (unfortunately still unknown) other factors, such as the relation of intelligence to marriage rate, complete childlessness of marriage, death rates[7] before reproduction age, regression to the mean, and so forth, might counteract the main birth rate effect, or, if marked, even slightly reverse it. On retesting across the same age group in the same city 13 years, and making a small

(b) Effects

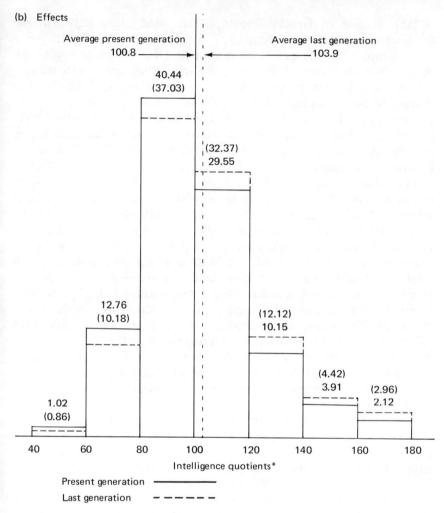

Present generation ──────────

Last generation ── ── ── ──

Percentages in each category.
Present generation thus .18; last generation thus .(15).
*Calculated alteration of distribution of intelligence. Present adults to present ten-year-olds (1936). Urban area isolating the effects of differential birth rate only, and without regression allowance.

allowance in the result for increased pupil *test sophistication* occurring between the thirties and forties, the present writer concluded that the predicted drop had not occurred (1950, 1974). We thus remain "up in the air" as to this possible source of change in modern societies—a source, however, absurdly and studiously neglected in understanding the last decade's findings of declining school performance scores (see analysis in Cattell, 1954, 1974). But historians if not all social psychologists have seriously examined it as a probable cause of the decline of Greek, Roman, Aztec, and other cultures (see Darlington, 1969; Huntington, 1927, 1964; and Weyl, (1973).

Community changes from migration (No. 5 above, resembling again a somatic type of change in the individual) have been studied by sociologists, far more than the genetic changes, in the United States, Britain, Australia and elsewhere. Urban-rural migration and counter migration have been thoroughly documented in regard both to attitude and intelligence selections, and some information is available also on migration selection between nations (see for example Eysenck's discussion, (1971). Two main considerations are: "Does the decision to migrate itself cause selection?" and "Does the process of migration, through differing survival rates, cause additional selection?" Huntington (1928) answers the latter by reference to the long migration that produced the high civilization of Ankor Wat, and on a small scale one could examine in the U.S. what selection took place in the persecution of the Mormons and their migrations to Utah. We could consider also the likelihood of selective survival with respect to the Jewish exodus; the sea migrations of the English and Norse to England; and the frightful death rate shown in the graveyards of Plymouth, Massachusetts in 1612 to 1630. Nowadays selection *en route* is scarcely important, but the question, say, whether the more or less successful farmers migrate to cities typifies the issue. The "brain drain" from Europe to the United States during the last 30 years at least gives a name to the popular conclusion as to what is happening.

Very little data exist on the magnitude and direction of such effects, so far as specific personality and ability traits are concerned, but certain general principles can be noted. A recent joke among psychologists that the movement of a certain professor from a leading American university to a particular university in Britain raised the level of both institutions, illustrates the complexity of the issues! What section migrates, and between what countries or classes, determines the whole nature of the effect. Virtually the only research bearing on population movement, done with adequate instruments and samples tends to be on children and school performance, and here both Eysenck's report (1975) in England, Jensen's (1973) in the United States, and Thorndike's regional studies (1949, 1951) point to the possibility of fairly marked changes in norms with migration. Obviously, since there is two-way causal actions of syntality and personality dimensions, migration can be an important modifier of syntality, and the action of the final cultural syntality on population personality will, through the migrating fraction, affect the native, nonimmigrant population fraction also. With small immigrations such effects are likely to be gradual and escape observation, but large immigration produces a clash of cultures, which occurs in Britain today with the West Indies immigrations; in the American Indiann culture, and to Hawaiian culture with the European influx, as it did for the ancient Britons in the Saxon invasions.

Clash of cultures as such, and its relation to personality, is picked up later, for here we need to turn to the sixth and last of the sources of group syntality change: that due to *synergy transfers* between co-active groups, that is groups sharing common members. Even groups that are not mutually in conflict as groups, for example, the family and the school, may be passively or actively competitive for the interest and loyalty of the same individuals. The total synergy of a group, which determines among other things its capacity to survive, vis-à-vis nature and other groups depends on these shares of individual investments. As we have seen in the basic dynamic definition of a group it disperses when its synergy, as the sum of dynamic vectors of members' attitudes, reaches zero, and any individual member leaves a group when his own dynamic specification equation for his group drops to a zero sum across ergs and sentiments, thus:

$$a_{gi} = \overset{x=p}{\Sigma} b_{gx} E_{xi} + \overset{y=q}{\Sigma} b_{gy} M_{yi} = 0 \qquad (7\text{-}11)$$

there being p ergs (E's) and q sentiments (M's) that can be involved in his belonging attitude to the group, a_{gi}. The condition for dissolution of the group could be stated in an equation which sums (7-11) across n members.

However, even when the attitude interest for an individual is nowhere near zero, there can be conflict in the *indurated* attitude to the group, for that individual, expressed just as for any other conflict in an attitude, on p. 124. And from the usual summation of this across all dynamic structures, now carried across all group members a value can be derived for the inherent degree of conflict characteristic of a particular group synergy, thus:

$$c_g = \overset{i=n}{\Sigma} \overset{x=p}{\Sigma} \frac{\overset{(-)}{b_{gx}} E_{xi}}{\underset{(+)}{b_{gx}} E_{xi}} + \overset{i=n}{\Sigma} \overset{y=q}{\Sigma} \frac{\overset{(-)}{b_{gy}} M_{yi}}{\underset{(+)}{b_{gy}} M_{yi}} \qquad (7\text{-}12a)$$

where $\overset{(-)}{b}$ is a negative loading $\overset{(+)}{b}$ a positive and there are n people in the group g.

If (7-11) were put in the form of attitude strength and summed over people and then compared with (7-12a) it would be evident that total group synergy and total group conflict are different and that the latter can be substantial without the former falling to zero. However, there would be the usual algebraic tendency for a/b to correlate with $(a - b)$ and, when both terms in c_g reach unity, synergy reaches zero. It seems reasonable to hypothesize that just as total synergy, in small groups, comes out, apparently, as a primary syntality dimension of morale, so c_g will be found to have some syntality factor corresponding to the degree of indurated conflict in its members. Indeed, we have already considered what might be called the *co-synergy law* that with n individuals in m coactive (co-member) groups—that is all n individuals each belonging in some degree to all m groups—the sum of group synergies must equal a value which is the sum of the n individuals' energies other than what goes into non-group interests. In situations where the latter is constant the total synergies summed for all groups must be constant, and therefore a growth gain in any group must be accompanied by shrinkage of synergy in one or more others.[8]

Now any such change in synergy distribution has to be considered from the standpoint both of groups and individuals. The simple conflict for the individual between desires to belong to two groups is formulatable in the same form as that for *active decision* conflict between any two courses of action (p. 122). That conflict was there treated as an "all or nothing" satisfaction of either course of action. But there—and still more frequently in the between groups conflict—it is more precisely expressed as going rather more into this and rather less into that.[9] Since the satisfactions will change continuously in character as one goes more into a group the mathematical problem becomes one of determining the possible intersection of two curves and of integrating over them for comparable gains over time.

As regards the group aspect of synergy competition, it would seem from even a casual survey of corporations, teams, churches, and nations to be an empirical law that groups and their leaders normally strive to increase their synergy, by adding fresh services, attracting more members, and clarifying to members what the group can do for their needs. The last includes reducing the conflict measure (7-12a) that has been characteristics of the group.

The social power of groups being substantially a function of their synergy resources (which sometimes boils down in large part to economic resources) it is not surprising that the competition among groups often becomes explicit and overtly combative even among co-member groups, and one consequence of this is the introduction of a corresponding conflict within the individual sentiment systems of members. Millions of minds must have suffered such conflicts in the Renaissance battle of rising nationalisms with the Christian church. To the above (7-12a) conflict index concerning belonging to any one group, could be added a value for an index to express conflict in the individual arising from the different groups to which he belongs. This sum would bring a necessary third term to add to *deflection strain* and *long-circuiting-complexity* in appraising the stressfulness of a given culture. Although this new term—of indurated conflict in belonging to a given culture—has two facets, requiring formulations of conflict with respect to each subgroup and between subgroups, in such a brief overview as is here possible let us represent it by a single term : *group sentiment conflict* (ergic conflict in the ergic investments of the sentiments).

Our discussion has necessarily moved to and fro between a static and a kinetic analysis of the group syntality-individual personality relation. We began with the static situation of a tolerably adjusted adult personality in relation to a group culture in equilibrium, and found various relations holding between them. We then asked what types of change could occur in groups and analyzed six possible sources of such change. The corresponding question of developmental changes in the individual personality has been dealt with throughout this second volume, but not intensively in relation to group change. At this point we recognize that the true complexity finally to be faced in personality study is the kinetic analysis of an individual moving through a personal history in relation to a group culture moving through world history. This can be realistically handled only in a systems model.

The structure of a model for such analysis can merely be hinted here, and we will do so by considering, in brief snapshots from the wisdom of history, some of the relations to be considered, beginning with change stepped up to revolutionary extremes, in order to accentuate the issues. Our view of group change in so far as it occurs through learning, is that all individual learning principles are at work, and particularly means-end (operant) learning by trial and error (insight in so complex a domain being unusual, and, when claimed, often turning out later to have been trial and error!). Granted this, we recognize further that neither a group nor an individual learns unless the organism is in a state of dissatisfaction, usually through some established, learned response failing in a changed situation.

Change for change's sake, occurring in a perfectly adjusted system, is rare, and is usually motivated by the erg of curiosity operating as intellectual speculation and perceiving still better ways of satisfying wants already tolerably satisfied in the existing equilibrium. To be strong enough to move a culture it must generally be buttressed by more immediate needs. Ferdinand and Isabella did not finance Columbus to give his seamen an educational tour or to settle disputes among scholars. And a growing pinch of necessity has usually been the mother of invention, as when Watts shaped the steam engine to permit miners to go deeper, without drowning, in their pursuit of ore. Under whatever need pressures change occurs, that change is recognized by historians as proceeding either by evolutionary steps, altering now this and now that piece of social machinery, or by revolution. Rate and magnitude of change have distinguished these for most writers, but the difference may, psychologically, be more than a difference of pace. There are biological parallels worth studying here as between the "evolutionary" growth of the vertebrate organisms and the revolutionary pattern of the crustaceans and insects who are rigid for substantial periods, with short crises of growth as they cast off a skeletal shell that is too small and take on a larger one.

Naturalistic observers of cultural change, as seen in historians, or social psychologists, such as Fairweather (1972) and sociologists such as Boulding (1970) and Sorokhin (1937), point to innovation as requiring (1) discontent, (2) a formulator of new ideas, and (3) a "salesman" to get to the main population with those ideas. These components are seen, they would argue, most clearly in revolutionary change, as in the French and Russian revolutions. Our own formulation, as the above six-fold analysis indicates (p. 533), would describe social change in all forms, evolutionary or revolutionary, as multiply determined, but here, in *rapid* change, we are dealing largely with two sources: true learning, which begins with a dissatisfaction, and synergic changes, involving conflict and changes of sentiments within the individual.

If our analysis of the "burden" of a culture, that is, the psychological cost of reaching its demands with acceptable amounts of total ergic satisfaction, is correct, the determiners of that burden are *dynamic complexity, ergic deflection strain, amount of long-circuiting,* and *loss of ergic satisfaction in indurated conflict.* All these have been formulated in such a way that they could be measured so that social research can put theory to the test. Further, we have indicated certain cultural syntality dimensions, notably *cultural pressure, intelligent affluence* and *vigorous technical development* which would be expected to relate to the above population (average) dynamic indices in a culture.

What is new, relative to the sociological approach to revolution is (a) the introduction of the above indices and (b) the recognition that the mean traits of the population vector play a part in the proneness to revolution. One would think that the latter would not need to be substantiated as a general principle by psychological measures, for historians and travelers have made consistent observations. For example, Julius Caesar in 51 B.C. (*Comentarii de bello Gallico*) explicitly noted the higher surgency of the Gauls (in quite a good description of F factor!), and right through to the French revolution and after other observers and writers, including Napoleon, have noted the same population temperament trait. That population traits play a part in reaction to cultural pressure is supported by the recent evidence of two kinds or phases of reaction to cultural pressure (Cattell, Woliver, & Graham, 1978). In the second factor the greater frequency of riots, political clashes with other countries, strikes, and participation in wars is notable. The role assigned in change and revolution to "new ideas" (for example by Boulding, Fairweather, & Sorokhin above, and others) is discounted by the psychologist relative to the emotional reaction to the existing cultural frustration, which reaction is partly determined by the cultural burden indices and partly by population traits. New social ideas may wait for centuries without revolutions, and revolutions may occur without essentially changing social values. When dissatisfaction ferments in a particular section of the population, it tends, quite systematically, to bring together those who, in personality and intellect, are ahead of their time in their perception of improved possibilities of satisfaction, and those who are atavistically behind it. For the latter are, by personality distance from culture, already "rebels without a cause" finding the necessary cultural complexities too great for them to tolerate. The crucifixion of Christ between thieves is symbolic. A common result of this bimodality is that the passions of the maladjusted take over from the ideals of the progressive in "smashing this sorry scheme of things entire"; and there arises the danger that the ideational revolutionist will get burnt by what he hoped to use only as fuel for his attack (as happened with the Jacobins in 1794 and various Russian intellectuals in 1917). Since this large section of the maladjusted, intolerant even of the existing complexity, aims emotionally at something more primitive, revolution as opposed to evolution may end in what is ideationally more regressive than what previously existed. Both the Terror that ruled by guillotine in France, and in the excesses that caused a substantial fraction of Russian intellectuals to sicken over what they had started, the interest in destruction rather than construction is evident. Even for the average man and when real psychological progress is made, the new complexities and restraints may be only briefly supportable, as when the English "Revolution" ultimately backed away from Cromwellian austerity and efficiency. History is inclined to record the political revolutions which, though not as progressive as the non-political agricultural, industrial, and cybernetic "revolutions" introduced something progressive, whereas a straight count of all revolutions might show more instances of a mere change of governments, or a temporary giving rein to anarchists, or a debacle like the Paris Communes of 1871.

As to the particular ergic frustration most involved (apart from the general deflection stress), the popular idea thereof is shown in the hungry, cold, and ragged mobs depicted by Hollywood scenes. But deeper and more pervasive is the intolerance of cultural inhibitions of any kind (explicit in 19th century anarchist parties—and in criminals of all centuries). Although this is less obvious in the well-known progressive revolution of recent centuries than in the endless historical lesser ones that have ended in mere destruction, it is still always present.

As Crane Brinton and other investigators have pointed out, if hunger and cold and other basic frustrations go far enough, revolution does not occur. At some point of recovery from a cowed and highly deprived condition, when some aspiration standards are held with confidence, action begins—for evolution or revolution. The men who solemnly condemned Charles I to the scaffold were, typically, prosperous farmers, who disliked disorder and the breakdown of authority as much as anyone. Although the psychological motives in a revolution may lie partly in the thwarting of basic ergs of hunger and security-seeking, yet self-assertion, and possessiveness are probably in the end more important. Weyl (1975) and some other students of power shifts have stressed the importance of self assertion that is, desire for personal control and power. As Weyl has well documented, some of the biggest massacres of a ruling class, such as those of Carthage, appear motivated by sheer envy. As modern scientific productivity wipes out extensive hunger and need of shelter, less basic and material needs would be expected to take charge of the direction in those protests against any "establishment"—protests that in part result from frustration by complexity and the inhibitions of long circuiting. The move to free divorce decisions entirely, and the interest in movements like women's liberation and environmental protection, over the last generation, would scarcely have occurred to the Medieval and Renaissance populations, whose frustrations struck at more viscerogenic ergs.

Turning to the second sense of revolution we meet less dramatic and spectacular events (largely political, military and power seeking) which an older generation of historians ignored. When historians now speak of the agricultural, industrial, and cybernetic revolutions, they insist that they are essentially more important than the political changes of power, and that in suddenness and magnitude they *are* revolutions.[10] These revolutions within evolution seem to come at an increasing pace; from 10,000 years for the agricultural revolution, to 500 for the industrial revolution; and down to the recent 10 decades for the communication cybernetic revolution of telegraph, telephone, radio, and computer. It is now widely recognized that technical revolutions that make human satisfactions easier almost invariably create secondary maladjustments (unemployment, damage to environment, new diseases), as a beneficient new drug commonly has side effects. In popular terms this has been powerfully described in Toffler's (1970) *Future Shock*.

What Toffler describes in detail is essentially the pattern we have factored out in national syntalities as reaction to cultural pressure (Table 7-1). For the attainment of ergic goals, for example eating more easily and dependably, is not the same thing as reduction of long circuiting or deflection strain. As we stressed in Chapters 2 and 5, goodness of adaptation and goodness of adjustment are not the same thing. Other syntality factors such as *developed-vs-undeveloped state*, *enlightened affluence*, and *simple life morale* (reversed) also contain variables compatible with a concept of "future" shock, but *reaction to cultural pressure* seems most clearly to represent the primary syntality-behavior connected with a psychological reaction to complexity of new demands, and long circuiting.

From certain theoretical points of view one would expect, at least over some time intervals, a positive feedback from the initial responses to adjustive demands through the "side effects" creating still further needs for adjustment. In our terms we would say that the deflection strain from the new adjustment creates frustration responses demanding further adjustment. In the last generation several social scientists have supposed that there is in this age a positive acceleration (not just a high speed) in social change and have speculated whether a catastrophic "explosion" might not impend. It is more likely that we have a temporary phenomenon here, but, regardless of the historical question, it is clear that personality research has to be aware, more than it would have in the age of Confucius or Chaucer, of the personality effects of a fast tempo of cultural change.

A component in the cultural pressure pattern that has received more attention lately—and justly so since it came initially as an empirical suprise rather than from subjective theories—is the effect of population overcrowding. By Calhoun's (1962) experiments on rats, Bruce (1966) and Kessler's (1975) on mice, and ethologists (Jay, Ripley, Sujiyama: see Wilson, 1975) on monkeys, as well as Ehrlich's analysis (1968) of the social psychology of human crowding, we have learned that unusually crowded conditions increase insecurity and hostility, reduce female fertility and (in animals) nesting behavior and care of the young, break down the stable hierarchical family structure, increase anarchic "gang" behavior in young males, and induce more homosexual relations. This "behavioral sink" as Calhoun has described it, in his most crowded rat communities, may be accompanied by such signs of physiological stress as Christian (1961) and others observed in lemmings, deer, and other groups in nature, such as stunted growth and over-sized adrenals.

In both men and animals the abolition of "personal space" and intimate property rights apparently creates insecurity, threats to various subtle instinctual expectations, with resulting frustration and pugnacity and inhibition of sexual and parental protective ergs. Excessive and rapid population growth thus produces, long before the Malthusian nemesis of hunger and physical disease is reached, a state of psychological disease. Those rightly concerned about risk of uncontrolled world population growth have viewed it as a problem in itself, and of a dramatic nature, but the evidence of cultural syntality analysis is that it is a component part of the demonstrated cultural pressure factor continuously active in some degrees over the last century. In that total pattern as Table 7-2 shows, high density of population, as witnessed by percent in cities over 20,000, high divorce rate, higher ratio of tertiary occupations, high suicide (and, we may expect, higher drug addiction and homosexuality) combine the ergic deflection stress of crowding with other psychological influences to produce breakdown of domestic life and other pathologies.

In this connection it is noteworthy that P-technique studies of the cultural pressure factor in Britain (Cattell 1953), the U.S.A. (Cattell & Adelson, 1951) and Australia (Gibb 1956) show a steep rise (with population density *and* several other variables such as technical complexity) in the 19th and 20th centuries (which incidentally, continues its steep climb in the U.S. a decade after that rise has ceased in Britain).

Just as we recognized psychopathology in individuals by measures on certain source trait factors such as anxiety, depression, reduction of C factor (ego strength), and so forth, so changes in national syntality measures may monitor pathology in a cultural group. In both, doubt must arise as to what changes are pathogical, but in groups a fall on the morale morality factor (Cattell & Gorsuch, 1963) must be so considered and also a rise in the pattern of Calhoun's "behavioral sink."

In the context of this chapter the question naturally arises as to the relation of group pathologies to the pathology of individual personalities. Granted that the pathologies of organized groups constitutes an important topic of study, their relations to personality urgently need to be investigated. Let us, therefore, take a brief glance at them. If by pathological we mean something that may lead to death, then the primary pathology of a society is the decay of its synergy to the point at which its structure fails and it falls apart. When that happens it must be ceasing—or *seeming* to cease—to provide the satisfactions individuals need. ("Seeming" is necessary because individuals—like children who run away from home—do not always at the moment realize how much they get from the society.) Security and order form one immediate service society provides, and we see that when the Roman Empire ceased to be able to provide them it broke into the many relatively culturally degenerate medieval feudal societies.

A second major pathology is a decay of morale and moral standards (group morale and average *individual* morality are closely related). In the recent concept of *Beyondism* (Cattell, 1972), although diverse group cultural adventure gives some diversity of values, it is shown that a scientific basis for inferring moral values can be found that up to a point is the same for all groups. These are the citizen behavior values that permit the group to survive. This role of mean superego strength level in maintaining group synergy is so far most clearly quantitatively shown in the above small-group experiments. But insofar as we can trust the nonmetric, clinical type of conclusion from history, it is clear there too that through undermining of religions and in other ways a general decline of ethical standards occurs from time to time with well nigh fatal results. The nature-nurture evidence (Chapter 1) shows that superego strength has a genetic component, and in human history a million years of small group competition would be expected to have produced and increased such endowment. But it needs its environmental support and direction too. In both primitive and modern groups the punishment of expulsion from the group, with loss of all the satisfactions, has deterred the worst exhibitions of low morality; but other and generally religious institutions have been necessary for positive teaching, and the rationalist destruction of many religious beliefs may basically be responsible for current apparent decline of superego development.

A third form of pathology lies in genetic decay, such as would occur if the differential birth rate in intelligence (Figure 7-6 above) persisted dysgenically, without counteracting inferences, for three or four generations. Data on this and discussion of the sequences involved are available elsewhere (Cattell, 1937, 1974) and are handled in a broader perspective by Burt (1946), Cavallho-Sforza (1970), Darlington (1969), Graham (1970), Huxley (1953), McDougall (1935), and others.

Finally, because age is a fatal disease, there is a pathology of aging in groups, constantly instanced by the historian, as in the ancient culture of Egypt, the classical cultures of Greece and Rome, and others much nearer to our own time. Inherent in most organism designs there is a limit of growth. Insects cannot grow as large as vertebrates because the oxyen-exchange design for their blood is by diffusion through spiracles, not by a pump, as in vertebrates. Trees cannot exceed a certain size because of similar impacts of natural laws connected with pressures required to raise sap. Larger societies require more complex organizations and educational systems than small ones to maintain all necessary communication channels among parts. A bureaucracy is thus needed but may become top-heavy (as in ancient Egypt's priest class) and too expensive for the productive power of the community. (Think of the man-hours of very capable minds that are abstracted every year from production in completing income tax forms!)

The complications of a higher society can be seen to limit, by their cost, gain from increased productivity, incidentally thus systematically contributing to inflation, but do they necessarily lead to moribund conditions and ultimate decease of the culture, as complexity seems to lead to aging and death of biological organisms above the single cell level? One reason for increased likelihood of ultimate breakdown of a complex organism is that the more complicated a system becomes the more there is in it to go wrong. And, keeping systems theory in mind, we recognize that something going wrong in one part produces extra strains in others. It is sometimes said that rigidity in the organism's repertoire of physiological responses is the cause of aging in biological organisms. But in social organisms this is a secondary consequence of the complication that puts beyond the intelligence of leaders (or the adaptive strategies programmed in the organism) any ability to readapt the organism as a whole to the challenges presented by accidental error in the parts. Part of the adjustment problem we discussed as "future shock" is a special case, made apparent by unusual speed, of the problems of society and the individual in adjusting to the widespread repercussions of each local change in a complex system.

Yet another probable expression of pathology in social organisms needs to be investigated as the decline of what we have called *effective synergy* (p. 514) relative to *maintenance synergy*. Obviously the fraction of the received synergy available for effective synergy will be reduced by internal friction in maintenance synergy, poor structure and the development of narcistic behavior in the members. We have instanced charitable societies the officials of which are so expensive that only perhaps 10% of intake reaches the objects of charity, and one could instance occasional scientific and other culturally supportive societies which in time become mere social clubs.

Technical advance regarding social pathology, like that concerning general syntality must rest on analyses of relations of syntality, structure and population values for both large and small, traditional and neonate groups, such as has given us glimpses of significant correlations in the work above.

7-10. Systems Theory, the Life of Groups, and the Philosophy of Science

It has been recognized that personality and environment constitute a closed system. And since a system involves, by definition, always, an ongoing series of adjustments, with terms for each moment in various processes, a personality today contains in some degree all history. One aspect of this we expressed above by saying that our formulae have to deal with the relations of a moving personality to a moving society. Let us begin by a concrete illustration of this relation and pursue the systems analysis further into development of relationships between changing subgroups.

The habit of the personality psychologist of considering the individual as developing under the control of a massive and therefore virtually unchanging social culture may be excused, as a legitimate first approximation, akin to the rocketeers ignoring the recoil of the whole earth when a rocket is fired. However, all individuals to some degree and a few individuals to a high degree *do* shift the culture, and all have their growth and being in a culture which, especially in the last century, has a fairly rapid movement of its own. The point has been well made by Churchill when he responded to the requests of the curious in *If I Lived My Life Again!* (1974) as follows; "I should not be living my life again. I should be living another life in a world whose structure and history would diverge (from those into which I was born").

The principles basically involved in calculation of the interaction can best be simply introduced in regard to the concrete and investigated instance of determining normal age curves of development in personality (Cattell & Schuerger, 1978, p. 149) and abilities. Only 40 ago it was thought sufficient in plotting age curves (for example, the intelligence age curves of Miles, 1934; Jones & Conrad, 1933; and others) to take groups, one at 10, another at 20, another at 30 years of age, and so on, and to average the group's raw scores, for each decade taken, and plot them. More recently, the analyses and methods of Baltes (1968), Cattell (1969), Horn and Donaldson (1976), and Schaie and Strother (1968) have recognized the need to separate the normal, average human life trend from the intruding trends particular to an epoch. The approach to this analysis begins with supplementation of the above *cross-sectional* data with *cursive* data, from measuring one and the same group of same-age people— a "cohort"—as they advance in age from decade to decade. The age curves of, for example, intelligence, have been rather badly misunderstood prior to recognition of these two distinct contributors. Tuddenham's (1948) comparison of army drafts of 1917 and 1942, Finch's succession of measures in Illinois schools (1946), and other studies show that the mean scores of people on traditional crystallized intelligence tests, have soared, presumably as a consequence of educational changes, in a single generation, in a remarkable fashion. (This has not happened, incidentally, for culture-fair tests.) There is a lesson for practitioners here in terms of psychometrics in that the standardizations, on however large a sample, of traditional intelligence tests, such as the WAIS and the WISC, are out of date from the day of publication! On the other hand the present writer (1949) found virtually no change, over more than a dozen years, in the fluid intelligence of a population measured by the Culture-Fair Intelligence Scales (IPAT, 1949, 1970), which thus retain their standardization.

That this epoch effect intrudes disturbingly upon the work of the practical psychologist shows that the resolution of curves into what we may call *prevailing* (averaged over all epochs of measurement) or *ecogenic* curves and *epochal* or *epogenic* curves (the contribution peculiar to an epoch—say, the period of history started by free and compulsory education) is more than an academic refinement. The need to separate *epogenic* (effects due to an epoch) from *ecogenic* (those natural to average, ordinary human ecology) curves almost certainly is highly relevant also to personality measurement. The age curves for primary and secondary personality source traits yet available (Cattell, 1973, Cattell & Schuerger, 1978) are of the cross sectional type. But there are a few (as yet statistically untested) *ecogenic* observations strongly suggesting that G, superego strength, has dropped since about 1950, and that surgency, F, and dominance, E, have risen in the span of this generation.

For lack of text space we shall leave the compact Table 7-8 to explain the methods of gathering observations to make the conceptual separations defined and labeled therein. Incidentally, it will be noticed from the analysis shown in this table that an investigator does not have to wait 50 years to get a 50 year curve of the cursive type, that is, on what happens to the same actual individuals. He can measure in one and the same calendar year several groups, each at a decade point in age, and wait, say, only 5 years to retest all of them. His short line plots will give tangents that can be fitted together for a 50 year curve of changes in the same people (as if of the same age cohort). However, in terms of analyzing out epogenic and ecogenic curves this cursive curve is not equivalent to that from the 50 year wait, and must be differently named and treated as Table 7-8 states.

The main separation—epogenic from ecogenic (or prevailing)—can finally be made only if there are measures over several epochs since ecogenic is defined as epoch-free. Naturally, other separations can be made in the data of the curve beyond the principal one here considered between the typical life history of the individual in *any* epoch and the effects of the movement of society in a given epoch. As we know from the analysis of change (Chapters 1 and 2), we can, for example, aim to distinguish the total environmental change from the total genetic, volutional change. And, within the former, the threptic component (Chapter 1), we can at least theoretically distinguish *learning* from *transformation* (due to *direct* effects on the organism). The methodology of these further distinctions, which would yield no fewer than six differently conceived and calculated component curves from gross data gathered as in Table 7-8 is approached elsewhere (Cattell, 1973).

It has been said, from Anaximander on, that the only constant thing in our lives is change. The importance of keeping this in mind in psychology has been well stated in qualitative terms by many philosophers of psychology, for example, Riegel (1972) and Royce (1973, 1977). The real creative task, however, lies ahead in the discovery of particular concepts, the development of mathematical models that fit them, and the pursuit of sophisticated experimental methods to check them.

As regards the two partners in this dance of evolution we can surely claim to have gone far enough already in defining the individual in a quantitative picture of reality-tested concepts, and it remains to see whether we can yet focus the cultural society with that equality of sharpness necessary to direct quantitative experiment on their final coordination. The answer, of course, is that social psychology and its branches in economics, cultural anthropology, sociology and political science have not yet progressed to sufficient integration. Nevertheless, the broader of the concepts we have put into a model and a method for the organism we call the individual have proved in this last chapter to fit much of the behavior of the social organism. The VIDA developments in personality began with a taxonomy of behavior expressed in vectors of source traits. They proceeded to processes related to structures in persons and situations,

TABLE 7-8. Tables and Modes of Separation of Ecogenic, Epogenic, Exogenous, and Endogenous Components in Life Span Change

(a)   Possible Combinations of Observations

	Same age at testing		Different age at testing	
	Same birthday	Different birthday	Same birthday	Different birthday
Same year of testing	No series	Impossible	Impossible	SC
Different year of testing	Impossible	FCE	SL and CL	FE

Note: Only one category permits a further subdivision into same subjects or different subjects (from the same age group), namely, SL and CL.

(b)   Resulting Series

Calendar year of birth

Different persons tested

Age at testing

	10	20	30	40	50	60	
1910	1920	1930	1940	1950	1960	1970	SL
1900	1910	1920	1930	1940	1950	1960	
1890	1900	1910	1920	1930	1940	1950	
1880	1890	1900	1910	1920	1930	1940	FE
1870	1880	1890	1900	1910	1920	1930	SC
1860	1870	1880	1890	1900	1910	1920	
1850	1860	1870	1880	1890	1900	1910	

FCE

Same persons tested

Age at testing

	10	20	30	40	50	60	
1910	1920	1930	1940	1950	1960	1970	CL_1
1900	1910	1920	1930	1940	1950	1960	
1890	1900	1910	1920	1930	1940	1950	CL_2

TABLE 7-8. *(continued)*

Suggested Designations of Six Major Experimental Series

SL *Simple Longitudinal* series: same birth year, different subjects, different ages, different testing dates.

CL *Cursive (or Cohort) Longitudinal* series: same birth year, same subjects, different ages, different testing dates. Two sub-series, $CL_{(1)}$ and $CL_{(2)}$ are put in here because one may test *all* of the cohort at every point, as proposed, designated $CL_{(1)}$; or test all at age 10, divide into five groups, and retest each at a different decade, to avoid retesting effects (practice), as in $CL_{(2)}$.

SC *Simple (Fixed-date) Cross-Sectional* series: different birth years, different ages, same testing date.

FCE *Fixed Age Changing Epoch Cross-Sectional* series: different birth years, same age, different testing data.

FE *Fixed Epoch* series: different birth years, different age at testing, different testing date, but with life span centered on the same calendar year (epoch).

CCL *Combined Cursive Longitudinal* series: same as CL above, except that for a planned collation of results for several different age groups in the same epoch.

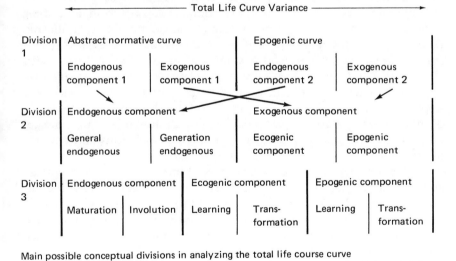

Main possible conceptual divisions in analyzing the total life course curve

representable as trajectories in state spaces. The environment being given vector representation in this process, and differential equations being introduced (pp. 404, 429) to handle learning and other changes from moment to moment, a systems model (VIDAS) was developed placing personality and socio-physical environment in a closed system.

Let us now look at the other partner: that major section of the environment that we call society, with its structures and traditions. Here too a taxonomy has proved possible, representable in vectors of syntality and synergy. But the greater variety of groups, as to size, type of member, volume and antiquity of tradition, and form of internal structure, will require many more years than personality study required to get a reasonably comprehensive taxonomy. They present also the new phenomenon of co-active membership, opening up a whole new territory of concepts and models not paralleled in personality. Nevertheless, we have been able to establish conceptual relations between the personality and dynamics of individuals and the syntalities and synergies of groups, with empirical checks, on the basic relations in $S = f(R \cdot P)$.

As we come to the final problem here—the changing individual in relation to the changing group—it is evident that we have an adequate analysis to handle group learning, group volution, and other forms of group change. Unfortunately, we do not have applicable data (in spite of P-technique studies of 3 nations, and experiment on small groups) to support and develop our group change model with the precision of our change curves and structured learning principles for individuals. Nevertheless, in the last two sections we have explained various kinds of group change: evolution and revolution, genetic change, pathological change, population migration change, and, especially, the new kinds of synergy competitions and cooperations that produce change in group systems.

It would be desirable to tidy up and integrate the group change concepts in the last two sections in a general model as a basis for the group-individual change problem, and the present writer is confident, or at least optimistic that this could usefully be done, but space precludes the necessary digression from personality aspects wholly and intensively into group aspects.

Certain basic propositions can be readily stated, and though basic they deserve brief formulation; for they are not of that philosophical generality or self-evidence that make it unecessary to recite them to an experimenter. First there are quantitative statements about physical and other growth in organisms that would be expected to give us a first fit to growth of populations and dimensions of syntality. Young plants, and some animals, for example, grow in such parameters as heights, weight and strength, over certain periods, at a weight proportional to their existing size. This could become an explosive growth, as in some germ colonies, or as is approximated in some populations to pressure catastrophes we have discussed. (Even in plants this can be disastrous as in a well known weed killer which applies hormones that disorganize internally by stimulating excessively rapid growth.) However, if there are no internal problems and the environment offers all necessary food or energy, there are some three or four main possibilities of predicting the syntality trait, for example, gross national product, S_t at time t_2, namely a simple linear growth:

$$S_{t2} = S_{t1} + kt_{(2-1)} \tag{7-13a}$$

where $t_{(2-1)}$ is the elapsed time from the initial size at S_{t1}, or with an acceleration due to time, like that of a falling stone

$$S_{t2} = S_{t1} + kt_{(2-1)}^2 \tag{7-13b}$$

where k is a constant.

The growth dependent on internal properties of the group is more likely to be a function of its *size* at any point than simply of time. It is also likely to be a function of its degree of internal differentiation and an interesting pioneer model in this direction was recently proposed by Blau (1970). Dealing with a function of sheer numbers, however, and recognizing that with a fixed rate of biological reproduction human populations would become enormous, Malthus's classical work pointed with alarm to the effect in human societies of what we often now speak of as a positive feedback system, and represent by equation (7-14):

$$S_{t2} = S_{t1}e^{t(2-1)^k} \tag{7-14}$$

where S_{t1} is the size of the population at the starting point, t is time, k is a constant, and e is exponential e. He recognized, however, an opposing negative feedback from the same term—the total size— which in this case (as human populations had actually up to that time increased but little) he considered could be identified with poverty, famine, disease, and natural catastrophy. Some of these setbacks would be environmental, but others a function of crowding, and so a second—negative-feedback—formula could be considered to impose its curve on the first, thus:

$$S_{t2} = S_{t1}\bar{e}^t(2\text{-}1)^m \tag{7-15}$$

where a new constant such as m would be introduced. The actual observed curve and its final outcome (if conditions permitted equilibrium) or at some arbitrary point, would be the summed effect of these positive and negative feedbacks.

Such growth curves as we have illustrated are those of groups sheltered from the impact of other groups, or such unexpected environmental demands as may occur in any open system. If one asks what determines the constants in such growth curves the answer is in the first place that they represent such features as numbers of members, rate of addition of members, and dynamic units of ergic sources drawn upon. For example, a proselytizing religious group might for a time have a growth of synergy proportional to the number of members it attracts and the fervor it can evoke. But a group that caters to one particular ergic need—say, security, as in an insurance company—is likely sooner to come to a definite limit (granted a fixed membership) to its synergy, since it restricts itself to drawing on only one need. The more general course of events in the jockeying of groups for position—their competition and symbiosis—is that leaders often find ways of drawing on other needs and interests than those the group originally satisfied. The group synergy then expands, as in the examples above, by drawing a larger and more diverse fraction of the ergic satisfaction of existing members into the group, as when a society with a charter to accomplish a limited service begins to supply other services. For example, monasteries have developed wine businesses; police forces have developed football teams for youths in delinquent areas; and corporations have "diversified" their services.

However, although through such synergy expansion a church may, in historical instances, have become a state, a football team or a university has not been known to do so. The first reason for this capacity of some groups to grow synergically while others do not is that the latter fix their structures by constitution, by traditions, or in other ways defining their purposes from the beginning as applying to only a certain profile of ergic satisfactions and cognitive activities. As we move from isolated groups to those in a system of groups a second restriction is that other groups are for situational reasons more efficient in meeting certain needs that might otherwise be "poached" by the first group. A third reason is probably the inherent rigidity, especially after a certain age, in the earlier rewarded sentiment structures—the dynamic lattices—in *individual* personalities. This is only one of many (the percolation range effect is another) that would illustrate the importance of personality parameters as such setting limits and rates to cultural movement.

To encompass in one summary equation all the types of influence we have discussed determining systems changes in a group is a more difficult task than in our corresponding equation for the individual. In the latter we included weights on the existing traits of the individual (which included genetic change therein) and terms for *ME* (*CR*II) learning by reward and *CE* learning by coexcitation (p. (p. 284).

These could be considered to estimate change on a specific behavior, change on a trait, or change on a sub-system in a systems representation. The changes in a particular *S*, which we can consider either a syntality trait or a subsystem or institution in the group will, in a summary, need, similarly, terms for other syntality and structural traits, for rewards attached to the situation (*ME*), for cognitive events (*CE*), and for genetic changes in population. But additionally it will need terms for synergy changes through co-action. Using a generally descriptive equation, with all syntality traits shown briefly as one *S*, all population personality and motivation as one *P*, all structure wrapped in one *R*, and *ME* and *CE* for learning, with *b*'s for behaviors indices for learning, we should have, analogously to personality gain (equation 4-10, p. 276) on a particular trait, the following change per unit time on a syntality trait:

$$\frac{dS_x}{dt} = b_sS + b_pP + b_rR + b_mME + b_cCE + b_{sx}S_x \qquad (7\text{-}16)$$

S_x could be included in *S*, but is placed alone because it reminds us that the action of S_x itself could be prominent, as in (7-14). This, however, is the simplest linear, additive statement of what would eventually almost certainly require interaction terms—notably of reward, *ME*, with the structure of the group which with varying efficiency filters the reward to the effective individuals.

Now in accordance with the move to a systems theory of interaction of subsystems which we began on encountering the ME and EM terms in the VIDA model we would have to recognize here that while the dS_x/dt change is going on, with S_x as a dependent variable, a similar change is going on in P_y, as a dependent variable. And in the P_y, equation *S* has joined *R* and other independent "predictor" variables. For, as stated our model is a complete reticular one in which every element in the system interacts with every other with two way causal action. If we take all *S*'s en bloc as a single term in place of S_x and similarly for *R*'s and *P*'s there will be six equations like (7-16). (If instead we take each term as actually a series of terms, say *p* social structure parameters like *R* and *q* incidents of reward like *ME*, there will actually be decidedly more.)

For neater representation these six (or more) simultaneous equations would be placed in a square (6 × 6 or more) matrix, with the specific values—S_x, etc.—down the diagonal. Some difficult mathematical and logical decisions would follow if one attempted, knowing empirically the growth rates, such as dS_x/dt, to solve these equations for the unknowns. Assuming one had other empirical ways of knowing the values one might most logically proceed, as was suggested in what we have called the "*ME* and *EM*" problem, by adding the growth of S_x in the first equation *over one short unit of time* to the initial S_x value in equation one, inserting this in equation two, and proceeding similarly for one round with all the six equations, substituting P, R, etc.

The population values, P's, are only one, and probably not the most important, in the determination of group change in (7-16); but they concern most our problem of relating the moving individual to the moving society. The problem concerns, however, the single individual, not the average population values in (7-16), and here we must assume (except for individuals like Christ, Mohammed, Newton, and Hitler) that his effect on society is negligible compared to the effect on him of the society into which he is born. Here, therefore, we deal with one equation, not a set of simultaneous equations, in which the personality change in the individual (in some source trait T_x) is the dependent variable.

Now we have already set out in equations (4-9), (4-10), (4-11), the change in behavior in an individual (written here as $a_{hijk}a_{hijkt2}$ or as dT/dt, or as the underlying engram increment, n) as a function of all that needs to go into such an estimate, namely, the various existing traits of the individual, the reward to *ME* (*CR*II) "operant" response and the coexcitation, *CE*, effects. Where does the cultural environment enter here? Like any environment it is present first in the vector of b values (behavioral indices; in (4-9) given as vs's). Secondly, it is present in the *ME* rewards accorded to various behaviors in the culture (the fourth term in 4-9) and in the contingencies of cognitive experiences offered by the culture, in the last term in (4-10). The transformation from the S, P, and R terms in (7-16) to personality effects is therefore not going to be easy, and still more complex will be the relating of social change (involving the further terms in (7-16) as dS/dt) to co-existing individual change dT/dt.

What seems certain, from our discovery that the description of learning requires both the events during the learning period and the parameters of the preceding condition including the momentum, is that individual personality change prediction and understanding will require *in toto* (including the culture and cultural change) the following five contributors, based on the relevant group changes reviewed on p. 553:

1. The prior existing trait scores of the individuals, with the b weights upon them determined by the dimensions of the culture. For b weights are general cultural properties related to the cultural dimensions as in (7-17)—if we adopt a simple weighted linear formula. The changes in an individual's traits through joining the culture will be the end result of the b changes on sets of a_{hjk}'s.

$$b_{hjk} = f_{hjk}(\Sigma y_s S + \Sigma y_r R + \Sigma y_p P) \tag{7-17}$$

2. If, as we suppose, cultural change is also occurring and that change itself has an effect, an expression (contingently as a product of S, R, and P) must be added to (7-17) as in (7-18):

$$b_{hjk} = f_{hjk} (\Sigma y_s S + \Sigma y_r R + \Sigma y_p P)$$
$$+ f_{hjk}\left(\frac{d(SRP)}{dt}\right) \tag{7-18}$$

3. Change, however, includes soma effects (p. 159) besides learning, through, for example, level of nutrition, climatic temperature, proportion of sedentary jobs, with weights (w's) which, unlike (7-17) and (7-18), will apply directly to the traits, for example, T_x, as in (7-19).

$$\frac{dT_x}{d_c} = w_x (\Sigma w_s S + \Sigma w_r R + \Sigma w_p P)$$
$$+ w'_x\left(\frac{d(SRP)}{dt}\right) \tag{7-19}$$

where d_c represents the cultural level and its change.

4. The volutional, genetic change in personality, which will be a function only of the genetics of the trait T_g and the age of the subject and can be written dT_g/dt.

5. The contribution to the learning (so far given on b's only from personality and syntality traits) from the two main learning principles, ME and CE. These are largely idiosyncratic to the individual's life: he happens to make this operant reponse which is rewarded or

to encounter that contiguity with certain contingencies. Even so, if these are recorded as in (4-9) purely in individual terms, their effects could to some degree be modified according to the cultural field in which they occur. Consequently *ME*, which we will use here to represent the whole reward expression in (4-9) could have the modifications from syntality and change in syntality, represented additively, thus:

$$f_{me}ME + f_{meds}\left(\frac{d(SRP)}{dt}\right)ME \tag{7-20}$$

and the whole coexcitation effect similarly as:

$$f_{ce}CE + f_{ceds}\left(\frac{d(SRP)}{dt}\right)CE \tag{7-21}$$

It will be noted that the f terms above mean "functions of," and must not be assumed to be simple weights. Each has a different subscript to indicate its particularity. If we wish now to put all together, to remind us of the total set of influences we could set it out as in (7-22). It will be understood that this is what we have called a schematic equation, in which there are different condensations and "understood subscripts" from those used when there is space to deal with the terms in isolation. Moreover, the engram gain has been substituted (as change in T_x) for the behavioral index gain, from (7-18) the first line in (7-22) which is assumed to sum the specific behaviors by which T_x is scored, deriving from the b's and T_a to T_z.

$$\frac{dT_x}{dt} = \sum^{a=z} f_{Tx}(\Sigma y_s s + \Sigma y_r R + \Sigma y_p P)T_a + f_{Tx}\left(\frac{d(SRP)}{dt}\right)$$
$$+ f(\Sigma w_s S + \Sigma w_r R + \Sigma w_p P) + f\left(\frac{d(SRP)}{dt}\right) + \frac{dT_g}{dt}$$
$$+ f_{me}ME + f_{meds}\left(\frac{d(SRP)}{dt}\right) + f_{ce}CE + f_{ceds}\left(\frac{d(SRP)}{dt}\right)CE$$

$$(7-22)$$

In review, (7-22) is essentially no different from our general learning equations (4-9), (4-10) for one person, etc., analyzing gain as due to the personality (including dynamics) of the learner and the reward and contiguity experiences he encounters. The expansions are (1) recognizing the terms —notably the y's, S's, R's, P's, and w's— where the character of the culture intrudes, and (2) considering the effect of the change in culture in the time period in which the individual is changing.

The closed system of personality and environment with which we have operated throughout is therefore finally expressed to include both the previous actualities of both parts and the ongoing changes in both.

An important final perspective here concerns the role we have given to controlling integrating mechanisms in the two parts: the ego in the individual; the existing government in the major group. Each is in control with the aim of maximizing adaptation to environment—the physical and international universe for the group, the physical universe *and* the group for the individual. These controlling and integrating mechanisms for the two open subsystems are only of moderate efficiency and there is no controlling mechanism for the whole, unless one steps into the realm of reasoning which assumes a deity. At this mystery of an adventurous, apparently uncontrolled ongoing process we must presently stop.

It is generally agreed by effective scientists that as their various sciences broke loose—as natural philosophy—from the apron strings of Mother Philosophy further development has required great wariness to prevent attempts to re-attach the strings, for mother's guileful fondness is unabated. The social sciences in particular have suffered, for example, in the Hegelian mysticism which, in psychology, came out in McDougall's teleological "group mind" and in Karl Marx's dependence on the "dialectic" process. As far as the present writer's reaction is concerned, the dialectic thinking ritual of emergence from opposites (thesis and antithesis) is a kind of verbal superstition, like that of the ancient philosophers' belief that since a circle is the most "perfect" figure, and since the heavens are perfect, heavenly bodies must move in perfect circles. Saying goodbye to all that, we nevertheless have to recognize a very different sense in which psychology and the social sciences definitely need to think harder about "philosophy," namely in regard to epistemology and the properties of a human brain, an instrument still not much above that of the apes.

The life sciences have intelligently and faithfully pursued the methods of investigation and canons of "truth" proven so effective in the physical sciences. The fact that they have had less success than the latter in reaping an impressive harvest of basic laws could be ascribed to various causes (a late start; a slowness to recognize the new need for multivariate rather than bivariate experiment; and having further to go from local specifications and a plethora of descriptive detail to fundamentals). We shall see that there may be more to the problem than this, but let us consider for a moment this difficulty in getting down from local and temporary laws to more basic laws and generalizations. For example, to the chemist and physicist, the properties assigned to sodium remain constant, and Ohm's law holds for electrical conduction over most ranges. By contrast, a statesman who asks an economist for a prediction on some economic measure is referred to a law known only to apply to an advanced industrial country, in the twentieth century, when surrounded by undeveloped countries.

The same circumstantial uncertainty—or intrusion of trivial localism—holds for probably a majority of psychological generalizations that we like to think of as current laws in our science. Learning curves and their constants alter radically with different species and even different breeds of rats as well as with the many possible varieties of learning problems. The correlation of intelligence with school performance changes with age, social group, and the approved teaching style at the time. And so on. Yet the ultimate aim of scientific research is accepted by most scientists as getting to unchanging elements in fundamental and universal laws. In physiology, a generalization about erythrocytin and its capacity for oxygen transport to the brain will vary from species to species, because its chemical composition is somewhat different in different species. Nevertheless, researchers in social and biological sciences continue to be encouraged by glimpses of a genuine, slow but sure reduction of the more local generalizations to unchanging physical and chemical laws.

Yet this reduction is not enough. For further consideration shows that the problem is not that of getting down to basic laws but of getting upward from knowledge of the basic laws to the more complex situations. In discussing "emergents" in population interactions (p. 530) we took the simple instance of predicting from the basically known properties of sodium and chlorine the fact that NaCl would have a salt taste and have a particular saturation solubility in water. It illustrates the fact that we do not know all about the ultimate properties of sodium and chlorine so long as we do not combine them. Similarly we do not know the full meaning of, say, the basic chemical laws until we see them in, say, neurological action in an organism. Or, to express it in another mode of definition, we cannot derive laws at the more complex level of expression without adding knowledge of higher interactional principles to our more basic laws. To speak thus of emergents is another way of saying that we do not know the part until we know the whole.

Pondering this, we run into a further difficulty: that up to any given point in time we cannot have experience of all the emergents that might exist. The inadequacy exists even in the physical sciences but is likely to strike us first in the social sciences where we deal with historically evolving systems that move toward greater complexity. There we see that there exist complexities and emergents, necessary to the full understanding of more basic properties and laws, that at present lie beyond the reach of our observation, in the future. If this is correct our knowledge—that is, our command of laws necessary to complete scientific prediction—must remain ineluctably imperfect. The fuller implications of this view may be expanded upon in four propositions in social science as follows, defining the epistemological limitations of personality and learning theory, and of their derivatives in future history.

1. *Not all emergents from elements and relations studied only to a given time point are predictable.* This states in summary form what we have discussed above. Emergents may be predicted from elements and relations that have *previously* been found to account for such emergents, for example 2 × 3 = 6. But since the properties of elements are fully known only when all emergents are known, and at a given point in history all emergents will *not* be known, the emergents from new combinations of known elements may not be predictable by known laws. This says that the observation "History repeats itself" can in most instances refer to only an approximate repetition.

In term of curves of relationship this means that we can *interpolate* missing points in a curve, but not *extrapolate* to points beyond—a fact of life which many stock exchange theorists have painfully learned. Incidentally, no method of converting irregular curves to combinations of mathematically regular curves, as in a Fourier series, can overcome this difficulty.

2. *The sampling of social events can never be sufficient to permit fully accurate prediction.* This states that even when we predict and make estimates resting on laws and elements completely defined by past experience any sampling short of the population is unable to encompass any really complete and exact prediction because in general any one event outside laboratory control is affected by virtually all existing elements.

This principle is distinct from (1) above, though they overlap. Thus (1) might be considered within (2), sampling, in the sense that a sampling which cannot include future events is a badly biased sample.

3. *The logistics of information assembly prevents exact prediction—in the sense of foretelling—even if principles (1) and (2) did not already do so.* Prediction—often an ambiguous word—has been used throughout this book in the sense of mathematical, scientific prediction, which statistically is "estimation." Here we

distinguish *foretelling*, which means prediction ahead of time. The inability here may seem to consist only of the practical problem that in multivariate prediction—as all prediction is in the last resort—we may not be able to assemble existing values for all the predictor elements in time to predict before the event has occurred. The optimist may say that this is only a matter of developing sufficient speed of communication and calculation and is a practical rather than a theoretical limitation. It is hoped that the margin of error from this cause can be cut; but at least the possibility exists that there is an inherent limit. It will be remembered that the answer to the paradox of Maxwell's demon, who seemed to beat entropy by opening his trapdoor only to the faster molecules passing him, was that supplying him with bits of information about the speed of particular molecules would itself consume energy. Possibly some lemma on the laws of thermodynamics will deny us the possibility (even granted we know all necessary predictive laws) of ever bringing together before an event, even with the most efficient logistics, all the far flung partial determiners that need to enter into the foretelling.

4. *Though science is based on faith in causal determinism as we know it, regions are likely to be reached in which such determinism exists only in modified form.* Science necessarily and rightly proceeds on the postulate that determinism holds throughout the universe, and questions the postulate only if or when it fails. In this generation, however, the postulate has been shaken, even in the deterministic sanctuary of the physical sciences, by the discovery that time and place cannot simultaneously be accurately stated for an individual particle, that the observer affects what he sees, and that a statistical probability has to be substituted. The line from Willard Gibbs to Niels Bohr and Schrodinger accepts this view, but that from Kelvin to Einstein insists, as the latter said, that "God does not play dice." Oppenheimer's comment (1966) gives a useful perspective here.[11] Because the human mind was evolved to fit and bring survival only in a region covering a limited span of the existing size range between the electron and the stellar nebulae, it is conceivable that this evolved instrument does not have the logical equipment (that is, is bound to a false "self evidence" of propositions) to handle types of relationships yet to be encountered in new domains. For example, on the issue of the connection of neurological action with consciousness, the distinguished neurologist, Eccles, has said that the nervous system has features that suggest it is designed to be played, like a piano, by a spirit outside the machine. That is to say, we may have to abandon a simple psycho-physical parellelism of consciousness and neurological events.

Be that as it may, an open mind must recognize the possibility that forms of relationship beyond those of causal determinism as now understood may operate at the frontiers of our knowledge and we may suspect that such a frontier could be reached earlier in motivation research than elsewhere. Obviously the common-sense strategy of the scientist is not to lose heart at insufficiently investigated apparent failures of determinism but to proceed with deterministic assumptions until they unmistakably break down. Our methods and measurements in psychology are not so advanced that any failure of prediction today justifies speculating that we may have reached the frontiers of determinism. But intuition suggests that if such frontiers are reached it will be in the domain of the dynamic calculus of decision and group decision. The fact that concepts of personality are inextricably intertwined with those of the social group, as this chapter has tried to illuminate, means that the scientific study of personality must ultimately become alert to what we have called above the four epistemological limitations.

These limitations, within a scientific framework, however, are very different from the many naive objections to the social sciences, for example, on the grounds that values intrude into them, and that "values are beyond science." One must agree with these critics that values must be clearly dissected from the scientific inferences of social science, as the present writer (1938, 1944, 1948, 1950), has long urged. But ethical values themselves can also be scientifically studied, not only (1) in their operation, as in our analysis of sentiments, but also (2) in their *origins* as scientifically derivable injunctions from the facts of evolution, as instanced in the arguments of Beyondism (Cattell, 1972).

7-11. Summary

1. As fully recognized initially in Chapter 6, Volume 1 the individual personality system has to be considered in relation to the full system of environment, the two creating a closed system. The most important part of environment, on which we expand here, concerns the social groups and culture to which the individual belongs. A digression must therefore be made into social psychology, and we begin with the basic psychological definition of a group as *a set of people (or other organisms) whose behaviors are so inter-related that the group contributes positively to the satisfactions of all members.* A group is thus a particular kind of means-end instrument in individual satisfactions.

2. If we are to study interpersonal relationships comprehensively, we have to cover those of (a) persons to persons (b) persons to groups and vice versa, and (c) groups to groups. This requires a precision in describing groups equivalent to that so far gained in describing individual personalities.

3. The description and measurement of a group requires values for three "panels": *syntality* (*S*), *structure* (*R*), and *population* (*P*). Syntality is the analogue of personality in the individual, and is defined for any group as a vector of scores on dimensions discovered by factoring the behaviors of groups *as* groups, that is, taking *groups* as subjects for correlation. This must be done afresh for each *type* of group, however, from neonate to national, because dimensions of each type could be very different, and type differences loom larger than in personality measurement. Examples of such discovered group dimensions (both for small neonate and for national groups) show they are psychologically meaningful, helping us penetrate the nature of group dynamics. A subset of syntality dimensions, those corresponding to *dynamic* traits in the individual personality, are best analyzed and discussed separately because of their special properties. These constitute the vector of group *synergy*, normally a section within the syntality vector.

4. In one direction of causal action (when we hold up consideration of feedback), syntality can be regarded as a function of structure and population characteristics, as in equation (7-1): $S = f(RP)$. For anything beyond a moment of observation, however, we also must consider feedback circularities in this equation. In particular, P can have two meanings: population qualities *before* the group is formed, and population qualities formed after the group reaches equilibrium on R and S.

5. The dynamic relationship of the individual to the group can be considered like any other sentiment attachment, operationally defined as "In these life circumstances I want so much to belong to group X." Like any other sentiment it can have its total interest analyzed into a specification equation in which E and M terms are most important, though temperament and ability terms may also enter. The summed ergic and engram strengths represent the totality of satisfaction the individual gets from the various participating courses of action (attitudes) in the group activities. As with any attitudes about a single sentiment object these sum to the individual's total sentiment vector. The sum of these sentiment vectors across all members (whose vectors are typically by no means identical) yields a measure of total *synergy* for the *group*, as such.

6. Normally every individual is simultaneously a member of several groups. If we grant that dealing with the physical environment is (in

all but Robinson Crusoes) part of a group activity, then the sum total of an individual's group affiliative sentiment vectors adds up to the individual's total psychological "energy." (Energy has yet not been defined in its full connotation, but initially is operationally defined as the sum of b_eE and b_mME terms in the system—attitude, sentiment, person.) It follows that if the energy of each individual may be considered constant, and the number of persons affiliated to a set of coactive groups remains the same (coactive meaning sharing membership with other groups), the total group synergies must be constant. This basic group synergy theorem has several corollaries, expressible in other formulae, one of which is that one group can grow in synergy only at the expense of another, so that the typical state of affairs is one of changing equilibria among their synergies.

7. There is an enormous variety of groups, and an objective taxonomy of them—which must locate types as a preliminary to factoring the within-type dimensions—is theoretically best obtained by the same methods as have been developed for individuals and physical objects. This requires the classifying of the natural diversity of social groups by their syntality profiles into species types, by r_p and the Taxonome method and program. The profiles must rest on a preliminary ascertainment of factor dimensions and scores. Sociologists such as Sorokin and Boulding have given tentative group classifications but these are crude and subjective. One is encouraged, by the consistency and historical meaningfulness of the results of typing modern nations by Taxonome on a basis of syntality vectors to conclude that more comprehensive, more exact, and less subjective "types" could now be more profitably made the center of research and theory. At least it is already evident that when national syntality profiles are objectively sorted by the Taxonome, using r_p, they fall into cultural type groups that agree essentially with those of historians of culture.

8. The internal structure (R) of any group is defined largely by roles, emotional-dynamic ties, communication networks, the pattern of interacting subgroups, the status dimension, and possibly other dimensions of "fields" determining social action at a given position. Within this internal structure, just as in the systems analysis of the individual, various adjustments go on, basically mediating between the genetic composition of the group and the adaptive demands presented by the environment. The rates of flow in relation to classes, economic exchanges, roles and educational streams are central in the systems description of a group. Here social mobility between classes is taken as a field effect about which psychology has already sufficient data to reach some conclusions.

9. Much of the structure of groups is accounted for by roles, and by

the traditional rules and mores that define and utilize them. The scientific definition of a role requires simultaneous approach from four different angles of perception, notably (a) as an acquired sentiment structure similarly repeated in a class of individuals, and representable as a factor, that is, as a matrix of loadings on a broad sample of behaviors, as set out in Chapter 6, Volume 1; (b) as a pattern of social expectations in the group member, determinable by survey methods; (c) as a map of the role's typical network of communication ties with persons in other roles; and (d) as a tangible contribution to effectiveness of group life, measurable by effects on group syntality and synergy. The last is measurable in principle by the *successive abstraction* method, and, incidentally, provides one of the best objective operational definitions of the important role we call that of a leader. The leader is operationally defined as the person whose abstraction from the group produces a greater change in syntality than the loss of any other member.

10.   The exploration of networks has been carried to a considerable precision of formulation by communication science, handling transactions largely in flow of units of information. The transactional ties between one individual and another, however, are channels for emotional as well as cognitive traffic, and an adequate formulation thus has to embrace also the emotional, dynamic exchanges. This is a considerable challenge, but it can be met if we recognize that the activity ordinarily measured in an attitude course of action contains both cognitive and dynamic behavior and measurement terms. Consequently, and especially for purposes of role definition and synergy transactions, representation of a tie by the dynamic specification equations of the attitude of person A to B, and B to A, covers a great deal of the transactional tie between them. Because we have recognized (in 9) that one way of representing a role is by its communication network, it seems that this description could now be enriched by representing the ties additionally with the usual dynamic specification information.

Transactional ties in organized groups have been extensively explored in networks with regard to concrete exchange data, such as business research naturally deals with; but so far no study has been made in which a network has been described in two-directional attitudes expressed in ergic and sentiment loadings. There is surely little doubt that study of relations in such a network—analogous to the dynamic lattice but with people as nodes instead of sentiment objects—would lead to interesting advances in group use of the dynamic calculus.

11.   Factor analytically, socioeconomic status variables on individuals yield many dimensions but when taken on occupations are

accounted for largely by a single dimension, at the center of which lies *prestige*, with salary, education, housing, and so on, as definitely of lower loadings. In modern society, when the calculation is made on occupations, the intelligence levels of the occupations correlates most highly with this prestige. We may hypothesize fairly safely that this prestige characteristic will be central in all societies, whereas the appurtenances and evokers of prestige may vary from academic degrees to shark-tooth collections. The drives to status in the individual are complex combinations of assertive, narcistic, and security ergs, and the superego and self-sentiments. Selection operating in the steady stream of social promotion produces significant correlations of psychological traits, and thus of combinations of traits, with social class.

12. To grasp the full dynamic relations of individual personalities to any group it is necessary to recognize relationships of groups to groups, notably (a) their symbiotic patterns, in which one group reciprocally serves the purposes of another, creating a lattice in form like the dynamic lattice, but with groups instead of subgoals for nodes; (b) intergroup conflict. The latter is of two kinds, *direct* in various forms, and *indirect*, by competition of coactive groups for interest and membership increase, aiming at synergy growth. The individual, as distinct from management, normally has little concern with this subsequent use of the energy he bestows on a group, except if he is consciously interested in the *effective synergy* (see 13). Because the pattern of his sentiment formation is that produced by the groups to which he directly belongs, however, conflict of sentiments can be created within individuals by social conflict of the groups to which their sentiments have become attached. Among other forms this can take the form of one group virtually forbidding its members to belong to another group. Since the rounded and adequate satisfaction of an individual's needs is often dependent on his wise choice of a set of groups providing supplementing satisfactions, group conflict can lead to individual conflict and ambivalent attitudes to groups joined. Such conflict is perennial, because it seems to be an empirical law that most groups try to increase their synergy, by catering to more people and catering to more kinds of satisfaction than initially brought the group together ("imperialism").

13. The energy investment in a group, which can be expressed as a particular ergic vector, can be cut into functional parts from the standpoint of the group, yielding *intrinsic* and *effective* synergy. The satisfaction any individual gets from a group can be broken down according to situation stimulus, into segments which will partly agree with the former. Those parts are: (a) his contribution to *effective synergy*—his interest in what the group purposes to do over and

above merely maintaining itself as a group; (b) *intrinsic* synergy—the satisfactions from direct interactions, for example, gregarious, sexual, security-giving, with congenial members; (c) *status* satisfactions from a group role; (d) *personal activity* satisfactions; (e) *personal*, non-group-specific (usually monetary) reward. These distinct components have relevance to calculations among groups as well as among individuals. A cardinal consideration in analyzing the relation of summed individual to total group synergy and its disposal is that means of exchange between individuals, notably money, upset what would otherwise be necessary relations between the ergic quality of what individuals put into the group and the ergic quality of the synergy expended by the group through action of its leadership.

14. Groups persist by a more or less deliberate, and institutionally complex machinery of education for molding individuals to their values. The first major generalization evident between group and individual structure is that much of the sentiment structure of the individual will be essentially a replica of the number and nature of group institutions (subgroups). This can be called *the law of person-society isomorphism*. The second important generalization has been called *the law of coercion to the biosocial norm*. It states that in any trait a pressure will be exerted on the individual proportional to his original (largely genetic) score distance from the approved value for the social norm. This distance, in individual or group we call the *genetic-cultural gap* or lag. Sometimes the ideal level is consciously embraced in education (for example, as to the superego level) and then it generally deviates for everyone in one direction from the genetic average; in other cases it is unconscious and defined more by the biological and social behavior *mean* of the given group.

15. In studying the relation of group syntality to the dynamic adjustments of the population important concepts are *deflection strain, the dynamic complexity of a culture, long circuiting* and *cultural pressure*. Deflection strain can be formulated and measured as the degree of deviation of cultural stimuli and required response from the tendency long inherited in ergs. Dynamic complexity can be formulated and measured from the loadings of behavior specification equations of attitudes sampling the culture. Due to the general isomorphism of population sentiment structures and cultural institutions the more complex the society the larger the number of groups to which the individual belongs and the higher the number of roles the average member of the society has to learn and manage. Long circuiting is counted by time or subgoals in the ergic path and is probably highly correlated across cultures with the complexity index. The syntality dimension "cultural pressure" is hypothesized to relate highly to these indices, and as far as can be inferred from

population personality measures on high cultural pressure nations it does so.

16. Significant *population trait-syntality dimension* correlations have been found for several syntality dimensions and fit psychological expectations, with a few exceptions. Relations of syntality to personality and motivation variables are also known in both small neonate groups just as in national groups. For example, neurotic traits in individuals seem to reduce the morale score in small groups. Between national syntality dimensions and population measures, in addition to the above relations to *cultural pressure I*, a relation is found to *cultural pressure II* of the population "toughness, self-assuredness" dimension, (*O-*). Community differences in intelligence as studied by Lynn, Jensen, and others also seem to show significant relations to syntality variables, such as educational level, infantile death rate, average real income, and so on.

17. Group change arises from six causes, of which only one can strictly be called learning. They are: *learning; volution* (age maturations in the population as individuals); somatic change in the population, for example, disease; *genetic change* through internal selection; genetic and cultural change through *in- and out-migration;* and *synergy change* through change of investment of individuals in regard to their dynamic structures. The first three are principles seen also in individual personality change, but the last three are peculiar to group changes.

18. All forms of group learning, as measured in *syntality* change, involve simultaneous changes in *structure, population* or both. Some instances of these are examined. Steady trends over half a century or more have been plotted in dimensions of national syntality and can be related to observations in history, though the syntality of a group seems more stable than more superficial, dramatic historical events might suggest. In the last resort all group learning *depends on*, but cannot *be reduced to*, learning in individuals by the usual principles of coexcitation, means-end learning, and integration learning (and possibly the two other principles active in individuals). It cannot be so reduced because group learning or change can result from change of structure (roles, interaction networks) with comparatively little change in population parameters per se. Comparatively large emergents in syntality can depend on disproportionately small population changes, even without structural change, though the latter is usually present as an effect of status hierarchy, of degree of formalized leadership, and of the form of the transmission network for conveying group rewards to various roles, and so on. (*Law of emergence*, p. 530.)

19. The learning of a group as a group, as directly seen in syntality

and synergy changes, rests on reward, for trial and error (*ME*, *CR*II) or insightful learning, and also on the *CE* principle. However, the learning of an organized group acting as a group is far slower than individual learning because the reward has to be distributed to individuals in such a way as to change their individual behavior (as well as structural relations) in a *pattern* to fit the new group response).

A fully developed model for this can scarcely be presented until more experiment with dynamic calculus concepts in a group setting has been examined. However, existing experiment shows group learning adaptation to depend both on structure and population properties. The former is shown by inferior performance experimentally in leaderless groups and by correlations of performance with personality traits of the leader which favor individual members' confidence, and good communication. The role of members' traits shows in several significant correlations, both in small neonate groups and in nations, between syntality and performance measures and the mean population scores on personality traits. Thus sociological and economics theories which treat individuals as equal, faceless units are inadequate. One way in which the ability and personality trait mean and distribution in populations can affect syntality is illustrated in terms of communication processes under the concept of the *percolation range* of ideas and motivations.

20. The last three forms of group change are instanced in influences changing the mean IQ; in monitored selection by migration; and in historical and current examples of changing synergy investments following the interests of the population. Equations are given for indurated conflict in group synergy; for calculating the point of group dissolution; and for "group sentiment conflict." The relation of group conflict to individual conflict varies from simple isomorphism to quite complex derivations. The properties of the individual mind— for example its degree of rigidity and of intelligence— necessarily affect the speed and manner of change in group syntality and the rate of modification of the structure. In particular the distributions of personality properties affect the stability of institutions and the "percolation range" of ideas on which action depends.

The basic isomorphism found between sentiment structure and the structure of social institutions has several implications. (a) It requires educational aids in institutions, to produce and maintain the isomorphism. Social psychologists correlating the values in individuals with those in groups have sometimes ranked institutions as to the magnitude of their educational influence on individuals, generally concluding that home is more important than church or school. (b) When change occurs in either, change is produced in the other, for example, personality sentiment change means change in the above synergy distribution. (c) Conflicts between the institution groups as such produce conflict in the individual.

21. Groups as such learn by reinforcement of operant (sometimes insightful) behavior, and coexcitation, plus additional structural change, as covered in summaries 18 and 19 above. When change begins in the group, as an organism, being forced upon it by environmental change, etc., it may be unpleasant to the population, by heightening the continually present deflection stress (deflection strain, ergic complication, and long circuiting), conflict and ergic frustration. When rapid, such change has been called "future shock". In part the stress can be viewed as a discrepancy of cultural demands and genetic endowments. Under stresses evolution may turn into revolution, which may have pathological features.

22. It seems possible to define a variety of social pathologies, and with more research these should be recognizable and diagnosable by certain extreme syntality scores. Pathologies are manifested by genetic-cultural dissonance (by birth rates and migrations), by dissolution of internal structure, by loss of morale closely associated with loss of individual morality; by rigidities from an aging population or excessive traditionalism; by excessive fractions of synergy going to maintenance synergy, and by narcistic individual adjustments reducing total synergy. Social pathology and individual (population) pathology are nevertheless different concepts. Both may tend to occur together (as in the finding in small groups that more neurotics lower group performance). But what by most standards would measure up as a decadent or moribund society can exist with "happily adjusted" individuals. On the other hand a rapidly progressing or vigorous society may excite resistance in individuals, defense mechanisms, overt pugnacity and revolt, and neurotic maladjustments, that is, individual pathology, as in the *reaction to cultural pressure* dimension of syntality.

23. The individual personality and the group are sub-systems within a total closed system, which includes the physical environment constituted by the universe. The elements and relations within the individual system have been indicated in some detail in personality structure, but in the group structure more sketchily, appropriate to the present state of social sciences. The ongoing process of the individual personality system can only be finally understood and predicted by recognizing that we deal with a changing personality in a changing society. The methodology of separating the epogenic contribution of society from the normal ecogenic pattern of change in the average person is illustrated.

For understanding change in the social group system a series of simultaneous differential equations are proposed, as numerous as the syntality, structure, population, and learning experience elements in the system. But, assuming the traits of most individuals can only be *dependent* variables in relation to the massive movement of the total cultural group, that is, action is one sided as far as an individual (but not the whole population, *P*) is concerned, a formula can be developed for assessing change in a unit time in the individual from change in society in the same brief interval, that is, in a time differential equation. The predictors are (1) the original vector of personality scores (2) the original vector of syntality scores, which enter first into determining the *b*'s of the personal behavior equation (3) the *soma* change effect of the culture. (4) The syntality *change* has specific effects on individual learning, over and above absolute level effects. (5) The rewards and coexcitations normally added to prediction of learning from traits alone are here again functions of the cultural and cultural change dimensions in the society the individual joins.

Considered as separate systems the individual and the group alike have adaptation and survival as the goal and use control subsystems as the means. But the closed total system apparently has only what can be descriptively and broadly called an uncontrolled evolutionary goal, and like all closed systems is subject to increasing entropy.

24. Pursued far enough, the psychology of individual and group finds itself marching side by side with the study of history. However, it has no need to loosen its quantitative models and experimental methods in a misguided attempt to amalgamate with current historical methods, or to embrace the quasi-philosophical approaches (Hegelian dialectics, Carlyle's leadership by heroes, Toynbee's "yin and yang," Spengler's "inevitable decline," or certain economic theories) that have permeated historical theories, Multivariate analysis of historical happenings and manipulative experiment with psychologically measured small groups will develop entirely new general theory in history.

Nevertheless, the psychologist has to recognize that in encompassing the personality-syntality system he may be approaching four epistemological limits to his powers of scientific generalization and prediction. They are: the inadequacy of sampling, for truly refined prediction; the practical logistic limits of speed and completeness of data assembly for predictive calculations on *immediately* ensuing events; the impossibility of finding out the laws determining emergents from presently known elements when the most complex emergents have not yet been experienced at this point in history; and the possibility that the deterministic mode of thought acquired by the human mind at this stage of evolution may fail (as in present nuclear physics) in exploring the most complex motivational and social phenomena that we come to study.

On the other hand, the confusions of social sciences with "revealed," dogmatic ethical systems can be clearly solved by recognizing the derivation of ethics from observations of evolution, as specifically proposed in the Beyondist system.

NOTES

[1] Several voices have been raised recently, deploring that sociology and economics have not made, over the last 40 years, the progress toward effective sciences that had been expected of them. There are several reasons for this. (a) Sociology has almost necessarily stayed at the level of a *descriptive* discipline, because *explanation* could come only by involving the psychology of organism-environment interaction. (b) Until the last decade sociology lagged behind psychology in its methodology, notably in regard to use of psychometric measures and multivariate experimental methods. (c) Sociologists have tended to be concerned with immediate practical applications, in what they assumed to be progressive measures. This has produced, on the one hand, an intellectually repugnant and useless mixture of science with local social values (as in Marxism, or a papal encyclical), and, on the other, absence of attention to knowledge for its own sake, and the larger syntheses that go therewith.

[2] A distinction might advantageously be drawn between *pristine* population characteristics, present before joining the group and necessarily independent variables as they could be in (7-1), and *adjustive* population variables, after the group has formed, which are both causes and consequences of S and R.

[3] Although the self-assertive erg comes out very clearly in factoring objective motivation measures the self-submissive pattern is, mainly for lack of checking researches, not yet so well established on this basis. But from its presence in primates and other mammals, and from admiration, hero-worship, and the capacity for reverence in human behavior, there can surely be little doubt that satisfaction in worship makes the dominance or status hierarchy workable, by generating innate satisfactions at *both* ends of such relations.

[4] Whenever words are used—which is in all tests but culture fair intelligence tests—the effect of translation on the factor weight of the items and on the standardization has to be taken into account. Two way translation, equivalent sampling of items (Cattell, 1973), and the use of bicultural groups for comparing standardizations, are useful. In the last resort, however, a theoretically accurate cross cultural comparison will require the methods of *isopodic* and *equipotent methods* (Cattell, 1969, 1970) of scoring.

[5] In the development of the dynamic specification equation we have already stated the theoretical model that any cultural situation, besides its acquired action on ergs by learned M in the ME term, can have some direct action innately on an erg. This supposes there are elements in cultural situations that are also primitive, that is that happen to have innate cue characters—as

when a man notices that the woman cashier in a bank has sex appeal. But cultural situations and courses of action generally can show greater or lesser resemblance to the innate patterns, and thus involve less or more deflection strain in the perhaps distinct sense of requiring less or more departure from the innate pattern of a million years. The problem is that we have no easy and direct way of ascertaining those patterns. To define "innate" as what is present and manifest at birth is useless, as we saw in behavior genetics. All actual, realized, cultural behavior already has achieved degrees of deviation from such patterns, so that their presence and nature is only to be inferred from the comparative difficulties in teaching people particular perceptual attentions and behaviors that constitute the various deviations from the innately preferred. An attempt to define experimentally the degrees of difficulty in acquiring various deviations is an approach that should not be neglected. For example, instead of snatching his hand away from an approaching red hot poker a person might be taught to call out a number as a condition of its withdrawal. The readiness of reversion from each of several taught solutions to the innate one might prove a measure of their difficulty (inverted). However, if factor analysis is able cleanly to pull out the ergic factors then we have directly available in the straight loading of some given S-R attitude on the erg (as distinct from that on the ME term) a measure of the extent to which the given situation and response involve the erg innately. It has already been recognized that these loadings get higher the closer the S-R attitude is to the consummatory goal. However, if this theory is correct it should be possible also to recognize high innate involvements in some behaviors that are remote from the consummatory goal but which happen to be similar to earlier parts of the biologically innate path and its environment.

[6] A case of slow learning in channeling group reward to the organs and roles responsible is widespread over the 110 countries in UNO today. The syntality advances of the last 100 years in health, longevity and gross national product, and so on has not been due to any change in the personalities or methods of politicians, businessmen, religious leaders, or trade unions, but to the efforts of an elite of about 10,000 scientists in the whole world. The feedback of support to their endeavors has been a miserable fraction of the group gain. So far as one can ascertain from conflicting figures, Germany and Russia are the countries (out of the 110) coming anywhere near directing, in status and resources, an optimum fraction of the national product back to this subgroup.

[7] There is no adequate information even today on the relation of death rate to intelligence. The shrewdist guess from bits of evidence here and there is that the more intelligent survive (to reproduce) longer, as Shakespeare implied in Macbeth in "All our yesterdays . . .".

[8] That synergy will expand through increasing numbers is obvious, and simply expressed by our first synergy equation. A striking example of synergic expansion learning would be the East India Company, which began as a trading company and finished by being virtually the government of India. As far as this writer knows, there is no record of any shareholder successfully objecting to this expansion, though other outside groups did, as Clive and Warren Hastings realized. Indeed, it seems to be remarkably rare for the governing body in a group to object to the synergic expansion change form of learning through increase of the population under its control. Power and greed have often caused politicians and industrialists to import what has been virtually slave labor without regard to quality and future effects on the culture. Growth of synergy by "robbing" coactive groups (other groups to which individuals belong) is most often relative—a shift of degrees of interest such as seems to have occurred be-

tween the primary family and various secondary groups such as insurance companies, which in a few generations have taken over part of the family's functions. We see in the change of individual sentiment structure here—a change sometimes accompanied by conflict—the association with the second form of group conflict. The process readily expresses itself for measurement in economic terms in finance and industry.

A man might sell his stock in company B and buy that of A if A offers better dividends when company A diversifies its products (a form of synergy expansion, as well as of insurance), and A thus trespasses on company B. Looking at essentials, we can see that the main recurring theme in history is this competitive interaction of group synergies (1) in direct group conflict and maneuvering, and (2) in competition for members. It has been conspicuous, for example, among great religions. In theory there is no limit to the synergic expansion of a group until the sum of all individual energies is reached and one group caters for all needs. Some totalitarian socialist countries which forbid religions and other competing groups, approach this. Incidentally, if this were achieved, it would put an end to that trial-and-error variation among many smaller groups, and the ensuing natural selection, that are indispensable to varied cultural evolution. Evolution could then occur only through international competition.

[9] For completeness this active conflict between an individual's wish to belong to two groups having some degree of practical incompatibility of simultaneous realization we may repeat (6-8) in group form as:

$$c_{gi(A)} = w_1 \left(\overset{x=p}{\Sigma} b_{g1x} D_{xi} + \overset{x=p}{\Sigma} b_{g2x} D_{xi} \right) +$$

$$+ w_2 \left(\overset{x=p}{\Sigma} b_{g1x} D_{xi} - \overset{x=p}{\Sigma} b_{g2x} D_{xi} \right) \tag{7-12b}$$

where w_1 and w_2 are weights respectively for the joint magnitude of the interests in conflict and for the fineness of the difference. (We *could* use a ratio rather than a difference.) The b_{g1}'s are loadings for the larger and the b_{g2}'s for the smaller strength of loyalty.

[10] Nevertheless, popular ideas of what happens in major social change still remain too dramatically "revolution preoccupied," partly inherited from the philosophical mysticism of the Hegelian "antithesis," partly expressing a vicarious satisfaction for humanity's constant pugnacity against its cultural burden.

The emphasis in understanding change is now, as Boulding (1970), Huntington (1927, 1945), Toynbee (1947), and many others point out, more on evolution rather than revolution. Nevertheless, the agricultural, industrial, and communications (cybernetic) "revolutions" deserve that name by reason of the completeness of change of patterns. But clearly, in this sense, the word means something very different from the Paris mob under Marat and Robespierre and from political revolutions that change very little but the party in power. Indeed, although the psychological aggressions and defenses generated by the gap (deflection strain) between our genetic makeup and what we have defined as the complexities of the culture as evident in the cultural pressure factor, keep up a constant head of revolutionary steam, probably at higher pressure in the less-adapted lower-status groups, at least as many revolutions come from the top as the bottom of the status dimension (Vide the Shah of Iran in 1978!). In view of the pervasive tendency in the mass media to dramatic oversimplification, it is still necessary to emphasize that the transforming revolutions begin in the "small back room" of the laboratory and the inventor's attic—with Faraday, Watt, and Shockley—and the pressures generated by the resulting great stresses on older habits are handled by more literary, journalistic and political recipes.

[11] "These two ways of thinking, the way of time and history, and the way of eternity and timelessness, are both part of man's efforts to comprehend the world in which he lives. Neither is comprehended in the other nor reducable to it." Oppenheimer, 1966, p. 69. In the present writer's analysis, above, however, these are not two different categories. "The way of eternity" is the knowledge the scientist would like to have, and theoretically could have, by his methods, *with infinite time.* The way of history (which is scientific knowledge to date) is the fraction of this total, consisting of the same *kind* of knowledge, that he is permitted to have at a given time.

BIBLIOGRAPHY

Ach, N. *Über die Willenstatigkeit und das Denken; ihre experimentelle Unter-suchung, mit einem Anhange über das Hippsche Chronoscop,* Göttingen, Springer, 1905.

Adams, J. A. *Human memory,* New York, McGraw-Hill, 1967.

Adelson, M. A study of ergic tension patterns through the effects of water deprivation in humans. Unpublished Ph.D. thesis, University of Illinois at Urbana, 1952.

Aird, J., et al. Association between ABO groups and peptic ulceration. British Medical Journal, 1954, 2, 315.

Alker, R. Is personality situationally specific or intrapsychically consistent. *J. of Personality,* 1972, 40, 1-16.

Allport, G. W. *Pattern and growth in personality.* New York: Holt, Rinehart & Winston, 1961.

Allport, G. W., & Odbert, H. S. Trait-names: a psycholexical study. *Psychological Monograph,* 1936, 47, 171-220.

Altman, I. *The environment and social behaviour: privacy and personal space, territory, and crowding.* New York, Brooks Co., 1975.

Amarel, S. An approach to automatic theory formation, Pp. 104-130 in Von Foerster, H., & Zopf, G. W. (Eds.), *Principles of self organization,* London: Pergamon Press, 1962.

Ammons, R. B. Effects on knowledge of performance: A survey and tentative theoretical formulation. *Journal of Genetic Psychology,* 1956, 54, 279-299.

Amsel, A., & Cole, K. F. Generalization of fear motivated interference with water intake. *Journal of Experimental Psychology,* 1953, 46, 243-247.

Anastasi, A. A., Fuller, J. L., Scott, J. P., & Schmitt, J. R. A factor analysis of the performance of dogs on certain learning tests, *Zoologica,* 1955, 40-50.

Anderson, B. F. *Cognitive Psychology,* New York: Academic Press, 1975.

Anderson, E. E. the interrelationship of drives in the male albino rat. III. Among measures of emotional, sexual and exploratory behavior. *Journal of Genetic Psychology,* 1938, 53, 335-352.

Anderson, E. E. The externalization of drive; IV. The effect of prefeeding on the maze performance of hungry non-rewarded rats. *Journal of Comparative Psychology,* 1941, 31, 349-353.

Angermeier, W. F. Some basic aspects of social reinforcements in albino rats. *Journal of Comparative Physiological Psychology,* 1960, 53, 364-367.

Anokhin, P. K. *Biology and neurophysiology of the conditioned reflex and its role in adaptive behavior.* New York: Pergamon Press, 1974.

Applezweig, M. H. Response potential as a function of effort. *Journal of Comparative Physiological Psychology*, 1951, *44*, 225-235.

Ardrey, R. A. *The territorial imperative.* New York: Dell, 1966.

Ardrey, R. A. *The social contract.* New York, Athenaeum, 1970.

Argyle, M., & Little, B. R. Do personality traits apply to social behavior? *Journal of Theory in Social Behavior*, 1972, *2*, 1-35.

Arnoult, M. D. Predictions of perceptual responses from structural characteristics of the stimulus. *Perceptual and Motor Skills*, 1960, *11*, 261-268.

Asch, S. E. *Social Psychology*, New York: Prentice Hall, 1952.

Ashby, W. R. Principles of the self organizing system. In Von Foerster, H., & Zopf, G. W. (Eds.), *Principles of self organization*, Pp. 225-278. New York: Macmillan, 1962.

Ashem, B. A. and Proser, E. G. (Eds.) *Adaptive learning: behavior modification with children.* London, Pergamon, 1973.

Attneave, F. Physical determinants of the judged complexity of shapes. *Journal of Experimental Psychology*, 1957, *53*, 221-227.

Aveling, F. P. The conative indications of the psychogalvanic phenomenon. *8th International Congress of Psychology*, Groningen, 1926. Pp. 232.

Aveling, F. P. *Personality and will.* New York: Appleton, 1931.

Ayllon, T., & Azrin, T. H. The measurement and reinforcement of behavior of psychotics. *J. of the experiental analysis of behavior*, 356-383. 1965.

Bacon, F. *Selected essays.* (Ed., J. M. Patrick). New York, Appleton Century, 1948.

Baddeley, A. D. Retrieval rules and semantic coding in short term memory. *Psychological Bulletin*, 1971, *78*, 379-385.

Baddeley, A. D. *The psychology of memory.* New York: Basic Books, 1976.

Baddeley, A. D., & Warrington, E. K. Amnesia and the distinction between long term and short term memory. *Journal of Verbal Learning and Verbal Behavior*, 1970, *9*, 176-189.

Baker, J. R. *Race.* New York: Oxford University Press, 1974.

Bales, R. F. *Interaction process analysis: A method for the study of small groups.* Cambridge, Mass: Addison Wesley, 1950.

Bales, R. F. and Strodtbeck, F. L. Phases in group problem solving. *Journal of Abnormal and Social Psychology*, 1951, *46*, 425-495.

Ballard, P. B. Oblivescence and reminiscence. *British Journal of Psychology*, *Monograph Supplements*, 1927. Vol. 1, Supplement No. 2.

Baltes, P. B. Longitudinal and cross sectional sequences in the study of age and generation effects. *Human Development*, 1968, *11*, 145-171.

Baltes, P. B., & Nesselroade, J. R. The developmental analysis of individual differences on multiple measures. In Nesselroade, J. R., & Reese, H. W. (Eds.), *Life span developmental psychology.* New York: Academic Press, 1973.

Baltes, P. B., Nesselroade, J. R., & Cornelius, S. W. Toward an explanation of multivariate structural change in development: A simulation. In Shanan, J. (Ed.), *Transitional phases in human development.* New York: Academic Press (in press, 1976).

Baltes, P. B. & K. W. Schaie, On the plasticity of intelligence in adulthood and old age. *American Psychologist*, 1976, *31*, 720-725.

Bandura, A. Social learning through imitation. In Jones, M. R. (Ed.), *Nebraska Symposium on Motivation.* Lincoln: University of Nebraska Press, 1962.

Bandura, A. Vicarious processes, a case of no-trial learning. In Berkowitz, L. (Ed.), *Advances in experimental social psychology.* Vol. II. New York: Academic Press, 1965.

Bandura, A. & Kupers, C. J. Transmission of patterns of self-reinforcement through modelling. *Journal of Abnormal and Social Psychology*, 1964, *69*, 1-9.

Bandura, A. & Perloff, B. Relative efficacy of self-monitored and externally imposed reinforcement systems. *Journal of Personality and Social Psychology*, 1967, 7, 111-116.

Bandura, A. & Walters, R. H. *Social learning and personality development*. New York: Holt, Rinehart & Winston, 1963.

Barker, R. G. Ecological psychology: Concepts and methods for studying the environment of human learning. Stanford: Stanford University Press, 1968.

Barlow, J. A. Secondary motivation through classical conditioning: A reconsideration of the nature of backward conditioning. *Psychological Review*, 1956, *63*, 406-408.

Barton, K., & Cattell, R. B. Personality before and after a chronic illness. *Journal of Clinical Psychology*, 1972(a), *28*, 464-467.

Barton, K., & Cattell, R. B. Personality factors related to job promotion and turnover. *Journal of Counseling Psychology*, 1972(b), *19*, 430-435.

Barton, K., & Cattell, R. B. Personality factors of husbands and wives, as predictors of own and partner's marital dimensions. *Canadian Journal of Behavioral Science*, 1973, *5*, 83-92.

Barton, K., & Cattell, R. B. Changes in personality over a 5-year period. Relationship of change to life events. *JSAS Catalogue of Selected Documents in Psychology*, 1975.

Barton, K., & Cattell, R. B. *The Core Trait and State (CTS) Battery*. Champaign Ill.: Institute for Personality and Ability Testing, 1978.

Barton, K., Cattell, R. B., & Vaughan, G. M. Changes in personality as a function of college attendance or work experience. *Journal of Counselling Psychology*, 1973, *20*, 162-165.

Barton, K., Dielman, T. E., & Cattell, R. B. Personality, motivation and I.Q. measures as predictors of school achievement and grades. *Psychology in the School*, 9, 47-51, 1972.

Bartsch, T. W. Changes of attitudes as function of interest patterns in learning, 1973.

Bartsch, T. W., Barton, K., & Cattell, R. B. A repeated measures investigation of the relation of the School Motivation Analysis Test to academic achievement. *Psychological Reports*, 1973, *33*, 743-748.

Bass, B. M. *Organizational psychology*. Boston: Allyn & Bacon, 1965.

Bavelas, A. Communications in task-oriented groups. In Cartwright, D., & Zander, A. (Eds.), *Group dynamics, research and theory*. Pp. 29-38. New York: Row & Peterson, 1953.

Bavelas, A., Hastorf, A. H., Gross, A. E., & Kite, W. R. Experiments on the alteration of group structure. *Journal of Experimental and Social Psychology*, 1965, *1*, 55-70.

Beach, T. A., & Jordan, L. Sexual exhaustion and recovery in the male rat. *Quarterly Journal of Experimental Psychology*, 1956, *8*, 121-133.

Beck, A. *Depression: its clinical, experimental and theoretical aspects*. New York: Hoeber, Med. Div., 1967.

Becker, J. *Depression: theory and research*. Washington, D.C.: Winston, 1974.

Berrien, F. K. *General and social systems*. New Brunswick, N. J. Rutgers University Press, 1968.

Bertalanffy, L. von. *Robots, men and minds: Psychology in the modern world*. New York: Braziller, 1967.

Bertalanffy, L. von. *General systems theory: foundations, developments, application.* New York: Braziller, 1969.

Beurle, R. L. Functional organization in random networks. In Von Foerster, H., & Zopf, G. W. (Eds.), *Principles of self organization.* Pp. 291-314. New York: Macmillan, 1962.

Beveridge, W. *The art of scientific investigation.* New York: Norton, 1951.

Birkett, H. & Cattell, R. B. Diagnosis of the dynamic roots of a clinical symptom by P-technique: a case of episodic alcoholism. *Multivariate Experimental Clinical Research*, 1978, *3*, 173-194.

Birkett, H. & Cattell, R. B. The psychological significance of similarities and differences of motivation structure in process (P-technique) and individual difference (R-technique). (In preparation)

Birkett, H. & Cattell, R. B. *The new psychotherapy: from structured learning theory.* (In preparation).

Birkun, M. M., Kessen, M. L., & Miller, N. E. Hunger reducing effects of food by stomach fistula, versus food by mouth measured by a consummatory response. *Journal of Comparative Physiological Psychology*, 1952, *45*, 550-554.

Bitterman, M. E. Learning in animals. In Helson, H., & Bevan, W. (Eds.), *Contemporary approaches to psychology.* Chapter 4. Princeton: Van Nostrand, 1967.

Bitterman, M. E., Reed, P. C., & Kubala, A. L. The strength of sensory preconditioning. *Journal of Experimental Psychology*, 1953, *56*, 178-182.

Bitterman, M. E., & Schoel, W. M. Instrumental learning in animals: Parameters of reinforcement. In *Annual Review of Psychology*, chap. 10, 1970, *21*, 367-433.

Blacker, C. P. *The chances of morbid inheritance.* London: Lewis, 1934.

Blakeslee, A. T., & Fox, A. L. Our different taste worlds. *Journal of Heredity*, 1932, *23*, 96-110.

Blalock, H. M. *Causal inferences in non-experimental research.* New York: Norton, 1971.

Bleuler, M. The delimitation of influences of environment and heredity on mental disposition. *Character and Personality*, 1933, *1*, 286-300.

Block, J. Some reasons for the apparent inconsistency of personality. *Psychological Bulletin*, 1968, *70*, 210-212.

Block, J. *Lives through time.* Berkeley, Cal., Bancroft Books, 1971.

Blodgett, H. C. The effect of introduction of reward upon the maze performance of rats. *University of California Publications in Psychology*, 1929, *4*, 113-134.

Bogoslovski, A. I. An attempt at creating sensory conditioned reflexes in humans. *Journal of Experimental Psychology*, 1937, *21*, 403-422.

Bolitho, W. *Twelve against the gods.* New York, Simon and Schuster, 1929.

Bolles, R. C. Reinforcement, expectancy and learning. *Psychological Review*, 1972, *79*, 394-409.

Bolton, B. Evidence for the 16 PF primary and secondary factors. *Multivariate Experimental Clinical Research.* 3, 1-15, 1977.

Borgatta, E. G., & Cottrell, L. S. On the classification of groups. *Sociometry*, 1956, *18*, 665-678.

Borgatta, E. G., Cottrell, L. L., & Mann, J. H. The spectrum of individual interaction characteristics: An inter-dimensional analysis. *Psychological Reports*, 1958, *4*, 279-319.

Borgatta, E. F., & Meyer, H. I. *Sociological theory.* New York: Knopf, 1956.

Boulding, K. E. *The organizational revolution.* New York, Harper, 1953.

Boulding, K. E. *A primer of social dynamics.* New York: Free Press, 1970.

Bousfield, W. A. The problem of meaning in verbal learning. In Cofer, C. N. (Ed.), *Verbal learning and verbal behavior.* New York, McGraw Hill, 1961.

Bower, G. H., Monteiro, K. P., and Gilligan, S. G. Emotional mood as a context for learning and recall. *J. of Verbal Learning and Verbal Recall.* 1978, 17, 573-585.

Brady, J. V. The effect of electroconvulsive shock on a conditioned emotional response: The significance of the internal. *Journal of Comparative Physiological Psychology,* 1951, 44, 507-511.

Bramblett, C. A. Patterns of primate behavior. New York: 1976.

Brams, S. J. Transaction flows in the international system. *American Political Science Review,* 1966, 60, 880-898.

Brand, D. A. Games theory, decision processes, and man-made interaction. Chap. 13, Pp. 417-437 in Cattell, R. B. (Ed.), *Handbook of Multivariate Experimental Psychology.* Chicago, Rand McNally, 1966.

Broadbent, D. E. A mechanical model for human attention and immediate memory. *Psychological Review,* 1957, 64, 205-215.

Broadbent, D. E. *Perception and communication.* New York, Pergamon.

Broadbent, D. E. Distinctions among various types of memory, 1958. In Kimble, D. P. (Ed.), *The organization of recall.* New York, New York Academy of Sciences, 1967.

Broadhurst, P. S. Application of biometric genetics to behavior in rats. *Nature,* 1959, 184, 1517-1518.

Broadhurst, P. L. & Jinks, J. L. Psychological genetics, from the study of animal behavior. In Cattell, R. B., & Dreger, R. M. (Eds.), *Handbook of modern personality theory.* Chap. 12. New York: Hemisphere, 1977.

Brogden, W. J. Sensory pre-conditioning. *Journal of Experimental Psychology,* 1939, 25, 323-332.

Brookover, W. B., & Gottlieb, D. *A sociology of education.* 2nd ed. New York: American Book, 1964.

Bruce, H. M. Smell as an exteroceptive factor. *J. of Animal Science,* 1966, 25, 83-89.

Brunswick, E. Perception and the representative design of psychological experiments. Berkeley: University of California Press, 1956.

Burdsal, C. A. Jr., & Schwartz, S. A. The relationship of personality traits as measured in the questionnaire medium and by self-ratings. *Journal of Psychology,* 1975, 91, 173-182.

Burt, C. L. *The young delinquent;* London: University of London Press, 1923.

Burt, C. L. *Intelligence and fertility.* London: Hamilton, 1946.

Burt, C. D., & Howard, M. The multi-factorial theory of inheritance and its application to intelligence. *British Journal of Statistical Psychology,* 1956, 9, 95-131.

Buss, A. R. Learning, transfer and changes in ability factors: A multivariate model. *Psychological Bulletin,* 1973, 80, 106-112.

Buss, A. R. A general developmental model for inter-individual differences, intra-individual differences, and intra-individual changes. *Developmental Psychology,* 1974a, 10, 70-78.

Buss, A. R. A recursive non-recursive factor model and developmental causal networks. *Human Development,* 1974b, 17, 139-151.

Buss, A. R. & Poley, W. *Individual differences: traits and factors.* New York, Gardner Press, 1976.

Butcher, J. Three multivariate experiments throwing light on dynamic structure in eleven-year-old children. Adv. Public, No. 12, 1963, Lab. of Person Assess.: University of Illinois, Urbana, Ill.

Calhoun, J. B. Population density and social pathology. *Scientific American*, 1962, *206*, 139-148.

Campbell, B. A., & Kraeling, D. Response strength as a function of drive level and amount of drive reduction. *Journal of Experimental Psychology*, 1953, *45*, 101-103.

Cancro, R. (Ed.). *Intelligence: Genetic and environmental influence.* New York: Grune and Stratton, 1921.

Cannon, W. B. *Bodily changes in pain, hunger, fear and rage.* 2nd ed. New York: Appleton, 1929.

Carlton, P. L. Response strength as a function of delay of reward and physical confinement. Unpublished M.A. Thesis, University of Iowa, 1954.

Carpenter, C. R. *Social behavior of non-human primates.* University Park, Penn.: Pennsylvania State University Press, 1952.

Cartwright, D. *Theories and models of personality.* Dubuque, Iowa; W. C. Brown Co., 1978.

Cartwright, D. S., & Cartwright, C. F. *Psychological adjustment: Behavior in the inner world.* Chicago: Rand McNally, 1971.

Cattell, R. B. The significance of the actual resistances in psychogalvanic experiments. *British J. of psychology.* 1928, *19*, 34-43.

Cattell, R. B. Experiments on the psychical correlate of the G.S.R. *British Journal of Psychology*, 1929, *19*, 357-386.

Cattell, R. B. *The subjective character of cognition and the pre-sensational development of perception.* Cambridge, Cambridge University Press, 1930.

Cattell, R. B. Temperament tests, II. *British Journal of Psychology*, 1933, *24*, 20-49.

Cattell, R. B. Friends and enemies: a psychological study of character and temperament. *Character and Personality.* 1934, *3*, 54-63.

Cattell, R. B. Perseveration and personality: Some experiments and a hypothesis. *Journal of Mental Science*, 1935(a), *61*, 151-167.

Cattell, R. B. The measurement of interest. *Character and Personality*, 1935(b), *4*, 147-169.

Cattell, R. B. *The fight for our national intelligence.* London, King, 1937.

Cattell, R. B. Some changes in social life in a community with a falling intelligence quotient. *British Journal of Psychology*, 1938, *28*, 430-450.

Cattell, R. B. The concept of social status. *Journal of Social Psychology*, 1942, *15*, 293-308.

Cattell, R. B. Fluctuations of sentiments and attitudes as a measure of character integration and of temperament. *American Journal of Psychology*, 1943, *56*, 195-216.

Cattell, R. B. The cultural functions of social stratification; regarding the genetic bases of society. *J. of social psychology*, 1945, *21*, 3-23.

Cattell, R. B. *Description and measurement of personality.* New York: World Book, 1946.

Cattell, R. B. Concepts and methods in the measurement of group syntality. *Psychological Review*, 1948, *55*, 48-63.

Cattell, R. B. The dimensions of culture patterns by factorization of national characters. *Journal of Abnormal and Social Psychology*, 1949, *14*, 443-469.

Cattell, R. B. The discovery of ergic structure in man in terms of common attitudes. *Journal of Abnormal and Social Psychology*, 1950(a), *45*, 598-618.

Cattell, R. B. The fate of national intelligence: Test of a thirteen year prediction. *Eugenics Revue*, 1950(b), *42*, 136-148.

Cattell, R. B. *Personality, a systematic theoretical and factual study.* New York: McGraw-Hill, 1950(c).

Cattell, R. B. The principal culture patterns discoverable in the syntal dimensions of existing nations. *Journal of Social Psychology,* 1950(d), *32,* 215-253.

Cattell, R. B. New concepts for measuring leadership in terms of group syntality. *Human Relations,* 1951, *4,* 161-184.

Cattell, R. B. Research designs in psychological genetics with special reference to the multiple variance method. *American Journal of Human Genetics,* 1953(a), *5,* 76-93.

Cattell, R. B. On the theory of group learning. *Journal of Social Psychology,* 1953(b), *37,* 27-52.

Cattell, R. B. A quantitative analysis of the changes in the culture pattern of Great Britain 1837-1937, by P-technique. *Acta Psychologica,* 1953(c), *9,* 99-121.

Cattell, R. B. Personality structures as learning and motivation patterns: A theme for the integration of methodologies. In *Learning theory, personality theory and clinical research.* Kentucky Symposium. Lexington: University of Kentucky Press, 1954.

Cattell, R. B. A mathematical model for the leadership role and other personality role relations. In Sherif, M., & Wilson, M. O. (Eds.), *Emerging problems in social psychology.* Pp. 207-229. Norman: University of Oklahoma Press, 1957(a).

Cattell, R. B. *Personality and motivation structure and measurement.* New York: World Book, 1957(b).

Cattell, R. B. The dynamic calculus: Concepts and crucial experiments. In Jones, M. R. (Ed.), *The Nebraska symposium on motivation.* Pp. 84-134. Lincoln: University of Nebraska Press, 1959.

Cattell, R. B. The dimensional measurement of anxiety, excitement, effort, stress, and other mood reaction patterns. In Uhr, L. and Miller, J. G. (Eds.), *Drugs and Behavior,* New York, Wiley, 1960a.

Cattell, R. B. The multiple abstract variance analysis equations and solutions: For nature-nurture research on continuous variables. *Psychological Review,* 1960b, *67,* 353-372.

Cattell, R. B. Group theory, personality and role: A model for experimental researches. In Geldard, J. (Ed.), *Defense Psychology.* Pp. 209-258. New York: Pergamon Press, 1961(a).

Cattell, R. B. Factor analytic evidence on the dynamic structure of the ego. *Acta Psychologica,* 1961(b), *17,* 244-245.

Cattell, R. B. The basis of recognition and interpretation of factors. *Educational and psychological measurement,* 1962, *26,* 667-697.

Cattell, R. B. The interaction of hereditary and environmental influences. *British Journal of Statistical Psychology,* 1963(a), *16,* 191-210.

Cattell, R. B. Personality, role mood and situation-perception, a unifying theory of modulators. *Psychological Review,* 1963(b), *70,* 1-18.

Cattell, R. B. The structuring of change by P-technique and differential R-technique. In Harris, C. W. (Ed.), *Problems in measuring change.* Pp. 167-198. Madison: University of Wisconsin Press, 1963(c).

Cattell, R. B. Formulating the environmental situation and its perception in behavior theory. In S. B. Sells (Ed.), *Stimulus determinants of behavior.* New York, Ronald, 1963(d), 46-75.

Cattell, R. B. The parental early repressiveness hypothesis for the authoritarian personality factor, U.1.28. *Journal of Genetic Psychology,* 1964, *106,* 332-349.

Cattell, R. B. Methodological and conceptual advances in evaluating hereditary and environmental influences and their interaction. In Vandenberg, S. G.

(Ed.), *Methods and goals in human behavior genetics.* Pp. 95–140. New York: Academic Press, 1965.

Cattell, R. B. Patterns of change: Measurement in relation to state-dimension, trait change, liability and process concepts. In Cattell, R. B. (Ed.), *Handbook of multivariate experimental psychology.* Chapter 11. Chicago: Rand McNally, 1966(a).

Cattell, R. B. (Ed.), *Handbook of multivariate experimental psychology.* Chicago: Rand McNally, 1966(b).

Cattell, R. B. Taxonomic principles for locating and using types (and the Taxonome program). In Kleinmuntz, B. (Ed.), *Formal representation of human judgment.* Pp. 99–148. Pittsburgh: Pittsburgh University Press, 1968(a).

Cattell, R. B. Trait view theory of perturbation in ratings and self-ratings (L [BR] and Q data). Its application to obtaining pure trait scores estimates in questionnaires. *Psychological Review,* 1968(b), *75,* 96–113.

Cattell, R. B. Comparing factor trait and state scores across ages and cultures. *Journal of Gerontology,* 1969, *24,* 348–360.

Cattell, R. B. The isopodic and equipotent principles for comparing factor scores across different populations. *British Journal of Mathematical and Statistical Psychology,* 1970(a), *23,* 23–24.

Cattell, R. B. Separating endogenous, exogenous, ecogenic and epogenic component curves in developmental data. *Developmental Psychology,* 1970(b), *3,* 151–162.

Cattell, R. B. *Abilities: Their structure, growth and action.* Boston: Houghton-Mifflin, 1971(a).

Cattell, R. B. Estimating modulator indices and state liabilities. *Multivariate Behavioral Research,* 1971(b), *6,* 7–33.

Cattell, R. B. The interpretation of Pavlov's typology and the arousal concept, in replicated trait and state factors. In Gray, J. A. (Ed.), *Biological bases of individual behavior.* Pp. 141–164. New York: Academic Press, 1972a.

Cattell, R. B. Real base, true zero factor analysis. *Multivariate Behavioral Research Psychology Monogram* No. 72–1, 1972b. Fort Worth: Texas Christian University Press.

Cattell, R. B. *A new morality from science: Beyondism.* New York, Pergamon, 1972c.

Cattell, R. B. *Personality and mood by questionnaire.* San Francisco: Jossey Bass, 1973(a).

Cattell, R. B. Unravelling maturational and learning developments by the comparative MAVA and structured learning approaches. In Nesselroade, J. R., & Reese, J. (Eds.), *Life span developmental psychology.* Pp. 111–144. New York: Academic Press, 1973(b).

Cattell, R. B. An analysis of state and trait change factors in pathology by dR technique on the CAQ. *Indian Journal of Clinical Psychology,* 1974(a), *1,* 34–40.

Cattell, R. B. How good is the modern questionnaire: General Principles for evaluation. *Journal of Personality Assessment,* 1974(b), *38,* 115–129.

Cattell, R. B. Differential fertility and natural selection for I.Q.: some required conditions in their investigation. *Social Biology,* 1974(c), *21,* 168–177.

Cattell, R. B. A second order analysis of state and trait change factors by dR technique on the CAQ. Laboratory of Personality and Group Analysis. University of Illinois Advanced Publication No. 21, 1974(d).

Cattell, R. B. Structured learning theory applied to personality change. In Cattell, R. B., & Dreger, R. M. (Eds.), *Handbook of modern personality theory.* Chapter 18. Pp. 433–472. Washington, Hemisphere, and New York, Halsted, 1976(a).

Cattell, R. B. Personality and culture: General concepts and methodological problems. In Cattell, R. B., & Dreger, R. M. (Eds.), *Handbook of modern personality theory.* Pp. 473–476. Washington, Hemisphere, and New York: Halsted, 1976(b).

Cattell, R. B. The grammar of science and the evolution of personality theory. Chapter 1 in Cattell, R. B., & Dreger, R. M. (Eds.), *Handbook of Modern Personality Theory.* New York, Wiley, 1977a.

Cattell, R. B. Lernfahigkeit, Persönalichkeitstruktur und die Theorie des strukturienten Lernens. In Nissen, G. (Ed.), *Intelligentz, Lernen und Lernstorungen.* Berlin, Springer Verlag, 1977b.

Cattell, R. B. *The scientific use of factor analysis.* New York: Plenum Press, 1978.

Cattell, R. B. Adolescent age trends in primary personality factors measured in *T*-data; a contribution to the use of standardized measures in practice. *J. of Adolescence,* 1979, 2, 1–16.

Cattell, R. B. Second order structure among motivation strength primaries: further evidence on the nature of the Unintegrated and Integrated components. In preparation, 1980(a).

Cattell, R. B. The higher order organization of dynamic traits. In preparation, 1980(b).

Cattell, R. B., & Adelson, M. The dimensions of social change in the U.S.A. as determined by P-technique. *Social Forces,* 1951, *30,* 190–201.

Cattell, R. B., & Baggaley, A. R. A confirmation of ergic and engram structures in attitudes objectively measured. *Australian Journal of Psychology,* 1958, *10,* 287–318.

Cattell, R. B., & Bartlett, H. W. An R-dR technique operational distinction of the states of anxiety, stress, fear, etc. *Australian Journal of Psychology,* 1971, *23,* 105–123.

Cattell, R. B., & Barton, K. Changes in psychological state measures and time of day. *Psychological Reports,* 1974, *35,* 219–222.

Cattell, R. B., & Bjersted, A. The structure of depression by factoring Q-data in relation to general personality source traits. *Scandinavian Journal of Psychology,* 1967, *8,* 17–24.

Cattell, R. B., Blewett, D. B., & Beloff, J. R. The inheritance of personality: A multiple variance analysis determination of approximate nature-nurture ratios for primary personality factors in Q-data. *American Journal of Human Genetics,* 1955, 7, 122–146.

Cattell, R. B., Breul, H., & Hartman, H. P. An attempt at more refined definition of the cultural dimensions of syntality in modern nations. *American Sociological Review,* 1952, *17,* 408–421.

Cattell, R. B., & Butcher, J. *The prediction of achievement and creativity.* Indianapolis: Bobbs-Merrill, 1968.

Cattell, R. B., & Child, D. *Motivation and dynamic structure.* New York: Wiley-Halsted, 1975.

Cattell, R. B., & Coulter, M. A. Principles of behavioral taxonomy and the mathematical basis of the taxonome computer program. *British Journal of Mathematical and Statistical Psychology,* 1966, *19,* 237–269.

Cattell, R. B., Coulter, M. A., & Tsujioka, B. The taxonometric recognition of types and functional emergents. In Cattell, R. B. (Ed.), *Handbook of multivariate experimental psychology.* Chapter 9. Chicago: Rand McNally, 1966.

Cattell, R. B., De Young, G., & Barton, K. A check on the validity of motivation component measures of ergic tension, by manipulation of the hunger erg. In Press, 1978.

Cattell, R. B., De Young, G. E., & Horn, J. L. Human motives as dynamic states: A dR analysis of objective motivation measures. *Journal of Multivariate Experimental Personality and Clinical Psychology*, 1974, *1*, 58-78.

Cattell, R. B., & Dielman, T. E. The structure of motivational manifestation as measured in the laboratory rat: An examination of motivation component theory. *Social Behavior and Personality*, 1974, *2*, 10-24.

Cattell, R. B., & Dreger, R. M. *Handbook of modern personality theory*. New York: Hemisphere, 1977.

Cattell, R. B., Eber, H. W., & Tatsuoka, M. *The 16 personality factor test handbook*. Champaign, Ill.: Institute for Personality and Ability Testing, 1970.

Cattell, R. B., Graham, R. K., & Woliver, R. E. A re-assessment of the factorial cultural dimensions of modern nations. *Journal of Social Psychology*. 1979, 108, 241-258.

Cattell, R. B., & Horn, J. L. An integrating study of the factor structure of adult attitude interests. *Genetic Psychological Monograph*, 1963, *67*, 89-149.

Cattell, R. B., Horn, J. L., Radcliffe, J., & Sweney, A. B. The nature and measurement of components of motivation. Genetic Psychology Monographs, 1963, *68*, 49-211.

Cattell, R. B., Horn, J. L., Sweney, A. B., & Radcliffe, J. *The motivation analysis test, MAT*. Champaign, Ill.: Institute for Personality and Ability Testing, 1964.

Cattell, R. B., & Horowitz, J. Objective personality tests investigating the structure of altruism in relation to the source traits A, H and L. *Journal of Personality*, 1952, *21*, 103-117.

Cattell, R. B., Kawash, G. F., & De Young, G. E. Validation of objective measures of ergic tension: Response of the sex erg to visual stimulation. *Journal of Experimental Research in Personality*, 1972, *6*, 76-83.

Cattell, R. B. & Killian, L. R. The pattern of objective test personality differences in schizophrenia and the character disorders. *Journal of clinical psychology*, 1967, *23*, 343-348.

Cattell, R. B., & Klein, T. W. A check on hypothetical personality structures, and their theoretical interpretation at 14-16 years, in T-data. *British Journal of Psychology*, 1975, *66*, 131-151.

Cattell, R. B., Klein, T. W., & Schuerger, J. M. Heritabilities by the MAVA method and the objective test measures, of personality traits U.I.23, capacity to mobilize; U.I.24, anxiety; U.I.26, narcistic ego; and U.I.28, asthenia. (In press, 1979).

Cattell, R. B., & Kline, P. *The scientific study of personality and motivation*. New York, Academic Press, 1977.

Cattell, R. B., & Korth, B. The isolation of temperament dimensions in dogs. *Behavioral Biology*, 1973, *9*, 15-30.

Cattell, R. B., Korth, B., & Bolz, C. R. Behavioral types on pure bred dogs objectively determined by taxonome. *Behavioral Genetics*, 1973, *3*, 205-216.

Cattell, R. B., Lawlis, F., McGill, J., & McGraw. A check on the structure and meaning of primary motivation components. *Multivariate Experimental Clinical Research*. 1979, 4, 33-52.

Cattell, R. B., & Molteno, E. V. Contributions concerning mental inheritance. II. Temperament. *Journal of Genetic Psychology*, 1940, *57*, 31-47.

Cattell, R. B., & Nesselroade, J. R. Likeness and completeness theories examined by 16 P.F. measures on stably and unstably married couples. *Journal of Personality and Social Psychology*, 1967, *7*, 351-361.

Cattell, R. B., & Nesselroade, J. R. The discovery of the anxiety state pattern in Q-data and its distinction in the LM model from depression, effort stress and fatigue. *Multivariate Behavioral Research,* 1976, *11*, 27-46.

Cattell, R. B., Pierson, G., & Finkbeiner, C. Proof of alignment of personality source trait factors from questionnaires and observer ratings: The theory of instrument-free patterns. *Multivariate Experimental Clinical Psychology,* 1976, *4*, 1-31.

Cattell, R. B., Price, P. L., & Patrick, S. V. Diagnosis of depression by four source trait measures from the O-A Battery Kit: U.I.19, 20, 25, and 30. (In press, 1979).

Cattell, R. B., Radcliffe, J., & Sweney, A. B. The nature and measurement of components of motivation. *Genetic Psychological Monograph,* 1963, *68*, 49-211.

Cattell, R. B., Rickels, K., Weise, C., Gray, B., & Yee, R. The effects of psychotherapy upon measured anxiety and regression. *American Journal of Psychotherapy,* 1966, *20*, 261-269.

Cattell, R. B., Saunders, D. R., & Stice, G. F. The dimensions of syntality in small groups. *Human Relations,* 1953, *6*, 331-356.

Cattell, R. B., & Scheier, J. H. *The meaning and measurement of neuroticism and anxiety.* New York: Ronald Press, 1961.

Cattell, R. B., Schmidt, L. R., & Bjersted, A. Clinical diagnosis by the objective-analytic personality batteries. *Journal of Clinical Psychological Monograph Supplements* No. 34, 1972.

Cattell, R. B., Schmidt, L. R., & Pawlik, K. Cross cultural comparison (U.S.A., Japan, Austria) of the personality structures of 10 to 14 year olds in objective tests. *Social Behavior and Personality,* 1973, *1*, 182-211.

Cattell, R. B., & Schuerger, J. *Personality theory in action: The objective analytic (O-A) personality factor kit.* Champaign, Ill.: Institute for Personality and Ability Testing, 1978.

Cattell, R. B., Schuerger, J. M., & Klein, T. W. The degree of inheritance in the control triumvirate: ego strength (C), super ego strength (G), and the self sentiment investment (Q_3); by MAVA and Q-data. (In press, 1979).

Cattell, R. B., Shrader, R. B., & Barton, K. The definition and measurement of anxiety as a trait and state in the 12-17 year range. *British Journal of Social and Clinical Psychology,* 1974, *13*, 173-182.

Cattell, R. B., & Stice, G. F. *The dimensions of groups and their relations to the behavior of members.* Champaign, Ill.: Institute for Personality and Ability Testing, 1953. Republished Ann Arbor, Michigan, University Microfilms International, 1976.

Cattell, R. B., Stice, G. F., & Kristy, N. F. A first approximation to nature-nurture ratios for eleven personality factors in objective tests. *Journal of Abnormal and Social Psychology,* 1957, *54*, 143-159.

Cattell, R. B., & Sweney, A. B. Components measurable in manifestations of mental conflict. *Journal of Abnormal and Social Psychology,* 1964, *68*, 479-490.

Cattell, R. B., & Tatro, D. F. The personality factors, objectively measured, which distinguish psychotics from normals. *Behavioral Research and Therapy,* 1966, *4*, 39-57.

Cattell, R. B., & Vogelmann, S. Second-order personality factors in combined questionnaire and rating data. *Multivariate Experimental Clinical Research,* 1976, *3*, 40-64.

Cattell, R. B., & Warburton, F. W. Objective personality and motivation tests: A theoretical introduction and practical compendium. Champaign Ill.: University of Illinois Press, 1967.

Cattell, R. B., & Wenig, P. Dynamic and cognitive factors controlling misperception. *Journal of Abnormal and Social Psychology*, 1952, *47*, 797–809.

Cattell, R. B., & Williams, H. F. P-technique: A new statistical device for analyzing functional unities in the intact organism. *British Journal of Preventive and Social Medicine*, 1953, *7*, 141–153.

Cattell, R. B., & Wispe, L. G. The dimensions of syntality in small groups. *Journal of Social Psychology*, 1948, *28*, 57–78.

Cattell, R. B., & Woliver, R. E. The relations of syntality dimensions of modern nations to the personality dimensions of their populations. *International J. of Intercultural Relations*, 1979 (In Press).

Cattell, R. B., & Woliver, R. E. A classificatory grouping of the culture patterns of modern nations, using the Taxonome program on 100 countries. (In press, 1980).

Cattell, R. B., Young, H. B., & Hundleby, J. D. Blood groups and personality traits. *American Journal of Human Genetics*, 1964, *16*, 397–402.

Cavalli-Sforza, L. H., & Bodmer, W. F. *The genetics of human populations.* San Francisco: Freeman, 1971.

Chadwick, R. W. Steps toward a probabilistic theory of political behavior, with special reference to integration theory. In Alker, H. R., et al (Eds.), *Quantitative and mathematical methods in political science.* Pp. 72–88. Amsterdam: Elsevier, 1971.

Chambers, R. M. Some physiological bases for reinforcing properties of reward infections. *Journal of Comparative Physiological Psychology*, 1956, *49*, 545–560.

Christian, J. J. Phenomena associated with population density. *Proceedings of the National Academy of Sciences*, U.S.A., 1961, *47*, 422–449.

Churchill, W. S. (Ed. J. Fishman.), *If I lived my life again.* London, Allen, 1974.

Clemans, W. V. An analytical and empirical examination of some properties of ipsative scores. *Psychometric Monographs* No. 14, Pp. 87. 1966.

Clore, G. L., & Byrne, D. The process of personality interaction. Chap. 22, pp. 530–550, in Cattell, R. B., & Dreger, R. M. (Eds.), *Handbook of Modern Personality Theory*, Washington, D.C. Hemisphere Books, 1977.

Coan, R. W. *The optimal personality.* New York: Columbia University Press, 1974.

Cohen, M. R., & Nagel, E. *An introduction to logic and scientific method.* New York: Harcourt Brace, 1934.

Collins, A. M., & Loftus, E. F. A spreading activation theory of semantic processing. *Psych. Review*, 1975, *82*, 407–428.

Collins, A. M., & Quillian, M. R. Retrieval time from semantic memory. *Journal of Verbal Learning and Verbal Behavior*, 1969, *8*, 240–248.

Collins, A. M., & Quillian, M. R., Experiments on semantic memory and language comprehension. In L. W. Gregg (Ed.), *Cognition in learning and memory.* New York: Wiley, 1972.

Cortes, T., Pryeworski, A., & Sprague, J. *Systems analysis for social scientists.* New York: Wiley, 1974.

Craighead, W. E., Kazdin, A. E., & Mahoney, M. J. *Behavior modification: Principles, issues and applications.* Boston, Houghton Mifflin, 1976.

Craik, K. H. *Environmental psychology.* Chap. in *Annual Review of Psychology.* Washington, D.C. A.P.A. 1973.

Crespi, L. P. Quantitative variation of incentive and performance in the white rat. *American Journal of Psychology*, 1942, *55*, 467–517.

Cronbach, L. J. The two disciplines of scientific psychology. *American Psychologist*, 1957, *12*, 671–684.

Cronbach, L. J. *Educational Psychology.* New York, Harcourt Brace, 1964.

Cronbach, L. F., Gleser, G. C., Nanda, H., & Rajaratnam, N. *The dependability of behavior measurements: Theory of generalizability for scores and profiles.* New York: Wiley, 1972.

Cross, K. P. Determination of the ergic structure of common attitudes by P-technique. Unpublished M.A. thesis, University of Illinois at Urbana, 1951.

Curran, J. P. Dimensions of state change, in Q-data, by chain P-technique on twenty women. Unpublished M.A. thesis, University of Illinois at Urbana, 1968.

Curran, J. P., & Cattell, R. B. *Handbook for the 8 state battery.* Champaign, Ill.: Institute for Personality and Ability Testing, 1976.

D'Amato, M. R. *Experimental psychology: Methodology, psychophysics, and learning.* New York: McGraw-Hill, 1970.

Darlington, C. D. *The evolution of man and society.* New York: Simon & Schuster, 1969.

Das, R. S. An investigation of attitude structure and some hypothesized personality correlates. Unpublished Ph.D. thesis, University of Illinois at Urbana, 1955.

Davison, G. C., & Valens, S. Maintenance of self-attributed and long-attributed behavior change. *Journal of Personality and Social Psychology,* 1969, *11,* 25–33.

Deese, J., & Hulse, S. H. *The psychology of learning.* 3rd ed. New York: McGraw-Hill, 1967.

Delhees, K., Cattell, R. B., & Sweney, A. B. The structure of parents' intra-familial attitudes and sentiments measured by objective tests and a vector model. *Journal of Social Psychology,* 1970, *82,* 231–252.

Denny, M. R., & King, G. F. Differential response learning on the basis of differential size of reward. *Journal of Genetic Psychology,* 1955, *87,* 317–320.

Deutsch, K. W. *The analysis of interactional relations.* Englewood Cliffs, N.J.: Prentice-Hall, 1968.

Deutsch, M. The effects of cooperation and competition upon group success. In Cartwright, D., & Zander, A. (Eds.), *Group dynamic research and theory.* Pp. 319–353. New York: Row Peterson, 1953.

Deutsch, M. *Social class, race and psychological development.* New York: Holt, Rinehart & Winston, 1965.

De Young, G. E. A causal model of effects of personality and marital role factors upon diary reported sexual behavior. Convention Handbook, 81st annual convention of the APA. Montreal, Canada, 1973, *8,* 357–358.

De Young, G. E., Yoon, G. H. Y., & Cattell, R. B. Sexual motivation: comparison of drive, reinforcement and random response models. In press, 1978.

De Young, G. E., Cattell, R. B., & Gaborit, M. and Barton, K. A. Causal model of effects of personality and marital role factors upon diary reported sexual behavior. Proceedings of the 81st annual convention of the APA, Montreal, Canada, 1973, *8,* 357–358.

Dielman, T. E., Cattell, R. B., and Kawash, G. F. Three studies of manipulation of the fear erg. Laboratory of Personality and Group Analysis. University of Illinois Advanced Publication No. 14, 1971.

Dielman, T. E., & Krug, S. E. Trait description and measurement in motivation and dynamic structure. In Cattell, R. B., & Dreger, R. M. (Eds.), *Handbook of modern personality theory.* Chapter 5. New York: Hemisphere, 1976.

Dreger, R. M. Developmental structural changes in the child's personality. Chap. 17. In Cattell, R. B., & Dreger, R. M. (Eds.).

Duffy, E. The psychological significance of the concept of "arousal" or "activation." *Psychological Review,* 1957, *64,* 265–275.

Dulany, D. E. Awareness, rules and propositional control: a confrontation with

S-R behavior theory. In Dixon, T. R., & Horton, D. L. (Eds.), *Verbal behavior and general behavior theory.* Englewood Cliffs, N.J., Prentice Hall, 1968.

Eaves, L. J. The genetic analysis of continuous variation: A comparison of experimental designs applicable to human data. *British Journal of Mathematical and Statistical Psychology,* 1969, *22,* 130–147.

Ebbinghaus, H. *Memory: a contribution to experimental psychology.* 1885 (Transl. Reiger, H. A., 1913). New York, Columbia University Press.

Edwards, A. L. *The social desirability variable in personality assessment and research.* New York: Holt, 1957.

Egger, M. D., & Miller, N. E. When is reward reinforcing? An experimental study of the information hypothesis. *Journal of Comparative and Physiological Psychology,* 1963, *56,* 132–137.

Ehrlich, P. R. *Population bombs.* New York: Ballantine Books, 1968.

Elliot, M. H. The effect of change of reward on the maze performance of rats. *University of California Publications in Psychology,* 1928, *4,* 19–30.

Ellis, A. *Reason and emotion in psychotherapy.* New York: Lyle Stuart Inc., 1962.

Endler, N. S., & Magnusson, D. *Interactional psychology and personality.* Washington, D.C.: Hemisphere Pub. Co., 1976.

Estes, W. K. Stimulus response theory of drive. In Jones, M. R. (Ed.), *Nebraska Symposium on Motivation.* Pp. 71–94. Lincoln: University of Nebraska Press, 1958.

Estes, W. K. The statistical approach to learning theory. In Koch, S. (Ed.), *Psychology the study of a science.* Pp. 103–135. Vol. 2. New York: McGraw-Hill, 1959.

Estes, W. K., Burke, C. J., Atkinson, R. C., & Frankmann, J. B. Probabilistic discrimination learning. *Journal of Experimental Psychology,* 1957, *47,* 225–234.

Eysenck, H. J. *Psychology and Politics.* London, Routledge and Kegan Paul, 1954.

Eysenck, H. J. *The structure of human personality.* London: Methuen, 1960.

Eysenck, H. J. *The biological basis of personality.* Springfield, Ill.: Thomas, 1967.

Eysenck, H. J. *Race, intelligence and education.* London, Temple Smith, 1971.

Eysenck, H. J. Multivariate analysis and experimental psychology. In Dreger, R. M. *Contributions to the understanding of psychology in honor of Raymond Cattell.* Baton Rouge, La., Claitor Publisher, 1972.

Eysenck, H. J., & Prell, D. B. The inheritance of neuroticism. *Journal of Mental Science,* 1951, *97,* 441–265.

Eysenck, H. J., & Rachman, S. *The causes and cures of neurosis: an introduction to modern behavior therapy based on learning theory and the principles of conditioning.* San Diego: Knapp, 1965.

Eysenck, H. J., & Rachman, S. *The effects of psychotherapy.* New York: International Science Press, 1966.

Eysenck, H. J., & Wilson, G. S. *The experimental study of Freudian theories.* London: Methuen, 1973.

Eysenck, S. B. G. Neurosis and psychosis: An experimental analysis. *Journal of Mental Science,* 1956, *102,* 512–529.

Fahrenberg, J. Physiological concepts in personality research. Chap. 25. Pp. 585–614. In Cattell, R. B., & Dreger, R. M. 1977.

Fairweather, Y. W. *Social change: the challenge to survival.* Lauriston, N.J.: General Learning Co., 1972.

Falconer, D. S. *Introduction to quantitative genetics.* New York: Ronald Press, 1960.

Farber, I. E. Anxiety as a drive state. In M. R. Jones (Ed.), *Current theory and research on motivation.* Nebraska Symposium on Motivation. Lincoln, Nebraska: University of Nebraska Press, 1954.

Feigenbaum, E. A., & Feldman, J. *Computers and thought.* New York: McGraw-Hill, 1964.

Ferguson, G. A. On transfer and the abilities of man. *Canadian Journal of Psychology,* 1956, *10,* 121-131.

Ferster, C. B. Sustained behavior under delayed reinforcement. *Journal of Experimental Psychology,* 1953, *45,* 218-224.

Festinger, L. Laboratory experiments: The role of group belongingness. In Miller, J. G. (Ed.), *Experiments in social process.* New York: McGraw-Hill, 1950.

Festinger, L. *A theory of cognitive dissonance.* Rev. ed. Stanford: Stanford University Press, 1962.

Fiedler, F. *Leader attitudes and group effectiveness.* Urbana: University of Illinois Press, 1958.

Fiedler, F. *A theory of leadership effectiveness.* New York: McGraw-Hill, 1967.

Finch, F. H. Enrolment increases and changes in the mental level of the high school population. *Applied Psychological Monograph,* 1946, *10,* 75.

Fischbein, M. Attitude and the prediction of behavior. In Fischbein, M. (Ed.), *Readings in attitude theory and measurement.* New York: Wiley, 1967.

Fisher, R. A. *The genetical theory of natural selection.* Oxford: Clarendon, 1930.

Fleishman, E. A. Individual differences in motor learning. In Gagne, R. M. (Ed.), *Learning and individual differences.* Columbus, O.: Merrill, 1967(a).

Fleishman, E. A. Development of a behavior taxonomy for describing human tasks: a correlational-experimental approach. *Journal of Applied Psychology,* 1967(b), *51,* 1-10.

Forgus, R. H. Early visual and motor experience as determiner of complex maze learning ability. *Journal of Comparative Physiological Psychology,* 1955, *48,* 215-220.

Fowler, H., & Trapold, M. A. Escape performance as a function of delay or reinforcement. *Journal of Experimental Psychology,* 1962, *63,* 464-467.

Frederikson, C. H. Abilities, transfer and information retrieval in verbal learning. *Multivariate Behavioral Research Monograph,* No. 69-72, 1969.

Frederiksen, N. Toward a taxonomy of situations. *American Psychologist,* 1972, *27,* 114-123.

Frederiksen, N., Jensen, O., & Beaton, A. E. *Prediction of Organizational Behavior.* New York: Pergamon Press, 1972.

Freeman, G. L., & Katzoff, E. T. Individual differences in physiological reactions to stimulation and their relations to other measures of emotionality. *Journal of Experimental Psychology,* 1942, *31,* 527-537.

Frenkel-Brunswick, E. Meaning of psychoanalytic concepts and confirmation of psychoanalytic theories. *Science Monitor,* 1954, *79,* 203-300.

Freud, A. *The ego and the mechanisms of defense.* London: Hogarth, 1937.

Freud, S. *General introduction to psychoanalysis.* New York: Liverright, 1920.

Freud, S. *Outline of psychoanalysis.* New York: Norton, 1949.

Friedman, J., & Katz, J. *The psychology of depression.* 1975.

Friedman, W. F. *The index of coincidence and its application to cryptography.* Washington. Riverbank Publications, U.S. Army, No. 22. 1920.

Fulker, D. W. A biometrical genetic approach to intelligence and schizophrenia. *Social Biology,* 1973, *20,* 266-275.

Fuller, J. L., & Thompson, W. R. *Behavioral genetics.* New York: Wiley, 1960.

Gage, N. L. (Ed.). *Handbook of research on teaching*. Chicago: Rand McNally, 1963.

Gagne, R. M. (Ed.). *Learning and individual differences*. Columbus, O.: Merrill, 1967.

Garcia, J., Ervic, F. R., & Koelling, R. A. Learning with prolonged delay of reinforcement. *Psychonomic Science*, 1966, *5*, 121-122.

Gantt, W. H. Pavlov's system. Pp. 127-149. In Wolman, W. B., & Nagel, E. (Eds.), *Scientific Psychology*. New York: Basic Books, 1965.

Gavin, J. Organisational climate as a function of personal and organizational variables. *Journal of applied psychology*, 1975, *60*, 135-159.

George, F. H. *Cybernetics and biology*. London: Oliver & Boyd, 1965.

Geer, J. H. The effect of fear upon task performance and verbal behavior. *Journal of Abnormal Psychology*, 1966, *71*, 119-123.

Gibb, C. A. The emergence of leadership in small temporary groups of men. Unpublished Ph.D. Thesis, University of Illinois, 1949.

Gibb, C. A. Changes in the culture pattern of Australia, 1906-1946, as determined by P-technique. *Journal of Social Psychology*, 1956, *43*, 225-238.

Gibbon, E. *The decline and fall of the Roman empire*. London, Dent, 1910.

Glass, G., & Hakstian, A. R. Measures of association in comparative experiments: Their development and interpretation. *American Educational Research Journal*, 1969, *6*, 403-414.

Glass, G., Willson, V., & Gottman, J. *Design and analysis of time series experiments*. Boulder: University of Colorado Associated Press, 1975.

Glickman, S. E., & Schiff, B. R. A biological theory of reinforcement. *Psychological Review*, 1967, 81-108.

Goldberg, L. R. *Language and personality; toward a taxonomy of trait descriptive terms*. Society for Multivariate Experimental Psychology, Annual meeting, Oregon, 1975.

Goldfried, M. R., & Merbaum, M. *Behavior change through self control*. New York: Holt, Rinehart & Winston, 1973.

Gorsuch, R. L. The clarification of some factors in the area of super ego behavior. Unpublished M.A. thesis, University of Illinois at Urbana, 1965.

Gorsuch, R. L., & Cattell, R. B. Personality and socio-ethical value: The structure of self and super ego. In Cattell, R. B., & Dreger, R. M. (Eds.), *Handbook of modern personality theory*. Chapter 29. New York: Hemisphere, 1977.

Gottesman, I. I., & Shields, J. Contributions of twin studies to perspectives on schizophrenia. In B. A. Maher (Ed.), *Progress in experimental personality research*. New York: Academic Press, 1966.

Graham, R. K. *The future of man*. North Quincy, Christopher, 1970.

Grice, G. R. An experimental study of the gradient of reinforcement in maze learning. *Journal of Experimental Psychology*, 1942, *30*, 475-489.

Grindley, G. C. Experiments on the influence of the amount of reward on learning in young chickens. *British Journal of Psychology*, 1929, *20*, 173-180.

Gruenberg, M. M. The distinction between short-term memory and long-term memory. *Bulletin of the British Psychological Society*, 1976, *29*, 327-333.

Guetzkow, H. An analysis of the operation of set in problem-solving behavior. Unpublished Ph.D. thesis, University of Michigan, 1948.

Guetzkow, H. Multiple loyalties: A theoretical approach to a problem in international organization. *Center for World Political Research Report No. 4*, Princeton University, 1955.

Guetzkow, H. A use of simulation in the study of internation relationships. *Behavioral Science*, 1959, *4*, 183-191.

Guetzkow, H., & Simon, H. A. The impact of certain communication nets upon organization and performance in task-oriented groups. *Management Science*, 1955, *1*, 233-250.

Gulliksen, H., & Voneida, T. An attempt to obtain replicate learning curves. Educational Test Service. No. RB 73-46, Princeton, 1973.

Guthrie, E. R. *The psychology of learning*. New York: Harper, 1952.

Guttman, G. Neuropsychologie Aspekte des Lernens. In Nissen, G. (Ed.). *Intelligenty, Lernen und Leadstorungen*. Berlin: Springer Verlag, 1977.

Hake, H. W. The study of perception in the light of multivariate methods. In Cattell, R. B. (Ed.), *Handbook of multivariate experimental psychology*, 502-534. Chicago: Rand McNally, 1966.

Hakstian, A. R., & Cattell, R. B. The checking of primary ability structure on a broader basis of performance. *British Journal of Educational Psychology*, 1974, *44*, 140-154.

Hakstian, A. R., & Cattell, R. B. *The comprehensive ability battery*. Champaign, Ill.: Institute for Personality and Ability Testing, 1976.

Hall, C. S. The inheritance of emotionality in the rat. *Psychological Bulletin*, 1940, *37*, 432.

Hall, J. F., & Kubrick, J. L. The relationship between the measures of response strength. *Journal of Comparative Physiological Psychology*, 1952, *45*, 280-282.

Hammer, A. G. *Elementary matrix algebra for psychologists and social scientists*. New York, Pergamon Press, 1971.

Hardin, G. The cybernetics of competition: a biologist's view of society. In *Perspectives in Biology and Medicine*. Autumn, 1963, *3*, 10-31.

Harker, G. S. Delay of reward and performance of an instrumental response. *Journal of Experimental Psychology*, 1956, *51*, 303-310.

Harlow, H. F. The formation of learning sets. *Psychological Review*, 1949, *56*, 51-65.

Harlow, H. F., & Harlow, M. K. The affectional systems. In Schrier, A.M., Harlow, H. F., & Stollnitz, F. (Eds.), *Behavior of non-human primates*. New York, Academic Press, 1965.

Harris, C. W. (Ed.). *Problems in measuring change*. Madison: University of Wisconsin Press, 1963.

Harris, E. L., Lemke, E. A., & Rumery, R. E. Generalized learning curves and their ability and personality correlates. *Multivariate Behavioral Research*, 1974, *9*, 21-35.

Haverland, E. M. The application of an analytical solution for proportional profiles rotation to a box problem and to the drive structure in rats. Unpublished Ph.D. thesis 1954, University of Illinois.

Haythorne, W. The influence of individual members on the behavior of co-workers and on the characteristics of groups. Unpublished Ph.D. thesis, University of Rochester, 1952.

Haythorne, W. The influence of individual members on the characteristics of small groups. *Journal of Abnormal and Social Psychology*, 1953, *48*, 276-284.

Hebb, D. O. *The organization of behavior*. New York: Wiley, 1949.

Hempel, W. E., & Fleishman, E. A. A factor analysis of physical proficiency and manipulative skill. *Journal of Applied Psychology*, 1955, *39*, 12-16.

Hemphill, J. K., & Weste, C. M. The measurement of group dimensions. *Journal of Psychology*, 1950, *29*, 325-342.

Hendricks, B. C. The sensitivity of the dynamic calculus to short term change in interest structure. Unpublished M.A. thesis, University of Illinois at Urbana, 1971.

Hernandez-Peon, R. Attention, sleep, motivation, and behavior. In Baken, P. (Ed.), *Attention*, 88-107. New York: Van Nostrand, 1966.

Herbart, J. F. *Sammtliche Werke*. Gottingen, 1852.

Herrmann, T., & Stapf, A. Personality and culture: the family. In Cattell, R. B., & Dreger, R. M. (Eds.), *Handbook of modern personality theory*. Pp. 477-495. New York: Hemisphere, 1977.

Herriot, P. *Attributes of memory*. London: Methuen, 1974.

Herrnstein, R. J. Secondary reinforcement and the rate of primary reinforcement. *Journal of Experimental Analytical Behavior*, 1964, 7, 27-36.

Herrnstein, R. J., & Morse, W. H. A conjunctive schedule of reinforcement. *Journal of Experimental Analytical Behavior*, 1958, 1, 15-24.

Herton, W. W., & Iverson, I. H. Classical conditioning and operant conditioning: a response pattern analysis. Springer Verlag. New York, 1978.

Hess, E. H. Imprinting in animals. *Scientific American*, 1958, 198, 81-90.

Hollander, E. P., & Willis, R. H. Some current issues in the psychology of conformity and non-conformity. Pp. 412-428 in Borgatta, E. F. (Ed.), *Social Psychology, readings and perspective*. Chicago, Rand McNally, 1969.

Horn, J. L. Structure in measures of self sentiment, ego and super-ego concepts. Unpublished master's thesis, University of Illinois, 1961.

Horn, J. L. Motivation and dynamic calculus concepts from multivariate experiment. In Cattell, R. B. (Ed.), *Handbook of multivariate experimental psychology*. Pp. 611-641. Chicago: Rand-McNally, 1966.

Horn, J. L. Organization of data on life span development of human abilities. In Goulet, L. R., & Baltes, P. B. (Eds.), *Life span developmental psychology*. New York: Academic Press, 1970.

Horn, J. L. State, trait and change dimensions of intelligence. *British Journal of Educational Psychology*, 1972, 42, 159-185.

Horn, J. L., & Cattell, R. B. Age differences in primary mental abilities. *Journal of Gerontology*, 1966, 21, 210-220.

Horn, J. L., & Cattell, R. B. Studies of adulthood development of intellectual abilities and cognitive processes. *Journal of Educational Measurement*, 1979. (In press)

Horn, J. L., & Donaldson, G. On the myth of intellectual decline in adulthood. *American Psychologist*, 1976, 31, 701-719.

Horn, J. L., & Donaldson, G. Faith is not enough: a response to the Baltes-Schaie sermon that intelligence will not wane. *American Psychologist*, 1978.

Horn, J. L., & Sweney, A. B. The dynamic calculus model for motivation and its use in understanding the individual case. In A. R. Mahrer (Ed.), *New approaches to psychodiagnostic systems*. New York, 1968.

Horst, P. *Factor analysis of data matrices*. New York: Holt, 1965.

Horst, P. An overview of the essentials of multivariate analysis methods. In Cattell, R. B. (Ed.), *Handbook of multivariate experimental psychology*. Pp. 129-152. Chicago: Rand McNally, 1966.

Hess, E. H. The relationship between imprinting and motivation. In M. R. Jones (Ed.), *Nebraska symposium on motivation*. Lincoln, University of Nebraska Press, 1959, 47-77.

Hess, E. H. Ethology, an approach towards the complete analysis of behavior. In R. Brown, E. Galanter, E. H. Hess, & G. Mandler, *New directions in psychology*. New York: Holt, 1962.

Higgins, J. V., Reed, S. W., & Reed, S. C. Intelligence and family size. A paradox resolved. *Eugenics Quarterly*, 1962, 9, 84-90.

Hilgard, E. R., & Bower, G. H. *Theories of learning*. 3rd ed. New York: Appleton-Century-Crofts, 1966.

Hilgard, E. R., & Marquis, D. G. *Conditioning and learning.* New York: Appleton-Century, Crofts, 1940.

Hill, W. F. *Learning: A survey of psychological interpretations.* San Francisco: Chandler, 1963.

Hinde, R. A. *Animal behavior: A synthesis of ethology and comparative psychology.* New York: McGraw-Hill, 1970.

Hirsch, J. Intelligence: Genetic and environmental influences. In Cancro, R. (Ed.), *Intelligence: Genetic and environmental.* Pp. 88-106. New York: Grune & Stratton, 1971.

Hobbes, T. *Leviathan, or the matter, form and power of a commonwealth.* London, 1651.

Hoffeld, D. R., Thompson, R. T., & Brogden, W. J. Effect of stimulus-time relation during pre-conditioning training upon the magnitude of sensory pre-conditioning. *Journal of Experimental Psychology,* 1958, *56,* 437-442.

Hoffman, M. Identification and conscience development. *Child Development,* 1971, *42,* 1071-1082.

Hogben, L. Astroglossa, or first steps in celestial syntax. *Journal of British Interplanetary Society,* Nov. 1952, *11,* 258-274.

Hull, C. L. A functional interpretation of the conditioned reflex. *Psychological Review,* 1929, *36,* 498-511.

Hull, C. L. *Essentials of behavior.* New Haven: Yale University Press, 1951.

Hull, C. L. *A behavior system.* New Haven: Yale University Press, 1952.

Hull, C. L., Felsinger, J. M., Gladstone, A., & Yamaguchi, H. G. A proposed quantification of habit strength. *Psychological Review,* 1947, *54,* 237-254.

Humphreys, L. G. The effect of random alternation of reinforcement on the acquisition and extinction of conditioned eyelid reactions. *Journal of Experimental Psychology,* 1939, *25,* 141-158.

Humphreys, L. G. Measurement of strength of conditioned eyelid responses. *Journal of Experimental Psychology,* 1943, *29,* 101-111.

Hundleby, J., Pawlik, K., & Cattell, R. B. *Personality factors in objective test devices.* San Diego: Knapp, 1965.

Hunt, J. McV., Ewing, T. N., Laforge, R., & Gilbert, W. M. An integrated approach to research on therapeutic counselling, with samples of results. *Journal of Counselling Psychology,* 1959, *6,* 46-54.

Huntington, E. *The character of races.* New York: Scribner, 1927.

Huntington, E. *Mainsprings of civilization.* 3rd ed. New York: Wiley, 1964.

Huxley, J. *Evolution in action.* London: Chatto and Windus, 1953.

Inhelder, B., & Piaget, J. *The growth of logical thinking from childhood to adolescence.* New York: Basic Books, 1958.

Insel, P. M., & Moos, R. H. Psychological environments: expanding the scope of human ecology. *American Psychologist,* 1974, *29,* 179-188.

IPAT. *The IPAT culture-fair intelligence scales, 1, 2, and 3.* Champaign, Ill.: Institute for Personality and Ability Testing, 1949, 1955, 1975.

Irwin, D. A., Knott, J. R., McAdams, D. W., & Rebert, C. S. Motivational determinants of the "contingent negative variation." *Electroencephalography and clinical neurophysiology,* 1966, *21,* 538-541.

Ittelson, W. H., Proshansky, H. M., Rivlin, L. Y., & Winkel, Y. K. *An introduction to environmental psychology.* New York: Holt, Rinehart & Winston, 1974.

Jackson, P. C. *Introduction to artificial intelligence.* New York: Petrocelli, 1974.

James, L. R., & Jones, A. P. Organizational climate: a review of theory and research. *Psychological Bulletin.* 1974, *81,* 1096-1112.

James, W. *Principles of psychology.* New York: Henry Holt, 1890.

James, W. *Pragmatism: and four essays from "The meaning of truth".* New York: Meridian Books, 1960.

Jencks, E. et al. *Inequality: A reassessment of the effect of family and schooling in America.* New York: Harper, 1972.

Jensen, A. R. How much can we boost I.Q. and scholastic achievement? *Harvard Educational Review,* 1969, *39,* 1-123.

Jensen, A. R. *Educability and group differences.* New York: Harper & Row, 1973.

Jensen, A. R., & Figueroa, R. A. Forward and backward digit span interaction with race and I.Q.: predictions from Jensen's theory. *Journal of Educational Psychology,* 1975, *67,* 882-893.

Jinks, J. L., & Fulker, D. W. Comparison of the biometrical-genetic, MAVA, and classical approaches to the analyses of human behavior. *Psychological Bulletin,* 1970, *73,* 311-349.

Johnson, C. F. Chunking and organization in the process of recall. In Bowen, E. H. (Ed.). *The psychology of learning and motivation.* 4. New York: Academic Press, 1970.

Johnson, D. M., Johnson, R. C., & Mark, A. L. A mathematical analysis of verbal fluency. *Journal of Genetic Psychology,* 1951, *44,* 121-128.

Johnson, R. C. A study of children's moral judgments. *Child development,* 1962, *33,* 327-354.

Jones, H. E., & Conrad, H. S. The growth and decline of intelligence. *Genetic Psychological Monograph,* 1933, *13,* 223-298.

Jöreskog, K. G. Some contributions to maximum likelihood factor analysis. *Psychometrika,* 1967, *32,* 443-482.

Jung, C. G. *Symbols of Transformation.* Collected Works, Vol. 5. Ballinger Series, Pringle, N. J.: Princeton University Press, 1911.

Kallman, T. J. *Heredity in health and mental disorders.* New York: Norton, 1953.

Kameoka, V. The nature of the psychological state measures in the Clinical Analysis Questionnaire: A comparison of a dR-technique with an R-technique factoring. (In press, 1979.)

Kamin, R. J. The gradient delay of secondary reward in avoidance learning. *Journal of Comparative Physiological Psychology,* 1957, *50,* 445-449.

Kanfer, F. H., & Phillips, J. S. *Learning foundations of behavior theory.* New York, Wiley, 1970.

Karson, S., & O'Dell, M. *The clinical use of the 16 P.F.* Champaign, Ill.: Institute for Personality and Ability Testing, 1976.

Kawash, G. W., Dielman, T. E., & Cattell, R. B. Changes in objective measures of fear motivation as a function of laboratory-controlled manipulation. *Psychological Reports,* 1972, *30,* 59-63.

Keller, F. S. *Learning: reinforcement theory.* New York: Random, 1969.

Kelley, H. P., & Thibaut, J. W. Group problem solving. In Lindzey, G., & Aronson, E. (Eds.), *Handbook of social psychology.* Vol. 4. Reading, Mass.: Addison Wesley, 1969.

Kelley, H. P. *A factor analysis of memory ability.* Princeton: ETS Research Bulletin, 1954, 54-57.

Kelly, E. L. A preliminary report on psychological factors in assortative mating. *Psychological Bulletin,* 1937, *34,* 749.

Kempthorne, O. *An introduction to genetic statistics.* Ames.: Iowa State University Press, 1969.

Kendall, D. G. Stochastic Processes occurring in the theory of queues. *Annals of Mathematical Statistics,* 1953, *24,* 338-354.

Kendler, H. H., & Kanver, J. H. A further test of the ability of rats to learn the location of food when motivated by thirst. *Journal of Experimental Psychology,* 1950, *40,* 762–765.

Kendler, H. H., & Law, F. E. An experimental test of the selective principle of association of drive stimuli. *Journal of Experimental Psychology,* 1950, *40,* 299–304.

Kentucky Symposium. *Learning theory, personality theory and clinical research.* New York: Wiley, 1954.

Kessler, F. M., Crocker, M. J., & Price, A. J. *Noise and Noise Control.* Cleveland, CRC Press, 1975.

Kety, S. S., Rosenthal, D., Wender, P. H., & Schulsinger, T. The types and prevalence of mental illness in the biological and adoptive families of adopted schizophrenics. *Journal of Psychiatric Research,* 1968, *6,* 345–362.

Kimble, D. P. (Ed.). *The organization of recall.* New York: New York Academy of Science, 1967.

Kimble, G. A. Behavior strength as a function of the intensity of the hunger drive. *Journal of Experimental Psychology,* 1951, *41,* 341–348.

Kimble, G. A. See Hilgard, E. R., & Marquis, D. (Eds.), *Conditioning and learning.* Second Edition. In particular Chapter 7 on Secondary Reinforcement. New York: Appleton-Century-Crofts, 1961.

King, R. C. *Genetics.* New York: Oxford University Press, 1965.

Klein, T., & Cattell, R. B. Heritabilities of high school personality questionnaire factors from intro-class correlations on twins and sibs. Paper at *Behavior Genetics Association* meeting, 1972. Available from T. Klein, University of Hawaii, Psychol. Dept., Honolulu.

Kleinrock, L. *Communication nets.* New York: Dover, 1964.

Kleinsmith, L. J., & Kaplin, S. Interaction of arousal and recall interval in nonsense syllable paired associate learning. *Journal of Experimental Psychology,* 1964, *67,* 124–126.

Kline, P., & Grindley, J. A 28 day case study with the MAT. *Journal of Multivariate Experimental Personality and Clinical Psychology,* 1974, *1,* 13–22.

Klir, G. J. (Ed.), *Trends in general systems theory.* New York: Wiley-Interscience, 1972.

Kohlberg, L. Moralization; the cognitive development approach. In Baltes, P. B. & Schaie, K. W. (Eds.). *Life Span Developmental Psychology.* New York: Adademic Press, 1973.

Konorski, J. *Conditioned reflexes and neuron organization.* Cambridge: Cambridge University Press, 1948.

Korth, B. Attitude change in relation to reward and initial dynamic structure. Unpublished M.A. thesis. University of Illinois, 1970.

Krause, M. S. Use of social situations for research purposes. *American Psychologist,* 1974, *29,* 179–188.

Kretschmer, E. *Korperbau und Charakter.* (Translated as *Physique and character).* New York, Harcourt Brace, 1925.

Krug, S. E. An experimental alteration of motivation levels in adolescents. *Multivariate Experimental Clinical Research.* 1977(a), *3,* 43–51.

Krug. S. E. *Personality assessment in psychological medicine.* Champaign, Ill.: Institute of Personality and Ability Testing, 1977(b).

Krug, S. E., & Cattell, A. K. S. Second order structure among primary ergs and sentiments. In press, 1978.

Krug, S. E., & Kulhavy, R. W. Personality differences across regions of the United States. *Journal of Social Psychology,* 1973, *91,* 75–79.

Kuhn, T. S. *The structure of scientific revolutions.* Chicago: University of Chicago Press, 1962.

Labouvie, E. W. An extension of developmental models; a reply to Buss. *Psychological Bulletin,* 1975, *82,* 165–169.

Lanzetta, J. T., & Roby, T. B. Group learning and communication as a function of task and structure demands. *Journal of Abnormal Social Psychology,* 1957, *55,* 121–131.

Lashley, K. S. The problem of serial order in behavior. In L. A. Jeffress (Eds.), *Cerebral mechanisms in behavior.* New York: Wiley, 1951.

Laszlo, W. *System, structure, and experience: Toward a scientific theory of mind.* New York: Gordon & Brasch, 1969.

Laughlin, J. Prediction of action decisions from the dynamic calculus. Unpublished M.A. thesis, University of Illinois at Urbana, 1973.

Lawlis, G. F. Motivational aspects of the chronically unemployed. Unpublished Ph.D. thesis, Texas Technological College, 1968.

Lawlis, G. F. Motivational factors reflecting employment stability. *Journal of Social Psychology,* 1971, *84,* 215–225.

Lazarus, R. S. *Psychological stress the coping process.* New York: McGraw-Hill, 1966.

Lazarus, R. S., & Fonda, C. F. Personality dynamics and auditory perceptual recognition. *Journal of Personality.* 1951, *19,* 472–482.

Lebo, M. A., & Nesselroade, J. R. Individual differences: dimensions of mood change during pregnancy, identified in 5 P-technique analyses. *Journal of research in personality.* 1978, *12,* 205–224.

Lecritt, H. J. Some effects of certain communication patterns upon group performance. *Journal of Abnormal and Social Psychology,* 1951, *46,* 38–50.

Lentz, T. F. Relation of I.Q. to size of family. *Journal of educational psychology,* 1927, *18,* 486–496.

Leonard, D. W., & Capaldi, E. J. Successive acquisitions and extinctions in the rat as a function of the number of non-rewards in each extinction session. *Journal of comparative and physiological psychology,* 1971, *74,* 102–107.

Leontieff, A. N. Ponyatie otrazheniya i ego znachenie dlyz psikhologii. (The concept of reflection and its significance for psychology.) *Voprosy Filosofii,* 1966, *20,* 48–56.

Lerner, I. S. *Heredity, evolution and society.* San Francisco: Freeman, 1968.

Levine, R., Chein, I., & Murphy, G. The relation of the intensity of a need to the amount of perceptual distortion: A preliminary report. *Journal of Psychology,* 1942, *13,* 283–293.

Li, C. C. *Human genetics.* Chicago: University of Chicago Press, 1961.

Li, C. C. *An introduction to path coefficients.* New York: McGraw-Hill, 1976.

Lindzey, G. *Assessment of human motives.* New York: Rinehart, 1958.

Lindzey, G. General discussion of behavior genetic contributions. In Vandenberg, S. G. (Ed.). *Methods and goals in human behavior genetics.* New York: Academic Press, 1965.

Lindzey, G., & Hall, C. S. *Theories of personality.* New York: Wiley, 1975.

Linton, R. *The study of man.* New York: Appleton-Century, 1936.

Loehlin, J. C. A computer program that simulates personality. In Tomkins, S. S., & Messick, S. (Eds.). *Computer simulation of personality.* New York: Wiley, 1963.

Loehlin, J. C. Some methodological problems in Cattell's multiple abstract variance analysis. *Psychological Review,* 1965, *72,* 156–161.

Loehlin, J. C. Psychological genetics from the study of human behavior. In

Cattell, R. B., & Dreger, R. M. (Eds.). *Handbook of modern personality theory.* Chapter 13. New York: Hemisphere, 1978a.

Loehlin, J. C. Combining data from different groups in human behavior genetics. Banff Conference on Human Behavior Genetics. Oct., 1978b.

Loehlin, J. C., Lindzey, G., & Spuhler, I. N. *Race differences in intelligence.* San Francisco: W. H. Freeman, 1975.

Loehlin, J. C., & Vandenberg, S. G. Genetic and environmental components in the covariation of cognitive abilities. In Vandenberg, S. G. (Ed.), *Progress in human genetics.* Pp. 261-281. Baltimore: Johns hopkins Press, 1968.

Loevinger, J. Theories of ego development. In Breger, L. (Ed.), *Clinical-cognitive psychology: Models and integrations.* Pp. 162-180. Englewood Cliffs, N. J.: Prentice-Hall, 1969.

Logan, F. A. *Incentive: How the conditions of reinforcement affect the performance of rats.* New Haven: Yale University Press, 1960.

Logan, F. A., & Wagner, A. R. *Reward and punishment.* Boston: Allyn and Bacon, 1965.

Lorenz, C. *On aggression.* New York: Harcourt, 1966.

Lorenz, C., & Leyhausen, G. *Motivation in animals and men.* New York: Van Nostrand, 1970.

Lorge, I., & Thorndike, E. L. The influence of delay in the after-effect of a connection. *Journal of Experimental Psychology,* 1935, *18,* 186-194.

Luria, A. R. The nature of human conflicts: Or emotion, conflict and will. An objective study of disorganization and control of human behavior. Trans. from the Russian and ed. by Gantt, W. H. New York:Liveright, 1932.

Lynn, D. B. The process of learning parental and sex role identification. Pp. 223-230, In Borgatta, E. F. (Ed.). *Social psychology; Readings and perspective.* 1969, Chicago, Rand McNally, 1969.

Lynn, R. *Personality and national character.* Oxford: Pergamon Press, 1971.

Lynn, R. The intelligence of the Japanese. *Bulletin of the British Psychology Society,* 1977, *30,* 69-72.

Lynn, R. The social ecology of intelligence in the British Isles. *British Journal of Social and Clinical Psychology.* (In press, 1978).

MacCorquodale, K., & Meehl, P. On the elimination of blind entries without obvious reinforcement. *Journal of Comparative Physiological Psychology,* 1957, *44,* 367-371.

Macfarlane, J. W. From infancy to childhood. In Mussen, M., Conger, J., & Kagen, M. (Eds.). *Basic and contemporary issues in child development.* New York: Harper and Row, 1965.

MacKay, D. M. Toward an information flow model of human behavior. *British Journal of Psychology,* 1956, *47,* 11-30.

MacKay, D. M. *Geographical mobility and the brain drain.* London: Allen & Unwin, 1969.

Mackintosh, N. J. *The psychology of animal learning.* New York: Academic Press, 1974.

MacLeish, J., Matheson, W., & Park, J. *The psychology of the learning group.* London: Hutchinson, 1973.

Madsen, K. B. The formal properties of Cattellian personality theory. In Cattell, R. B., & Dreger, R. M. (Eds.). *Handbook of modern personality theory.* Chapter 31. Washington: Hemisphere, New York; Halsted, 1977.

Magnusson, D. The person and the situation in an interactional model of behavior. *Scand. J. Psychol.,* 1976, *17,* 253-271.

Magnusson, D., & Ekehammar, B. Anxiety profiles based on both situation and response factors. *Multivariate Behavioral Research,* 1975(a), *10,* 27–44.

Magnuson, D., & Ekehammar, B. Perception of and reaction to stressful situations. *Journal of personality and social psychology,* 1975(b), *31,* 1147–1154.

Malecot, G. *Les mathematiques de l'heredite.* Paris: Masson, 1948.

Malmo, R. B. Activation; a neurophysiological dimension. *Psychological Review,* 1959, *66,* 367–386.

Manosewitz, M., Lindzey, Y., & Thiessen, D. *Behavior genetics: method and research.* New York: Appleton Century, 1909.

Mariotto, P. M., & Paul, G. Persons versus situations in the real-life functioning of chronically institutionalized mental patients. *Journal of Abnormal Psychology,* 1975, *84* (5), 483–493.

Marsella, A. Diagnostic type, gender and consistency versus specificity in behavior. *Journal of Clinical Psychology,* 1974, *30,* 484–488.

Maslow, A. H. Appetites and hungers in animal motivation. *Journal of Comparative Psychology,* 1935, *20,* 75–83.

Maslow, A. H., & Flanyb, M. S. The role of dominance in the social and sexual behavior of infra-human primates. *Journal of Genetic Psychology,* 1936, *48,* 310–338.

Mather, K., & Jinks, I. *Biometrical genetics: Study of continuous variations.* San Francisco: Freeman, 1975.

Maxwell, J. *The level and trend of national intelligence.* London: London University Press, 1969.

May, David R. An application of the taxonome method to a plasmode. *Multivariate Behavioral Research,* 1973, *8,* 503–510.

May, J. M. The effects of electric shock therapy on repression and other phenomena related to personality, motivation and repression. Unpublished Ph.D. thesis, Texas Technological University, 1964.

May, J. M., & Sweney, A. B. Personality and motivation changes observed in the treatment of psychotic patients. Paper from the *Southwest Psychological Society,* 1965.

McAdam, D. W. Increase in CNS excitability during negative cortical slow potentials in man. *Electroencaphic Clinical Neurophysiological,* 1969, *26,* 216–219.

McClearn, G. E., & DeFries, I. C. *Introduction to behavioral genetics.* San Francisco: Freeman, 1973.

McClelland, D. C., Atkinson, I. W., Clark, R. A., & Lowell, E. L. *The achievement motive.* New York: Appleton-Century-Crofts, 1953.

McDougall, W. *National welfare and national decay.* London: Methuen, 1920.

McDougall, W. *The energies of men.* London: Methuen, 1932.

McKusick, V. A. *Human genetics.* Englewood Cliffs, N.J.: Prentice-Hall, 1958.

McKusick, V. A. *Mendelian inheritance in man: Catalogue of autosomal recessives and X-linked phenotypes.* Baltimore: Johns Hopkins Press, 1966.

McNemar, Q. *Psychological statistics.* New York: Wiley, 1962.

Mead, M. Anthropological data on the problem of instinct. *Psychosomatic Medicine,* 1942, *4,* 396–397.

Mead, M. *Coming of age in Samoa: a psychological study of primitive youth for Western Civilization.* New York: New American Library, 1949.

Mead, M. *Culture patterns and technological change.* New York: New American Library, 1955.

Meehl, P. E., & MacCorquodale, K. A further study of latent learning in the T-maze. *Journal of Comparative Physiological Psychology,* 1948, *41,* 372–396.

Meichenbaum, D. H., & Goodman, J. Training impulsive children to talk to themselves; a means of developing self control. *Journal of abnormal psychology*, 1971, 77, 115-126.

Meredith, G. M. Observations on the origins and current status of the ego assertive personality factor U.I. 16. *Journal of Genetic Psychology*, 1967, *110*, 269-286.

Messick, S. Beyond structure: In search of functional models of psychological process. *Psychometrika*, 1972, *37*, 357-375.

Messick, S. Multivariate models of cognition and personality: the need for both process and structure in psychological theory and measurement. In Royce, J. R. (Ed.), *Multivariate Analysis and Psychological Theory*. Pp. 265-303. London: Academic Press, 1973.

Michotte, A. *Études de psychologie*. Paris: Alcan, 1914.

Miles, C. C. The influence of speed and age on intelligence scores of adults. *Journal of General Psychology*, 1934, *10*, 208-210.

Miller, N. E. Experimental studies of conflict. In Hunt, J. McV. (Ed.), *Personality and the behavior disorders*. Pp. 431-465. New York: Ronald Press, 1944.

Miller, N. E. Liberalization of basic S-R concepts. Extensions to conflict behavior, motivation and social learning. In Koch, S. (Ed.), *Psychology: A study of a science*. Vol. 2. Pp. 550-589. New York: McGraw-Hill, 1959.

Miller, N. E. Some reflections on the law of effect to produce a new alternative to drive reduction. In Jones, M. R. (Ed.), *Nebraska symposium on motivation*, 1963, *11*, 65-112.

Miller, J. G. *Living systems*. New York: McGraw-Hill, 1978.

Miller, J. Y., Galanter, E., & Pribram, K. H. *Plans and the structure of behavior*. New York: Holt, Rinehart, Winston, 1960.

Milton, G. A. A factor analytic study of child rearing behavior. *Child Development*, 1958, *29*, 381-392.

Mischel, W. Continuity and change in personality. *Am. Psy.* 1969, *24*, 1012-1018.

Mischel, W. Toward a cognitive social learning reconceptualization of personality. *Psychological Review*, 1973, *53*, 49-61.

Montgomery, K. C. The effect of hunger and thirst drives upon exploratory behavior. *Journal of Comparative Physiological Psychology*, 1953, *46*, 315-319.

Moos, R. H. Conceptualization of human environments. *American Psychologist*, 1973, *28*, 652-665.

Morgan, C. L. *An introduction to comparative psychology*. London: Scott, 1894.

Morrell, F. Electrophysiological contributions to the neural basis of learning. *Physiological Review*, 1961, *41*, 443-494.

Morton, N. E. Analysis of family resemblance. I: Introduction. *American Journal of Human Genetics*, 1974, *26*, 318-330.

Mowrer, O. H. Animal studies in the genesis of personality. *Transactions of the New York Academy of Science*, 1938, *56*, 273-288.

Mowrer, O. H. A stimulus response analysis of anxiety and its role as a reinforcing agent. *Psychological Review*, 1939, *46*, 553-565.

Mowrer, O. H. Two-factor learning theory reconsidered, with special reference to secondary reinforcement and the concept of habit. *Psychological Review*, 1956, *63*, 114-128.

Mowrer, O. H. *Learning theory and behavior*. New York: Wiley, 1960a.

Mowrer, O. H. *Learning theory and the symbolic processes*. New York: Wiley, 1960b.

Muktanada, B. *Play of consciousness*. Los Angeles, Cal.: Ashram, 1974.

Murray, H. A., et al. Explorations in personality. New York: Oxford University Press, 1938.

Myrdal, G. *Asian drama: an enquiry into the poverty of nations*. New York: Pantheon, 1968.

Napalkov, A. V. Tsepi dvigatelnykh uslovnykh refleksov u golubel. (Chains of conditioned motor reflexes in pigeons.) *Zh. vyssh. nervn. Deiatel.*, 1959, 6, 615-621.

Nesselroade, J. R. *The seven state objective test battery*. Champaign, Ill.: Institute for Personality and Ability Testing, 1960.

Nesselroade, J. R. A comparison of cross product and differential R-factoring regarding cross study stability of change patterns. Unpublished Ph.D. thesis, University of Illinois, 1967.

Nesselroade, J. R., & Bartsch, T. W. Multivariate perspectives on the validity of the trait-state distinction. In Cattell, R. B., & Dreger, R. M. (Eds.), *Handbook of modern personality theory*. Chapter 8. New York: Hemisphere, 1977.

Nesselroade, J. R., & Reese, J. (Eds.). *Life span developmental psychology*. New York: Academic Press, 1973.

Nissen, G. *Intelligenz, Lernen und Lernstörungen*. Berlin: Springer-Verlag, 1977.

Noble, C. E., & Alcock, W. T. Human delayed-reward learning with different lengths of task. *Journal of Experimental Psychology*, 1958, 56, 407-412.

O'Kelly, L. I., & Heyer, A. W. Studies in motivation and retention. V. The influences of need duration on retention of a maze habit. *Comparative Psychological Monograph*, 1951, 20, 287-301.

Olds, J. Neuro-physiology of drive. *Psychiatric Research Reports*, 1956, 6, 15-20.

Oppenheimer, R. *Science and the human understanding*. New York: Simon & Schuster, 1966.

Pan, S. The influence of context upon learning and recall. *Journal of Experimental Psychology*, 1926, 9, 468-491.

Parker, J. B., & Spielberger, C. D. Frequency of blood types in a homogeneous group of manic-depressives. *Journal of Mental Science*, 1961, 107, 936-942.

Pattee, H. H. *Hierarchical theory*. New York: Braziller, 1973.

Patterson, G. R. Changes in status of family members as controlling stimuli. In Hammerlynck, L. A. et al. *Behavior change: methodology, concepts and practice*. Champaign, Ill.: Research Press, 1973.

Pavlov, I. P. *Lectures on conditioned reflexes*. New York: International Press, 1928.

Pavlov, I. P. *Selected works*. Moscow: Foreign Languages Publishing House, 1955.

Pawlik, K., & Cattell, R. B. Third order factors in objective personality tests. *British Journal of Psychology*, 1964, 55, 1-18.

Penman, A. S. Factors influencing learning and problem solving in small groups. Unpublished Ph.D. thesis, University of Illinois at Urbana, 1951.

Perin, C. T. A quantitative investigation of the delay-of-reinforcement gradient. *Journal of Experimental Psychology*, 1943, 32, 37-51.

Perkins, C. C. J. An analysis of the concept of reinforcement. *Psychological Review*, 1968, 75, 155-172.

Pervin, L. A. A free-response description approach to the analysis of person-situation interaction. Princeton: *ETS Bulletin* RB-75-22, 1975(a).

Pervin, L. A. Definitions, measurements and classifications of stimuli situations and environments. Princeton: *ETS Bulletin* RB-75-23, 1975(b).

Pervin, L. A. *Personality: Theory, assessment and research*. New York: Wiley, 1975c.

Pierson, G. R., Barton, V., & Hey, G. SMAT motivation factors as predictions of academic achievement of delinquent boys. *Journal of Psychology*, 1964, 57, 243-249.

Porter, L. W., & Miller, N. E. Training under two drives alternately present vs. training under a single drive. *Journal of Experimental Psychology*, 1957, 54, 1-7.

Postman, L., & Adams, P. A. Studies in incidental learning. IV. The interaction of orienting tasks and stimulus occasions. *Journal of Experimental Psychology*, 1956, 51, 329-333.

Premack, D. Toward empirical behavior laws. I. Postive reinforcement. *Psychological Review*, 1959, 66, 219-233.

Prosser, C. L. Comparative neurophysiology. In A. D. Bass (Ed.), *Evolution of nervous control*. Publication No. 52 American Association for the Advance of Science. Washington, D.C., 1959.

Purkey, W. W. *Self concept and school achievement*. Englewood Cliffs, N. J.: Prentice-Hall, 1970.

Rachman, S., & Teasdale, J. D. Aversion therapy; an appraisal. In Franks, C. M. (Ed.), *Behavior therapy: appraisal and status*. New York: McGraw-Hill, 1969.

Rainio, K. *A stochastic model of social interation*. Copenhagen: Munkgaard, 1961.

Rao, C. R., Morton, N. E., & Yee, S. Resolution of cultural and biological inheritance by path analysis. *American Journal of Human Genetics*, 1976, 28, 228-242.

Rao, D. C., & Morton, N. E. Path analysis of family resemblances in the presence of gene-environment interaction. *J. of human genetics*, 1974, 26, 767-772.

Rapoport, A. Mathematics and cybernetics. In Arieti, S. (Ed.), *American handbook of psychiatry*. Pp. 705-740 New York: Basic Books, 1974.

Razran, G. Backward conditioning. *Psychological Bulletin*, 1956, 53, 55-69.

Razran, G. The dominance contiguity theory of the acquisition of classical conditioning. *Psychological Bulletin*, 1957, 54, 1-46.

Reade, Winwood. *The Martyrdom of Man*. London: Watts & Co., 1948.

Reese, H. W. Models of memory and models of development. *Human Development*, 1974.

Renner, K. E. Temporal integration: Relative value of rewards and punishments as a function of their temporal distance from the response. *Journal of Experimental Psychology*, 1966, 71, 902-907.

Renner, K. E. Temporal integration: Modification of the incentive value of a food reward by early experience with deprivation. *Journal of Experimental Psychology*, 1967, 75, 400-407.

Rescorla, R. A. Pavlovian conditioning and its proper control procedures. *Psychological Review*, 1967, 74, 71-80.

Rescorla, R. A., & Solomon, R. C. Two-process learning theory: Relationships between Pavlovian conditioning and instrumental learning. *Psychological Review*, 1967, 74, 151-182.

Ribot, T. *Diseases of memory* London: Dent, 1882.

Ribot, T. *La psychologie des sentiments*. Paris; Alcan, 1896.

Ricardo, D. *The principles of political economy and taxation*. London: Dent, 1817.

Richardson, L. F. *Statistics of deadly quarrels*. Pittsburgh: Boxwood Press, 1960.

Rickels, K., et al. Drug response and important external events in the patients's life. *Diseases of the Nervous System*, 1965, 26, 782-786.

Rickels, K., & Cattell, R. B. The relationship of clinical symptoms and the IPAT factored tests of anxiety, regression and asthenia: A factor analytic study. *Journal of Nervous and Mental Disease*, 1968, *146*, 147-160.

Rickels, K., Cattell, R. B., Wiese, C., Gray, B., & Yee, R. Controlled psychopharmacological research in private psychiatric medicine. *Psychopharmacologia*, 1966, *9*, 288-306.

Riegel, K. F. Developmental psychology and society: Some historical and ethical considerations. In Nesselroade, J. R., & Reese, H. W. (Eds.). *Life span developmental psychology*. Pp. 1-24. New York: Academic Press, 1973.

Riordan, J. *Stochastic service systems*. New York: Wiley, 1961.

Rips, L. J., Shohen, E. J., & Smith, E. E. Semantic distance and the verification of semantic relations. *Journal of Verbal Learning and Verbal Behavior*, 1973, *12*, 1-20.

Roby, T. B. On the measurement and description of groups. *Behavioral Science*, 1957, *2*, 119-127.

Roff, M. A factorial study of the Fels parent behavior scales. *Child Development*, 1949, *20*, 29-45.

Rogers, C. R. *A therapist's view of personal goals*. Wallingford, Pa.: Pendle Hill, 1960.

Rohner, J. H. A motivational state resulting from non-reward. *Journal of Comparative Physiological Psychology*, 1949, *42*, 476–485.

Rokeach, Milton. *The open and closed mind*. New York: Basic Books, 1960.

Rosenthal, D. *Genetic theory and abnormal behavior*. New York: McGraw-Hill, 1970.

Ross, J. Mean performance and the factor analysis of learning data. *Psychometrika*, 1964, *29*, 67-70.

Ross, J. F., & McDermott, J. K. A multi-dimensional system dynamics model of affect. *Motivation and Education*, 1977, *1*, 193-223.

Rotter, J. B. Generalized expectancies for internal versus external control of reinforcement. *Psychological Monographs*, 1966, *80*, No. 1.

Royce, J. R. Factor theory and genetics. *Educational and Psychological Measurement*, 1957, *17*, 361-376.

Royce, J. R. Concepts generated from comparative and physiological observations. In Cattell, R. B. (Ed.), *Handbook of multivariate experimental psychology*. Pp. 682-683. Chicago: Rand McNally, 1966.

Royce, J. R. (Ed.). *Multivariate analysis and psychological theory*. London: Academic Press, 1973.

Royce, J. R. The relationship between factors and psychological processes. In Scandura, J., and Brainerd, C. J. *Structural Process Theories of Complex Human Behavior*, Leiden, Holland: Sijthoff International Publishing Company, 1977.

Royce, J. R., & Buss, A. R. The role of general systems and information theory in multi-factor individuality theory. *Canadian Psychological Review*, 1976, *17*, 1-21.

Royce, J. R., & Covington, M. Genetic differences in the avoidance conditioning of mice. *Journal of Comparative Physiological Psychology*, 1960, *53*, 197-200.

Ruggles-Gates, A. *Human heredity*. New York: Macmillan, 1946.

Rummel, R. J. Dimensions of conflict behavior within and between nations. *General Systems Yearbook of Society for General Systems Study*, 1963, *8*, 1-50.

Rummel, R. J. Domestic attributes and foreign conflict. In Singer, J. D. (Ed.), *Quantitative international politics*. Pp. 43-85. New York: Free Press, 1968.

Rummel, R. J. Indicators of cross national and international patterns. *American Political Science Review*, 1969, *63*, 1-5.

Rummel, R. J. *Applied factor analysis.* Evanston: Northwest University Press, 1970.

Rummel, R. J. *The dimensions of nations.* Beverly Hills, Calif.: Sage Publications, 1972.

Rummel, R. J. *Understanding conflict and war.* New York: Halstead, 1975.

Rummel, R. J. *Field theory evolving.* Beverley Hills, Cal., Sage Publ., 1977.

Rummel, R. J. *National attitudes and behavior linkage dimensions.* Beverley Hills, Cal., Sage Publ., 1978.

Rundquist, E. E. Inheritance of spontaneous activity in rats. *Journal of Comparative Psychology,* 1933, *16,* 1-30.

Rusak, B., & Zucker, I. Biological rhythms and animal behavior. *Annual Review of Psychology,* 1975, *26,* 137-171.

Russett, B. M. *International regions and the international system.* Chicago: Rand McNally, 1967.

Ryckman, R. *Theories of personality.* New York: Van Nostrand, 1978.

Saltzman, I. J. Mase learning in the absence of primary reinforcement: A study of secondary reinforcement. *Journal of Comparative Physiological Psychology,* 1949, *42,* 161-173.

Saltzman, I. J., & Koch, S. The effect of low intensities of hunger on behavior mediated by a habit of maximum strength. *Journal of Experimental Psychology,* 1948, *38,* 347-370.

Sarason, S. B. The measurement of anxiety in children: Some questions and problems. In Spielberger, C. D. (Ed.), *Anxiety and behavior.* Pp. 63-80. New York: Academic Press, 1966.

Sawyer, J. Dimensions of nations: Size, wealth and politics. *American Journal of Sociology,* 1967, *73,* 145-172.

Sayre, K. M., & Crosson, F. J. *The modelling of mind.* Notre Dame: University of Notre Dame Press, 1963.

Schachter, S. *The psychology of affiliation.* Stanford, Cal., Stanford University Press, 1959.

Schachter, S., & Singer, J. E. Cognitive social and physiological determinants of emotional state. *Psychological Review,* 1962, *65,* 121-128.

Schaie, K. W., & Goulet, L. R. Trait theory and verbal learning processes. In Cattell, R. B., & Dreger, R. M. (Eds.), *Handbook of modern personality theory.* Chapter 24, pp. 567-584. New York: Hemisphere, 1977.

Schaie, K. W., & Strother, C. R. A cross-sequential study of age changes in cognitive behavior. *Psychological Bulletin,* 1968, *68,* 10-25.

Scheier, I. H. *The eight parallel form anxiety battery.* Champaign, Ill.: Institute for Personality and Ability Testing, 1959.

Schludt, W. Über die spontaneitat von Erbkoordinationen. *Zur Tierspychologie,* 1963, *21,* 235-256.

Schneewind, K. R. Personality and perception. In Cattell, R. B., & Dreger, R. M. (Eds.), *Handbook of modern personality theory.* Chapter 23, pp. 551-566. New York: Hemisphere, 1977.

Schoeck, H. *Envy: a theory of social behavior.* New York: Harcourt Brace and World, 1969.

Scott, J. P., Fuller, J. L., & King. J.A. The inheritance of animal breeding cycles in hybrid basenji-cocker spaniel dogs. *Journal of Heredity,* 1959, *50,* 254-261.

Scriven, M. The mechanical concept of mind. In Sayne, K. M., & Crosson, F. J. (Eds.), *The modelling of mind.* Pp. 243-254. Notre Dame: University of Notre Dame Press, 1963.

Seidel, R. J. A review of sensory pre-conditioning. *Psychological Bulletin,* 1959, *56,* 58–73.

Sells, S. B. The nature of organizational climate. In Taguiri, R. and Litwin, G. (Eds.), *Organizational climate: explorations of a concept*. Boston: Harvard University Press, 1968.

Seward, J. P. Drive, incentive and reinforcement. *Psychological Review*, 1956, *63*, 195-203.

Shannon, C. C., & Weaver, W. *The mathematical theory of communication*. Urbana: University of Illinois Press, 1949.

Sheffield, F. D. Theoretical considerations in the learning of complex sequential task from demonstration and practice. In Lumsdaine, A. A. (Ed.), *Student response in programmed instruction*. Washington, D.C.: National Research Council, Publication No. 943, 1961.

Sheffield, F. D. Relation between classical conditioning and instrumental learning. In Prokasy, W. F. (Ed.), *Classical conditioning: A symposium*. New York: Appleton-Century, 1965.

Sheffield, F. D. New evidence on the drive reduction theory of reinforcement. In Haber, R. N. (Ed.), *Current research in motivation*. Pp. 30-52. New York: Holt, Rinehart & Winston, 1966.

Sheffield, F. D., & Roby, T. B. Reward value of a non-nutritive sweet taste. *Journal of Comparative Physiological Psychology*, 1950, *43*, 471-482.

Sheffield, F. D., Wulff, J. J., & Backer, R. Reward value of copulation without sex drive reduction. *Journal of Comparative Physiological Psychology*, 1951, *44*, 3-8.

Sheldon, W. H., & Stevens, S. S. *The varieties of temperament: A psychology of constitutional differences*. New York: Harper, 1942.

Sherif, C. W., Sherif, M., & Nabergill, R. E. *Attitude and attitude change: The social judgment-involvement approach*. Philadelphia: Saunders, 1965.

Siegelman, M. College student personality correlates of early parent-child relationships. *J. of consulting psychology*, 1965, m, *29*, 559-564.

Simmel, G. *"Conflict"* and *"The web of group affiliations."* Wolff, K. H., & Bendix. R., trans. Glencoe: Free Press, 1969.

Singer, J. D. *Quantitative international politics: Insights and evidence*. New York: Free Press, 1968.

Sjoberg, L. Thurstonian methods in the measurement of learning. *Scandinavian Journal of Psychology*, 1965, *6*, 33-48.

Skinner, B. F. *The behavior of organisms*. New York: Appleton, 1938.

Skinner, B. F. "Superstition" in the pigeon. *Journal of Experimental Psychology*, 1948, *38*, 168-172.

Skinner, B. F. Are theories of learning necessary? *Psychological Review*, 1950, *57*, 193-216.

Skinner, B. F. *Contingencies of reinforcement*. New York: Appleton-Century-Crofts, 1969.

Slater, E. The inheritance of mental disorder. *Eugenics Review*, 1937, *28*, 1-16.

Smith, E. E., Shoben, E. J., & Rips, L. J. Structure and process in semantic memory. A feature model for semantic decisions. *Psych. Review*, 1974, *81*, 214-241.

Smuts, J. *Holism and evolution*. New York: Macmillan Company, 1926.

Solomon, R. L., & Wynne, L. C. Traumatic avoidance learning: The principles of anxiety conservation and partial irreversibility. *Psychological Review*, 1954, *61*, 353-388.

Sorokin, P. *Social and cultural dynamics*. New York: American Book Company, 1937.

Sorokin, P. "Basic trends." *World Union Goodwill Congress*, December, 1973.

Spear, N. E. Verbal learning and retention. In D'Amato, M. R. (Ed.), *Experimental Psychology*. Chapter 12. New York: McGraw Hill, 1970.

Spearman, C. E. *The nature of intelligence and the principles of cognition*. London: Macmillan, 1923.

Spearman, C. E. *Creative mind*. London: Macmillan, 1927.

Spence, K. W. Cognitive-vs.-stimulus response theories of learning. *Psychological Review*, 1950, *57*, 159-172.

Spence, K. W. *Behavior theory and conditioning*. New Haven: Yale University Press, 1956.

Spence, K. W. A theory of emotionally based drive (D) and its relation to performance in simple learning situations. *American Psychologist*, 1958, *13*, 131-141,

Spence, K. W., & Spence, J. T. *The psychology of learning and motivation*. New York: Academic Press, 1967.

St. Claire Smith, R. Blocking of punishment. Paper presented at the Eastern Psychological Association, Atlantic City, 1970.

Spence, K. W., & Taylor, J. Anxiety and strength of the UCS as determiners of the amount of eyelid conditioning. *Journal of Experimental Psychology*, 1951, *42*, 183-188.

Spielberger, C. B. *Anxiety and behavior*. New York: Academic Press, 1966.

Spielberger, C. B. *Anxiety: Current trends in theory and research*. New York: Academic Press, 1973.

Staats, A. W. *Social behaviorism*. London: Irwin-Dorsey, 1975.

Staats, A. W., Staats, C. K., Heard, W. G., & Finley, J. R. Operant conditioning of factor analytic personality traits. *Journal of General Psychology*, 1962, *66*, 101-114.

Staats, A. W., & Warren, D. R. Motivation and three function learning: Food deprivation and approach-avoidance to food words. *Journal of Experimental Psychology*, 1974, *103*, 1191-1199.

Stake, R. E. Learning parameters, attitudes, and achievements. *Psychometric Monograph No. 9*, 1961.

Stewart, R. A. C. Cross cultural personality research and basic cultural dimensions through factor analysis. *Personality*, 1971, *2*, 45-71.

Stogdill, R. M. Leadership, membership and organization. *Psychological Bulletin*, 1950, *47*, 1-14.

Stogdill, R. M. Leadership and morale in organized groups. In Hullett, J., & Stagner, R. (Eds.), *Problems in Social Psychology*. Pp. 140-152. Urbana: University of Illinois Press, 1952.

Stogdill, R. M., & Koehler, K. *Measures of leadership structure and organization change*. Columbus: Ohio State University Research Foundation, 1952.

Stricker, L. J. Indexes of social stratification: some cautionary findings. Princeton, N.J. E. T. S. Report RM-78-5. 1978(a).

Stricker, L. J. Dimensions of social stratification for whites and blacks. Princeton, N.J. E. T. S. Report RM-78-6. 1978(b).

Studman, L. G. Studies in experimental psychiatry. W and f factors in relation to traits of personality. *Journal of Mental Science*, 1935, *81*, 107-137.

Sturtevant, A. H. *A history of genetics*. New York: Harper & Row, 1965.

Sutherland, H. E. G., & Thomson, G. H. The correlation between intelligence and family size. *British Journal of Psychology*, 1927, *41*, *17*, 81-92.

Swan, D. A., & Hawkins, G. The dermatoglyphics of South Missisippi Anglo-Saxon school children. *Mankind Quarterly*, 1978, *18*, 163-185.

Sweney, A. B. Objective measurement of strength of dynamic structure factors. In Cattell, R. B., & Warburton, F. (Eds.), *Objective personality and motiv-*

ation tests: A theoretical introduction and a practical compendium. Pp. 127-185. Champaign, Ill.: University of Illinois Press, 1967.

Sweney, A. B. *Descriptive manual for individual assessment by the motivation analysis test.* Champaign, Ill.: Institute for Personality and Ability Testing, 1969.

Sweney, A. B., & Cattell, R. B. Dynamic factors in 12-year-old children as revealed in measures of integrated motivation. *Journal of Clinical Psychology*, 1961, *17*, 360-369.

Sweney, A. B., & Cattell, R. B. Relations integrated and unintegrated motivational components examined by objective tests. *Journal of Social Psychology*, 1962, *57*, 217-226.

Tapp, J. (Ed.). *Reinforcement and behavior.* New York: Academic Press, 1969.

Tatro, D. F. The utility of source traits measured by the O-A (Objective-Analytic) Battery in mental hospital diagnosis. *Multivariate Behavioral Research*, 1968, Special 3, 133-150.

Taylor, C. W., & Barron, F. (Ed.). *The identification of creative scientific talent.* New York: Wiley, 1963.

Taylor J. A. The relationship of anxiety to conditional eyelid response. *Journal of Experimental Psychology*, 1951, *41*, 81-92.

Thayer, R. E. Toward a psychological theory of multidimensional activation (arousal). *Motivation and emotion*, 1978, *2*, 1-34.

Thomas, E. J., & Fink, C. F., Effects of group size. Pp. 653-666. In Borgatta, E. F. (Ed.), *Social psychology, Readings and perspective.* Chicago, Rand McNally, 1969.

Thompson, R. F. The search for the engram. *American Psychologist*, 1976, *31*, 209-227.

Thompson, W. R. Traits, factors and genes. *Eugenics Quarterly*, 1957, *4*, 8-16.

Thompson, W. R. Multivariate experiment in behavior genetics. In Cattell, R. B. (Ed.), *Handbook of multivariate experimental psychology.* Pp. 711-731. Chicago: Rand McNally, 1966.

Thorndike, E. L. *Fundamentals of learning.* New York: Teachers' College, 1932.

Thorndike, E. L. The interests of adults: 2. The inter-relations of adult interest. *Journal of Educational Psychology*, 1935a, *26*, 497-507.

Thorndike, E. L. *The psychology of wants, interests and attitudes.* New York: Appleton-Century-Crofts, 1935(b).

Thorndike, E. L., & Woodyard, E. Differences within and between communities in the intelligence of children. *Journal of Educational Psychology*, 1942, *33*, 641-656.

Thorndike, R. L. The effect of discussion upon the correctness of group decisions, when the factor of majority influence is allowed for. *Journal of Social Psychology*, 1938, *9*, 343-362(a).

Thorndike, R. L. On what type of task will a group do well? *Journal of Abnormal Psychology*, 1938(b), *33*, 409-413.

Thorndike, R. L. Norms and the individual community. In *Proceedings of the 1948 Conference on Test Problems.* Pp. 79-80. Princeton: Educational Testing Service, 1949.

Thorndike, R. L. Community variables as predictors of intelligence and academic achievement. *Journal of Educational Psychology*, 1951, *42*, 321-338.

Thurstone, L. L. The stimulus response fallacy in psychology. *Psychological Review*, 1923, *30*, 354-369.

Thurstone, L. L. A multiple factor study of vocational interests. *Journal of Personality*, 1935, *10*, 198-205.

Thurstone, L. L. *A factorial study of perception.* Chicago: University of Chicago Press, 1946.

Tinbergen, N. *The study of instinct.* Oxford: Clarendon Press, 1951.

Tinbergen, N. *Social behavior in animals.* New York: Wiley, 1953.

Toffler, A. *Future shock.* New York: Random House, 1970.

Tolman, E. C. The determiners of behavior at a choice point. *Psychological Review,* 1938, *45,* 1–41.

Tolman, E. C. Cognitive maps in rats and men. *Psychological Review,* 1948, *55,* 189–208.

Tombaugh, T. N. The overtraining extinction effect with a discrete trial bar-press procedure. *Journal of experimental psychology,* 1967, *73,* 632–634.

Toynbee, A. J. *A study of history.* New York: Oxford University Press, 1947.

Trapold, M. A., & Overmier, J. B. The second learning process in instrumental learning. In Black, H., & Prokasy, W. F. (Eds.), *Classical conditioning II: Current research theory.* New York: Appleton-Century-Crofts, 1972.

Tryon, R. C. Genetic differences in maze-learning ability in rats. 39th Yearbook, National Society for Research on Education, Part 1. Pp. 111–119. Bloomington, Ill.: Public School Publication Company, 1940.

Tsujioka, B., & Cattell, R. B. A cross cultural comparison of second stratum questionnaire personality factor structures in anxiety and extraversion, in America and Japan. *British Journal of Social and Clinical Psychology,* 1965, *4,* 287–297.

Tsushima, Y. Failure stress in examinations related to anxiety factor scores. Unpublished M.A. thesis, University of Illinois, Urbana, 1957.

Tucker, L. R. Some mathematical notes on three-mode factor analysis. *Psychometrika,* 1966, *31,* 279–311.

Tuddenham, R. D. Soldier intelligence in World Wars I and II. *American Psychologist,* 1948, *3,* 54–56.

Underwood, B. J. *Experimental psychology.* 2nd Ed. New York: Appleton-Century-Crofts, 1966.

Undheim, J. D. Ability structure in 10–11 year old children and the theory of fluid and crystallized intelligence. *Journal of Educational Psychology,* 1976, *68,* 411–423.

Vandenberg, S. G. The primary mental abilities of Chinese students: A comparative study of the stability of a factor structure. *Annals of the New York Academy of Science,* 1959, *79,* 257–304.

Vandenberg, S. G. The hereditary abilities study: Hereditary components in a psychological test battery. *American Journal of Human Genetics,* 1962, *14,* 220–237.

Vandenberg, S. G. The primary mental abilities of South American students: a second comparative study of the generality of a cognitive factor structure. *Multivariate Behavioral Research,* 1967, *2,* 175–198.

Vandenberg, S. G. Assortive mating, or who marries whom? *Behavior Genetics,* 1972, *2,* 127–157.

Vandenberg, S. G. Second order factors—fluid and crystallized abilities, etc.—among primary abilities (In press) 1980.

Van den Daele, L. F. Infrastructure and transition in developmental analysis. Educational Testing Service, No. RB-73-49. Princeton, N.J., 1973.

Van Egeren, L. F. Experimental determination by P-technique of functional unities of depression and other psychological states. Unpublished M.A. thesis, University of Illinois, 1963.

Van Egeren, L. F. Multivariate research on the psychoses. In Cattell, R. B., & Dreger, R. M. (Eds.), *Handbook of modern personality theory.* Pp. 653–674. New York: Hemisphere, 1977.

Vaughan, D. S. *A test of Cattell's structured learning theory.* M.A. thesis, University of Illinois Library, University of Illinois, Urbana, Ill., 1971.

Vaughan D. S., & Cattell, R. B. The search for common personality factors in questionnaire and objective test media. Advanced publication No. 63. Laboratory of personality and Group Behavior, 1973.

Vaughan, G. M. Personality and small group behavior. In Cattell, R. B., & Dreger, R. M. (Eds.), *Handbook of modern personality theory*. Chapter 21. New York: Hemisphere, 1977.

Vernon, P. E. *Intelligence and cultural environment*. London: Methuen, 1969.

Von Foerster, H., & Zopf, G. W. *Principles of self organization*. New York: Macmillan, 1962.

Von Neumann, J. The general and logical theory of automata. In Jeffress, L. A. (Ed.), *Cerebral mechanisms in behavior*. Pp. 68–85. New York: Wiley, 1955.

Vygotski, L. S. The problem of the cultural development of the child. *Journal of Genetic Psychology*, 1929, *36*, 415–434.

Vygotsky, L. S. *Thought and language*. New York: Wiley, 1962.

Waddington, C. H. *The strategy of the genes*. London: Macmillan, 1957.

Waddington, C. H. New patterns in genetics and development. New York: Columbia University Press, 1962.

Walker, E. L., & Tarte, R. D. Memory storage as a function of time, with homogeneous and heterogeneous lists. *Journal of Verbal Learning and Verbal Behavior*, 1963, *2*, 113–119.

Walter, W. G. Effects on anterior brain responses of an expected association between stimuli. *Journal Psychosomatic Research*, 1963, *10*, 1–18.

Walter, W. G. et al. Contingent negative variation: An elective sign of sensorimotor association and expectancy in the human brain. *Nature* (London), 1964, *203*, 300–304.

Wardell, D., & Yeudall, T. *A multidimensional approach to forensic disorders. 1. The factor analysis*. Edmonton, Alberta: Department of Neuro-Psychology, Alberta Hospital, 1976.

Warden, C. J. *Animal motivation studies: The albino rat*. New York: Columbia University Press, 1931.

Waters, L.R., Roach, D., & Batlis, N. Organizational climate dimensions and job-related attitudes. *Personnel Psychology*, 1974, *27*, 465–476.

Watson, D. L., & Tharp, R. G. *Self-directed behavior and self modification of personal adjustment*. New York: Wadsworth, 1972.

Watson, J. B. *Behavior: an introduction to comparative psychology*. New York: Holt, Rinehart and Winston, 1914.

Webb, W. B. Drive stimuli as cues. *Psychological Review*, 1955, *1*, 287–298.

Weckowicz, T. E., Cropley, A., & Muir, W. An attempt to replicate the results of a factor analytic study in depressed patients. *Journal of Clinical Psychology*, 1971, *27*, 30–31.

Wedding, D. A comparison of meditation and progressive relaxation in the treatment of anxiety in college students. M.A. thesis, University of Hawaii Library, Honolulu, 1977.

Weiner, B. Effects of motivation on the availability and retrieval of memory traces. *Psychological Bulletin*, 1966, *65*, 24–37.

Weir, M. Developmental changes in problem solving strategies. *Psychological Review*, 1964, *71*, 473–491.

Weiss, P. A. (Ed.), *Hierarchically organized systems in theory and practice*. New York: Hofner, 1971.

Weizmann, F. Learning theory, personality and the S-R paradigm. In Cattell, R. B., & Dreger, R. M. (Eds.), *Handbook of modern personality theory*. Pp. 377–388. New York: Hemisphere, 1977.

Wenger, M. G. Inter-relations among some physiological variables. *Psychological Bulletin*, 1940, *37*, 466-476.

Wenig, P. The relative roles of naive, autistic, cognitive and press compatibility misperception and ego defense operations in tests on misperception. Unpublished M.A. thesis, University of Illinois at Urbana, 1952.

Wertheimer, M. *Productive Thinking*. New York: Harpers, 1959.

Wessman, A. E., & Ricks, D. F. *Mood and personality*. New York: Holt, Rinehart & Winston, 1966.

Weyl, N. Some possible genetic implications of Carthaginian child sacrifice. In Bresler, (Ed.), *Genetics and Society*. New York, 1973.

Weyl, N. The geography of stupidity in the U.S.A. *Mankind Quarterly*, 1975, *15*, 117-123.

Wherry, R. J. Determination of the specific components of maze ability for Tryon's bright and dull rats by factorial analysis. *Journal of Comparative Psychology*, 1941, *32*, 237-252.

Wickelgren, W. The long and the short memory. *Psychological Bulletin*, 1973, *80*, 425-438.

Wickens, D. D., & Snide, J. D. The influence of non-reinforcement of a complex stimulus on resistance to extinction of the complex itself. *Journal of Experimental Psychology*, 1955, *49*, 257-259.

Wickens, D. D., & Wickens, C. D. Some factors relating to pseudo-conditioning. *Journal of Experimental Psychology*, 1942, *31*, 518-526.

Wiener, N. Time, communication, and the nervous system. Annals of the New York Academy of Sciences, 1948(a), *50 (4)*, 197-220.

Wiener, N. *Cybernetics*. New York: Wiley, 1948(b).

Wiggins, J. S. *Personality and prediction: Principles of personality assessment*. London: Addison Wesley, 1973.

Williams, J. R. *The definition and measurement of conflict in terms of P-technique: A test of validity*. Unpublished Ph.D. thesis, University of Illinois at Urbana, 1958.

Williams, J. R. A test of the validity of the P-technique in the measurement of internal conflict. *Journal of Personality*, 1959, *27*, 418-437.

Wilson, E. O. *Sociobiology*. Cambridge, Mass.: Belknap, Harvard University Press, 1975.

Wohlwill, J. F. The emerging discipline of environmental psychology. *American Psychologist*, 1970, *303*, 25.

Wolfe, J. B., & Kaplon, M. D. Effect of amount of reward and consummative activity on learning in chickens. *Journal of Comparative and Physiological Psychology*, 1941, *31*, 353-361.

Woodfield, A. *Teleology*. Cambridge University Press, 1976.

Wright, S. The interpretation of multivariate systems. In Kempthorne, O., et al. (Eds.), Statistics and mathematics in biology. Pp. 120-147. Ames: Iowa State College Press, 1954.

Wylie, R. C. *The self concept: A critical survey of pertinent research literature*. Lincoln: University of Nebraska Press, 1961.

Wynne, J. D., & Brogden, W. J. Effect upon sensory pre-conditioning of backward, forward and trace pre-conditioning training. *Journal of Experimental Psychology*, 1962, *64*, 422-423.

Yamaguchi, H. G. Drive (D) as a function of hours of hunger (h). *Journal of Experimental Psychology*, 1951, *42*, 108-186.

Yerkes, R. M. Social behavior of chimpanzees. *Journal of Comparative Psychology*, 1940, *30*, 147-186.

Young, P. T. *Motivation and emotion*. New York: Wiley, 1961.

Zeaman, D. Response intensity as a function of the amount of reinforcement. *Journal of Experimental Psychology*, 1949, *39*, 446–483.

Zeaman, J., & Wegner, N. The role of drive reduction in the classical conditioning of an autonomically mediated response. *Journal of Experimental Psychology*, 1954, *48*, 349–354.

Zeeman, E. C. Catastrophe theory. *Scientific American*, 1976, *221*, 65–83.

Ach, N., 337, 390
Adams, J. A., 184, 269, 270
Adelson, M., 534, 536, 556
Aird, J., 5
Alcock, W. T., 231
Alker, R., 88, 534
Allport, G. W., xx, 75, 146, 365, 421
Amarel, S., 396
Ammons, R. B., 229
Anastasi, A. A., 245
Anderson, B. F., xxiv, 184, 282
Anderson, E. E., 245
Angermeier, W. F., 242, 371
Anokhin, P. K., ix, 242
Ardrey, R. A., 476, 505, 516
Arggle, M., 383
Aristotle, 7, 87
Arsenian, S., 524
Asch, S. E., 537
Ashem, B. A., 401
Ashley, M., 422
Atkinson, R. C., 154, 167, 222, 272, 285
Aveling, F. P., 87, 222, 390
Ayllon, T., 402
Azrin, T. H., 402

Backer, 113
Baddeley, A. D., 268
Baggaley, A. R., 124
Bain, A., 163
Bales, R. F., 490
Ballard, P. B., 236
Baltes, P. B., 158, 380, 544, 560
Bandura, A., 166, 182, 218, 370, 371, 402
Barlow, J. A., 182, 184
Barron, F., 237

Bartlett, H. W., 288
Barton, K., xxiv, 34, 36, 85, 92, 140, 200, 237, 261, 263, 288, 289, 295, 296, 305, 360, 362, 372
Bartsch, T. W., 85, 349, 362
Barelas, A., 491
Beck, A., 416
Beloff, H., 13, 21, 25, 28, 49, 139
Berg, I., xxiii
Berlyne, D. E., 289
Bertalanffy, L. von, 219, 422, 431
Beveridge, W., 237
Birkett, H., xxii, 99, 131, 132, 199, 237, 261, 262, 289, 295, 305, 336, 355, 373, 380, 390, 393, 419, 459
Bitterman, M. E., 184, 315, 232, 233, 239
Bjersted, A., 146, 400
Blacker, C. P., 3
Blain, D., xxii
Blakeslee, A. T., 3
Blalock, H. M., 440
Blau, T., 565
Bleuler, M., 3
Blewett, D. B., 13, 21, 25, 28, 49, 139
Blodgett, H. C., 231, 243, 287
Bodmer, W. F., 41, 509
Bogoslovski, A. I., 218
Bolitho, W., 372
Bolles, R. C., 242
Bolz, C., xxv, 5
Borgatta, E. G., 466, 491
Boulding, K. E., 483, 484, 500, 519, 552, 553, 577, 587
Bower, G. H., 182, 184, 230, 236, 271, 280
Brackenridge, C., 5

Brahe, T., xiii
Brams, S. J., 486
Brennan, J., 416, 419
Brentano, F., x
Breul, H., 467, 486, 525, 535
Broadbent, D. E., 231, 268, 269
Broadhurst, P. S., 4, 52
Broca, P., 49
Brogden, W. J., 166, 223, 225
Brookover, W. B., 136
Brown, W., 540
Bruce, H. M., 555
Brunswik, E., 199
Buerle, W., 422
Burdsal, C. A. Jr., 136
Burke, C. J., 167, 222, 272
Burt, C. L., 31, 46, 52, 135, 545, 557
Buss, A. R., 396, 422, 431, 458
Butcher, J., xxiv, 175, 237, 315, 361, 362, 388, 413, 506, 532

Calhoun, J. B., 555, 556
Campbell, B. A., 228
Cannon, W. B., 412
Capaldi, H., 428
Carlton, P. L., 230
Carpenter, C. R., 505
Carroll, D. G., 349
Cartwright, C. F., 305, 306
Cartwright, D. S., xxiv, 305, 306
Cattell, A. K. S., 262
Cavalli-Sforza, L. H., 4, 41, 509, 557
Chadwick, R. W., 486, 534
Chein, I., 71
Child, D., 63, 65, 85, 92, 103, 117, 118, 133, 137, 175, 191, 194, 200, 245, 250, 261, 263, 306, 324, 336, 364, 371, 373, 388, 427, 505
Christian, J. J., 556
Clemans, W. V., 342, 343
Coan, R. W., 72, 145
Cohen, M. R., 305
Collins, A. M., 336
Conrad, H. S., 559
Cottrell, L. S., 466, 491
Covington, R., 4
Craighead, W. E., 458
Crespi, L. P., 228, 232, 234, 243, 287
Cronbach, L. J., 166, 534, 535

Cross, K. P., 336
Crossen, W., 422
Curran, J. P., 262, 288, 289, 408, 414, 415, 418, 419

D'Amato, M. R. 223, 236
Darlington, C. D., 4, 508, 509, 533, 545, 557
Darwin, C., 178, 247
Das, R. S., 145, 394
Davison, G. C., 403
Deese, J., 161, 175, 243
DeFries, J., 4, 41, 52
Delhees, K., 263
Denny, M. R., 228
Deutsch, M., 486, 534
DeYoung, G. E., 88, 200, 261, 263, 289
Dielman, T. E., xxiv, 4, 65, 85, 174, 245, 246, 282, 362, 372
Digman, J., 132
Dodson, A., 413
Donaldson, G., 560
Dreger, R. M., xxiii, 420
Duffy, E., 262, 289
Dulaney, D. E., 229

Eaves, L. J., 41
Eber, H. W., 133, 136, 140, 154, 199, 248, 300, 361, 362, 380, 382, 398, 494, 521, 524, 527, 543, 544
Ebbinghaus, H., 218
Eccles, J. C., 422
Edwards, A. L., 502
Egger, M. D., 184, 223
Ehrlich, P. R., 555
Einstein, A., 219
Elliot, M. H., 243
Ellis, R., 371, 380
Ervic, F. R., 396
Estes, W. K., 163, 166, 167, 222, 272, 285, 287
Eysenck, H. J., xii, xvii, xviii, xxi, 146, 175, 199, 237, 270, 305, 413, 458, 543, 548
Eysenck, S. B. G., 146

Fahrenberg, J., 220
Fairweather, Y. W., 552, 553
Falconer, D. S., 4, 52
Feigenbaum, E. A., 422

Feldman, J., 422
Ferster, C. B., 230
Festinger, L., 72, 145
Fiedler, F., 541
Finch, F. H., 545, 560
Finkbeiner, C., 133, 369, 502
Fischbein, M., 71, 72, 148
Fisher, R. A., xxi, 27, 52, 508, 509
Fleishman, E. A., 199, 295
Fonda, C. F., 98
Forgus, R. H., 192
Fowler, H., 231
Fox, A. L., 3
Frankmann, J. B., 222
Fredericksen, N., 491
Freeman, G. L., 412
Frenkel-Brunswik, E., 237
Freud, A., 130, 397, 400
Freud, S., xxi, 64, 75, 106, 112, 127,
    246, 361, 378, 381, 400, 408,
    409, 410, 426, 472
Fried, J., 524
Friedman, W. F., 180, 356
Fulker, D. W., 13, 21, 31, 32, 38, 52
Fuller, J. L., 4, 174

Gage, N. L., 534
Gagné, R. M., 349
Galanter, E., 322
Galen, 7
Galileo, G., xxiv
Galton, F., ix, x
Gantt, W. H., 242
Garcia, J., 396
Gates, R., 396
Geer, J. H., 387
George, F. H., 422
Gerard, J., 422
Gerardin, R., 422
Gibb, C. A., 466, 467, 534, 536, 541,
    556
Gibbon, E., 524
Gleser, G. S., 535
Goldfried, M. R., 377
Goodman, J., 392
Gorsuch, R. L., 50, 132, 147, 200,
    361, 362, 556
Gottesman, I. I., 14
Gottlieb, D., 136
Graham, R. K., 467, 469, 479, 484,
    525, 526, 553, 557
Grice, G. R., 215, 230

Grindley, G. C., 229
Grindley, J., 261
Gruenberg, M. M., 268
Guetzkow, H., 486, 537, 541
Guilford, xii, 175
Guthrie, E. R., 163, 164, 166, 167,
    272, 287, 401
Guttman, G., 186, 220

Hakstian, A. R., 268, 380, 385, 436,
    517
Haldane, J. B. S., 52
Hall, C. S., 4, 65
Hall, S., 365, 372
Hammer, A. G., 200, 296
Hardin, G., 500
Harker, G. S., 231
Harlow, H. F., 70, 102, 103
Harris, C. W., 322
Harris, E. L., 322
Hartman, H. P., 467, 486, 525, 535
Harvey, W., xxiv
Haverland, E. M., xxiv, 245, 282
Hawkins, G., 5
Haythorne, W., 466
Hebb, D. O., 422, 445
Helson, H., xviii
Hempel, W. E., 199
Hemphill, J. K., 466
Hendricks, B. C., 199, 203, 295
Hernandez-Peon, R., 280
Herrnstein, R. J., 236, 241
Herton, W.,W., 166
Hess, E. H., 5, 8, 98, 102, 192
Hey, J., 92
Heyer, A. W., 277
Higgins, J. V., 23, 545
Hilgard, E. R., 182, 184, 230, 236,
    287
Hinde, R. A., 286
Hirsch, J.,, 42
Hobbes, T., 476, 505, 506
Horn, J. L., xxii, 65, 85, 88, 92, 99,
    107, 119, 124, 131, 132, 136,
    147, 158, 206, 268, 318, 356,
    361, 362, 376, 380, 385, 445,
    544, 560
Horst, P., 200, 296
Howard, K., 31, 46, 52, 518
Hudson, W. W., xxi
Hull, C. L., ix, 93, 112, 125, 150,
    163, 165, 175, 189, 228, 231,

233, 235, 241, 253, 254, 257, 282, 287
Hulse, S. H., 161, 175, 243
Hume, D., 222
Hundleby, J., 5, 72, 145, 175, 271, 349, 387, 500
Hunt, J. McV., 146, 200
Huntington, E., 3, 4, 544, 548, 587
Huxley, J., 524, 557

Inhelder, B., 371
Irwin, D. A., 186, 220
Iverson, I. H., 166

Jackson, P. C., 422
James, W., xxi, 146, 328, 369, 377, 407, 426
Jensen, A. R., 36, 268, 548, 581
Jinks, J. L., 13, 21, 31, 32, 52
Johnson, C. F., 269
Johnson, D. M., 263, 441
Johnson, R. C., 263, 392, 441
Johnson, S., 3
Jones, H. E., 559
Jung, C., 64, 193, 259, 260, 369, 385, 426, 457, 515, 516

Kallmann, T. J., 3
Kameoka, V., 419
Kamin, R. J., 230
Kanfer, F. H., 400
Kaplan, M. D., 229
Karson, S., 140, 305, 362
Katzoff, E. T., 412
Kawash, G. F., 200, 263
Kazdin, A. E., 458
Kelley, H. P., 268, 380, 385, 436
Kelly, E. L., 509
Kempthorne, O., 41
Kendall, D. G., 490
Kendler, H. H., 226
Kepler, J., xiii
Kessler, F. M., 555
Kety, S. S., 14
Kimble, G. A., 98, 164, 215, 287
King, G. F., 228
King, R. C., 52
Klein, T., 13, 16, 21, 28, 49, 57, 139, 524
Kleinrock, L., 80, 84, 490
Kline, P., 261, 306

Klir, G. J., 422
Knott, J. R., 186
Koch, S., 228
Koelling, R. A., 396
Kohlberg, L., 363
Kohler, W., 218
Konorski, J., 223
Korth, B., xxv, 5, 174, 245
Kraeling, D., 228
Kretschmer, E., 5
Kristy, N., 13, 21, 28, 49
Krug, S., E., xxii, 129, 199, 237, 261, 262, 263, 289, 305, 415
Kubala, A, L., 184, 232
Kuhn, T. S., xxiii, 237, 238
Kulpe, x, 337
Kupers, C. J., 402

Labouvie, E. W., 396
Lacey, M., 288, 289
Lange, J., 407
Lashley, K. S., 445
Laszlo, W., 422, 431
Laughlin, J., 122, 123, 154, 199, 295, 419
Lawlis, G. F., 65, 73, 117, 118, 119, 508
Lazarus, R. S., 98, 140
Lebo, M. A., 419
Leighton, 524
Lemke, E. A., 322
Lentz, T. F., 545
Leontiv, A. N., 185
Leonard, K., 428
Lerner, I. S., 52
Levine, R., 71
Lewin, K., 353
Leyhausen, G., 102
Li, C. C., 4, 52, 56
Liebent, G., 402
Lindzey, G., 5, 52, 57, 65, 241
Linnaeus, K., 178
Little, B. R., 383
Loehlin, J. C., 5, 13, 39, 41, 46, 50, 52, 56, 57, 423
Loevinger, J., 371
Logan, F. A., 229, 230
Lorenz, C., 94, 102
Lorge, I., 230
Lucas, G., 422
Luria, A. R., 185, 392

Lynn, R., 382, 411, 469, 470, 507, 527, 528, 533, 545, 581

MacCorquodale, K., 68, 177, 194, 226, 232
Mach, E., x
MacKay, D. M., 422, 431, 528
MacKintosh, N. J., 172, 182, 215, 223, 225, 232, 236, 243, 249, 396, 428
MacLeish, J., 534
Madsen, K. B., xix
Mahrer, A. R., 305
Malecot, G., 52
Malmo, R. B., 262, 288
Mark, A. L., 263, 441
Marquis, D. G., 182
Marsella, A., 524
Maslow, A. H., 505
Mather, K., 31, 52
Matheson, W., 534
Maxwell, J., 528, 545
May, D. R., 414, 457
May, J. M., 131, 414
McAdam, D. W., 220
McClearn, G. E., 4, 41, 52
McClelland, D. C., 154
McCulloch, J., 422
McDougall, W., 94, 136, 146, 328, 353, 368, 369, 426, 444, 457, 505, 557
McFarlane, R., 383
McGill, J., 6, 73, 117, 118, 119
McGrath, P., 65
McGraw, T. C., 65, 73, 117, 118, 119
McKeen, J., x
McKusick, V.,A., 4
McNemar, Q., 54
Mead, M., 102, 472, 517, 524, 527
Meehl, P., 176, 194, 226, 232
Meichenbaum, D. H., 392
Meinong, H., 337
Merbaum, M., 377
Messick, S., 349, 353
Meyer, H. I., 491
Miles, C. C., 559
Mill, J. S., 163, 222
Miller, J. Y., 322, 422, 423
Miller, N. E., 163, 184, 223, 253, 254, 287
Mischel, W., 402

Mitchell, H., xxiv
Molteno, E. V., 5
Monteiro, J., 271
Morgan, C. L., xix, 163, 164, 184, 537
Morrell, F., 218
Morse, W. H., 236
Morton, N. E., 35, 52, 56, 57, 80, 440
Mowrer, O. H., ix, 162, 166, 176, 184, 207, 229, 230, 233, 241, 250, 257, 287, 288, 367, 412
Muktananda, B., 193
Murphy, G., 71
Murray, H. A., 66
Myrdal, G., 525

Nabergill, R. E., 71
Nanda, H., 535
Napalkov, A. V., 69
Nesselroade, J. R., xxii, xvii, 32, 34, 36, 37, 55, 85, 262, 288, 289, 349, 396, 416, 419, 509
Newton, xiii, 29
Nissen, G., 186
Noble, C. E., 231
Nunnally, J., 535

O'Dell, J. W., 140, 362
O'Kelly, L. I., 277
Olds, J., 243, 288, 289, 422
Oppenheimer, R., 574, 588
Overmeier, J. B., 166

Park, J., 534
Parker, J. B., 5, 524
Pasteur, L., xxiv
Patrick, S. V., 415
Pavlov, I. P., ix, x, 64, 67, 87, 120, 160 160, 163, 164, 168, 170, 175, 181, 185, 215, 226, 235, 242, 287, 293
Pawlik, K., 72, 145, 175, 271, 349, 376, 387, 400, 527
Penman, A. S., 535
Perin, C. T., 230
Perkins, C. C. J., 182
Perloff, B., 402
Pervin, L. A., 65
Phillips, J. S., 400
Piaget, J., 86, 352, 357, 371
Pierson, G. R., 92, 133, 369, 502

Platt, R., 422
Poser, E. G., 401
Premack, D., 242
Pribram, K. H., 322, 422
Price, P. L., 415
Purkey, W. W., 136

Quillian, M. R., 336

Rachman, S., 237, 458
Radcliffe, J., 65, 71, 92, 119, 124,
    131, 356
Rajaratnam, N., 535
Rao, D. C., 35, 52, 56, 57, 440
Rapoport, A., 400, 422
Rashevsky, R., 422
Razran, G., 166, 184
Read, W., 524
Reed, P. C., 184, 232
Reed, S. C., 23, 545
Reed, S. W., 23, 545
Reese, H. W., 55, 396
Reid, J., 163
Rescoria, R. A., 184, 232, 241, 243
Rican, P., 245
Ricardo, D., 498
Richardson, L., 478
Rickels, K., 146, 199, 200, 237, 403,
    408
Ricks, D. F., 415
Riegel, K. F., 561
Riordan, J., 490
Rips, L. J., 336
Roby, T. B., 113, 466
Rogers, C. R., 136
Rokeach, M., 72
Rosenblueth, J. E., 412
Rosenthal, D., 3, 14
Ross, J., 201
Rotter, J. B., 72
Rousseau, J. J., 476
Royce, J. R., xii, 4, 41, 174, 245,
    282, 349, 353, 396, 407, 422,
    431, 458
Ruggles-Gates, A., 3
Rummell, R. J., 356, 467, 471, 479,
    481, 486, 498, 525, 534, 535
Rundquist, E.,E., 4
Russell, B., x, 486

Saltzman, I. J., 69, 228

Sarason, S. B., 409, 413
Saunders, D. R., 466
Saville, P., 527
Sawyer, J., 486
Sayre, M., 422
Schacter, S., 378, 454
Schaie, K. W., 158, 380, 544, 560
Scheier, J. H., xviii, 146, 262, 288,
    306, 387, 408, 409, 411, 412,
    414, 518
Schlosberg, J., 163, 165
Schmidt, L. R., 146, 400, 527
Schneewind, K. R., 245
Schuerger, J., 13, 16, 21, 28, 50, 57,
    58, 287, 380, 393, 544, 559,
    560
Schwartz, S. A., 136
Scott, J. P., 4, 174
Scriven, M., 422
Seidel, R. J., 182, 218
Sweard, J. P., 228
Shannon, C. C., 422, 426, 490
Sheffield, F. D., 113, 120, 163, 218
Sheldon, W. H., 5
Sherif, C. W., 71
Sherif, M., 71
Sherman, J., 336
Shields, J., 14
Shohen, E. J., 336
Shotwell, A., 289
Sigurdson, J., xxii, 172
Simmel, G., 486, 541
Sine, L., xxii
Singer, J. D., 378, 454, 486, 534
Sjoberg, L., 198
Skinner, B. F., ix, x, 64, 68, 86, 161,
    163, 178, 194, 215, 219, 230,
    236, 265, 287, 288, 292, 302,
    314, 391, 401
Slater, E., 3
Smith, E. E., 336
Smith, St. C., 223
Smuts, J., 421
Solomon, R. C., 232, 241, 242
Sorokin, P., 483, 552, 553, 577
Spearman, C. E., ix, x, 47, 218, 222,
    237, 380, 426, 445, 540, 542
Spence, K. W., ix, 165, 176, 215, 229,
    230, 287, 408, 412, 416
Spencer, H., viii
Spielberger, C. B., 5, 289, 409, 416

Spuhler, J. N., 5, 52, 57
Staats, A. W., 87, 164, 207, 232, 257, 264, 265, 371
Stevens, S. S., 5
Stice, G. F., 13, 21, 28, 49, 466, 490, 494, 540
Stogdill, R. M., 466, 491
Stricker, L. J., 503
Strother, C. R., 560
Studman, L. G., 262
Sturtevant, A. H., 3, 4
Sutherland, H. E. G., 545
Swan, D. A., 5
Sweney, A. B., xxii, 65, 71, 85, 92, 99, 107, 119, 122, 124, 129, 131, 132, 250, 295, 315, 356, 386, 414, 508, 519

Tarte, R. D., 269
Tatro, D. F., 146, 379, 380
Tatsuoka, M., 133, 136, 140, 155, 248, 300, 361, 362, 380, 382, 398, 494, 521, 524, 527, 543, 544
Taylor, C. W., 237, 416
Teasdale, F., 458
Terman, L., 396
Thayer, R. E., 261
Thompson, W. R., 4, 41
Thomson, G. H., 545
Thorndike, E. L., 164, 165, 223, 228, 230, 233, 237, 241, 244, 287, 527, 540, 548
Thurstone, L. L., ix, 49, 86, 380, 436, 517
Tinbergen, N., 94
Titchener, E. B., x, 337
Toffler, A., 519, 555
Tolman, E. C., ix, 68, 163, 164, 176, 184, 226, 232, 233, 257, 287, 288
Tombaugh, M., 428
Toynbee, A. J., 478, 484, 587
Trappold, M. A., 166, 231
Tryon, R. C., 4, 174, 245
Tsujioka, B., 527
Tsushima, Y., 416
Tucker, L. R., 216, 246, 342
Tuddenham, R. D., 545, 560

Underwood, B. J., 164, 218, 230
Undheim, J. D., 206, 527

Valens, S., 403
Vandenberg, S. G., 41, 46, 49, 50, 509, 527
Van Egeren, L. F., 288, 305, 416
Vaughan, G. M., 200, 295
Verbeck, K., 422
Vigotsky, L. S., 371
Vogelmann, S., 502
von Foerster, H., 422
von Neumann, J., 422, 426

Waddington, C. H., 4, 52
Wagner, A. R., 230
Walker, E. L., 269
Walter, W. G., 186, 371
Warburton, F. W., xvii, 36, 38, 145, 154, 154, 316, 349, 353, 356
Wardell, D., 368
Warden, C. J., 120, 249
Warrington, E. K., 268
Watson, D. L., x, xxiii, 95, 158, 163, 215, 516
Weaver, W., 490
Weckowitz, T. E., 416
Wedding, D., 416, 419
Weiner, B., 98, 277
Weir, M., 380
Weiss, P. A., 396
Wells, H. G., 219
Wenger, M. G., 409
Wenig, P., 130, 400
Wetheimer, M., 421
Wessman, A. E., 415
Weste, C. M., 466
Weyl, N., 548, 554
Wherry, R. J., 199, 295
Wickelgren, W., 269
Wickens, C. D., 215
Wickens, D. D., 215
Wiener, N., 422, 423, 459, 487, 490
Wiggins, J. S., 305, 502
Williams, J. R., 128, 144, 336
Wilson, E. O., 94, 102, 458, 505, 515, 555
Wispe, L. G., 466, 535
Witkin, H. A., xviii
Wolfe, J. B., 229
Woliver, R. E., 382, 467, 469, 470, 479, 484, 486, 525, 526, 529, 532, 534, 535, 553
Woodfield, A., 68

Woodworth, x, xxiii, 407
Woodyard, E., 527
Wright, S., 52, 80
Wulff, J., 113
Wundt, W., ix, x, 407
Wylie, R. C., 136
Wynne, J. D., 223, 225, 242

Yee, S., 35, 56, 57, 440
Yerkes, R. M., 4, 413
Yeudall, T., 368
Yoon, G. H. Y., 261
Young, P. T., 5, 253, 254

Zeaman, D., 228, 232

Activation
  distinguished from arousal, 163,
    263
  in engram formation, 321
  formula for rate of activation, 263
  general and structurally specific,
    204
  as a general state, 417
  relation to cortertia as a trait, 262
Adaptation
  in adjustment process analysis, xxv
  distinguished from adjustment, 247
  and inhibition, 247
  and integration learning, 247
Adjustment
  and conflict frustration, 250
  distinguished from adaptation, 247
  and integration learning, 247
Adjustment process analysis (APA)
  anxiety in (Chiasm 5), 307
  APA chart for analyzing *any* dyna-
    mic root, 308
  APA chart, determiner-potency
    matrix, 210
  and depression, 417
  frustration in (Chiasm 2), 307
  and inhibition, 250
  learning path potency for single
    trait, 311
  in learning texts, xxv
  path determiners for given trait,
    310
  pugnacity in (Chiasm 3), 307
Aging: life span change
  cross sectional and cursive analyses
    of, 560
  epogenic curves, 561
  erogenous and endogenous curves,
    563

Ambient situation, as term in speci-
    fication, xxiii
Anxiety
  action as a general state, 407
  correlation with depression, 419
  disturbance of cognition, 413
  fear of control loss, 410
  formulae for origin of, 412
  and motivation, 418
  relation to dynamic traits, 407
  relation to measured conflict, 420
  situation of deprivation, 409, 411
Arousal
  as a general state, 417
  in means-end learning, 257
  relation to activation, 163, 202
  of specific ergs, 101
Assortive mating correlations
  as genetic r related to σ^2_{wg}, 31
  of husbands and wives, 37
  and social range of traits, 509
  and social status, 508
Attitudes
  attitude chains, determination of
    sequences, 278
  dimensions of, 72, 148
  dissection from hierarchy, 70
  distinction from polling attitude, 71
  "evoked" type from nodes, 83
  toward group belonging, 475
  as integral calculus derivates from
    reflex actions, 350
  "serving" type to nodes, 83
  stability of, 60
  in stimulus response terms, 71
  in subsidiations, 67
  summation of attitude vectors, 108
  taxonomy of, 291, 356
  as unit in dynamic analysis, 291

Aversive drives
  or aversive behavior?, 239
  and learning, 253

Behavioral sink
  and cultural pressure, 556
  features of, 556
Behavior change, four origins of, 157, 159
Behavior genetics research, strategy in, 60
Behavioral indices
  changes in, related to trait change, 206
  splitting into four varieties, 200
Behaviorism, correct and incorrect use of term, 168
Bivariate methods, limitations in personality research, 459
Blocking, reflexological concept in coexcitation setting, 223, 236

Chain reflex, its distinction from tract in dynamic lattice, 327
Chiasms, as six choice points in APA, 307
Coexcitation, *CE*
  cognitive and dynamic components, 217
  essence of action deferred, 185
  as a foundation for *ME* action, 222
  four possible forms of, 183
  objection to strong immediate effect of, 185, 221
  in perspective of specification equation, 275
  relation to *CR*I, 281
  relation to neural events, 225
  role of contiguity in, 219
  role of education in, 210
  and sentiment formation, 226
  varieties of directional quality, 224
Cognitive activation
  as basis of dynamic control, 385
  relation to repression, 387
  relation to *U* and *I* components, 387
Cognitive structure
  as basis of control, 449
  importance in *CET*, 391, 449
  not only in engrams, 74

Common Schedule learning, and sentiment formations, 314
Comparative MAVA (CMVE)
  light of on threptic-environmental correlations, 53, 55
  revelation of, of genetic component in a trait in one individual, 54
Concept definitions on bivariate and multivariate basis, xvi, xvii
Conflict
  in active form, 121, 122, 124
  calculation of, 124, 125, 128
  definition, 120
  in indurated form, 121
  relation to clinical data, 131
  relation to *U* and *I*, 131
Controlling structures
  comparison of *C*, *G*, and Q_3, 360
  and the general states, 418
  in personality, 359
  the superego, *G*, 360
  in the VIDAS model, 433
Correlations and covariances
  causal inference in dynamics, 453
  list of possible *r*'s in families, 23
Coercion to the biosocial norm
  evidence for, 521
  stress in, 522
Covariance and interaction distinguished, 9
*CR*I: Classical conditioning
  incorporation in structured learning theory, 237
  as Pavlovian paradigm, 161
  relation to contiguity and coexcitation, 163
*CR*II: Operant conditioning (*see* Means-end learning, *ME*)
  attempt to unite with *CR*I, 166
  incorporation in structured learning, 175, 237
  possibly false extensions, 161
  principles beyond *CR*II, 169
  reconceived as means-end learning, *ME*, 163
  separation of description and explanation of, 163
  as a Skinnerian paradigm, 161
Cross-cultural comparisons, translation problems, 585
Cue evocation of traits (*CET*)

its action in implementing decisions, 378, 383
its action in sensing needs, 378–379
CET as orchestra conduction, 389
equation as flunction of ego, 386, 390
equation for generation of cognitive evocators, 385
as form of self-directed stimulus control, 391
relation to repression, 387
relation to *U* and *I* components, 387
Culture
change in, 553
change and personality change, 565
dimensions of, 480
growth formulae for, 566
patterns of, 481
transmission agencies, 521
Cultural diffusion
the percolation range concept, 542
and social distribution properties, 542
Cultural learning and change, *see* group learning and change
Cultural pressure
factor pattern of, 470
personality relations of, 526
Cumulative learning and common schedule action, 320
Cybernetics and systems theory, 423

Decision, calculus of, 119
Defense mechanisms, identification of, 130
Deflection strain
cultural indices for, 531
problem of defining innate, 586
Depression
as general state pattern, 407
in the APA chart, 417
Determiner potency analysis
relation to ecometrics, 305
relation to PLA, 301
Determiner potency analysis (DPA) and learning laws, 302
Determinism
as a hypothesis or postulate in science, xix

ambiguous status of in "emergents," xix
Differential birth rate, effect on group intelligence, 547
Drive strength, defined re need strength, ergic tension, and arousal, 111
Drive reduction hypothesis
incorporation of in arousal and activation, 252
the paradox in, 255
of reward, 252
Drives and drive strength, *see* ergs and ergic tension
Dynamic calculus
and structured learning theory, xxiv
foundation of human learning, 63
incorporation of reflexology in, 246
Dynamic equivalents, in lattice, 84
Dynamic lattice
basis in reward stability, 74
dendritic form of, 77
distal and proximal parts, 75
end goals in subsidiations, 77
methods of investigating, 80
nodes in, 78
subgoals in subsidiations, 75
Dynamic structure, investigation of, 63

Ecometric situation, indices of, 302
Economics and psychology
ability supply and demand theory, 501
equilibria in price of goods, 499
equivalence of dynamic diversity, 497
marginal utility, 479
supply and demand and earnings, 503
Eduction, role of in coexcitation learning in humans, 220
Ego Structure, *C*
action in integration, 142
and attitude fluctuation, 394
CET action and *C* as a second order, 388
CET emphasizing cognitive panel, 389

Ego Structure *(cont.)*
  as a *(CET)* modifier of other senti-
    ment actions, 404
  and conflict, 394
  Cue evocation of traits in, 378
  and defense mechanisms, 400
  equation for "simple" ego action,
    383
  as factor in three media, 376
  four "panels" of action of, 378,
    395
  and general emotionality, 395
  growth, 402
  heritable component of, 377
  and inhibition, 249
  origins of, 140
  pervasiveness of loadings on be-
    havior, 390
  relation to control, UI(T)19,
    QVIII, 392
  relation to integration index, 145
  relation to intelligence, 145, 249,
    380
  relation of to T-data factors, 146
  relation to UI(T)16, 17, 19, 20, 23,
    26, 27, and 34, 392
  stages in panel action, 405–406
  summary on, 447
  summary of C's empirical relations,
    377
  two modes of control by, 449
Eidolon model in nature-nurture interactions, 47, 52
Energy-saving (Rest-seeking erg), as a
  principle in learning, 194
Engrams
  as acquired cognitive-dynamic
    structures, 93
  acquired as function of need
    arousal reduction, 267
  changes in, 204
  engram formation principles, 283
  formula for learning, 268
  persistence of, 285
  rate of acquisition, perviance, and
    other qualities, 244
  specificity of ergic investment in,
    243
  storage of and brain damage, 270
  unengrammed engrams as innate
    cognitive connections, 259

Engram storage, reservoir in VIDAS,
  432
Epistemology of social prediction
  four limitations to prediction,
    573
  possible limits of determinism, 574
Environmental support systems, reflex-
    ological conclusion thereon vitia-
    ted, 401
Ergic deflection strain
  defined, 524
  relation to long circuiting, 530
Ergic goal modification learning
  defined and illustrated, 192
  relative to deflection strain, 586
Experimental paradigms in $C R$I and
    $C R$II, their difference from ex-
    planatory principles, 209
Ergic modulation
  more than "emotional condition-
    ing," 206
  as s_{hk} indices, 196
Ergic tension
  and the hypothalamus, 260
  as need strength plus arousal, 256
  not measurable by one variable, 245
  related to progress to a goal, 255,
    266
Ergic investment of an engram
  calculation of, 104
  concept of, 92
  expression for, 99
  generator terms as ergic convokers,
    268
  as magnitude of a sentiment, 106
  as a vector, 108, 258
Ergic tension
  distinguished from need strength,
    94
  involved in cognitive recall, 98
  relation to need strength and
    arousal, 101
Ergs
  evidence for structures, xvi, and
    Vol. 1.
  absence of subfactors in, 276
  erg-engram interaction, 280
  and innate cognitive paths, 102,
    276
  "isomorphism" to evolutionary
    environment, 352

and Jungian archetypes, 102
manifold paths to, in lattice, 77
Evoked attitudes, at lattice nodes, 83
Experimental psychology, bivariate
form, and definitions, xviii
Extinction, related to *ME* principle,
234

Family, and sentiment tradition formation, 520
Family constellations, used in MAVA,
16
Feedback loops
between E and M terms, 443
and "runaway action," 444
in systems theory, 423
Field independence in perception, as
an expression of independence,
Five basic learning principles, possible
reduction of, 209
Five vector learning descriptive
as radical departure from
reflexology, 313
simultaneous measurement of behavioral index and trait
change in, 216
Five vector description of learning
change
defined analytically, 195
determination of values in, 201
matrix treatment of, 202
Functional autonomy
questioned, 75
in relation to superego, 365

General states
anxiety and depression, 409
depression, 418
and integrative action of ego, 414
proof of patterns, 407
regression, 417
role in the VIDAS model, 432
as secondaries, *T*-data, 415
Genetic-cultural gap, and deflection
strain, 580
Genic causes and genetic effects, 8
Genothreptic
causes of genothreptic correlations,
24-29, 33-37

correlations to be expected among
relatives, 31
list of correlations for families, 23
models of environmental interaction, 6
nonlinear correlations in, 24
rationale for possible correlations,
22
Goal modification learning, GM,
possible reduction of, 209
Groups
difference from personality in
factoring, 465
differing synergies of, 475
group predominance, 482
overlapping groups, 476
panels of syntality, structure, and
population, 576
pathology of aging in, 558
psychological definition of, 463,
575
relation of roles to structure, 578
subsidiations among, 486, 519
supply-demand equilibria among,
496
and systems theory, 559
types of, 479, 483
Group learning and change
equations for, 568
evolution and revolution in, 587
forms of, 533, 544
and historical observation, 535
and migration effects, 548
and personality change, 532, 565,
584
plots of syntality changes, 539
as population learning, 536
relation to *ME* learning, 537
slowness through reward distribution, 582
as structural change, 541
summary of varieties of, 582
Group organizations
internal structure of, 577
by taxonome, 480
types of, 479
varieties of, 577

Habituation
animal manipulative method, 4

Habituation *(cont.)*
  clinical-geneological method, 3
  convarkin methods, 5
  and *ME* learning, 234, 235
  parent-child relations, 29
  physical linkage method, 4
Heritability, *H*
  attempts to relate to genome, 45
  calculation of, 40
  for each of several personality fac-
    tors, 50, 58
  effect of environmental cultural
    range on, 43
  effect of population age and other
    properties on, 44
  models for (summary), 59
History
  differences of method, 584
  and social psychology, 584
  timelessness and, 588
Hydraulic model, 84, 163

Imitation of models, for ego and
  self-sentiment, 402
Individual conflicts, over group application, 587
Inherent growth agency, as sentiment
  producer, 314
Inhibition
  and integration learning, 247
  as Pavlovian concept, 235
  as reactive inhibition, 235
  related to *ME* learning, 236
Innate, distinction from congenital
  and inherited, 42
Integration, definition and calculation
  of, 129
Integration learning, *N*
  calculation of learning gain, 251
  defined, 190
  and intelligence, 249
  relation to adjustment and adapta-
    tion, 247
  relation to confluence learning, 190
Intelligent affluence
  as a cultural dimension, 471
  its personality associations, 525
Involvement index, *v*, as part of *b*,
  94
Involution, as part of volution, 158
Isomophism

of dynamic vectors at learning and
    retrieval, 280
  of sentiments institutions, 85

Kinetic, distinguished from dynamic,
  457

Law of emergence, never complete,
  581
Learning law matrix, solved by PLA,
  296
Leadership
  and group learning, 540
  as morale factor, 468
  personality profile of, 495
Learning of the ego structure
  acquisition of second panel, 397
  acquisition of third panel, 398
  adjusting exercise to control dif-
    ficulty, 397
  cognitive generalization of control,
    396
  heritable basis in impulse control,
    395
  through life experiences, 402
  reward to *C* by control, 399, 403
  trial and error quality in, 398
Learning as engramming
  basic formula in dynamic terms,
    273
  specification equation for, 284
  summary of processes in, 269
Learning score change
  difference of performance change
    from engram change, 214
  on personality factors: experimen-
    tal results, 200
Limboid activity
  computer models for, 277
  in short distance memory, 269
Logistics of applying knowledge, in-
    evitable lag in "prediction," xx
Long cicuiting of ergs, and dynamic
    complexity of culture, 530

Manipulative experiment, for investi-
    gating the lattice, 83
Maintenance synergy
  disproportion to effective synergy,
    558
  relation to intrinsic synergy, 579

Maturation
  as part of volution, 158
  relation to genetic factors, 58
MAVA (Multiple abstract variance
    analysis)
  as comparative MAVA, 53
  eleven equation, six constellation
    form, 18
  model with and without inter-
    action, 12
  rationale of equations for, 20
  summary of, 59
Means-end learning, *ME*
  arousal and reward in, 267
  definition of, 186–190
  ergic specificity of *ME* engrams,
    233
  modifying s_{hk} modulator, 207
  nine empirical evidences for four
    animal learning, 228
  reasons for preferring to *CR*II, 98,
    181
  relation to *CE* processes, 217, 232
  relation to drive shift and reward
    shift, 232
  relation to drive strength, 228
  relation to goal distance, 230
  relation to insight, 211
  relation to reflexology, 211
  relative role of trial and error and
    of insight, 292
  and sentiment formation, 321
Mental energy
  definition and measurement, 428
  persistence in psychological theory,
    426
  relation to MAT measures, 430
Modulator index, *s*, as part of *b*,
    94
Modalities of traits, objective basis
    for distinguishing three, 366
Modelling (*see also* Imitation), in
    life and literature, 453
Morale
  as congeniality, 469
  as leadership, 468
Morality
  decay of, 557
  relation to moral, 557
Motivation components, m.c.'s
  hypothetical relation to arousal,

activation, and need strength,
    117
  as seven primaries, 73
Motivation strength measurement,
    objective devices for, 64
Multivariate experiment, manipula-
    tive and nonmanipulative, xii

National cultures
  differences in intelligence among,
    529
  dimensions of, 480
Nature-nurture ratio, *N*
  calculation of, 39
Need strength
  in the drive reduction model, 253
  equation for, 113
  relation to drive strength and
    arousal, 283
Networks of communication
  and roles, 490
  and structure, 578
Nodes in lattice
  as sentiments, 83
  as subgoal-stimulus probability
    situation, 325

Operant conditioning *CR*II, synony-
    mous with means-end learning,
    ME, 98
Operationism, on multi- and bi-variate
    bases, xxiv
Overshadowing, as reflex learning idea,
    236

Panels of ego action
  halting, 405
  implementation of decision, 404,
    406
  scanning and retrieval, 406
  sensing, 405
P-technique
  cumulative for individual quanti-
    fied process matrix, 345
  chain, distinguished from *common*,
    357
Path coefficients, in investigation of
    threptic-genetic relations, 56
Path learning analysis (PLA)
  determiner constitution of path,
    305

Path learning analysis (PLA) *(cont.)*
  determiner constitution of path as ecometric construction, 305
  matrix represenation of, 296
  path experience matrix, 296–299
  path potency matrix, 299, 312
  with *P*-technique, 297
  regarding *p, r, i, s,* and *T* changes, 295
  relation to DPA, 351
Perception, in the VIDAS system, 436
Percolation range, and the action function in group learning, 542
Personality factor change
  by learning 200
  by modelling, 371
Physiological structure, check on behavioral structure, xxiii
Population characters
  difference between pristine and adjustive, 505
  and syntality change, 565
Population genetics and tracing *H*'s to genes, 52
Processes
  as multiple quantity or stochastic structure, 354
  relay action in, 340, 355
  similar in ergs and sentiments, 352
  structure of sentiment process, 331, 354
Punishment, basic meaning as deprivation, 240
Process analysis, to determine dynamic goals, 180

Random responses
  re Skinner's operants, 288
  true nature of, 286
Reflexological learning theory
  contrasted with information in five vector learning laws, 198
  some demolitions required for building, 242–245
  difference from general behaviorism x
  failure to account for rise of structure, 161
  failure to correlate learning gain measures, 246

frequency, spacing, regularity of reward in, 236
  methods related to concepts in, 172
  risky metaphorical extensions of, 215
  tenets of, 160
Reflexology as a model
  historical sign of exhaustion of, 238
  ignoring of drive specificity, 242
  misleading pedantry in, 239, 241
Regression,
  as de-cathestion in U.I.23
  as a general state, 417
Reinforcement, ambiguity of, 170
Relations of form of genetic
  genetic factors and single genes, 46
  genetic factors and multiple genes: eidolon model, 47
  the indepence model, 49
  and threptic factor patterns, 46
Reminiscence
  and *ME* learning, 234
  and retrieval, 268
Response proficiency index, *r*, and engram formation, 313
Retrieval (Recall)
  as action recall, 244
  and behavior reinstatement, 277
  dynamic roots of, 270
  equation for retrieval, with ego action, 383
  partial formula for, 263
Reverberation
  and activation-arousal, 264
  in reverberation-fixation action, 285, 312
  and short-distance memory, 269
Revolution
  and ergic deflection strain, 352
  and level of frustration, 555
  and temperament, 553
Reward
  and consummatory goal activities, 291
  effect in engramming, 267
Roles
  alternative definitions of, 487
  defined in tie matrix, 493

Scientific status of psychology, comparison of training with physical science and medicine, viii
Secondary drives, as superfluous concepts, 242
Secondary emotions, relation to derived, 457
Self concept, and self sentiment, 136
Self sentiment
    acquisition in learning, 368
    discrepancies from real self, 369
    motivational roots of, 138, 373
    in R-, dR-, and P-techniques, 132
    relation to ego and superego, 131, 360
    sources in social presses, 370, 372
    summary on, 447
    and values, 374
    and vicarious learning, 371
Sentiments
    ergic mandates of expressed, 100
    ergic mandates of as influence vectors, 258
    indispensable concepts in human emotional learning, 349
    isomorphism with institutions, 85
    in the lattice structure, 79
    origins in common learning schedule, 85, 314
    origins in common subsidiation, or budding, 88, 316
    origins in inherent growth agency, 86, 314
    phasic and direct growth in, 396
    relation of activation to engram, 101
    relation to Tolman's "cognitive map," 226
    research on acquisition of unfolding adaptive process, 346
    spread of activation in m's and M's, 227, 333, 336
    three processes in acquiring, 352
    as unfolding adaptive processes, 279, 322
Sentiment structure
    and learning texts, xvi
    demonstrated in dR activation, 163
    equation for engram formation, 320
    as network of n-links, 262

Situational definition, ecometric and psychometric differences, 302
Social institutions
    isomorphism of and subsidiation, 517
    Jungian archetypes in, 515
    as molders of sentiments, 352, 516
Social status
    and authority hierarchy, 506
    dimensions of, 504
    and personality differences, 508
    and prestige, 579
    profile on MAT of low status, 511
    and social desirability, 502
S-R and S-O-R models contrasted, xi
Stability and control
    from G, C, and Q_3, 133
    role of sentiments, 134
Social pathologies, difference from individual maladjustment, 583
States, *see* general states
Stimulus, confusion with cause, 165, 215
Structure-based systems theory
    basis of term, 458
    (*see also* VIDAS)
Structured learning theory
    as broader approach to learning, x, 171
    closer psychological and statistical analysis of, 203
    and dynamic calculus, xi
    five vector formulation of change, 195
    four main departures from reflexology, 173, 210
    going beyond immediate peripheralism, 176
    introduced, 64
    introducing modification of vector of behavioral indices, 190
    all learning changes whole personality, 197
    more parsimonious account of CRII findings, 281
    scattered nature of publications on, xiv
Stimulus control of behavior
    discriminative, 391

Stimulus control of behavior *(cont.)*
  as self-directed or *CET*, 391
Subgoal structures, *m*'s
  activation of, 332
  arousal at, 335
  and focal stimuli in, 330
  investigation by factoring, 341
  overriding of by M's, 334
  in sentiments, 329
Subsidiation of chains
  of attitudes, 67
  and chain reflex, 66
  constancy of motive in, 69, 84
  ending in ergic consummations, 77
Subgoals
  as satisfactions, 76
  as sources of stimulation, 76
Superego
  causes for persistence of, 366
  and the control second order, 148
  ergic forces in, 364
  ideational rewarders in, 365
  influences in learning of, 362
  family and social origins of, 139
  as an *L-Q* data factor, 133
  relation to *C* and *Q*$_3$, 360
  summary on, 446
Symbol manipulation, cognitive gap
  affecting animal-human transfer of learning styles, 211
Syntality
  defined, 466
  function of *R* and *P*, 467
  personality-syntality transactions,
  512
  plots of age change in, 539
Synergy
  defined, by formula, 474
  effective synergy, 485
  extraneous reward synergy, 515
  group goal synergy, 513
  intrinsic synergy, 513
  law of vector conservation, 478
  laws of in equations, 477
  personal activity synergy, 514
  status synergy, 514
  as sum of attitudes, 473
  synergy competition of group, 550
  transfers between co-active groups,
  549
Systems theory
  basic nature of concepts, 422–423

beginnings in VIDA model, 421
  not necessarily homeostatic, 424
  organization of, vii, x
  relation to process analysis, 421
  simplest behavioral model, 424

Teaching, present book's need for
  elaborations, xx
Terminology
  setbacks from impression in, x
  problems of new nomenclature,
  xxi
  semantic confusions avoidable,
  xxiii
Theoretical integration, resistances
  to, vii
Theory
  untutored use of term, xiii
  and "empiricism," xiv
Threptic effects and environmental
  causes, 10
Ties
  in defining a role, 489
  matrix in roles, 493
  and motivation vector in, 490
Tracts
  defined in the dynamic lattice, 324
  expressed in algebraic terms, 330
  h and *k* sequences in, 326
Tri-partite learning equation, personality, *CE*, and *ME* joined,
  317
Twin method of research, as limited
  form of MAVA, 13

Unfolding adaptive processes
  acquisition by learning, 340
  diagram of relay action in, 340
  equation for action in given path,
  339
  in ergic and sentiment structures,
  322
  h's and *k*'s in activation process,
  348
  inclusion of environmental factors
  in, 347
  mechanisms determining paths,
  331
  structure found by factoring, 344
UI(T)21, Exhuberance, formula in
  systems theory, 441
UI(T)23, Mobilization-vs-Regression,

and general states of adjustment,
418
Unity-producing learning processes
effects on *p, r, i,* and *s* indices, 313
for sentiments, 312, 456
relation to tripartite learning
equation, 317

Values
difference from "valencies," 374
not "free-floating," 375
as part of self-sentiment, 374
Vigorous development
as a culture dimension, 525
personality relations to, 525
Variances
within family, formulae, and
kinds, 16
four basic kinds in MAVA, 14
VIDAS, structure-based model
diagram of flow in, 434
inferring internal structure in, 439,
452

information and energy in, 426
and path coefficients, 440
as psychological systems model,
424
relation to specification equation,
443–444, 459
relation to VIDA model, 421,
440, 451
reservoirs and physiological
sources, 445
seven subsystems in, 431
six main concepts in, 425
summarized, 451
Viscerogenic ergs, appetitive quality
in, 240
Volution
defined, 158
maturation and involution as different aspects of, 208

Watsonian tradition, opposition to
innate path components, 95,
102